The Life and Letters of
Emily Chubbuck Judson
{Fanny Forester}

VOLUME 4

MERCER
UNIVERSITY PRESS

Endowed by

TOM WATSON BROWN

and

THE WATSON-BROWN FOUNDATION, INC.

The Life and Letters of Emily Chubbuck Judson {Fanny Forester}

Volume 4

January 1848–September 1851

EDITED BY
George H. Tooze

Published in cooperation with the American Baptist Historical Society

Mercer University Press
Macon, Georgia

MUP/H803

First Edition

Books published by Mercer University Press are printed on acid-free paper that meets the requirements of American National Standard for Information Sciences—Permanence of Paper for Printed Library Materials.

Mercer University Press is a member of Green Press Initiative (greenpressinitiative.org), a nonprofit organization working to help publishers and printers increase their use of recycled paper and decrease their use of fiber derived from endangered forests. This book is printed on recycled paper.

ISBN 978-0-88146-189-3

Letters

The American Baptist Historical Society, Atlanta, Georgia (1,217 letters)
The Hanna family files, Dr. Stanley Hanna, Palo Alta, California (384 letters); Mr. David Hanna, Phoenix, Arizona
Jerome Walker Chubbuck Collection, Wisconsin Historical Society Archives, Madison, Wisconsin (24 letters)
The First Baptist Church of Malden, Massachusetts (3 letters, 1 poem)
Franklin Trask Library, Andover Newton Theological School, Newton Centre, Massachusetts (3 letters)
Special Collections, Colgate University, Hamilton, New York (1 letter)

Pictures

The New York Public Library, New York, New York (12 portraits)
The Hanna family files, Dr. Stanley Hanna, Palo Alta, California (16 pictures); Mr. David Hanna, Phoenix, Arizona
The American Baptist Historical Society, Atlanta, Georgia (14 pictures)

Cataloging-in-Publication Data is available from the Library of Congress

Book design by Burt&Burt

To

Catherine Anne Tooze Tolbert

Ethan Wade Tolbert

Lelia Lucile Tolbert

Nora Louise Tolbert

Campbell Wade Tolbert

With boundless thanks for all
that you bring to our life together.
You light up our lives!

This engraving by Crosscoe and West Engraving Company appears in *Emily C. Judson. A Memorial,* by Walter N. Wyeth, published in Philadelphia in 1890.

It is a colorful, informal portrait, different from many of the earlier engravings. Emily is wearing something in her hair and a bright scarf around her neck.

Contents

Preface

This is volume 4 of *The Life and Letters of Emily E. Chubbuck (Fanny Forester)*.

The letters in this volume begin on January 1, 1848. This was a good year for the Judson family; they were relatively healthy, they were living in Maulmain in a comfortable setting, and they had but few problems throughout the year. Emily wrote descriptive letters to her friends in the United States about the wonderful life that she shared with "Dear Papa" and the children, including the newly born Emily Frances Judson.

Letters from friends and family in the United States are long and rambling. They were often started, set aside, added to, and finally finished and forwarded to the Mission Rooms in Boston, the headquarters of the American Baptist Missionary Union so that they could be included in the monthly shipment to the far-off mission shores. The letters provide a window into the family life of Miss Cynthia Sheldon and Miss Anna Maria Anable; Miss Sheldon was Emily's most significant mentor, and Anna Maria her dearest friend. In summer 1848, this family moved from the Utica Female Academy in Utica, New York, to establish the Misses Anables' School in Philadelphia, Pennsylvania.

In 1849, illness reared its ugly head, and Emily was so sick that, for a time, Adoniram Judson despaired for her life. She recovered, only to see Adoniram begin his final illness toward the end of that year. One poignant letter from this time was written by Elizabeth Stevens, a missionary with the Judsons in Maulmain. She asks if some of the mission wives could stop by the Judson household on their way to prayer meeting to look in on Adoniram Judson and catch a glimpse of his face, to feel his presence. His stature in the mission community was that of a beloved saint.

By February 1850, Adoniram and Emily took a quick sea voyage, spent some time in the supposedly healthier climate of Amherst, and planned a lengthier sea voyage for Adoniram; Dr. Morton told them that Adoniram definitely would not survive if he stayed in Maulmain, so the sea voyage offered the only possibility, however remote it was, of his survival. Emily could not go with him because of her pregnancy; she wrote of his departure on April 3, of her daily visits to the boat as it slowly made its way seaward, and of the last time she was able to see him on April 6, 1851 as the *Aristide Marie* reached the open ocean. The letters from Emily reflect her personal pain; in a number of them, she relates the stillborn birth of their son Charley, named after her father Charles Chubbuck. They also reflect her concern for Adoniram and the heartache of not knowing what was happening. Adoniram died on April 12, but Emily did not learn it until the middle of August when she received the news in a letter from the Reverend W. S. MacKay, a missionary of the Free Church in Scotland who resided in Calcutta.

From this point, letters reflect an outpouring of love from her friends, the mission family, and the churches. They also reveal her dilemma about going home or staying in Burmah. The Judson family's need to be together finally brought her to the point of leaving Burmah, the land that had given her so much, the land that she had come to love, and the land that had taken so much from her.

The need of the family was critical, for the Judsons were scattered. George Dana Boardman, the son of George and Sarah Hall Boardman, was at Brown University. As to the children of Adoniram and Sarah Hall Boardman Judson: Abby Ann Judson was at Bradford Academy in Bradford, Massachusetts, under the guidance of the Hasseltine family; Adoniram and Elnathan were in Worcester, Massachusetts, with Dr. and Mrs. Calvin Newton; and Henry and Edward were returning from Burmah to the United States with Emily. Emily Frances Judson, the daughter of Adoniram and Emily Judson, was three and a half years old at this time. Their dream of being together on a permanent basis never happened; the children gathered at the homestead in Hamilton, New York, in summer 1852 and 1853, but Emily's failing health prevented more than that.

On her return voyage, Emily temporarily enjoyed renewed health. She wrote of gaining weight and of leaving the ship at one of its stops and going into the community for supper. She found warm companionship with Captain Lay, in charge of the *Tudor* and its long voyage, and her fellow passengers, even writing a poem to the absent husband of one of her companions. When they arrived in England, Emily spent approximately a month there, and the letters show the hospitality she was accorded by these old friends of the mission movement, but new friends to Emily and her family.

Volume 4 ends with Emily's arrival in Boston at the end of September 1851. With her, in addition to Edward, Henry, and Emily Frances Judson, is Nancy, a Malayan woman who came as a faithful friend, servant, and companion to take care of Emily and to help with the children.

After some visits with family and friends, Emily began the work of gathering resources for the Judson memoir and moving to Providence, Rhode Island, so that she could work closely with Dr. Francis Wayland, who wrote it in close collaboration with her. This will begin volume 5.

Again and again, Emily Chubbuck Judson pulls us into her circle of life and shows that she was an extraordinary woman growing into missionary life and motherhood beyond all expectations. As she prepares to leave Burmah for a return to her native land, home, and family, she makes an amazing statement in an October 20, 1850, letter to best friend Anna Maria Anable—that she is finding it far more difficult to leave Burmah than when, in 1846, she had left the United States. Through the wonderful grace of God, she had come to love the work, the people, and the mission.

So her ministry to God's church and God's kingdom continues to take shape, and in that wonderful mystery of God's grace, we find our souls too taking sustenance from the overflow of her limited energy and timeless love.

George H. Tooze
Indianapolis, Indiana

Acknowledgments

The editor wishes to express his deepest appreciation to the following for granting permission to use original letters and pictures for these volumes.

Letters

The American Baptist Historical Society, Atlanta, Georgia

The Hanna family files, Dr. Stanley Hanna, Palo Alta, California; Mr. David Hanna, Phoenix, Arizona

Jerome Walker Chubbuck Collection, Wisconsin Historical Society Archives, Madison, Wisconsin

The First Baptist Church of Malden, Massachusetts

Franklin Trask Library, Andover Newton Theological School, Newton Centre, Massachusetts

Special Collections, Colgate University, Hamilton, New York

Pictures

The New York Public Library, New York, New York

The Hanna family files, Dr. Stanley Hanna, Palo Alta, California; Mr. David Hanna, Phoenix, Arizona

The American Baptist Historical Society, Atlanta, Georgia

Letters

January–June 1848

Emily Frances Judson (Adoniram Judson) to Anna Maria Anable, January 1, 1848[1]

A happy new year to you, dear Aunt and to all my Utica and Hamilton relatives and friends. Room for me somewhere in your seminary, for I'm a clear go-a-head-on. They will have to lengthen my basket soon. That's poz [sic]. And as to Mamma, I have eaten her out of house and home, so they have been obliged to get a wet nurse for me. I have seen a good deal of company. Among the rest, Aunt Stevens[2] came and exclaimed, what a beautiful child! This sure is impartiality. And one Mrs. Hough[3] a sort of dashing, not over agreeable lady, but an old acquaintance of Papa, came and stared at me rather ill-mannerly and exclaimed—Why 'tis Judson all over. But I'm not sure whether this was very complimentary or not.

Source: Hanna family files.

Emily Frances Judson (Adoniram Judson) to Anna Maria Anable, January 2, 1848[4]

Now I'll tell you something funny—They have been trying to keep Mamma a-bed, because it is the fashion, I believe, in these parts. But she has contrived to baffle their vigilance two or three times and stepped into the next room. Today, Papa went to the native chapel to preach; and when all was quiet, Mamma got up and went scooting about the house, when lo and behold, she heard Blue-beard coming, and I tell'ee if she didn't run back to bed, like a well flogged flash of lightning. It's a pity and no mistake.

Source: Hanna family files.

[1] There are four addenda to the original letter of December 24, 1847; this is the first. The others are dated January 2, January 3, and January 13, 1848, and appear under those dates.

[2] Elizabeth Stevens arrived in Maulmain in February 1838; her husband was Edward Stevens. Elizabeth Stevens took six-month-old Edward Judson into her home when Sarah and Adoniram had to leave for the United States in 1845, and her care and nurture saved his life. She served forty-eight years in Burmah. She had extensive correspondence with Emily Judson, and her letters spoke of everyday life among the missionaries. When Emily returned to the United States, the letters from Mrs. Stevens brought news of friends and colleagues. Mrs. Stevens had a sister, Sarah Haven, in Massachusetts, who wrote a number of letters to Emily asking for information on the Stevens family.

[3] George and Phoebe Hough were the first missionaries to be wholly called by the American Baptist Missionary Union to work in Burmah with Adoniram and Ann Judson. Mr. Hough learned the printing trade from his father, and they set up a print shop to support the work of the mission. They arrived in Burmah in October 1816 and retired from missionary service in 1826; George Hough subsequently worked for the government as an interpreter and school superintendent, and Mrs. Hough worked as an educator. They remained friends with Adoniram Judson and many of the other missionaries. Their independence was problematical at times.

[4] There are four addenda to the original letter of December 24, 1847; this is the second. The others are dated January 1, January 3, and January 13, 1848, and appear under those dates.

Emily Frances Judson (Adoniram Judson) to Anna Maria Anable, January 3, 1848[5]

Well, here's another funny thing. On new year's day, Mamma contrived to get her account book and a pencil, and away she went at her old tricks. But Papa has just found her out, so I will copy off the lines, but in great confidence, for if I should be caught betraying the family secrets, I should get a dreadful trouncing—

"*My Bird*"[6]

Ere last year's moon had left the sky,
 A birdling sought my Indian nest,
And folded, oh so lovingly!
 Her tiny wings upon my breast.
From morn till evening's purple tinge,
 In winsome helplessness she lies,
Two rare leaves with a silken fringe,
 Shut softly on her starry eyes.

There's not in Ind a lovelier bird,—
 Broad earth owns not a happier nest,—
Oh God! Thou hast a fountain stirred,
 Whose waters nevermore shall rest.

This beautiful, mysterious thing,
 This seeming visitant from heaven,
This bird with the immortal wing,
 To me—to me, thy hand has given.

The pulse first caught its tiny stroke,
 The blood its crimson hue, from mine;—
This life which I have dared invoke—
 Henceforth is parallel with thine.

A silent awe is in my room,
 I tremble with delicious fear,

[5] There are four addenda to the original letter of December 24, 1847; this is the third. The others are dated January 1, January 2, and January 13, 1848, and appear under those dates.

[6] There is another copy of this poem in the Hanna family files with the title "Fanny Forester's Bird."

The future, with its light and gloom,
Time and eternity are here.

Doubts—hopes, in eager tumult, rise—
Hear, oh my God! One earnest prayer;—
Room for my bird in Paradise,
And give her angel plumage there!

Source: Hanna family files.

Emily Frances Judson (Adoniram Judson) to Anna Maria Anable, January 13, 1848[7]

Well, I am promoted at last. My basket is not lengthened, it is true, for there is still quite an unexplored tract at the bottom; but it has been placed in a swinging cot and when I cry, they have a trick of swinging it, and I am such a jiggy, that I forget myself and go to sleep. And Mamma has moved into her withdrawing room, where we have a carpet and two windows and live ( ). Many people have come to see me, and among the rest, Mrs. Ranney,[8]—rather prim and critical, so when I heard her stepping, I scribbled some lines (for I take after my mother)—pin on the back of her cap; and here they are—

Tum in, tum in, doody Yanney, Tum & theede jitter Panny;
Yarb you peep erth up tho bwight, And wiew de thun by pardin lights.

A pretty considerable beginning, isn't it, for this child? However, I see that Mamma is taking to writing; so that I suppose Miss Othella's occupation's gone, and she has nothing else to do, but to wipe the ink off her fingers, and snuggle down in her basket and remain

Your affectionate and dutiful niece,

Frances Judson

Enclosed is a lock of my fine hair, which I flatter myself you will have made into a bracelet, as Mamma tells me you are rather fond of such vanities—

Source: Hanna family files.

[7] There are four addenda to the original letter of December 24, 1847; this is the fourth. The others are dated January 1, January 2, and January 3, 1848, and appear under those dates.

[8] Maria Gager Ranney arrived in Maulmain in May 1844. Her husband Thomas was the superintendent of the printing press and business manager for the missionary compound. A letter from Lydia Lillybridge reveals that Mrs. Ranney had some responsibilities in the mission schools. She had no children; Maria Ranney died on April 26, 1857.

Emily C. Judson to her family, January 13, 1848—Maulmain

Dear father, mother, Kitty and Peter,

I beg leave to introduce to your notice one Miss Frances Judson,[9] usually mentioned in these parts as Fanny Forester,[10] or Fanny *gelee*, (little Fanny) and who claims to be your grand-daughter and niece. She is a very nice little affair—is my black-eyed baby, and oh so fat and healthy! She beats all the babies in the mission, (and there are plenty of them, I assure you) in size. "Such a head!" everybody says too, and "how handsome she is!" and all that sort of thing; and as she don't [sic] know enough to be vain, I have to be vain for her. Seriously though, we have a very fine child, who, if God spares her life, may be a great comfort to all of us—you as well as me. And such a happy house as ours has been for the three last weeks (she is three weeks old today) I think could be found scarce anywhere else in the world. I was followed by the bowel complaint so fatal in this climate and so exceedingly dangerous in such circumstances, up to the very day of her birth, and we all trembled for the result. But, as you will guess by my being up writing now, I have done uncommonly well—better than any of my neighbours [sic], and am entirely cured of the bowel complaint. Don't you think we have more reason than anybody else in the world to be grateful? Mrs. Wade[11] will tell you what a happy family we are, but even she saw us under a cloud, for we couldn't help looking to the future with some dread. Now everything is sunshine.

You will naturally inquire whom Miss Fanny resembles. I will enclose a little lock of the black hair which was as thick as mine when she was born. The shape of her head, her forehead and eyes are mine. The lower part of her face, nose, and mouth and chin—it takes longer to develop, you know, but we think they are Judsonian. In the breadth of her face and general plumpness of her person she is very far removed from our, that is, your family, but her little hands, thin and long-fingered are perfect patterns of my own. Did I call the nose Judsonian? Well, so the natives consider it, but I have some slight suspicion that the little gypsy stole ( ). I must own that neither nose nor mouth are at present *very* pretty and her complexion must have been taken from our side of the fence—it is quite as brunnette-ish as her

[9] Emily Frances Judson was born December 24, 1847.

[10] Emily Chubbuck wrote under the *nom de plume* Fanny Forester. Asked about it once, she said, "Would anyone buy a book written by Emily E. Chubbuck?"

[11] Deborah Wade was a missionary to Burmah; with her husband, Jonathan, they were appointed in 1823. Adoniram Judson called them "his dearest and best of friends." Much of their work was in the jungle communities following the path of George Boardman. They left for the United States on December 22, 1847. From the Hamilton, New York, area, they stayed not far from the home of Emily's parents and sister; they visited the Anable-Sheldon families in Philadelphia. With a large group, they had left Boston on July 25, 1850, and returned to Burmah in February 1851.

aunt Kitty's.[12] If she should be near-sighted too! think of that! Those little round black eyes are alarmingly like her poor blind mamma's. Well! we will wait and see. She is beautiful now—[Note: Two thirds of a line is crossed out by Emily.] I have not yet told you that we have been obliged to employ a wet-nurse, because I came near starving the poor thing. We have a young healthy Burman woman to whom we are obliged to pay $10 per month, beside board and other perquisites, but it is one of those expenses that cannot be avoided. I must give up my drives and some other things which I can spare, now I am well. Besides, to tell you a little secret, the last year was much less expensive than we imagined, and we came out on the sunny side of debt. When the Doct. told me I was so surprised that I would not believe it and made him bring his accounts to my bed to look over, lest he had somehow missed a figure. But no; all was right; and we had not only lived within our salaries but actually paid something on an old debt. When we went to Rangoon[13] we believed it would be money out of pocket, but we thought it wrong to allow that consideration any weight. Living there was very expensive—then my health required various comforts, after we came here, which, if I had been well I sh'd not have dreamed of spending money on—then we had all sorts of little losses—our furniture knocked to pieces at sea, our clothes ruined by Rangoon washermen, sacrifices made in selling things which we thought we should not want in Rangoon, and various other things, beside the fire.[14] Well, we supposed that we had very much over-run our salary, but resolved to economize and make up another year. Now do you know we consider this something like the *widow's cruse of oil*; and we are really superstitious enough to believe if we had tho't more of money and less of doing our duty, the result would have been different. We have used money as freely as we needed it (not wastefully) and put ourselves in circumstances to use a great deal, while I know several mission families that have lived here quietly have economized and economized and fretted and worried and after all overrun their salaries. Don't you think we have a right to believe ourselves especially cared for? You must help us be thankful, for nobody in the world is so completely hedged in by blessings.

[12] Sarah Catharine Chubbuck, "Kate," "Kit," or "Kitty" was Emily's older sister by ten months. Outside of the two terms at the Utica Female Academy, which Emily arranged for her, Catharine always lived at home with her parents in Hamilton, New York. The letters indicate opportunities for marriage, but she, for unknown reasons, remained single. She later helped to care for Henry and Edward Judson after their return from Burmah in fall 1851 when they moved into the Hamilton home with their "aunt" and "grandparents," and she was remembered by them as "dear old Aunt Kate—a dear friend."

[13] Adoniram and Emily had left Maulmain for Rangoon on February 15, 1847; it was Judson's hope that this would be a prelude to moving on to the capital city of Ava, and the ability to bring the gospel to the king, his court, and the governmental authorities. Promoting toleration for the Burmese Church was yet another consideration. Living in Rangoon was both expensive and difficult, and they often felt threatened by the authorities. Emily's pregnancy was certainly a factor that brought them back to Maulmain the first week of September, as was the paucity of funds available from the mission board.

[14] On February 17, 1847, shortly after they left Maulmain for Rangoon, a fire in the mission compound at Maulmain destroyed all of Adoniram and Emily's household and personal articles; much of the loss had been personal gifts of great sentimental value. Emily estimated the loss at five hundred to a thousand dollars.

How I wish you could come and dine with us today. John[15] should get you a nice dinner, and we would bring birdy Fanny out,[16] and little fat Edward[17] would clamber over your knees and play with your nose and eyebrows, while
[Written in the left margin of the address page:] he teazed [sic] you to "do and wals" with him, or "dive" him "a ittle dirl dolly" [sic] and Henry[18] would play bo-peep behind your chair and laugh till the old house should sing again and I, why I would make the tea as is proper for such a sedate matron, and HE should carve. Massey! What a time we would have! Won't come, eh? Well, you may see the time you will be glad to if the old hall *is* shockingly out at the elbows and if everybody *does* say the house looks as dismal as a barn. It is pleasant to us.

[Written in the right margin of the address page:] I am very, *very* glad you are to see Mrs. Wade; she can tell you so much that I can't write. And now do I beg send me long letters and tell me all about yourselves. You seem to forget that I have hundreds of letters to write where you have only me. Then you hear of me from various sources, while I hear of you only through your own letters. Sleepy Fanny will send you a kiss as soon as she is big enough and in the meantime you must content yourselves with love from your own

Nemmy[19]

Source: Hanna family files.

[15] John was the family cook.

[16] Eight days after the birth of Emily Frances Judson, Emily wrote a seven-stanza poem, "My Bird."

[17] Edward Judson, born December 27, 1844, in Maulmain, Burmah, was the eighth child of Adoniram and Sarah Hall Boardman Judson and the fifth of their children to survive. Only a few months old when Sarah and Adoniram returned to America, Edward's life was saved by the nurture and care he received from Elizabeth Stevens. He loved Emily as the only "Mama" he had ever known and returned with her to the United States in October 1851. Edward, who was Eddy to his family, became a minister; he did mission work with the immigrants in New York City, and with the aid of the Rockefeller Family, he built the Judson Memorial Baptist Church in what is now Washington Park.

[18] Henry Hall Judson, born July 8, 1842, was the son of Adoniram and Sarah Hall Boardman Judson. Henry was the sixth of their eight children and the fourth of five who survived. He remained in Burmah in 1845 when Adoniram and Sarah returned to the United States with the three older children. He returned with Emily in 1851 and went to live with her family in Hamilton, New York. Henry attended Brown University and Williams Collage; he enlisted in the army at the time of the Civil War in January 1864. Later that year, he experienced a debilitating accident attributed either to sunstroke or a horse kicking him in the head. He was married once—unhappily according to his own correspondence—and he eventually died in a veteran's home in 1918, the last of his siblings to die. Of this, the chaplain noted, "The end was a genuine example of Christian fortitude." See Rosalie Hall Hunt, *Bless God and Take Courage, The Judson Legacy* (Valley Forge PA: Judson Press, 2005) 291.

[19] "Nem" or "Nemmy" was a name of endearment given to Emily by a small group of her intimate friends at the Utica Female Academy. Anna Maria Anable was "Ninny."

Emily C. Judson to Miss Jane Kelly,[20] February 7, 1848[21]—Maulmain

Dear Jenny,—

I have seen my two fine boys[22] safe in their nests, and taken a peep into baby's[23] little swing-cot,[24] and as the worser-half is out tea-ing it, I am all alone. All alone! Bless me, how indifferent we can be brought to feel to the presence of humans! There is Granny Grunter (alias wet-nurse, alias Mah Bya, who does nothing but eat and sleep alternately (she is eating now) during the twenty-four hours, and who would invent a machine to lift the child and carry it to her breast if she were a Yankee. Then there is his impship, teetotum John, an old Bengalee dwarf, with a smoke-colored face, no teeth, a vermilion tongue, that looks precisely like a snake's, and muscles all on the outside of his dried-up body. No monkey ever practiced more grimaces, no goose was ever half so much of a fool, or hissed with more effect, and no other blackamoor, I am sure, *could* love "Massa" and" Missish" so well, or be so useful and faithful. In addition to all his other qualifications, our John[25] (the missionaries named him John because his heathen name was too wicked to speak) is that wonder of wonders in this climate, an active man. Well, John is rattling the teacups on the veranda; and in my door, erect as a sentinel, stands Sir Oily Long-legs—a Bengalee of the first water—Jessingh by his heathen appellation, and lady's factotum, at least at present. He is a fine-looking six-footer, with a turban which makes him appear at least six inches taller. And what do you think he does—this magnificent specimen of humanity, with his quick eye, graceful figure, and smooth tongue? Why, any thing and every thing [sic] "mamma" pleases, and as deliberately and superficially as Jessingh pleases. He bathes the boys, dresses and undresses them, sweeps the floors, waxes the tables, puts "mamma's" things to rights, even in her dressing-room, runs of errands, and lastly, though far from least sews on all needed strings and buttons. Isn't he a useful man, this Jessingh? Too costly, however, is he for common use, and so when Miss Frank is a week or two older, I shall have to dismiss him. Do you wonder why he stands there in the door so like a statue? Why, in these parts, where every man sleeps with a spear at his bed's head,

[20] Jane Kelly had been a teacher with Emily at the Utica Female Academy as well as a friend. In 1844 she had become the Literary Principal and then in fall 1848, following the removal of the Sheldon-Anable families to Philadelphia to start the Misses Anable's School, Jane Kelly would take full responsibility for the academy, replacing Miss Cynthia Sheldon.

[21] There is an addendum to this letter dated February 10, 1848.

[22] Henry Hall Judson (almost six years old) and Edward Judson (just over three years old) were the two youngest surviving children of Adoniram and Sarah Hall Boardman Judson. Because of their ages, they were left in Burmah when Adoniram, Sarah, and the older children returned to the United States in the hopes that Sarah could regain her health. She died on the trip home on September 1, 1845, at the Isle of St. Helena, and in November 1846, Adoniram Judson returned to Burmah with Emily, the boys' "new mamma."

[23] Emily Frances Judson, the daughter of Adoniram and Emily Chubbuck Judson, was born December 24, 1847.

[24] See the letter written by Emily Frances Judson dated January 13, 1848, in which she explains this "swing-cot." Adoniram was writing in her name.

[25] John was the Judson family cook.

women people do not stay alone as in your land of safety. So, when master goes out, Long-legs stands guard, and if mamma chances to want a pocket-handkerchief or string, searches creation over but it is found, and then presents it with such a reverence as you never saw in America. Such offices are what these fellows like, but all work they detest. What would you think, Jenny, of having this same Sir Oily hooking your frock, making your bed, and performing other like offices? Mind, I do not say that I so employ him; but if you want to learn to think just nothing at all of men and women, why, come out here and employ Bengalee servants. The Burmese are a little different.

Source: A. C. Kendrick, *The Life and Letters of Mrs. Emily C. Judson*, 288–90.

Emily C. Judson to Miss Jane Kelly, February 10, 1848[26]

The scene is changed' since writing the above. It is just half past twelve and painfully light (nobody darkens houses here). I have just basted a hem for a Burmese girl—my only seamstress—and she is poking over it. Sir Oily has been missing since nine o'clock, and my mouth is drawn into scolding order. Wet-nurse asleep, as usual; factotum gone to buy dinner; little Master Henry[27] at his lesson, which I must hear very soon; Edward[28] rolling on the carpet, with his heels in the air, and spelling " b-a ba," with all his might; husband, as usual, digging at his dictionary, with his two assistants; and I by just such a confused, littered up table as you used to see at home, with baby[29] asleep on my knees (baby is sick to-day, and I have been dosing her), my port-folio in a chair on one side, and a half dozen Burman books on the other. Do you think you see us? Not a bit of it. The bare floors in every room but this of mine, the unglazed windows, the high roof, through which the daylight peeps so boldly, the frame-work of the house standing out from the boards after the fashion of a barn, the screen-like partitions, the strips of awning, hung here and there, to answer the purpose of a ceiling, and waving in the wind—these, and a thousand other oddities, I am sure you could not see if you were to try.

"Not quite yet." That was not said to you, but in answer to a call from the next room—"Lovey, will you have Ko-shway-doke now?" Ko-shway-doke is my Burmese teacher, a fine, gentlemanly fellow, who always covers his knees with his silk waist cloth, and when he comes to my room sits in a chair.

Don't expect a decent letter from me, for I have scarce a minute that I can call my own. Just before we left Rangoon, I gave you a long description of the different

[26] This is an addendum to a letter started February 10, 1848.

[27] See vol. 1, "Cast of Characters," s.v. "Judson, Henry Hall."

[28] See vol. 1, "Cast of Characters," s.v. "Judson, Edward."

[29] Emily Frances Judson, the daughter of Adoniram and Emily Chubbuck Judson, was born December 24, 1847.

costumes which I saw in the course of the day—Burmese, Mussulman, Chinese, Jewish, and Armenian. The Karen and Shan are very much like the Burmese, and the Portuguese are caricatures of the English. Think of men walking the streets with English pantaloons, and jackets, made of silk striped in crimson, yellow, bright green, etc. The better sort of Armenian ladies adopt English fashions, and procure their *go-abroad dresses* from Calcutta. They, of course, want the nicest articles out, and so get *party* dresses. It is ridiculous to see one of these pretty, liquid eyed madams, parading our narrow, dirty streets, with a train of Burmese women (lady's maids) at her heels, and arrayed according to her extravagant taste. The richest silks, crimson, green, gold, etc., are worn, but rich laces and lisses, with short sleeves, low necks, and short over-skirts are most in vogue; and wouldn't you laugh to see the mountain of *a bishop*? They do not wear bonnets, but decorate their heads in various ways, and load themselves with jewelry. A lady called on me in the day-time, who would have been elegant in a ball-room, but altogether over-dressed in a Utica party—

Source: A. C. Kendrick, *The Life and Letters of Mrs. Emily C. Judson*, 288–90.

Emily C. Judson to the Maulmain Mission Community,[30] 1848[31]

On the Death of a Sister

Sad are we since thou hast left us,
Sadder far than words can tell;
Tho' a kind Hand has bereft us,
Tho' in glory thou dost dwell.
Oh, with grief our hearts are riven,
To us thou were so, *so* dear!
Hope and faith in vain have striven,
To repress the rising tear.
All in vain: we can but mourn thee,
For we miss thee everywhere;
Since away from us they've borne thee,
All things bright a shadow wear.

[30] This poem was obviously written at the time of a death in the mission community in Burmah. In the years that Emily served in Maulmain, a number of the mission women died; it could have been written any time between 1847 and 1849, so it is placed generally in 1848. It was found in the Hanna Family files; with lines crossed out and words written over, it is obviously a work in progress. There is no record of its ever having been published. In her published and unpublished poems, death was a common subject, either generally as something all the human family faces in time or specifically coming to a member of the family or community.

[31] There is no date for this poem, but it is clustered here with a poem on a similar theme—the death of a child ("Little Lincoln")—and a poem "Song of Maulmain." These three poems were probably written in 1848.

But 'tis Jesus hath bereft us,
And to his own will we bend;
Frail are we—thou has left us,
For a sinless, glorious Friend.

Jesus, Saviour, in our weakness,
Lowly bow we at thy throne,
Cling to thee in faith and meekness.
Make us—make us all thine own!
And when on some future morrow,
We too turn at Death's behest,
From this world of sin and sorrow,
May we in thy bosom rest.

Emily C. Judson to the Maulmain Mission Community, 1848[32]

Little Lincoln[33]

A mound in the graveyard,
    A short and narrow bed,
No grass yet springing on it,
    And no marble at its head.
Ye may go and weep beside it,
    Ye may kneel and kiss the sod,
But you'll find no balm for sorrow,
    In the cold and silent clod.

There is anguish in the household,
    It is desolate and lone;
For a fondly cherished nursling,
    From the parent nest has flown;

[32] This poem is not dated. It is clustered here with a poem on a similar theme (On The Death of a Sister) and a poem titled "Song of Maulmain." These three poems were probably written in 1848. This poem is the second stanza in a poem printed in Emily Judson's *An Olio of Domestic Verses* under the title "Little Children in Heaven" ([New York: Lewish and Colby, 1852] 182–90).

[33] The missionary records of this time do not refer to a child "Lincoln" who died. There are many reports that simply indicate that a "boy" died. There is also not a complete record of all of the missionaries who were in Maulmain.

A little form is missing,
    A heart has ceased to beat,
And the chain of love lies shattered,
    At the Desolator's feet.

Remove the empty cradle,
    His clothing put away,
And all his little playthings
    With your choicest treasures lay;—
Strive not to check the tear-drops,
    Which fall like summer rain,
For the sum of hopes shines through them,—
    Ye shall see his face again.

Oh, think where rests your darling!—
    Not in his cradle bed;
Not in the distant graveyard,
    With the still and mouldering dead;
But in a heavenly mansion,
    Upon the Saviour's breast,
With his brother's arms about him
    He takes his sainted rest

He has put on robes of glory,
    For the little robes ye wrought,
And he fingers golden harp-strings,
    For the toys his sister's brought;—
Oh, weep! But with rejoicing,—
    A heart-gem have ye given,
And behold! Its glorious setting
    Is the diadem of heaven.

Source: Arabella M. Wilson, *Lives of the Three Mrs. Judsons*, 328–29; Emily C. Judson, *An Olio of Domestic Verses*, 184–86.

Emily C. Judson to the Maulmain Mission Community, 1848[34]

Song of Maulmain.

Ply the lever, pioneers!
Many a waiting angel cheers;
Christ above is interceding,
Here the Holy Ghost is pleading,
          And the promise of Jehovah,
                    Stands upon his blessed book.
Cheerly, cheerly ply the lever!
Pause not—faint not—falter never
Course the river, thrid the alley,
From the hill-top to the valley,
          Go this barren border over,
                    Scattering seed in every nook.
Gifted with a little wing,
Far the seed shall float and spring,
Spring and bloom in Burmah's centre,
Till life-giving fragrance enter,
          Even the sacred groves of Boodha [sic],
                    And the monarch's golden hall.
Plant the seed, and ply the lever!
Pause not—faint not—falter never!
With a trusting heart and humble,
Toil till Boodha's [sic] throne shall crumble,
          Monastery and pagoda
                    Reel before the Cross and fall.

Source: Emily C. Judson, *An Olio of Domestic Verses*, 159–61; Emily Judson, *The Kathayan Slave and Other Papers*, 56–57.

[34] This poem is undated. It is grouped here with two other poems—"On the Death of a Sister" and "Little Lincoln." These three poems were probably written in 1848. In Emily's *An Olio of Domestic Verses* ([New York: Lewish and Colby, 1852]), this poem immediately follows "My Bird," which was written around January 1, 1848, to celebrate the birth of Emily Frances Judson.

Emily C. Judson to Anna Maria Anable, February 20, 1848[35]—Maulmain

My dear Ninny,[36]

The steamer came last night with the letters and among them your wee note. It is really a great consolation to see you as you are there, though darling grandmother with nice soft loving eyes—oh, that is sad! I wonder if you are really as happy as we are here—it seems to me that nobody can be, though we have nothing to make us happy but God and each other. We are almost worn out with change, but we are hoping for some rest soon. Have you ever considered how we have been chasing ourselves around like a cat after her own tail for the last year—well we are near the end. Next week we change houses with the Stevens[37] and get into our own nest again at last, the house next the chapel [sic] in which we planted ourselves on landing. Three movings[38] in one year occurring after the great move of a five month's voyage is not a thing to be sneezed at. It is said that three removes are equal to one fire. We have had the removals and the fire too,[39]and I might mention some other things. (We have lost $250, in America—not my affairs, the Doctor's. Then, you knew he had some money—his mother's legacy. A bank in Calcutta has failed and 3,600 rupees have gone to the winds. This news came by the last streamer—last night. There are other things, comparative trifles of course, which I might tell you of, but it is no matter.) We are not distressed at these disappointments, indeed we are really happy because we think we see a Father's hand in all. It is our intention to fling ourselves upon the current, knowing it is the breath of God which stirs it, and be drifted as He pleases. The Doctor will not immediately resume the pastorship of the church, though from his vicinity to it he will probably do quite as much good. His Dictionary[40] is progressing rapidly. He has performed his daily task ever since our arrival, making up nights where we were well what he has lost by illness, and losing no time except in going to Rangoon and back. For myself, I have as yet done

[35] This letter was mailed to the mission rooms in Boston of the American Baptist Missionary Union, and postage shows that it was received and forwarded by them on May 22, 1848.

[36] "Ninny" was a name of endearment given to Anna Maria Anable by her most intimate friends at the Utica Female Academy. Emily was "Nemmy."

[37] Edward and Elizabeth Stevens were missionaries to Burmah. They arrived in Maulmain, Burmah, in February 1838. There are twenty-four letters in the correspondence from them. Mrs. Stevens took Edward Judson into her home when Sarah and Adoniram had to leave for the United States in 1845, and her care and nurture saved his life. The home of Elizabeth and Edward Stevens burned to the ground in 1847, and two trunks being stored for Adoniram and Emily were destroyed; these trunks held all of their excess clothes and precious mementos, which they had not wanted to bring to Rangoon with them. Mr. Stevens buried Charles Chubbuck (Emily's "Angel Charley") in April 1850. Edward Stevens also accepted the responsibility of finishing the dictionary after the death of Adoniram Judson.

[38] Adoniram and Emily moved to Rangoon in February 1847, returning to temporary quarters the first week of September 1847. Now, they were moving into a permanent residence.

[39] On February 17, 1847, a fire in the mission compound at Maulmain destroyed all of Adoniram and Emily's household and personal articles. Emily estimated the loss at between five hundred and a thousand dollars.

[40] The Burmese-English dictionary was the monumental work of Adoniram Judson after the Burmese Bible.

nothing. Family cares, the preparation of the Memoir,[41] and the state of my health have conspired to prevent my gaining a knowledge of the language, but now I am once more well, I do not mean to allow of hindrances. Ninny, my darling husband and I both feel as though God was inducing us by gentle chastisements to give ourselves up to him more entirely. We are glad he has done what he has, and trust it will be for our good, as we know it was intended. Do pray for us dear, for a missionary life is by no means free from temptations. When we get into our own house we intend to watch for opportunities to benefit *somebody*—English, American (missionary) or heathen—no matter who, it shall be our object to do good. How I wish you could come and live with us. Everything, except proper care of the children, is to yield to my getting the language—English writing I must wholly abandon—even letters, to a very great extent. The little cords that bind one to country and home are hard to break, but they are great trammels. I think hereafter I shall seldom send letters anywhere but to Utica and Hamilton. I am about breaking with the *Columbian*,[42] and shall do the same with religious publications. I begin to feel that "life is real, life is earnest" and must not be frittered even on good things. I do not say that I never shall write any more [sic]—I shall make no calculation on writing, be under no engagements, and strive to forget there is anybody in America out of my two homes. Don't you approve this plan? It has been suggesting itself to me gradually for the last six months, and now that I am well enough to study and begin to love the language, I've nothing else for me to do. The children[43] necessarily take up a great deal of my time, as I have to teach them to read, cut and baste all their clothes etc. etc. and the servants take some, so you see it is a moiety that I devote to my books after all. I seldom see company, and never go out. I have called only on one English lady since I have been in the country. People think it is because I am not well enough, but the secret reason is I am too busy. (Do you know whether Mrs. Stevens[44] wrote anything to her friends about Mrs. Bullard, now Mrs. Mason?[45] I ask only out of curiosity, and there is nothing pending either way on the answer. It seems everybody got by the cars while we were in Rangoon. I don't know whether

[41] Emily completed the memoir of Sarah Hall Boardman Judson, the second wife of Adoniram Judson.

[42] The *Columbian* magazine was published first by John Inman and then by Robert West. By early 1844, the *Columbian* was printing Emily's stories; this was before N. P. Willis and the *New Mirror* made her famous. With Graham (of *Graham's Magazine*), they readily agreed to pay her a top rate of five dollars a page for anything that she would write, and on several occasions, they tried to get Emily to write exclusively for them. They finally succeeded in this when she went to Burmah, for they obtained exclusive rights to all that she would send them at fifty dollars a story.

[43] See vol. 1, "Cast of Characters," s.v. "Judson, Henry Hall," "Judson, Edward," and "Judson, Emily Frances."

[44] See vol. 1, "Cast of Characters," s.v. "Stevens, Elizabeth 'Bessie.'"

[45] Francis Mason arrived in Maulmain in November 1830 and transferred to Tavoy in 1831. His first wife died, and he married Helen Maria Griggs just before leaving the United States. She died in Burmah in 1846; they were the parents of four children. A skilled linguist, Mr. Mason was fluent in twelve languages and translated the Scripture into two of the Karen dialects. In spring 1847, Mr. Mason was seriously ill, and the other missionaries were concerned about him. On September 25, 1847, Mr. Mason had married Ellen Huntley Bullard, the widow of missionary Edwin B. Bullard. Adoniram Judson had officiated at the ceremony.

the Vintons[46] will say anything queer about anybody, but if they should, you are to remember there has been a regular row here, and Mr. V. on one side and Lydia's Mr. Howard[47] on the other (both excellent men by the way) headed it. Oh, you don't know how Lydia[48] has changed. She queens it after a grand sort, and is a great belle. Mrs. Commissioner it seems has adopted her as her special pet—takes her out riding, invites her to tea, and makes a deal of her. She has grown handsome, dresses elegantly and is changed in everything but real goodness of heart. There she is Lydia still. Certainly I knew Mr. Jones tried his best to get her, and Mr. Ingalls[49]

[Written in the right margin of the address page:] has made another awkward attempt, but though I approve of the course she took in both of those cases I would give all the frocks I have got left (Lydia gave me two) if she was well married. This about Lydia is the only part of my letter not *private*. That about our losses is especially so. Don't even mention it in your letter to me.)

[Written in the left margin of the address page:] Please go and have a little chat with grandfather[50] and ask him to pray for us and tell him how happy we shall all be when we get together in heaven. Did it ever occur to you, darling, that our loves will be continued in heaven and that all earthly affection if sanctified and cemented

[46] Justus Hatch Vinton was born in Willington, Connecticut, in 1806. He attended the theological school at Hamilton, New York, and was ordained in June 1834. In July that same year, he sailed as a missionary to Burmah. His wife was Calista Holman Vinton; they were married April 9, 1834. They worked with the Karens at Chummerah, Newville, and Maulmain, where he had charge of the Karen theological seminary. At the end of 1847, they left for the United States, returning to Burmah and work at Rangoon in July 1850. Justus Vinton died in Kemendine, Burmah, on March 31, 1858. His wife, Calista Holman Vinton, died in Rangoon, Burmah December 20, 1864. Mrs. Vinton taught the Karen women and was the author of several hymnbooks in their language.

[47] Hosea Howard first sailed for Burmah in 1834, arriving in December that year. His wife was Theresa, and they had been married just before departure. Hosea Howard was a recent graduate of the Theological Seminary in Hamilton, New York. They were stationed in Maulmain as missionaries with Adoniram Judson, and he was to claim in a letter to Emily that he had worked there with Adoniram longer than any other missionary. Mr. Howard's responsibility was to run schools that the mission maintained, a task in which he was ably assisted by his wife. It was to Mr. and Mrs. Howard that Lydia Lillybridge was responsible when she arrived in November 1846. Mr. and Mrs. Howard left Maulmain for the United States in February 1850.

[48] Lydia Lillybridge was one of Emily's closest friends at the Utica Female Academy. When Emily made the decision to go to Burmah as the wife of Adoniram Judson and as a missionary, Lydia wanted to go with them. Emily spoke to Adoniram Judson of Lydia's extraordinary abilities, and Adoniram advocated her appointment before Dr. Solomon Peck and the Board of the American Baptist Missionary Union. Lydia was commissioned to go with them, in spite of the fact that she remained single. Always independent, outspoken, and unafraid to cause ripples in the missionary community, Lydia served on the mission field for twenty-eight years. She married missionary Thomas Simons in May 1851. See the timeline on the life and service of Lydia Lillybridge Simons in vol. 1.

[49] Lovel Ingalls was born August 21, 1808, in Worcester, New York. He was ordained October 2, 1834, in Boston, New York, and graduated from the Hamilton Literary and Theological Institute in 1837. In September 1834, he married Marcia Dawes of Cummington, Massachusetts; Miss Dawes had been educated at Cummington Academy. They first sailed for Burmah in 1835, arriving at Amherst February 20, 1836. They were stationed at Mergui and then Maulmain in May 1845; Marcia Dawes Ingalls died on November 9, 1845, at Maulmain. Lovel and Marcia Ingalls were the parents of three children. Mr. Ingalls went to Akyab in 1846 and returned to the United States beginning May 1850. He went back to Burmah in December 1851. His second wife was Marilla Amelia Baker, and they married December 23, 1850, at Troy, New York. Mr. Ingalls died at sea on March 14, 1856.

[50] Deacon Asa Sheldon was the father of Miss Cynthia Sheldon, Urania Sheldon Nott, and Alma Sheldon Anable. Deacon and Mrs. Sheldon lived with their daughters and grandchildren as a part of the Utica Female Academy community. Isabell Low Sheldon died January 29, 1847. Deacon Asa Sheldon continued to have a room at the Utica Female Academy, where he died in March 1848. For many years, he led mealtime prayers for the academy family, and Deacon and Mrs. Sheldon were popular with the students, who often looked in on him.

by a higher love will make us far happier there. Then, if not before, we will sit down together and tell the things we cannot now write and love on forever. Don't your pulse quicken at the prospect

EJ

Source: Hanna family files.

Miss Cynthia Sheldon to Emily C. Judson, February 20, 1848[51]—Utica

Dear dear Emmy,

Oh! That we could peer through this hazy distance and discover in your far off house, all that can be seen of domestic felicity—It is Sabbath Morn—I know you are not in public worship, because you cannot have gained strength for it by this time—do you know we have a little stranger Charley Gratiot since 12th of Dec.[52]—well in mind I make you and Cousin Ann[53] visits together try to think the Mothers and twin babies are doing finely—you know she is very delicate but has come up from this so nicely and the baby grows so fast that I shall keep you in mind by the same process—hoping all the time you and yours are keeping pace with her—but Oh if the letters could only get here to make it sure—would we not have a day of rejoicing—Heaven grant we may realize it soon. I am sitting by dear father's[54] table with shawl on and face muffled—The rest have gone to Church—a series of deeply interesting meetings are now going on in our Church—five are to be baptized this Morn'g—they are the gathering of last winter's revival—Many more of the same character are standing between the porch and the altar and we hope many are now being pricked in the heart—Mr. Westcott[55] is a very impressive preacher—Mr.

[51] This letter has an addendum dated February 25, 1848.

[52] In her letter of December 28, 1847, Anna Maria Anable has clearly written the date of Charley Gratiot's birth as December 23, 1847. In this letter, there is no doubt that Miss Sheldon has the date as the 12th.

[53] Ann Sheldon was a younger cousin of Miss Cynthia Sheldon, Mrs. Alma Sheldon Anable, and Mrs. Urania Sheldon Nott. She married Charles Gratiot, the son of a prominent army officer and engineer who opened the port of St. Louis. Because Charles and Ann Gratiot often lived with the Sheldon-Anable families, both at Utica and in Philadelphia after 1848, they were often mentioned in the correspondence. They had six children, one of whom was born very close to the birth of Emily Frances Judson. The letters reveal how Ann coped in her husband's absence when he went west during the gold rush to seek his fortune.

[54] See vol. 1, "Cast of Characters," s.v. "Sheldon, Deacon Asa and Isabell Low."

[55] Dr. Westcott was mentioned in a number of letters from Utica in early 1847. He was likely a preacher and was preaching in the Utica Baptist Church where Mr. Corey was the pastor and where a revival was taking place that touched the lives of many of the Anable-Sheldon families.

Corey[56] grows stronger and really stands very high in the city—We have just had finished a new basement room—and find two more can be made under our Church—They will serve Bible classes and rooms for candidates when done—rendering the baptistery very convenient—at present it is useful especially so, on a rainy day like this—very little snow this winter—

Dear Emmy I know when Anna M.[57] is writing I can tell you very little in addition—Your letter to her was full of interest—one thing I have regretted every moment since it came—that is to think so much unmade cloth was on the way there—when every inch of it should have been made—had I known what I now do about the necessity for it—thus much have I profited by the instructions given to dear Anna M.—too late for the past—but my future course will be regulated by them.

The dear girl is full of energy—she is now making her own path through a school of her own in prospect[58]—I do think it will come round, but really feel sad disappointment in not having the girls together again with us—Ann M. [sic] feels that I should at once decide to withdraw from this school and live easy—however pleasant such a course might be—it is a grave question to settle—to draw myself up into a nutshell would be comparatively easy—but I should want to be where I could see the young acorns shooting forth—and if need be clear away the knot grass for them—I know that ten more years here would not yield me gold to draw back upon—but I could scatter some more in that time—there are in truth a thousand considerations. One is how can I make dear father's room seem the same to him—

[56] Mr. Corey was the pastor of the Bleecker Street Baptist Church near the Utica Female Academy, and Miss Sheldon and many of the girls from the academy attended worship there. (Cynthia Sheldon, Alma Anable, Deacon Asa and Isabell Sheldon, Edward Bright, and Horace Hawley had been charter members of the church in 1838.) In April 1844, he wrote to Emily, expressing dismay that at a school program one of the girls had read a composition justifying dancing as exercise; he spoke of this as a roadblock to the salvation of many. Then, on March 10, 1846, Emily indicated in a letter to Anna Maria that Mr. Corey had been critical of her relationship and impending marriage to Adoniram Judson. Miss Cynthia Sheldon wrote a number of times expressing Mr. Corey's regret and support, and in 1847, there were letters of reconciliation between Emily and Mr. Corey. In spring 1848, letters reveal that Mr. Corey's wife had died of consumption, her condition exacerbated by recent childbirth. She had left behind four children. In July 1849, Anna Maria Anable wrote of his impending marriage to Jane Backus, a good choice for this "rising man." Mr. Corey remained popular with the Sheldon-Anable families even after their move to Philadelphia in 1848. A March 2, 1852, letter from Charles B. Stout told of Mr. Corey's call to the Stanton Street Church in New York City, which Mr. Corey did not accept. Finally, in 1854, there was a pastoral letter from Mr. Corey to Emily on her illness and her possible death. He preached at the Bleecker Street Church as late as January 1867.

[57] Anna Maria Anable was the niece of the Misses Urania and Cynthia Sheldon and the daughter of Joseph and Alma Sheldon Anable. Emily first met Anna Maria in fall 1840 when she went as a student to the Utica Female Academy; both Emily and Anna Maria became members of the faculty there. In these years, Anna Maria became Emily's dearest friend, and the extensive correspondence between the two reflects sensitive, flirtatious spirits and a deep intimacy. Emily was "Nemmy" to Anna Maria's "Ninny." In 1848, Anna Maria Anable, with the help of her extended family, moved to Philadelphia and started the Misses Anable's School in Philadelphia. At Emily's death in 1854, Anna Maria was given guardianship of Emily Frances Judson, daughter of Emily and Adoniram Judson.

[58] This is the first inkling of Anna Maria's plans to start her own school. From July 1846 when Adoniram and Emily sailed from Boston, Anna Maria's letters suggested her interest in joining them on the mission field. In summer 1847 she underwent painful medical procedures to straighten her spine so as not to be disqualified for missionary service. This is a dramatic shift; by August, the Anable and Sheldon families moved to Philadelphia to start the Misses Anable's School. Her sisters Harriet, Mary, and Fanny were teachers there, and her mother and Miss Sheldon were on hand in reduced capacities.

we cannot leave Utica—the spot is hallowed[59]—what can I do here independent of a school to secure our present comforts—The Lord will in His good providence make my path plain. I thought three weeks ago when the varialoid [sic] broke out in school that if the Trustees did not come forward to relieve me in part in sustaining the school—I should consider it a plain indication to withdraw in Aug.—Well they stood aloof—but the panic has so far subsided that it is not likely to effect the school as we feared—thus we see how much better the Lord is than our fears many times—I do feel that my hold on life is very precarious for since an extreme sickness twenty six years ago—my days seemed lengthened only to smooth the pathway of my dear parents to the grave—To me my restoration was like a miracle—it had in its healing beams the voice of God—Thy days are lengthened—and since that time the faith of assurance has been mine for an earthly inheritance while my dear parents needed earthly comforts—not longer—I do think dear Anna M. is wonderfully furnished with right views and right feelings for extensive usefulness—If her plan in Baltimore succeeds I think on many accounts she would enjoy life better there than here—but we cannot in this world have every thing [sic] as we would like—and the dear child will find it so in whatever circumstances.—It has been my a'—[sic] only to avoid the greater evils—and I hope to be directed by this view in deciding about giving up the school.—

Our people have been home and gone again—They said the Church was crowded—and very solemn during the ordinance.—

The want of snow has prevented Anna M. from seeing your dear Mother[60]—I feel very anxious she should before these letters go—We have just seen that your Memoir[61] is out—and read a beautiful extract in the *Macedonian*[62]—I am crazy to get hold of it—were in hopes it would have come yesterday—were it here to day [sic] this sheet would be blank—dear Emmy your comfortless voyage back to Maulmain haunts me—and I cannot know how many discomforts you have even in Maulmain—greatly fear your own house is shorne [sic] of many goodly things by the removal as well as fire[63]—do write every thing [sic]—I shall leave this till near the time Anna M. wants to close—Heaven bless you—I shall ever bless the Lord

[59] Miss Sheldon's mother, Isabell Low Sheldon, died January 29, 1847.

[60] Emily's mother, Lavinia Richards Chubbuck, was born June 1, 1785, at Goffstown, New Hampshire, the eldest of thirteen children. She married Charles Chubbuck on November 17, 1805, at Goffstown, New Hampshire. Four of her children were born at Goffstown, and moved with Charles and Lavinia Chubbuck to Eaton, New York, in September 1816; they were Lavinia, Benjamin, Harriet, and John Walker. Sarah Catharine, Emily, and Wallace were all born in Eaton.

[61] Fanny Forester, *Memoir of Sarah B. Judson, Member of the American Mission to Burmah* (New York: L. Colby and Company, 1848).

[62] *The Macedonian* was a magazine published by the American Baptist Missionary Union. Emily was often asked to write articles for it.

[63] Shortly after Adoniram and Emily left Maulmain for Rangoon in February 1847, a fire destroyed the home of missionaries Edward and Elizabeth Stevens, consuming as well the household and personal articles that the Judsons had left in storage with them, a loss that was estimated between five hundred and a thousand dollars.

for making you the helpmeet [sic] of so *good* a man as your Doct.—future generations will bless the Lord for the same.

Source: American Baptist Historical Society, AJ 20, no. 1001.

Gould, Kendall and Lincoln to Adoniram Judson, February 22, 1848—Boston

Dear Sir:

We have too long neglected to write to you respecting the edition of your work on Baptism which we published soon after you left the country. The work was not sold as well as we had hoped, a considerable portion of the edition is still on hand; and taking this—in connection with the fact that the whole work, with exception of the few pages which you added at the end, and which we think has rather *retarded* the sale—was not copyrighted and therefore free for any one [sic] to publish who pleased.—we think it right and fair to allow you *twenty five dollars* and we have accordingly passed to your credit this amount, which will be held subject to your order. Could we have come out with the edition when you first came to the country we should doubtless have soon sold off the ed. and hence could have afforded to pay you more than we now propose. We think however so far as the cause of Missions is concerned it was wise to withhold it until you left the country. You will doubtless remember that we addressed you a note soon after your arrival here, proposing to publish a Memoir of the 2d Mrs. Judson, provided you, or any one [sic] else, would prepare one; and that subsequently you call'd at our store where we had considerable conversation as to the size, type, style etc;[64] and that you stated that you should not be able to do it until your return to Burmah etc; since you left, we have been waiting very patiently to hear from you on the subject, when to our great astonishment we saw it announced, some weeks since, as *in press by Lewis Colby and Co.* New York! The work has just appeared, and we think it will have a very rapid and wide spread circulation. Although the Mem. of the *first* Mrs. Judson was an *old book*,[65] and many thousand copies had been sold, when *we* commenced business, *we* find on looking over, that we have printed *ten thousand copies*: on which we have paid a premium to the late Prof. Knowles and to his widow *five hundred and twenty five dollars*.[66] We have just published a Memoir of the late Wm G. Crocker Missionary to Africa a copy of which we shall send you per first opportunity.

[64] This is the first indication that Adoniram Judson spoke with the publishing firm of Gould, Kendall and Lincoln about the publication of the memoir of Sarah Hall Boardman Judson.

[65] Lincoln and Edmands, an earlier version of Gould, Kendall and Lincoln, published the *Memoir of Mrs. Ann H. Judson, Late Missionary to Burmah. Including a History of the American Baptist Mission in the Burman Empire* by James D. Knowles.

[66] In this not-so-subtle way, the publishers were telling Adoniram Judson that if they had printed the memoir of Sarah Judson, her family would have been extremely well compensated.

We remain very
Respectfully Your
Friend

Gould,[67] Kendall and Lincoln[68]

Source: American Baptist Historical Society, AJ 6, no. 95.

Gould, Kendall and Lincoln to Emily C. Judson, February 22, 1848[69] —Boston

Dear Madam:

We understood when you left the country that it was your wish and intention to write, what your other engagements would allow, for the American press. Presuming that you may not have made an arrangement with any publishing house, we take the liberty to say that we shall be happy to publish any work you may write and think proper to send us for that purpose, in good style, and pay you a premium of *twenty per cent* on the price of the book, (which is *twice* the usual price paid) on all copies which may be sold;[70] or should you prefer, we should be willing to pay you a fair compensation for the copyright.

We think a work on Scenes in Burmah, or, recollections of scenes in America, or some kindred subjects, would take well. We presume however you will not be at all troubled for subjects to write upon.

May we not hope, and long to receive a volume for publication from your gifted pen;

Please communicate with us on the subject, and much oblige
Your friend

Gould,[71] Kendall and Lincoln[72]

Source: American Baptist Historical Society, AJ 6, no. 95.

[67] In October 1850, Charles Gould married Sarah Bell Wheeler, Emily's intimate friend from the Utica Female Academy. Sarah Bell was teaching at the academy in 1848. When Emily Judson returned from Burmah in October 1851, she stayed at the home of Charles and Sarah Bell Gould.

[68] Joshua Lincoln was a prominent Baptist layman in Boston. Anna Maria Anable lived with Mr. and Mrs. Lincoln in summer 1848 when she went to Boston for medical treatments to correct deficiencies in her shoulder and spine.

[69] See two letters to Adoniram Judson from Gould, Kendall and Lincoln dated February 22, 1848, and March 8, 1848. They published a book on *Baptism* by Adoniram Judson, and as Lincoln and Edmands, they had also published in 1829 the *Memoir of Ann Judson*.

[70] In a letter written on June 29, 1847, Anna Maria Anable, who was living in Boston with Mr. and Mrs. Joshua Lincoln, spoke on behalf of Mr. Lincoln and of Gould, Kendall and Lincoln, saying that they would like to publish anything Emily would write for them and would pay her the premium of 20 percent. She also mentioned that they had published the earlier *Memoir of Ann Hasseltine Judson*.

[71] See vol. 1, "Cast of Characters," s.v. "Gould, Charles."

[72] See vol. 1, "Cast of Characters," s.v. "Lincoln, Joshua and Mrs."

Emily C. Judson to Catharine Chubbuck, February 24, 1848 —Maulmain

Dear Kitty,

Our little Frank[73] is just two months old today, and *such* a jewel! It would take you a month to see how handsome she is. No wonder; her 'spectable parents you know are both beauties. Ah, but Kate[74] you don't know what a dear little lady she is, with her cunning little smile, her head stuck coquettishly on one side and her ever-lasting "a-coo, a-coo." Every body [sic] says she looks and acts at least four months old. Well, seein' is knowin', that's all. Doc' is out walking this morning in one direction, and Henry and Edward[75] under the care of a long-legged Bengalese in another, baby and nurse are both asleep and nobody but teetotum [sic] John[76] is stirring. We hav'nt [sic] had the pleasure of settling ourselves down but three times since we left the *Faneuil Hall*, and so just for the fun of the thing, we contemplate another remove next week. We have whirled and chased ourselves around for all the world like a cat after her own tale [Note: "Tale" is crossed out and over it is written "Whew! tail, I meant."] until we have got back to our old starting point—the doc's own house by the chapel. We have been living in Mr. Simons',[77] you know. By the way, what ( ) ( ) ( ) told you of Rangoon *as it was*, was doubtless true. Things are very much changed. When Kincaid[78] and Simons and various others were in (

[73] Emily Frances Judson, the daughter of Adoniram and Emily Chubbuck Judson, was born December 24, 1847. Emily married the Reverend Thomas Alexander Thomson (T. A. T.) Hanna in 1870, and they had eight children, two of whom served as missionaries in Burmah.

[74] See vol. 1, "Cast of Characters," s.v. "Chubbuck, Sarah Catharine."

[75] Henry Hall Judson, (almost six years old at this time) and Edward Judson (three years old) were the two youngest surviving children of Adoniram and Sarah Hall Boardman Judson. They were left in Burmah because of their age when Adoniram, Sarah, and the older children returned to the United States in the hope that Sarah could regain her health. Sarah died on the trip home at the Isle of St. Helena on September 1, 1845, and in November 1846, Adoniram Judson returned to Burmah with Emily, the boys' "new mamma."

[76] A Burman, John was the Judson family cook.

[77] Thomas Simons was born in Wales. He was ordained on December 18, 1831, after graduation from the Newton Theological Institute and was appointed to missionary service on March 7, 1831. He sailed for Burmah on June 29, 1832, arriving in Maulmain on January 1, 1833. On June 23, 1833, he married Caroline Jenks Harrington in Maulmain, probably the widow of a missionary who had died, and between 1834 and March 1843, they had six children, two of whom died in June 1839. Caroline Simons died on May 1, 1843. Mr. Simons returned to America in May 1846. While in the United States, he visited with Abby Ann Judson at Bradford Academy; she would have known him from her years in Burmah. He returned to Burmah in November 1847, arriving in Maulmain April 19, 1848. His second wife was Lydia Lillybridge, who had sailed to Burmah with Adoniram and Emily Judson; they were married in Maulmain in 1851.

[78] Born in 1797, educated at the seminary in Hamilton, New York, and ordained in 1822, the Reverend Eugenio Kincaid served several churches before being appointed as a missionary to Burmah in February 1830. His first wife died soon after their arrival. His second wife was Barbara McBain, and they were married in 1833. In these years, they served in Rangoon, Ava, Saduja, and Akyab. The Reverend and Mrs. Kincaid returned to the United States in 1843; because of her persistent health problems, they were not reappointed in 1846. While in the United States, Rev. Kincaid became instrumental in the establishment of the University of Lewisberg (later Bucknell University). Upon Mrs. Kincaid's restoration, they returned to Burmah, arriving in February 1851 just as Emily Judson was embarking for her return voyage. With his knowledge of the language and customs, Rev. Kincaid was able to establish himself in work with the Burmese government at Ava. With one more trip home (in 1857, on an official mission for the King of Burmah to President Buchanan of the United States), they retired to Gerard, Kansas, in 1866. Of Rev. Kincaid, the correspondence indicates a man of convictions and occasional independent action.

)h there was an English resident at Ava, which of course made everything different. When the English resident left, Kincaid and Simons left too and they do say that the former, in his fright ran so hard that he could'nt [sic] stop himself till he reached the farther end of the Provinces.

Since then Stevens,[79] Vinton[80] and Ingalls[81] made a trip to Rangoon and got ordered back again and then we cut our flourish. But the country is growing worse all the time, and if the money had'nt [sic] failed us just as it did,[82] we should very likely had got into great trouble, for the king is carrying on like mad since we left. Don't be troubled, we shan't try the ( ) ( ) at present.

What under the sun have you and mother[83] been spending your money to make me frocks and such gimerackerus [sic] for? Did'nt [sic] you know that I would take the will for the deed. Well, what must be must, and I will think of you every time I put on the alapaca. By the way it is just the thing, and will really be far more useful to me than the merino, because I shall not feel quite so saving of it. Aunt C.[84] sent me an inventory of the Utica things this month, and we also had news that we are to have a valuable box from Roxbury.[85] If that church sets out they will beat all others, for they are rich, people of taste and fashion, and they love us both—me as well as they can a stranger they have seen so little of, and the doc' entirely. Last month I gave you some account of our doings the past year in the cash line; well, nothing is certain in this world. A bank in Calcutta has failed and we have lost 3,600 Rupees—something like $1,800. It was laid by for the children, so although it has made us sad it does not really distress us. This matter of the money is secret which you must'nt [sic] mention to anybody, but father and mother. We don't expect the American ship these two months yet.

[79] Edward Stevens arrived in Maulmain in February 1838; his wife was Elizabeth Stevens. Mr. Stevens was responsible for the native churches that were associated with the mission. He took on the work of finishing the dictionary after the death of Adoniram Judson, and he buried "Angel Charley" in the chapel compound after his birth in April 1850. Mr. Stevens was in Burmah for forty-eight years.

[80] See vol. 1, "Cast of Characters," s.v. "Vinton, The Reverend Doctor Justus Hatch and Calista."

[81] See vol. 1, "Cast of Characters," s.v. "Ingalls, The Reverend Lovel."

[82] While they were in Rangoon, the board of the American Baptist Missionary Union reduced, without warning, the funds available to the mission in Burmah, and rather than following the plans to move on to Ava, Adoniram and Emily instead returned to Maulmain.

[83] Emily's mother. See vol. 1, "Cast of Characters," s.v. "Chubbuck, Lavinia Richards."

[84] Miss Cynthia Sheldon was in charge of the administrative and financial departments of the Utica Female Academy. Miss Sheldon and her sister Urania, who was literary principal, gave Emily Chubbuck a place at the academy in October 1840. They had deferred any cost to a future time when Emily could afford to reimburse them. Upon Miss Urania Sheldon's marriage in late summer 1842 to the Reverend Doctor Eliphalet Nott, the president of Union College, and her subsequent move to Schenectady, Miss Cynthia Sheldon assumed a larger leadership role at the academy. Active and well-known in Baptist circles, Miss Cynthia was to become an important mentor, advisor, and friend to Emily until the time of Emily's death in 1854. She was the aunt of Emily's best friend, Anna Maria Anable, and was addressed by most as "Aunt Cynthia." In 1848, Miss Sheldon moved to Philadelphia to help Miss Anable with the startup of the Misses Anable's School.

[85] Dr. and Mrs. Edward Bright lived in Roxbury, a suburb of Boston, and Adoniram and Elnathan lived with them when Emily returned from Burmah in October 1851. Mr. Bright was the corresponding secretary of the American Baptist Missionary Union.

Lewis Colby[86] writes us that he had published all my little books and they sell like smoke. He says also that he sells *Alderbrook*[87] as fast as the publishers. The Memoir[88] must be in press about this time and we flatter ourselves that it will be very popular. I shall not write much more for the *Columbian*[89] or anything else. [Note: A sentence of a line and a half is crossed out here.]

Did you receive a couple of loose engravings with your copy of *Alderbrook* and have you put one in the miniature frame? If you did'nt [sic] get any let father[90] write Ticknor and Co. for it.

The steamer goes today and I have several letters to write so good-bye and all good be wi' ye!

Your loving sister

Nemmy[91]

Source: Hanna family files.

Miss Cynthia Sheldon to Emily C. Judson, February 25, 1848[92]

Dear Emmy This must go to night [sic]—I have just seen in the Magazine for March—your Dr.'s letter to the Board 19th Sep.—your own house occupied—and you quartered in Mr. Simons[93] house[94]—I hope in all favor he will not find quarters with you—I suppose he will always owe me a grudge—

[86] Lewis Colby was a publisher in New York. In agreeing to publish the *Memoir of Sarah Hall Boardman Judson*, they had also agreed to republish some of Emily's earlier books. Lewis Colby also published *An Olio of Domestic Verses* ([New York: Lewish and Colby, 1852]).

[87] A sequel to *Trippings in Author-land*, *Alderbrook* was a collection of Fanny Forester's stories, poems, and sketches. It was published by Ticknor and Company (later Ticknor, Reed and Fields), and the first edition came out in December 1846. By April 1847, it was in its fourth edition.

[88] Fanny Forester, *Memoir of Sarah B. Judson, Member of the American Mission to Burmah* (New York: L. Colby and Company, 1848).

[89] See vol. 1, "Places, Events, Organizations, and Magazines," s.v. "*Columbian* Magazine." They had recently published a long article by Emily written on the *Faneuil Hall* on the trip from Boston to Burmah; this was titled "Outward Bound." This article appears in the correspondence (vol. 3) under the date "Fall 1846."

[90] Emily's father, Charles Chubbuck, was born at Bedford, New Hampshire, on March 3, 1780; he was married to Lavinia Richards in Goffstown, New Hampshire, on November 17, 1805. They were to have seven children. Though he held varying jobs over the years, he failed at many of them, and Emily was the main support of the family after she purchased a home for her family in fall 1842.

[91] "Nem" or "Nemmy" was a name of endearment given to Emily by a small group of her intimate friends at the Utica Female Academy. Anna Maria Anable was "Ninny."

[92] This letter is an addendum to a letter dated February 20, 1848.

[93] See vol. 1, "Cast of Characters," s.v. "Lillybridge, Lydia." Also, "A Timeline of the Life and Mission of Lydia Lillybridge Simons."

[94] See the letter of Emily C. Judson to Anna Maria Anable dated February 20, 1848.

[Written along the bottom of the address page:] Now I am as you see close run for paper—Urania[95] writes that she had read your book[96] to the Doct.—they were both deeply interested—indeed she said a great many fine things about it. It is too bad that we cannot yet get hold of it—

In the political world—rumour [sic] says negotiations are going on for peace with Mexico—but the funeral obsequies of John Quincy Adams are now occupying the cabinet—he was

[Written along the top of the address page:] seized with paralysis in the senate chamber last Saturday and died on Wed'y—Sarah Johnson was spending the winter with them in Washington—her father goes for her—Dr. and Mrs. Coventry left in Dec. for France mostly on account of his health—their little Mary was buried yesterday—Mrs. Corey[97] is very ill—to day [sic] there is great apprehension for her—Mrs. Anable[98] was there this aft'n, and thinks she has faded since yesterday—Poor Mr. Corey[99]—and the three children—what will they do—Martha[100] sent a full letter to Lydia[101] yesterday—give my love to her—tell her Martha is good as the Bank—

[Written along the left margin of the address page:] Heaven bless you and yours—the dear little boys[102] we love them much—I was told dear E. their grandmother Hall[103] was in great distress on account of not receiving a letter from the

[95] Urania Sheldon had been the literary principal of the Utica Female Academy in fall 1840 when Emily Chubbuck came to study there. Emily was able to afford this wonderful education through the generous offer of Miss Sheldon and her sister Cynthia, the executive and financial head of the academy, to defer tuition. Urania Sheldon left in late summer 1842 upon her marriage to the Reverend Doctor Eliphalet Nott, the president of Union College in Schenectady, New York. Because of the distance separating them, Emily's relationship with Urania Sheldon Nott did not develop the intimacy that grew between Emily and Miss Cynthia Sheldon. Urania Sheldon Nott remained a mentor, advisor, and friend to Emily in the years of her writing, her missionary endeavors, and upon her return to America in 1851. She was also the aunt of Anna Maria Anable.

[96] Fanny Forester, *Memoir of Sarah B. Judson, Member of the American Mission to Burmah* (New York: L. Colby and Company, 1848).

[97] Mrs. Corey was the wife of D. G. Corey, minister at the Bleeker Street Baptist church in Utica where many of those at the Utica Female Academy attended worship.

[98] Alma Sheldon Anable was the sister of Miss Cynthia Sheldon and Urania Sheldon Nott. Genealogy sources show that she married Joseph Hubbell Anable in Troy, New York, on July 28, 1814, and that it was the second marriage for Mr. Anable. Born in 1773, he was forty-one at the time of the marriage, and Alma was likely considerably younger. He died in 1831, which explains why Alma Anable and her family lived and worked first at the Utica Female Seminary and then later at the Misses Anable's school in Philadelphia. Joseph and Alma Anable were the parents of nine children: Henry Sheldon Anable (b. June 21, 1815); William Stewart Anable (b. November 6, 1816); Anna Maria Stafford Anable (b. September 30, 1818), Cynthia Jane Anable (b. January 28, 1820); Samuel Low Anable (b. November 28, 1821); Harriet Isabella Anable, also known as Hatty or Hattie (b. December 18, 1823); Courtland Wilcox Anable (b. July 28, 1825); Frances Alma Anable, or Fanny (b. April 12, 1828); and Mary Juliet Anable (b. February 18, 1830).

[99] See vol. 1, "Cast of Characters," s.v. "Corey, The Reverend D. G."

[100] Martha Lillybridge was the sister of Lydia Lillybridge, who went to Burmah with Emily and Adoniram Judson. Martha was at the Utica Female Academy. On May 28, 1848, Anna Maria wrote, "Martha is a very fine looking girl—but she lacks energy. I think we shall have her take Fanny's (Anna Maria's sister) place at Miss Martin's. It will suit her as she has no desire to shine as a teacher in a school."

[101] See vol. 1, "Cast of Characters," s.v. "Lillybridge, Lydia." See also "A Timeline of the Life and Mission of Lydia Lillybridge Simons."

[102] See vol. 1, "Cast of Characters," s.v. "Judson, Henry Hall" and "Judson, Edward."

[103] This was the mother of Sarah Hall Boardman Judson. Adoniram Judson visited the Boardman-Hall families while he was in the United States looking for funds to support the education of George Dana Boardman, the son of George Dana Boardman and Sarah Hall Boardman.

Dr. since he left the country—Heaven bless you and yours—your ever truly affectionate friend

C. Sheldon

Source: American Baptist Historical Society, AJ 20, no. 1001.

Emily Elizabeth Blucker to Emily C. Judson, February 26, 1848

My dear Mrs. Judson

It was an unexpected gratification to me, to receive a few days since, the little volume you have just written,[104] especially as I find it was sent me, at your request. Many thanks for the gift—which I prize most highly, not only for the sake of the sainted subject of the memoir, but as a remembrance of her, who has thus thought of me, in a far-distant land. I have read the work, with such deep interest, that I cannot but regard you, my dear Mrs. Judson as highly priviledged [sic], thus to be able to touch many hearts and awaken a tenderer, deeper feeling, in the Missionary cause.

My Mother and sisters write with me, in expressions of affectionate regard for yourself and Dr. Judson, and believe me to be

Yours truly

Emily Elizabeth Blucker

Source: American Baptist Historical Society, AJ 12, no. 318.

Anna Maria Anable to Emily C. Judson, February 28, 1848—Utica

Dear, dear Emily

Your good long candid and consoling letter in answer to my fidgety, flighty sort of a Missionary epistle[105] came about a fortnight since and relieved me not a little. I have regretted time and again that I had written as I did, fearing you would be anxious about me. Otherwise I am glad I wrote so, for I really felt last Summer that if there was a prospect of increased usefulness and I could persuade myself I was fit

[104] Fanny Forester, *Memoir of Sarah B. Judson, Member of the American Mission to Burmah* (New York: L. Colby and Company, 1848).

[105] As Anna Maria struggled with her call to be a missionary, always in the background was her commitment to the Utica Female Academy, the way that her Aunt Cynthia depended on her, and her responsibilities within the family. Being in Boston, however, for serious medical treatment to treat some skeletal problems with her shoulder and spine had made Anna Maria realize that it would be vain to think of anything but going out as a missionary. Having prayed for six of her children (she had nine) and having those prayers answered in so many ways, her mother would not criticize her and there would be no question if God called her daughter for such service. She remarks that everyone in Boston seems to think that she would be going. A later letter from Miss Sheldon (August 22, 1847) states that she thought it utter foolishness for Anna Maria to think of missionary service. In the end, the family moved to Philadelphia in late summer 1848 to start the Misses Anable's School, with Anna Maria in charge, a responsibility of which she spoke in terms of her calling.

to assume such a responsibility I would perhaps do so. Now Nemmy[106] darling I am going to tell you of another plan of mine which may end as the last one. If I write at all I must write about all such nonsense, just as we used to talk.

May be [sic] you don't know that since last Sept. I have been teaching Reading, Rhetoric and Drawing, and that I am now teaching Intellectual Philosophy in the Utica Fem. Acad. Well I am—and what's more I am so puffed up with my success, and so delighted with training young ideas to shoot right that I think seriously of starting out on *my own hooks* as Eugenia[107] used to say. The truth is I am tired of having Hatty[108] off South so long, and she won't return here to teach, for she thinks, and not without reason that Aunt C.[109] barely meets her expenses, and that one of these days we shall be left with ourselves and Mother[110] and Aunt C. to look after and not a cent to do it with.

I have no such forebodings as the latter one, but the truth is this great establishment is entirely too much for Aunt C. and mother's work is quite too arduous for her, at her age. Couldn't we have a darling little family school somewhere? Aunt U.[111] is entirely in favor of it and we have the Summer before us to nurture the plan. We are thinking some of Baltimore. That would be far enough South to suit Harriet's constitution, and besides that I am told there is a very good Society of Baptists there. Dr. Fuller[112] was North last Summer while I was in Boston and he staid [sic] a day or two here, and struck up a great friendship and intimacy with Grandpa[113] and the whole

[106] "Nem" or "Nemmy" was a name of endearment given to Emily by a small group of her intimate friends at the Utica Female Academy. Anna Maria Anable was "Ninny."

[107] Eugenia Damaux had been part of Emily's intimate circle of friends at the Utica Female Academy. Living in New York City, Eugenia suffered from some kind of eye problem that made life difficult at times; this was a matter of comment in many of the letters exchanged between the girls themselves and with Miss Cynthia Sheldon. In 1848, Eugenia was in New York living "at Mrs. Brown's—the same warm-hearted French girl as ever." In 1849, she married Johnny Edmonds, described as rich and pious, and they lived in Utica.

[108] Harriet or "Hatty" or "Hattie" or "Hat" Anable was one of nine children born to Joseph and Alma Anable, and was a niece to Miss Cynthia Sheldon and Mrs. Urania Sheldon Nott. In 1841, she had added a note to a letter written by Miss Cynthia Sheldon to Emily. As early as November 1842 she was away, and a letter from Emily to Catharine Chubbuck said that "she (Miss Sheldon) expected that Hat would return as accomplished as Anna Maria." Her trips away were both educational and employment, as she worked as a private tutor in families that would bring her into their homes. In August 1843, she had just returned from Beonsen, in the vicinity of New Orleans, and was engaged to go again. A letter from Anna Maria on January 6, 1845, said that she would stay South for another year. About this time Miss Cynthia Sheldon mentioned her concern for Hatty's spiritual health. In May 1845 she was in New Orleans. She was home again in summer 1846, but a September 27 letter from Anna Maria said she had been asked by Mr. Roman with some urgency to return and she thought that she should. She was to return home from New Orleans in January 1849 after Anna Maria Anable had started the Misses Anable's School in Philadelphia in fall 1848. Harriet was fluent in French, having placed herself earlier in a French environment in New Orleans. Hatty died in 1858.

[109] See vol. 1, "Cast of Characters," s.v. "Sheldon, Miss Cynthia."

[110] See vol. 1, "Cast of Characters," s.v. "Sheldon, Alma and Joseph Hubbell."

[111] See vol. 1, "Cast of Characters," s.v. "Sheldon, Urania."

[112] Dr. Richard Fuller was born in Beaufort, South Carolina, in April 1804, and he became the pastor of a church in Baltimore in 1846. Of him, William Cathcart said in *The Baptist Encyclopaedia* ([Philadelphia: Louis H. Everts, 1881] 423): "One of the conditions of his removing to Baltimore was that a new church edifice should be built, and accordingly a house of worship was erected on Paca and Saratoga Streets, where thronged congregations listened for so many years to his eloquent and impressive preaching, and where such large numbers were added to the church."

[113] See vol. 1, "Cast of Characters," s.v. "Sheldon, Deacon Asa and Isabell Low."

family. He writes that he hopes we will find it for our interest to come, as the Roman Catholics are educating quite too many of their young ladies. Don't you feel like smiling audibly when you think of Ninny's[114] presiding over a seminary of learning? By the way, ask the Dr. if in case I sh'd arrive at such distinction in the world, my name could not be changed? I think there is Scripture authority for it at least.

I think you would smile, could you see the voluminous tomes by which my room is littered. I have collected all the big works that have ever been written on Int. P. You never see such a thing as *Graham*[115] or the *Columbian*[116] in my room, now *I guess* unless perhaps there may be an article from Mrs. J. in the latter. Even Court[117] tries to make me pedantic for the boy will insist on coming to my room every aft—and of late he has taken it into his head to read me the *Iliad* that I may admire the euphony of the Greek language. I am so provoked that I cannot get hold of your Memoir[118] yet. Aunt U. had it a week ago, and writes that she and the Dr. are quite fascinated with it. It has not come to our town yet.

Mr. Westcott[119] is here again holding a protracted meeting with us. It does seem as if ours is a good little church which God means to bless. Mr. Corey[120] is certainly one of the most earnest, devoted pastors that are I know, and he is universally respected. Poor Mrs. C.[121] I am afraid is dying of consumption. She has not been well since the birth of a little child this winter, and now she does not sit up more than an hour or two in the day.

Grandpa is very well this Winter—he goes out to meeting every aft. and eve'g. He cried when I read your little message, and said he did always ( ) to remember you. I have written on so far dear Nemmy and said nothing of the little stranger who must before this time have taken his (or her) place in your household.[122] I

[114] "Ninny" was a name of endearment given to Anna Maria Anable by her most intimate friends at the Utica Female Academy. Emily was "Nemmy."

[115] George Graham was the editor of *Graham's Magazine*, one of the preeminent literary magazines of Emily's time. He took an interest in Emily Chubbuck as Fanny Forester; he mentored her and published every piece of writing that she could submit to him, and for it all, he remunerated her with the astounding sum of five dollars a page. In April 1845, when Emily was staying in Philadelphia with the Reverend and Mrs. A. D. Gillette, Mr. and Mrs. Graham were frequent visitors, often inviting Emily to tour parts of the city with them in their elegant carriage. That relationship picked up again when Emily returned to Philadelphia in fall 1845.

[116] See vol. 1, "Places, Events, Organizations, and Magazines," s.v. "*Columbian* Magazine."

[117] Courtland Anable was a younger brother of Anna Maria Anable. He held several positions over the years, and he studied at Hamilton College while he boarded for a time with Emily's parents. In 1853, he returned to Philadelphia where he preached his first sermon at the Eleventh Baptist Church. He was "Uncle Court" to Emily Frances Judson. In 1880, Courtland Anable was listed in the Massachusetts Census as an ordained minister serving in a church.

[118] Fanny Forester, *Memoir of Sarah B. Judson, Member of the American Mission to Burmah* (New York: L. Colby and Company, 1848).

[119] See vol. 1, "Cast of Characters," s.v. "Westcott, Doctor."

[120] See vol. 1, "Cast of Characters," s.v. "Corey, The Reverend D. G."

[121] Mrs. Corey, the wife of the Reverend D. G. Corey.

[122] See vol. 1, "Cast of Characters," s.v. "Judson, Emily Frances."

cannot but hope that all as gone well with you, and that your home is gladdened by its baby innocence. It seems a long time to wait, before I can hear.

Jul[123] and Sarah Bell[124] send lots of love. Jul is happy in Casswell's[125] increased prosperity and usefulness, but poor Sarah I am afraid will all her be disappointed [sic] in John[126]—The last instance of fickleness in him is his turning Presbyterian.

Jane[127] is growing more and more popular as a principal—indeed she is very much admired both physically and mentally. When I look at her I feel encouraged to think that I may accomplish something yet. Now I told you that Dr. Nott[128] has been suffering all Winter from inflammatory rheumatism and that he is practicing hydropathy. Poor man! he is completely drenched 6 times a day and laid away in wet sheets.[129] I don't think he can complain of exposure from immersion hereafter. I must stop. Good bye. I am dying of impatience to hear from you.

[123] Julia Look was a student of Emily's at the Utica Female Academy and later a fellow teacher. A November 22, 1845, letter from Anna Maria encouraged Emily to stay in Philadelphia for the winter for her health and remarked that Julia had the hardest part because she was teaching Emily's composition class, and the students kept asking for Emily. In a September 1847 letter, she was listed as one of the teachers at the Utica Female Academy. On September 23, 1849, Anna Maria wrote that Julia and Albert B. Casswell were married and came to visit with her. In one 1849 letter Julia spoke of another teacher who was teaching "our composition class." On October 27, 1850, Anna Maria Anable noted that she had had a son. She was one of a small number of people who addressed Emily as "Emily" and as "Nemmy" in her letters.

[124] Sarah Bell Wheeler was a teacher at the Utica Female Academy, an intimate of Emily Chubbuck, and one of the few who addressed Emily as Nemmy. In a September 1847 letter, she was listed as one of the teachers at the Utica Female Academy. There are a number of letters from Sarah Bell before and after her marriage to Charles Gould of Boston in October 1850. There are several letters clustered in the year or two after Emily left for Burmah and a number at the time of her return to America. Emily stayed with Charles and Sarah Bell Gould in October 1851 when she arrived in Boston after the long sea voyage from Burmah and then England. She stayed there a number of times following that. In 1851, Anna Maria Anable wrote of Sarah Bell: "Sarah is grown so lovely in person as well as character that she must assert a blessed influence on all with whom she comes in contact."

[125] In 1849, Mr. Albert B. Casswell married Julia Look, one of Emily's intimate friends from the Utica Female Academy. Mr. Casswell wrote in April 1853 acknowledging two checks totaling more than $1000 that Emily sent to him to invest on her behalf. In another letter of May 1853, he apologizes for her misunderstanding that he would work on her behalf gratis. He charged her a 3 percent fee and said that it was customary: "Thus I have acted quite professionally in this matter and am under obligation to you for giving me the opportunity of making a respectable little fee without much labor—and shall be ever glad to repay by any acts of friendship in my power." He then sends regards from his wife Julia. Because of the long term relationship between Julia and Emily, she thought the transaction would be a gift to her; many other people were willing to help Emily with the responsibilities for the Judson children. Mr. Casswell obviously saw it as no more than a profitable (to him) business transaction.

[126] On November 26, 1847, Sarah Bell wrote, "Speaking of marriage reminds me of myself Nemmy. I don't know when that happy (wedding day I mean) is coming to me. My friend is in Galena, so I know I shall live west one of these days. Nemmy I hope you will pray for me that I may be a useful humble Christian. John has met with a great change and I trust he will remain steadfast to his profession." John Sheldon was a cousin of Anna Maria Anable and a nephew of Miss Cynthia Sheldon. In October 1850, Sarah Bell married Mr. Charles Gould of Boston, a widower with small children.

[127] Miss Jane Kelly was Emily Chubbuck's friend at the Utica Female Academy, and then she became a teacher with Emily at that institution. Miss Kelly became the literary principal in 1844 with the retirement of Mr. and Mrs. James Nichols from that position. During a period of Miss Kelly's illness in 1844, Emily filled in the position for her. Then, in 1848, when Miss Cynthia Sheldon moved to Philadelphia to help start the Misses Anable's School, Miss Kelly became the "headmistress" of the academy and successfully brought it into the future, though not without some initial disparagement from the Sheldon-Anable families.

[128] The Reverend Doctor Eliphalet Nott was the president of Union College in Schenectady, New York. An ordained Presbyterian minister, he was married to Urania Sheldon Nott, the sister of Miss Cynthia Sheldon and Mrs. Alma Anable and the aunt of Anna Maria Anable.

[129] In her letters over the years, criticism of Dr. Nott's choices and this form of treatment are constant themes in Miss Cynthia Sheldon's letters.

[Written in the right margin of page 4:] Tell Lydia[130] I meant to write to her by this mail, but shall not have time. She does not desire many letters to be sure, but I am of a generous make in the letter line and besides I believe I wrote a kind of a naughty letter to her the last time. Martha[131] is doing admirably in every thing [sic]. She only needs to have her energy called out to make a grand woman. She is quite handsome withal.

[Written in the left margin of page 4:] Tell the Dr. I am much obliged for the kind endorsements he sends occasionally to your epistles. I do feel grateful for the interest you both take in my welfare. I do not see why it is I should have such dear good friends, God grant that if I do not see you again in this world, I may so live that we may spend an eternity together.

Adieu. Anna M.

[Written in the left and top margins of page 1:] Mary Spencer has just returned from Albany. It is said she is engaged to John James, a handsome young widower with three children, and two or three hundred thousand $'s. He is brother to our friend Rev. W. James. This is but rumour [sic]. I have not seen Mary yet.

Source: American Baptist Historical Society, AJ 13, no. 495.

Gould, Kendall and Lincoln to Adoniram Judson, March 8, 1848

Dear Sir

Your communication of the 21st Nov./47 has just reached us. We had written the foregoing letter,[132] and it was laying at the Mission Rooms, waiting an opportunity to send, when yours came to hand. We have obtained the sheet; and hasten to reply, and shall forward it per Over-land mail, instead of waiting for a vessel. We were certainly greatly surprised to learn that you had not rec'd any copies of your work on Baptism; we supposed we had sent you some, and can hardly account for the omission, it was certainly entirely accidental and we beg pardon for the neglect. We will send you fifty copies per first opportunity, and will furnish more in future, if you wish, and we will also put in same package a few copies of the first Mrs. Judson's Mem. and Boardman's Memoir.[133] We are selling about *one hundred Copies* of the 2nd Mrs. Judson's Mem. *per day*.[134]

[130] See vol. 1, "Cast of Characters," s.v. "Lillybridge, Lydia." Also, "A Timeline of the Life and mission of Lydia Lillybridge Simons."

[131] See vol. 1, "Cast of Characters," s.v. "Lillybridge, Martha."

[132] See the letter from Gould, Kendall and Lincoln to Adoniram Judson dated February 22, 1848, and their letter to Emily C. Judson of the same date.

[133] Lincoln and Edmands, the predecessor firm to Gould, Kendall and Lincoln, had published the *Memoir of Ann H. Judson* in 1829 and later the *Memoir of George Dana Boardman*.

[134] Fanny Forester, *Memoir of Sarah B. Judson, Member of the American Mission to Burmah* (New York: L. Colby and Company, 1848).

We are glad to learn of your continued good health. May the Lord continue and prosper you for very many long years to come.

We are very respectfully your friend
And brethren in Christ

Gould,[135] Kendall and Lincoln[136]

Source: American Baptist Historical Society, AJ 6, no. 95.

Mrs. Elizabeth L. Stevens to Emily C. Judson, March 1848[137]

My dear Sister

Saturday is my picking up and putting to rights day. And among other things to go to their lawful owners is this volume; you must have thought it an unreasonably long time for copying "Speak Gently" and "We are Leven [sic]" and must suppose the book worn out by such long use—but it has had a *very long* "resting spell" safe in the bottom of a box snug and quiet.

If you will forgive me this time I'll promise to be better in future [sic].

I was thinking this morning of the dear little bombees [sic] I lent you once—I suppose you had an ample supply made so that it would be no use for me to ask you if you would like the whole or a part of them. Although the dear little lamb never wore them, I had so long had them laid aside as *his 1st future*. I associate them with his little dear frocks. I should enjoy giving some of both frocks and bombees to your baby,[138] unless you have had as many made up as she will be able to wear out before they are outgrown. You can judge how long they will fit her. As it is some time since you had them I will send some

[Written along left and top margins of page 1:] for you to try on. Now do be kind enough to write as plainly as I have done and let me know how many of each you can make use of.

Affy

E. L. S.

Source: American Baptist Historical Society, AJ 19, no. 909.

[135] See vol. 1, "Cast of Characters," s.v. "Gould, Charles."

[136] See vol. 1, "Cast of Characters," s.v. "Lincoln, Joshua and Mrs."

[137] This letter is undated. Because of its reference to Emily's baby, it is placed several months after the birth of Emily Frances Judson.

[138] See vol. 1, "Cast of Characters," s.v. "Judson, Emily Frances."

Emily C. Judson to Catharine Chubbuck, March 19, 1848[139]—Maulmain

Well Kitty,[140] what would you give to look in upon me this blessed March day and see what I am about. Well, I'll tell you. I'm in a room with two windows, two doors, one child's cot, one book case, one writing-desk, one couch, two tables, four chairs, two Burman boxes about twice as big as yours and one moorah which serves me for a writing-stool. In the next room—the dinning-hall, sits doc at a clumsy looking, but exceedingly convenient place of a writing-table and on the veranda are three children at play—or rather two are playing *to* the third. There are two beautiful blue-eyed boys,[141] making themselves agreeable to a black-eyed, black-haired little girl[142] no less beautiful; and she opens her little lips with a smile and shows her little toothless gums in a very pretty sort of a way. Don't you wish you had been introduced to your little niece sooner so that you could have sent her a keepsake?

Source: Hanna family files.

Emily C. Judson to Mrs. Mary Brayton, March 20, 1848—Maulmain

My Dear Mrs. Brayton,—

I fully appreciate your kindness in "advocating my cause,"[143] but after all, my dear sister, of what consequence are the opinions of men? Why should I spend the few precious hours allotted me here in trying to convince people away in America that I am a good missionary? If I walk humbly and prayerfully before God, try to do all the good in my power, and leave my reputation in His hands, I am not afraid that I shall suffer. But for this trust I should scarce have ventured to put myself in a position to be criticized, as I very well knew I was doing when I consented to come to Burmah. Formerly I used the little talent that God had given me for what I believed a legitimate object, and I can but believe that I was blessed in so doing. As soon as that object was accomplished, He opened a wider field of usefulness, and I entered it. That I am unfit for the work I very well know; that I may be fitted for it I pray daily. But will it fit me any better—shall I be any more diligent and prayerful, if I distract my mind and divide my attention between what Americans think of me, and what Burmans think of my Saviour? No, no, my dear sister; though many may think ill of me, I already have more credit than I deserve, and my little, small,

[139] This letter has an addendum dated March 22, 1848.

[140] See vol. 1, "Cast of Characters," s.v. "Chubbuck, Sarah Catharine."

[141] See vol. 1, "Cast of Characters," s.v. "Judson, Henry Hall" and "Judson, Edward."

[142] See vol. 1, "Cast of Characters," s.v. "Judson, Emily Frances."

[143] Mary Brayton, a missionary to Burmah with her husband, Durlin, returned to the United States. On December 28, 1847, Mrs. Brayton said to Emily in a letter: "I am asked a thousand questions about the present Mrs. Judson. Excuse my frankness. I always freely and conscientiously advocate your cause."

insignificant self is not worth the ink that would be wasted on a vindication, explanation, or whatever you may choose to call it.

If you were here I could tell you many interesting—all of them to me interesting—stories of the children; but though my partial tongue may move very fast, I must put some restraint on my pen. Yet I will relate one little anecdote of Edward,[144] which you may tell to Mary[145] if you like. When you left, I believe the little fellow could not talk, but now he has become the veriest chatterbox in the mission. While we resided in Rangoon the children became great cowards (I suppose they caught the infection from us), and when we came over here, I was obliged to take great pains to break it up. One night Edward, who slept in a little room by himself, called out that he was "afraid," and would not be comforted. I have never taught them a prayer to repeat, because I do not like the formality, but I assist them in discovering what they need, and then have them repeat the words after me. So I prayed with little E., kissed him good night, and left him apparently satisfied. Pretty soon, however, I heard him call out, as though in great distress, "O, Dod!" The poor little fellow had not sufficient acquaintance with language to know what to say next ; but this up-lifting of the heart evidently relieved him, for in a few minutes after he again called out, "O, Dod!" but in a tone much softened. I stepped to the door but hesitated about entering. In a few minutes he again repeated "O, Dod !" but in a tone so confiding that I thought I had better go back to my room, and leave him with his Great Protector. I heard no more of him for some time, when I at last went in and found him on his knees fast asleep. He never fails now to remind me of asking "Dod to tate tare of him," if I neglect it, and I have never heard him say a word since of being afraid.

I am very busy with the language, having got on but slowly during the past year. You know it is not everyone who comes out that begins with a family of children, and so I am obliged to be doubly diligent. There is not much that is encouraging in the church or among the natives, and but for faith, I am afraid that the hearts of the missionaries would sink. By reports from Rangoon, Burmah seems more effectually closed against us than ever. But one thing we do know, that the day will come when "the earth shall be filled with His glory!"

Most truly and affectionately yours,

Emily C. Judson

Source: A. C. Kendrick, *The Life and Letters of Mrs. Emily C. Judson*, 291–92.

[144] See vol. 1, "Cast of Characters," s.v. "Judson, Edward."

[145] Durlin and Mary Brayton had a daughter Mary, who would have been almost seven years old at this time.

Emily C. Judson to Catharine Chubbuck, March 22, 1848[146]

I have just come in from my Burmese prayer-meeting and doc. says "Well, lovey, I hope your letters are ready—I have just sealed up mine." My letters! I tell you what it is, Kate,[147] if you had the babies, and 11 ty thousand[148] other botherations on your hands, it is precious few letters you would write. There is madam wet-nurse now has walked off—left the poor half-starved baby screaming at the top of her voice. "Write—write away and I'll take care of her," doc. says. You would'nt [sic] think that if you could see Miss Frances[149] that she was starved. She is as fat as a roll of butter.

This is an interesting letter to travel so far, but it will say that we are well, and I suppose that is the principal [sic] thing you want to know. Tell Mrs. Wade[150] that I meant to have written her this month, but have no time. Tell her that we have got back into our old house—the doctor holds meetings twice during the week and preaches once on the Sabbath—and I have got so that I can read well enough to manage the female prayer meeting, though I don't venture to pray yet.

Here is another *ahmoo* as the Burmans say. Edward[151] has been stuffing himself with green guavas, and the poor fellow has got to take a whipping as well as the sickness. So, good-bye and look out that you don't get any whipping yourself.

Your loving sister,

Nemmy[152]

Source: Hanna family files.

Miss Louisa B. Marble to Emily C. Judson, March 30, 1848—Utica

My dear Mrs. Judson,

Anna Maria[153] has just stopped at my room to tell me that she is to send off a package of letters for you tomorrow. So I have begged the privilege of sending a "wee bit" word to you—away over in Burmah! How strangely that would have sounded some four or five years ago, but the strangeness of it is all over now, though it always slips off the end of my pen rather reluctantly.—

[146] This letter is an addendum to a letter dated March 19, 1848.

[147] See vol. 1, "Cast of Characters," s.v. "Chubbuck, Sarah Catharine."

[148] Likely "11 ty thousand" is a colloquialism ("eleven-ty thousand"), i.e., a large amount.

[149] See vol. 1, "Cast of Characters," s.v. "Judson, Emily Frances."

[150] See vol. 1, "Cast of Characters," s.v. "Wade, Jonathan and Deborah." The Wades were in the Hamilton, New York, area at the time.

[151] See vol. 1, "Cast of Characters," s.v. "Judson, Edward."

[152] "Nem" or "Nemmy" was a name of endearment given to Emily by a small group of her intimate friends at the Utica Female Academy. Anna Maria Anable was "Ninny."

[153] See vol. 1, "Cast of Characters," s.v. "Anable, Anna Maria."

Oh! how delighted we were to hear from you! Could you have been seated last Wednesday in the old room you used to have, just over Miss Kelly's[154] where I am now, you would have heard the words repeated joyfully throughout the halls, "letters from Burmah!" "letters from Burmah!" Then you might have seen something of a rush down to Miss Cynthia's[155] room and could you have caught a glimpse of the anxious faces; some pale, some flushed, as letter after letter was opened, why, *perhaps* you might have been sorry (for half a minute *only*!) that you ever forsook such dear, kind friends. I have pored over the incidents of your voyage most *devouringly*, and have opened my mouth and eyes in perfect astonishment that our pet, "Fanny Forester"[156] ever lived to describe such scenes. But leaving out all the sea-sickness and other uncomfortable things—was'nt [sic] it grand, sublime to feel that a ( ) wee mortal could find herself permitted to take in such draughts of the beautiful, the infinite? Oh! could I have borrowed a pair of poet's spectacles, how I'd like to have stood beside you as you were dancing over the billows, to have seen what poets see.—[157]

Things have not changed much yet at the Seminary, except that dear Grand-Ma Sheldon[158] has dropped from among us. The light of life melted away in her mild blue eyes as day melts into twilight, and she had gone! Then there were heart-sobbings and prayers—a gathering in the halls—and a coffin was carried out, followed by many mourners. I never believed much in broken hearts before, but I believe most firmly now, when I see poor Grand-Pa[159] Sheldon sitting alone by his quiet fireside, that he has most emphatically and truly a "broken heart."

While I am writing, I hear merry voices in the halls—snatches of songs, and bursts of laughter just as when you were here a little while ago—Perhaps you wonder that I am still at the Seminary. I have been playing "parlor-boards" this winter, and I've been trying to *write* a little too for amusement. But I shall never have ambition enough to make myself comfortably miserable—that *famous*—not I. My black-eyed sister whom perhaps you will recollect, has gone home to prepare for her bridal the coming summer. She loved you and "Alderbrook"[160] most devotedly. How welcome was that long looked for book which some of the editors call a "posthumous work."

[154] See vol. 1, "Cast of Characters," s.v. "Kelly, Miss Jane."

[155] See vol. 1, "Cast of Characters," s.v. "Sheldon, Miss Cynthia."

[156] Emily Chubbuck wrote under the *nom de plume* Fanny Forester. Asked about it once, she said, "Would anyone buy a book written by Emily E. Chubbuck?"

[157] The reference here is to the article "Outward Bound," which Emily wrote on the voyage from Boston to Maulmain, and which appeared in the *Columbian* magazine.

[158] Isabell Low Sheldon was the mother of Miss Cynthia Sheldon, Mrs. Urania Sheldon Nott, and Mrs. Alma Anable and the grandmother of Anna Maria Anable and her eight siblings. She lived at the Utica Female Academy. She and her husband were fixtures, and much beloved by the faculty and students. Isabell Low Sheldon died January 29, 1847.

[159] See vol. 1, "Cast of Characters," s.v. "Sheldon, Deacon Asa and Isabell Low."

[160] *Alderbrook* was a collection of Fanny Forester's stories, poems, and sketches and was a sequel to *Trippings in Author-land*. Published by Ticknor and Company (later Ticknor, Reed and Fields), the first edition came out in December 1846, and by April 1847, it was in its fourth edition.

I read "Dora"[161] most conscientiously once a month. You remember Nora Westcott?[162] We have just heard of her *death*—of consumption—poor—dear child. But I am wearying you, and I am fearful my note will have but little interest for you—but oh! if you knew how differently *Burmah* looks to me now, from the country I used to hunt out on the map—in my Geography lesson! And Rangoon—can you, *must* you go there?[163] Yet *God* will protect you and yours wherever you may go. Oh! it is a glorious thing to labor for Him!—I cannot tell you how acceptable even a very *few* lines from *you* would be to your old pupil and friend—nor dare I ask them.

May God bless you! Yours most affectionately and sincerely

L. B. Marble

[Written along the left margin of page 3:] You may kiss your sweet little boy[164] for me—will you? Louise B. Marble

Source: American Baptist Historical Society, AJ 17, no. 744.

Mrs. Mary L. Colby to Emily C. Judson, April 3, 1848—Newton Centre

My dear Mrs. Judson

I received your letter of the 18th Oct last with very great pleasure, the more perhaps from having looked for it so long. I found it hard to persuade myself that you had really forgotten me and often thought I would write to you and then it occurred to me that you probably had many correspondents who were older friends than myself, and I would not intrude my poor letter upon your notice or take up your valuable time, I am exceedingly gratified by your kind remembrance of us all, and that the recollection of your visit at our house is pleasant to you.[165] It will always be a green spot in my memory if I should live many years. Time has flown rapidly with me since then. I can hardly realize that nearly two years have passed away. A large part of that time my health has been very feeble, but since our removal to the country[166] it has

[161] Dora was a fictional character in one of Emily's stories that was released in fall 1844. The artist Flagg was moved by the story, and N. P. Willis commissioned himto do a portrait of her; details of the painting slowly came out. For more information, see the letter dated November 20, 1844, from N. P. Willis to Emily E. Chubbuck. The painting was shipped in the Christmas season, and Anna Maria Anable wrote to Emily on December 30, 1844, that they had retrieved it from the express office. Apparently, between the time Willis had received the painting and brought it to the express office, it had been on display, and he told Emily that thousands had seen and admired it.

[162] Nora Westcott was one of the girls from the Utica Female Academy. On January 17, 1847, Anna Maria Anable noted that Nora was in Mississippi, though dying of consumption. In November 1849, Sarah Hinckley spoke of her death.

[163] Emily and Adoniram returned to Maulmain from Rangoon on September 5, 1847.

[164] This is a reference either to Henry Judson (almost six years old) or Edward Judson (three years old).

[165] Adoniram and Emily Judson were the guests of Gardner and Mary Colby in the days before they sailed from Boston to Maulmain.

[166] Gardner and Mary Colby moved from their home in Pemberton Square, Boston, to temporary lodgings near the Newton Theological Seminary, and they were waiting to move to a small farm when their house was ready.

improved gradually, and I am now enjoying comparatively good health, this blessing of which I hope I should appreciate more than ever. I wish that you would have written that you were quite well, for surely you need to be if any body [sic]. I wonder how you could have lived through the privations and suffering you experienced at Rangoon[167] and did fondly hope that when your good Husband was returned to Burmah he would escape any more such trials as he has in former times had to pass through but I suppose a Missionary life is always subject to suffering and trials. I feel exceedingly anxious to hear from you again, as I suppose before this you have passed through a season of peculiar trial, which I do hope has resulted favorable in every way.[168] I shall not be at ease about you until I hear that this is the case. I am all prepared to love any little body who may have come for its Mother's sake.

I regret that you did not while in Boston have a better opportunity to visit Newton that you might be able to form some idea of our situation here. The house we now occupy is directly at the foot of the hill on which the Institution[169] stands. But before summer is past I expect our own house will be completed and we shall remove from here and I hope take up a permanent abode on a farm, not that I expect to make butter and cheese or be in a degree a good farmer's wife. I have no fancy for country life myself, but my husband and children are so much happier than when living in the city that I cannot but prefer it, and I must acknowledge that I find a great many pleasant things about it now that I am here. Our Society is very choice though limited. In the Institution my husband and I feel a deep interest. A fine class of sixteen students entered last autumn and the Family and friends of the Institution feel encouraged to hope that there will soon be a better state of things than has been known for a long time past. The students have interested themselves more than usual in the village church and Sabbath school and have made our prayer meetings very interesting. About twenty conversions have occurred among the children, and young people, and the religious state of the congregation is very pleasant. Our excellent pastor Mr. S. F. Smith[170] I think the Doct. will remember, and if you would form an idea of the quality of the preaching we are favored with, you can do so by reading a sermon entitled the "Missionary covenant" published in the Feb. and March number of the *Missionary Magazine*. We are truly favored with great priv-

[167] Emily and Adoniram Judson were in Rangoon, Burmah, from mid-February until the end of August 1847, and Emily's letters from that time are filled with wonderful stories of their lives, trials, and privations.

[168] This is a reference to Emily Frances Judson, who was born December 24, 1847.

[169] Newton Theological Institution. Gardner Colby was on the board of this seminary and of the American Baptist Missionary Union.

[170] An ordained Baptist minister, Samuel Francis Smith served as the pastor of the First Baptist Church of Waterville, Maine, and professor of modern languages at Waterville College. He became the editor of the *Christian Review* and then the editor of the publications of the American Baptist Missionary Union. He held the latter position at the time of his correspondence with Emily C. Judson. On April 8, 1852, Rev. Smith wrote to Emily, offering to proofread her book, *An Olio of Domestic Verses*, before publication. The manuscript was submitted in May and published in August. Rev. Smith lived in Newton Center, Massachusetts, and was a friend of Gardner Colby. He was the author of the national hymn "My Country, 'tis of Thee," the great missionary hymn "The Morning Light Is Breaking," and numerous other hymns, poems, and publications.

ileges and ought to be more grateful than we are, and humbled that we improve them so poorly.

I had a letter a little while since from Miss Anable[171] in which she speaks of having studied hard all winter

[Written in the right margin of the address page:] with the view of establishing a school somewhere next fall. I wish for your sake, that it might be in your neighborhood wherever that may be. I am not surprised that you want her with you, and I am sure should she propose herself to the Board my husband would do everything he could to accomplish your wishes. She is truly an excellent girl, and during her stay with us last summer[172] I learned to love her very much. Last week I received a paper from Utica in which I saw the death of Dea. Sheldon.[173] He has soon followed his companion, their meeting doubtless was joyful. I was exceedingly interested in them when at Utica more than a year

[Written in the left margin of the address page:] since and have often thought how happily they seemed to be passing down the hill of life together.

I enjoyed a little visit from Sarah Haven[174] a short time since. I presume you have heard through Mrs. Stevens[175] that they move into the country soon. I am very sorry that they find it necessary to do so. Persons of Mr. and Mrs. Haven's years do not generally enjoy such changes, but I sincerely hope they will realize all their wishes.

[Written in the top margin of page 1 across the text:] You see I have filled my sheet and must soon close. I hear very pleasing accounts of Abby Ann[176] and the little boys.[177] Mr. Swaim[178] spoke most-decidedly of Elnathan's conversion when

[171] See vol. 1, "Cast of Characters," s.v. "Anable, Anna Maria."

[172] Thinking of possible missionary service, Anna Maria Anable spent summer 1847 in Boston, Massachusetts, taking some very painful medical treatments to correct a skeletal condition with her spine and shoulder. See her letter of June 19, 1847, for a description of these treatments. On April 26, 1848, she wrote, "My shoulder is quite strong and my shape is very much improved."

[173] See vol. 1, "Cast of Characters," s.v. "Sheldon, Deacon Asa and Isabell Low."

[174] Sarah Haven was the sister of Elizabeth Stevens, missionary to Burmah and colleague of Adoniram and Emily Judson. There are seven letters to Emily in the correspondence from her.

[175] See vol. 1, "Cast of Characters," s.v. "Stevens, Elizabeth 'Bessie.'"

[176] Abby Ann Judson, the first daughter and oldest child of Adoniram and Sarah Hall Boardman Judson, was born September 26, 1835. She saw her mother die on the Isle of St. Helena as they returned to the United States from Burmah. Just before leaving for Burmah with Emily, Adoniram Judson placed Abby Ann at Bradford Academy for her education. The family of Ann Hasseltine Judson was generous to Abby Ann and supportive of her interests and her future. On October 15, 1851, Abby Ann started a course of study at the Misses Anable's School in Philadelphia, and in fall 1853, she moved to New York City to take a teaching position in the home of Mrs. Maria Brown, a former missionary to Siam. She enjoyed a warm relationship with Emily, and her letters show that the two could speak freely with each other.

[177] At this time Adoniram "Pwen" or "Addy" Judson was eleven years old; his brother Elnathan "Elly" Judson was almost ten. They lived in Worcester, Massachusetts, with Dr. and Mrs. Calvin Newton.

[178] The Reverend Doctor Samuel Swaim was born in Pemberton, New Jersey, in June 1809. He finished his college courses at Brown University and then entered Newton Theological Institution. He taught college studies in Granville, Ohio, before receiving a call as pastor of the First Baptist Church in Worcester, Massachusetts. In October 1851, just as she was returning to America, Dr. Swaim wrote Emily about the possible baptism of Elnathan. He spoke of Elnathan's coming to faith and of his meeting with the church requesting baptism, and he was obviously trying to schedule this important event at a time when Emily could be present.

here sometime since. I was very happy to hear it, and trust we may soon hear the same of the others.

Mother[179] has been spending the winter with her daughter in Danvers though she has occasionally made me short visits—her health is very good. My Sister Fanny has also been away with my Brothers and Sisters in Brooklyn, N.Y. so that I have been almost alone this winter. My husband and children write with me in most affectionate regards for yourself and husband. Remember me kindly to Miss Lillybridge[180] and ask her if she cannot write me one little note. I should be so happy to hear from her. Please also to give my love to Mrs. ( ) Binney[181] and all in Maulmain who remember me. Be kind enough to write again when you can take time and you will very much gratify your warm friend

M. L. Colby

[Written in the left margin of page 1 and across the text:] P.S. I had almost forgotten to thank you for the pretty volume[182] I rec'd from F. F.[183] Be assured I read it eagerly and with delight both for the sake of the Subject and the Author and as far as I hear of it, it give [sic] universal pleasure. Perhaps if I were writing to some persons I should make many apologies for this letter, but as it is to yourself I shall make none but send it as it is begging you to remember that my heart loves you, and nothing would give me more pleasure than to serve you in every possible way.

Yours

M. L. Colby

Source: American Baptist Historical Society, AJ 15, no. 631.

Anna Maria Anable to Emily Frances Judson,[184] April 25, 1848—Utica

My dear little niece Fanny

Your letter dated Dec. 24th reached me this morning, and could you begin to know with how much anxiety I have awaited this fine intelligence from your dear little self you would know how very welcome your letter was. Let me first congrat-

[179] Mrs. Sarah Colby was the mother of Gardner Colby. See her letter of September 1, 1847.

[180] See vol. 1, "Cast of Characters," s.v. "Lillybridge, Lydia." See also "A Timeline of the Life and Mission of Lydia Lillybridge Simons."

[181] Juliette Binney arrived in Burmah in April 1844. Her husband was Joseph Binney, who opened the Karen Theological School in Maulmain for training indigenous pastors for the Burmese Church. They both worked in establishing general education possibilities for the Burmese people. She returned to the United States in 1850 because of her health. He returned in 1859, moving the seminary to Rangoon.

[182] Fanny Forester, *Memoir of Sarah B. Judson, Member of the American Mission to Burmah* (New York: L. Colby and Company, 1848).

[183] Emily Chubbuck wrote under the *nom de plume* Fanny Forester. Asked about it once, she said, "Would anyone buy a book written by Emily E. Chubbuck?"

[184] See the letters from "Emily Frances" to "Aunt Anna Maria" on December 24, 1847, and January 1, 2, 3, and 13, 1848.

ulate you on the composition of your letter, so remarkable for so young a Miss—and next upon the kindness of heart you manifested in telling me all about your dear Mama, for you know of course that I am deeply interested in what concerns her. I see at a glance that you are a prodigy and bound to make a sensation in the world you have so lately entered. Thinking the Utica Fem. Acad. will hardly furnish facilities for accomplish( ) so bright a little being as yourself, I intend opening a new school in the city of Philadelphia,[185] in which you can every possible advantage [sic] which the country affords for the further development of your talents. Many thanks for the pains you were at to copy those beautiful verses of your dear Mama,[186] and also for the lock of hair you sent me. When I get to Philadelphia I shall have it made into a little ring which I shall wear until you come to see me your own dear little self. Do you know darling I can imagine just how you look, for we have little Charley Gratiot[187] with us who is only one day older than you are. He too is a remarkable child, which is not at all strange, for was he not born in the Academy? Remember me affectionately to your dear papa, mama and Aunt Lydia.[188] Your loving Aunt

Anna M.

Source: American Baptist Historical Society, AJ 13, no. 494.

Miss Cynthia Sheldon to Emily C. Judson, April 26, 1848

My dear dear friends—

The good news contained in the *pet* letter to day [sic], has given us more real pleasure than can be expressed[189]—we will thank God together—and invoke his protecting care hence forward [sic] for the dear one—I am delighted that you call her Fanny—and the poetry dear E.[190]—do say it may be published some where [sic] when you write again—and now tell the good people—Sadie, Aunty, all, named as guests and friends of the wondering prodigy—that Aunt C.[191] now feels sure the Mother is among civilized people—Anna M.[192] is telling you all about her Philadel-

[185] In letters to Emily, Anna Maria and Cynthia Sheldon spoke of establishing a school. To this point, Anna Maria had been talking of Baltimore; this is the first indication that the school would be in Philadelphia.

[186] This was the poem "My Bird" that Emily Judson had written on January 1, 1848.

[187] Charley Gratiot, son of Anne and Charles Gratiot, was born December 23, 1847, a day prior to the birth of Emily Frances Judson. Anne Gratiot was a Sheldon cousin, and at this time the family was living with the Anable-Sheldon family at the Utica Female Academy.

[188] See vol. 1, "Cast of Characters," s.v. "Lillybridge, Lydia." See also "A Timeline of the Life and Mission of Lydia Lillybridge Simons."

[189] This was the letter announcing the birth of Emily Frances Judson on December 24, 1847.

[190] Emily wrote the poem "My Bird" on January 1, 1848.

[191] See vol. 1, "Cast of Characters," s.v. "Sheldon, Miss Cynthia."

[192] See vol. 1, "Cast of Characters," s.v. "Anable, Anna Maria."

phia enterprise[193]—I am sure it will gladden your heart to know the prospect for a change—the great change to our family dear E. has made this house so desolate to me that I do feel thankful to God for this opening in providence—after dear father was gone[194]—my mind was soon made up—and the 2d day of April I left home—spent one night with Urania[195]—two days in new York visiting the most popular schools—merely to see the style of furniture etc.—on Sat. arrived at P. Mr. G.[196] met me at the wharf—they were all kindness—just three years before do you remember our landing there for the first time to each of us[197]—Mrs. G.[198] was all kindness to me—her four boys are remarkably fine children—the youngest 20 months only—but quite the man—Mrs. Robarts[199] was very attentive—Mr. R. was quite sick at that time—Well, many had been engaged for our removal—and I found them engaged too in making up a box for "dear Dr. and Mrs. Judson"—Mrs. Robarts told me all about her *feelings*[200]—and how they had changed—the Misses Eerp [sic] enquired [sic] kindly after you—They are in deep affliction—a dear brother is in the Insane Hospital—Mrs. E. had been with him to England and just returned

[193] After thinking of missionary service, Anna Maria Anable was processing a lot of information. After picking up new responsibilities at the Utica Female Academy, she was becoming aware of her love of and her gift for teaching. Her mother and her Aunt Cynthia must begin to slow down as the burdens of the academy were increasingly too heavy for them. Only by going on her own could she achieve the financial stability that would enable her to support her aunt and her mother in the future. Speaking first of going to Baltimore, the final decision was made for Philadelphia, and by the end of August 1848, Miss Anable was writing from Philadelphia in her new home and her new school. From an April 26, 1848, letter, it is apparent that Miss Cynthia Sheldon had an important role in choosing Philadelphia as their new home.

[194] See vol. 1, "Cast of Characters," s.v. "Sheldon, Deacon Asa and Isabell Low." A letter from Mary Colby to Emily dated April 3, 1848, tells of his death.

[195] See vol. 1, "Cast of Characters," s.v. "Sheldon, Urania."

[196] Following several successful pastorates, the Reverend A. D. Gillette was the founding pastor of the flourishing Eleventh Baptist Church in Philadelphia in 1839. With his wife Hannah and several children (they would eventually have six), he graciously opened their home to Emily Chubbuck when she came to Philadelphia at the end of March 1845 for her health. The connection had been made through Miss Cynthia Sheldon, a family friend of Mr. Gillette and his parents. A prominent Baptist, Mr. Gillette journeyed to Boston in December 1845 to accompany Adoniram Judson to Philadelphia for meetings, and on Christmas Day, he introduced Dr. Judson to Emily Chubbuck with the hope that Fanny Forester could be persuaded to write the memoir of Sarah Hall Boardman Judson. A. D. Gillette and his wife Hannah remained valued and trusted friends, not only with Emily, but with the Sheldon and Anable families. He moved from Philadelphia to New York in 1852.

[197] On March 29, 1845, Miss Sheldon and Emily arrived in Philadelphia as Emily sought a milder climate for her health.

[198] Hannah Gillette was the wife of the Reverend A. D. Gillette, pastor of the Eleventh Baptist Church in Philadelphia.

[199] Mr. and Mrs. W. S. Robarts were active in Philadelphia Baptist circles. They were frequent visitors to the home of the Reverend and Mrs. A. D. Gillette and later to the Misses Anable's School, which Anna Maria Anable and her extended family had started in Philadelphia in 1848. In his biography of his father, Edward Judson mentioned that Adoniram Judson stayed at the. Robarts's home when he came to Philadelphia in December 1845 when he met Emily Chubbuck. A. C. Kendrick said, "(Mr. Gillette and Dr. Judson) arrived in (or out of) due time in Philadelphia, and Dr. Judson was welcomed to the house of Mr. and Mrs. W. S. Robarts, who became warm personal friends, as they were already active friends of the mission cause." (A. C. Kendrick, *The Life and Letters of Mrs. Emily C. Judson* [New York: Sheldon and Company, 1862] 142.) In 1846, with the engagement of Adoniram Judson and Emily Chubbuck, the correspondence indicates some hard feelings toward Mrs. Robarts for comments disparaging the coming marriage and missionary service. This is found in Emily's letter to Adoniram dated February 6, 1846; Mrs. Robarts seemed to be accusing Emily of worldliness when all the time, Emily was quick to say, Mrs. Robarts was engaging in the same activity of which she was accused. The correspondence also indicates a satisfactory healing of the relationship. In January 1849, Miss Sheldon told Emily that Mrs. Robarts had placed their daughter Mary in the Misses Anable's School.

[200] Mrs. Robarts said some things following Emily's engagement to Adoniram Judson that had deeply distressed Emily. She judged Emily's Christian character; see the above footnote with its comments on this matter.

without the least benefit—did they live in Girard block when you was [sic] there—if so you may know we have the same kind of house—311 Walnut St.—very near the same range—just below 11th St—the aristocratic part—Schools and boarding houses prohibited in that Section—you may well ask how I come to be favored above others—a kind providence (not to say a lucky star) directed the owner of it a widow to yield—the house was new two years since and vacated by the decease of the owner—Your next dear E. must be directed to the number I have named—I shall write to Mrs. Gillette in the Morn'g telling the good news—for they are all anxiety in that quarter—shall beg them to hurry off the box—

When I was there Mr. Graham[201] had promised $20—we conclude to send your commission to Mrs. Gillette—have her expend that money—and tear up the draft on the board—you must not fail to adjust your account accordingly—Heaven keep you in health—and encircle you and yours with rich blessings—

Yours with great affection

C. Sheldon

P.S. I have just been in Cousin Ann's room[202]—her baby boy is a prodigy[203]—just one day older than Miss Fanny—if I could stand God-Mother's now to both—do not you think they would probably have a *great liking* for each other when in their teens—just learn her [sic] to say Charley Gratiot as one step.—

Mr. Corey[204] is often in he feels sad enough about our going away—his lone life sits very hard on him—he laments his loss in the death of his dear wife most truly—but our Church is now in great prosperity—112 added during the year just closed—15 more are waiting baptism—we can leave the church with less concern than ever before.

Source: American Baptist Historical Society, AJ 20, no. 1000.

Anna Maria Anable to Emily C. Judson, April 26, 1848—Utica

Dear Emily

I was so delighted and agitated when I saw the letter in the Dr.'s hand writing[205] that I could scarcely go on with my Abercrombie class. I did manage to keep quiet however till the lesson was over for somehow I have felt all the time that all would

[201] See vol. 1, "Cast of Characters," s.v. "Graham, George."

[202] See vol. 1, "Cast of Characters," s.v. "Gratiot, Charles and Ann."

[203] Ibid.

[204] See vol. 1, "Cast of Characters," s.v. "Corey, The Reverend D. G."

[205] See the letter from Adoniram Judson dated December 24, 1847, January 1, 2, 3, and 13, 1848.

go well with you. I am surprised that you have not rec'd my letters yet. For fear you have not—I will tell you now that I was very much improved by my visit to Boston.[206] My shoulder is quite strong and my shape is very much improved. To return to little Fanny[207]—remember you promised her to me Nemmy,[208] and one of these days I am going to claim her.[209] Last month I did not write for we were so engrossed with family matters immediately after dear Grandpa's death[210] that I wrote no letters. He was seized with another paralysis while Aunt U.[211] was on her last visit here. The day preceding his attack he had been out to church, and enjoyed the services very much. He came home a good deal exhausted and passed a restless night—but the next morning was as well as usual until this attack. He lay in a state of stupor from Monday till the next Sabbath morn'g.

You cannot conceive how we miss him. Their room looks so desolate now.

Grandpa's death has made a great change in our plans for the future. For a year or more I have been anxious to have Aunt Cynthia[212] give up the charge of this great establishment, and now she has decided to do it. All our plans are fixed. We have rented a beautiful house in Philadelphia—311 Walnut St. and in Sep. we are to commence a school. I will send our circular when it is published and from that you will see what we design to do. This Ninny[213] don't [sic] mean to be second to any one [sic] in what ever she undertakes if she can help it. You will see at once that Phil. will afford every thing [sic] which we cannot supply ourselves. Harriet[214] will come home and take the French department for she speaks it like a Parisian the French say of her. She has been in a family where she spoke nothing but French for two years.

[206] See vol. 1, "Cast of Characters," s.v. "Anable, Anna Maria."

[207] See vol. 1, "Cast of Characters," s.v. "Judson, Emily Frances."

[208] "Nem" or "Nemmy" was a name of endearment given to Emily by a small group of her intimate friends at the Utica Female Academy. Anna Maria Anable was "Ninny."

[209] Sadly, this statement is prophetic. After the death of Emily Judson in June 1854, the six-and-a-half-year-old Emily Frances Judson went to live with her "Aunty Anna Maria" in Philadelphia, and Anna Maria Anable raised her.

[210] See vol. 1, "Cast of Characters," s.v. "Sheldon, Deacon Asa and Isabell Low." In an April 3, 1848, letter, Mrs. Mary Colby reported that she had read of his death in the Utica paper.

[211] See vol. 1, "Cast of Characters," s.v. "Sheldon, Urania."

[212] See vol. 1, "Cast of Characters," s.v. "Sheldon, Miss Cynthia."

[213] "Ninny" was a name of endearment given to Anna Maria Anable by her most intimate friends at the Utica Female Academy. Emily was "Nemmy."

[214] See vol. 1, "Cast of Characters," s.v. "Anable, Harriet."

[215] Mary Juliet Anable was born February 18, 1830, in Bethlehem, Albany County, New York, one of nine children born to Alma and Joseph Anable. She went to New Orleans with Hatty in 1847, but she returned home early in March 1848, and by 1849, she was working with Anna Maria in the Misses Anable's School in Philadelphia. Writing in March 1849, Hatty said of Mary, "She paints and draws, speaks French, plays the piano, sings, dances and is our mathematician. What should we ever do without her? She laughs from morning till night, and it is really refreshing to be with her." On December 26, 1860, she was married to Pierre Jacques Darey, the officiating minister being the Rev. Dr. Eliphalet Nott, her uncle. Mary died at the age of sixty-eight on April 20, 1898, in Ottawa, Ontario, Canada.

Mary[215] returned from the South last month. She has grown very graceful, and has been away just long enough to rub off the rusticity of early girlhood without losing any of its freshness. Fanny[216] has gone to Willow brook on Owasco lake with Mrs. Martin. She is to take charge of her children for the Summer. She writes that she is delightfully situated. It is one of the pleasantest county seats in Central New York, built and improved by Gov. Throop, Mr. Martin's uncle, who made it his hobby for years. We shall all come together I hope in Sept. and won't we be happy? It has been the darling wish of my life to get mother[217] away from this place where she would not have to work so hard. I am afraid the plan is too good to succeed.

Do you ask where my Missionary fever has gone?[218] I do not suppose I sh'd ever have thought I could engage in such an undertaking as the present had I not first made up my mind to do any thing [sic] and every thing [sic] that came to hand. I do not what they are going to do here [sic]. Jane[219] is evidently glad to get affairs of the school in her own hands, as she probably will. She thinks she can make money and it is a little humbling to her ambitions to think that she is hired by Aunt C.

Source: American Baptist Historical Society, AJ 13, no. 493.

Miss Mary Anna Longstreth to Emily C. Judson, May 1848—Philadelphia

My dear friend,

I can not [sic] allow the present opportunity to pass without sending thee a few lines, expressions of my affectionate interest and sympathy, and especially to thank thee for thy kind remembrance in sending me the delightful Memoir of Sarah B. Judson which is doubly valuable as thy gift. She was, indeed, a gem of the purest brilliancy; and it must have been a pleasing, as well as a mournful task to study and delineate her character, and preserve for the contemplation and imitation of future

[216] Fanny Anable was one of nine children born to Joseph and Alma Anable and was a niece of Miss Cynthia Sheldon and Mrs. Urania Sheldon Nott. The correspondence indicates that in April 1845 she was away from home studying and taking music lessons. These spring letters indicate that she was in Philadelphia, working in the home of and with the family of the Reverend A. D. Gillette. See Miss Sheldon's letter to Emily of November 30, 1845, in which she spoke of all that Fanny was doing to improve herself in the field of music, but also her concern for Fanny's interest in the party life and the "vanitie" which surround her." A March 30, 1847, letter from Anna Maria Anable told of Fanny's conversion following her grandmother's death. In September 1847, she was listed as one of the teachers at the Utica Female Academy. Fanny became a teacher with her sisters in the Misses Anable's School in Philadelphia.

[217] See vol. 1, "Cast of Characters," s.v. "Sheldon, Alma and Joseph Hubbell."

[218] For about a year and a half after Emily's marriage to Adoniram Judson, Anna Maria spoke of the possibility of having a call to missions and joining Adoniram and Emily in Burmah. On March 31, 1847, Sarah Bell Wheeler said that Anna Maria was a devoted Christian, and she thought that one day she would go to Burmah. She obviously put a lot of prayer and thought into the matter. The painful medical treatments she underwent in summer 1847 were likely intended to improve her general health (see her letter of June 19, 1847). In summer 1848, she decided that her call was to remain a teacher, and Anna Maria moved to Philadelphia and opened the Misses Anable's School with her family where she raised Emily Francis Judson. Anna Maria remained there until her death.

[219] See vol. 1, "Cast of Characters," s.v. "Kelly, Miss Jane."

times the recollection of her loveliness and Christian excellence, which "like a dew drop, sparkled, was exhaled, and went to Heaven." To succeed two such women as Ann and Sarah Judson must have felt somewhat formidable to thee—(although perfect love casteth out fear) but I must confess I trembled for thee, dear Emily, soon after the commencement of thy missionary life, when I found that the newspapers were publishing parts of thy letters which could not have been intended for the public eye, and I thought it was very unkind in the Editors—especially as thou wast so remote as not to be able to know of such publication and have an opportunity to explain thyself more fully. I can not [sic] now recall the expressions, but the idea conveyed, was that thou hadst not a missionary spirit, in the ordinary acceptation of the term—and other remarks which might be construed by some as an admission that in going to Burmah thou was not activated by an ardent love for souls. I was of course unwilling to think that such was the case, though such an impression was made upon some minds—parts of letters often convey a very imperfect idea of the writer's meaning. For it seems to me that *all* who really love their Saviour [sic] *must be imbued with a missionary spirit*—must love the souls for whom he died—and though duties plainly assigned to them by Providence prevent many from going in person to the benighted heathen with the glad tidings of salvation, the hearts of all true Christians must expand in love, and the *Spirit* to go, if they have not the ability.

It is delightful to think of the comfort and solace thy society must be to thy beloved husband—he must so need the influence of a buoyant, sunny spirit, as the shades of evening begin to gather around him—and it seems as if the hand of Providence had been remarkably with him in selecting all the partners of his cares, anxieties and labours [sic]—each one so peculiarly adapted for the period of his life during which her lot was united with his—so qualified to share its trials, and sooth his sorrows. And his dear little boys[220]—how much they must enjoy thy maternal kindness.

We have just heard of the arrival of thy little babe[221]—and doubt not it is felt to be a treasure.

I thought I could not send thee any thing [sic] more useful than thread and needles and articles of that kind—which are probably very dear in Burmah. The Memoir of Margaret Mercer will interest thee, I hope. Please accept it and *Gurney's Hymns* with my kindest wishes and the assurance of my very affection interest.

Sincerely thy friend,

M. A. Longstreth

Source: American Baptist Historical Society, AJ 17, no. 768.

[220] See vol. 1, "Cast of Characters," s.v. "Judson, Henry Hall" and "Judson, Edward."

[221] Emily Frances Judson, the daughter of Adoniram and Emily Chubbuck Judson, was born December 24, 1847.

Emily C. Judson to Anna Maria Anable, May 20, 1848—Maulmain

Dear Ninny,[222]

It makes me sad to think how you must have worked and sweated over these nice things that you have sent me; and moreover what a draft you made upon your purse. Blessings on you, darling, for thinking so much of poor good-for-nothing Nemmy[223]—it is a sad thing to be away off here, where it takes months for any news to reach us; and a sweet thing to be remembered by those left behind.

The shawl is a perfect beauty and precisely what I want. It is much prettier than Mrs. Stevens.[224] But what do you think?—that missionary babies can afford to wear so much cloth in their frocks—that is a length. I shall cut the shirts in the middle and make two of each! We got a small box from Roxbury[225]—the children and I, and I had several pretty things from Sarah Haven,[226] a handsome bag from Mrs. Kilham, a collar from Mrs. Lincoln[227] and some baby frocks from Mrs. Colby.[228]

I shall write a note for the Mr. Anderson[229] of yours, which please seal and forward to him. I have taken a great fancy, and sh'd like him exceedingly for a cousin-in-law.

I am writing in the red wrapper you made. Oh, it is *so* soft, and *so* comfortable, and *so* nice! But there is a great struggle in my mind about it, for baby is wanting it dre'fully. I *shall* be obliged to cut it up notwithstanding doc. protests, if I can't make a dicker with Mrs. Stevens. She has four yards for her three babies (her sixth child

[222] "Ninny" was a name of endearment given to Anna Maria Anable by her most intimate friends at the Utica Female Academy. Emily was "Nemmy."

[223] "Nem" or "Nemmy" was a name of endearment given to Emily by a small group of her intimate friends at the Utica Female Academy. Anna Maria Anable was "Ninny."

[224] See vol. 1, "Cast of Characters," s.v. "Stevens, Elizabeth 'Bessie.'"

[225] Roxbury was a suburb of Boston, Massachusetts. Dr. and Mrs. Edward Bright lived there; Mr. Bright was the corresponding secretary of the American Baptist Missionary Union. Mrs. Bright was active with the women of the local Baptist church in support of missions.

[226] See vol. 1, "Cast of Characters," s.v. "Haven, Sarah L." She took an active interest in missions, and especially in the affairs of her sister and family. In 1852, when Emily was living in Providence, Rhode Island, working with Dr. Francis Wayland on the Judson Memoir, Mrs. Haven was one of her visitors.

[227] Mrs. Lincoln was the wife of Joshua Lincoln, a prominent Baptist layman and a partner in Gould, Kendall and Lincoln. Anna Maria Anable boarded with Mr. and Mrs. Lincoln when she stayed in Boston in summer 1847 for medical treatments. Mrs. Lincoln was a strong supporter of missions.

[228] Mary Colby was the wife of Gardner Colby, a prominent businessman and active Baptist layman. Mr. Colby was a member of the Board of the American Baptist Missionary Union and an avid supporter of the missionary movement. In a letter after they sailed from Boston to Burmah, Emily mentions the extravagant hospitality extended to them in early July as they waited for the *Faneuil Hall* to embark. Adoniram and then Emily stayed with the Colby family quite frequently over the years. Mrs. Colby was an active correspondent with Emily and supported her, her family, and the cause of missions.

[229] Anna Maria Anable says that Mr. Anderson was a professor whom she met at a social gathering at Gardner and Mary Colby's in summer 1847. She became enamored with him and said that she thought she was losing her heart to him. He used the stories of Fanny Forester to teach religious topics to his classes, and he collaborated with Anna Maria on sending some books to Emily. See Anna Maria's letters of August 25 and September 27, 1847. In her letter of August 27, 1848, she says that she has heard nothing from him since their "desperate flirtation." She then mentions that she has heard of his engagement and brings this up again on November 27, 1848. He did send Emily some books, and the reference here is to a "thank you" note that Emily sends to Anna Maria to forward. In the November letter, Anna Maria says that she has sent the letter on.

is about coming on the carpet) and I think a yard apiece is a great plenty in these sea'ce [sic] times. At any rate, I shall try hard before I spoil a little the nicest contrivance for a body cover that I ever owned yet. Well, darlin' keep a-thinking of me, though the subject be a bad one; and one day—do you know, *one day*—sometime in the near hereafter we shall live together again.

Adieu,

Nemmy

Source: Hanna family files.

Emily C. Judson to Mrs. Mary Colby, May 20, 1848—Maulmain

My very dear Mrs. Colby,

I am sure baby[230] thanks you for the very nice things you sent although she is so cross today that I must own she don't [sic] look very thankful. I have been trying for the last two hours to get her asleep so that I could write you and she now lies in the cradle but will be still only as I swing it with my foot. She is a very stout healthy child but is commencing her teething, and moreover for three or four days has been troubled with sore eyes that must excuse her ill humor.

I had almost given up all hope of being remembered by you when your welcome package arrived. Now I am still more greedy and want a letter. I cannot picture you in your new home, and Mr. Judson is sure there is no place on earth like Pemberton Square.[231] Do you have pleasant society, and do the children love racing in the fields catching bees and butterflies, knocking off thistleheads, making dandelion curls and such fine sport? Please tell me everything, for didn't I once love weeks at your house; and don't I feel too grateful for your kindness, not to want to know all about you hereafter? You who go on every day making new friends, feeling new interests in your great whirlpool of America, cannot imagine how we are constantly turning back to the past, for all we have now to love or interest (except our work) is within our own walls. Oh how we talk over the times we had at your house, recounting every little anecdote, dwelling on it with pleasure and quitting it with a sigh.

And now my dear Mrs. Colby let me tell you what you have a right above others to know, how dearly I love being a missionary. It is a sweet work a glorious one too, and God has been far better to me than my fears. When I left America I did not dare make any professions of interest, for I was afraid I might afterwards fail, but if

230 See vol. 1, "Cast of Characters," s.v. "Judson, Emily Frances."

231 Gardner and Mary Colby lived in a home at Pemberton Square, Boston, where Adoniram and Emily stayed before leaving for Burmah. From Pemberton Square, they moved to Newton Centre and lived for a brief period in temporary housing at the bottom of the hill from the Newton Theological Institution. They lived there until they could move into their new house, which was built on the small farm that they had purchased.

I wore the crown of Victoria, I would lay it down for what is now within my reach I know I would. Oh I was so happy in Rangoon notwithstanding our various trials for I felt as each suffering came "this is undoubtedly, this is decidedly for the sake of Christ." Then too my husband (is it silly for me to praise him) is so much better than I at first knew, so prayerful and so self-sacrificing, I should be very wicked not to love the work he loves so much. The mission at present is in a very discouraging state to all outward view, but we are not discouraged and Christians at home who live by faith will not be discouraged for we know who will at last gain the victory.

Did I once tell you I would write you about my housekeeping. Well, what with training and teaching my little ones,[232] having them always with me from morning until night, studying Burmese etc. I don't keep house much, and what I do is often a very homely fashion. But I manage to get on. In fact I have discovered that many things I had been accustomed to count on among the necessaries of life are my luxuries and so we do without them.

Please give my love to your sister and your mother when you see her, and remember me most kindly to Mr. Colby.[233] I have his face as it appeared at the wharf the day we left so distinctly—and yours too—complete daguerreotypes. I hope you pray for us—do! And love us at least a little.

Most affec'y

Emily Judson

Source: Hanna family files.

Mr. Charles B. Stout[234] to Emily C. Judson, May 21, 1848—New York

My Dear Friend

Your favor of Feb. 21st was received a week since, and has been read repeatedly and with pleasure. We learned some months ago that you had left Rangoon and your reasons for so doing. It has worked for good, however, and God be praised. I

[232] Henry Hall Judson, almost six years old; Edward Judson, three and a half years old; and Emily Frances Judson, five months old.

[233] A prominent businessman, Gardner Colby and his family lived in Pemberton Square in Boston before moving "to the country," Newton Centre, Massachusetts. Mr. Colby was a member of the Board of the American Baptist Missionary Union and an avid supporter of the missionary movement. In a letter after they sailed from Boston to Burmah, Emily mentions the extravagant hospitality extended to them in early July as they waited for the *Faneuil Hall* to embark. Adoniram and Emily stayed with the Colby family frequently.

[234] Mr. Charles Stout first wrote to Emily on January 1, 1847. He received a letter from her in July the previous year as she was leaving Boston; apparently, it went to his wife, but it was inadvertently addressed to "Mr. Stout" instead of "Mrs." He identified himself as one who was interested in missions and as the secretary of the Young Men's Mission Society of the Stanton Street Baptist Church. His letters in 1852, of which there were three, had to do with helping to secure materials that would be helpful to the writing of the memoir. "Charles B. Stout was born at Flemington, N. J, in 1824. spent his youth in New Brunswick, became an active member of the Stanton Street Baptist church, New York; has been for years connected with the First or with the Remsen Avenue church in New Brunswick. He is the author of several books which have had an extensive sale; was one of the first to use the blackboard in Sunday-schools, and is widely known in the Sunday-school work as an able speaker and contributor to the magazines" (William Cathcart, *The Baptist Encyclopaedia* [Philadelphia: Louis H. Everts, 1881] 1114).

judge from your letter that it will not be prudent to return until there is a change in the government, or its officers. Meantime I doubt not, you labour [sic] as cheerfully at Maulmain as you would in the capital itself. "*So busy*" you say, but do you not rejoice that it is your Master's business? The busier the better I sometimes think. My mind frequently follows you in your wanderings, and I have not ceased to pray that the blessing of him who "giveth the increase" may accompany you. Jesus is with you, and as Harriet Newell[235] said "It is sweet to be a stranger and a wanderer for such a friend as this." Labour [sic] on Dear sister and the seed thou sowest, water with thy tears; God is faithful, and will give thee answer to thy prayers.

"Wait in hope—the morning dawneth;
When the night is gone;
And a peaceful rest awaits thee
When thy work is done."[236]

Employed gloriously thou art, but my poor efforts deserve not a name. But there must be hewers of wood and drawers of water; as well as preachers and physicians. And it is some consolation to think, that if not in the fore-front of the battle, we sustain those who *are* there. Let me hold on then with a firm grasp till death shall unnerve the arm, and palsy the willing hand.

A Missionary in Arracan (Bro. Ingalls)[237] thus writes—"I am more and more persuaded that the church wants light"; so I am not alone in my opinion. We are not destitute of intelligence from heathen lands, but that we have is not always of the precise character we could wish. In view of these facts, I called for information, and you will pardon me for naming it again. "Let us do what we can (Amen!) and *do it in the dark*." This noble sentiment is alike worthy of the cause and of the writer; but there is *light ahead*, and I fondly believe that a better and brighter day is to dawn upon the world. For this I have both laboured [sic] and prayed, and with this hope before me pledged myself to the Heaven blessed cause of Missions. The "Columbian"[238] for June says

"Ere last year's moon had left the sky,
A birdling sought my Indian nest"

[235] Harriet Atwood Newell was a longtime friend of Ann Hasseltine. They met at Bradford Academy some ten years before Adoniram Judson and Samuel Newell appeared on the scene. Harriet married Samuel Newell, and they were part of that small group of missionaries who embarked on the ship *Caravan* from Salem Harbor in 1812.

[236] This is a poem written by Mrs. Margaret Bailey. For many years in the mid-nineteenth century, Mrs. Bailey was the publisher of *The Youth's Monthly Visitor.*

[237] See vol. 1, "Cast of Characters," s.v. "Ingalls, The Reverend Lovel."

[238] See vol. 1, "Places, Events, Organizations, and Magazines," s.v. "*Columbian* Magazine."

—and the city papers have chronicled the same event as occurring in M. Nov. 24, 1847.[239] Long may the mother live to shelter her immortal bird! Please tell us how that good old soldier Dr. Judson is, and how employed. I should be happy to hear what success attends the labour [sic] of Sister Lillybridge,[240] and what above all things ( )eded for Burmah? The "Memoir" of Mrs. S. B. Judson[241] has been sometime before the public and I believe will accomplish much good. Men, and women too, are made better by reading such books; and, what is very desirable, they are called to consider the trials of those who "go far hence to the gentiles."

The American Tract Society has recently published "Thoughts on Missions" by the late Rev. Sheldon Bibble, fourteen years missionary in the Sandwich Is. Soul stirring that they are too, and good must follow their perusal. 100 copies of the work were sold during the meeting of the Am. Bap. Miss. Union at N. Troy, and numbers are circulating in the city. As you will see the official account of the Union meeting, I will only say here, that it was a blessed and an encouraging one. I think the home work will be prosecuted with renewed energy and increased zeal.

The little Society[242] whose servant I am, has given, since Jan. 1848 $200 to the Union, $50 to the Am. Bap. Home Miss. Soc. and fifty more are soon to be paid over to the latter Society. And this is in a church, which five years since contributed but fifty dollars for missions of any kind. The contribution this year will not fall short of $500. I trust you will see in this ground for encouragement; if all the churches in the land were to make the same advance in the next five years, the mission treasuries would soon be filled—then indeed would the wilderness and the solitary place be glad for us, and the desert rejoice and blossom as the rose!

In "thoughts on Missions" it is strongly urged that laymen go to heathen lands, farmers, mechanics, civilians, and teachers, and the reasons given are worthy of consideration. Permit me to ask, what, in your opinion would be the result if six Christian families, comprising 12 or 15 individuals, filled with the love of Christ and ardently desiring to promote his glory and the good of souls, what if these at their own expense should come to M. or any other station? Would it add to the strength of the Mission—would it be possible for the families to support themselves and have much time left to do good? And in view of the loss and gain, think you such a moment is desirable? I have proposed the question, because you are on the ground, and have greater facilities for deciding than we at home can possibly have. It looks

[239] These lines begin Emily's "My Bird," a poem written on January 1, 1848, shortly after Emily Frances Judson was born. The date of her birth given here is incorrect; she was born December 24, 1847.

[240] See vol. 1, "Cast of Characters," s.v. "Lillybridge, Lydia." See also "A Timeline of the Life and Mission of Lydia Lillybridge Simons."

[241] Fanny Forester, *Memoir of Sarah B. Judson, Member of the American Mission to Burmah* (New York: L. Colby and Company, 1848).

[242] Mr. Stout was the secretary of the Young Men's Mission Society of the Stanton Street Baptist Church, New York, New York.

to me like a question of some importance and ( ) good may be done in this way, the sooner we know it the better.

It is a bright breezy morning,

"I feel a newer life in every gale;
The winds, that fan the flowers,
And with their welcome breathings fill the sail,
Tell of serener hours;—
Of hours that glide unfelt away
Beneath the sky of May."

Thus singeth a sweet poet[243] of the passing month, and a brother bard characterizes it, as an—

"Emblem of the life to come
And an every-blooming home"

But my narrowing span admonishes me to be brief. Your notes were delivered at the residences of the gifted gentlemen to whom they were addressed as I was unwilling to subject them to the delay of a P.O. delivery. In hope of hearing from you soon again, and praying that God may bless you and yours, I subscribe myself

Yours affectionately

C. B. Stout 185 Allen St. N.Y.

Source: American Baptist Historical Society, AJ 19, no. 887.

Anna Maria Anable to Emily C. Judson, May 28, 1848—Utica

Your letter dear Nemmy[244] containing the particulars of your accouchement came last week just three months after date. Well, I am thankful [sic] you are well over it but I wish you had told me how you are now, or rather I wish I could know. I can see the dear "yittle [sic] Fanny"[245] just as if she was before me—from her own letter to me[246] I can see her whisking about from place to place, cutting up all sorts of pranks, and getting in all sorts of mischief. I guess miss—is, we have had great baby times here this Winter as well as you there. We have had dear little Charley[247]

[243] The above lines are from a poem titled "May" by James Gates Percival. Mr. Stout quoted the first of four stanzas.

[244] "Nem" or "Nemmy" was a name of endearment given to Emily by a small group of her intimate friends at the Utica Female Academy. Anna Maria Anable was "Ninny."

[245] See vol. 1, "Cast of Characters," s.v. "Judson, Emily Frances."

[246] See the letters written by Adoniram Judson in the name of Emily Frances Judson, dated December 24, 1847, and January 1, 2, 3, and 13, 1848.

[247] See vol. 1, "Cast of Characters," s.v. "Gratiot, Charles and Ann."

all Winter (he is just a day older than your Fanny) and now we have Olivia[248] and her little 'Bel—who is some three weeks younger. This last little cherub is the fattest, straightest, healthiest little thing you ever saw—she looks just like Will[249] and of course makes no pretensions to beauty, but she is so smart she attracts more attention than twenty beauties. She is so much stronger than little Charley that, we think she is quite a prodigy. She will sit in her little tub while her mother washes her like a child a year old. Livy is going to spend the Summer with us. She once in a while gets lonesome 'cause Will isn't here, but she is the most sensible cheerful—hearted little thing I know of. Will perfectly dotes on her yet, and I think he showed a deal of courage in letting her make so long a visit. Her mother has been miserable all winter and they thought now while somebody is building a house for them would be a good time to visit. Laura Baldwin is here making a long visit too, and Anna (Fred's wife)[250] has been down from Rome making us a visit of a few days. We expect to have a houseful all Summer, but we have lots of room for their accommodation. We want to see all our friends before we leave this part of the country.[251] Mary[252] has nothing to do but make herself agreeable, and she does that very well. You can hardly imagine what a difference a French toilet makes in the appearance of a girl. Mary is positively handsome with her tall, slender and graceful figure, notwithstanding the freckles which adhere to her as ( ) as of yore. What do you think of our project for Phila—? Does it seem wild to you from the uncertainty attending it? You know I always had a taste for wild things. It is not half so wild as my Missionary project[253] and to my view far more practicable. I am going to wage a war (though without pretending to) against the Roman Catholic French Schools which have abounded so in our century. There is some uncertainty about Hatty's[254] being able to come on by Sept. She has made an engagement with Mad. Roman till Dec. but "never say die" say I, with the ( )—I am great in an emergency you know, but what I shall do in this I have not yet quite discerned. How many things there are just now that I want to tell you, but

[248] Olivia Williams Anable was married to William Stewart Anable, the second child and second son of Joseph and Alma Sheldon Anable. See the letter written by Anna Maria Anable on September 27, 1846. They lived in Sheboygan, Wisconsin, where Will Anable was in charge of a retail store. They had at least two children: Judson, and 'Bel.

[249] Born on November 6, 1816, in Albany, New York, William Stewart Anable was the second child and the second son of Joseph and Alma Sheldon Anable. In an August 31, 1844, letter, Miss Cynthia Sheldon reported to Emily that William had returned home, having "doff'd his sailor garb for age." He married Olivia Williams on September 24, 1846, according to a letter written on September 27 by Anna Maria Anable. They moved to Sheboygan, Wisconsin, where Will opened a store. William died February 9, 1863, in Virginia, California.

[250] Fred Sheldon lived in Rome, New York, where he opened a grocery store. This is likely the next generation to Fred and Martha Sheldon from Troy.

[251] In August, the Anable-Sheldon families moved to Philadelphia, where Anna Maria started the Misses Anable's School. See Miss Cynthia Sheldon's letter of April 26, 1848, about the house at 311 Walnut Street in Philadelphia.

[252] See vol. 1, "Cast of Characters," s.v. "Anable, Miss Mary Juliet."

[253] See vol. 1, "Cast of Characters," s.v. "Anable, Miss Anna Maria." Anna Maria had thought of becoming a missionary and joining Adoniram and Emily in Burmah.

[254] See vol. 1, "Cast of Characters," s.v. "Anable, Harriet."

which I cannot. It is just as well for you that I cannot, for my head is full of plans, and Grammar and Arithmetic. After stuffing it with mental and Moral Philosophy all Winter, I have concluded to rely on my own mentals—and morals, and study only the elements. Bah! I must write about something besides myself. The women folks must have some thing [sic] or other to egotize [sic] about. If it is not our house, our husband and our babies, it will be our school, our pupils and our plans. Do you suppose Nemmy we shall ever have any of those grand long talks we used to have. I do. Won't you one of these days be bringing little Fanny over to be educated? And then won't we have lots of things to talk about? I suppose you will require that I should imagine I broke my tooth for the little creature, before you'll think I can possibly have maternal instinct enough to be trusted with her. Well, we'll see.

You ask about Mrs. Mason.[255] I never have heard anything of her marriage 'cept from you. The Boston people were amazingly interested for her last Summer but I cannot tell what they think now. I never could swallow down the affected romance of her letters. I hope her friends will not give her up just because she is married again. I am glad Lydia[256] is so much admired. She will have some thing [sic] to think of out of School, besides her duties. I mean to be admired too when I go to P. Martha Lilly[257]—is a very fine looking

[Written in the right and top margin of page 1:] girl—but she lacks energy. I think we shall have her take Fanny's place at Miss Martin's. It will just suit her as she has no desire to shine as a teacher in a school.

[Written on page 4:] The Bennetts[258] we shall take with us, unless Mrs. Wade[259] has some other plan to reveal. Anna M. is improving constantly. Nelly not so much so. You don't know how perfectly lovely Utica looks this Spring. I do hate to leave it. Our court yard [sic] is beautiful. The trees have grown wonderfully within two years. The Rowan or Mountain Ash before our window reaches above the second story. We are perfectly sheltered from the street by the trees. *N'importe*, I mean to find pretty trees and pleasant people in P. too.

[255] This is the third "Mrs. Mason." The second wife of missionary Francis Mason died in 1846, and the people of the mission were greatly concerned for his health. There was considerable mention of his returning to the United States. Then. in September 1847, he remarried, and Adoniram Judson officiated the ceremony. His third wife was Ellen Huntley Bullard; originally from Vermont, she was the widow of Edwin Bullard, missionary to Burmah.

[256] See vol. 1, "Cast of Characters," s.v. "Lillybridge, Lydia." See also "A Timeline of the Life and Mission of Lydia Lillybridge Simons."

[257] See vol. 1, "Cast of Characters," s.v. "Lillybridge, Martha."

[258] Anna Maria is speaking here of the daughters of Cephas and Stella Bennett, missionaries to Burmah. The Bennetts arrived in Burmah in January 1830, and Mr. Bennett remained the superintendent of the Baptist Press there for more than fifty years. From the Utica area, they sent their children back and the girls were educated at the Utica Female Academy and later the Misses Anable's School in Philadelphia. The girls included Elsina (April 1828), Mary (November 1829), Ann (August 1833), Ellen (June 1835) and Sarah (June 1837).

[259] See vol. 1, "Cast of Characters," s.v. "Wade, Jonathan and Deborah." The Wades were in the Hamilton, New York, area at the time.

So you think Miss Fanny Forester[260] that you will give up writing![261] I should like to see you do it. I think a person who writes poetry when her child is ten days[262] old is likely to give up writing. Your book I hear sells very well, but the critics lash you unmercifully. They are mortally offended ( ) because you are still Fanny Forester.[263] I have not seen any of these articles but I hear the worst one is the *New York Recorder* the paper that Colby publishes.[264] Don't you mind them Nemmy—I believe they are bound to find fault with you always. You will hear by the papers all about Hamilton's going to Rochester,[265] and that Union did last week in Troy.[266] Aunt C.[267] went down. It was a glorious meeting. If Dr. Sears[268] was a widower now, I'd offer myself to him and go with him on a Mission to Germany. Would n't [sic] that be grand? Those European Missions are becoming excessively interesting but I think the Asiatics [sic] need not fear the ( ) of the people go for the copper-color. Mr. Linton lashed the Union unmercifully

[Written along the left margin and across the text of page 4:] but they took it in good part. I have written this since breakfast and I am afraid you cannot read it.

[260] Emily Chubbuck wrote under the *nom de plume* Fanny Forester. Asked about it once, she said, "Would anyone buy a book written by Emily E. Chubbuck?"

[261] See the letter of Emily C. Judson to Anna Maria Anable dated February 20, 1848. In that letter, Emily said that she planned to stop writing for the *Columbian* and the other religious publications.

[262] To celebrate the birth of Emily Frances Judson, Emily wrote a poem titled "My Bird."

[263] Fanny Forester, *Memoir of Sarah B. Judson, Member of the American Mission to Burmah* (New York: L. Colby and Company, 1848).

[264] Lewis Colby also published the *Memoir of Sarah B. Judson*. Anna Maria Anable is suggesting a contradiction here, with one arm of the publisher not supporting something that another arm had printed.

[265] The school that became Madison University was founded in 1817 by the Baptist Education Society of New York State for the purpose of educating ministers. Two of its first students, Jonathan Wade and Eugenio Kincaid and their wives, were the first missionaries to join Adoniram and Ann Judson in Burmah. The Wades arrived in 1823, and the Kincaids in 1830. In 1834, the school was organized as a seminary, college, and academy called the Hamilton Literary and Theological Institution. In 1846, it was chartered as Madison University, drawing upon all of the history and good will in its former existence. In 1847, attempts were made to remove the university to the more urban setting of Rochester, and after three years of stressful turmoil that did tremendous damage to the prospects of the university, the courts decided the case in favor of those who wished the university to remain in Hamilton. Letters of the early 1850s show that the university soon made a remarkable recovery, and the university and seminary were later named for philanthropist Samuel Colgate.

Dr. Nathaniel Kendrick was one of the venerated leaders at the school while also serving as the beloved pastor of the youthful Emily Chubbuck. He officiated at the marriage of Adoniram and Emily on June 2, 1846, his last official act in his seriously declining health. After the commitment to stay in Hamilton, Dr. Stephen Taylor was elected as the second president, and later in 1856, George Eaton became the third president. Dr. A. C. Kendrick, the nephew of Nathaniel Kendrick and the biographer of Emily Chubbuck Judson, was one of the professors who left Hamilton in 1850 to teach at the University of Rochester. Numerous graduates were called for service on the mission field, and many churches were blessed through the pastoral ministry of those who had been trained there. One such minister was Courtland Anable, the brother of Emily's best friend Anna Maria Anable; Courtland Anable was there during Emily's final illness and death in 1854.

[266] This is a reference to a meeting of the American Baptist Missionary Union. See the letter of Charles Stout on May 21, 1848.

[267] See vol. 1, "Cast of Characters," s.v. "Sheldon, Miss Cynthia."

[268] Dr. Barnas Sears was a professor at the Hamilton Literary and Theological Institution until he went to Germany in 1833 to pursue theological studies. Upon his return, he became a professor in the Newton Theological Institution, and in 1848, he was chosen "secretary and executive agent of the Massachusetts board of education, in which position his wide and varied experience of methods of education in Europe made him especially useful." (William Cathcart, *The Baptist Encyclopaedia* [Philadelphia: Louis H. Everts, 1881] 1038). He later followed Dr. Francis Wayland as the president of Brown University.

I hope Sally has put in all the sentiment that belongs to it. Poor child! She is all sentiment just now. I don't believe she will marry John.[269]

Love to Lydia and the Dr. and kisses for little Fanny and yourself.

From Ninny

Source: American Baptist Historical Society, AJ 13, no. 491.

Emily C. Judson to Miss Cynthia Sheldon, May 29, 1848[270]—Maulmain

My Dear Miss Cynthia.—

The rain is falling with a charmingly cooling sound tonight, a grateful sort of music with which we have been favored for the last two or three weeks. Would you **ever** have believed that *I* would ever like rainy weather, such as divides the streets into gutters, washes the color and perfume from the flowers, and mantles everything within doors with mildew? Yet I do. What a wonderful elasticity must **our minds must** (the mind) possess, **since we** (which) can accommodate itself to circumstances so readily! Mr. J. is digging at his tedious dictionary to-night, as usual; the three little people are fast asleep[271] under their mosquito curtains, and so, the day's work done, I am at liberty to come to you. And now do you see me, nestled down in the corner of the big couch, there where I have been a hundred times before. Not see? O, **I wish** (would) that I could be there with eyes and tongue, as I am in spirit, for I want to look upon you once again, and to tell you a great many things. And first, I would tell you—for you would inquire—why my complexion and figure are so changed. I **sh'd** (should) scarce be called pale [Note: Written and crossed out is "I am so stout—my colour so changed."] (and thin now), I am so, *so* well! What do you think of a walk of three miles before breakfast? Is there no sound of health and vigor in that? Do not tell me that, in such a case, I have an additional talent to account for. I am feeling it most deeply just now.

But **we should have more interesting subjects** (there are more interesting matters) than any which pertain to my little self—just those things (which) it is

[269] We believe this to be a mention of Sarah Bell Wheeler and John Sheldon. See the letter of Sarah Bell Wheeler to Emily C. Juson dated November 26, 1847, and the letter of Anna Maria to Emily C. Judson dated February 28, 1848.

[270] There are two versions of this letter: the original as written by Emily E. Chubbuck and the edited version published by Dr. A. C. Kendrick in his biography, *The Life and Letters of Mrs. Emily C. Judson* (New York: Sheldon and Company, 1831). Additions made by Dr. Kendrick are in parentheses, and words in the original left out by Dr. Kendrick have been added in bold. There are significant changes and omissions. In a note in his book, Dr. Kendrick explained that interest, purpose, and propriety sometimes led to these changes and exclusions, "I remark here that in giving Miss Chubbuck's letters, I do not always indicate unimportant omissions. Real letters must always contain much which should not meet the public eye; and Emily's were real letters, dashed off hastily amidst pressing cares and duties. Written also after the exhausting labors of the day, they by no means do uniform justice to her epistolary powers." He later added, "In giving a few extracts from his and Miss Chubbuck's correspondence at this time, I have no wish to minister to a prurient curiosity, not to violate that principle which would generally place letters written during the period of an 'engagement' under the shelter of inviolate secrecy."

[271] Henry Hall Judson, almost six years old; Edward Judson, three and a half years old; and Emily Frances Judson, five months old.

impossible to write down. Since my first letters (all written *running*), I have been censured more than I deserve for being a negligent correspondent. Now, there are two special reasons why I write so little. The first is want of time. When I first landed I was a *spectator*; now I am a *worker*—in the smallest of all ways, to be sure, but still I am busy. Every moment **of time** seems inexpressibly precious. **Just think** (and) how **very** few the days before we shall be in the grave; and, Aunt C.,[272] I do want to be made the instrument of some little good before I die.

My other reason for not writing is that I can not [sic]. I lack the **graphic** power to **make you see** (paint to you) things as they really exist. We breathe a different atmosphere from yours, and its peculiarities are not transferable, at least by my pen—**we see things in a different light and** if we attempt to present them to you, they fall in distorted shapes on your vision. I have felt this most painfully when **I have sat** (sitting) down to write to you. "How interested Aunt C. would be in this story! But no. I **should be obliged to** must explain that—and that—and that; and then it would **be only a dull bit** (prove but a common-place bit) of missionary intelligence after all." **the like of which she has heard twenty times before. And I have told you of some little personal concern instead.** To be interesting, a writer must be met half way [sic]—half on the paper, half in the reader's heart. Now, though the great cause of missions **may be** (is) in your heart, and dear as your life, the **particulars** (special details) are not there, and can not [sic] be put there. Imagination is a fine painter; but it is past associations, simple memories, that stir up feeling. "Give us light," one earnest generous-spirited correspondent writes to me, "and we will give you money." Now, if I believed it possible, by dint of severe labor, to furnish the necessary light, I would work much harder than in days gone by, when you used to come to me at midnight with the refreshing draught and kind words; for money is the thing just now most needed. **For one, I can see no use in sending out men while those that are already in the field have so little freedom to work. Pity that such grievous burdens should be bound on any Mo( )men shoulders. I suppose some people really think that the bare support, the food and clothing of missionaries is the great desideratum of expense, that you know a small part. Perhaps too in this view of things when people hear such urgent appeals made for money, their deafness may in part arise from supporting the appellants influenced by selfish motions. Now what selfishness is there in asking for that which will increase one's cares and labours [sic], the only way in which personal comfort is at all concerned in the matters. Of course missionaries must have their bread and will make no difference so far as that is concerned whether the coffers of the board are full or empty; that they are sent out with their hands tied, and their hearts do ache so ( ), I assure you. Missionaries have very**

[272] See vol. 1, "Cast of Characters," s.v. "Sheldon, Miss Cynthia."

different trials from what I used to suppose, and severe enough to crush any nature gifted with sensibility. If I were sitting by you, I could give you some personal experience. I would tell you of a time when we were hungry for want of palatable food; when we were ill, and had neither comforts nor physician; when we were surrounded by the spies of a jealous (and) unscrupulous government, without **an** (any) earthly friend to assist us, or any way of escape. But there are circumstances in which (even) such trials assume a minor importance. My first *real* missionary trial—(you would believe me could you hear me speak the words, though it may sound common-place on paper)—was when, amidst sufferings such as I have described, a letter came telling of retrenchments. Schools, with the life already nearly pressed out of them, must be cramped still more; assistants must be cut off; the workmen's hands must be tied a little tighter; and then, if they could succeed in making bricks without straw, the churches at home were ready to rejoice in their success. This intelligence, of course, **built** (reared) a wall directly across our own path; for how could we carry out our plan of going to Ava, while we lacked even the means of remaining where we were? There was nothing left us but to retrace our steps; so we came back to good, comfortable, pleasant Maulmain, making a decided gain in the Egyptian "leek and onion" line. **And (one of us at least) another gain—a lesson in things of which I had previously known too little.** I do not wish, dear Aunt C., to say an unkind word **or think an unkind tho't**; but do, please, tell me your own opinion. Is not the great interest in missions, which makes so much noise at the present day, very much a matter of moonshine—more on the tongue than in the heart? It is not becoming in me, **however** (perhaps), to write of this; but I think, if some of our rich American Baptists could occupy our point of vision for a little while, it would plant a most salutary thorn in their consciences.[273]

I have made my letter so long that I have only room, etc.

Source: A. C. Kendrick, *The Life and Letters of Mrs. Emily C. Judson*, 293–95; Hanna family files.

[273] In this paragraph, Emily is speaking of their experience in Rangoon, from approximately February 1847 through August that same year. They endured the privations because they felt that being there would be but a prelude to moving on to Ava and dialogue with the Burmese government. Perhaps with this effort they could have religious toleration extended to the Burman churches and Christians, opening doors and possibilities for future evangelism. With those preparations in hand, however, they were notified by the Board of the American Baptist Missionary Union that funds were being cut back and that moving on to Ava was out of the question. Adoniram, Emily, and the children moved back to Maulmain, stung by what they saw as the lack of faith and of support of the churches in the United States. Some of that bitterness is evident in these words written by Emily in this letter.

Emily C. Judson to the Reverend Dr. Nathaniel Kendrick, June 20, 1848—Maulmain

My Very Dear Father and Friend,

You have so long been apparently within a step of heaven, and have been so happy in that position, that you will not be shocked when I say I should have written you before, but that I supposed you would be beyond the reach of letters before mine could cross the ocean. God, however, has been very merciful to those who love you, and has kept you with them; and I can not [sic] but hope you will still remain much longer, though for yourself "to depart and be with Christ," is doubtless "far better."

Since, my dear Dr. Kendrick,[274] you were the first, and indeed the only one to whom I communicated my early impressions with regard to missions, it is fitting that I should tell you something of my views since I have actually entered upon the field. I was very young when I opened my heart to you—full of the enthusiastic romance of girlhood, and the undisciplined zeal of a young Christian. When I remember this, I almost wonder that you should have spoken so kindly and encouragingly—indeed, your most judicious letter, though not understood at the time, was invaluable to me afterward. Your advice to "await the openings of Providence," had a calming effect; and I am glad I learned so long ago how good it is to *wait*, for this is a much more difficult part of Christian duty than to *labor*. God led me in a mysterious way afterward—perhaps to show me more of my own heart, and more of the completely unsatisfying nature of this world, even in its brightest guises, than I should otherwise have learned. My early impressions did not wear away gradually, as you would naturally suppose; but circumstances seemed to force me into another path of life; and so, not without a severe struggle, I deliberately gave up the hope—perhaps I should say dream—of years. But my regret was short-lived. I entered upon my new plans—every thing [sic] prospered that my hand touched—and I grew very worldly—so worldly that I used sometimes to laugh within myself at my own early folly, and to be ashamed to meet you, because I knew you were acquainted with it. In the midst of this, though I did not "await the openings of Providence," the door opened; but by this time it was like death for me to enter.

Of myself, I never could have resolved on the great step, but God strengthened me, and after that first resolve, I found it comparatively easy to break the innumerable ties which I had been so long and so industriously gathering about me. And now I can not [sic] be too thankful that I am here. I do not know that God has

[274] When Emily Chubbuck was in her teens, Dr. Nathaniel Kendrick was the pastor of the Baptist church in Eaton and also a professor in a local theological school. With dawning religious conviction, Emily spoke with him early in her life about becoming a missionary. Dr. Kendrick cautioned her to wait until the Providence of God opened the door to her. Dr. Kendrick officiated at the marriage of Adoniram and Emily on June 2, 1847. He died on September 11, 1848, before Emily returned home.

given me any work to do—I am certain that I do not *deserve* any such honor; but I mean to stand ready, and I daily feel, more and more, that it is a precious privilege to be in the *field*. The work of missions is continually becoming dearer, and assuming increased glory and magnitude in my eyes; and now, though I am the least of laborers, too small to be included in the number, I would not exchange my position for any thing [sic] on earth.

The letter which, thirteen years ago, you slid into my hand as you were passing our door in Morrisville, tattered and somewhat faded, lies before me now. It opens with the remark, "The day is wonderful in which we live;" and the time that has elapsed since those words were written has only rendered their truth still more striking. The day is indeed wonderful, and each passing moment unfolds new wonders. Perhaps the strangest feature of all is that rulers and statesmen, and political revolutionists, without being in the least aware of it, are actually cooperating with the Church of Christ in setting up His kingdom; and as "the angel having the everlasting gospel to preach" wings his flight, they are opening the way before him. It is better to be a willing instrument in the hands of God, though it is to accomplish comparatively small things, than an unconscious one; and it is my earnest desire to have grace to "act well my part," whatever it may be. You used often to pray by the bedside of my now sainted sister Lavinia;[275] will you not from your own bed of suffering pray for me also, since you know that I stand greatly in need of your prayers?

My dear husband joins in most affectionate regards.

Emily C. Judson

Source: A. C. Kendrick, *The Life and Letters of Mrs. Emily C. Judson*, 295–97.

Emily C. Judson to J. Walker Chubbuck, June 21, 1848—Maulmain

My very dear brother,

I have been looking back on the past, and in doing so have tho't a great deal of you. There was a time when I almost doted on you, and worried about you night and day, but I am sorry to say it was more for your worldly interests than your eternal ones. I know you sometimes think seriously and you know all about the externals of religion and what is necessary to your salvation—then why is it that you are not a true believer? Do you consider how very near the grave is? And how soon you and I will meet on the other side of it—*must* it be to be separated again forever? I *do*

[275] Lavinia Richards Chubbuck was the oldest of the Chubbuck children, born in Bedford, New Hampshire, on September 28, 1806. She died in Pratt's Hollow, New York, on June 22, 1829, just short of her twenty-third birthday. Her illness and death had a lasting impact on her sister Emily, who was younger by eleven years. In July 1853, Emily memorialized her in the book "My Two Sisters," which spoke of Lavinia and Harriet and their untimely deaths. In his letter telling of Emily's baptism in 1834, Dr. William Dean spoke of Lavinia's death and the influence it had at that time on Emily and her religious convictions.

hope in Christ that he will save me, and I *do* tremble for you;—not that you are wickeder, but you will not avail yourself of the merits of our Great Sacrifice. I do beg you just to stop one minute—and weigh this world as it deserves to be weighed. Suppose you could gain wealth—you cannot take it to the grave with you. Suppose yourself possessed of honours [sic]—are Webster the orator, Polk the president, or Taylor the successful general men to be envied? Seriously, and tho'tfully, are earthly honours [sic] worth the seeking? And what is there that fills the heart and satisfies it? Anything that you have yet found? I tell you truly that religion properly rec'd and properly enjoyed (but very few thus receive and enjoy it) is elevating and glorious; and aside from all cant, is just what the heart of man needs to sustain him here, by furnishing him with an object suited to his original capacity. We are fallen and utterly depraved; but, with all our littleness, and meanness, there is something great about us; and we cannot be satisfied with these daily follies to which we are sacrificing ourselves. But after all, it matters little in the comparison whether we are happy here or not; but it does matter whether we please God, and on that our Eternity depends.

You would like to be a Christian? I know you *think* you would; but you, after all, care very little about it. Are you willing to pray for it day after day, and year after year? Are you willing to learn of anyone who is possessed of this one pearl of wisdom, though he may be in other respects a fool? Are you willing *to* tell all with whom you come in contact, that you are striving to become reconciled to God through Christ? Are you willing to fix upon this as the great object of your life and make every other thing yield to it? Are you willing to make it the subject of conversation during the day and of meditation at night? Are you ready to resolve, I will try to serve God to the very utmost of my ability and leave the event in his hands? Oh do make this resolution—mingle with the Christians—talk and pray with them and let the matter of your salvation rest, if you find difficulty in settling it. Don't think I am getting crazy. I know the difficulties in your way; and I know that you would appear very odd and singular. But one thing is certain—God always blesses such a course; and is there anything would weigh in the balance against his blessing? Perhaps you are teaching—if you were faithful you might lose your school, or, on the contrary, you might be the means of converting half your pupils. And "he that turneth many to righteousness shall shine as the stars forever and ever." Praying earnestly and sincerely that *you*, at least, may "turn and live," I am

Forever
Your affectionate sister

Emily C. Judson

Source: Hanna family files.

Anna Maria Anable to Emily C. Judson, June 28, 1848—Utica

Dear Nemmy[276]

It does seem as if I never should get time to write again. All Creation is visiting us this Summer. No sooner does one party go than another comes in the same train. So it has been for two months past and so it is likely to be till we get fairly away, which I hope will be by the 12th of August.[277] How can I give you any idea of what we are about? You will see what *we* propose to do by the circular—my great anxiety is that we shall not have any scholars to teach. I do not suffer myself to grow thin with apprehension however, for I know I shall have as much prosperity as I desire.

Matters here look rather dubious. Notwithstanding Miss Kelly's[278] repeated assertions that "the trustees never would allow the school to go down," [ ] allow her to leave, that same corporation have concluded that without a Miss Sheldon[279] to sift all the expenses of the school they can do nothing. The case is this. There is a mortgage on the house of six thousand dollars, and in order to induce any one [sic] else to come in, they must raise enough to pay that off, and pay Aunt C. for fixtures she has added, besides getting new things to start fresh with. There is not public spirit enough here to do *all that* and the building will probably be sold to pay off the mortgage. Mr. and Mrs. Allen proposed some time ago to come in and take Aunt Cynthia's place, but Miss Kelly refused to co-operate with them, tho' the trustees urged it. She wanted the control of the tuition and besides, I think she feels a little jealous of *Baptist* influences. I sincerely hope that Mrs. Allen will purchase the house and build up a new interest here, for Jane has given up all hope of going on with the school herself. I think you would laugh if you could hear some of the wise plans which have been broached with respect to the boarding department. Miss Kelly presented Jimmy Blodgett to the trustees, at their last meeting, as a desirable one to take Aunt Cynthia's place. I would not say anything about these matters if you did not know Jane so well. She has tried for two years to "put down" Aunt C. more than she ever tried to put you and me down.

[276] "Nem" or "Nemmy" was a name of endearment given to Emily by a small group of her intimate friends at the Utica Female Academy. Anna Maria Anable was "Ninny."

[277] The Anable-Sheldon families were in the process of leaving Utica and the Utica Female Academy to move to Philadelphia, where Anna Maria Anable started the Misses Anable's School, assisted by her sisters Harriet, Mary and Fanny, her mother Alma Sheldon Anable, and her Aunt, Miss Cynthia Sheldon.

[278] See vol. 1, "Cast of Characters," s.v. "Kelly, Miss Jane."

[279] See vol. 1, "Cast of Characters," s.v. "Sheldon, Miss Cynthia."

Your brother[280] has been here for a week attending the Barnburner's Convention. He is a very fine looking chap and talks remarkably well. I expect Kate[281] to come down next week. I want to see her ever so much. I am going spend a week [sic] in Hamilton at the close of the term with Mrs. Eaton, Kate

[Written across the left side of the page, perpendicular to and across the lines of text of page 4:] and the rest of the good folks. Dr. Eaton[282] is here trying to get a subscription for ( ) too. I hope he will succeed. Give a sweet kiss to the Dr. and tell him not to think I am a saucy girl because I send some irrelevant messages to him occasionally. I forget he is Dr. Judson and think of him as my little Nemmy's husband. I suspect I sh'd devour that "gittle Ponny [sic]"

Anna M.

Give my love to Lydia[283] and tell her Martha[284] is going to a nice place.

[Written across the left side of the page, perpendicular to and across the lines of text of page 3:] What do you think of my circular? It is my first attempt at authorship, but I never thought of being bashful till Dr. Eaton complimented it the other evening.

Source: American Baptist Historical Society, AJ 13, no. 490.

[280] Born January 1, 1824, William Wallace Chubbuck was six years younger than Emily. During these years of Emily's correspondence, Wallace was living at home, or near home, working at different occupations including printing, office work, and teaching. Emily wrote of him as very capable in many areas but seeming to lack ambition at times. He proved to be a strong support for the Chubbuck family over these years, and, at the time of her death in 1854, Wallace had become one of Emily's primary care-givers. After February 1854, he wrote, at her dictation, all of her letters because of her failing strength. Wallace married Julia Allin Throwbridge on July 18, 1854. He died on August 13, 1861, at the age of thirty-seven. The obituary in the Utica *Herald* noted that Wallace had trained as a printer in Morrisville and had gained some astute political skills. He was "possessed of one of the brightest of intellects, and wield[ed] one of the most trenchant of pens." He had served as a justice of the peace and as clerk to one of the legislative committees in Albany.

[281] See vol. 1, "Cast of Characters," s.v. "Chubbuck, Sarah Catharine."

[282] The Reverend Doctor George W. Eaton was a distinguished professor and future president of Madison University and the Hamilton Theological Institution. He had a warm relationship with the Sheldon-Anable families, especially while they were at the Utica Female Academy. Mrs. Eaton was his wife.

[283] See vol. 1, "Cast of Characters," s.v. "Lillybridge, Lydia." See also "A Timeline of the Life and Mission of Lydia Lillybridge Simons."

[284] See vol. 1, "Cast of Characters," s.v. "Lillybridge, Martha."

Letters

July–December 1848

Anna Maria Anable to Emily C. Judson, July 29, 1848—Utica

Dear Emily

I returned last evening from Hamilton where I have spent a week delightfully. Sarah[1] and I left here a week to day [sic]. We *slept* at Mrs. Eaton's[2] but were on the go to other places constantly. Hamilton sure looked so lovely—your house is improving in appearance every year, and the lot on the right looks as if it was made the most of. Your mother[3] told me they raised every thing [sic] they wanted, and *I know* that they live as comfortably as any family in the village.[4] Every thing [sic] within and without is as neat as a pin and they all look contented and cheerful. Wallace[5] is doing great execution for the University in his paper, and by taking such a decided position he comes in contact with the ablest men in the village and is considered *one of them*. Every one [sic] considers him a man of talent, bound to rise in the world, but he is also thought a little wild. His associating on terms of equality with great and good men will of course make him careful of his reputation. Indeed I think he got up his name for wildness some time ago perhaps before you left, for he has been at Peterboro a good while, and I should think he was perfectly staid there. He is on committees with Dr. Kendrick,[6] Dr. Eaton, etc. and while he is hail fellow with them I don't think there is much danger of his returning to other associates whom he must feel to be beneath him. Your mother thinks he is more

[1] Sarah Bell Wheeler was a teacher at the Utica Female Academy, an intimate of Emily Chubbuck, and one of the few who addressed Emily as Nemmy. In a September 1847 letter, she was listed as one of the teachers at the Utica Female Academy. There are a number of letters from Sarah Bell before and after her marriage to Charles Gould of Boston in October 1850. There are several letters clustered in the year or two after Emily left for Burmah and a number at the time of her return to America. Emily stayed with Charles and Sarah Bell Gould in October 1851 when she arrived in Boston after the long sea voyage from Burmah and then England. She stayed there a number of times following that. In 1851, Anna Maria Anable wrote of Sarah Bell: "Sarah is grown so lovely in person as well as character that she must assert a blessed influence on all with whom she comes in contact."

[2] The Reverend Doctor George W. Eaton was a distinguished professor and future president of Madison University and the Hamilton Theological Institution. He had a warm relationship with the Sheldon-Anable families, especially while they were at the Utica Female Academy. Mrs. Eaton was his wife.

[3] Emily's mother, Lavinia Richards Chubbuck, was born June 1, 1785, at Goffstown, New Hampshire, the eldest of thirteen children. She married Charles Chubbuck on November 17, 1805, at Goffstown, New Hampshire. Four of her children were born at Goffstown, and moved with Charles and Lavinia Chubbuck to Eaton, New York, in September 1816; they were Lavinia, Benjamin, Harriet, and John Walker. Sarah Catharine, Emily, and Wallace were all born in Eaton.

[4] In late summer 1842, Emily purchased a new home for her parents using the proceeds from her writing; she seemed to be a mainstay of support for her mother, father, and sister Kate. Upon her return to Hamilton in spring 1852, she purchased a home large enough to keep her parents and her "children" together.

[5] Born January 1, 1824, William Wallace Chubbuck was six years younger than Emily. During these years of Emily's correspondence, Wallace lived at or near home and worked at different occupations including printing, office work, and teaching. Emily wrote of him as capable in many areas, but seeming to lack ambition at times. He proved to be a strong support for the Chubbuck family over these years, and at the time of her death in 1854, Wallace had become one of Emily's primary caregivers. After February 1854, she dictated all her letters to him because of her failing strength. Wallace married Julia Allin Throwbridge on July 18, 1854. He died on August 13, 1861, at the age of thirty-seven. The obituary in the Utica *Herald* noted that Wallace had trained as a printer in Morrisville and had gained very astute political skills. He was "possessed of one of the brightest of intellects, and wield[ed] one of the most trenchant of pens." He had served as a justice of the peace and as clerk to one of the legislative committees in Albany.

[6] Asahel C. Kendrick was a distinguished professor of Greek at Hamilton University. In 1860, he wrote the definitive *The Life and Letters of Mrs. Emily C. Judson* (New York: Sheldon and Company, 1831).

serious than she has ever known him, and I assure you he has improved wonderfully. Mrs. Eaton gave a sociable for me and invited all the faculty and your family. They all came and seemed to enjoy the visit very much. I took your mother all about the grounds (she had never been on the hill before) and she enjoyed the scenery highly. There is a pretty cousin of yours from the east visiting your folks. Her name is Woodleiegh [sic] and she is intelligent, graceful and genteel, and received a good deal of attention.

Dr. Eaton is here now on a soliciting expedition—I sh'd think he had spent a month or six weeks at our house this Summer while attending to University business. He is (a) dear good man, and he and I have got to be the greatest cronies you can imagine. Mrs. Conant[7] with all her talent I have found out to be a thoroughly selfish woman, so I don't mean to like her any more. Anne Wayland wrote that criticism on your Memoir[8] which appeared in the *N.Y. Recorder*. I have not seen it.

Now Nemmy[9] if you could see the hullabaloo in which I am writing you would ( ) away in less than no time. Our ( ) takes place to morrow in our school room. Miss Kelly[10] takes the entire school in her own hands, and is going to furnish *anew*—She is (in) New York now, buying furniture. She will have to incur a debt of $3000 dollars. Every body [sic] was surprised at her taking the school, but all are disposed to help all they can. All the people wonder at her not buying our furniture however. *N'importe*. This error lies in the head more than in the heart I verily believe.

[Written in the right margin of the address page:] I hope you can make out to read this scrawl. I should not have written this morning had I not told your folks I would. Do write me Nemmy and tell me if you have rec'd that box. I should like to know how the picture books got to you before the other things.

[7] Anna Maria's comments about Mrs. Conant in her letter of July 31, 1848, are quite interesting, if not surprising. In a May 1846 letter, Emily said that she had found Mrs. Conant quite "agreeable." In spite of Anna Maria's feelings, Mrs. Conant was an accomplished scholar. She wrote a number of articles and books about the Bible and was considered competent in the biblical field. Earlier letters indicate that she called on Emily a number of times when she was in Hamilton, and the references are always very cordial. When Emily returned to the United States, a warm letter from Mrs. Conant invited her to stay with her should she come to Rochester. After the publication of the Judson memoir, written by Francis Wayland in collaboration with Emily Judson, Emily planned to write an abridgement of those two volumes as a more popular offering. As Emily's health deteriorated in late 1853 and it became increasingly obvious that she would be unable to take on such a task, Mrs. Conant was asked to take the responsibility for that project and it was published as *The Earnest Man: A Memoir of Adoniram Judson, D.D., First Missionary to Burmah*.

[8] Fanny Forester, *Memoir of Sarah B. Judson, Member of the American Mission to Burmah* (New York: L. Colby and Company, 1848).

[9] "Nem" or "Nemmy" was a name of endearment given to Emily by a small group of her intimate friends at the Utica Female Academy. Anna Maria Anable was "Ninny."

[10] Miss Jane Kelly was Emily Chubbuck's friend at the Utica Female Academy, and then she became a teacher with Emily at that institution. Miss Kelly became the literary principal in 1844 with the retirement of Mr. and Mrs. James Nichols from that position. During a period of Miss Kelly's illness in 1844, Emily filled in the position for her. Then, in 1848, when Miss Cynthia Sheldon moved to Philadelphia to help start the Misses Anable's School, Miss Kelly became the "headmistress" of the academy and successfully brought it into the future, though not without some initial disparagement from the Sheldon-Anable families.

[Written in the left margin of the address page:] Give my best love to the Dr. and Lydia[11] and tell the latter I sh'd have written this month—but for the hurry.

Affectionately

Ninny[12]

Source: American Baptist Historical Society, AJ 13, no. 489.

Emily C. Judson to Miss Cynthia Sheldon, July 31, 1848[13]

Dear Aunt C.

Miss Emily Frances[14] (the young lady of late rec'd the dignity of two names) has just been grabbing my paper, so you will consider the rumpling of this corner the work of her dear little hand.

I am glad you are going to Phil.[15] for all your own sakes, and that, you are to be a united family. God in his infinite mercy guide you.

Lydia[16] told me of the death of dear grandfather, and, after the first page was over, I felt relieved by it. It used to make me very sad to think of him in that room which I knew must be very desolate without grandmother,[17] and he has gone only a little while before the rest of us. What changes have taken place since I left! And you have seen enough of the world to know it will always be so. You know that you will not be without trials in your new position, and A. M.[18] especially must be

[11] Lydia Lillybridge was one of Emily's closest friends at the Utica Female Academy. When Emily made the decision to go to Burmah as the wife of Adoniram Judson and as a missionary, Lydia wanted to go with them. Emily spoke to Adoniram Judson of Lydia's extraordinary abilities, and Adoniram advocated her appointment before Dr. Solomon Peck and the Board of the American Baptist Missionary Union. Lydia was commissioned to go with them, in spite of the fact that she remained single. Always independent, outspoken, and unafraid to cause ripples in the missionary community, Lydia served on the mission field for twenty-eight years. She married missionary Thomas Simons in May 1851. See the timeline on the life and service of Lydia Lillybridge Simons in vol. 1.

[12] "Ninny" was a name of endearment given to Anna Maria Anable by her most intimate friends at the Utica Female Academy. Emily was "Nemmy."

[13] This is an undated letter. The arrangements for the Misses Anable were made by early April, and Miss Cynthia Sheldon wrote at the end of April as did Anna Maria Anable. There was a three-month period for a letter to travel from the United States to Burmah, so the earliest this could have been written would be the end of July, and this is where it is placed.

[14] Emily Frances Judson, the daughter of Adoniram and Emily Chubbuck Judson, was born December 24, 1847. Emily married the Reverend Thomas Alexander Thomson (T. A. T.) Hanna in 1870, and they had eight children, two of whom served as missionaries in Burmah.

[15] The Anable-Sheldon families were in the process of leaving Utica and the Utica Female Academy to move to Philadelphia, where Anna Maria Anable started the Misses Anable's School, assisted by her sisters Harriet, Mary and Fanny, her mother Alma Sheldon Anable, and her Aunt, Miss Cynthia Sheldon.

[16] See vol. 1, "Cast of Characters," s.v. "Lillybridge, Lydia." See also "A Timeline of the Life and Mission of Lydia Lillybridge Simons."

[17] On February 15, 1847, Anna Maria Anable wrote to Emily about Grandmother Sheldon's death on January 29, 1847, and expressed their great desolation at this terrible loss. She repeatedly mentioned the terrible loneliness of Grandfather Sheldon, who was a great favorite with the students and faculty of the Utica Female Academy.

[18] Anna Maria Anable was the niece of the Misses Urania and Cynthia Sheldon and the daughter of Joseph and Alma Sheldon Anable. Emily first met Anna Maria in fall 1840 when she went as a student to the Utica Female Academy; both Emily and Anna Maria became members of the faculty there. In these years, Anna Maria became Emily's dearest friend, and the extensive correspondence between the two reflects sensitive, flirtatious spirits and a deep intimacy. Emily was "Nemmy" to Anna Maria's "Ninny." In 1848, Anna Maria Anable, with the help of her extended family, moved to Philadelphia and started the Misses Anable's School in Philadelphia. At Emily's death in 1854, Anna Maria was given guardianship of Emily Frances Judson, daughter of Emily and Adoniram Judson.

prepared to meet them. You will have various little troubles if no great ones; and by and by death will again come among you. How nicely planned this probation of ours is to keep us dependent on God.

I am not much of a missionary, dear Aunt C.,[19] though I think I have advanced rapidly in the language since my confinement. I can read and write it better than Lydia, though from her being always in school she can speak more words than I can. Anna M. would speak it beautifully, I know. It requires a limber tongue. By the way, don't feel too certain that you are to keep A. M. with you always. I wrote to her very frankly. Perhaps it might sound discouraging, because I was willing to leave the matter for God to bring about in his own wise providences. I am pretty certain she will be a missionary yet.[20] You will readily believe that I love her and Kate[21] above all persons in America. Now I would rather see both of them doing even a small work on mission-ground, though I knew they must undergo much suffering, than in any other position on earth. I pray that my own little Frances may be a missionary.

Do not think now that I shall ever make the least effort to get Anna M. out here, though Mrs. Colby[22] writes that her husband would manage the matter for her with the Board.[23] I doubt whether it is quite the duty of an unmarried woman to come; and I cannot see the way clear for her at present. But when I do, aunt C.—when I do! Then won't you scratch about and get her ready to send off in a twinkling? This missionary business is to be the great work of the church you know, by and by—I forgot that all my letters to you, from my own permission, are liable to

[19] Miss Cynthia Sheldon was in charge of the administrative and financial departments of the Utica Female Academy. Miss Sheldon and her sister Urania, who was literary principal, gave Emily Chubbuck a place at the academy in October 1840. They had deferred any cost to a future time when Emily could afford to reimburse them. Upon Miss Urania Sheldon's marriage in late summer 1842 to the Reverend Doctor Eliphalet Nott, the president of Union College, and her subsequent move to Schenectady, Miss Cynthia Sheldon assumed a larger leadership role at the academy. Active and well-known in Baptist circles, Miss Cynthia was to become an important mentor, advisor, and friend to Emily until the time of Emily's death in 1854. She was the aunt of Emily's best friend, Anna Maria Anable, and was addressed by most as "Aunt Cynthia." In 1848, Miss Sheldon moved to Philadelphia to help Miss Anable with the startup of the Misses Anable's School.

[20] For about a year and a half after Emily's marriage to Adoniram Judson, Anna Maria spoke of the possibility of having a call to missions and joining Adoniram and Emily in Burmah. On March 31, 1847, Sarah Bell Wheeler said that Anna Maria was a devoted Christian, and she thought that one day she would go to Burmah. She obviously put a lot of prayer and thought into the matter. The painful medical treatments she underwent in summer 1847 were likely intended to improve her general health (see her letter of June 19, 1847). In summer 1848, she decided that her call was to remain a teacher, and Anna Maria moved to Philadelphia and opened the Misses Anable's School with her family. She remained there until her death.

[21] Sarah Catharine Chubbuck, "Kate," "Kit," or "Kitty" was Emily's older sister by ten months. Outside of the two terms at the Utica Female Academy, which Emily arranged for her, Catharine always lived at home with her parents in Hamilton, New York. The letters indicate opportunities for marriage, but she, for unknown reasons, remained single. She later helped to care for Henry and Edward Judson after their return from Burmah in fall 1851 when they moved into the Hamilton home with their "aunt" and "grandparents," and she was remembered by them as "dear old Aunt Kate—a dear friend."

[22] Mary Colby was the wife of Gardner Colby, a prominent businessman and active Baptist layman. Mr. Colby was a member of the Board of the American Baptist Missionary Union and an avid supporter of the missionary movement. In a letter after they sailed from Boston to Burmah, Emily mentions the extravagant hospitality extended to them in early July as they waited for the *Faneuil Hall* to embark. Adoniram and then Emily stayed with the Colby family quite frequently over the years. Mrs. Colby was an active correspondent with Emily and supported her, her family, and the cause of missions.

[23] See the letter of Mary Colby to Emily C. Judson dated April 3, 1848.

publication;[24] but as I don't think there is any danger of this getting into the papers, I will venture to see it off.

God in heaven bless you all!

Affectionately

E. C. Judson

Source: Hanna family files.

Adoniram "Addy" Judson[25] to Emily and Adoniram Judson, August 15, 1848—Worcester

My own Father and Mother

I am rejoiced to make you acquaintted [sic] with the fact that our sister Abbie[26] has made her first visit to her brothers[27] since you departed from the New World.[28] She arrived on Monday morning and is to stay till tomorrow. We are enjoying the luxuries of a summer vacation which is 7 weeks in duration. I went to a lecture on Chemistry by Dr. Colton.[29] Among the things exhibited was a circular track and an engine and a little car with the royal family inside; they had little flags in their hats. The train was propelled by electrifying the track instead of steam, which is a new discovery. Dr. Colton put a shilling into a basin containing water which he electrified and then said that six of the boys might try to take out the money and that the one who could take it out might have it to keep. All of them tried it; but one only was able to get it and he was the youngest. Give my best to mama and accept a great deal yourself from

Your most affect. son

A. B. Judson

Source: American Baptist Historical Society, AJ 10, no. 257.

[24] In a letter written August 29, 1847, Miss Sheldon said, "Mr. Beebee called yesterday to see if we had letters from you by the last steamer—he is very greedy—and says the extracts he took from your letter to Mrs. Jones is lauded every where [sic] and he hopes you will rest assured that such communication is just what every body wants—the cause would be advanced ten fold if our Missionaries understood giving out such details." Mr. Beebee was the publisher of the *Baptist Register*. Recipients of Emily and Adoniram's correspondence were quite willing to share their letters with the public press.

[25] Adoniram was eleven years old when he wrote this letter.

[26] Abby Ann Judson, the first daughter and oldest child of Adoniram and Sarah Hall Boardman Judson, was born September 26, 1835. She saw her mother die on the Isle of St. Helena as they returned to the United States from Burmah. Just before leaving for Burmah with Emily, Adoniram Judson placed Abby Ann at Bradford Academy for her education. The family of Ann Hasseltine Judson was generous to Abby Ann and supportive of her interests and her future. On October 15, 1851, Abby Ann started a course of study at the Misses Anable's School in Philadelphia, and in fall 1853, she moved to New York City to take a teaching position in the home of Mrs. Maria Brown, a former missionary to Siam. She enjoyed a warm relationship with Emily, and her letters show that the two could speak freely with each other.

[27] Adoniram and Elnathan Judson were living in Worcester, Massachusetts, with Dr. and Mrs. Calvin Newton. The Newtons had also taken in George Boardman in 1835 when he returned from Burmah as a young child.

[28] Adoniram and Emily left in July 1846.

[29] This is also mentioned in Elnathan's letter of August 16, 1848.

Elnathan "Elly" Judson[30] to Emily and Adoniram Judson, August 16, 1848—Worcester

My dear Father and Mother,

I hope you do not think I have forgotten you for I have not. Yesterday I went to hear Dr. Colton[31] and to [Note: "Find" is written and crossed out.] see some experiments which he did. But I forgot to say that Abbie[32] was here and went with us. this [sic] afternoon we expect to go to the exhibition of the institute to which George[33] used to go. We expect to go to Dudley and Sturbridge the 18th of this month and anticipate fine times. We can go a fishing and everything mosts [sic]. We are to have a new suit of clothes before we go to Sturbridge or Dudley we have had a beautiful gray squirrel given us lately by Mr. Buxton he has grown to be very tame and will allow us to stroke him he is so timid that he will seldom eat, while we are present. Uncle Newton[34] has bought us a little wheelbarrow.

This morning we we [sic] went to see some little rabbits. We are going a fishing this afternoon with Mr. Herrey [sic], one of the boarders, we expect to go to Long pond; but as it is not convenient we are to go to Sabshery's [sic] Pond, and anticipate fine times. Abbie who has never been fishing before is going with us. But hear [sic] I must stop.

Your affectionate son,

Elnathan Judson

Source: American Baptist Historical Society, AJ 11, no. 458.

[30] Elnathan Judson was ten years old when he wrote this letter.

[31] See the reference to Dr. Colton in Adoniram's letter of August 15, 1848.

[32] See vol. 1, "Cast of Characters," s.v. "Judson, Abby Ann."

[33] George Dana Boardman, the son of George Dana Boardman and Sarah Hall Boardman, was born August 18, 1828, in Tavoy, Burmah. George returned to the United States in 1844 at the age of six and lived with Dr. and Mrs. Calvin Newton in Worcester, Massachusetts. He attended Brown University in Providence, Rhode Island, graduating after taking a few years off for travel in the West. He attended the Newton Theological Institute, and in 1855, he married Miss Ella Covell. He served two churches before settling into the First Baptist Church of Philadelphia, where he served with distinction for thirty years. He formed a close relationship with Emily upon her return in 1851; when she gave him a copy of *An Olio of Domestic Verses*, she addressed it "Georgie—from Mamma."

[34] Dr. Calvin Newton, after some theological training, went to medical school to become a physician. He apparently had differing ideas about medicine, and he became a part of what was known as the Eclectic School of Medicine; with that background, he established the Worcester Medical Institute. In 1835, Dr. and Mrs. Newton received into their home the young George Dana Boardman, just returned from Burmah for his education. Adoniram and Elnathan went there in fall 1845 when they returned to the United States with their father, and they remained there under the Newton's care until Emily's return in October 1851. At that time, Mrs. Newton had become ill, and the boys went to live with Dr. and Mrs. Edward Bright.

Anna Maria Anable to Emily C. Judson, August 27, 1848—Philadelphia

It is a beautiful Sabbath afternoon dear Nemmy[35] but as I am tired and Mr. Gillette[36] had no service in his church, I shall ( ) myself to you instead of going out. Do you notice my darling the place whence I write? We arrived here ten days ago and are now *almost* settled.[37] Imagine us in one of the finest houses on Walnut St. The exterior is a kind of stucco imitation of grey stone very much in vogue, with marble door steps casings etc. giving the house an aspect singularly neat even for Philadelphia. The hall is like all the halls in this city—the first door to the right opens into a couple of rooms the size of Mrs. Gillette's parlors. They are prettily carpeted, and we use the front one for a music room, recitations, and occasional sitting room for the boarders. The back room is the library, and for the present it is also Courtland's[38] room, tho' we use it in the day time for recitations. A sofa bedstand [sic] and ( ) wash-stand of black walnut prevent its looking too much like a bed-room. These rooms can be thrown into one by folding doors and used for our French Soirees. The kitchen is on the same floor and the conveniences are such as to make Patty our colored cook's eyes dance. There is a fine large cellar below in which among other comforts etc. a furnace which heats nearly the whole house. Now we will go back and ascend the stair case [sic] heading from the front entrance—the first flight lands you on the parlor hall. The parlors are splendid rooms connected by folding doors and as they cover the whole front of the house you cannot get into the front one without going thro' the back one. They are carpeted with a handsome drab and crimson and furnished with black walnut sofa, chairs and tables, an ottoman, divans etc. of rosewood. The halls are graced with very pretty pictures I assure you and the space between the front windows is adorned

[35] "Nem" or "Nemmy" was a name of endearment given to Emily by a small group of her intimate friends at the Utica Female Academy. Anna Maria Anable was "Ninny."

[36] Following several successful pastorates, the Reverend A. D. Gillette was the founding pastor of the flourishing Eleventh Baptist Church in Philadelphia in 1839. With his wife Hannah and several children (they would eventually have six), he graciously opened their home to Emily Chubbuck when she came to Philadelphia at the end of March 1845 for her health. The connection had been made through Miss Cynthia Sheldon, a family friend of Mr. Gillette and his parents. A prominent Baptist, Mr. Gillette journeyed to Boston in December 1845 to accompany Adoniram Judson to Philadelphia for meetings, and on Christmas Day, he introduced Dr. Judson to Emily Chubbuck with the hope that Fanny Forester could be persuaded to write the memoir of Sarah Hall Boardman Judson. A. D. Gillette and his wife Hannah remained valued and trusted friends, not only with Emily, but with the Sheldon and Anable families. He moved from Philadelphia to New York in 1852.

[37] After thinking of missionary service, Anna Maria Anable was processing a lot of information. After picking up new responsibilities at the Utica Female Academy, she was becoming aware of her love of and her gift for teaching. Her mother and her Aunt Cynthia must begin to slow down as the burdens of the academy were increasingly too heavy for them. Only by going on her own could she achieve the financial stability that would enable her to support her aunt and her mother in the future. Speaking first of going to Baltimore, the final decision was made for Philadelphia, and by the end of August 1848, Miss Anable was writing from Philadelphia in her new home and her new school. From an April 1848 letter, it is apparent that Miss Cynthia Sheldon had an important role in choosing Philadelphia as their new home.

[38] Courtland Anable was a younger brother of Anna Maria Anable. He held several positions over the years, and he studied at Hamilton College while he boarded for a time with Emily's parents. In 1853, he returned to Philadelphia where he preached his first sermon at the Eleventh Baptist Church. He was "Uncle Court" to Emily Frances Judson. In 1880, Courtland Anable was listed in the Massachusetts Census as an ordained minister serving in a church.

by Mrs. Judson.[39] These two windows by the way lead out upon a balcony with iron railings—a pleasant arrangement for a Summer evening. In the back parlor are the shell cases which adorned our library in Utica, but you would not recognize them in the garb in which our Mr. Pollard had dressed them. They are very handsome affairs and we put in them all our ( ), knick-knacks etc. besides the shells. I am sitting on the settee which stood in Jane Kelly's[40] room which is covered with a pretty English chintz. The dining room, and four bedrooms and my room are outfitted with the old parlor carpets. I wish you were here with your little Fanny,[41] would n't [sic] we have a fine frolic? I sh'd want the Dr. by too, for I would give more to see his dear face again than that of any other man living. You need not tell him that however for he has had plenty of such roses already. Poor Dr. Nott[42] I am afraid will never be better, tho' he is thought to be so just at present. He has suffered every thing [sic] with inflammatory rheumatism. Dear old man! I wish he would look at me and pet me as he used to, but his illness to which he is so unaccustomed renders him inpatient and during the short visit I have made there since my return from Boston[43] I saw but little of him. He is very kind as you will see by the circular,[44] most of the testimonies for which were procured by him.

[39] P. F. Rothermel was a well-known portrait painter in the Philadelphia area. In a letter of February 15, 1846, Emily said that she had been to see Mr. Rothermel and that he was painting a portrait of her for Anna Maria Anable.

[40] See vol. 1, "Cast of Characters," s.v. "Kelly, Miss Jane."

[41] See vol. 1, "Cast of Characters," s.v. "Judson, Emily Frances."

[42] The Reverend Doctor Eliphalet Nott was the president of Union College in Schenectady, New York. An ordained Presbyterian minister, he was married to Urania Sheldon Nott, the sister of Miss Cynthia Sheldon and Mrs. Alma Anable and the aunt of Anna Maria Anable.

[43] Thinking of possible missionary service, Anna Maria Anable spent summer 1847 in Boston, Massachusetts, taking some very painful medical treatments to correct a skeletal condition with her spine and shoulder. See her letter of June 19, 1847, for a description of these treatments. On April 26, 1848, she wrote, "My shoulder is quite stron and my shape is very much improved."

[44] The reference is to a circular that described Anna Maria's new school in Philadelphia and included testimonials from credible sources about her qualifications and abilities. One contributor was N. P. Willis, former mentor, benefactor, and romantic interest of Emily Chubbuck.

[45] Mr. and Mrs. W. S. Robarts were active in Philadelphia Baptist circles. They were frequent visitors to the home of the Reverend and Mrs. A. D. Gillette and later to the Misses Anable's School, which Anna Maria Anable and her extended family had started in Philadelphia in 1848. In his biography of his father, Edward Judson mentioned that Adoniram Judson stayed at the. Robarts's home when he came to Philadelphia in December 1845 when he met Emily Chubbuck. A. C. Kendrick said, "(Mr. Gillette and Dr. Judson) arrived in (or out of) due time in Philadelphia, and Dr. Judson was welcomed to the house of Mr. and Mrs. W. S. Robarts, who became warm personal friends, as they were already active friends of the mission cause." (A. C. Kendrick, *The Life and Letters of Mrs. Emily C. Judson* [New York: Sheldon and Company, 1862] 142). In 1846, with the engagement of Adoniram Judson and Emily Chubbuck, the correspondence indicates some hard feelings toward Mrs. Robarts for comments disparaging the coming marriage and missionary service. This is found in Emily's letter to Adoniram dated February 6, 1846; Mrs. Robarts seemed to be accusing Emily of worldliness when all the time, Emily was quick to say, Mrs. Robarts was engaging in the same activity of which she was accused. The correspondence also indicates a satisfactory healing of the relationship. In January 1849, Miss Sheldon told Emily that Mrs. Robarts had placed their daughter Mary in the Misses Anable's School.

Eve'g. I have just returned from church Nemmy and Mrs. Robarts[45] says your box is to be closed on Tuesday. Mrs. Gillette[46] gave me last Friday twenty dollars which I have expended as nearly as you directed as was possible on so short notice. I supposed every thing [sic] would have been purchased and sent

[Written along the left margin of page 3:] to you before we came on.

The mirrors we had in Utica hang on the Mantles and the gas fixtures descend from the ceilings—altogether the parlors are handsome rooms. The dining room is at the other end (of) the hall in the back part of the house. It is a long handsome room with folding doors opening into a small room which Aunt C.[47] and Mother[48] occupy. There is a fine cup-closet opening from the hall and dining room containing a dumb-waiter, hot and cold water and plenty of shelves. The next flight of stairs lands you into *our* parlor over the dining room and *our* bed room over Mother's room. Over the parlors are the school rooms and spare bed-rooms. Just by our door and over the cup closet is the bathing room—and water closet. In the fourth story are three fine rooms for the Boarders. The kitchen stairs run at the center of the house by the cup closet and bathing room, so that scholars can descend them and spare our front stair-cases and halls which are handsomely carpeted. Now Nemmy whether you care for this minute description or not I want you to keep it in mind for I shall take you hereafter to any part of the house I please—just as if you had been there.

Your letter dated May 17th came on the 25th of this month and I was so glad to hear of your health, that it is so good, and that you think *you* can be contented in Maulmain. Your notes to the girls I shall forward immediately, but poor Fanny[49] looked quite "down in the mouth" when she found that the "little curtsy" which

[46] Hannah Gillette was the wife of the Reverend A. D. Gillette, pastor of the Eleventh Baptist Church in Philadelphia. Emily stayed with them when she came to Philadelphia in spring 1845 for her health, and she returned in November. In the parlor of their home, she met Adoniram Judson on Christmas Day 1845. Mr. and Mrs. Gillette became strong friends and supporters; Mrs. Gillette played an important part in getting Emily's outfit together for her life in Burmah.

[47] See vol. 1, "Cast of Characters," s.v. "Sheldon, Miss Cynthia."

[48] Alma Sheldon Anable was the sister of Miss Cynthia Sheldon and Urania Sheldon Nott. Genealogy sources show that she married Joseph Hubbell Anable in Troy, New York, on July 28, 1814, and that it was the second marriage for Mr. Anable. Born in 1773, he was forty-one at the time of the marriage, and Alma was likely considerably younger. He died in 1831, which explains why Alma Anable and her family lived and worked first at the Utica Female Seminary and then later at the Misses Anable's school in Philadelphia. Joseph and Alma Anable were the parents of nine children: Henry Sheldon Anable (b. June 21, 1815); William Stewart Anable (b. November 6, 1816); Anna Maria Stafford Anable (b. September 30, 1818), Cynthia Jane Anable (b. January 28, 1820); Samuel Low Anable (b. November 28, 1821); Harriet Isabella Anable, also known as Hatty or Hattie (b. December 18, 1823); Courtland Wilcox Anable (b. July 28, 1825); Frances Alma Anable, or Fanny (b. April 12, 1828); and Mary Juliet Anable (b. February 18, 1830).

[49] Fanny Anable was one of nine children born to Joseph and Alma Anable and was a niece of Miss Cynthia Sheldon and Mrs. Urania Sheldon Nott. The correspondence indicates that in April 1845 she was away from home studying and taking music lessons. These spring letters indicate that she was in Philadelphia, working in the home of and with the family of the Reverend A. D. Gillette. See Miss Sheldon's letter to Emily of November 30, 1845, in which she spoke of all that Fanny was doing to improve herself in the field of music, but also her concern for Fanny's interest in the party life and the "vanitie" which surround her." A March 30, 1847, letter from Anna Maria Anable told of Fanny's conversion following her grandmother's death. In September 1847, she was listed as one of the teachers at the Utica Female Academy. Fanny became a teacher with her sisters in the Misses Anable's School in Philadelphia.

should have been made to her was trained for Sarah Bell.[50] She took great pride in working that blanket. I am glad you like the shawl, and sorry that you sh'd have to cut up the wrapper if you liked it. If I had time now I would make another to go out in this box.

Did you receive a set of spoons I sent you? I hope they were not stolen out at any of the custom houses. I am glad Anderson[51] sent you those books. I have not heard a word from him since our "desperate flirtation" and I was afraid he had not left them at the Rooms[52] as I told him. Mrs. Lincoln[53] had the unkindness to tell me in her last letter that he was engaged to a Miss Brown, ( ) while on ( ) in Providence. I wish you would tell me when you receive this box if I have purchased the right things for you, you forgot to say anything about the things you commissioned me to get, and I am more anxious to execute your commissions to your mind than anything else.

Whether you ever wrote "A Dream" or not Graham[54] published one as yours and he paid twenty five dollars for that and some other scraps, twenty of which I have aside for you, instead of making use of the draft on the board which the Dr. sent me. I intended to send this letter in the box with the other things, but I guess you will want to hear from me this month, so I will put it in the mail.

Why do you use thick paper Nemmy? I like the thin better for your letters keep longer on the thin paper.

Adieu. All good be with you

Anna M.

Source: American Baptist Historical Society, AJ 13, no. 488.

[50] See vol. 1, "Cast of Characters," s.v. "Wheeler, Sarah Bell."

[51] According to Anna Maria in a letter of August 25, 1847, Mr. Anderson was "the drollest genius of a professor from way down east"; Anna Maria Anable says that Mr. Anderson was a professor whom she met at a social gathering at Gardner and Mary Colby's in summer 1847. She became enamored with him and said that she thought she was losing her heart to him. He used the stories of Fanny Forester to teach religious topics to his classes, and he collaborated with Anna Maria on sending some books to Emily. See Anna Maria's letters of August 25 and September 27, 1847. In her letter of August 27, 1848, she says that she has heard nothing from him since their "desperate flirtation." She then mentions that she has heard of his engagement and brings this up again on November 27, 1845. He did send Emily some books, and the reference here is to a "thank you" note that Emily sends to Anna Maria to forward. In the November letter, Anna Maria says that she has sent the letter on.

[52] The "Rooms" are the Boston offices of the American Baptist Missionary Union; materials were collected there to be sent to the foreign missions and missionaries.

[53] In summer 1847, when Anna Maria was in Boston for medical treatments, she boarded with Mr. and Mrs. Lincoln; he was a publisher and prominent Baptist layperson.

[54] The copy of the original letter cut off the end of the lines on each of the two pages, accounting for the larger than usual amount of omissions.

Anna Maria Anable to Emily C. Judson, August 29, 1848—Philadelphia

Dear Nemmy[55]

I have just been around to Mrs. Erp's [sic] when I met Mrs. Robarts.[56] I was going up to her house to carry the little box of things, wh I have purchased for you but she told me to come to-morrow and I would meet Mrs. Longstreth.[57] I am anxious to make the acquaintance of Mrs. L. for I have heard the Dr. speak so often of her and Miss Marianna. Mrs. Robarts has taken us under her wing and I conform to all her notions for the present. We are only *teachers* just now—whether the life and Robarts connection look upon us simply as fact I do not care, for I know that I can find my lead wherever I am, only give me time. I like Philadelphia and I mean to have a first-rate school here if such a thing is possible. That is my great object for the present, and I do not trouble myself about society.

I hope your pin will suit you. The cameos are rarer. The one with a ( ) is Dante, but the others I do not know. I supposed the box was to close last Saturday. If I had known I could have had so much time I perhaps had ordered a plainer one made, but it would be hardly possible and secure anything tasteful.

The handkerchief and collar I purchased for the sake of spending all the money.

Good night Nemmy darling, I wrote you a long letter yesterday which I sent overland.

Anna M.

Source: American Baptist Historical Society, AJ 13, no. 487.

Miss Cynthia Sheldon to Emily C. Judson, September 6, 1848—Philadelphia

Dear Emily,

Your cheering note May 21st met us here on the 20th of Aug.—how little you dreamed when penning it that it would be lodged elsewhere than at the old house where in a trice each note could find its owner—and a general gathering follow as quickly—now excepting Anna M.[58] and my own all were remailed—but never can your letters do us more good—only think we had taken possession of the house—

[55] "Nem" or "Nemmy" was a name of endearment given to Emily by a small group of her intimate friends at the Utica Female Academy. Anna Maria Anable was "Ninny."

[56] See vol. 1, "Cast of Characters," s.v. "Robarts, Mr. and Mrs. W. S."

[57] Mary Anna Longstreth was a Quaker who lived in Philadelphia and who took an extraordinary interest in Adoniram and Emily Judson. She lived with her extended family, and they are frequently mentioned in her letters. Apparently, she ran a private school much like the one Anna Maria Anable started. Her letter of May 1848 paints a strong picture of her character, her faith, and her sensitivity. In this letter, she remarks on the particular strengths of each of the wives of Adoniram Judson.

[58] See vol. 1, "Cast of Characters," s.v. "Anable, Anna Maria."

Minus all our household goods—in some respects our discomforts were not unlike your siege in Bat Castle[59]—in others nothing worth the same of discomforts—the girls[60] and Courtland[61] really enjoyed the romance of being minus chairs, ( ) etc.—but Mrs. Gillette[62] prevented our being incommoded long, they are all kindness—would scarce consent to our coming from their house before we were settled. The delay of our goods was rather trying—still when we found they had a very narrow escape from the large fire in Albany,—we felt grateful to God, for getting them at all—only 24 hours before the fire they were in the Warehouse that was consumed with 400 buildings in that part of the city—why were we preserved from loss—It would have destroyed our hopes about school on such a tender thread is our temporary *all* ( ) and yet our comforts are many—we know who only is able to continue them—The 1st Sabbath Morn'g here—before any thing [sic] had found its permanent place—was our family altar erected—Courtland took the lead in our devotions—from the canvass in the dining room (on all such occasions) are those loving eyes beaming upon us[63]—and now dear E. methinks they are full of kindness while my pen is moving for you. These mementos are not needed to remind us, but how gratifying to *have* them—the feeling their spirits are near and around us gives comfort too—knowing as we do know that their bliss is complete is an *enduring abiding* comfort—The fear I had, that home would be no more home has vanished—I find enough to interest me—and in reality it is like beginning new in the world—Our girls are delighted with the house—it would do your heart good to see the taste and appropriateness of the furniture how well our antique tables, glasses etc. set off the rooms—Our shell cases are made perfect showcases—much admired—

I have received a line from Urania[64] written in Utica Monday—where she had just arrived on a visit to Dr. Foster Dentist—she felt lonely and sad—she had visited the twin graves[65]—the only relic of our home—dear Emily—what changes two short years have made—I feel that in them I have lived an age—could you have seen the poor old house shorn of every thing [sic]—by an auction—sales incredibly low—I

[59] See Emily Judson's letters from Rangoon, Burmah, dated March 13 and 15, 1847.

[60] Anna Maria's sisters Fanny and Mary. Harriet, or "Hattie," was still in New Orleans.

[61] See vol. 1, "Cast of Characters," s.v. "Anable, Courtland."

[62] See vol. 1, "Cast of Characters," s.v. "Gillette, The Reverend A. (Abram) D. (Dunn) and Hannah."

[63] See vol. 1, "Cast of Characters," s.v. "Rothermel, P. F."

[64] Urania Sheldon had been the literary principal of the Utica Female Academy in fall 1840 when Emily Chubbuck came to study there. Emily was able to afford this wonderful education through the generous offer of Miss Sheldon and her sister Cynthia, the executive and financial head of the academy, to defer tuition. Urania Sheldon left in late summer 1842 upon her marriage to the Reverend Doctor Eliphalet Nott, the president of Union College in Schenectady, New York. Because of the distance separating them, Emily's relationship with Urania Sheldon Nott did not develop the intimacy that grew between Emily and Miss Cynthia Sheldon. Urania Sheldon Nott remained a mentor, advisor, and friend to Emily in the years of her writing, her missionary endeavors, and upon her return to America in 1851. She was also the aunt of Anna Maria Anable.

[65] Isabell Low was the mother of Urania Sheldon Nott, Alma Sheldon Anable, and Miss Cynthia Sheldon. She died January 29, 1847, and Deacon Asa Sheldon, their father, died in March 1848.

was heartsick—the loss very great—Miss Kelly[66] had jumped at a conclusion to have *new—new*—throughout—at first she thought a very few hundred would refurnish in style—but when too late—found it would cost as many thousands—and not then have the wanted comforts of the old house—she spent the two first weeks of vacation in New York making purchases—returned just as we came away—poor thing I pity her as no one else can pity. This having every body's [sic] troubles and your own too with tremendous weight, crushing debts—I feel dear E. like one scathed to the very tendons—just now perfectly still—believeing [sic] *time* with the blessing of God will heal the bruises as far as best for me—Mrs. Anable[67] came on Saturday last—The Bennetts[68] came with her—we have only two other boarders—we hope to have four more, five day scholars—do you think we can make a live [sic] on five—we shall have I do believe four times this number when the box reaches you—the good people here talk of small beginnings as the sure road to success—we shall all strive hard to keep our pleasant home—only think what a cosey [sic] table we have—Mrs. Anable and myself feel overwhelmed with our present comfort with the children—Hatty[69] writes in good spirits about coming home in Dec.—her last letter yesterday speaks of a nice gold watch Mr. Roman had ordered for her before his death—they are very kind, but we have thought very selfish in holding her so fast—however providence has provided—Matilda Berthoud[70] is every thing [sic]

[66] See vol. 1, "Cast of Characters," s.v. "Kelly, Miss Jane."

[67] See vol. 1, "Cast of Characters," s.v. "Sheldon, Alma and Joseph Hubbell."

[68] The reference here is to two of the daughters (Ann or "Anna" and Ellen, called "Nelly") of Cephas and Stella Bennett, missionaries to Burmah. Mr. and Mrs. Bennett arrived in Burmah in January 1830. Mr. Bennett remained the superintendent of the Baptist Press there for more than fifty years. From the Utica area, they sent their children back, and the girls were educated at the Utica Female Academy. The girls included Elsina (April 1828), Mary (November 1829), Ann (August 1833), Ellen (June 1835), and Sarah (June 1837).

[69] Harriet or "Hatty" or "Hattie" or "Hat" Anable was one of nine children born to Joseph and Alma Anable, and was a niece to Miss Cynthia Sheldon and Mrs. Urania Sheldon Nott. In 1841, she had added a note to a letter written by Miss Cynthia Sheldon to Emily. As early as November 1842 she was away, and a letter from Emily to Catharine Chubbuck said that "she (Miss Sheldon) expected that Hat would return as accomplished as Anna Maria." Her trips away were both educational and employment, as she worked as a private tutor in families that would bring her into their homes. In August 1843, she had just returned from Beonsen, in the vicinity of New Orleans, and was engaged to go again. A letter from Anna Maria on January 6, 1845, said that she would stay South for another year. About this time Miss Cynthia Sheldon mentioned her concern for Hatty's spiritual health. In May 1845 she was in New Orleans. She was home again in summer 1846, but a September 27 letter from Anna Maria said she had been asked by Mr. Roman with some urgency to return and she thought that she should. She was to return home from New Orleans in January 1849 after Anna Maria Anable had started the Misses Anable's School in Philadelphia in fall 1848. Harriet was fluent in French, having placed herself earlier in a French environment in New Orleans. Hatty died in 1858.

[70] Matilda Berthoud was a friend of Anna Maria Anable and probably of Emily as well, for Anna Maria's and Miss Sheldon's letters refer to her. In one letter, Miss Sheldon tells how Anna Maria had gone to visit Matilda, and while there, Matilda's brother had taken Anna Maria for a buggy ride. Somehow the horse got frightened, and Anna Maria and her host were taken on a wild ride, which they survived by the heroic actions of the brother, the undaunted courage of Anna Maria, and the providence of God. In a letter shortly after their move to Philadelphia in 1848, Miss Sheldon says that Matilda is everything to them. She is perfectly happy being with them, and she adds that she is a "host in French." When Henry and Edward went to Hamilton to live with Emily's parents and sister, Matilda was one of the individuals considered to be employed to help with work around the house and with the care of the family.

to us—and perfectly happy here—she is a host in French—we expect Julia Look[71] here on her way to Utica—she and Mary Barber[72] will represent the Baptists in that school—poor Mr. Corey[73] has felt too sad about our leaving, his family situation at home makes him feel it much more—I do pity him—almost fear he will not stay—the Church will not be likely to have his place made good if he should leave—at this time the Church is strong in numbers—and among them many young families—the aged are few—good Mr. and Mrs. Seaton still fill their seats in Chh—

The girls had some feeling about connecting with Mr. Gillette's[74] Chh here—but Mr. G. is so much like a brother and his people so kind that this feeling will no doubt be hushed before our letters are required—we did not bring them—chose to defer it.

Our friends find us here—Mr. and Mrs. Thos Sheldon of Detroit were here Tuesday and Wed-y—Mrs. Lincoln[75] of Boston too—in both cases they have friends here—who I hope will be friends of the school—Anna M. does step forward beauti-

[71] Julia Look was a student of Emily's at the Utica Female Academy and later a fellow teacher. A November 22, 1845, letter from Anna Maria encouraged Emily to stay in Philadelphia for the winter for her health and remarked that Julia had the hardest part because she was teaching Emily's composition class, and the students kept asking for Emily. In a September 1847 letter, she was listed as one of the teachers at the Utica Female Academy. On September 23, 1849, Anna Maria wrote that Julia and Albert B. Casswell were married and came to visit with her. In one 1849 letter Julia spoke of another teacher who was teaching "our composition class." On October 27, 1850, Anna Maria Anable noted that she had had a son. She was one of a small number of people who addressed Emily as "Emily" and as "Nemmy" in her letters.

[72] Mary Barber was mentioned frequently in the Emily Chubbuck Judson letters; she was a student and then a teacher at the Utica Female Academy. There were ups and downs to that relationship; in fall 1845, apparently Mary had written to someone expressing what Anna Maria Anable called "ingratitude," and Mary had been banned from the Academy until she made proper apologies to Miss Sheldon. In a September 7, 1845, letter from Anna Maria, we learn that her remarks had been about Miss Cynthia Sheldon. In November 1847 Jane Kelly remarked that they had not heard from Mary in more than a year. In 1848 Mary Barber was back at the Utica Female Seminary teaching with Jane Kelly. Though at this time Miss Sheldon had moved to Philadelphia, Mary Barber had been able to reconcile with her, and in later years we find Mary very close to the Sheldon-Anable families; later, there was considerable consternation on Miss Cynthia Sheldon's part in her correspondence with Emily about Mary's health, the seriousness of it, and Mary's impending death. These letters were written in April 1852. Miss Sheldon went to help transfer Mary to Albany in June 1852, where she would be better situated and perhaps have access to better doctors. On September 9, 1852, Anna Maria Anable wrote to Emily of Mary Barber's death.

[73] Mr. Corey was the pastor of the Bleecker Street Baptist Church near the Utica Female Academy, and Miss Sheldon and many of the girls from the academy attended worship there. (Cynthia Sheldon, Alma Anable, Deacon Asa and Isabell Sheldon, Edward Bright, and Horace Hawley had been charter members of the church in 1838.) In April 1844, he wrote to Emily expressing dismay that at a school program one of the girls had read a composition justifying dancing as exercise; he spoke of this as a roadblock to the salvation of many. Then, on March 10, 1846, Emily indicated in a letter to Anna Maria that Mr. Corey had been critical of her relationship and impending marriage to Adoniram Judson. Miss Cynthia Sheldon wrote a number of times expressing Mr. Corey's regret and support, and in 1847, there were letters of reconciliation between Emily and Mr. Corey. In spring 1848, letters reveal that Mr. Corey's wife had died of consumption, her condition exacerbated by recent childbirth. She had left behind four children. In July 1849, Anna Maria Anable wrote of his impending marriage to Jane Backus, a good choice for this "rising man." Mr. Corey remained popular with the Sheldon-Anable families even after their move to Philadelphia in 1848. A March 2, 1852, letter from Charles B. Stout told of Mr. Corey's call to the Stanton Street Church in New York City, which Mr. Corey did not accept. Finally, in 1854, there was a pastoral letter from Mr. Corey to Emily on her illness and her possible death. He preached at the Bleecker Street Church as late as January 1867.

[74] See vol. 1, "Cast of Characters," s.v. "Gillette, The Reverend Abram Dunn."

[75] Mrs. Lincoln was the wife of Joshua Lincoln, a prominent Baptist layman and a partner in Gould, Kendall and Lincoln. Anna Maria Anable boarded with Mr. and Mrs. Lincoln when she stayed in Boston in summer 1847 for medical treatments. Mrs. Lincoln was a strong supporter of missions.

fully—Fanny[76] and Mary,[77] too—the three school rooms are finely fitted up—it was thought good policy to carpet and have fine desks and chairs—which will take off this year's profits—fortunately Harriet could send on five hundred to furnish with—

Oh dear E. how often I wish you were here to enjoy the benefit of our fine market—you know what it is—this season is fine, melons, peaches etc. are enormous and abundant—

I was quite vexed to find this box had not gone—but glad to find so much good feeling about it—wish we had something to add. The little iron has been fated to be left—I close this now for fear the box will be closed—I did design to write every thing [sic] that would interest you and Lydia[78]—but the nights have been too warm and my head too much wearied to do so—let Lydia know it—still I would not complain of the weather—Mrs. Anable—the girls—Courtland and myself do think the climate and every thing [sic] about us proposes more comfort than we have ever before had—Heaven bless you and yours—from your ever affectionate friend.

C. Sheldon

Source: American Baptist Historical Society, AJ 20, no. 999.

Emily C. Judson to Catharine Chubbuck, September 21, 1848—Maulamin

Another mail!—no letter! July—no letter! August—no letter! September no letter! Surely poor absent Nemmy[79] has reason to believe herself remembered has'nt [sic] she? Ah, well-a-day—Dogs must be thankful for a bone, when they get it, and when they don't get it they must be thankful that they did'nt [sic] get a kick—I suppose. I tell you what, Miss Lazy Kate[80] if you don't tell me every thing [sic] about every body [sic] and that every month too, I'll make will and cut you off with a shilling. By the way, we have a Katy here. The boys have a favourite [sic] pup that they have named "Katy" (I believe their papa first put it into their head because he said she looked like you) and when they are particularly affectionate they call her

[76] See vol. 1, "Cast of Characters," s.v. "Anable, Fanny."

[77] Mary Juliet Anable was born February 18, 1830, in Bethlehem, Albany County, New York, one of nine children born to Alma and Joseph Anable. She went to New Orleans with Hatty in 1847, but she returned home early in March 1848, and by 1849, she was working with Anna Maria in the Misses Anable's School in Philadelphia. Writing in March 1849, Hatty said of Mary, "She paints and draws, speaks French, plays the piano, sings, dances and is our mathematician. What should we ever do without her? She laughs from morning till night, and it is really refreshing to be with her." On December 26, 1860, she was married to Pierre Jacques Darey, the officiating minister being the Rev. Dr. Eliphalet Nott, her uncle. Mary died at the age of sixty-eight on April 20, 1898, in Ottawa, Ontario, Canada.

[78] See vol. 1, "Cast of Characters," s.v. "Lillybridge, Lydia." See also "A Timeline of the Life and Mission of Lydia Lillybridge Simons."

[79] "Nem" or "Nemmy" was a name of endearment given to Emily by a small group of her intimate friends at the Utica Female Academy. Anna Maria Anable was "Ninny."

[80] See vol. 1, "Cast of Characters," s.v. "Chubbuck, Sarah Catharine."

"Aunt Katy." And every little while poor little fat sober-faced Edward[81] with his great solemn eyes comes along—"Ho, Mamma!" (this *ho* is an interjection they got from the Burmese and it prefaces everything) "wat twok shall I put on? Aunt Katy which twok, or Aunt Anna[82] which twok!" Thereupon Master Henry[83] takes it upon himself to answer, "Ho mamma! Edward don't [sic] know anything. It is not a 'which frock' it is the frock *which Aunt Katy* or Aunt Anna sent. I like Aunt Katy's frock best—shall I wear that mamma?" Aunt Anna is Anna Maria you know of course.

Oh the children are *so well* and *so handsome* and *so loveable* and *so good*! I really don't believe anybody ever had such a happy family before. I am just putting Henry, who is six and a half years old,[84] on the Latin grammar. I am very glad that I got a little smattering of Latin and Greek in my aforetime studies; for really I see no reason why I should'nt [sic] fit the boys for college. Henry has learned very rapidly since he first took to it; and Edward who is 3 1/2 reads in words of three letters. Children need much more care to teach them here than in America, and seldom learn to read at so early an age. If I succeed well in training the boys I mean to put baby on the same tack, and try to have it carried out with her in after life. I see no reason why girls should not pursue the same course of study as boys. By the way, have I told you yet that baby's name is *Emily* Frances?[85] She is now about nine months old and climbs up by a chair and when she has somebody to support her, walks in grand style, setting one foot before the other with the utmost precision. She is a jewel, she is, and the Burman women spin long yarns about her always concluding with, "she has great wisdom." Twenty times in a day I hear "*tai na lee the*," that is, "she is very *understanding*." She has a strong will and violent temper, so much so that she was whipped three times once by her papa and twice by me before she was six months old. We hope hope [sic] however to do up all our whipping in her baby-hood, for she has been whipped but once, and that very slightly, since she was six months,

[81] Edward Judson, born December 27, 1844, in Maulmain, Burmah, was the eighth child of Adoniram and Sarah Hall Boardman Judson and the fifth of their children to survive. Only a few months old when Sarah and Adoniram returned to America, Edward's life was saved by the nurture and care he received from Elizabeth Stevens. He loved Emily as the only "Mama" he had ever known and returned with her to the United States in October 1851. Edward, who was Eddy to his family, became a minister; he did mission work with the immigrants in New York City, and with the aid of the Rockefeller Family, he built the Judson Memorial Baptist Church in what is now Washington Park.

[82] See vol. 1, "Cast of Characters," s.v. "Anable, Anna Maria."

[83] Henry Hall Judson, born July 8, 1842, was the son of Adoniram and Sarah Hall Boardman Judson. Henry was the sixth of their eight children and the fourth of five who survived. He remained in Burmah in 1845 when Adoniram and Sarah returned to the United States with the three older children. He returned with Emily in 1851 and went to live with her family in Hamilton, New York. Henry attended Brown University and Williams Collage; he enlisted in the army at the time of the Civil War in January 1864. Later that year, he experienced a debilitating accident attributed either to sunstroke or a horse kicking him in the head. He was married once—unhappily according to his own correspondence—and he eventually died in a veteran's home in 1918, the last of his siblings to die. Of this, the chaplain noted, "The end was a genuine example of Christian fortitude." See Rosalie Hall Hunt, *Bless God and Take Courage, The Judson Legacy* (Valley Forge: Judson, 2005) 291.

[84] Henry Hall Judson was born July 8, 1842; on the day this was written, he would have been approximately six years and two months old.

[85] See vol. 1, "Cast of Characters," s.v. "Judson, Emily Frances."

and then it seemed really to break her heart. I think she is uncommonly affectionate; the doc' says he never had a child like her and her nurse is all the time telling me she is "very loving." The Burmans are ready to eat her up. She is very fat and healthy; and every body [sic] says she don't [sic] look at all like me; so I was particularly gratified when Abbott[86] screamed out at first seeing her, "the exact picture of her mother"—"a perfect copy of her grandfather—of her *grandmother*." I sh'd have sooner said for her eyes are just like mother's but she is so fresh and strong that she don't [sic] resemble any of us much. She has three cunning little white teeth and is trying to *scold* the fourth through.

I have filled this whole letter with the children for they are more interesting than we are.

Give my best love to dear Mrs. Wade and her good husband[87] and remember me to Nicky Pierce.

God bless you all! Lovingly etc.

E. C. Judson

I have some fear that I don't get all the letters you write. Your best way to direct is "Mrs. Dr. Judson, Maulmain, Burmah Care of Rev. S. Peck, Baptist Mission Rooms, Boston." And be sure to write in a conspicuous place, "*Over Land*"

Source: Hanna family files.

Emily C. Judson to Dr. Solomon Peck, September 21, 1848—Maulmain

My dear Mr. Peck,

I should have written you before this, but that I have nothing to tell which you would be interested in hearing. I find it no trifling matter to step from America to a land so totally unlike it in all the common affairs of life, as well as the more important—a strange land, peopled by strange men, subject to strange customs, and speaking a strange tongue. I say it is no small thing to step at once into such a new

[86] Elisha Abbott was born October 23, 1809, in Cazenovia, New York. He graduated from the Hamilton Theological Institute and was ordained August 25, 1835. He wife was Ann P. Gardner, and they were married April 2, 1837. Though they were appointed for work in Telagus, India, that changed upon their arrival, and they went to Maulmain in April 1837. They continued on to Rangoon shortly after that. In March 1840, they established the station at Sandoway. Mrs. Abbott died in Sandoway on January 27, 1845. Mr. Abbott left for the United States in November 1845, returning in August 1847. At one point in the correspondence, Mr. Abbott was mentioned as a possible husband for Lydia Lillybridge.

[87] Jonathan and Deborah Wade were appointed missionaries to Burmah in 1823. Their relationship with Adoniram Judson was especially dear because of the early experiences they shared, including the death of Ann Judson. When she died and Adoniram returned to Amherst, he never forgot the sight of Deborah Wade standing on the veranda holding little Maria in her arms. Much of their work was spent in the Karen jungle communities following the path of George Boardman. They returned home to America on December 22, 1847, and went back to Burmah in January 1851, just as Emily was returning to the United States. They were from the Hamilton, New York, area. They left for Burmah on July 25, 1850, and were in Maulmain by February 1851. Both died in Burmah; Deborah died at Maulmain in 1868, and Jonathan died in Rangoon in 1872.

life; and then in addition to this to find myself in so short a time the mother of three little children,[88] who cannot be sent to school during six hours in the day, nor even shut away in a nursery. I do not mean to intimate that this is not all very pleasant, but I do not think the "Secretary of the Board" would be particularly interested in the daily routine. Yet with all my heart do I thank my Heavenly Father for having brought me hither; and more, that in doing it, he took me from a position of increasing worldliness, and which might afterwards have proved an irresistible whirlpool. "It is not in man that walketh to direct his steps"; but we have a privilege more precious still—to love the Hand which leads us into pleasant paths. If I have opportunity to do, as Brainerd expressed it, any "little chore for Christ," I trust I shall not be found a laggard; and hoping for some such opportunity, I am endeavoring to make what progress I may in the language, though it is necessarily very slow.

I thank you for the permission you have given my poor pen to employ itself occasionally in the Magazine; but you will see from what I have said above, that under present circumstances anything of the kind would be inconsistent with more pressing duties. It is considerably more than a year since I have written anything for the American Press, except an occasional poem when I was too ill to do anything else; and I see no prospect of being more at leisure in (the) future.

Speaking of health mine has very much improved of late; and is now better I think than at any time during the last three or four years.

Please present my kind regards to Mrs. Peck.

Believe me,

Most sincerely yours

Emily C. Judson

Source: American Baptist Historical Society, AJ 12, no. 383

[88] Henry Hall Judson (six years old at this time) and Edward Judson (three and a half years old) were the two youngest surviving children of Adoniram and Sarah Hall Boardman Judson. They were left in Burmah because of their age when Adoniram, Sarah, and the older children returned to the United States in the hope that Sarah could regain her health. Sarah died on the trip home at the Isle of St. Helena on September 1, 1845, and in November 1846, Adoniram Judson returned to Burmah with Emily, the boys' "new mamma." Emily Frances Judson, born December 24, 1847, was nine months old at this time.

Miss Rebecca Ann "Bessie" Rhees to Adoniram Judson, October 1, 1848[89]—Philadelphia

When I recollect, dear Dr. Judson, how long it is since you have seen me, or perhaps thought of me, and how many and how important are your engagements, I almost hesitate as to the propriety of again claiming your notice, or hoping to find myself remembered. But I do so long to hold converse with you once more that, having an opportunity of sending a letter by missionaries, going out, (for a wonder) from Phila I must avail myself of the occasion, at least to tell you how warmly you are remembered, how constantly prayed for.

You have *not* quite forgotten me, dear brother? You promised to remember and to pray for me, and very often since, when weary and sad, I have recalled that promise, and been cheered by the thought that I was not forgotten by you at the throne of grace. Now do not think I have turned Romanist, and am depending on the intercession of the saints, instead of trying to work out my own salvation. I know that even *your* prayers will not stand me in stead [sic] of my own exertions and supplications, but I know too that "the fervent effectual prayer of the righteous man availeth much" and there is no one in the world whose prayers I would so gladly have as yours.

I have never willingly omitted to attend the Monthly Concert of Prayer, since you were here, and I generally go to one of the Baptist churches, in hope of hearing tidings from you. I am quite a Baptist in all missionary matters, thanks to my intercourse with you, and know more about Burmah, Arracan, and Siam, than about any of the mission stations of my own church. I wish that the pastors of churches generally would take more pains to make the Monthly Concert interesting; if I were a clergyman I do think I would find a way to make the people attend; for their own gratification, if they would not from a sense of duty.

[89] Miss Rebecca Ann Rhees, who wrote this and four other letters to Adoniram Judson, also wrote three letters to Emily C. Judson beginning in September 1850 with the death of Adoniram. Miss Rhees met Adoniram, she said, while he was traveling on deputation in 1846 and transcribed several of his sermons and remarks for publication.

On March 6, 1846, Adoniram wrote to Emily about a letter he had received from a female admirer and said he would share it with her; then, he added, "And that also of R. A. Rhees, one of the few flames I have had since you left."

In her first letter to Emily, she spoke of her grief at Adoniram Judson's death as inconsolable. A second letter followed in December 1851 in which she commented on meeting Emily briefly at Miss Sheldon's in Philadelphia, probably when Emily traveled there after her return to America. This letter was in response to Emily's request for materials for the Judson memoir. Here, Miss Rhees implored that she be allowed to address her as "Emily," and she obviously was hoping to establish a relationship. Apparently, she was unsuccessful, for in the third letter, she said, "I will not ask you again to write to me." It appears that she had sent something to Emily, who had returned it to her, for after saying the above, she went on to ask Emily to excuse her for sending it along. In not getting what she hoped for from Emily, a hard edge emerges, suggesting that there was more to the request than what was seen on the surface.

The letters of Rebecca A. Rhees ("Bessie") to Adoniram are included in the correspondence to fill in some background information. Their dates are February 19, 1846; May 8 and 10, 1846; October 1, 1848; and November 25, 1849. There are currents emerging that are expressed in a multitude of ways; it seems evident that Miss Rhees would today be called a "groupie" with a strong need for attachment to a famous figure. There is an unfolding story of unrequited love that forms an interesting subchapter to the life of Adoniram and Emily.

Mr. Gillette[90] said to me a few evenings since, seeing me at a missionary meeting, "You still retain your missionary thirst, I find," and I thought "I do not see how I could lose that, and retain a Christian Spirit." The one appeared to me to be inseparable from the other. Oh! I do love the cause of Missions, and my inability to join those who have gone forth to obey Christ's last command, is a source of continued grief—a perpetual cross to me.

Once, last winter, I thought that the time *had* come when I might hope to keep the promise made to you, when I saw you last, that if my family was ever in a situation to dispense with my exertions, I would strive to join you in the heathen land I still consider as my home. They had removed from Phila, and I was here alone teaching; I felt that I was doing very little to contribute to their comfort—that they could do without me, and I wrote to my sister, "O! if Dr. Judson were only here, or if when he was here, I had been placed as I now am! I would not hesitate as to my duty, were the way open to me now." But while I debated as to what steps I should take for the accomplishment of my wishes, my health, for a short time precious, usually good, failed me entirely and from that time to the present, I have never, for a single day, felt well enough to venture to talk to any one [sic] of going out as a missionary. I am sometimes almost discouraged; indeed, since you are gone, no one ever encourages me to think of such a thing. And yet I can not [sic] entirely resign to hope that the way will one day be opened before me, and health and strength given to me to walk in it. Will you still pray for me dear friend, that this may be?

I am still a member of the Episcopal church, and love her Liturgy, articles, and order as well as when you smiled at my ardent expression of affection for them. But more even than that I love the common cause, the work in which you are engaged, and I know that you do not refuse me your fellowship and Christian affection, because I do not belong to the same branch of the church catholic, with yourself. You, to whom I am but one among the many who loves you here, can scarcely realize how precious to me is the memory of my few brief interviews with you;—how distinctly I recollect almost, if not quite, every word I heard you utter. The lines you wrote me, the book you gave me, are my most valued treasures; were it not for these, I should sometimes scarcely persuade myself that my intercourse with you, vividly as I recall it, was not all a dream.

I did not ask you to write to me when you went away; I felt that many would ask it, whose claims were superior to mine, and I feared to seem to presume upon your kindness. But I will tell you what I *had* the vanity to hope for—a message, a word of remembrance through Mr. Gillette, and I have seldom shed more bitter tears than at the Monthly Concert, April, 1847, when he read the letters announcing your arrival at Maulmain, and I found that I was forgotten. Forgive my

[90] See vol. 1, "Cast of Characters," s.v. "Gillette, The Reverend Abram Dunn."

presumptuous hopes; I think you would, if you could have seen my disappointment, and, dear friend, if it is not asking quite too much, will you not some day [sic], write me, if it is but a word or two? I fear the request is a selfish one; I know your time is very precious, your dearer friends very numerous, but indeed I do not think there is any one [sic] in America to whom a line from you would give more delight.

You will be weary of this rambling epistle, which it is indeed full time to close. I have attempted to give you no news; your brethren no doubt keep you supplied with intelligence from home. I write simply from the impulse of an affection which the memory of your kindness when here renders, perhaps too presuming.

Pray present my best and warmest regards to Mrs. Judson; if I knew nothing of her but that she bears your name, this would be in itself a claim on my affection, and her writings have so often awaked an answering chord in my heart that I almost fancy I know her as a friend.

Will you think me very foolish, if I enclose a few simple lines, written while you were "afar upon the sea." They lay no claim to poetic merit, but as an expression of deep feeling, you will not judge them harshly.

Farewell, dear, dear brother; may the blessing of the God you serve, our common Father, rest ever upon you. I never kneel without remembering you; may I hope that you will sometimes think of me in prayer? A modern author says, "Angels are round the good man when he prays, and fly to minister to those for whom he pleads."

With sentiments of the deepest respect, esteem and affection, I remain

Ever yours

R. A. Rhees

Rev. A. Judson

Afar upon the sea, dear friend! Afar upon the sea!
Yet across that waste of waters, my soul communes with thee,
And when thy spirit soars above, borne on the wings of prayer,
In thought I'm kneeling by thy side—in heart am with thee there.

Afar upon the sea, dear friend! The wild and stormy main,
O'er whose darkly tossing billows thou wilt never sail again,
We know that on this weary earth we shall see thy face no more,
Nor clasp thy hand in welcome warm on this thy native shore.

Afar upon the sea, dear friend! Yet thou art not alone,
Dear ones are near thee—round thy way the light of love is thrown
Kindred in Christ, and for His sake, beloved, are by thy side,
And thy chosen one is with thee there, thy young and gentle bride.

Afar upon the sea, dear friend! The shining ones above
Hover around thy floating home with an untiring love,
Unseen, unheard, perchance unfelt, yet whispering words of cheer,
And God, thy covenant keeping God himself, is ever near.

Afar upon the sea, dear friend! Beyond it lies thy home,
The heathen's cry for help is borne across the ocean foam,
And mingling with it comes a sound of weeping and of prayer,
Thy brethren wait thy coming, and thy people need thee there.

Afar upon the sea, dear friend! And far behind thee lies
Another home to which thy heart is bound by tenderest ties
Whence many a warm and glowing wish thy onward way attends,
And round many a Christian hearth, for thee the fervent prayer ascends.

Afar upon the sea, dear friend! And alas! Afar from *me*!
Would it had been the Master's will to send me forth with thee!
I hear no more thy gentle tone, nor meet thy kindly glance,
Severed from thee by stormy seas, and the wide world's expanse.

Afar upon the sea, dear friend! Would that the hour were come,
When all who love one common Lord, shall have one common home,
Earth's separations, sad Farewells, and partings cease to be,
And tears no more be shed for those afar upon the sea.

Bessie

Mrs. Mary L. Colby to Emily C. Judson, October 9, 1848—Newton Centre

Your letter My dear Mrs. Judson, I received about six weeks since.[91] It was a great gratification to me and I am exceedingly obliged to you for taking time to write to me, aside from the pleasure I have in hearing from you myself is that of being able to answer satisfactorily the many inquiries which are constantly made of me as to your health and happiness, the people all taking it for granted that I know all about it. I can't tell you how glad I am that you *really do* enjoy a missionary life, the more I hear and read of it, the more am I persuaded that I could not endure, what

[91] See the letter of Emily C. Judson to Mary Colby dated May 20, 1848.

a mercy I never was called to that work, but if I know my own heart I am willing and glad to do what I can at home to promote it.

We have within a few weeks moved into our new home[92] and are now I trust permanently settled and I am becoming quite a lover of country life. I know you will be glad to know it and count me very wicked and as having no taste not to like it before but such as [sic] been my infirmity. You enquire if the children love country sports. I assure you they do, and the abundance of exercise they take in the open air keeps them in good health. We have not needed a Physician for a year which is great cause of thankfulness and somewhat remarkable when there are four little children. Mr. Colby's sister has recently buried the third child, it died of Whooping cough. Mother[93] is still at Danvers with Eme, but I expect she will spend the winter with us. How I should love to see your dear little one.[94] It is delightful is it not, notwithstanding all the responsibility, to be a mother; I trust she is getting along well with her teeth, and ( ) weak eyes I hope will not be a permanent trouble.

Mr. and Mrs. Wade[95] spent two nights and a day with us a few weeks since. It was a delightful visit to us. Mrs. Wade is a sweet woman and all who see her are so much pleased, she is so considerate of every ones' [sic] feelings, when we know she must think we are doing wrong in many things, she reproves no one. I have great veneration and respect for her character but now I love her too. You may be sure we talked a great deal about you and yours and I almost felt as if I could look into your pleasant home, and see you taking care of your little ones.

I went to Boston last evening to attend the meeting for the designation of Missionaries. Two of them have been students here, both most excellent young men. Mr. Benjamin,[96] who I understand is to be at Tavoy we think much of, and if we do not mistake he will be very efficient; his lady has been teacher of the school belonging to "Children's' Friend Society" in which Mother has been for many years deeply interested. She is highly esteemed by all who know her and I hope will make a good Missionary. I wish Mr. Benjamin would have remained at home another year

[92] The Colbys lived in a home at Pemberton Square, Boston, and Adoniram and Emily stayed with them before leaving for Burmah. From Pemberton Square, the Colbys moved to Newton Centre and lived in temporary housing at the bottom of the hill from the Newton Theological Institution for a brief period. They lived there until they could move into their new house, which was built on the small farm they purchased.

[93] Sarah Colby was the mother of Gardner Colby, Mary Colby's husband. There are two letters in the correspondence from Sarah Colby.

[94] See vol. 1, "Cast of Characters," s.v. "Judson, Emily Frances."

[95] See vol. 1, "Cast of Characters," s.v. "Wade, The Reverend Doctor Jonathan and Deborah."

[96] Judson Benjamin was born February 2, 1819, in Rodman, New York. He was baptized in Franklin, Indiana; graduated from Brown University and Newton Theological Seminary; and was ordained on October 13, 1848, in Providence, Rhode Island. He married Susan Ruggles Stone on September 3, 1848, and they departed for Tavoy, Burma, on October 21, 1848. They arrived at Tavoy in April 1849; in March 1850, they were sent to Mergui. Mr. Benjamin collected a vocabulary of 1,200 Salong words. They sailed from Rangoon to Boston on January 21, 1854, and Rev. Benjamin died in Boston of pulmonary disease in February 1855. Susan Benjamin remarried William Ward, and they left from Boston in June 1860 to return to Burmah.

and finished his course of study at the Institution. Dr. Sears[97] has resigned his office as President here to take the secretaryship [sic] of the State Education Society, and Dr. Pattison[98] of Covington Theological Seminary, has been elected in his place. I fear however that Dr. Sears' office will not be easily filled. He is a man of rare ability.

Please accept the accompanying parcel. The contents are not of much value, they are such as I happened to have in the house and I hope may be of some use to you. In the country we cannot shop as easily as in town, we are a mile from any store, and those as near as that are very poor. The piece of muslin will supply the place of the burnt dress perhaps.

Give my affectionate regards to your dear husband and all the friends around you who remember me not forgetting Miss Lillybridge.[99] I don't know but I shall do well to be angry with her that she never sends me a line. I surely thought she would. My husband and sister send much love. Kiss the dear babe for me. I trust she will be spared to be a great comfort to you, and if at any time in the midst of your numerous cares and labours [sic] you can afford to write me be assured you will greatly please your

sincere friend Mary L. Colby.

Source: American Baptist Historical Society, AJ 15, no. 632.

Miss Cynthia Sheldon to Emily C. Judson, October 28, 1848—Philadelphia

My dear Emily,

How cheering your late letter—you can scarce imagine what a load of anxiety about your health they have dissipated—we are now fixing our minds on your happy Burman home—can see you now giving toys or a bent to children's play; next giving orders for the day in Burmese all the time your paper is before you gaining impressions as by magic—were it otherwise I am sure your Burmese b( ) would be at a stand still—we do feel to praise God for all he is doing with you, and by you—go

[97] Dr. Barnas Sears was a professor at the Hamilton Literary and Theological Institution until he went to Germany in 1833 to pursue theological studies. Upon his return, he became a professor in the Newton Theological Institution, and in 1848, he was chosen "secretary and executive agent of the Massachusetts board of education, in which position his wide and varied experience of methods of education in Europe made him especially useful." (William Cathcart, *The Baptist Encyclopaedia* [Philadelphia: Louis H. Everts, 1881] 1038). He later followed Dr. Francis Wayland as the president of Brown University.

[98] Dr. Robert E. Pattison had a varied early career. He was pastor of several churches; a tutor at Columbian College in Washington, DC; a professor at Waterville College; the secretary of the Home Department of the American Baptist Missionary Union; and the president of the Western Baptist Theological Institute in Lexington, Kentucky. For six years, he was a professor at Newton Theological Seminary. Following Newton, he became the president of Waterville College, which later became Colby College, named after Gardner Colby of Newton Centre, who was a trustee of both the American Baptist Missionary Union and Newton Theological Seminary. (William Cathcart, *The Baptist Encyclopaedia* [Philadelphia: Louis H. Everts, 1881]).

[99] See vol. 1, "Cast of Characters," s.v. "Lillybridge, Lydia." See also "A Timeline of the Life and Mission of Lydia Lillybridge Simons."

on—but not to Ava till these perilous times have past [sic]—do we not see the strongest evidence we could wish to have, that Infinite Wisdom has set a hedge round about you—by closing the door to Ava when your health could have suffered, and perils oft might have ended your valuable life ere this—not that I justify the niggardly course of American Churches at that crisis of your operations saying plainly to your good Doct. turn back,[100] but while we shall be punished it shall be the exaltation of the oppressed. My faith is strong that great good will come from it—Now I see you watching for a glimmer of light—a beacon, some kind of providence by which duty can be made more clear—and when you do venture—I firmly believe that Israel's God will work for you and with you—This going to Ava is a mighty work—The Churches will yet see it so, and be astonished—

Anna M.[101] is filling a sheet for you—but you cannot gather from anything we can say how we look, or act here—She is now engaged with her Bible Class, from five to six o'clock Sabbath—Matilda,[102] Fanny[103] and Mary[104] have gone into the front parlor to watch the pedestrians; we have a fine balcony screen before the windows. I am now at the round table by gas light in the back parlour [sic]—heard Mr. Gillette[105] in the morning, Dr. Cuyler this aft'n—our long walks to Church, make us all very tired—but we sometimes hear Mr. G. in the evening. I have been to Utica since we wrote you and providentially met Catharine[106]—she was looking very well—and said your Mother[107] was quite better—I was delighted to meet Catharine—should have gone to Hamilton if it had been possible—In Utica my time was mostly occupied with business—and some of it perplexing—It was Saturday E-g 10 o'clock (the cars were detained 2 hours) when I did set down at the old house—Mary Barber[108] was in train to greet me—she had been there only three days and distressedly [sic] homesick—you would have thought her mother dear had suddenly let down among them—well every thing [sic] passed for what it was worth all round—Jane's[109] Mother and three sisters find as much to do as they wish—things were rightly straight—The Trustees have expended some $1200 on the house—but Jane has been obliged to run into debt more than $3000—which she now thinks can be cleared in three years—ministers and every body [sic] must

[100] In February 1847, Adoniram, Emily, Henry, and Edward moved to Rangoon as a stepping stone for eventual ministry in Ava. They were forced to return to Maulmain in September 1847 due to reductions in funding to the mission by the Board of the American Baptist Missionary Union.

[101] See vol. 1, "Cast of Characters," s.v. "Anable, Anna Maria."

[102] See vol. 1, "Cast of Characters," s.v. "Berthoud, Matilda."

[103] See vol. 1, "Cast of Characters," s.v. "Anable, Fanny."

[104] See vol. 1, "Cast of Characters," s.v. "Anable, Miss Mary Juliet."

[105] See vol. 1, "Cast of Characters," s.v. "Gillette, The Reverend Abram Dunn."

[106] See vol. 1, "Cast of Characters," s.v. "Chubbuck, Sarah Catharine."

[107] Emily's mother. See vol. 1, "Cast of Characters," s.v. "Chubbuck, Lavinia Richards."

[108] See vol. 1, "Cast of Characters," s.v. "Barber, Mary."

[109] See vol. 1, "Cast of Characters," s.v. "Kelly, Miss Jane."

pay now—The Trustees treated me very shabbily in not allowing claims—they feel it too—That is all the redress I should ever get—One thing is certain I am thankful to be *quit* of them—at the same time ready to meet them any where [sic]. On the Sabbath Morn'g Mr. Corey[110] gave us one of his best sermons—Aft'n Communion. Mary Barber went with me to the grave yard [sic] endeared spot[111]—we took tea at Dea. Bailey's—Evening attended the Tract Meeting in the 1st Pres. Chh—house full—reports interesting—Mr. Corey made an address to be remembered—numbers spoke to me about it afterwards—inquiringly said, how could you leave such a Minister—do you find his equal—every thing [sic] to show me that he is rising in Utica—poor man he feels very desolate there I fear[112]—he will not stay long—After Sabbath night I staid [sic] altogether at Mr. Cyrus Clark's—every body [sic] was so glad I could tell them of your feats in walking—you have friends there now—The Hawleys[113] paid court to me—they understand the tie is to Lennie only—and Mary Jones looks very feeble[114]—and her husband is much worse than when you left[115]—my heart aches for them—wish he could find some thing here to do for a good living—I begged him to come on and see if there was not some thing [sic]. A change in his circumstances might work wonder in his health—Mr. and Mrs. Crafts[116] and a host of such people were all kindness to me—our good friend Mrs. Ford—Dr. and Mrs. James[117]—with a very few others were the choice spirits of olden friendship I met. My visit ended there on Friday, returned then to Schenectady—poor Dr.

[110] See vol. 1, "Cast of Characters," s.v. "Corey, The Reverend D. G."

[111] Deacon and Mrs. Sheldon recently died. Mrs. Sheldon died on January 29, 1847, and Deacon Asa Sheldon died in March 1848. They were buried in Utica.

[112] Mr. Corey's wife recently died of consumption. The correspondence indicated that her condition was exacerbated by the birth of a child several months previous to her death.

[113] Mr. Horace H. Hawley enjoyed a family relationship with the Sheldons. A letter Emily wrote on May 7, 1841, reveals that he was to marry a niece of Misses Cynthia and Urania Sheldon and Mrs. Alma Sheldon Anable, the daughter of their brother John Sheldon. Through the help of Miss Cynthia Sheldon, he was introduced into the life of Emily Chubbuck. A member of a publishing firm, he also worked with Alexander Beebee in publishing the *Baptist Register*. Beginning in 1841 with the publication of *Charles Linn*, Mr. Hawley was enormously helpful to Emily Chubbuck as she was publishing her early stories and books. There are numerous references to his help and his generosity.

[114] See the letter of Anna Maria Anable to Emily Judson dated June 19, 1847, and the letter of Morven M. Jones to Emily dated December 9, 1848. Both describe the collapse of a bridge over the Mohawk River. It fell under the weight of a crowd from Mr. Corey's church that had gathered to watch a number of candidates be baptized. One man was killed, and a number were injured; Mrs. Jones was severely injured, and the family feared for her life. Anna Maria tells of how her sister Fanny was standing next to Mrs. Jones, but she had her parasol open and that helped to break her fall.

[115] In his letter of December 9, 1848, Mr. Jones describes his difficulties and how he has been in less-than-perfect health since fall 1846.

[116] Augusta Crafts is mentioned frequently in the letters written from the Utica Female Academy. A number of references chronicle her very strong opinions; many of these were spoken against N. P. Willis and Emily's relationship to him (Mrs. Crafts did not approve of either). In an April 30, 1845, letter Anna Maria Anable said, "The Dr. is not engaged nor isn't going to be to Mary Spencer I imagine, and tho' Mrs. Crafts intimated very strongly that there was *some one* he had his eye upon, he denied it to me strongly and scolded about Mrs. Crafts gossiping tongue."

[117] Dr. James was a trusted physician, who attended the students and faculty of the Utica Female Academy. He is mentioned frequently in the correspondence as having been consulted for varying medical complaints, and his advice was always welcomed and highly regarded.

Nott[118] is not only a sufferer with Rheumatism but I fear will be, or is a martyr to Hydropathy—plunge baths and "packing"—Urania[119] was to have come home with me for the first visit here—but she could not leave him then—she however got here and was delighted with every thing [sic]—even Anna Maria's teaching and government met decided approval—The Referees with whom she was acquainted passed an evening here, all had an effect—they are becoming interested—by and by we shall live by the *school*—Dear Emily—in Mrs. Wade[120] you have a friend indeed—she kindly filled a sheet for me after she got in her quiet home at Eaton. I can hardly wait for the Union Meeting in May to see them—It is possible Anna M. Bennett[121] may go back with them—she is thinking of it. Heaven grant health to yourself and dear little ones[122]—Love to all—tell dear Lydia[123] to write me—affectionately and truly your friend

C. Sheldon

Source: American Baptist Historical Society, AJ 20, no. 998.

The Reverend Doctor Solomon Peck to Emily C. Judson, October 29, 1848—Rooms

My dear Mrs. Judson,

Having written to your husband about you, I find in it an additional reason for writing to you. It would pain me not a little, if by any thing [sic] there expressed I were to give you pain. Since the day that I met you in the parlor at Utica,[124] I have

[118] See vol. 1, "Cast of Characters," s.v. "Nott, The Reverend Doctor Eliphalet."

[119] See vol. 1, "Cast of Characters," s.v. "Sheldon, Urania."

[120] Deborah Wade was a missionary to Burmah; with her husband Jonathan, they were appointed in 1823. Adoniram Judson called them "his dearest and best of friends." Much of their work was in the jungle communities following the path of George Boardman. They left for the United States on December 22, 1847. From the Hamilton, New York, area, they stayed not far from the home of Emily's parents and sister; they visited the Anable-Sheldon families in Philadelphia. With a large group, they had left Boston on July 25, 1850, and returned to Burmah in February 1851.

[121] Anna Bennett was the daughter of Cephas and Stella Bennett, missionaries to Burmah. They arrived in 1830; Anna was born in August 1833. She returned to the United States for her education and was enrolled at the Utica Female Academy; she would have been fifteen years old at this time.

[122] Henry Hall Judson, six years old; Edward Judson, almost four years old; and Emily Frances Judson, almost a year old.

[123] See vol. 1, "Cast of Characters," s.v. "Lillybridge, Lydia." See also "A Timeline of the Life and Mission of Lydia Lillybridge Simons."

[124] After Lydia Lillybridge was accepted to missionary service by the Board of the American Baptist Missionary Union, Dr. Solomon Peck traveled to Utica to meet with her and with Emily at the same time, though he admitted to Adoniram Judson that his meeting with Emily was for his own interest and was not required by the board. See Adoniram Judson's letter of April 20, 1846, written to Emily to hide "Anna Maria up into the attic or some other hiding place—and any other of your community who has such a wicked face and is addicted to such carryings on—Be quick, or he will be upon you. And put on a quantity sufficient of longitude of face yourself and pitch all the 'bracelets and anklets' into the oven—for he is coming—father Peck—not old father Peck—but the great hideous, the Corresponding Sec. of the ABBFMN—which means the American Baptist Board of Foreign Missions, even the Rev. Solomon Peck—he is coming—not the subdued, meek man that lately visited you—no—no—but Solomon Peck, the organ of the board, a man to take the shins off of you, before you can get your stockings mended—."

See also the not-so-sympathetic letter that Dr. Peck wrote to Emily after that meeting, sternly admonishing her of the need to put things behind her. It was strongly moralistic and judgmental. After all, she was the person—Fanny Forester—who wrote those books he did not think the denomination should reprint.

been substantially of one mind, not being by nature "given to change." And I still cherish the kind and good thoughts concerning you which I had then. And I have others in addition. God began before you left this country to prove to you his abiding faithfulness; and since your departure He has given many infallible proofs that He is with you still. Yet I am left in the weakness of my faith to a painful solicitude lest trial and suffering break your health and spirit. I say weakness of faith, for God is *able* to make all grace abound unto you according to your utmost need. I pray most fervently that He will *do* according to his power; and that you may be filled with the fullness of his strength, wisdom, and consolation and joy. It will give me great pleasure to receive a letter from you. And be assured that, whatever you write to me, will come to one who, divine grace assisting, will not turn your confidence to causeless sorrow, but will endeavor in all circumstances to imitate *Him* who a*bide*th faithful.

Truly your brother

S. Peck

Source: American Baptist Historical Society, AJ 19, no. 949.

Anna Maria Anable to Emily C. Judson, October 29, 1848—Philadelphia

Dear Nemmy[125]

It seems a great while since I have written to you and yet it is only two months. In those months I have set up for school ma'am in very deed [sic]. We have only twelve scholars as yet, but we are all as busy as bees, and I can assure you that our school is delightful. I am much obliged for the good advice in your last letter and shall try to profit by it. In all matters pertaining to the religious instruction of the school, I find my task easier than I had anticipated. Shall I tell you what we do from 9 till 2, which are school hours?

At nine I read and have prayers, occupying about ten minutes—then follows the French class which continues two hours. The rest of the day we devote to the different English classes, Music, drawing etc. At present I am teaching only Ahnorombic [sic] Rhetoric and English Grammar, but I expect to have much more to do another year. Mary[126] has the Mathematical, drawing, and geographical departments and Fanny[127] takes the little ones in every thing [sic]. Hatty[128] will take the

[125] "Nem" or "Nemmy" was a name of endearment given to Emily by a small group of her intimate friends at the Utica Female Academy. Anna Maria Anable was "Ninny."

[126] See vol. 1, "Cast of Characters," s.v. "Anable, Miss Mary Juliet."

[127] See vol. 1, "Cast of Characters," s.v. "Anable, Fanny."

[128] See vol. 1, "Cast of Characters," s.v. "Anable, Harriet."

French and History when she comes, which we expect will be by the last of Dec.[129] Our scholars all look interested in their school and I assure you Emily it is a great pleasure to have a school just to your own liking. We have children from the very most respected families in the city for instance—the great-granddaughter of Chas. Carroll of Carrolton, and the daughters of Senator Bayard, whose mother "hopes to be of some service to us in introducing us to a large circle of acquaintances." She is a brilliant woman of the world, but wishes her daughters not only to be accomplished but thoroughly educated. Then we have the grand-daughter of old Matthew Casey, who made the finest collection of paintings and statuary in the city. Her mother has succeeded to the old gentleman's house and paintings, so that we have access to the gallery whenever we please. A daughter of Dr. Duaguson [sic], Pres. of the Medical College and one of Mr. George Earp make up the list of aristocrats. These children are electioneering for us every where [sic]. They seem as much pleased with us, as we are with them. As for the discipline of the school—we have no rules at all. The children are with the teachers all the time and we think we can manage them better without rules. I have erased from the present circulars the remarks upon self-government, for the more I thought of introducing the daily report into our school the more convinced I became that it tended to make little hypocrites. Now Nemmy what do you think the Baptists are about that they pay no attention to us? Dr. Ide[130] has not been near us, and not until this week has Mr. R( ) called. We have not a Baptist scholar from the city with the exception of young miss from Sansom St. church. Mrs. Brooks and Mrs. Robarts[131] have called and Mrs. R. means to send Mary in the Spring. It is a little amusing to me after all that was said in Utica about our wishing to establish a Baptist School.

Drs Bethume [sic], Cayler, and Luddon are very friendly and I go very often to hear Dr. Bethume preach. He is a man after my own heart and if I attend Mr. Gillette's[132] church twice a day, I must recharge myself in the Music Service. The Dr. has sent me books twice, so you see he means to be cordial. Many pleasant people have called, but not a solitary Baptist. You know I do not like this—for tho' I do not wish to be sectarian as far as society goes, yet I know that there is in this

[129] See the letter from Hatty Anable to Emily C. Judson dated March 26, 1849. Hatty made a commitment to a family in New Orleans through the end of December, and though there was hope she could be released from it, it appears that this did not happen.

[130] Dr. George Ide was born in Coventry, Vermont, in 1804. Though his father was a minister, George Ide tended toward skepticism and developed a reputation for being quite vocal in sharing his dissident views. After a powerful religious experience of conversion, he gave himself to revivalism, preaching in a number of smaller churches throughout Vermont before being called to Albany, New York. Over the years, he had a series of successful pastorates, including the Clarendon Street Church in Boston. He was at the First Baptist Church of Philadelphia for sixteen years and at the First Baptist Church of Springfield, Massachusetts, for twenty. He was the author of two volumes of sermons and a Sunday school book titled *Green Hollow*. Dr. Ide is mentioned in an October 29, 1848, letter from Anna Maria Anable, and an August 7, 1852, letter of Miss Cynthia Sheldon to Emily Judson. (William Cathcart, *The Baptist Encyclopaedia* [Philadelphia: Louis H. Everts, 1881] 568.)

[131] See vol. 1, "Cast of Characters," s.v. "Robarts, Mr. and Mrs. W. S."

[132] See vol. 1, "Cast of Characters," s.v. "Gillette, The Reverend Abram Dunn."

city very superior society of our own denomination, and I hope some time [sic] or other to get acquainted with it.

It is only two months since we came so I do not mean to complain—only I wish Baptists any where [sic], were a little more independent—I believe they wait always to see the *Pedo* stamp. Ah, Nemmy, if you could see how pleasant our home is for Mother[133] you would be glad with us. Her room is just across the hall from the parlor, and with her knitting she spends every evening with us, and it really seems as if she is likely to have some rest and enjoyment in the old age.

Some old ladies (neighbors) have called upon her, and I am quite sure she will enjoy the society here better than she ever did any where [sic], except in Troy. Aunt U.[134] has made us a visit, and she seemed really pleased with all of our arrangements. She thinks the house delightful and says she knows we are going to have a grand school. When we get to making money Nemmy I hope I sha'nt [sic] forget the Missionary cause.[135] Give a kiss to Miss Emily Frances[136] and tell her I should have written her this time, but it is most eleven o'clock at night, and our future school ma'am must be regular in her habits or she'll be worn out before Miss ( ) comes over. How glad I am that you are so well! Do take good care of yourself and keep so, for I shall hope to see you yet in our home. Give love to Lydia[137] and tell her she is in my debt, and I mean to expect the uttermost farthing for my engagements now are as pressing as hers.

Adieu. Anna M.

Source: American Baptist Historical Society, AJ 13, no. 486.

[133] See vol. 1, "Cast of Characters," s.v. "Sheldon, Alma and Joseph Hubbell."

[134] See vol. 1, "Cast of Characters," s.v. "Sheldon, Urania."

[135] See vol. 1, "Cast of Characters," s.v. "Anable, Miss Anna Maria."

[136] See vol. 1, "Cast of Characters," s.v. "Judson, Emily Frances."

[137] See vol. 1, "Cast of Characters," s.v. "Lillybridge, Lydia." See also "A Timeline of the Life and Mission of Lydia Lillybridge Simons."

Adoniram Judson to Abby Ann Judson,[138] November 26, 1848—Maulmain[139]

My Dear Daughter,

I waited long for a letter from you, and at last yours of April 21st and August 11th both came together a few days ago. I am sorry that I let so long time pass without writing to you; but I was expecting a letter every month, and the months passed away more rapidly than I was aware. The whole past year I have been working on the dictionary, and I expect to put the first volume, the English and Burmese part, to press in a very short time. The other part will cost me at least two years more. Your little sister Emily Frances[140] is a fine healthy child. She has got your teeth and can almost stand alone, being now eleven months old. It is generally said, that she looks like you. Henry[141] can read children's books pretty readily. Edward[142] is a stout chunky fellow, another John Bull, like Elnathan,[143] though Henry has Elnathan's face. We are a deliciously happy family; but we think much of the three

[138] One of the themes of this letter to Abby Ann is her salvation and that of her brothers Adoniram and Elnathan. It was not an uncommon theme for Adoniram Judson.

An earlier letter to Adoniram and Elnathan, probably written in late fall 1845 after he left them with Dr. and Mrs. Newton in Worcester, Massachusetts, states:

> You know not how much I love you, and how much I think of you. I pray for you every time I pray for myself. I hear that there are revivals of religion beginning to appear in different parts of the country. It would be a blessed thing if you should both experience religion, and have the privilege of beginning a revival in Worcester. Cherish this desire in your hearts and pray in faith that the blessing may come. If you begin to feel sorry for your sins, and afraid of the wrath to come, and begin to love the dear Saviour, because he has died to save you, and feel some desire to commit your immortal souls to him, and be forgiven and accepted, you may begin to hope the grace of God is reaching you, and that the blessed work is just beginning. Hold on, then, and cherish those impressions, until you get full light and hope.
>
> Dear children, remember your father in his solitary wanderings, and forget not your dear mother, whom we buried at St. Helena. Pray for your sister, and your little brothers beyond the sea. You ever affectionate father, A. Judson (Francis Wayland, *A Memoir of the Life and Labors of the Rev. Adoniram Judson, D. D.* [Boston: Phillips, Sampson, and Co., 1853] 241).

Then, in May 1848, he wrote again to Adoniram and Elnathan:

> My dear sons: Is it possible that I have letters from you at last? I had waited so long that I began to think it never would be. And I am so glad to hear of your welfare, and especially that you have both been under religious impressions, and that Elnathan begins to entertain a hope in Christ! O, this is the most blessed news. Go on, my dear boys, and not rest until you have made your calling and election sure. I believe that you both and Abby Ann will become true Christians, and meet me in heaven; for I never pray without praying for your conversion, and I think I pray in faith. Go to school, attend to your studies, be good scholars, try to get a good education; but, O, heaven is all. Life, life, eternal life! Without this, without an interest in the Lord of life, you are lost, lost forever. Dear Adoniram, give your heart at once to the Saviour. Don't go to sleep without doing it. You may wake up in hell. Try, try for your life. Don't mind what any body [sic] may say to the contrary, nor how much foolish boys may laugh at you. Love the dear Saviour, who has loved you unto death. Dear sons, so soon as you have a good hope in Christ that your sins are pardoned, and that Christ loves you, urge your pastor and the church to baptize and receive you into communion. They will hold back, thinking you are too young, and must give more evidence. But don't be discouraged. Push on. Determine to do it. Determine to stand by Christ, come what will. That is the way to get to heaven—Will Elnathan tell me what little book it was that was so much blessed to him? I have forgotten what I sent him. I have sent you copies of your mother's Memoir. You will be delighted to read it, so beautifully and so truthfully is it written. Ever love to cherish the memory of your own dear mother,—how much she loved you to the last gasp;—and prepare to follow her to heaven. Your fond father, A. Judson. (Francis Wayland, *A Memoir of the Life and Labors of the Rev. Adoniram Judson, D. D.* [Boston: Phillips, Sampson, and Co., 1853] 307–308)

dear absent ones,[144] and my tears frequently fall for your dear dear mother in her lone bed at St. Helena.[145] And every time I enter the burial place here, I see the white grave-stone of poor little black-eyed Charley.[146] Ah, we had to leave the poor little fellow to die in the arms of Mrs. Osgood.[147] It was hard, but we could not help it. God's will be done. He is now happy with his mother. If you should die, would you go to them too? O that I would hear of your and your brother's conversion. I did have some hope for Elnathan a few months ago. He wrote me as follows: "I have felt a change for the last fortnight. Our minister Mr. Swaim[148] has been to see me, and I have been to see him. When all of a sudden I felt changed. I felt happy and loved to pray. I loved to read the Bible, and I never felt so happy in my life. The

[139] This letter originally came from Mrs. Marjorie Carson Hanna Shipman, a great-granddaughter of Adoniram and Emily Judson. Her father was Thomas Carson Hanna. Mrs. Shipman gave this letter and two others, as well as other Judson artifacts, to the First Baptist Church of Malden, Massachusetts, thinking that the Baptist Church in the city of Adoniram Judson's birth would be a good repository. These letters and artifacts are now on loan to the American Baptist Churches Board of International Ministries, held by the American Baptist Historical Society. This editor was the pastor of that historic church from 1977 to 1983.

[140] See vol. 1, "Cast of Characters," s.v. "Judson, Emily Frances."

[141] See vol. 1, "Cast of Characters," s.v. "Judson, Henry Hall."

[142] See vol. 1, "Cast of Characters," s.v. "Judson, Edward."

[143] Elnathan "Elly" Judson was born July 15, 1838, the third child and second son of Adoniram and Sarah Hall Boardman Judson. From November 1845 to October 1851, he lived with Dr. and Mrs. Calvin Newton in Worcester, Massachusetts. He then spent a year with Dr. and Mrs. Edward Bright in Roxbury, Massachusetts, and before entering Brown University, he spent two years at Pierce Academy in Middleboro, Massachusetts. There are strong indications that Elnathan planned to become a minister, and in fact, he did graduate from Union Seminary. In 1860, however, he suffered a serious sunstroke that subsequently caused serious mental impairment. For much of his life, Elnathan was confined to mental institutions. He died after a second paralyzing stroke in 1896; in the last years of his life, Elnathan was lovingly cared for by his sister Abby Ann Judson.

[144] Adoniram and Elnathan Judson were living in Worcester, Massachusetts, with Dr. and Mrs. Calvin Newton. Abby Ann was living at Bradford Academy, where she was intimately involved with the Hasseltine family.

[145] Sarah Hall Boardman Judson was the mother of George Dana Boardman, Abby Ann, Adoniram, Elnathan, Henry, and Edward Judson. A first Henry Judson died at one and a half years old; Luther Judson was stillborn, and Charles Judson died at one and a half years old. The family left Burmah for the United States on account of Sarah's health in 1845; she died at the Isle of St. Helena on September 1, 1845, and she was buried there.

[146] Because he was so young and frail, Charles Judson was left in the care of one of the missionary families in Burmah, along with Henry and Edward, when Adoniram, Sarah, and the older children left for the United States. He had died a few months after their departure, and Adoniram did not learn of his death until a letter reached him on November 28, 1845.

[147] Rev. Sewall Osgood was a missionary in Maulmain who worked with and lived by Adoniram Judson. Judson and Osgood occupied two of the four homes in the mission compound and lived so close that it "allowed me the pleasure and profit of almost hourly intercourse." He arrived in Burmah in 1834. His first wife Elhira Brown Osgood died on October 5, 1837, in Maulmain. On July 8, 1838, he married Sarah Thomas, the widow of the Reverend Jacob Thomas, with Adoniram Judson officiating at the wedding. He spoke in the letters to Emily, of which there are five between July 1850 and April 1852, of Adoniram Judson as his "most intimate friend." He never personally met Emily, as he had returned from the field prior to 1846. At the time of his letters, he was working with the American Baptist Missionary Union as a district secretary. In 1845, just as they were leaving for the United States, Sarah and Adoniram Judson gave care of Charley, too young to make the trip, to Mr. and Mrs. Osgood. Charley died not long after their departure. Mr. Osgood visted Adoniram, Elnathan, and Abby Ann in the United States. His third wife was Caroline Wait; they were married December 30, 1850, at Saratoga, New York. With all of his suggestions of "intimacy" and "his most intimate friend," Mr. Osgood stated that his life was so busy that he simply did not have the time to look through his papers for anything that would be helpful in writing the Judson memoir.

[148] The Reverend Doctor Samuel Swaim was born in Pemberton, New Jersey, in June 1809. He finished his college courses at Brown University and then entered Newton Theological Institution. He taught college studies in Granville, Ohio, before receiving a call as pastor of the First Baptist Church in Worcester, Massachusetts. In October 1851, just as she was returning to America, Dr. Swaim wrote Emily about the possible baptism of Elnathan. He spoke of Elnathan's coming to faith and of his meeting with the church requesting baptism, and he was obviously trying to schedule this important event at a time when Emily could be present.

impressions made on my mind, from one of the books which you sent me has remained written on my heart, and that little book has led me to think on these things. You cannot think how much good that little book has done for me. It has aided me to be a Christian. It has showed me the way to paradise." And when Mr. Brayton[149] saw him just before leaving America, he thought he gave some evidence of being born again. But alas! Since that, I have heard nothing more, and in two later letters, he says nothing on the subject of religion. Morning cloud and early dew, I am afraid. And yet I cannot but hope that the seed is sown which will yet spring up to life eternal.

I am very much pleased with all (you) say about your studies, and the progress you make, and the prospects you have of getting a good education. And I am much pleased with the account you have given of your visit to Framingham and Worcester.[150] Did your brothers say anything to you on the subject of religion? Dr. and Mrs. Newton[151] wrote me some months ago, that Adoniram[152] seems to have as deep religious impressions as Elnathan, but I have heard nothing else. Emily and Mary Howard[153] and Eddy Stevens[154] were all baptized a few weeks ago. They appear to be true Christians. Emily thinks that she experienced a change of heart, as much as five years ago, though she said nothing about it, except to her mother. She is, you know, one day older than you. Eddy is, I believe, not as old as Elnathan. He is very clear in his expressions and very consistent and humble in his ( ) and quiet deportment. Lydia Pascal and Judson Pascal and several ( ) scholars from Mr. Howard's school, have also been baptized. Oh, if you and your brothers had staid [sic] here among the heathen, perhaps you would have got grace,—but now at Bradford and Worcester, in the midst of light privileges, it may be said of you as of Capernaum—

[149] The Reverend Durlin L. Brayton was born in Hubbardton, Vermont, on October 27, 1808. He graduated from Brown University and then the Newton Theological Seminary in 1837, at which time he was appointed to missionary service. On October 2, 1837, he married Mary Hawley Fuller, and they sailed for Burmah on October 28, 1837. They arrived in April 1838 and, passing through Amherst and Maulmain, arrived at Mergui in April 1840. In February 1847, they departed Maulmain for America due to Mrs. Brayton's ill health. Mr. Brayton returned to Burmah the following November, and Mrs. Brayton remained in America until arriving back in Burmah in March 1850. They had one daughter, Mary. Mary (Mrs. Durlin) Brayton died December 16, 1890, in Rangoon; Durlin Brayton died April 23, 1900, also in Rangoon.

[150] See letters from Adoniram "Addy" Judson and Elnathan "Elly" Judson dated August 15 and 16, 1848, as they describe this visit and some of their activities.

[151] See vol. 1, "Cast of Characters," s.v. "Newton, Doctor Calvin and Mrs. M. I."

[152] Adoniram "Addy" Judson was born April 7, 1837, the second child and first son of Adoniram and Sarah Hall Boardman Judson. From November 1845 to October 1851, he lived with Dr. and Mrs. Calvin Newton in Worcester, Massachusetts. He then spent a year with Dr. and Mrs. Edward Bright in Roxbury, Massachusetts, and before entering Brown University, he was two years at Pierce Academy in Middleboro, Massachusetts. After his education and medical school, Adoniram served as a surgeon in the Civil War and became a prominent orthopedic surgeon with several books to his credit. He died in 1916. Over the years, he became vocal about the separation of missionary children from their parents.

[153] Emily and Mary Howard were the daughters of Hosea and Theresa Howard, missionaries to Burmah. The Howards were responsible for a Burman school maintained by the mission, and Lydia Lillybridge reported to Mr. Howard.

[154] Edward Stevens was the son of Edward and Elizabeth Stevens, missionaries to Burmah. Edward was born in Burmah on December 17, 1838.

exalted to heaven—but at last, cast down to hell! James Haswell[155] is under ( ), but gives no satisfactory evidence. Little David ( ) gives some evidence, and Sarah Stilson's[156] mother thinks that she has got grace; the Howards[157] are not going home at present as she is rather better. But the Haswell's[158] are going very soon. He has preached his farewell discourse to the native church, and now the whole care of the church devolves on me again except that I expect some assistance from Mr. Stevens.[159] You can never know how much I want to see you—how much I think of you—how much I pray for you always when I pray for myself. O my dear daughter, my motherless daughter, meet me at the throne of grace—meet me in the bosom of Jesus, and we shall meet in his blessed presence on high, together with your dear mother, lost to us for a time, but not forever—whose spirit ever watches over you and will rejoice with joy yet unfelt, when you turn to the Saviour and give your heart to him.[160]

Your longing, hoping father.

A. Judson

[155] James Haswell was the son of James and Jane Haswell, missionaries to Burmah. Arriving early in 1836, the Haswells served for more than forty years. Young James Haswell was born in Burmah in September 1836.

[156] Sarah Stilson was the daughter of Lyman and Hannah Stilson. The Stilsons arrived in Burmah in February 1838. Sarah Stilson was born in Burmah in August 1839.

[157] Hosea and Theresa Howard first sailed for Burmah in 1834, arriving in December that year. Hosea Howard was a recent graduate of the theological seminary in Hamilton, New York. They were stationed in Maulmain as missionaries with Adoniram Judson, and he claimed in a letter to Emily that he worked there with Adoniram longer than any other missionary. Mr. Howard's responsibility was to run schools that the mission maintained, a task in which he was ably assisted by his wife. Lydia Lillybridge was responsible to Mr. and Mrs. Howard when she arrived in November 1846. Mr. and Mrs. Howard left Maulmain for the United States in February 1850.

[158] James Madison Haswell was born February 4, 1810, in Bennington, Vermont. He was married to Jane Matilda Mason of Cheshire, Massachusetts. The Haswells sailed for Burmah on September 23, 1835, to work with the Talaings. They arrived at Amherst in February 1836. The Haswells became partners with Adoniram and Sarah Hall Boardman Judson; Sarah turned over the translation of the Peguan scripture to Mr. Haswell after Elnathan and Adoniram were born, and her energies were focused elsewhere. When Sarah and Adoniram sailed for America in 1845, the Haswells took care of Henry until Adoniram returned in 1847 with Emily. The Haswells left Burmah in December 1848 and arrived in America in 1849; they remained in the United States until September 1852, when they again sailed for Burmah.

[159] Edward Stevens arrived in Maulmain in February 1838; his wife was Elizabeth Stevens. Mr. Stevens was responsible for the native churches that were associated with the mission. He took on the work of finishing the dictionary after the death of Adoniram Judson, and he buried "Angel Charley" in the chapel compound after his birth in April 1850. Mr. Stevens was in Burmah for forty-eight years.

[160] Adoniram Judson was a missionary and was called to proclaim the gospel to those in foreign lands who would never have an opportunity to turn to Jesus Christ and the salvation that was offered through grace. He had this same passion for his family, and this letter reflects Adoniram Judson's questions and concerns about his three children in the United States and the state of their souls. Similarly, Emily sent her brother J. Walker Chubbuck a letter on June 21, 1848, as she clearly presented the gospel to him and inquired as to his spiritual condition. We would note as well the letters from Miss Cynthia Sheldon and Miss Anna Maria Anable at the end of March 1847; a revival was happening in the local church. Fanny and Henry, a sister and brother to Anna Maria and a niece and nephew of Miss Sheldon, had come to faith in Jesus Christ; several other members of the household had also been touched, and others were struggling with the issues in the midst of much family concern and prayer. Then in 1852–1853, there were multiple letters from Mr. A. C. Osborn. A student at Hamilton College, Mr. Osborn moved into the Chubbuck home to help with Henry and Edward Judson, who at that time would have been ten and eight years old. Mr. Osborn wrote continually of their spiritual condition, their "almost converted" moments, and the extent of his own personal efforts to bring them into the presence of saving grace.

P.S. I write this on a separate paper, as more suitable for your eyes alone, though I know of no objection to its being seen by others, if you have none. I have thought it possible, that seeing so many praises bestowed upon me, you might feel somewhat elated, thinking that you are the daughter of such a man. Bear in mind, that I am only a poor missionary; and that most of the praises I receive are occasioned by the good missionary feeling that prevails among the churches, and their forwardness to patronize and encourage every enterprise that aims at convicting the work. Bear in mind also, that however highly you may regard your father, and however gratified you may be, that he has attained some degree of distinction, it will be in the eyes of others anything but lovely and amiable for you to appear proud of it, or put on any airs in that account. Remember, rather, that mere meekness, and humility and virtue of every kind will be expected of you, than if you were the daughter of a person of no distinction at all.

One thing more—perhaps as I have not been at hand to explain the matter to you—you may not be aware of the obligations we are under to the family at Bradford, nor feel sufficiently thankful for their kindness to you. I think I have mentioned before, that Dr. Newton gets $100 a year for each of your brothers whereas we pay nothing for your board and tuition, nor for this kindness, which has admitted you into the family as one of themselves. This kindness might have been expected, if you had been the daughter of their sister Ann; but your mother was no relative of the family, nor your father, except through a former marriage. And yet they allow you to call them aunt and cousins and—and they treat you like a daughter and give you such advantages, that I know of no situation in the whole country to which I should be willing to remove you. Do, therefore, be obedient and grateful and kind to them all and our hope that the time will come, when you will be able in some way to make even return for all the kindness they bestow upon you. As soon as I am able, I intend to send you some money to give your cousins N( ) and Ellen.

Source: Marjorie Hanna Shipman, the First Baptist Church, Malden, Massachusetts

Anna Maria Anable to Emily C. Judson, November 27, 1848—Philadelphia

Your letter dear Emily which I received last week made me feel too provoked at myself for anything. Why need I go and tell you what Mrs. Grundy petted at, when the more you humour [sic] the old lady the more she frets. I was all taken aback by your giving up so meekly. I wanted you to come out in wrath upon them, but you have done best. Did I ever tell you that the writer of the criticism in the *Recorder*, which by the way I never saw, was Anne Wayland?[161]

[161] This was a review of Emily's recently published book: *Memoir of Sarah B. Judson, Member of the American Mission to Burmah* (New York: L. Colby and Company, 1848).

I *guess* you will have to give up my being a Missionary[162] Nemmy,[163] for my little school[164] takes a strong hold on my interest and affection, and I begin to feel too old to think of "toting" across the waters. The fact is I feel less and less inclined to make the sacrifice of friends, home, (now that I have one) and the comforts of life; and the more I feel so, the more I am afraid I shall have to come to it one of these days. I'll tell you what—I mean to be always willing, and then may be I shall not have to.

I forwarded your note to Prof. Anderson.[165] The man has been engaged long ago, and ought to have been married, to set the hearts of single maidens at rest.

I have just had a delightful visit from Mr. and Mrs. Colby.[166] They are just the nicest folks I know of and I always feel ever so much obliged to your good husband for making me acquainted with them. I have seen Mr. Lincoln[167] also since we have been here, and brother Heman[168] comes to see us whenever he comes to town.

We are a great deal more in the way of seeing people than when in Utica. Mr. Hill of New York, Mr. and Mrs. Gillette[169] and Mr. and Mrs. Colby took tea with us on Sat. evening. The Gillettes are as kind as they can be, and Mr. G. trumpets us every where [sic] he goes, but his trumpeting does not get us any scholars.

[162] See vol. 1, "Cast of Characters," s.v. "Anable, Miss Anna Maria."

[163] "Nem" or "Nemmy" was a name of endearment given to Emily by a small group of her intimate friends at the Utica Female Academy. Anna Maria Anable was "Ninny."

[164] After leaving the Utica Female Academy in August 1848, Anna Maria Anable started the Misses Anable's School in Philadelphia with help from her sisters, her Aunt Cynthia Sheldon, and her mother.

[165] See vol. 1, "Cast of Characters," s.v. "Anderson, Mr."

[166] A prominent businessman, Gardner Colby and his family lived in Pemberton Square in Boston before moving "to the country," Newton Centre, Massachusetts. Mr. Colby was a member of the Board of the American Baptist Missionary Union and an avid supporter of the missionary movement. In a letter after they sailed from Boston to Burmah, Emily mentions the extravagant hospitality extended to them in early July as they waited for the *Faneuil Hall* to embark. Adoniram and Emily stayed with the Colby family frequently.

[167] Mr. Joshua Lincoln was a prominent Baptist in the Boston area. In summer 1847, when Anna Maria was in Boston for medical treatments, she boarded with the Lincoln family, and their names appear in a number of subsequent letters. Mr. Lincoln was in partnership with Charles Gould in the firm Gould, Kendall and Lincoln. This company published the memoirs of Ann Hasseltine Judson and George Dana Boardman and a book on baptism in 1846 by Adoniram Judson. There are three letters in the collection from the firm; Adoniram Judson had spoken to them about publishing the memoir of Sarah Hall Boardman Judson, and the letters state their surprise when they noticed the publication coming from the Lewis Colby Company of New York. They also sought material from Emily C. Judson for publication in their 1848 letters. Joshua Lincoln was a brother of Heman Lincoln. Mrs. Lincoln was a sister to Charles Gould.

[168] Born in 1821, Dr. Heman Lincoln was ordained in 1845 when Adoniram Judson was returning to the United States. He was in New Britain, Pennsylvania, and then in 1850, he moved to Philadelphia to pastor the Franklin Square church. Many of the letters from Anna Maria Anable and Miss Cynthia Sheldon contain references to Mr. Lincoln or Mr. and Mrs. Lincoln, and through this relationship, he became acquainted with Emily. There are three letters from Mr. Lincoln written in October 1851, just as Emily is returning to America. He is close enough to Emily so that they had a ride together before she returned to Hamilton. He was known to Emily's friends, Miss Cynthia Sheldon, Dr. Edward Bright, and Dr. Francis Wayland. In the second letter, he asks for clarification of their conversation as to her remarks on who would write the Judson memoir. The third letter thanks her for her reply to his second letter, and he speaks of the qualifications of Dr. Wayland. He was a brother to Joshua Lincoln.

[169] See vol. 1, "Cast of Characters," s.v. "Gillette, The Reverend Abram Dunn."

Have I told you how our family are all scattered? Sarah Bell[170] is at home in Cleveland, attending to her throat. She writes in good spirits, but is homesick for Aunt Cynthia.[171] Jul Look[172] is in Virginia doing nobody knows what besides teaching for she never writes. Eugenia Damaux[173] is still in New York at Mrs. Brown's—the same warm-hearted French girl as ever. She always wants to know what I hear from you. Mary Adams[174] has gone back South this Fall, and Mary Barber[175] is in Utica with her dear friend Jane.[176] They have quite a snug little set there at the old place. Miss M. Incan [sic], Jimmy Blodgett,[177] Mary, Jane etc. but I do not suppose I should go there in years. I am heartily provoked at all the people, though *they* don't know it. I may wish we had a good preacher here; somehow I long for a sermon of brother Corey's[178] once in Phila.

I go to hear Dr. Bethume [sic] very often. Yesterday he preached on baptism—the design and base of it, and one of these days, he will preach on the *mode*. Wouldn't I clap my hands if he would only learn what the true mode is! If I dared I should lend him a little book that I know of[179]—but he would think me impertinent and very likely set it down as another instance of the bigotry and infatuation of the sect. He is a blessed man nevertheless, and were I not so sure that I am right, he would sooner than any other minister draw me back to my Dutch kin. Last evening we spent at Dr. Caylers—very pleasantly. There are four girls—all sociable and very cordial to us. One of them is coming to school next Monday. We were all invited last week to Mrs. Potter's, to meet all the school teachers under the Bishop's patronage and some of the most distinguished patrons of schools. Our school is

[170] See vol. 1, "Cast of Characters," s.v. "Wheeler, Sarah Bell."

[171] See vol. 1, "Cast of Characters," s.v. "Sheldon, Miss Cynthia."

[172] See vol. 1, "Cast of Characters," s.v. "Look, Julia."

[173] Eugenia Damaux had been part of Emily's intimate circle of friends at the Utica Female Academy. Living in New York City, Eugenia suffered from some kind of eye problem that made life difficult at times; this was a matter of comment in many of the letters exchanged between the girls themselves and with Miss Cynthia Sheldon. In 1848, Eugenia was in New York living "at Mrs. Brown's—the same warm-hearted French girl as ever." In 1849, she married Johnny Edmonds, described as rich and pious, and they lived in Utica.

[174] Mary Adams was related to the Utica Female Academy. Her letter to Emily in October 1845 was almost a whimsical piece of fantasy with literary pretensions. It would reflect a fairly close relationship. A second letter in December 1845 was similar. The letters were written from New Orleans, and she spoke of Hatty Anable as being near to her. On January 29, 1849, Anna Maria Anable wrote, "Hatty says Mary Adams is going to marry Gardner Green of Norwich,—a very fine young man, of invention, fortune, piety and all that Mary's heart was sighed for." On July 8, 1850, Mrs. Urania Sheldon Nott spoke of attending this wedding in New York.

[175] See vol. 1, "Cast of Characters," s.v. "Barber, Mary."

[176] See vol. 1, "Cast of Characters," s.v. "Kelly, Miss Jane."

[177] Jimmy Blodgett had been mentioned in Anna Maria's letter dated June 28, 1848, as having been proposed by Jane Kelly for an administrative position at the Utica Female Academy after the departure of Miss Cynthia Sheldon. The letter suggested surprise that such a nomination would be made.

[178] See vol. 1, "Cast of Characters," s.v. "Corey, The Reverend D. G."

[179] Adoniram Judson wrote a book on baptism; it was the subject of letters to him in February and March 1848 from Gould, Kendall and Lincoln.

slowly increasing, we have fifteen now. Molly[180] and Matilda[181] are having a great frolic by my side, over a guitar lesson. Fanny[182] sings very sweetly now—she has gone to give a lesson. Altogether we manage to keep quite busy.

Cortland[183] has gone to Hartford and Boston on business, and we feel quite lonesome without him. I must send off this wretched scrawl or it will not get mailed till next month. If you did not tell me once in a while that you cared for a letter, I should not think mine worth the sending. Kiss little sis[184] for me, and

[Written in the left margin and across the text of page 4:] tell the Dr. when I get amiable and humble, may be I'll tell some more news.

Lovingly as ever

Anna M.

[Written in the left margin and across the text of page 1:] Elder Leonard is here making people pay up what they owe to their master for the "bible society." He wants to send fifty thousand bibles into Austria at once. Mr. Hill is looking after a young brother Wheeler who is going on a mission to San Francisco in California.

Source: American Baptist Historical Society, AJ 13, no. 485.

Mr. Morven M. Jones[185] to Emily C. Judson,[186] December 9, 1848[187]—Utica

My Dear and much Eternal Friend.

Pardon such an apparently cold and formal introduction and which so feebly expresses the true sentiments of *our* heart as "Very dear" etc. but it the best [sic] I dare choose especially with the fact of my long silence staring me in the face—Two years and a half are but a small dot on the great circle of Eternity; a short, unimportant line upon the pages of the worlds [sic] history, but how long a portion, how important in events and consequences are they in the allotment of frail, feeble and finite man—a period possibly in which he views all the little of which he ever gained of worldly immortality, or gains an humble hope of an eternal present before the

[180] See vol. 1, "Cast of Characters," s.v. "Anable, Miss Mary Juliet."

[181] See vol. 1, "Cast of Characters," s.v. "Berthoud, Matilda."

[182] See vol. 1, "Cast of Characters," s.v. "Anable, Fanny."

[183] See vol. 1, "Cast of Characters," s.v. "Anable, Courtland."

[184] See vol. 1, "Cast of Characters," s.v. "Judson, Emily Frances."

[185] Morven Jones lived in Utica, New York, and was an active member of the Bleecker Street Baptist Church. His wife, Mary, was seriously injured in the collapse of a bridge while the church was baptizing a number of new members in the Mohawk River. He wrote Emily several letters over the years and was an enthusiastic cheerleader for her missionary career.

[186] This letter from Morven M. Jones, written over three days, is probably the longest letter in the correspondence. It is four large pages of small handwriting.

[187] There are two addenda to this letter, dated December 21 and 22, 1848.

Throne.—But we should not talk thus were we to meet either upon the banks of the pagoda lined views of India or Church lined views of N. York—How *do* you do? How does that little bamboo-cradled pet fledgling do?[188] Ah—we hope and pray the great Giver that the answer is a cheerful, smiling, happy "all is well"—Is the primitive sentiment drawn from a residence among souls clad in sin and darkness, fraught with happiness? Yes, we trustfully reply in your stead.—

We parted laughing at Mr. Colby's July 2, 1846[189]—In the fall of that year my health failed gradually until I was unable to leave my house and for about eight months I was unable to do anything—until mid-summer of 1847—Since then I have gained very slowly sometimes better for a few days—then worse—then better again and in the aggregate I am in some better health than a year ago—Thus much for my own ills—How garrulous one is apt to become as to his ailments (especially if those all live on one's nerves) if he is for a long time "under the weather"—Now as to Mary—You probably read an account of the accident—On 9th May, 47 while Mr. Corey[190] was baptizing where Dr. Judson baptized Miss Anable, the side walk [sic] of the bridge fell and precipitated about 30 persons men, women and children upon the rocks and into the river below—a distance of about 15 feet[191]—My Mary was more seriously injured than any other, except Mr. Smith who was killed—

Her left shoulder blade was broken across above the middle and the lower part broken into 3 or 4 pieces. Two or three of her ribs were cracked as was also the shoulder cap—But worse than all the rest was the injury to her lungs by being crushed—The shoulder blade could not be set, because she could not (even for months) support the least bandaging, not even a sheet across her chest, and the broken pieces settled down nearly under her arm where they grew together in a lump, but when dressed her figure is not changed for the worse, for she says that shoulder is improved and talks of breaking the other to better its shape—Thanks to a kind Providence which directed Homoeopathy with its Arnica etc. there was very little inflammation—To this day however her side and lungs are very weak and at times very sore—When she was brot [sic] home (I was at home ill) the Dr. feared the worst as to her life[192]—In a few weeks she took her place in the gallery at

[188] See vol. 1, "Cast of Characters," s.v. "Judson, Emily Frances."

[189] Emily and Adoniram Judson stayed at the Colby home in Pemberton Square, Boston, prior to their departure for Burmah on July 11, 1846. Mr. Colby was a member of the Board of the American Baptist Missionary Union and an avid supporter of the missionary movement. After they sailed from Boston to Burmah, Emily writes of the extravagant hospitality extended to them in early July as they waited for the *Faneuil Hall* to embark. Adoniram and then Emily stayed with the Colby family quite frequently over the years.

[190] See vol. 1, "Cast of Characters," s.v. "Corey, The Reverend D. G."

[191] In her letter to Emily Judson dated June 19, 1847, Anna Maria Anable tells this story in some detail. She says that the baptism was taking place in the Mohawk River, and it was the same place where she had been baptized by Adoniram Judson on June 7, 1846.

[192] On October 28, 1848, Miss Sheldon wrote to Emily: "Mary Jones looks very feeble—and her husband is much worse than when you left—my heart aches for them—wish he could find some thing here (in Philadelphia) to do for a good living—I begged him to come on and see if there was not some thing a change in his circumstances might work wonder in his health."

Church, pretending to be as well as ever, but a trial of her lungs told a different story, and after another similar effort with similar results she came down to sit with her larger 1/2 where she still is obliged to remain, although H. H. H.[193] has at various times summoned her back—With great care she may yet become comparatively sound, but never as well before—This I have attempted to answer a few of those natural questions which you might ask were you and she to meet—

I should have ere this have replied to the Dr's letter enclosing a draft on the Mission Treas'y for $41, in Miss Sheldon's[194] favor which came safely and was attended to with pleasure—I would invite any other commissions which either you or the Dr. might wish attended to in this country as it would give me much pleasure to be able to serve you in any way—Suspecting (as the event justified) that if I gave the order to Miss. S. her generous heart would cause her to burn it without drawing upon the Treas'y I got it cashed and gave her the proceeds—upon explaining how I came by it, she said she was not thus to be thwarted and the money would go into the Lord's Treas'y some other way—

We have to thank you for the valuable and much valued presents—the beauty of a tea pot and the Burmah Bible—We did drink your health—health—peace and prosperity in the pretty tiny tea-pot—yes we drank from it more than once—How much it has been admired and talked about—and the Bible that is *mine*—Ah you know my penchant aye passion for such things—and that Bible is a great thing—Last year when the NYBMS Convention met here by request I took it to the Register Office[195] where all the *dominies* in the State did it reverence, and occasionally one more wise than the rest would exclaim "Wall, who'd a think [sic] any body [sic] could even learn to read such a language" never once dreaming but that the "Roman Antiquities" upon which they strained their noddles in their a-b-c-darian days were then natural characters—Then the autographs[196] you sent me have long demanded my thanks—I think as much as ever of such humanities—but have collected but few in a year or two past.

I suppose others have kept you advised as to the progress and condition of our church, that we purchased the Bleecker St. house[197] in Feb. 1847 for $6250, on favorable credit—Since then that square-toed spire has had its alitude [sic] and

[193] See vol. 1, "Cast of Characters," s.v. "Hawley, Horace H."

[194] See vol. 1, "Cast of Characters," s.v. "Sheldon, Miss Cynthia."

[195] The *Baptist Register* was a local Baptist paper in central New York that grew into regional prominence. Published by Alexander Beebee, it had significant influence in Baptist circles. The *Baptist Register* was a natural outlet for some of Emily's work as a budding writer. Later, in 1846 and the immediate time after her engagement and marriage to Adoniram Judson, there was conflict between Emily Judson and Mr. Beebee, who was less than enthusiastic about Emily's suitability for missionary service, reflecting the attitude of many in the wider Church. Emily was, after all, a secular, popular writer, and Adoniram Judson was the venerable missionary held in awesome respect. Eventually, Emily and Mr. Beebee were reconciled, and Mr. Beebee was often mentioned in letters from Miss Cynthia Sheldon as Emily's strongest supporter.

[196] See the letter dated October 17, 1845, from Morven Jones to Emily E. Chubbuck.

[197] Miss Cynthia Sheldon mentioned this purchase in her March 30, 1847, letter to Emily.

proportions improved, the roof has been re-shingled, the whole church painted a beautiful dark chocolate or reddish brown, a fence made upon the Bleecker and Charlotte Sts. sides with trees in the enclosures, a baptistery under the pulpit which pulpit has a new front that slides down to leave the view unobstructed etc. etc.—Our financial affairs are now quite easy and as prosperous as could be expected—Surely God has been pleased to prosper us beyond our hopes—In ten years we have been built up to a large church, with a full house, attentive audiences and commanding the respect and attention of all for a people who were once scorned and ridiculed as "ignorant, mean close-communion Baptists [sic]"—How does our prosperity call for gratitude to Him who is our Head, and for humility and faith in view of our nothingness and His mighty works—On 1st Sept. last we reported to the Association 320 members, 86 baptized in last year etc.—We are all united in and love Eld. Corey as much as ever—Still we bow under God's afflictive providence—Our very aged members have nearly all departed—Good old father and Mother Sheldon[198] have left their places to be taken, not filled, by their juniors—Then this fall aged Mother Barker (who resided in Whitestown and usually sat in Dea. Sheldon's seat, but maybe you did not know her) has been called home and lastly father Seaton has gone to that better country—Then again the loss of Miss Sheldon and the Fem. Acad. Family[199] is irreparable—Chas. Walker and family who were here a short time have gone to Chicago, Capt. Davidson is gone to Virginia this winter where he has purchased a plantation, and we fear that Mr. Cyrus Clark will remove to Buffalo where Mr. Gratiot[200] and wife have already gone—(I forgot to mention also the death of the Excellent Mrs. Corey)[201]—So you see we have need of additions to make good our hopes—Most of those baptized within two years are young and with but small means—I have sent you our Association minutes for 3 years past, the *Register* and divers other things, some of which I hope have made their voyage in safety—I also forgot to say that we have a Seraphina in our church a sort of piano-organ machine upon which Mrs. Jane P. Hawley[202] discourses

[198] Deacon and Isabell Low Sheldon were the parents of Miss Cynthia Sheldon, Mrs. Urania Sheldon Nott, and Mrs. Alma Sheldon Anable. Mother Sheldon died January 29, 1847, and Deacon Asa Sheldon died in March 1848.

[199] This is a reference to the Sheldon-Anable family's move to Philadelphia when Anna Maria was to start the Misses Anable's School in fall 1848.

[200] Charles Gratiot grew up in St. Louis, where his father was an army engineer responsible for developing the Port of St. Louis. He married Ann Sheldon, who was a cousin of Miss Cynthia Sheldon, Mrs. Urania Sheldon Nott, and Alma Sheldon Anable. Together, Charles and Ann Gratiot had six children. Because they often lived with the Sheldon family, their letters contain a great deal of him. Letters in 1847 speak of his religious awakening; those of 1849 speak of his leaving for the California gold fields. In 1853, Charles Gratiot applied for a grant of 400 acres in Illinois, and he already owned 148 acres.

[201] Mrs. Corey died of consumption in spring 1848, the complications following recent childbirth. She left four children. Miss Sheldon mentioned her death in an April 26, 1848, letter.

[202] Jane Sheldon Hawley was the daughter of John Sheldon and was a niece of Miss Cynthia Sheldon, Mrs. Urania Sheldon Nott, and Mrs. Alma Shelton Anable. She married Horace H. Hawley in 1841. Miss Sheldon was leaving for Wisconsin where the wedding took place, and Emily wrote of this on May 7, 1841. Horace H. Hawley worked in the publishing business and was instrumental in helping Emily with the publication of her earlier books as well as giving her guidance as she struggled with publishers, copyright issues, and other matters relating to publication.

good music—I do hope this long yarn will possess sufficient interest to repay you for untwisting it—I do wish I knew how much news and how many particulars and minutiae you receive, especially regarding Utica and vicinity and then I should know what to communicate.

The Broad St. Church has recently completed a very beautiful Chapel on the site of the old one which had been removed back and fitted up and now used for a miserable low and short lived Theatre—A Mr. Tarney has lately become their pastor (the church's) they having been for more than a year destitute of one, subsequent to Mr. Loring's death—As for Hamilton, Oh, Oh I would not mention her name and you have doubtless seen enough in the papers to make one's heart sick—I am glad good Dr. Kendrick has gone to "that rest"[203]—I understand Miss Cynthia is doing as well as she could have expected thus far in Philada [sic]—How Miss. [sic] Kelly[204] will do I know not—She did not think it worth her while to court the favor of Utica people, having imported all her furniture from N. York—not buying a cent's worth of Miss. [sic] Sheldon—I think the Trustees were guilty of the most niggardly meanness towards Miss. [sic] Sheldon[205] to enable them to be very liberal with Miss. [sic] Kelly, but time will show how long their liberality will last, which I think must *last* to enable Miss. [sic] K. to carry out her original plans—Maybe new furniture entire was necessary to get out all that hated *Baptist influence* which has with some people always been a bug-bear or bear-bug in that concern—There are yet some people in Utica who are so far behind the age as still to think that the Baptists are a weak, unimportant despicable and to be despised people and entitled to the same treatment which a arattan-pointed whiskerando [sic] generally awards to a *man*—I have just received in behalf of our church an excellent letter from Mrs. Maria M. *Slafter* Brown[206] of Bangkok Siam, who with her husband went out about ten years ago as members of our church, but upon her marriage with Mr. Brown, a Scotch

[203] When Emily Chubbuck was in her teens, Dr. Nathaniel Kendrick was the pastor of the Baptist church in Eaton and also a professor in a local theological school; she spoke with him early in life about becoming a missionary. Dr. Kendrick gave her the wise counsel of discernment, patience, and waiting. Adoniram and Emily turned to Dr. Kendrick to officiate at their marriage. He married Adoniram and Emily on June 2, 1846. A. C. Kendrick, in *the Life and Letters of Mrs. Emily C. Judson*, says that the marriage of Emily and Adoniram Judson was the last service for which Dr. Kendrick was able to leave his home. Other correspondents mention his continued frailty. He died on September 11, 1848.

[204] See vol. 1, "Cast of Characters," s.v. "Kelly, Miss Jane."

[205] This feeling about the action of the trustees is expressed in two letters to Emily from Miss Sheldon, the first dated September 6, 1848, and the second dated October 28, 1848. The second letter is especially bitter.

[206] Maria Brown was born October 3, 1818, in Oxford, New York. On August 19, 1838, she married the Rev. Corodon H. Slafter, who had been appointed to missionary work; they sailed for Siam in 1838. Rev. Slafter died there in 1841. On November 2, 1843, Maria Slafter married Captain Daniel Brown, a ship captain from Scotland who owned his own vessel and sailed between Bangkok and Liverpool. Their residence was in Bangkok, and Maria lived there until his death on September 30, 1850. She then returned to New York with her two daughters to live with her parents. In fall 1853, she employed Abby Ann Judson, who had recently completed her education at the Misses Anable's School in Philadelphia, as a teacher for her girls and some other children from her extended family in New York. Abby Ann's letters from this time are filled with the events in the household and of her first teaching experiences. In February and March 1854, Abby Ann wrote to Emily sharing the news that Dr. William Dean was calling regularly at the house and wondered at his intentions.

Merchant at Bangkok, she left the Mission, visited England, returned to Siam and now intends at some future day to remove to the United States—She enjoys the Society of Mess. Jones and Chandler and families who were well at date of her letter 30th August last—She wishes still to retain her standing in our Church—Her course to me was a singular one, especially after her engagement with Mr. Dean of China[207]—The all engrossing topic of conversation at present throughout this country, and in fact throughout N. and S. America, England, France, Sandwich Islands etc etc. is the immense amounts of *pure* gold being found in our New Territory of Upper California—The gold region covers an entire field over 200 miles square and at the last accounts about 4000 persons (whites and Indians) were engaged in washing gold, where they get from $20 to $300 of *pure* gold per diem, averaging $50 to $60 per man per day—As strange as this seems I suppose it is really true—Parties and individuals are starting for that Territory from all parts of the Country where gold dust is so plenty and every thing [sic] else so scarce, that it sells for 8 to $10 per oz. although worth $18 in coin, flour $100 per bbl, a shovel $30, labor $20 to $30, per day etc. etc.—

Source: American Baptist Historical Society, AJ 16, no. 652.

Mrs. H. H. Newton[208] to Emily C. Judson, December 14, 1848—New York

My dear Mrs. Judson, I have neglected you so long, I feel quite ashamed to write to you at all, but the truth is I dread your indulgance [sic] of a fear or thoughts that *perhaps* I might cease to remember you with the same friendship I was proud of many months ago, that at this late period, I have taken up my pen to say a few hurried things to you—

I must excuse myself a *very little*. My family cares, not very good health, and last tho not least no *genius* for expressing my ideas on paper, or any where [sic] else, but I think I can make out to show to you that I love you and often very often *thin*k of you; I am frequently with you in imagination—but it is always in Maulmain—that seems to me to be your Indian home—

[207] This seems to hint at an engagement between Mrs. Slafter and Dr. William Dean between the time she became a widow in 1841 and the time of her marriage to Daniel Brown in November 1843. Nothing is said about why that marriage did not take place, but if this is all true, it explains why William Dean began to call on her in New York City in early 1854, and they went on to be married in 1854, before going back to China.

[208] There are six letters in this correspondence from Mr. and Mrs. Newton of New York City. In a June 1846 letter Mrs. Newton indicated that they were "new friends" of Emily. They obviously had considerable wealth, which they shared generously with Adoniram and Emily through packages, and upon Adoniram's death, they immediately sent a check for five hundred dollars to Emily. Mr. Newton called Adoniram his "friend," and one of the letters invited Emily to stay with them in New York upon her return. A later letter indicates that Emily had indeed done that. On May 15, 1846, Adoniram Judson inscribed a dedication to Mrs. H. H. Newton on the fly-leaf of a volume of Burmese hymns that had been compiled by Mrs. Sarah B. Judson: "Mrs. H. H. Newton From A. Judson/ The wings ( ) ( ) /( ) are folded in St. Helena—New York—May 15th, 1846."

Your little mis[209] [sic], your "bird"[210]—how often I wish I could just *slip over* and see you all!

The thought has just darted through my mind, of what use is all this *profession* of love etc.—when I have apparently been so neglectful. Well! it relieves my own heart and that is the only answer I can make—I don't want to be a tax on your precious time but I should so love to have a *family* note from you—we are Mothers, and our Husbands and Children are our *green spot*—as we are separated from other earthly ties—so of course the brighter that spot. We have eight children and one *Grand* Child. George is the father—his health has some what [sic] improved the last few weeks their journey to Europe was of not very essential benefit to him. Frances is stouter than she was, her health is good—the six little ones are generally healthy with the exception of diseases incident to Children. Remember me with much aff to Dr. Judson—

My dear Husband[211] met with a very severe accident some few months since—he was thrown from a carriage and fractured or dislocated his right wrist—it is only now he has just commenced using his hand—I have felt so much thankfulness, that his life was spared and that the accident was no worse, that I scarcely felt, he was afflicted—I must now say adieu! My dear friend—accompanying this scrawl I send a trunk containing a few articles which I hope may be of some comfort to you—you will much oblige me by naming any thing [sic] would add to your comfort or any little thing you fancy—if any thing [sic] as to some colour [sic] etc. don't hesitate to let *me* know—because when I *find time* to think of you in this way—I may just as well *think* to some advantage to you—May that blessing which maketh *rich* rest upon *you*, My dear friend, and *your*s

Your aff friend

H. H. Newton

over

Your pretty blue vases have their *resting* place on our front parlour [sic] mantel—I am too choice of them to allow *natura*l flowers to be put in them fearing some accident may befall them—

And Dr. Judson's round box has its *resting* place by side of the fire place and every time I dust them my thoughts wander over the sea—all such little things are bright spots in this *dark* world—I suppose I know little of its darkness compared with you. Once more *good-bye*.

H. H. N.

[209] See vol. 1, "Cast of Characters," s.v. "Judson, Emily Frances."

[210] Emily Frances was born December 27, 1847. On January 1, 1848, Emily wrote the poem "My Bird."

[211] Mr. Isaac Newton.

The Trunk contains

12 Cotton Chemise	4 loose dresses	1 pink loose dress
12 Pocket hank'chs	11 Towels	12 White Cotton hose
2 pr Col-Cotton hose	3 Cotton petticoats	12 pairs of children's shoes

for Dr. Judson 2 pr cloth shoes—2 pr pumps—3 pr slippers—let me know if the size suits and the *style*. You will see some of my little Charley's *old* frocks—I thought they would save you a few *stitches* for the little one—2 Suits clothes for Dr. Judson
1 Muslin dress from Elizabeth Bl( )cker
1 Shawl and 1 Mantle from Mrs. G. Milbank
6 prs Cotton hose Muslin for two dresses and a few yards of White Cambric Muslin from Mrs. Sam'l Milbank
send the measure of your foot

Source: American Baptist Historical Society, AJ 18, no. 861.

The Reverend Ira M. Allen[212] to Emily C. Judson, December 18, 1848[213] —New York

My Dear Mrs. Judson

Before this brief letter meets your eye, you will have heard, probably, of the death of my dear wife.[214] Her useful life was terminated on the 15th of October last, by that most terrible disease, tubercular consumption. Its rapid progress subjected her to severe suffering from violent coughs, laboriousness of breathing, great feverishly agitation, and difficulty of speaking, all pressing upon her feeble, exhausted frame, and causing inability for any continued exercise of thought, which she painfully felt. In the entire stage of her disease she complained of great spiritual apathy, and insensibility to her condition and eternal prospects; but in August she experienced a great change in her feelings, and said in reference to it, "No tongue can tell the magnitude and blessedness of the ( ) I have experienced. I can never be sufficiently thankful for it. My soul is filled with peace and joy." Subsequently, in reply to my inquiries, she said "I feel as though I were floating in the ocean of God's love." Strong expressions, similar to that, she often used in reference to her feelings in view of death. Her faith was unwavering, and her hope of heaven cloudless.—Her mind, as already intimated, was much affected by the ravage of disease. Her thoughts, during the last few weeks of her life, were not unfrequently wandering [sic]—but generally in pleasant scenes and happy subjects. Her last night will ever be memorable to me. During all its hours, she was engaged in cheerful conversation,

[212] A note on the letter in a different handwriting says that Ira Allen was an ordained minister.

[213] There is an addendum to this letter written December 19, 1848.

in prayer, or in singing. Sometimes she was relating anecdotes and stories to her merry companions, and sometimes speaking of the Saviour [sic] and what he had done. Once, in a tune the most tender, sweet, and plaintive, she sung [sic] a most beautiful song about "the bird." A part of the words I remember were these:

"O the bird, the bird, the beautiful bird
With its shining, *shining* wing
It is mine, it is mine."

This I think was the result of impressions made in her mind by your poem, "My Bird,"[215] of which she speaks in the "jottings" of the July No of her Journal[216]—All her language in these mental wanderings was chaste, fine, and elegant, utterly with a fluency, warmth of feeling, and emphasis, that was most surprising.

In the morning she sung [sic] another song of heaven, while I was taking a little rest in sleep. Some of the words as remembered by Margaret who was with her were "Glory, glory, I am there; I am there." Shortly after this, I went to her. She had her reason perfectly, and whispered to me about her physical condition. Her power of speech then *failed*; but she continued rational to the last, as evinced by effort to speak, saying once "O the pride of the heart"—no more could be heard,—by her imploring look, and expressive gestures for relief from suffocation. I stood by her from eight in the morning till nearly two o'clock PM wetting her mouth frequently with a cloth dipped in weak brandy and water, as years ago she had requested me to do in case I survived her, and was present when she died. This was grateful to her, and was evidently recognized by her. Finally the adhesive matter in her lungs stopped her breath, and she fell asleep as gently as an infant on its mother's breast. In death her countenance was perfectly natural and pleasant as if it had been lighted up with heavenly emotions.

I am indeed a lonely sufferer. No relative of hers or mine was present when she died or at her funeral. Only a cousin has been with me a short time to assist in selling off most of my furniture, and making a division of my wife's clothing etc. among relatives, as she desired—This was my *second* trial. My *third* the sale of the Journal, and you will learn from the December number, which with the November and July

[214] Eliza Allen was the editor of the *Mother's Journal* and included material by Emily as early as 1843. Their correspondence went through spring 1846. In December 1848, Emily received a letter from Mrs. Allen's husband, the Reverend Ira Allen, describing in some detail the death of Eliza Allen. The *Mother's Journal* continued, and in an 1849 letter Anna Maria Anable informs Emily that a piece that she had written had appeared in the publication. In a letter to Emily during their courtship, Adoniram mentioned that he had met Mrs. Allen and went on to say that the *Mother's Journal* was considered to be a prestigious publication for the church. On May 27, 1846, after a meeting with her, Judson wrote: "I am afraid I shall get to dislike her. She is a woman that I could make some use of. She has a sharp, strong intellect—is a good critic in the rough, but not in the nice. No heart—no amiability—very severe and what is worse, glaringly envious."

[215] Emily wrote the poem "My Bird" on January 1, 1848, a little over a week after the December 24, 1847, birth of Emily Frances Judson. It was sent in a letter to Anna Maria Anable, and subsequently, it had appeared in the *Columbian* magazine.

[216] *The Mother's Journal*, of which Eliza Allen was editor.

I send you with this. I have got a small, kind family to come into my desolate house and board me for the rent till May next.

Hoping to receive a letter from you and your dear husband, to whom I send much love, and that you will also send something for the Journal, I remain affectionately yours in hope of eternal life

Ira M. Allen

Source: American Baptist Historical Society, AJ 12, no. 342.

The Reverend Ira M. Allen[217] to Emily C. Judson, December 19, 1848[218]

To the foregoing written at a very late hour last night I will add a few lines. When she made an extraordinary effort to speak and said in her dying moments "O the pride of the heart," I have thought she had reference to 1st John 2:15–17, and wished to impress the truth of those verses upon our minds. I think this is probable, because that chapter was by her request *twice* read to her by Margaret the day before. In the reading, Margaret stopped before she finished the chapter. The suffering listener said "Margaret, why do you stop there?" "I was afraid of wearing you" was the reply. "Read on Margaret," said she, "reading the Bible never wearies one." She then gave Margaret instruction and advice drawn from portions of that chapter. Among other things she said, as Margaret has since informed me, "Margaret, you are young, just setting out in life; and your path through this world is a narrow and straight one—like a single plant, thrown across a tremendous gulf, over which you are passing, and one step from a straight course to the right or left will plunge you in the awful chasm beneath and dash you to pieces."—In the November Journal you will find her obituary and in the December some remarks of mine relative to her devotion to the Journal to which she fell a martyr. I. M. A.

Source: American Baptist Historical Society, AJ 12, no. 342.

[217] A note on the letter in a different handwriting says that Ira Allen was an ordained minister.

[218] This is an addendum to a letter written on December 18, 1848.

Emily C. Judson to Anna Maria Anable, December 20, 1848—Maulmain

My dear Ninny,[219]

So you want to know how we poor missionary women spend our time and get "jagged out." Yesterday morning my first tho't on awaking was "now I will write A. M.[220] a nice long letter" and the first word I heard was, "walk this morning, lovey?" "Really, I don't believe I can unless Pinapah comes" (P. was away taking care of his sick wife) "for I don't like to trust baby[221] with the girls." "But you *must* go; you will have to sit till breakfast time and it will make you sick." My feet had just touched the floor when Miss Emmy Fan called "amah! amah!" and so the long and short of it is "amah" in the end lost her walk. At six o'clock bright and early in poured the women to a female prayer meeting and a nice time we had of it too, some of them being so affected that they sobbed right out. But oh, how the children worried me! I was obliged to go out several times to look after them and by the time breakfast came I was so hungry I could'nt [sic] eat. After breakfast I put Henry[222] to his lessons and baby asleep in her cot and at ten another company of Burman women came in to hold another prayer-meeting. I should have got on better, but I heard a low murmur from Henry's studying place which made me remember I had forgotten to explain his lesson and he could'nt [sic] learn it without. Edward[223] too troubled his papa by making a noise on the verandah and dictionary-making is hard enough with a quiet house.[224]

In the midst of the first prayer in came a girl to borrow my riding-cap for Mrs. B.[225] which of course nobody could get but myself; and I had just commenced reading a chapter when Mrs. R's[226] girl came in to know if I wanted to send for anything to Madras. I did, but there was no time to write so I lost the opportunity which comes only about twice a year. Meeting was not out for it was rather larger than usual when my teacher looked in at the window; and drew back to wait. Before the women got out of the house, I was explaining Henry's lesson, while John[227] stood waiting to give in his daily account, the tailor was waiting for buttons and the girl had a long *Cockrum* about poor Edward's doings in the bathing-room. Oh, my stars! I looked round, and caught my breath. "Here Edward, sit down in your little chair,

[219] "Ninny" was a name of endearment given to Anna Maria Anable by her most intimate friends at the Utica Female Academy. Emily was "Nemmy."

[220] See vol. 1, "Cast of Characters," s.v. "Anable, Anna Maria."

[221] See vol. 1, "Cast of Characters," s.v. "Judson, Emily Frances."

[222] See vol. 1, "Cast of Characters," s.v. "Judson, Henry Hall."

[223] See vol. 1, "Cast of Characters," s.v. "Judson, Edward."

[224] The English-Burmese Dictionary was a monumental achievement on the part of Adoniram Judson. He also translated the Bible into the Burmese language. Both publications continue to be in use in Burmah.

[225] This is likely Stella Bennett, the wife of Cephas Bennett. Mr. Bennett was superintendent of the Baptist Press.

[226] This is likely Maria Ranney, the wife of missionary Thomas Ranney. Mr. Ranney was Superintendent of the press in Maulmain, and the business manager for the missionaries there.

and Boke-song on the mat—I'll attend to you by and by." "John, make some lime-water." (That'll take him ten minutes, tho't I.) "Tailor, can you iron a dress." "Me! No, mamma!" his eyes standing out *a foot*. "Not iron!" "Who ever [sic] heard of a tailor that could'nt [sic] iron? What helpless fellows you Bengalis are, to be sure! Well, go and call the Dobie!" "Have you got the new book yet teacher?" "No, mamma, but it is of no consequence." "Oh, I want it very much. You had better get it now, and that will take you so late that I think I will not read to day [sic]." "As Mamma pleases." So I had a clear field—put Henry to his lesson with a light heart and by the time I got a good draught of lime-water (lemonade), was ready to take John's account without going crazy. I will not *bother* to tell you how the Dobie came without his tools and had to go back, all the time looking dreadfully sour because I wouldn't wait till tomorrow to have the only dress I could wear that evening ironed—nor how I managed about the tailor's buttons which I had to manufacture—nor how tired poor Henry had got and so how uncommonly troublesome he was—nor how the baby cried and clung to me and would'nt [sic] be taken care of by anybody else—*t'aint no use* [sic], you could'nt [sic] comprehend.—"Lovey, you look dreadfully tired—you will get sick. Don't mind the Memoir[228] darling," (I was trying to revise) "it is no killing matter to wait a month." True! I was relieved again, but *so* tired! My next move was to take a nap, so I sent the children to the chapel and doc. went off to his books. My head scarce touched the pillow when a phial was thrust in my face; medicine was wanted for a sick native child. Down again and a pretty voice, "is your mistress at home?" It was Mrs. Stevens.[229] She went away, the children were called and bathed, and then we sat down to dinner. But it was now half past four and I was obliged to swallow the mouthfuls whole for at five is our missionary female prayer-meeting and I never like to stay away from that. I was too tired to enjoy the meeting much, and it hung on dreadfully. I was too much worn out to *dress* when I got home, and I sat down and cried. "What is the matter, Mamma ?" asked Henry, putting his little soft hand on my wet cheek, "do you want to go to heaven?" "Not to leave you,"

[Written in the right margin of the address page:] I could not help saying, so I wiped away my tears, braided my hair, put on my pretty light silk frock, called a trusty Christian woman to take charge of the house, kissed the children under their

[227] John was the Judsons' cook.

[228] Fanny Forester, *Memoir of Sarah B. Judson, Member of the American Mission to Burmah* (New York: L. Colby and Company, 1848).

[229] Elizabeth Stevens arrived in Maulmain in February 1838; her husband was Edward Stevens. Elizabeth Stevens took six-month-old Edward Judson into her home when Sarah and Adoniram had to leave for the United States in 1845, and her care and nurture saved his life. She served forty-eight years in Burmah. She had extensive correspondence with Emily Judson, and her letters spoke of everyday life among the missionaries. When Emily returned to the United States, the letters from Mrs. Stevens brought news of friends and colleagues. Mrs. Stevens had a sister, Sarah Haven, in Massachusetts, who wrote a number of letters to Emily asking for information on the Stevens family.

mosquito curtains, and with my husband stepped into a carriage. Fifteen minutes after I was sitting in the handsome parlour [sic] of the Commissioner (governor) where we had been especially invited ("as a particular parting favour [sic] to *me*" came the Commissioner's note) to meet some very accomplished Calcutta ladies.

[Written in the left margin of the address page:] The ladies were very agreeable, but they have no idea that everybody in the world had not just as much *leisure* as themselves; and so I was obliged actually to be rude, to get rid of pointing out handsome views for sketching, and paying other impossible attentions. Today I have been obliged to dismiss my teacher again (what a learned woman *I shall* be!) and have also given Master Henry a holyday. This letter is written at a double gallop.

[Written perpendicular to the text across the top margin of page 1:] Dear, dear! Baby has torn my pattern in two, and I can't find the other piece. And the tailor is waiting for work. There! The clock striking two, the signal for the mail to close; the doc's letters are locked up and he is "po-Caiking" the Calcutta ladies. No! there he comes, as I live! We may get them in yet. Don't think I wrote this letter 'taint I—'tis some body [sic] else.

Source: Hanna family files.

Mr. Morven M. Jones to Emily C. Judson, December 21, 1848[230]

Eld. Corey[231] had his annual *donation* last evening, and his house was crowded with people and good things—He lives and boards with his children at his fathers on Blanding St.—Fanny you must know is married to Mr. Spring of *Noo*-Yawk [sic]—Unless you take the papers you will be surprised when I say that on 7th Nov. Maj. Gen. Zackary Taylor the hero of the Mexican War was elected President of U.S. for 4 years from 4th March next—Who's Gen. Taylor? is a question which would have been asked by at least 999 out of every 1000 voters in the US had he been named three years ago—He had never even *voted* at any election, had never held any civil office, even his politics were doubted and doubtful although he said he was "a Whig, but not an ultra Whig," all his notoriety and popularity were gained in a war which the Whig party had pronounced infamous, yet the great Whig party laid aside its idol Henry Clay and on the sole ground of availability, nominated "old Jack" "Old Whitey" and all and by the influence of drum and fife elected Gen. Taylor—The Whigs are however very anxious about the matter for they too well remember John Tyler and I shall be somewhat disappointed if Gen. Taylor does not take a pretty independent course and sometimes act independent of party and party

[230] This is the first addenda to a letter started December 9, 1848. The second was added December 22, 1848.

[231] See vol. 1, "Cast of Characters," s.v. "Corey, The Reverend D. G."

influences. So look out for breakers—The democrats nominated Lewis Cass and a better man in my view could not well have been selected—The *barnburners* of this state with the sore heads and disappointed of some other states organized a bolt, and for a hobby took up the *free soil*, Wilmot Proviso humbug and then united with the abolition party and to defeat Mr. Cass they nominated that embodiement [sic] of ingratitude and perfidy M. Van Buren and they succeeded but too well in their object—Out of the 290 votes given by 30 States Gen. Taylor rec. 163, Mr. Cass 127 and Van B. 0! After the thousand benefits conferred by the democrats upon the old Fox he sought revenge for not being nominated for Prest in 1844 or 48—but he is now despised and only named with Arnold except by the faction who thus attempted to mend their desperate fortunes—

Source: American Baptist Historical Society, AJ 16, no. 652.

Mr. Morven M. Jones to Emily C. Judson, December 22, 1848[232]

Thus far the season has been extremely mild and warm and pleasant more so than for many years, but last night snow came and to day [sic] is one of the roughest I ever saw, cold high winds and air full of snow—Ah, how different it must be with you—I wish I could winter with you to avoid this terrible climate—I some think of going to California after gold where the climate is milder!—I wish you would *also* write a letter to our *church* if not inconsistent with your feelings and duty, (you may think me selfish in this) and I am not sure but I should advise it were my advice asked—Such a communication as you would write would be recd, listened to and read with the most cordial pleasure and kindness by at least 320 including Mr. Corey[233] out of 320 members of the church and it would certainly (I believe) disarm a *few* active tongues of thick poison and confirm the confidence in you of many who do not know you—These are only my private notions and are offered with diffidence—There is one thing I have wished a thousand times I could tell you, but it cannot be told and much less written, but the evidence of it shall be *seen* and *heard*—Our good souled kind hearted Bro. Beebee[234] of the Register[235] is one of your

[232] This is the second addenda to a letter started December 9, 1848. The first addendum was added December 21, 1848.

[233] See vol. 1, "Cast of Characters," s.v. "Corey, The Reverend D. G."

[234] Alexander Beebee was trained as a lawyer, but after experiencing strong religious convictions after the death of his first child, he became active in a Baptist church near Skaneateles, New York. In 1824, he observed that the Baptist denomination had only a few credible newspapers in the United States, none of them being in New York. In 1825, he became the editor of the *Baptist Register*, and over the next thirty years, it became a strong foundation for the rapidly growing Baptist churches of Central New York. During the course of Emily's engagement to Adoniram, Mr. Beebee must have said something reflecting the religious wisdom or judgment strongly expressed by many about the marriage of Adoniram Judson and Emily Chubbuck. Many of Emily's letters reflect the antagonism she felt for him. In July 1849, she wrote him a confrontational letter about something he had said. Morven Jones and Miss Sheldon, through continued efforts, did bring about a truce. Morven said that Emily had "no better supporter" than Mr. Beebee.

[235] See vol. 1, "Places, Events, Organizations, and Magazines," s.v. "*Baptist Register*."

most zealous and sanguine advisors—indeed his admiration of you is of the most transcendent sort, altho, not withstanding the dozen thousand miles between you it is not of that sort which would excite the Dr's jealousy, but might were he merely human excite his sway—Bro. Beebee told me he did not "know but that it was well you wrote him that crusty womanish sort of note, or his regards for you might have amounted almost to adoration, and that you had thrown a bucket of water upon his high wrought feelings and cooled them down to a temperature more fitting a human object—that it was too bad after he had perfectly satisfied his doubts as the propriety of the Dr.'s (for the world held the Dr. as public property) course in marrying *Fanny Forester*[236] and while the whole Baptist denomination old and young, minister, deacons, laymen women and all were swayed by excitement one half maybe doubtfully yet calmly hoping for the best and the other half ready and a few weak ones anxious, to convince the Dr. of a very weak and silly thing and thus leave him to fall from the high moral position he had held so long, when you, although so favorably known to the literary and general world, were not really known at all to the world and only to a comparatively few personal friends, and while all were looking to Utica vicinity for an expression which should settle the whole question decidedly for weel or wo, while a few evil spirits were trying to show their consequence by giving an evil direction to public opinion, and under all these circumstances when he (Bro B.) was using his feeble exertions to insure you and the Dr. a cordial and proper reception, to receive such a repulse from you, it was too bad"—it was too bad—was it not? I have tried to clothe his ideas in his own language, and his *premises mainly too true*, and all his ardent temperament enlisted, as he told the story in glowing language, how I laughed! Twas too bad—too bad, really—But the wisdom of your self and others has made all to *end thus far* well (under a higher Wisdom) and now the *affaire* is among the things of the past—*Requiescat in peace*. Bro. B.'s sentiments towards you thus *tempered* are of the kindest and best sort—I doubt your thanking me for so saying any thing [sic] about that head, and indeed the story is ten times as long as I intended it should be.

The very latest news is that H. H. Hawley[237] and Co. (Horace and his mother) are going to remove to New York but you please say nothing at present as the matter is still *sub rosa*—and the last bit of scandal *connects* Eld. Corey and Miss M. E. Barber[238] now again teacher in Fem. Acady[239]—but of course this is all fudge—But time and patience fail and I must draw this uncouth hotch-potch [sic] to a close—

[236] Emily Chubbuck wrote under the *nom de plume* Fanny Forester. Asked about it once, she said, "Would anyone buy a book written by Emily E. Chubbuck?"

[237] See vol. 1, "Cast of Characters," s.v. "Hawley, Horace H."

[238] See vol. 1, "Cast of Characters," s.v. "Barber, Mary."

[239] The Utica Female Academy, where Emily had taught Composition under the guidance of Miss Cynthia Sheldon.

During my illness and some other periods I must confess a remissness in sending the *Register* and then have sent several at a time, but at this date Dec. 28. all the back Nos. have been mailed and if any are lost please charge the blame to Uncle Sam and John Bull or John Co. as the old gent, is called in the East—Long ere this you have doubtly heard the crashing and thundering of falling Kingdoms and dynasties and the clatter and discord attendant upon the breaking up of the moss grown and blood stained systems of Europe—Where that great moral, physical and political revolution will end, or when, Omniscience only knows.

Louis Phillips and his family, Guizot, Metternich, the Pope, kings, princes and nobles have taken refuge in strange lands—"A general war in Europe" is again feared—The heir to the throne of Napoleon Louis Bonaparte is doubtless at the head of the French republic, altho the results of the election of the 10th inst have not yet arrived—Foolish, fickle people! If Louis have but a tithe of his uncle's ambition, energy and military spirit the cap of Liberty may fall in the gore at the foot of the throne of a despot—But I will say no more or I may be guilty of inciting treason against the powers at Ava—

We beg and entreat that you will favor us with letters and epistles from the Dr. and yourself. Please write often and at length—Please pardon all faults in style, matter and workmanship in this long affair—I plead guilty to the charge of assurance and presumption in thus writing *such a letter* both in manner and matter to one who could and would have done so much better, but I have intended it all for the best—With our best wishes that you may all enjoy the richest of Heavens blessings spiritual and temporal and that the dark forms of paganism may all soon be replaced by the light and truths of the gospel of Christ. Believe me very Truly and Respectfully

Morven M. Jones

Mary[240] says "give my love *to her* and to *little Fanny*"[241] that she will write soon—

Source: The American Baptist Historical Society, AJ 16, Number 652.

[240] Mary Jones was the wife of Morven Jones. They lived in the Utica area and were intimately familiar with Miss Cynthia Sheldon and the staff and student body of the Utica Female Academy. Mr. and Mrs. Jones, as well as Miss Sheldon, were members of the Bleecker Street Baptist church where Mr. Corey was the pastor. In a December 1848 series of letters to Emily, Morven Jones described a terrible accident; a group from the church was standing on a bridge overlooking the Mohawk River, there to witness a baptism, and the bridge collapsed. At least one person died in that accident, and Mary Jones was severely injured.

[241] See vol. 1, "Cast of Characters," s.v. "Judson, Emily Frances."

Letters

January–June 1849

The Reverend Doctor William Dean to Emily C. Judson, January 17, 1849—Hong Kong

My dear Mrs. Judson

I was truly glad to hear from you by your letter of ( ). It was found on my table with many others, on my return a few weeks ago from a long visit to the north. After visiting Shanghai and ( ) I went to ( ) ( ) near the grand canal. A city as large as New York it contains as many people but as to houses and streets they differ ( ), as do the people from those of NY. I went to some of the tea and ( ) districts in the neighborhood of ( ) and learned some things new to me about the Chinese. I return to my work with new strength and a new relish—have just finished the "Notes on Mat." and a revision of "Acts with References"—am trying to put some explanatory notes to Genesis—the translation is substantially Mr. Goddards—i.e. so far as gone. He is perhaps ( ) at ( ) and we may help each other perhaps in aiding the people to a knowledge of the Bible. The Chinese Church here, as you prophetically suppose, is very different from the state in wh(ich) it was when I [Note: Most of line lost is in the fold.] now exclusions. So this is a queer world—and this is a queer people. They gave me a long face and a heavy heart at times but God is the same this year as last and therein I may rejoice.

I have heard indirectly of the arrival of the "blue eyes" and rejoice to learn that all, both "blues" and "blacks," the pets and their parents are so well. I sh [sic] enjoy a morning walk with you either over the hill of Maulmain or Hong Kong. The only advantage in favor of the latter is the cool weather we now have here and I have just this PM been on the hills rolling stones down into the Sea—my clerical employment! You may say—and so do I quite as clinical as to labor at the "Science of Circles" or the symbols of "( )." So you don't ( ) to say "*we* missionaries" eh? I suppose you class yourself with the class called "Home Missionaries." Very well, they are very useful in their way and perhaps all women would be as useful if they were to keep to that department—not that it is less important or honorable, or that I have any special objection to your teaching a class of old Burman women, or marking "Question Books" or reading or writing as much as you like, after you dry all those "blue eyes" and "blacks" from tears, and trying to keep sunny faces on all old and young within your own Burman Cottage then—as Confucius says "Children should *exhaust* their strength in filial piety and fraternal affection"—and then what then is *ours* should be spent in learning the Classics.

I have good news from my children monthly—and recently had a picture of the youngest wh [sic] has a place on my table is is [sic] subject to an occasional microscopic examination and an astronomer never examined a heavenly body with greater interest or with more satisfactory discoveries. If I were to intimate that I found more interest in examining my pictures than you do in looking at all those "blues" and "blacks" I might raise some indignant reply so I will save your temper and keep my suggestions to myself. May our gracious Father spare you the sorrow of looking at them only through their pictures, though this is no small comfort in that when you can't see their faces.

I found a good letter from Mrs. E. C. Allen[1] by the side of yours, awaiting my return from the north—also one from Mrs. ( ) Bacon of Washington, my good sisters at Rochester and Wyoming and from Prof. Richardson, Hamilton and my Brother at Morrisville.[2] At the latter place they have enjoyed a renewal—my br. baptized—now all are members of the Church—i.e. of my own mother's children. Many of their letters contain choice bits wh [sic] might interest you if you were there to hear them but I think of nothing more in there worthy of sending all the way to Burmah. Mrs. Allen was in poor health.

Madison University[3] ( ) still the object of struggle with many in that region. I hope you receive good news from your parents[4]—my love to them when you write home. Have you read Mr. ( ) "Thoughts on Missions"—I like it much and think it the best ( ) of its kind I have seen Harris' works not excepted.

[1] Mrs. Eliza Allen was the editor of the prominent Christian magazine *The Mother's Journal*. Her husband Ira Allen wrote to Emily Judson on December 18, 1848, of Mrs. Allen's tragic and painful death after a lingering illness. On May 27, 1846, after a meeting with Mrs. Allen, Adoniram Judson wrote, "I am afraid I shall get to dislike her. She is a woman that I could make some use of. She has a sharp, strong intellect—is a good critic in the rough, but not in the nice. No heart—no amiability—very severe and what is worse, glaringly envious."

[2] William Dean was the interim minister at the church in Morrisville, New York, in spring 1834, when he had baptized Emily Chubbuck. This was just prior to his leaving for the mission field.

[3] The school that became Madison University was founded in 1817 by the Baptist Education Society of New York State for the purpose of educating ministers. Two of its first students, Jonathan Wade and Eugenio Kincaid and their wives, were the first missionaries to join Adoniram and Ann Judson in Burmah. The Wades arrived in 1823, and the Kincaids in 1830. In 1834, the school was organized as a seminary, college, and academy called the Hamilton Literary and Theological Institution. In 1846, it was chartered as Madison University, drawing upon all of the history and good will in its former existence. In 1847, attempts were made to remove the university to the more urban setting of Rochester, and after three years of stressful turmoil that did tremendous damage to the prospects of the university, the courts decided the case in favor of those who wished the university to remain in Hamilton. Letters of the early 1850s show that the university soon made a remarkable recovery, and the university and seminary were later named for philanthropist Samuel Colgate.

Dr. Nathaniel Kendrick was one of the venerated leaders at the school while also serving as the beloved pastor of the youthful Emily Chubbuck. He officiated at the marriage of Adoniram and Emily on June 2, 1846, his last official act in his seriously declining health. After the commitment to stay in Hamilton, Dr. Stephen Taylor was elected as the second president, and later in 1856, George Eaton became the third president. Dr. A. C. Kendrick, the nephew of Nathaniel Kendrick and the biographer of Emily Chubbuck Judson, was one of the professors who left Hamilton in 1850 to teach at the University of Rochester. Numerous graduates were called for service on the mission field, and many churches were blessed through the pastoral ministry of those who had been trained there. One such minister was Courtland Anable, the brother of Emily's best friend Anna Maria Anable; Courtland Anable was there during Emily's final illness and death in 1854.

[4] Charles and Lavinia Richards Chubbuck lived in Hamilton, New York, in a home that Emily purchased for them in summer 1842. Catharine Chubbuck, Emily's sister, lived with them as well.

[5] Fanny Forester, *Memoir of Sarah B. Judson, Member of the American Mission to Burmah* (New York: L. Colby and Company, 1848).

I have just rec'd *Mrs. Judson*[5] by "Fanny Forester"[6] and ( ) over in thoughts the scenes with dear George.[7] Where is he and how is he to direct his future course? May I trouble you to mention my name to Bro. Howard and wife,[8] if they are with you, and any others I may know. So many have gone home, or to heaven, that I scarcely know who are remaining with you. I first came out with the Wades[9] and Newtons who are in US—the Comstocks ( ) ( ) ( ) who are above—Mrs. Osgood is also with them. Mr. Osgood[10] is in America. The Howards are all that remain of the party in Burmah—Mrs. Tracy of Singapore and Dr. Bradly of Siam were in the same ship who are now in U.S.—Mrs. Bradly with my own dear Matilda,[11] have joined the happy at home, and I am still encompassed with frailties and follies here—not I trust unhappy or discontented with my lot, but somewhat worn and worthless, not

[6] Emily Chubbuck wrote under the *nom de plume* Fanny Forester. Asked about it once, she said, "Would anyone buy a book written by Emily E. Chubbuck?"

[7] In 1834, while in Burmah on their way to Singapore, Dr. and Mrs. Dean took into their care six-year-old George Dana Boardman, who was being sent to America by his mother, recently married to Adoniram Judson. Fear for his health and hope for the best possible education available had brought Sarah Hall Boardman Judson to this decision. The group made it to Singapore, and while taking him to the ship on which he was to sail, Dr. Dean and Mr. Jones (another missionary) were savagely attacked by pirates, and while young George cowered under the seat, he watched both of the adults receive wounds from fishing spears carried by the pirates. After the pirates left with what they thought was a strongbox of money (instead it was letters and journals), the group was picked up by a fishing boat and taken back to Singapore. The next day George was safely put aboard the ship *Cashmere*.

[8] Hosea and Theresa Howard first sailed for Burmah in 1834, arriving in December that year. Hosea Howard was a recent graduate of the theological seminary in Hamilton, New York. They were stationed in Maulmain as missionaries with Adoniram Judson, and he claimed in a letter to Emily that he worked there with Adoniram longer than any other missionary. Mr. Howard's responsibility was to run schools that the mission maintained, a task in which he was ably assisted by his wife. Lydia Lillybridge was responsible to Mr. and Mrs. Howard when she arrived in November 1846. Mr. and Mrs. Howard left Maulmain for the United States in February 1850.

[9] Jonathan and Deborah Wade were appointed missionaries to Burmah in 1823. Their relationship with Adoniram Judson was especially dear because of the early experiences they shared, including the death of Ann Judson. When she died and Adoniram returned to Amherst, he never forgot the sight of Deborah Wade standing on the veranda holding little Maria in her arms. Much of their work was spent in the Karen jungle communities following the path of George Boardman. They returned home to America on December 22, 1847, and went back to Burmah in January 1851, just as Emily was returning to the United States. They were from the Hamilton, New York, area. They left for Burmah on July 25, 1850, and were in Maulmain by February 1851. Both died in Burmah; Deborah died at Maulmain in 1868, and Jonathan died in Rangoon in 1872.

[10] Rev. Sewall Osgood was a missionary in Maulmain who worked with and lived by Adoniram Judson. Judson and Osgood occupied two of the four homes in the mission compound and lived so close that it "allowed me the pleasure and profit of almost hourly intercourse." He arrived in Burmah in 1834. His first wife Elhira Brown Osgood died on October 5, 1837, in Maulmain. On July 8, 1838, he married Sarah Thomas, the widow of the Reverend Jacob Thomas, with Adoniram Judson officiating at the wedding. He spoke in the letters to Emily, of which there are five between July 1850 and April 1852, of Adoniram Judson as his "most intimate friend." He never personally met Emily, as he had returned from the field prior to 1846. At the time of his letters, he was working with the American Baptist Missionary Union as a district secretary. In 1845, just as they were leaving for the United States, Sarah and Adoniram Judson gave care of Charley, too young to make the trip, to Mr. and Mrs. Osgood. Charley died not long after their departure. Mr. Osgood visted Adoniram, Elnathan, and Abby Ann in the United States. His third wife was Caroline Wait; they were married December 30, 1850, at Saratoga, New York. With all of his suggestions of "intimacy" and "his most intimate friend," Mr. Osgood stated that his life was so busy that he simply did not have the time to look through his papers for anything that would be helpful in writing the Judson memoir.

[11] William Dean was married to Matilda Cowan on April 10, 1834, and they had one daughter, Matilda, born in February 1835. Mrs. Dean died in March 1835, shortly after her daughter's birth and before they reached their destination in Bangkok. They passed through Maulmain in December 1834 and through Singapore in January 1835. William Dean and his baby arrived in Bangkok in July 1835. Baby Matilda was adopted by Rev. Baron Stow.

long enough ( ) have worn out but long enough to have filled for greater usefulness than I fear will be accomplished by your old friend and fellow laborer,

W. Dean

[Written in the left of the first page top margin:] I enclose in this a ( ) plucked by my own hands about 20 miles from ( )

Source: American Baptist Historical Society, AJ 15, no. 587.

Miss Cynthia Sheldon to Emily C. Judson, January 28, 1849[12]—Philadelphia

My dear Emily

It is Sabbath evening near 10 o'clock—Our bevy of girls are chatting and have been in the front Parlor since Tea—Fanny[13] went with me to Church—we found them in the same spot on our return—Now they are making love to Spitzenberg [sic]—I wish we could just convey them to your side of the world—I would willingly do without for the next six months if it were possible to place them to your mouth—Anna M.[14] has of course told you all about Hatty's[15] return—but she brought a box

[12] This letter is dated January 28, but it does not reference the year. It is placed in 1849 because Miss Sheldon says that it has been two years since they learned that her mother would not recover from her illness. Her mother's death occurred January 29, 1847.

[13] Fanny Anable was one of nine children born to Joseph and Alma Anable and was a niece of Miss Cynthia Sheldon and Mrs. Urania Sheldon Nott. The correspondence indicates that in April 1845 she was away from home studying and taking music lessons. These spring letters indicate that she was in Philadelphia, working in the home of and with the family of the Reverend A. D. Gillette. See Miss Sheldon's letter to Emily of November 30, 1845, in which she spoke of all that Fanny was doing to improve herself in the field of music, but also her concern for Fanny's interest in the party life and the "vanitie" which surround her." A March 30, 1847, letter from Anna Maria Anable told of Fanny's conversion following her grandmother's death. In September 1847, she was listed as one of the teachers at the Utica Female Academy. Fanny became a teacher with her sisters in the Misses Anable's School in Philadelphia.

[14] Anna Maria Anable was the niece of the Misses Urania and Cynthia Sheldon and the daughter of Joseph and Alma Sheldon Anable. Emily first met Anna Maria in fall 1840 when she went as a student to the Utica Female Academy; both Emily and Anna Maria became members of the faculty there. In these years, Anna Maria became Emily's dearest friend, and the extensive correspondence between the two reflects sensitive, flirtatious spirits and a deep intimacy. Emily was "Nemmy" to Anna Maria's "Ninny." In 1848, Anna Maria Anable, with the help of her extended family, moved to Philadelphia and started the Misses Anable's School in Philadelphia. At Emily's death in 1854, Anna Maria was given guardianship of Emily Frances Judson, daughter of Emily and Adoniram Judson.

[15] Harriet or "Hatty" or "Hattie" or "Hat" Anable was one of nine children born to Joseph and Alma Anable, and was a niece to Miss Cynthia Sheldon and Mrs. Urania Sheldon Nott. In 1841, she had added a note to a letter written by Miss Cynthia Sheldon to Emily. As early as November 1842 she was away, and a letter from Emily to Catharine Chubbuck said that "she (Miss Sheldon) expected that Hat would return as accomplished as Anna Maria." Her trips away were both educational and employment, as she worked as a private tutor in families that would bring her into their homes. In August 1843, she had just returned from Beonsen, in the vicinity of New Orleans, and was engaged to go again. A letter from Anna Maria on January 6, 1845, said that she would stay South for another year. About this time Miss Cynthia Sheldon mentioned her concern for Hatty's spiritual health. In May 1845 she was in New Orleans. She was home again in summer 1846, but a September 27 letter from Anna Maria said she had been asked by Mr. Roman with some urgency to return and she thought that she should. She was to return home from New Orleans in January 1849 after Anna Maria Anable had started the Misses Anable's School in Philadelphia in fall 1848. Harriet was fluent in French, having placed herself earlier in a French environment in New Orleans. Hatty died in 1858.

of Pekan [sic] and ground nuts—bottles of figs and oranges preserved—which would do my heart good to transport again—

Even now dear E. such luxuries are seldom brought in my view, but I am reminded how much you would enjoy them—and how much more our dear distant Missionary friends deserve them than we do here—But you have the luxury of doing good, which yields the peaceable fruits of righteousness in abundance—making your lot on the whole an enviable one—Thus are the good things of this life more equally distributed, than we generally believe—

Our girls are happy indeed, and we are all happy in being relieved from the state of anxiety which her perils by Cholera, and by sea had for days absorbed our every thought—how much better is the Lord to us than our fears—Harriet is really in fine health, happy as possible to find herself at home again—My own *heart* responds to this feeling, although in it dwells sober thoughts—The days of this week are marked with past events which seem not to have gone by—At this time two years ago, we found the sickness of dear Mother was unto death!![16] Oh the two days that followed,—then the last past year this time, the deep drawn sighs of dear father seem even now sounding in my ears.[17] Those days of anguish are of course forgotten by many, but never can be by the children of such loved parents—Their sainted Spirits were soon reunited—How wonderful are the ways of providence. I was writing to Mrs. Clark of Utica last evening and took occasion to say after other things about liking this city—then there is an elevated tone of piety, a comminingling [sic] of minister and people which we much enjoy because they have been so very attentive and so free from treating us as bigots, or proselyters, because we are Baptists—I am sure the time has already come with us which proves a Baptist faculty has nothing to do with a sectarian school, we are known as such, yet Presbyterians, Episcopalians, Unitarians, Quakers and Catholics are among the patrons. Baptists too. The girls are all spirits, all heart, and all ready to benefit their pupils—I had an object in presenting this truthful tirade—some things have been borne in that community which will be remembered—and I verily believe such retribution and change of feeling at least will appear in this world—The Church there will ever share my sympathies—and we have friends who feel, and regard us as injured. All this however is of little moment—if we can have a conscience void of offense—all will end well.

[16] Mother Sheldon died on January 29, 1847. See the letter from Anna Maria Anable dated February 15, 1847.

[17] Deacon Asa Sheldon died in March 1848.

Mrs. Robarts[18] is all kindness to us. The school in which she had placed her young daughter and felt obligated to continue patronage has recently broken up, and she has secured to us three scholars with her Mary—Mr. and Mrs. Gillette[19] are all kindness too—he brought the transcript of your Sunday School book for Mary[20] to make a sketch or two for engravings—shall it be where Ex Gov. Leonard is whipping back his dog—and where he is again seen sleeping on the shoulder of a venerable Doct.—what think you—not likely to be very life like [sic] if sketched—no harm can come—how is dear Lydia[21]—I did mean to write to her at this time—but cannot—remember me to her with affection—We have been most sadly disappointed in not having letters from you for a long time—

May the blessings of heaven rest on you and yours—ever yours with affection

C. Sheldon

Source: American Baptist Historical Society, AJ 20, no. 953.

[18] Mr. and Mrs. W. S. Robarts were active in Philadelphia Baptist circles. They were frequent visitors to the home of the Reverend and Mrs. A. D. Gillette and later to the Misses Anable's School, which Anna Maria Anable and her extended family had started in Philadelphia in 1848. In his biography of his father, Edward Judson mentioned that Adoniram Judson stayed at the. Robarts's home when he came to Philadelphia in December 1845 when he met Emily Chubbuck. A. C. Kendrick said, "(Mr. Gillette and Dr. Judson) arrived in (or out of) due time in Philadelphia, and Dr. Judson was welcomed to the house of Mr. and Mrs. W. S. Robarts, who became warm personal friends, as they were already active friends of the mission cause." (A. C. Kendrick, *The Life and Letters of Mrs. Emily C. Judson* [New York: Sheldon and Company, 1862] 142.) In 1846, with the engagement of Adoniram Judson and Emily Chubbuck, the correspondence indicates some hard feelings toward Mrs. Robarts for comments disparaging the coming marriage and missionary service. This is found in Emily's letter to Adoniram dated February 6, 1846; Mrs. Robarts seemed to be accusing Emily of worldliness when all the time, Emily was quick to say, Mrs. Robarts was engaging in the same activity of which she was accused. The correspondence also indicates a satisfactory healing of the relationship. In January 1849, Miss Sheldon told Emily that Mrs. Robarts had placed their daughter Mary in the Misses Anable's School.

[19] Following several successful pastorates, the Reverend A. D. Gillette was the founding pastor of the flourishing Eleventh Baptist Church in Philadelphia in 1839. With his wife Hannah and several children (they would eventually have six), he graciously opened their home to Emily Chubbuck when she came to Philadelphia at the end of March 1845 for her health. The connection had been made through Miss Cynthia Sheldon, a family friend of Mr. Gillette and his parents. A prominent Baptist, Mr. Gillette journeyed to Boston in December 1845 to accompany Adoniram Judson to Philadelphia for meetings, and on Christmas Day, he introduced Dr. Judson to Emily Chubbuck with the hope that Fanny Forester could be persuaded to write the memoir of Sarah Hall Boardman Judson. A. D. Gillette and his wife Hannah remained valued and trusted friends, not only with Emily, but with the Sheldon and Anable families. He moved from Philadelphia to New York in 1852.

[20] Mary Juliet Anable was born February 18, 1830, in Bethlehem, Albany County, New York, one of nine children born to Alma and Joseph Anable. She went to New Orleans with Hatty in 1847, but she returned home early in March 1848, and by 1849, she was working with Anna Maria in the Misses Anable's School in Philadelphia. Writing in March 1849, Hatty said of Mary, "She paints and draws, speaks French, plays the piano, sings, dances and is our mathematician. What should we ever do without her? She laughs from morning till night, and it is really refreshing to be with her." On December 26, 1860, she was married to Pierre Jacques Darey, the officiating minister being the Rev. Dr. Eliphalet Nott, her uncle. Mary died at the age of sixty-eight on April 20, 1898, in Ottawa, Ontario, Canada.

[21] Lydia Lillybridge was one of Emily's closest friends at the Utica Female Academy. When Emily made the decision to go to Burmah as the wife of Adoniram Judson and as a missionary, Lydia wanted to go with them. Emily spoke to Adoniram Judson of Lydia's extraordinary abilities, and Adoniram advocated her appointment before Dr. Solomon Peck and the Board of the American Baptist Missionary Union. Lydia was commissioned to go with them, in spite of the fact that she remained single. Always independent, outspoken, and unafraid to cause ripples in the missionary community, Lydia served on the mission field for twenty-eight years. She married missionary Thomas Simons in May 1851. See the timeline on the life and service of Lydia Lillybridge Simons in vol. 1.

Anna Maria Anable to Emily C. Judson, January 29, 1849

Three months dear Nemmy[22] and no letter for me! In your epistolary retrenchment do you include me? If you do Madame Missionary I'll I'll [sic] do something desperate. Do you think you are the busiest little mortal in the universe? We show you [sic] by and by that you are by no means that most unenviable personage. As to my claims upon you—because I am an interesting correspondent myself, I make *none at all—at all*. I have burnt up more than one letter that I have written to you because it was flat, insipid, or so obscure that you could not I know make out what I was after saying. Indeed I wish you would write to me without my picking an answer. Come Nemmy darling—( ) ( ) of your benevolence—seems to me I would to you if I thought there would be any benevolence in such an act on my part. What would I not give to know what you are about this evening? And that blessed little baby of mine[23] that is more than a year old. I keep a running account of her age for I expect to have her (very) soon. She must by this time look like somebody. Who is it? Can she talk? She is a wonderful child with her fun, but that's not at all strange. I expect to get great glory for *developing* her one of these days.[24] By the way—have you any curiosity to know how this Ninny[25] gets along in the school? We close our first term next week, and we have twenty scholars. We are making great preparations for a musical Soiree, and a review in most of the classes. Just think of this child's setting up to conduct a recitation in Abercrombie [sic] or Astronomy before all our referrers [sic] and patrons. Drs. Roger and Ludlow both presidents of colleges, and one Bishop. Well, I don't expect to die under it for I have gone through more things in my day—indeed our girls do so beautifully that I begin to feel proud to show them off. Every body [sic], even Aunt Urania[26] who thinks I am such a ninny by nature as well as by name, says that we have a charming school. We have a reputation in the city for being thorough—and we are so. What do you suppose I do in the compo-

[22] "Nem" or "Nemmy" was a name of endearment given to Emily by a small group of her intimate friends at the Utica Female Academy. Anna Maria Anable was "Ninny."

[23] Emily Frances Judson, the daughter of Adoniram and Emily Chubbuck Judson, was born December 24, 1847. Emily married the Reverend Thomas Alexander Thomson (T. A. T.) Hanna in 1870, and they had eight children, two of whom served as missionaries in Burmah.

[24] There is tragic irony in these statements. Anna Maria took Emily Frances Judson, but not just as a student who was sent home from the mission field for education. Emily Frances Judson was six and a half years old when her mother died in June 1854. Under the arrangements of Emily Judson's will, Anna Maria Anable, her best friend, was given the responsibility of raising Emily Frances. Miss Anable filled this responsibility with passion and excellence.

[25] "Ninny" was a name of endearment given to Anna Maria Anable by her most intimate friends at the Utica Female Academy. Emily was "Nemmy."

[26] Urania Sheldon had been the literary principal of the Utica Female Academy in fall 1840 when Emily Chubbuck came to study there. Emily was able to afford this wonderful education through the generous offer of Miss Sheldon and her sister Cynthia, the executive and financial head of the academy, to defer tuition. Urania Sheldon left in late summer 1842 upon her marriage to the Reverend Doctor Eliphalet Nott, the president of Union College in Schenectady, New York. Because of the distance separating them, Emily's relationship with Urania Sheldon Nott did not develop the intimacy that grew between Emily and Miss Cynthia Sheldon. Urania Sheldon Nott remained a mentor, advisor, and friend to Emily in the years of her writing, her missionary endeavors, and upon her return to America in 1851. She was also the aunt of Anna Maria Anable.

sition class? I can't say much for that department; tho' my girls do well I feel that there are no thanks to me—'cept for making them think they can do. I suppose the children think I know every thing [sic] about writing, for ain't I a friend of yours—and don't I write to and get letters from you (sometimes)? The little things run to me every week for *Alderbrook*,[27] The Memoir,[28] or The Offering.[29] I am going to enclose a composition from one of my pupils for I want to know if you think it passes muster for school girls of fifteen. She is a sweet girl, who is to be with us some two or three years and I do not know but I like her so well as to like every thing [sic] she does. Now I'll have my hobby and tell you some news. Dear Hatty[30] returned from New Orleans this week, looking perfectly well. She is the same darling girl and now it seems as if all my hopes are to be realized. She is charmed with her new home and we are all charmed with her. Courtland[31] has a fine situation in a copper mining company which he can attend to at the same time that he is pursuing his law studies. We missed him a good deal at first, but we get along quite well without him now. He is twenty miles from us, and comes in often. The last news from Sarah Bell[32] was increasingly about her cough (her throat affliction) and Laura had a little son. Jul Look[33] is a wonderful favorite in the Episcopal school where she is. The school in

[27] *Alderbrook* was a collection of Fanny Forester's stories, poems, and sketches and was a sequel to *Trippings in Author-land*. Published by Ticknor and Company (later Ticknor, Reed and Fields), the first edition came out in December 1846, and by April 1847, it was in its fourth edition.

[28] Fanny Forester, *Memoir of Sarah B. Judson, Member of the American Mission to Burmah* (New York: L. Colby and Company, 1848).

[29] John Dowling, *The Judson Offering Intended as a Token of Christian Sympathy with the Living and a Memento of Christian Affection for the Dead* (New York: Lewis Colby and Company of New York, 1847).

[30] See vol. 1, "Cast of Characters," s.v. "Anable, Harriet."

[31] Courtland Anable was a younger brother of Anna Maria Anable. He held several positions over the years, and he studied at Hamilton College while he boarded for a time with Emily's parents. In 1853, he returned to Philadelphia where he preached his first sermon at the Eleventh Baptist Church. He was "Uncle Court" to Emily Frances Judson. In 1880, Courtland Anable was listed in the Massachusetts Census as an ordained minister serving in a church.

[32] Sarah Bell Wheeler was a teacher at the Utica Female Academy, an intimate of Emily Chubbuck, and one of the few who addressed Emily as Nemmy. In a September 1847 letter, she was listed as one of the teachers at the Utica Female Academy. There are a number of letters from Sarah Bell before and after her marriage to Charles Gould of Boston in October 1850. There are several letters clustered in the year or two after Emily left for Burmah and a number at the time of her return to America. Emily stayed with Charles and Sarah Bell Gould in October 1851 when she arrived in Boston after the long sea voyage from Burmah and then England. She stayed there a number of times following that. In 1851, Anna Maria Anable wrote of Sarah Bell: "Sarah is grown so lovely in person as well as character that she must assert a blessed influence on all with whom she comes in contact."

[33] Julia Look was a student of Emily's at the Utica Female Academy and later a fellow teacher. A November 22, 1845, letter from Anna Maria encouraged Emily to stay in Philadelphia for the winter for her health and remarked that Julia had the hardest part because she was teaching Emily's composition class, and the students kept asking for Emily. In a September 1847 letter, she was listed as one of the teachers at the Utica Female Academy. On September 23, 1849, Anna Maria wrote that Julia and Albert B. Casswell were married and came to visit with her. In one 1849 letter Julia spoke of another teacher who was teaching "our composition class." On October 27, 1850, Anna Maria Anable noted that she had had a son. She was one of a small number of people who addressed Emily as "Emily" and as "Nemmy" in her letters.

Utica is flourishing admirably under the present administration[34]—Mr. Lansing writes me that Mary Barber[35] is going to astonish us all—by some exploit matrimonial I presume. I have thought of every body [sic] in Utica but I cannot conceive (since Mr. Walcott and Mrs. Bagg are engaged) who there is for Mary to attack but Mr. Corey! [36] I have to stop and laugh at the very idea.[37] Hatty says Mary Adams[38] is going to marry Gardner Green of Norwich,—a very fine young man, of invention, fortune, piety and all that Mary's heart was sighed for. Hatty sends her very best love to you. Tell Lydia[39] I suppose she feels quite too grand now-a-days to answer any of my letters, but if I did not feel so stuffy I should write her nevertheless. Do write me darling—I am so afraid you are going to forget me.

Ninny

Source: American Baptist Historical Society, AJ 13, no. 484.

[34] This is an interesting reference, for in earlier letters, Anna Maria was gloomy over the prospects of success for Jane Kelly as the new headmistress of the Utica Female Academy. Miss Cynthia Sheldon also expressed some severe sentiments about the debt Miss Kelly had incurred in replacing much of what had been left behind and bitterness with the over-all treatment they had received from the trustees of the institution.

[35] Mary Barber was mentioned frequently in the Emily Chubbuck Judson letters; she was a student and then a teacher at the Utica Female Academy. There were ups and downs to that relationship; in fall 1845, apparently Mary had written to someone expressing what Anna Maria Anable called "ingratitude," and Mary had been banned from the Academy until she made proper apologies to Miss Sheldon. In a September 7, 1845, letter from Anna Maria, we learn that her remarks had been about Miss Cynthia Sheldon. In November 1847 Jane Kelly remarked that they had not heard from Mary in more than a year. In 1848 Mary Barber was back at the Utica Female Seminary teaching with Jane Kelly. Though at this time Miss Sheldon had moved to Philadelphia, Mary Barber had been able to reconcile with her, and in later years we find Mary very close to the Sheldon-Anable families; later, there was considerable consternation on Miss Cynthia Sheldon's part in her correspondence with Emily about Mary's health, the seriousness of it, and Mary's impending death. These letters were written in April 1852. Miss Sheldon went to help transfer Mary to Albany in June 1852, where she would be better situated and perhaps have access to better doctors. On September 9, 1852, Anna Maria Anable wrote to Emily of Mary Barber's death.

[36] Mr. Corey was the pastor of the Bleecker Street Baptist Church near the Utica Female Academy, and Miss Sheldon and many of the girls from the academy attended worship there. (Cynthia Sheldon, Alma Anable, Deacon Asa and Isabell Sheldon, Edward Bright, and Horace Hawley had been charter members of the church in 1838.) In April 1844, he wrote to Emily expressing dismay that at a school program one of the girls had read a composition justifying dancing as exercise; he spoke of this as a roadblock to the salvation of many. Then, on March 10, 1846, Emily indicated in a letter to Anna Maria that Mr. Corey had been critical of her relationship and impending marriage to Adoniram Judson. Miss Cynthia Sheldon wrote a number of times expressing Mr. Corey's regret and support, and in 1847, there were letters of reconciliation between Emily and Mr. Corey. In spring 1848, letters reveal that Mr. Corey's wife had died of consumption, her condition exacerbated by recent childbirth. She had left behind four children. In July 1849, Anna Maria Anable wrote of his impending marriage to Jane Backus, a good choice for this "rising man." Mr. Corey remained popular with the Sheldon-Anable families even after their move to Philadelphia in 1848. A March 2, 1852, letter from Charles B. Stout told of Mr. Corey's call to the Stanton Street Church in New York City, which Mr. Corey did not accept. Finally, in 1854, there was a pastoral letter from Mr. Corey to Emily on her illness and her possible death. He preached at the Bleecker Street Church as late as January 1867.

[37] On December 22, 1848, Morven Jones wrote to Emily Judson from Utica, and one of the rumors of which he spoke was a possible romance blossoming between Mary Barber and Mr. Corey, the pastor of the Bleecker Street Baptist church; Mr. Corey's wife died the previous spring.

[38] Mary Adams was related to the Utica Female Academy. Her letter to Emily in October 1845 was almost a whimsical piece of fantasy with literary pretensions. It would reflect a fairly close relationship. A second letter in December 1845 was similar. The letters were written from New Orleans, and she spoke of Hatty Anable as being near to her. On January 29, 1849, Anna Maria Anable wrote, "Hatty says Mary Adams is going to marry Gardner Green of Norwich,—a very fine young man, of invention, fortune, piety and all that Mary's heart was sighed for." On July 8, 1850, Mrs. Urania Sheldon Nott spoke of attending this wedding in New York.

[39] See vol. 1, "Cast of Characters," s.v. "Lillybridge, Lydia." See also "A Timeline of the Life and Mission of Lydia Lillybridge Simons."

Adoniram Judson—Last Will and Testament, January 31, 1849

Whereas I received by Bequest from my mother, a few years ago, the sum of $3,000, for the support and education of my children, and the money has been accumulating at interest, and by small accessions from other sources, I hope that notwithstanding the loss I have sustained, by the failure of the Union Bank in Calcutta (involving the loss of the donation of Mr. Douglas of Cavers, Scotland, committed to my trust) there will be enough at the time of my death, to meet the following bequests:—

Be it known, therefore, that by this my last Will and Testament, I bequeath—

1. To my daughter Abby Ann, Two Hundred Dollars a year, for the term of five years, beginning with Oct. 31st, 1851, when, if she live, she will be sixteen years of age, and Two Hundred and Fifty Dollars, when she is twenty one years of age.

2. To each of my sons Adoniram Brown and Elnathan, Twenty Dollars a year in addition to the Eighty Dollars a year paid for each by the ABMU until they are sixteen years of age, and from that period, Two hundred and Fifty Dollars a year, to defray the expenses of their education, until they come to the age of twenty-one, and whatever may remain unexpended to be paid them at that age.

3. To each of my sons Henry and Edward, Three hundred Rs. for their passage from India to America, and afterwards, the same as to their two older brothers, as specified in the 2nd article.

4. To my daughter Emily Frances, Three Hundred Rupees for her passage from India to America, Twenty Dollars a year from the time of her arriving in America, in addition to the Eighty Dollars a year from the ABMU until she is sixteen years of age, and from that time, Two hundred Dollars a year for five years, and Two Hundred and Fifty Dollars when she is twenty one years of age.

5. In regard to George D. Boardman, if he does not receive from various contributions, who are pledged to that purpose, enough to support himself four years at College, I bequeath him so much as may be necessary to supply the deficiency, at the discretion of the Executor.

6. I appoint my wife Emily C. Judson, the Executor of my Will, the Guardian of my children, and my residuary legatee.

7. As most of my property is and will remain vested in the Bank of Bengal, I direct, that if that bank stock prove insufficient to meet the bequests alone specified, they be all lessened in the same ratio, and to seek a degree as may be brought within the amount of the said bank stock.

8. And however small and insufficient that amount may be, I direct that no part of my immediate personal effects, such as Books, Household furniture, Wearing Apparel, etc.—nor the House and land situated in Hamilton, New York, the property of my wife, before her marriage, nor any other property not specified in this

instrument, be applied to make up the deficiency, but that all such property belong to the residuary legatee.

In witness whereof, I hereunto subscribe and set my hand and seal, at Maulmain, this thirty-first day of January, in the year of our Lord, One Thousand Eight Hundred and Forty nine.

(Signed) A. Judson

In the presence of
Thos S. Ranney
L. Stilson

Later Addendum:

We the undersigned, hereby solemnly affirm and declare that the foregoing is a true and faithful copy of the last Will and Testament of the late Rev. Adoniram Judson, D.D. who signed the same in our presence, both of us being present at the same time; and that we, in the presence of each other affixed our signatures thereto.

Thos S. Ranney
L. Stilson

Attest this 23rd day of December/ 1850
( ) Briggs
Maulmain omagh [sic]

Source: Hanna family files.

Emily C. Judson to Miss Cynthia Sheldon, February 17, 1849—Maulmain

Dear Aunt C.

I was glad to receive your kind note; for it is now sometime since I have heard from you, or written. Though I am more weaned from my beautiful native land than I ever expected to be; yet it makes me sad to think of the changes that have occurred since I left. I noted when you spoke of your visit to Utica,[40] and my imagination went with you, it seemed like walking among graves. I am glad you are in Philadelphia, however, and that everything looks so prosperous around you. I have never doubted but you would be richly blessed in whatever you undertook—and Anna Maria[41] too. I cannot imagine anything more charming than your whole establishment. Of course you will look for occasional reverses, but it seems to me as though you were in an admirable situation both for happiness and usefulness.

[40] See the letter of Miss Cynthia Sheldon to Emily C. Judson dated October 28, 1848.

[41] See vol. 1, "Cast of Characters," s.v. "Anable, Anna Maria."

We have had some trials since I wrote you last. God has given us a second time our precious Frances,[42] and we now value her if possible more than ever. She was attacked very suddenly with an *epidemic*, a species of *cholera*, and suffered greatly. Just as we began to entertain hopes of her recovery, the doctor startled us by his apprehensions of inflammation on the brain. This new disease, however, took a sudden turn; and she is now well and tolerably stout, though she had lost her roses. She toddles about the floor greatly to her own admiration; and is as full of her tricks as a monkey. She was an uncommonly heavy child when first taken ill, and I kept her in my arms constantly, though I suffered greatly while doing it with pain in the chest, and as soon as she was convalescent commenced the application of mustard poultices. But I had received a hurt not easily healed; and the result was an alarm (apprehensions of diseased lungs) from which we have scarcely yet recovered. I took to my bed, and called on the doctor; and though he helped me materially I am worth at best 10 percent less than before. I have been obliged to discontinue my long walks; and as the doctor recommends horse-back exercise my good husband has bought me a charming pony that canters like a cradle—a little better than a cradle. I am at present something of "a lame duck" it must be owned, but quite as well as I ever expected to be when I left America; and I am able beside taking care of my own family to do a little for the natives. Oh, Aunt C.[43] you have no idea how much strong efficient women are wanted here; for what with one thing and what with another, but little woman's work is done.

We are looking towards Ava anxiously, but Burmah is at present a mere den of robbers; and the king a puppet. The present war in the Punjaub [sic] makes the Burmese very impudent to foreigners.

I hope you will have all sorts of blessings there in Philadelphia. The Baptists will soon find you out. Perhaps it is your fashionable house and street that frightens them—perhaps your Pedo-recommendations. Don't mind—they have done you good unintentionally. I hope you will find time to write a little oftener now—at any rate to *think* often of

Yours ever affectionately

Emily C. Judson

Source: Hanna family files.

[42] See vol. 1, "Cast of Characters," s.v. "Judson, Emily Frances."

[43] Miss Cynthia Sheldon was in charge of the administrative and financial departments of the Utica Female Academy. Miss Sheldon and her sister Urania, who was literary principal, gave Emily Chubbuck a place at the academy in October 1840. They had deferred any cost to a future time when Emily could afford to reimburse them. Upon Miss Urania Sheldon's marriage in late summer 1842 to the Reverend Doctor Eliphalet Nott, the president of Union College, and her subsequent move to Schenectady, Miss Cynthia Sheldon assumed a larger leadership role at the academy. In the years that followed, Miss Sheldon and Emily developed an even stronger relationship. In 1848, Miss Sheldon moved to Philadelphia to help Miss Anable with the startup of the Misses Anable's School and to assume responsibilities in its operation. Active and well-known in Baptist circles, Miss Cynthia was one of Emily's most important mentors, advisors, and friends until the time of Emily's death in 1854. Miss Sheldon was the aunt of Anna Maria Anable.

Emily C. Judson to Mrs. Mary Colby, February 1849[44]

You cannot conceive what a quantity of warm clothing a person needs out here particularly a delicate person. As for the baby things, they were priceless. I pieced out the petticoat at top and made a nice white flannel frock, of which I have been more careful than I should have been of genuine Brussels. The frock with the pink spots is a special favorite with little Miss,[45] for she is true to her sex in all matters pertaining to pretty things. The child is indeed as you suggest a great comfort to me though (once I would not have believed this possible) no more so than her darling little brothers.[46] I can scarcely bring myself to believe that they are not mine in the strictest sense of the word. But I suppose it would be very silly for me to expatiate on my domestic happiness, in this or any other line, so I spare you.

I liked the appearance of the Benjamins[47] very much indeed—she in particular seemed to be a good common sense sort of a person; such as are rather rare nowadays; but I was so ill that I saw less of them than I could have wished. Miss Lillybridge[48] is very well, and now that she boards at Mr. Stilson's[49] is very happy. She has seen more of the "trials of missionary life" than she bargained for, poor thing, and certainly of a different kind, and in that perhaps she don't [sic] stand alone—among the *appointed* ones, I mean. We who receive our appointments from *private quarter* never have any trials, except with the babies. Have I ever mentioned to you what truly valuable people the Harrises,[50] who came out with us, are? I don't know

[44] The first page of this letter is missing. It is placed in February 1849 because when Emily says, "The child is indeed as you suggest a great comfort to me," she is picking up on a line from an October 9, 1848, letter of Mrs. Colby's, which would have taken several months to travel from Newton Centre, Massachusetts, to Maulmain, Burmah.

[45] See vol. 1, "Cast of Characters," s.v. "Judson, Emily Frances."

[46] Henry Hall Judson, (six and a half years old at this time) and Edward Judson (four years old) were the two youngest surviving children of Adoniram and Sarah Hall Boardman Judson. They were left in Burmah because of their age when Adoniram, Sarah, and the older children returned to the United States in the hope that Sarah could regain her health. Sarah died on the trip home at the Isle of St. Helena on September 1, 1845, and in November 1846, Adoniram Judson returned to Burmah with Emily, the boys' "new mamma."

[47] Judson Benjamin was born February 2, 1819, in Rodman, New York. He was baptized in Franklin, Indiana; graduated from Brown University and Newton Theological Seminary; and was ordained on October 13, 1848, in Providence, Rhode Island. He married Susan Ruggles Stone on September 3, 1848, and they departed for Tavoy, Burma, on October 21, 1848. They arrived at Tavoy in April 1849; in March 1850, they were sent to Mergui. Mr. Benjamin collected a vocabulary of 1,200 Salong words. They sailed from Rangoon to Boston on January 21, 1854, and Rev. Benjamin died in Boston of pulmonary disease in February 1855. Susan Benjamin remarried William Ward, and they left from Boston in June 1860 to return to Burmah.

[48] See vol. 1, "Cast of Characters," s.v. "Lillybridge, Lydia." See also "A Timeline of the Life and Mission of Lydia Lillybridge Simons."

[49] Lyman and Lucretia Stilson were missionaries to Burmah. They arrived in February 1838. There are five letters in the correspondence from them. Lucretia Stilson died in Maulmain on August 14, 1851.

[50] Norman Harris was born on February 19, 1813, in Becket, Massachusetts. He attended Columbia College and Hamilton Literary and Theological School, graduating in 1844. Olive Celina Wadsworth was also born in Becket, Massachusetts, on July 6, 1814. They were married on August 9, 1844, and were appointed to missionary service on October 28, 1844. In July 1846, they sailed to Burmah with the newly married Adoniram and Emily Judson. Olive Harris died in childbirth on November 23, 1853, in Shwegyin, Burma. In 1856, Norman Harris married for the second time; Miranda Harris died of fever in September that same year. Norman Harris left the mission field shortly after the death of his wife Miranda and returned to the United States. There, in June 1858, he married Julia Wadsworth Chapman, the sister of his first wife, Olive Celina Wadsworth. Norman and Julia Harris returned to Burmah in 1858, though not under the auspices of the American Baptist Missionary Union; they were reappointed as missionaries in 1861. Norman Harris died on March 1, 1884, in Hamilton, New York. Julia Harris died in September 1905.

much about them in the mission line, for they are Karens, but I cannot sufficiently admire their Christian character.—Poor Mrs. Cross[51] is up from Tavoy, ill, and with an almost dying child.

I wonder if you know Mrs. Benett[52] of Tavoy. She is just another Mrs. Wade,[53] only perhaps lacking Mrs. W's force of character. She is a real working missionary, and a spiritually minded Christian. I went down there for my health, and a most delightful visit did I have, though we both considered me on the verge of the grave. "Another salt of the earth" as Granny Randal would say, is Mrs. Stilson, though I am afraid we shall not have her with us long.—You will have heard from Mrs. Stevens[54] I hope. It was a terribly severe affliction, but they bore it with true Christian fortitude. I love Mrs. Stevens very much indeed. Mrs. Cross is staying with her.

I shall write to your mother by this mail. Give my love to your husband and sister. Oh, how I wish I could see all your faces once again—but don't forget me, will you?

Most affectionately,

Emily C. Judson

Source: Hanna family files.

[51] Edmund Cross was from Georgetown, New York, and graduated from the Hamilton Theological Institute in 1840. He was appointed to missionary service in Tavoy, Burmah, on November 28, 1842. Mr. and Mrs. Cross arrived in Maulmain on February 24, 1845, and at Tavoy a month later. His wife was Julia Ann Putman; they were married at Morrisville, New York, in August 1843. There are two letters in the correspondence from Mrs. Cross to Emily; both were written from Tavoy. Both of the letters have to do with helping Emily make preparations for her voyage, and the offering of arrowroot and soojer [sic] as medicines to take for the journey. Mrs. Cross is rather explicit in what soojer is for and how it works. Mrs. Cross died at Toungoo, Burmah in 1875; Mr. Cross died August 14, 1905, in Toungoo, Burmah.

[52] Stella Bennett was the wife of Cephas Bennett; they arrived in Burmah in January 1830. Mr. Bennett remained the superintendent of the Baptist Press there for more than fifty years. From the Utica area, they sent their children back, and the girls were educated at the Utica Female Academy and then the Misses Anable's School. The girls included Elsina (April 1828), Mary (November 1829), Ann (August 1833), Ellen (June 1835), and Sarah (June 1837).

[53] Deborah Wade was a missionary to Burmah; with her husband Jonathan, they were appointed in 1823. Adoniram Judson called them "his dearest and best of friends." Much of their work was in the jungle communities following the path of George Boardman. They left for the United States on December 22, 1847. From the Hamilton, New York, area, they stayed not far from the home of Emily's parents and sister; they visited the Anable-Sheldon families in Philadelphia. With a large group, they had left Boston on July 25, 1850, and returned to Burmah in February 1851.

[54] Elizabeth Stevens arrived in Maulmain in February 1838; her husband was Edward Stevens. Elizabeth Stevens took six-month-old Edward Judson into her home when Sarah and Adoniram had to leave for the United States in 1845, and her care and nurture saved his life. She served forty-eight years in Burmah. She had extensive correspondence with Emily Judson, and her letters spoke of everyday life among the missionaries. When Emily returned to the United States, the letters from Mrs. Stevens brought news of friends and colleagues. Mrs. Stevens had a sister, Sarah Haven, in Massachusetts, who wrote a number of letters to Emily asking for information on the Stevens family.

Emily C. Judson to Anna Maria Anable, February 20, 1849—Maulmain

My dear Ninny,[55]

Aunt C's[56] note[57] will plead my case for having been a negligent correspondent. I *did* intend to write you a long letter by this mail, but have put it off too long. The mail goes out tomorrow and I have two native female prayer-meetings to conduct in the morning. It is now nearly ten and I am not strong yet—how I wish you were here to help me. I have always regretted some things I wrote you from first impressions. I thought because a woman did little, there was little for them to do, but I was mistaken. Oh, if I only had free hands, a strong frame, and a holy heart! With *either* of the three alone, I might do more than now.

I am glad you are so nicely situated; and very thankful for all the minute particulars you have written.[58] I can see *everything* from your nice description. How I wish I could step in though I should'nt [sic] look much at anything except your darling face—all your faces. I hope Ninny that we—you and I—are not to have all our good things in this world—everything prospers in our hands; and we have everything to make us happy. Don't you think so? Oh, how I wish you could see my *sweet* home, made so by (I can say it to you, though it would not be proper to anyone else) my faultless, precious husband. Strange that God should so bless me, when I was and am still so undeserving. How true that everything is *of grace*. I wonder if your love for the Saviour [sic] has deepened any since I came away. If we were to meet now, though we might appear precisely the same as formerly to others, I think we should have some sweet talks that we did'nt [sic] use to have. Would'nt [sic] we? I want you all to pray for me a great deal. Give your mother[59] the commission with my love—I am so tired that I scarce know what I am writing, though I have got a heart-full to say—so a kiss, dear Ninny, and

Good-night

Nemmy C.J.

[55] "Ninny" was a name of endearment given to Anna Maria Anable by her most intimate friends at the Utica Female Academy. Emily was "Nemmy."

[56] See vol. 1, "Cast of Characters," s.v. "Sheldon, Miss Cynthia."

[57] See the letter of Emily C. Judson to Miss Cynthia Sheldon dated February 17, 1849.

[58] See the letter of Anna Maria Anable to Emily C. Judson dated October 29, 1848.

[59] Alma Sheldon Anable was the sister of Miss Cynthia Sheldon and Urania Sheldon Nott. Genealogy sources show that she married Joseph Hubbell Anable in Troy, New York, on July 28, 1814, and that it was the second marriage for Mr. Anable. Born in 1773, he was forty-one at the time of the marriage, and Alma was likely considerably younger. He died in 1831, which explains why Alma Anable and her family lived and worked first at the Utica Female Seminary and then later at the Misses Anable's school in Philadelphia. Joseph and Alma Anable were the parents of nine children: Henry Sheldon Anable (b. June 21, 1815); William Stewart Anable (b. November 6, 1816); Anna Maria Stafford Anable (b. September 30, 1818), Cynthia Jane Anable (b. January 28, 1820); Samuel Low Anable (b. November 28, 1821); Harriet Isabella Anable, also known as Hatty or Hattie (b. December 18, 1823); Courtland Wilcox Anable (b. July 28, 1825); Frances Alma Anable, or Fanny (b. April 12, 1828); and Mary Juliet Anable (b. February 18, 1830).

Give love to Matilda[60] and Mary.[61] I am glad to hear from Aunt C. that Courtland[62] is such a decided Christian—Give ever and ever so much love to the Gillettes.[63] Tell Mrs. G. I have just heard th( ) is a box for me from Phil on the way out. I shall write as soon as it is rec'd.

Source: Hanna family files.

The Reverend Doctor Solomon Peck to Emily C. Judson, February 20, 1849[64]—Baptist Mission Rooms, Boston

Mrs. E. C. Judson
My dear Sister

I was very much gratified to receive your letter of 21st Sept. The course of life which you are pursuing, is evidently working its effect—though possibly in some respects unnoticed by yourself—*the* effect which I anticipated and hoped for, and which will lead you yet more and more to thank your Heavenly Father for having brought you to Burmah.

But the way must and will often be rough and wearisome, and nothing will carry you safely through less than the almighty arm of Jehovah. *Jehovah jireih.* [sic]

I accept as you would have me, the explanation you give for not writing. But in doing so for the past, I must enter a new application for the time to come. You are about to accompany your husband to Ava.[65] Will it be too much to ask of you—

[60] Matilda Berthoud was a friend of Anna Maria Anable and probably of Emily as well, for Anna Maria's and Miss Sheldon's letters refer to her. In one letter, Miss Sheldon tells how Anna Maria had gone to visit Matilda, and while there, Matilda's brother had taken Anna Maria for a buggy ride. Somehow the horse got frightened, and Anna Maria and her host were taken on a wild ride, which they survived by the heroic actions of the brother, the undaunted courage of Anna Maria, and the providence of God. In a letter shortly after their move to Philadelphia in 1848, Miss Sheldon says that Matilda is everything to them. She is perfectly happy being with them, and she adds that she is a "host in French." When Henry and Edward went to Hamilton to live with Emily's parents and sister, Matilda was one of the individuals considered to be employed to help with work around the house and with the care of the family.

[61] See vol. 1, "Cast of Characters," s.v. "Anable, Miss Mary Juliet."

[62] See vol. 1, "Cast of Characters," s.v. "Anable, Courtland."

[63] See vol. 1, "Cast of Characters," s.v. "Gillette, The Reverend Abram Dunn."

[64] Emily answered this letter on July 18, 1849. Her reply was a blistering letter that runs for five pages of typewritten text in this correspondence; the handwritten pages are large sheets, and there are seven of them with a great deal of crossing out and underlining, showing the passionate force with which she wrote to justify her history, her style, and her work.

In Emily's biography by A. C. Kendrick, *The Life and Letters of Mrs. Emily C. Judson* (New York: Sheldon and Company, 1831), he sanitized her letter considerably. First, he showed it as having been written, not to Dr. Solomon Peck, executive secretary of the American Baptist Missionary Union, but to "a friend." Second, he removed all of the passion and strength and ends up with a bland letter that is more like a lecture. The editor strongly recommends that after reading this letter, the reader turn to the July 18, 1849, reply written by Emily. Both have been pulled together to show the original and the edited version.

[65] For years, Adoniram Judson tried to convince the mission board to allow him to go to Ava, the seat of power in the Burman empire, but lack of funding had always prevented approval. In February 1847, the Judsons went to Rangoon, and Emily and Adoniram were forced to return to Maulmain in September 1847 because of cutbacks in the funding from the board. Now, the board has approved such a move at the very time when Adoniram Judson was unable to go. Part of it was the work on the dictionary, which was better done with the help he had put together in Maulmain, and part were family and health reasons.

your husband relieving you of some of your cares by way of his own relaxation—to lay yourself out to give a descriptive narrative of your ascent of the Irrawaddy and of what you see at Ava. We in this country know very little, after all that has been written, of the interior of Burmah and of Ava. With your eye and pen you can give us almost an eye knowledge of that country, its people, their homes, employments etc. If you will consent to do this, I will find space in the Magazine. Only two things I venture to premise. One, that you bear in mind how sober and prosaic we are at the Magazine, and the other how sober and prosaic we should be were we our eyewitnesses of what you may describe.[66] To illustrate my meaning—I have sometimes queried whether I were to visit Hamilton[67] again,[68] I could find Alderbrook[69] and recognize it, with my matter of fact perception. (I shall make the experiment the first opportunity.) What we would most like would be sketches and outlines entitled to the faith of veritable history—yet drama by your graphic [sic] hand.

I write with fraternal freedom, and in so doing give the best proof in my power how truly you have from me a brother's confidence and affection. If I pain you *in the least*, I shall pain myself *far more*. I am writing—not as Secretary

But as
Truly and affectionately
Your brother

S. Peck

Source: American Baptist Historical Society, AJ 19, no. 947.

[66] Emily and Solomon Peck had never really hit it off. Peck saw Fanny Forester as a secular writer, and some of his stern, moralistic views in this regard can be seen in his April 30, 1846, letter, as he advocates for her, with a quote from the Bible, a new direction: "Forgetting the things that are behind and reaching forth to the things that are before." On May 8, 1846, in a letter to Anna Maria Anable, Emily reports that Dr. Peck deemed *Allen Lucas* to be an "evil book" and under no circumstances to be reprinted by the denomination. In this letter from Dr. Peck, the two conditions he imposes turn out to be the proverbial straw that broke the camel's back as far as Emily was concerned. He asked her to write about Ava for the mission magazine published by the denomination in a factual style instead of the more interpretative style she normally used. This brought to the surface all of the anger and frustrations about what she experienced as his perceptions of her past, which had been to date buried and unexpressed. Some of Emily's descriptive narrative can be found in her writings from August 1846 through March 1847. "Outward Bound" was written for the *Columbian* magazine and is a colorful portrayal of the voyage from the United States to sight of land in Burmah. Following that there are a number of letters to family and friends describing their first contact with Burmese coming out to meet the boat, the river trip up to Maulmain, and descriptions of the local populace.

[67] In late summer 1842, Emily E. Chubbuck had purchased a home in Hamilton, New York, for her parents, her sister Catharine, and her brother Wallace for the times when he was there.

[68] Dr. Solomon Peck traveled to Utica, New York, in spring 1846, following the decision of the Board of the American Baptist Missionary Union to accept Miss Lydia Lillybridge as a missionary candidate to go with Emily and Adoniram to Burmah. At that time, he had meetings with both Lydia and Emily. It was suspected at the time that he was far more interested in gaining an impression of Emily than he was of Lydia. Writing to Emily on April 20, 1846, Adoniram Judson said, "Mr. Peck said to me rather interestingly, that as he was going out to see Miss Lillybridge, he should be very glad to have an interview with the other lady. I said,—I supposed the Board would be pleased to have him do so. He replied—Not at all—her case was not even mentioned before the Board."

[69] The first volume of her collection of stories and sketches, which she had titled *Alderbrook*, includes a piece she named "Underhill Cottage." She described this cottage, the surrounding fields, and a brook lined with alders as idealic, for her a kind of "heaven on earth." In the second volume of *Alderbrook*, the last piece was titled "Farewell to Alderbrook."

Miss Cynthia Sheldon to Emily C. Judson, March 1849[70]

Dear Emily—

I do wish this box was of more value—indeed I am quite ashamed of its ( )grenes but believe it contains all the articles you requested Anna M.[71] to get—and a very few more—

We could not understand what kind of India Rubber Cloth you wanted—this is the lightest article to be found here—and fearing it would melt in the box, we concluded to get only the 1 1/2 yds to wrap the things in—There is a pitchy scent to it, quite disagreeable and we fear you will be disappointed altogether in it—I have given the price of materials—the work has been done most cheerfully by a few—

You may think it very strange, but we were misinformed about the Kincaids[72] going in April—and not till last week could we ascertain that they wait for the other Missionaries 1st of July—the box will be started for Boston tomorrow—and I do hope they will find an opportunity very soon to forward it—You will find some *light reading* in dilapidated state—purposely so—you will of course have letters before this reaches you containing more than I can not [sic] write—I shall put in all the reading matter we can now muster—hope to add some when the Missionaries go—heaven bless you and yours.

Love from all—affectionately yours

C. Sheldon

Mrs. Gillette[73] put most of the things in the way to be done—she is my admiration for a worker

Source: American Baptist Historical Society, AJ 20, no. 997.

[70] This letter is undated. It was a note accompanying a box of supplies sent to the Judsons. ABHS has it recorded as being written in 1849, so it is placed in March 1849.

[71] See vol. 1, "Cast of Characters," s.v. "Anable, Anna Maria."

[72] Born in 1797, educated at the seminary in Hamilton, New York, and ordained in 1822, the Reverend Eugenio Kincaid served several churches before being appointed as a missionary to Burmah in February 1830. His first wife died soon after their arrival. His second wife was Barbara McBain, and they were married in 1833. In these years, they served in Rangoon, Ava, Saduja, and Akyab. The Reverend and Mrs. Kincaid returned to the United States in 1843; because of her persistent health problems, they were not reappointed in 1846. While in the United States, Rev. Kincaid became instrumental in the establishment of the University of Lewisberg (later Bucknell University). Upon Mrs. Kincaid's restoration, they returned to Burmah, arriving in February 1851 just as Emily Judson was embarking for her return voyage. With his knowledge of the language and customs, Rev. Kincaid was able to establish himself in work with the Burmese government at Ava. With one more trip home (in 1857, on an official mission for the King of Burmah to President Buchanan of the United States), they retired to Gerard, Kansas, in 1866. Of Rev. Kincaid, the correspondence indicates a man of convictions and occasional independent action.

[73] Hannah Gillette was the wife of the Reverend A. D. Gillette, pastor of the Eleventh Baptist Church in Philadelphia. Emily stayed with them when she came to Philadelphia in spring 1845 for her health, and she returned in November. In the parlor of their home, she met Adoniram Judson on Christmas Day 1845. Mr. and Mrs. Gillette became strong friends and supporters; Mrs. Gillette played an important part in getting Emily's outfit together for her life in Burmah.

Mr. James T. Fields[74] to Emily C. Judson, March 2, 1849—Boston

Dear Mrs. Judson

I have been wishing a long time to write you and until now have delayed the pleasure that I might inform you of the publication of a xined [sic] edition of *Alderbrook*.[75] You will see in the receipt of a copy how far we have been able to comply with your wishes. We have printed all you suggest as additional matter, but have retained the story you thought might as well be omitted.[76] In a note appended with our signature we explain why we still print it. The reason we assign it is that it is too good to be left out. We find also it is a bad plan in a new issue of a popular book to leave out anything. The sale is sometimes checked in this way. However we doubt not you will forgive us for keeping alive an old favorite. It seemed really too bad to thrust out from among her companions, with whom she had shared so much honor, this unoffending maiden.

I really hope you will send us a mss. to print before long. We are confident that a new book from your far-home would meet with great success. We feel a particular interest, as the Publishers of *Alderbrook* (beside a strong partiality of friendship) that our house should issue your writings.[77] We know we can do as well (if not better) with any books you may hereafter write, as any publishing house in America. As regards terms we are always prepared to meet *your* wishes, and should allow no competition to interfere with arrangement between the author of *Alderbrook* and her original Publishers.

With my best wishes for your happiness wherever yr lot in life is cast, and my kindest remembrances to yr husband,

I remain
Yrs always most truly

James T. Fields

P.S. Allow me to add a line to Dr. Judson informing him that his Draft for $365.50 has been presented and paid.

Source: American Baptist Historical Society, AJ 16, no. 726.

[74] A publisher, editor, and author, Mr. Fields has six letters to Emily in this collection. He was a partner in Tichnor, Reed and Fields, which published *Alderbrook*, *The Kathayan Slave*, and *My Two Sisters*. He was editor of the *Atlantic Monthly* (1861–1870). There is a James T. Fields collection in the Houghton Library at Harvard, and it includes a letter, a portrait, and a poem of Emily Judson, along with memorabilia (letters, portraits, manuscripts) from his life's work in the publishing business.

[75] See vol. 1, "Places, Events, Organizations, and Magazines," s.v. "Alderbrook."

[76] See Emily's letter that has been approximately dated December 1847; this letter was included in the future editions of *Alderbrook*. Emily had written new material, which was added to subsequent editions, and the publishers elected to retain some material that she thought could be removed.

[77] Ticknor, Reed and Fields published two of Emily's future books, *My Two Sisters* and *The Kathayan Slave*. They worked hard to get the rights to Dr. Wayland's memoir of Adoniram Judson, but in a competitive environment, Dr. Wayland and Emily awarded the publication to a different publishing house (Phillips, Sampson, and Company).

Mrs. Urania Sheldon Nott to Emily C. Judson, March 15, 1849—Union College

My dear Emily,

A long time has passed since the rec't of your kind letter which arrived about the time that my husband[78] was violently attacked by inflammatory rheumatism—during one whole year he had very little rest and no cessation of pain night or day. Indeed we can at this time say that he has not known freedom from pain for a year and a half, altho' he is thro ( ) Providence comparatively better. His general health is perfect but his feet ( ) ( ) become free from disease, tho' they are gradually improving—He is able to walk about the house with a cane—as a substitute for his crutches which he has been obliged to use for a long time—he has not during this protracted illness lost more than one or two invitations—and attends to his college duties as usual. You may imagine dear Emily how constantly my hands have been occupied during this long period of trial—Indeed I have scarcely been able to write a letter during this time, except to my own family. Many changes have taken place within my own beloved home, since I last saw you—Death has been busy in our midst, and removed our loved and venerated parents to whom we were bound by peculiar ties[79]—the light has gone out in their dwelling, and the house once endeared by a thousand tender associations, has passed into stranger hands[80]—One spot alone remains in Utica, to which I am attached and that is a small but to me sacred enclosure containing all that is mortal of my beloved parents. There they lie side by side, and if my life is spared, thither I shall pay an annual visit to me a hallowed place—tho' I look with an eye of faith for visions in the skies—show beautifully their sun went down! May God grant that my last days be as peaceful—and thus "fade away into the light of peace."

I visited Philadelphia last ( ) to which my affections are now transferred, ( ) where I found all that remains of my own immediate family delightfully situated—the four sisters are again[81] after years of separation reunited—and are as happy as they well can be—they have a very excellent school in every sense[82]—that is steadily increasing—and which I doubt not will continue to flourish as long as their watering

[78] The Reverend Doctor Eliphalet Nott was the president of Union College in Schenectady, New York. An ordained Presbyterian minister, he was married to Urania Sheldon Nott, the sister of Miss Cynthia Sheldon and Mrs. Alma Anable and the aunt of Anna Maria Anable.

[79] Mother Sheldon died on January 29, 1847, and Deacon Asa Sheldon died in March 1848. They lived in rooms provided for them at the Utica Female Academy, where two of their daughters, Miss Cynthia Sheldon and Mrs. Alma Anable, were on the staff.

[80] Miss Cynthia Sheldon and the Anable family left the Utica Female Academy in August 1848 to start the Misses Anable's School in Philadelphia.

[81] Anna Maria Anable, Mary Anable, Fanny Anable, and Harriet " Hatty" Anable.

[82] On January 29, 1849, Anna Maria Anable wrote to Emily, "Everybody, even Aunt Urania who thinks I am such a ninny by nature as well as by name, says that we have a charming school."

efforts are continued to secure ( ) for prosperity—My sisters[83] are both comparatively free from care, and have time to breathe. It is pleasant to think of them thus emancipated from their bondage.[84] The little Bennetts[85] are little no longer—and are both girls of whom their good mother would be proud—Mrs. Pearson and her good husband and babies are very well—the youngest is about six months old and all of them are boys—Mary Barber[86] who is living with Miss Kelley[87] spent a week with her in Feb. She was in her usual spirits, and full of life. I am rejoiced to hear of your improved health since the birth of your little girl[88] who I doubt not contributes greatly to your happiness. I trust she will long be spared to bless her family and the world. Elisabeth Hoyt[89] died a few days since in New York at the house of her brother in law Mr. Beebee[90] where she had passed the winter. I met her in Nov. last on board the boat with Mr. James Colgate,[91] and was very much struck with her intelligence—and good sense—you will remember her as a very nice girl when in school—and it seems but a few days since she was an attentive beloved ( ) of ( ).

Now constantly death is aging this work and teaching us the great lessons of life (that we) too are mortal—oh, to be ready to die! What [Note: Due to a tear in the page, several words are lost.]—it ( ) be to die! to pass into that other world—so near (and) yet so distant—to stand before that Being who offered and [Note: Due to a tear in the page, several words are lost.] every day of our lives—What can prepare us for this dread event—but the righteousness of Jesus Christ—When [Note: Due to a tear in the page, several words are lost.] find a shelter but in the Rock of Ages—it was a humble [Note: Due to a tear in the page, a word is lost.]

[83] Miss Cynthia Sheldon and Mrs. Alma Anable

[84] One of Anna Maria's primary reasons for moving to Philadelphia was to relieve her mother and Aunt Cynthia from the overwhelming burden they had assumed at the Utica Female Academy.

[85] Cephas and Stella Bennett, were missionaries to Burmah. They arrived in Burmah in January 1830. Mr. Bennett remained the superintendent of the Baptist Press there for more than fifty years. From the Utica area, they sent their children back, and the girls were educated at the Utica Female Academy. The girls included Elsina (April 1828), Mary (November 1829), Ann (August 1833), Ellen (June 1835), and Sarah (June 1837). In 1849, the youngest of the girls would have been almost twelve years old.

[86] See vol. 1, "Cast of Characters," s.v. "Barber, Mary."

[87] Miss Jane Kelly was Emily Chubbuck's friend at the Utica Female Academy, and then she became a teacher with Emily at that institution. Miss Kelly became the literary principal in 1844 with the retirement of Mr. and Mrs. James Nichols from that position. During a period of Miss Kelly's illness in 1844, Emily filled in the position for her. Then, in 1848, when Miss Cynthia Sheldon moved to Philadelphia to help start the Misses Anable's School, Miss Kelly became the "headmistress" of the academy and successfully brought it into the future, though not without some initial disparagement from the Sheldon-Anable families.

[88] See vol. 1, "Cast of Characters," s.v. "Judson, Emily Frances."

[89] Elizabeth Hoyt was a student at the Utica Female Seminary; according to a July 20, 1849, letter from Emily, Elizabeth was one of her most "delightful" scholars. Anna Maria Anable wrote on March 17, 1849, of the death of Elizabeth Hoyt, saying that she had died of the same disease as her sister Mrs. Ellen Colgate. There is also evidence to connect both of these girls with Alexander Beebee of the *Baptist Register*; Emily writes to him of his terrible loss.

[90] Alexander Beebee, the editor of the *Baptist Register*, had a son, also Alexander M. Beebee, who in 1849 was pastor of a church in Jordan, New York. This would indicate that the son had married a sister of Ellen and Elizabeth Hoyt.

[91] A relationship likely existed between the Beebee and Colgate families. James Colgate was the son of William Colgate, the soap manufacturing giant; he was married to Ellen Hoyt Colgate, the sister of Elizabeth Hoyt. Ellen died in 1847 of the same disease that had taken Elizabeth Hoyt.

and confidence in this Saviour that my dear mother professed when called above to go through the river of death—and this I have no doubt my dear father would have said was his stay had he been permitted to speak when he lay aside his (bed of death). May we dear Emily be thus prepared when our summons shall come.

I ( ) ( ) from Hamilton—and regret to hear that the Institution is in a distracted state—growing out of the agitated question of its removal.[92] Prof. Eaton[93] was here not long since and is very much distracted about the notion. I sincerely hope the Inst. will not be removed—and I cannot believe it will be—it seems to me that it would be sacrilege to leave Hamilton.

I want you to say to your husband that we know ( ) ( ) ( ) was received

[Written in the right margin of the address page:] ( ) at the time that he was suffering the worst—he intended to answer as soon as he is able—Remember me most affectionately to Lydia Lillybridge,[94] who I doubt is very happy—as she must by this time be able to see for herself, that she is doing some good in the world. I do not know where you will be when this reaches you, as the papers ( ) said that you intend leaving Maulmain—but if any other of my friends are near you—remember me most affectionately ( ) ( )—I suppose you will be glad to know that ( ) ( ) ( )

[Written in the left margin of the address page:] is doing much better, that is, he is behaving quite sensibly and is grown very much in the estimation of the public—he is a great man in history but you know the proverb—"tho you bear a foot in a mortar" etc.—

Remember me most kindly to your husband whose devotion to the good ( ) will be followed sooner or later. I doubt not by the blessings of heaven—Wishing you every blessing in your new positions
I remain yours affectionately

U. E. Nott

Source: American Baptist Historical Society, AJ 25, no. 1228.

[92] See vol. 1, "Places, Events, Organizations, and Magazines," s.v. "Madison University."

[93] The Reverend Doctor George W. Eaton was a distinguished professor and future president of Madison University and the Hamilton Theological Institution. He had a warm relationship with the Sheldon-Anable families, especially while they were at the Utica Female Academy. Mrs. Eaton was his wife.

[94] See vol. 1, "Cast of Characters," s.v. "Lillybridge, Lydia." See also "A Timeline of the Life and Mission of Lydia Lillybridge Simons."

Anna Maria Anable to Emily C. Judson,[95] March 17, 1849[96]—Philadelphia

Dearest Nemmy[97]

I am beginning in season this month so as to have time to remember some news before the close. I generally send off my letters in such a hurry that I forget half that I meant to say, or say something I am ashamed of. At any rate Nemmy you know me for the same Ninny[98] that I ever was, for I cannot disguise to you what would I not give if you were only seated in this barrel (chair) by my side chatting as in olden times. How many things we should have to talk about! Do you think I have changed any? I fancy you have not, only to grow better. I don't grow better, but worse every day, and I feel that I must set about a reform in good earnest.

One piece of sad news that I read in the paper to day [sic] recalled old times very forcibly. Hoffman[99] is insane and confined now in a Lunatic Asylum. I can as yet learn nothing of the cause, but if I can find out I will of course tell you. Have you heard from him since you left? Poor fellow! I am afraid he has had some great sorrow.

Willis[100] too has been quite ill this Winter, so tell me if you know anything of him, for I never hear of him now a days.

[Note: The second page of this letter is missing.]

was invited.

[95] A page of this letter is missing; there may also be a page missing at the end of the March 25 addendum.

[96] There is an addendum to this letter dated March 25, 1849.

[97] "Nem" or "Nemmy" was a name of endearment given to Emily by a small group of her intimate friends at the Utica Female Academy. Anna Maria Anable was "Ninny."

[98] "Ninny" was a name of endearment given to Anna Maria Anable by her most intimate friends at the Utica Female Academy. Emily was "Nemmy."

[99] Charles Fenno Hoffman was a prominent literary figure in Philadelphia and New York, who was well known as an adventurer, an editor, a poet, and a writer of exceptional talent. In fall 1843, he wrote three letters to Emily Chubbuck addressed to "Laura Linden," for Emily had written to him under that name, asking his advice about love, fame, and fortune. Only one of these letters is in the correspondence. Hoffman was not to learn of Emily's identity until spring 1845; in a letter dated approximately April 7, 1845, he spoke of Laura having taken off her mask and revealing herself to him. There were four letters from Hoffman in April when Emily was in Philadelphia. There were another three in December 1845 when Emily again was in Philadelphia. See vol. 1, Cast of Characters:, Hoffman, Charles Fenno, and vol. 1, Places and Events, Laura Letters. Anna Maria Anable frequently intimated in her letters that Emily was interested in "Hoffy" as a beau.

[100] Nathaniel Parker Willis was the editor, with General George Morris, of the *New Mirror*, a prominent literary magazine in New York. His "discovery" of Emily in the June 8, 1844, edition of the *New Mirror* catapulted her into literary fame. Emily met him for the first time in New York in May 1844, when she went from Philadelphia back to her home in Hamilton and to the Female Academy in Utica. She wrote to her sister Kate that she had been with Willis practically ever day of the two-week period she was in New York. In June 1845, after the death of his wife in March, Willis left for Europe, and Emily spoke of going to Europe as a correspondent for the magazines, though illness had prevented it. Emily and Willis maintained an increasingly intimate correspondence, and when he returned in spring 1844 and found Emily engaged to Adoniram Judson, he wrote of it as "another death" in a letter edged in black. Subsequently, he sent additional letters in which he enclosed letters she had written to him; he underlined certain sections in red and noted that if she would read the marked sections, she would understand why he felt that he had a reasonable expectation that they would be married upon his return. She was forever grateful to Willis for his recognition of her literary genius and his encouragement to pursue it to the highest levels. After Emily and Adoniram left for Burmah, the *New Mirror* went out of business, and later Willis and General Morris forged a new partnership in a new publication. By January 1847, Willis married the ward of a United States senator, a woman, according to comments in the correspondence, who had substantial means.

I met Mrs. J. C. Neal[101] a few evenings since at a little sociable, but the stupid lady of the house did not introduce us and Mrs. N. is not sufficiently *au fait* of the ways of the world to know that she ought to make the first advance to a stranger. She is quite pretty and rather coquettish in her manners, and is on the whole quite an interesting young widow. Rumour [sic] says that Neal was harried out by her flirtations and finally took laudanum, but Mrs. Mitchell[102] told me that the dose was accidentally too large, that Mr. N. had not been very happy, but his wife was quite young, and society was so new to her it was not strange that if her head should have been a little turned by it. She told Fanny[103] she had often heard Mr. Neal speak of her. I suppose the truth is that Neal was very hypochondriacal [sic] and towards the last deranged. It seems as if nothing but sad news comes to my mind this evening. The *Register*[104] for the last two weeks has recorded first, the death of Elizabeth Hoyt,[105] of the same disease which took off her sister Mrs. Colgate,[106] and to night [sic] the death of Aunt Page, Grand pa's[107] sister aged 90 years. So we live and die, and "what is the use of all the labor that a man hath under the sun"? Verily I see none, except to fulfil [sic] our destiny, or appointed work I should say if I could feel that my work was appointed. I would ( ) out that last sentence if I could for I verily believe that my present work is appointed, and we are as happy as queens all together again, only as I told you I am growing wicked. Our school is prospering, the folks say, though we have had no additions since the first of Feb.

Source: American Baptist Historical Society, AJ 13, no. 483.

[101] Joseph Neal was a prominent member of the literary establishment in Philadelphia and became a part of Emily Chubbuck's circle of friends when she was there. Neal was well known and respected as a writer and editor; one of his best known works was the *Charcoal Sketches*. In 1842, he founded the *Saturday Gazette*, a successful publication that contained a great deal of humorous satire. Anna Maria Anable frequently referred to Neal as a beau for Emily. Mr. Neal married Alice Bradley in 1846; he died in 1847.

[102] Mr. and Mrs. Mitchell lived in Philadelphia; Mrs. Tyndale, Mrs. Mitchell's mother and the owner of a prosperous china shop in downtown Philadelphia, lived with them. In November 1845, as Emily was thinking of prolonging her stay in the city to last through the winter, the Mitchells generously offered to open their home to her, promising that they would do everything in their power to take good care of her: her own room, solitude or company as desired, the ability to write, and all of the comforts they could provide. Emily did express appreciation, saying that many of her friends told her what wonderful people they were and how sensitive they were to the needs of an invalid such as Emily was at that time. Her one serious reservation was that they were Unitarians. In the end Emily decided that she would stay with the Reverend and Mrs. Gillette, knowing from her past experience that she would be more than comfortable with them.

[103] See vol. 1, "Cast of Characters," s.v. "Anable, Fanny."

[104] The *Baptist Register* was a local Baptist paper in central New York that grew into regional prominence. Published by Alexander Beebee, it had significant influence in Baptist circles. The *Baptist Register* was a natural outlet for some of Emily's work as a budding writer. Later, in 1846 and the immediate time after her engagement and marriage to Adoniram Judson, there was conflict between Emily Judson and Mr. Beebee, who was less than enthusiastic about Emily's suitability for missionary service, reflecting the attitude of many in the wider Church. Emily was, after all, a secular, popular writer, and Adoniram Judson was the venerable missionary held in awesome respect. Eventually, Emily and Mr. Beebee were reconciled, and Mr. Beebee was often mentioned in letters from Miss Cynthia Sheldon as Emily's strongest supporter.

[105] See vol. 1, "Cast of Characters," s.v. "Hoyt, Elizabeth."

[106] A November 26, 1847, letter from Miss Cynthia Sheldon told of the death of Ellen Colgate, the wife of James Colgate, who was the son of the soap manufacturer William Colgate.

[107] Deacon Asa Sheldon was the grandfather of Anna Maria Anable and the father of Miss Cynthia Sheldon, Mrs. Urania Sheldon Nott, and Alma Sheldon Anable. He died in March 1848.

Adoniram Judson[108] to Anna Maria Anable,[109] March 18, 1849[110]—Maulmain

Dear Anna Maria:[111] (She is considerably better—see the last page)[112]

I know not how to begin to write you. A dark cloud is gathering around me. A crushing weight is upon me. I cannot *resist* the dreadful conviction that, dear Emily is in a settled and rapid decline. For nearly a year after the birth of baby,[113] she enjoyed pretty good health, and I flattered myself, that she would be spared for many years. But *thr*ee or four months ago, her appetite almost entirely failed her. Soon after, baby was taken very ill, and in the midst of it, our usual help left us, and she was obliged to undergo a great deal of severe fatigue; and I see now, that she has been declining ever since.[114] She soon became unable to take our usual walks, and I procured a pony for her, and she tried riding, but without any good effect. I next sent her to Tavoy in a steamer, on a visit to the missionaries there. She was gone ten days, and returned thinner in flesh and weaker than ever. I now take her out every morning in a chair, and this is all the exercise she can bear. She is under the care of a very skilful [sic] doctor, who appears to be making every possible effort to save her, but the symptoms are such, that I have *scarcely* any hope left. She is thinner than she has ever been—strength almost gone—no appetite—various pains in the region of the lungs—a dry cough, whh [sic] has hung on pertinaciously for two or three months. She was preparing some "Notes" to append to the Memoir,[115] but has been obliged to leave them unfinished, being unable to write or even read, without

[108] An edited version of this letter appears in A. C. Kendrick, *The Life and Letters of Mrs. Emily C. Judson* (New York: Sheldon and Co., 1862) 142.

[109] It was the custom of Miss Anna Maria Anable and her aunt, Miss Cynthia Sheldon, to share correspondence with Emily and Adoniram with the public press in order to support the mission movement with information on beloved missionaries. It also was a demonstration of the tremendous public interest in Adoniram and Emily Judson.

On Monday, September 3, 1849, the following article written by N. P. Willis appeared in the *Portland* (Maine) *Daily Advertiser*: "Mrs. Judson,—N. P. Willis notices the recent illness of Mrs. Judson, the missionary, in the following beautiful and touching manner:"

"That the constitution of this sweet child of genius was of consumptive tendency we knew; but had confidently hoped that the change of climate and the air of a warmer latitude would exercise the beneficial effects which they sometimes do, and give her better health than she had hitherto known. If she die there, her grave will be well placed, in a path of duty; but there are those here to whom a certainty of not seeing her again in this world will be heavy to bear. Her day will have been bright and brief but it sets with a rosy promise of a still fairer tomorrow; for the light of a soul like hers sends its brightness dawnlike, before her into heaven. It is short sighted to mourn over the pure spirit's decent below the horizon of the grave when we know that, as the light pales on this side of that dark limit to our vision, it kindles on the other side, in the glowing welcome of angels."

On Tuesday, October 4, 1849, a second article appeared in the *Portland Daily Advertiser*: "Fanny Forrester" [sic]— "Letters from Dr. Judson, dated June 20th, state that Mrs. Judson's health is infirm as to require her to lay aside her pen for the present, and of the possibility that she may never resume it again for the purpose of authorship."

[110] There is an addendum to this letter dated March 22, 1849. It reveals that Emily has taken a turn for the better.

[111] See vol. 1, "Cast of Characters," s.v. "Anable, Anna Maria."

[112] This is the addendum, which is dated March 22, 1849.

[113] See vol. 1, "Cast of Characters," s.v. "Judson, Emily Frances."

[114] On February 17, 1849, Emily wrote of the severe illness of Emily Frances.

[115] Fanny Forester, *Memoir of Sarah B. Judson, Member of the American Mission to Burmah* (New York: L. Colby and Company, 1848).

aggravating her pains. I look around in despair. If a change to any place [sic] promised the least relief, I would go any where [sic]. But we are here, in the healthiest part of India, and in the dry, warm season, and she suffers so much at sea, that a voyage could hardly be recommended for itself. My only hope is that the doctor, who, however, from principle, is known to be a great flatterer, declares that her lungs are not seriously effected [sic],[116] and that as soon as her system is fairly brought under the influence of the course of medicine he is now pursuing—digitalis being a principal ingredient—there will be a favorable result. I shall dissuade her from writing by the month's mail, though she has mentioned that she wants to write to you and to her family. Nor does she know that I am writing to you. Her family I don't want to distress at present. She may get better. But I suffer so much myself, that I felt it would be some relief to sit down and tell you all about it. You are the only person in the whole world beside myself, who knows how to appreciate her. We are the ones that will shed the bitterest tears over her grave. When she was at Tavoy, she made up her mind, that she must die soon; and that is now her prevailing expectation; but she contemplates the event with composure and resignation. Within a few months, she has grown much in devotional feeling and in longing desires to be wholly conformed to the will of Christ.[117] She had formerly some doubts about the genuineness of her early conversion, but they have all left her, and though she feels, that in her circumstances prolonged life is increasingly desirable, she is quite willing to leave all at the Savior's call. Praised be God for his love to her.

Yours affectly

A Judson

Source: Hanna family files.

Dr. Morton[118] to Emily C. Judson, March 1849[119]

My Dear Mrs. Judson

I have the greatest pleasure in answering your query frankly, as I am happy to say the symptom you allude to is of no serious consequence whatever but is perhaps in yr [sic] case *rather salutary than otherwise*. The blood you have ( ) up was evidently

[116] See the letter from Dr. Morton to Emily, which is dated approximately March 1849.

[117] The entries from Emily's journal, which will appear over the next month of the correspondence, speak eloquently of her struggle and her growth.

[118] Dr. Morton was the physician at the mission in Maulmain. There are many references to him, most notably that of May 20, 1850, when Emily wrote to Adoniram describing the birth of "Angel Charley" and Dr. Morton's part in that delivery. See also the letter of Adoniram Judson to Anna Maria Anable dated March 18, 1849, where he references Dr. Morton and his treatment of Emily.

[119] This is simply dated 1849. It is placed in March when Emily was ill and no doubt anxious about her health and alarming new symptoms.

from a *lower part* of the *mucous membrane* than that which lines the throat, but ( ) this membrane *extends* through the *whole* of the alimentary canal and it was from a lower portion of it or *that which lines the stomach* that the blood you raised this morning was derived. Your lungs I am happy to report are not in the least affected.

Believe me
Yours Sincerely

(Signature is illegible)

Source: American Baptist Historical Society, AJ 18, no. 875.

Adoniram Judson to Anna Maria Anable,[120] March 22, 1849[121]

[Written in the right margin of the address page:] Mch 22d—Glad I am that the mail is still open so that I can add, that Emily is better. The medicine seems really to have taken effect, and the crisis to have passed. But though the deadly pressure is a little removed from my heart, I do not venture to indulge very sanguine hopes, after what I have seen—; for a few days may prostrate all [written in the left margin of the address page] again. Do remember us in your prayers—I feel more than ever, that God heareth prayer.

The Philada Box has just arrived—I have opened it and shown Emily the things. May she be able to write next month and acknowledge the kindness of your presents.

Source: Hanna family files.

Anna Maria Anable to Emily C. Judson, March 25, 1849[122]

Mrs. Heman Lincoln[123] of Boston called on us last week and we had a delightful visit from her. She says that it is supposed that you will go to Ava,[124] and may be [sic] this letter will find you there. I don't like to have you go off there Nemmy,[125] but if

[120] Anna Maria Anable wrote a reply to this letter on June 25, 1849.

[121] This is an addendum to a letter Adoniram wrote on March 18, 1849.

[122] This letter is an addendum to a letter started March 17, 1849.

[123] Mrs. Lincoln was the wife of Heman Lincoln. Both were active in Baptist circles in Boston. See vol. 1, "Cast of Characters," s.v. "Lincoln, The Honorable Heman."

[124] In February 1847, Adoniram, Emily, Henry, and Edward moved to Rangoon as a stepping stone for eventual ministry in Ava. They were forced to return to Maulmain in September 1847 due to reductions in funding to the mission by the Board of the American Baptist Missionary Union. A February 20, 1849, letter from Dr. Solomon Peck, the executive secretary of the missionary union mentioned to Emily that she would be going to Ava; unfortunately, the opportunity arose when work on the dictionary was more effectively done in Maulmain and when debilitating illness prevented Emily or Adoniram from thinking of making a move.

[125] "Nem" or "Nemmy" was a name of endearment given to Emily by a small group of her intimate friends at the Utica Female Academy. Anna Maria Anable was "Ninny."

you go I hope it will be a good move all around. I want very much to hear from you; it seems as if news did not come half as often now as when we were in Utica.

Have I told you that Mrs. Denio is in the city? She has been here all winter and I suspect she must be writing something. Mary[126] is very delicate. Late news from Utica says that Geo. Spencer and Libby ( ) are engaged. The Academy[127] is flourishing finely under the new administration;[128] a little note from Mary Barber[129] complains of the *Scotch*iness of every thing [sic]. Mary is the only *one* who goes to the Baptist church now. Brother Corey[130] is going to stay with us, during the convention in May, and also Mr. and Mrs. Wade,[131] and perhaps Mrs. J. Lincoln[132] from Boston. If Bro. C. wants any further enlightenment [Note: The letter ends abruptly here—the next lines are in the margin of page 1. There may be a page missing.]

[Written in the left and top margins of page 1:] Do you know that you have never said anything about little Emily's coming to me since she was born? I mean always to have a daughter of some one [sic] of our missionaries in the school, that is, if they will let me.[133] I should like to have Mr. Vinton's,[134] but we cannot while we have Ellen,[135] as I am going to have one of my nieces here next fall, but my little Emily I want for my own special pet. Do let us hear from you often my darling, I thirst for news from you sometimes.

Adieu. Anna M.

Source: American Baptist Historical Society, AJ 13, no. 483.

[126] This is likely a reference to Mary Juliet Anable. See vol. 1, "Cast of Characters," s.v. "Anable, Mary Juliet."

[127] The Utica Female Academy, where Emily and Anna Maria taught together under the direction of Miss Cynthia Sheldon. Miss Jane Kelly had assumed resonsibility with the departure of the Sheldon-Anable families.

[128] When Anna Maria left Utica to start her school in Philadelphia, she made a series of negative remarks about Jane Kelly, the new headmistress of the academy, and the prospects for the future. Jane and the trustees incurred an enormous debt for new furnishings after Miss Sheldon had left. This note of success, then, is quite an admission. However, she does not mention Jane Kelly at all, and she follows her remark with a couple of negative comments.

[129] See vol. 1, "Cast of Characters," s.v. "Barber, Mary."

[130] See vol. 1, "Cast of Characters," s.v. "Corey, The Reverend D. G."

[131] See vol. 1, "Cast of Characters," s.v. "Wade, The Reverend Doctor Jonathan and Deborah."

[132] Mrs. Lincoln was the wife of Joshua Lincoln, a prominent Baptist layman and a partner in Gould, Kendall and Lincoln. Anna Maria Anable boarded with Mr. and Mrs. Lincoln when she stayed in Boston in summer 1847 for medical treatments. Mrs. Lincoln was a strong supporter of missions and a sister of Charles Gould, who would marry Sarah Bell Wheeler of the Utica Female Academy.

[133] Anna Maria has mentioned this possibility several times in previous letters. Anna Maria would have responsibility for Emily Frances, but under the tragic circumstances of Emily Judson's death in June 1854. Upon her death, Emily Judson assigned responsibility for Emily Frances to her dearest friend, Anna Maria Anable. Anna Maria became "Aunty" to Emily Frances and was a profound influence upon her life.

[134] Justus Hatch Vinton was born in Willington, Connecticut, in 1806. He attended the theological school at Hamilton, New York, and was ordained in June 1834. In July that same year, he sailed as a missionary to Burmah. His wife was Calista Holman Vinton; they were married April 9, 1834. They worked with the Karens at Chummerah, Newville, and Maulmain, where he had charge of the Karen theological seminary. At the end of 1847, they left for the United States, returning to Burmah and work at Rangoon in July 1850. Justus Vinton died in Kemendine, Burmah, on March 31, 1858. His wife, Calista Holman Vinton, died in Rangoon, Burmah December 20, 1864. Mrs. Vinton taught the Karen women and was the author of several hymnbooks in their language.

[135] This is likely a reference to Ellen Bennett, the daughter of Cephas and Stella Bennett, missionaries to Burmah. Several of the Bennett daughters attended the Utica Female Academy and now the Misses Anable's School. Ellen Bennett was born in Burmah on June 8, 1835.

Emily C. Judson to her Journal, March 25, 1849—Maulmain

I have been for some time past steadfastly looking into my grave; with the expectation of being shortly laid there; and there left—in silence, and darkness, and loneliness, till the resurrection morning. Only the shell, the cast-off garment there! Ay, but it is a shell into which the Son of God has seen fit to send back the principle of life, and which He will render immortal. Death is a curse—the most awful curse that divine justice could inflict; and though the blessed Saviour [sic] has deprived it of its sting, has gained a glorious victory for us, the triumph can not [sic] be complete till bone is gathered to bone, and sinew to sinew, and we rise to meet Him in the air. We naturally shrink from death, as the wounded man shrinks from the hand of the surgeon. Can this shrinking be entirely overcome? Have men actually risen so high by faith, as in the dying hour to be insensible to the pain and shame of their punishment , or are their beatific visions and their rejoicings to be in a degree ascribed to the peculiar state of the physical powers, the influence of the nervous system on the mind, in the moment of dissolution? It is a terrible thing to die! Am I, then, afraid? No, but I am filled with solemn awe.

Source: A. C. Kendrick, *Life and Letters of Mrs. Emily C. Judson*, 319–20.

Miss Cynthia Sheldon to Emily C. Judson, March 25, 1849[136]—Philadelphia

My dear Emily,

My thoughts are much with you since the Board took down the hindrances to your going to Ava[137]—could we but have the dear children with us while you were making the experiment and from the countless Philadelphia comforts fit you out for a year—it would then seem hard enough for your delicate nerves.—our thoughts and our prayers are with you—we think you will not go there till the hot season has passed, from that time till we hear from you all will again seem to us unsettled—We can think of you now in Maulmain as we could not in Rangoon—so it will be in regard to Ava—we know you will tell us all—still the treacherous Burmans may unsettle your plans long before the letter of consolation reaches us.—but why this distrust of the future, say you—it is not wise—the past bids us rest all with *Him who*

[136] No year is given for this letter. It is placed on March 25, 1849. Miss Sheldon's chronology of events in Emily's life is not correct at some points, but the date can be determined by other facts in the letter: the board has approved their going to Ava (February 1849), Mr. Corey is still not remarried (his engagement was announced in July), Mr. Hawley is moving to Hartford, the meeting of the missionary union in Philadelphia is in the future (May 1849). All of these facts conform with the March 1849 date.

[137] In February 1847, the Judsons moved to Rangoon as a stepping stone for eventual ministry in Ava. They were forced to return to Maulmain in early September 1847 due to reductions in funding, and when the opportunity arose again, work on the dictionary and illness prevented them from going.

sees the end from the beginning—I am just now fondly reminded that the month of March has way marks of the past, informing a deep lesson of trust for the future.—Do you remember that this month four years—our first visit was made to this city[138]—Then our God directed and blessed the jaunt to your restoration and even made *that the* pivot on which turned such momentous results—how little either of us thought while concocting that jaunt, just this time in the month, that one year from that date you would be returning, the second time from the goodly city, and *more*, betrothed to the Apostle of Modern Missions[139]—the next March you were in Rangoon[140]—the next my dear Mother had a few weeks previously, gone to Heaven[141]—the next my dear father joined her in that bright abode[142]—and now the remnant of our family[143] are here in Philadelphia—how marvelous—could you see our pleasant home you would rejoice greatly—my fears about the girls not feeling at home in the church and being kindly received in Society are ended—I presume Anna M.[144] tells you all about it—Mr. Heman Lincoln[145] has generally called when he has been in the city to attend their ministers meeting—Urania[146] took it into her head that he was calling rather too often—if Anna M. should be drawn off—the school must go over board—happily I could tell her in return that the girls had entered into a compact to remain unmarried five years, if all could get engaged in that time well—they would then have her Doct.[147] come, and marry all off at once—the truth is they are very happy—dear Hatty,[148] quite as much so as the rest—and I have full confidence they will continue as they are until the providence of God directs a change—they have two or three beaux to make fun over now—may their hearts ever be as light as at this time—

[138] In March 1845, four years before this letter, Emily, accompanied by Miss Sheldon, went to Philadelphia for health reasons for the first time. At that time, she lived with the Reverend and Mrs. A. D. Gillette.

[139] This would have been March 1846. Adoniram Judson's formal proposal of marriage, when he gave Emily the "charmed watch," was on January 20, 1846. She remained in Philadelphia as long as she could because of the weather, but she was impatient to return because of all that had to be done in preparing for her life in Burmah. Actually, Emily left Philadelphia on February 17, 1846, and arrived in Utica on February 20.

[140] This was March 1847.

[141] Mother Sheldon died on January 29, 1847. In this period, Emily and Adoniram were preparing for their move to Rangoon (February 1847). See the letter of Anna Maria Anable dated February 15, 1847, which speaks of her grandmother's death.

[142] Deacon Asa Sheldon died in March 1848, a little more than a year after his wife died. This was the same year that the Sheldon-Anable families made the decision to move to Philadelphia.

[143] Living in Philadelphia with Miss Cynthia Sheldon were her sister Alma Sheldon Anable and four of her nieces: Anna Maria, Harriet or "Hatty," Fanny, and Mary.

[144] See vol. 1, "Cast of Characters," s.v. "Anable, Anna Maria."

[145] This would be the minister son of the Honorable Heman Lincoln of Boston. In 1849 he would have been located in New Britain, Pennsylvania.

[146] See vol. 1, "Cast of Characters," s.v. "Sheldon, Urania."

[147] See vol. 1, "Cast of Characters," s.v. "Nott, The Reverend Doctor Eliphalet."

[148] See vol. 1, "Cast of Characters," s.v. "Anable, Harriet."

We learn by letters from Utica that Mr. Corey[149] moves the church forward prosperously—no talk of his getting married—Horace Hawley[150] is about moving to New York—the old people remain—Mrs. Gratiot[151] and children have returned to the Seminary, to stay while Mr. G.[152] makes his fortune in California—poor man. The world has gone hard with him the past year—but he is rich in grace. Mr. Jones and Mary[153] both have miserable health. I do wish they were in this city on many accounts—The Seminary[154] is prosperous—Mary Barber[155] passed the vacation in Schenectady and hated to go back—they were ever so *Scotchy* [sic]. Libby Upsom is engaged to Mr. George Spencer of Academy renown—Mrs. Denio and Mary are in the city and very friendly indeed—

Mrs. Pierson designs to be with us next Saturday, and Urania comes with the Doct. the next week—we know not how long they will stay—Moses comes with them to take care of the Doct. who can not [sic] yet walk without assistance—poor man—I do think he is a martyr to the hydropathic course—Dear Mrs. Wade[156] sent me a letter the first of the month—they had enjoyed a quiet winter with her friends—her letters are a treasure—we have just got our comfortable spare room ready for friends—the one we first filled with the Utica furniture was immediately occupied by a lady who could not go to the 4th story—Courtland[157] had the library, which is like Mrs. Gillette's[158] back parlor some larger—a settee bed step accommodated him—now the girls find they seldom need have a recitation there—and

[149] See vol. 1, "Cast of Characters," s.v. "Corey, The Reverend D. G."

[150] Mr. Horace H. Hawley enjoyed a family relationship with the Sheldons. A letter Emily wrote on May 7, 1841, reveals that he was to marry a niece of Misses Cynthia and Urania Sheldon and Mrs. Alma Sheldon Anable, the daughter of their brother John Sheldon. Through the help of Miss Cynthia Sheldon, he was introduced into the life of Emily Chubbuck. A member of a publishing firm, he also worked with Alexander Beebee in publishing the *Baptist Register*. Beginning in 1841 with the publication of *Charles Linn*, Mr. Hawley was enormously helpful to Emily Chubbuck as she was publishing her early stories and books. There are numerous references to his help and his generosity.

[151] Ann Sheldon was a younger cousin of Miss Cynthia Sheldon, Mrs. Alma Sheldon Anable, and Mrs. Urania Sheldon Nott. She married Charles Gratiot, the son of a prominent army officer and engineer who opened the port of St. Louis. Because Charles and Ann Gratiot often lived with the Sheldon-Anable families, both at Utica and in Philadelphia after 1848, they were often mentioned in the correspondence. They had six children, one of whom was born very close to the birth of Emily Frances Judson. The letters reveal how Ann coped in her husband's absence when he went west during the gold rush to seek his fortune.

[152] Charles Gratiot grew up in St Louis, where his father was an army engineer responsible for developing the Port of St. Louis. He married Ann Sheldon, who was a cousin of Miss Cynthia Sheldon, Mrs. Urania Sheldon Nott, and Alma Sheldon Anable. Together, Charles and Ann Gratiot had six children. Because they often lived with the Sheldon family, their letters contain a great deal of him. Letters in 1847 speak of his religious awakening; those of 1849 speak of his leaving for the California gold fields. In 1853, Charles Gratiot applied for a grant of 400 acres in Illinois, and he already owned 148 acres.

[153] Morven and Mary Jones from Utica. See his long letter written over December 9, 21, and 22, 1848. He speaks of his wife being severely injured to the point that they despaired for her life; the injuries were persistently disabling, and she never completely recovered. She had been standing on a bridge over the Mohawk River, part of a crowd watching a baptism, when the bridge collapsed. Mr. Jones had persistent health problems as well.

[154] The Utica Female Academy, where Miss Sheldon spent many years of her life in charge of Finance and Administration.

[155] See vol. 1, "Cast of Characters," s.v. "Barber, Mary."

[156] See vol. 1, "Cast of Characters," s.v. "Wade, Jonathan and Deborah."

[157] See vol. 1, "Cast of Characters," s.v. "Anable, Courtland."

[158] See vol. 1, "Cast of Characters," s.v. "Gillette, The Reverend A. (Abram) D. (Dunn) and Hannah."

we have placed bed—with all the necessaries for friends—we feel very comfortable in the view of having Mrs. Wade occupy it—Mr. Corey will take the front room at night only—Mrs. Lincoln will take up her abode with our girls, if her husband does not come—we may take care of more lady friends—but cannot of ministers—we are looking forward to the privileges of that meeting, with great interest. I shall write to Mrs. Wade this evening—when she is here we shall decide what course it is best for Anna Bennett[159] to pursue—Ellen[160] will remain with us if nothing happens till she is sixteen—Mrs. Bennett of Utica proposed to take Anna—were we able she should remain here one or more years longer, she is a very fine scholar and fine girl, and thinks much of going to Burmah some day—Mrs. W. will not go till next year—dear Emmie—my paper is gone—Heavens choicest blessings I cast upon you and yours—Mrs. A.[161] and all join in love to yourself—good Dr.—and Lydia.[162]

Affectionately your
friend C. Sheldon

Source: American Baptist Historical Society, AJ 20, no. 1005.

Mr. Smith to Emily C. Judson,[163] March 26, 1849

My Dear and Esteemed Lady

It will afford me the utmost pleasure in placing at your command a suitable sum for the erection of ten additional Mission stations and schools to be exclusively under your direction and superintendence.

You will be as good as furnish me through the medium of the British religious periodical press with a statement of the probable expense attending the ( ). Besides what I place at your command for this object the deep interest which you are held in by the Evangelical Churches of Europe furnish matter of the deepest interest. A

[159] Anna Bennett was the daughter of Cephas and Stella Bennett, missionaries to Burmah. She was born in August 1833. An 1850 letter said that beginning in April she would be teaching at a family school in a private home in the Philadelphia area.

[160] Ellen Bennett was the daughter of Cephas and Stella Bennett, missionaries to Burmah. She was born on June 8, 1835, so she would have been fourteen years old when this was written.

[161] See vol. 1, "Cast of Characters," s.v. "Sheldon, Alma and Joseph Hubbell."

[162] See vol. 1, "Cast of Characters," s.v. "Lillybridge, Lydia." See also "A Timeline of the Life and Mission of Lydia Lillybridge Simons."

[163] This letter is addressed to Mrs. Judson, Maulmain, Via Southampton, Calcutta. It is likely of British origin as the writer speaks of the Evangelical Churches of Europe; also, money is identified in pounds, and its postal imprint also has a crown imbedded in it

The letter is somewhat of a mystery. It offers significant amounts of money—five thousand pounds for mission stations and schools, a thousand pounds for a mission press; why it would be sent to Emily Judson, offering all of this to be under her direction, is not explained. There is no evidence that Emily ever gave that kind of leadership to the mission; these sorts of matters were clearly in the hands of others.

The writer and the group he represented likely felt that Emily's pen and her contributions to written material would bring considerable success in fundraising efforts. The writer does not identify himself; in his signature, he has just given the first letter of his first name, and it is unreadable.

separate appeal also proposed upon any other subject could not fail of being attended with the most happy—the most ( )—the most permanent results.

You will be as good in regards the former as ( ) the same ready at your earliest convenience. The interest of the Mission with your future plans for operation throughout all parts of the interior would be doubtless also greatly promoted with a public letter each month from your powerful pen.

Will you be enabled to carry out the opening of the ten stations with normal schools to each for training for five thousand pounds if not you will be so good as furnish me with the amount necessary.

I would contribute also one thousand pounds for the establishment of a powerful and well directed mission press for the pub. of small works in the various districts as well as for a special monthly issue of a Journal for friends in Europe as well as in America as regards the latter you will require to enter into full detail.

With much regard my highly esteemed Lady believe me—Yours in the best of bonds

( ) Smith

Source: American Baptist Historical Society, AJ 19, no. 920.

Miss Hatty Anable to Emily C. Judson, March 26, 1849

Do not think dearest Emily that I have forgotten you because I have never written, for often and often while away in my southern home[164] did I think of, and wish to write you, but knew not your directions. And now I am home again, home for life probably. I can hardly believe it, though I have already been here two months. And you cannot know just how pleasant it is to be here, how delightful home is to us now and how happy we are all together. We have become as quakerfied as all the Philadelphians—yet we enjoy solid comfort. Mary[165] our little Mary that "used to be" is our most useful and most accomplished teacher. She paints and draws, speaks French, plays the piano, sings, dances and is our mathematician. What should we ever do without her? She laughs from morning till night, and it is really refreshing to be with her. Anna Maria[166] appears (before the girls mind you) dignified, intellectual, and altogether a superior being, yet always interested in her scholars. Shall I tell you how she conducts herself up on our room? Just like a ninny as she always did. We tell her she is in her dotage—she has gone demented—but nothing will

[164] Hatty served with a family in the New Orleans area for a number of years; she learned to speak French fluently.

[165] See vol. 1, "Cast of Characters," s.v. "Anable, Miss Mary Juliet."

[166] See vol. 1, "Cast of Characters," s.v. "Anable, Anna Maria."

make her behave with becoming dignity unless it be the sight of a scholar. Fan[167] and I fill up the niches, she sings, and I am the French girl as to teaching other things than French and singing; we take what is given to us and manage not to disgrace the school.

This morning we had two new Scholars enter, and one application. Our wants are all provided for, and tho we are poor we are not in debt, so we are happy and grateful I believe. How much I wish dear Emily to see you again and your little "bird"[168] and husband too. I have been reading lately the Memoirs of "Mrs. Ann H. Judson," "Mrs. Sarah B. Judson" and the "Judson Offering," so I feel as if I know some thing of your dear husband, tho' I did not see him while he was in

[Written in the right margin and across the text of page 4:] this country. I should think you would perfectly worship him—

Kiss little Fanny[169] and receive the warmest love and a thousand kisses for yourself.

Your truly affectionate

Hatty Anable

Give my best love to Lydia.[170]

Source: American Baptist Historical Society, AJ 13, no. 482.

Emily C. Judson to her Journal, March 27, 1849

Am I afraid to die? My husband will lay me in the grave; and return to his house, leaving me away in that cold place, alone, beside the half mouldered [sic] bones of little Charlie.[171] He will be very sad and desolate—O, *too sad*! And yet my image will gradually fade from his mind—keep fading—fading—the tones of my voice will be lost, and our precious little conversations will mingle with the gray of the past, and become pleasant dreams.

My children will look about for their mother, and perhaps cry; and then they will forget me. They will be in trouble, and I can not [sic] help them; they will sin, and I can not [sic] teach and discipline them; they will feel sorrow for their sin, and

[167] See vol. 1, "Cast of Characters," s.v. "Anable, Fanny."

[168] Emily Frances Judson. After her birth on December 24, 1847, Emily Judson composed "My Bird," a poem that became famous. There are many references in the correspondence to Emily Frances as "Bird."

[169] See vol. 1, "Cast of Characters," s.v. "Judson, Emily Frances."

[170] See vol. 1, "Cast of Characters," s.v. "Lillybridge, Lydia." See also "A Timeline of the Life and Mission of Lydia Lillybridge Simons."

[171] Charles Judson, the son of Adoniram and Sarah Hall Boardman Judson, was born on December 18, 1843, and died in August 1845, after Adoniram and Sarah had left Burmah for America. Because of his young age, he was left in the care of Mr. and Mrs. Osgood.

I can not [sic] pray with them and point them away to Christ. I am not afraid to die, but I am very sad.

Source: A. C. Kendrick, *Life and Letters of Mrs. Emily C. Judson*, 320; Hanna family files.

Emily C. Judson to her Journal, March 28, 1849

Mah Zaat says I talk of death so calmly because my life has been so pure. Pure! Is there so great a sinner in the world as I? One who has sinned against such light? Converted in early childhood, educated amidst a blaze of gospel light, prayed for by a numerous company now in glory, and still prayed for by saints on earth. I have no doubt, but I shall get to heaven through Christ, but I have reason to believe that I shall occupy a very low place there. I can not [sic] condemn myself for idleness, mine has been a busy, working life, but such a waste of toil and vigor!—such a squandering of influence! How much good I might have done, if my heart had only been the dwelling-place of the Holy Spirit! I shudder and groan within myself when I think of it. Oh, I do long to live a little longer, and do good!"

Source: A. C. Kendrick, *Life and Letters of Mrs. Emily C. Judson*, 320; Hanna family files.

Emily C. Judson to her Journal, April 1, 1849

I am slowly gaining strength, and begin to weigh the probability of recovery. If it is the will of God, I should wish to live. He can soothe my husband's heart and be the Guardian of my children; and he can dispense with my weak, puny efforts in the Church. He can also lighten the dark passage of the grave, and make the prospect of going to my rest delicious to my soul. But I should count it an invaluable blessing to be allowed to maintain my place a little longer—to do something for Christ before I die. Perhaps my Heavenly Father designs to grant me this favor, perhaps the draught which we have long been preparing to drink in tearful submissiveness, may be withheld. "If it be possible, let this cup pass from me; nevertheless, not my will, but Thine, oh, God, be done"

Source: A. C. Kendrick, *Life and Letters of Mrs. Emily C. Judson*, 320–21; Hanna family files.

Emily C. Judson to her Journal, April 3, 1849

Mah Zaat has been asking about the *separate state*, and seems disappointed that I could tell her so little. I have had something like her feelings on this subject—if we had only been told as much about the dying as about the resurrection hour! This silence and mystery constitute much of the awfulness of death—horrible to the sinner, and a subject for the exercise of the Christian's faith. But since we shall be *with Christ*, what more need we to know? Sleep in Jesus!—be with him who died for us in Paradise! Perhaps it will be an unconscious sleep, and we shall seem to ourselves to step from our dying bed and weeping friends, to the glories of the resurrection. Perhaps it will be a conscious state of rest and subdued blissfulness—a baptism of the disembodied soul in Christ. We can scarcely suppose it a state of improvement or growth, or in any way a state of activity. Such a supposition would seem not in accordance with God's great plan. To be with Christ! My heart swells at the thought. I do long to be with Christ—to rest in His bosom. We shall need a long rest, after escaping from the shackles entailed by sin before we are in a state to enjoy the full fruition of the redeemed.

Source: A. C. Kendrick, *Life and Letters of Mrs. Emily C. Judson*, 321; Hanna family files.

Emily C. Judson to her Journal, April 4, 1849

Mah Zwoon came in to-day, and, after looking at me some time, shook her head sorrowfully and remarked, "I am afraid we never shall have the second part of *Pilgrim's Progress* now." Since I told the women there was another part about Christian's wife and children, they have been very anxious to obtain it, and I promised to translate it as soon as I was sufficiently versed in the language. The desire to live has grown stronger and stronger for a few weeks past. I do long for the privilege of doing something for Christ.

Source: A. C. Kendrick, *Life and Letters of Mrs. Emily C. Judson*, 321–22; Hanna family files.

Emily C. Judson to Adoniram Judson, April 1849[172]

Love's Last Wish

Thou say'st I'm fading day by day,
And in thy face I read thy fears;
It would be hard to pass away,
So soon, and leave thee to thy tears;
I hoped to linger by thy side,
Until thy homeward call was given,
Then silent to my pillow glide,
And wake upon thy breast in heaven.

And still I can but hope to stay;
But if the arrow should be sped,—
If I must weary by the way,
And rest so soon among the dead,—
I know thou needs must grieve to part
With one whom thou has loved so well;
But oh! let not thy living heart
Go with me to my silent cell.

I do not ask to be forgot,
I've read thy heart in every line,
And know that there one sacred spot,
Whate'er betide, will still be mine;
For death but lays its mystic spell,
Upon affection's earthliness,—
I know that though thou lov'st me well,
Thou lov'st thy sainted none the less.

And when I join that group above,
I would not leave thee here alone,
To struggle on, while trust and love,
Lie coffined where they had their throne;
'Twould make me happy, even now,
To know a lip as true as mine,

[172] In March 1849, Adoniram Judson wrote to Anna Maria Anable to say that Emily was desperately ill and that he doubted that she could survive. He added a note on March 22, 1849, that she was better, and he was more hopeful regarding her condition. This poem is dated near to this time, and it is clustered with three other poems that were likely written in this same time period. They are "The Choice," "Contentment," and "The Two Mammas."

When dust was gathering on my brow,
Should kiss the agony from thine.

It would be sweet to hover near,
And watch till thou again should'st smile;
And think'st thou not she would be dear,
Who could thy loneliness beguile?
And when at last we meet above,
Where marriage-vows are never spoken,
We all would form one chain of love,
Whose spirit-links could ne'er be broken.

Source: Arabella M. Wilson, *Lives of the Three Mrs. Judsons*, 366–67; Emily Judson, *An Olio of Domestic Verses*, 150–52.

Emily C. Judson to Adoniram Judson, April 1849[173]

The Choice.

The sultry day was almost done,
The grand old Myouk-ben hid the sun,
The fainting flowers looked cheerily up,
To catch the dew on lip and cup;
While from the rustic hall the sound
Of busy voices floated round,
And as with dream-inspiring swell,
Monotonous they rose and fell,
Though all uncouth the words and tone,
They softly melted into one,
As musically sweet and clear,
As ever soothed a sufferer's ear.
While wearily I strove to listen,
The evening star began to glisten;
Rippling the Salwen's silvery tide,

[173] Ibid. In her preface to "The Choice," Emily Judson writes, "The following fragment, which as it now stands, is given merely to connect the minor pieces, was originally intended as an introduction to something of higher aim, and greater length, if not more merit. The finished portions of it were penciled on scraps of paper, during a solitary illness, when some employment became almost a necessity; and the prosecution of the plan was interrupted by returning health."

Writing of it, Kendrick says: "'The Choice' is an ideal representation of the youthful Judson turning away from the lures of science, poesy, and eloquence, that he may devote himself to the divine work of bearing the message of spiritual life to the nations. The conception is happy, and though written because she was too ill to do any thing else, it is wrought with no little poetic power" (A. C. Kendrick said in *The Life and Letters of Mrs. Emily C. Judson* [New York: Sheldon and Company, 1831] 378).

From Zwai-ga-ben's wild mountain side [sic],
Deliciously the breezes crept,
Across my forehead, and I slept.
Then on the border of a wood,
Amid old moss-grown rocks I stood,
Where long and still the shadows lay,
        Where closed the flower, and drooped the bird,
For 'twas a slumberous summer day,
        And not a tiny leaf was stirred.
The rill, to gain a statelier tide,
Had leaped the distant mountain-side,
And seaward, with a silvery sweep,
Now rolled, a river broad and deep.
On this majestic flood afloat,
I marked full many a gallant boat;—
Some sculptured of the gems which glow,
In dim-lit palaces below;
Some, linked of stainless ocean-pearls,
Steered by pale, snowy-fingered girls;
And rose-lipped shells danced gayly there,
With children rosier and more fair.
The silver covering of the birch,
        Was fashioned to a light canoe,
The ring-dove's, and the eagle's perch,
        Alike to naval structures grew,
And oak, and elm, and cypress wood,
All balanced on the buoyant flood.

There waited many a child of Hope,
        Now in that radiant morning hour,
When glows her gay kaleidoscope,
        With fulness of warm life and power,
        When every sense is in its flower,
When, overhead, bright skies are bending,
With earth, in glorious beauty, blending.
Among them stood a stripling slight,
        The dark brown masses of his hair,
Flung backward from a forehead white,
        And on his face a beauty rare,

The soul new-fledged and hovering there;
An eye whose soft, love-beaming ray
Was caught from seraph lamps above,
And seemed forever back to stray,
As nestward turns the exiled dove.
Sweet is that hour when rosy dawn,
All earth in new-born life is steeping,
Just as the last gray mists are gone,
And still the flowers in dew are sleeping,—
Such dawn seemed o'er his clear brow creeping,
While beautiful the spirit lay,
In the first chastened beams of day.
Scarce more than child in form and face,
With all a child's unconscious grace,
He stood, as exquisitely bright
A thing, as ever Time may blight.
And yet, withal, he seemed to wear,
A more than dawning manliness,
A solemn thought, which was not care,
But deepened till 't was scarcely less;
And bending thus his bright young head,
Like flowers with glittering night-dews crowned,
A ray of light across it sped,
And circled in a halo round.

While still he mused, a deep, rich note
Swelled out upon the startled ear,
And where he stood, a curious boat,
In graceful curves came circling near;—
A strangely wrought and laden thing,—
There heavy tomes, half-mildewed lay,
With things of nameless fashioning,
All wetted by the careless spray.
O'er curious mechanism, wrought,
With dainty skill, through years of thought,
Hovered a swarm of golden stars
From heaven, and golden blocks and bars,
Ripped up from earth, and rainbows rare,
Torn hue from hue, were lying there.

All things o'er which the billows bound,
All that lie bedded in the ground,
All shapeless phantoms of the sky,
Things that ne'er lived, and things that die,
Or rich, or rare, or seeming mean,
Heaped strangely, pile on pile, were seen.

I said the voice was rich and deep,
And with a soft, enchanting swell,
It floated over vale and steep,
Till Nature quivered 'neath the spell,
And young Hilarion's pulses thrilled,[174]
To visions that his bosom filled,
As eagerly he bent his ear,
The magic minstrelsy to hear.

"Come, take thy way with me!
My hand guides not a pleasure-laden boat,
And dull may seem its noiseless track to thee,
Though by cool, shadowy islands it doth float,
Gems of the sea.

"With me the blue deep skim!
There is no pomp, no glitter in my way;
From solemn groves, in ancient grandeur dim,
Where murmuring brooks o'er mossy pebbles stray,
Upswells my hymn.

"I pierce to mysteries deep;
Fair Nature track through all her winding halls;
In subtle, quaint philosophies, I steep
My spirit, and in these Elysian thralls,
I sink to sleep.

"But, as the eagle shakes
The dust of drowsiness from his strong wing,
My spirit from its slumberous fetters breaks,

[174] On several occasions, in his correspondence with Emily Chubbuck, Adoniram Judson signed his letters as Hilarian Johnson or The Honorable Captain Hilarian Johnson. These include March 7, April 20, May 8 and 14, 1846.

My finger touches some deep-hidden spring,
Earth answering quakes.

"Then from my glory's blaze,
I shrink back to my solitary nooks,
Where the faint echoes of men's clamorous praise,
Come mingled with the sounds of birds and brooks,
In mellowed lays.

"If thou wouldst go with me,
First tune thy spirit with a child's meek hand,
For gentle feet will tread my groves with thee,
By no proud wing the soft pure airs be fanned,
No glare thou'lt see.

Then to my leafy cells!
Yon misty isles that purple the deep sea;—
In those dim solitudes where Wisdom dwells,
Tread reverently, and she shall cast for thee
Her deepest spells."

The voice was hushed;—the listener's eye,
At first no seeming answer bore,
But soon the lid drooped quiveringly,
And warm tears gushed its fringes o'er.
I knew some secret string was stirred,
But ere his lips had framed a word,
There gayly danced athwart his way,
A shallop [sic] of a lighter mould,
And trembling on the ripples lay,
While thus its glittering course was told.

"Come to my little boat,
My crimson shell!
Oh, bravely will it float,
Where breakers swell,
And wild wings dip;
There we will wreathe the pearls,
Dropped in their fleecy whirls,

With the rosy foam that curls
Each billow's lip,

"In paths of amber light,—
Far o'er the blue,
Where mirrored stars, at night,
Look smiling through,—
Where shadows play,—
Where beds of coral lie,
Where sea-maids peep and pry,—
Where caverned breezes sigh,
We'll take our way,

"Wide o'er the glorious deep,
In calm or storm,
And, wide o'er earth, we'll sweep;—
When stars are warm
With midnight fire,
When clouds in moonlight swing,
When birds fold up the wing,
We'll soar away and sing,
Sweeter and higher.

"We'll nestle in the heart,
Simple and pure;
Wherever tears may start,
Where follies lure,
Where woes are felt.—
We'll weave an airy charm,
A shield from grief and harm,
Cold. spirits we will warm,
The hardened melt.

"Mine is a gentle art,
And wisdom lies,
Most in the simplest part
My finger tries .
Yet hath it power;
Small are my lyre's light strings,

But high it sometimes rings,
As when a church-bell swings
    In some far tower.

"Then come! my shallop stays.
    If Poesy
Wreathe thy young brow with bays,
    All lovingly,
        Thy heart shall hold
Through life, its morning bloom,
Thy memory shall perfume
Thy hoary, moss-grown tomb,
    When thou art mould."

As with his morning wings half spread,
    The sky-lark, from his leafy nest,
Glad showers of music waits to shed
    Upon the fragrant couch he's pressed,
Flinging each wild, entrancing note,
Like molten silver; from his throat;
So fell this ringing silver shower,
On river's marge, and forest bower,
And trilled along the dimpling deep,
To barren wold and rugged steep.
So fell it on one waiting heart,
    But with a more enchanting spell;
For young Hilarion sat apart,
    Nor spoke but by the breathing swell
And quiver of his boyish frame,
As, with delicious tumult, came
A passionate, resistless throng
Of impulses, imprisoned long,
O'ermastered by one mighty thought,
That with remoulding power had brought,
A soul imperious, and wild,
Back to the meekness of a child.

But soon another voice was heard,
Now low, and warbling, like a bird,

Now swelling, as an anthem, high,
Now like a falling rose-leaf's sigh,
Anon, like some lone fountain gushing,
Then like the cataract, hounding, rushing,
Now tremulous, with love, or fears,
Triumphant now, then lost in tears.
At last it settled in a strain,
        Wild, bold, yet musically sweet,
Such as once heard we strive in vain,
        The lightest accent to repeat,
The fragment of a sound to save;
        And thus (as lisping echo's tell)
High o'er the sounding, emerald wave,
        Uprose its proud, impassioned swell.

"My voice in the forum! my voice in the hall!
In the green of proud nations—the rime of their fall—
Where golden spurs glitter-where moccasins tread,
As lightly as leaves from the autumn bough shed,—
My voice where the wise in their heaviness plod!
My awe-tempered voice at the altar of God!
My voice on the mountain—my voice o'er the lea—
        A wail for the slave, a huzza for the free.

"When wavers the council, my foot on the floor,
My finger uplifted,—it wavers no more.
I speak, and the fate of a nation is sealed,—
Quick flashes the blue steel, and purples the field;
Then, when blood bubbles hottest, and reels the mad brain,
My cooling words fall like the soft summer rain,
The sword to the smithy, the ox to the plow,
And the garland of peace on a nation's free brow!

"'T was the cry of my spirit—'Give freedom or Death!'
And noble the structure, which rose on the breath,
All Grecian in beauty,—the Saxon's stern power,
Joined the strength of the rock, to the grace of the flower.
When from her proud purity Liberty stoops,
When Virtue's foot falters, when Glory's plume droops,

I rend the soiled mantle, th' alarum I ring,
Give light to the spirit, and life to the wing.

"I seek not the silence of forest and bower;
I tread where men gather at day's stirring hour;
In the world's ceaseless battle, the struggle of life
I sound to the charge, and I cheer through the strife.
I speak, and proud multitudes gather to hear,
My thunder-tones quicken the dullard's cold ear;
The throng sways and murmurs, when breathed on by me,
Like the storm-wakened waves of the terrible sea.

"Wouldst thou shake mighty spirits, as night-blasts may stir,
The lightly poised aspen, or cone of the fir,
Wouldst thou reign, in true glory, the monarch of mind,
The darkness to scatter, the shackle unbind;
Wouldst thou shine, through all time, a magnificent star,
Whose light never dims though it travels from far—
Thy hand, and away to proud cities we glide,
On the wings of the wind, in the lap of the tide!"

Back from bold cliff and mountain side,
The wild strain rang and ringing died.—
The youth arose, nor trembled now,
        Though still his cheek was flushed and wet;
The beauteous calmness of his brow,
        Was as the mark by angels set,
When first they bent the glittering wing,
        To Eden's yet untrodden bowers,
And gazed upon the wondrous thing,
        Laid fast asleep among the flowers.
Calmly he spoke, though still a sigh,
Seemed on his breathing lip to lie:

"I know thy liquid track must be
        Scarce earthly in its gloriousness;—
Sweet were it to be blest with thee,
        Sublime, with thee, the world to bless;—
But I have seen woe's pallid hand,

Reach, beckoning, from a distant strand;
And o'er the dim, untrampled sea,
I mark, in faintest tracery,
Another pathway meant for me."
And then across his fair young face,
Stole back the shadowing weight of thought;
But lovelier, as some fresher grace,
On the soul's tablet had been wrought;
Or as again the angels, bending,
The brightness of their wings were lending.

* * * * *

He starts;
What wild sound rides the distant gale,
Like the last cry of anguished hearts,
A shriek in part, in part a wail?
"Woe ! woe! oh, woe !
Black graves below!
The foam for a shroud, and the billow a bier!
Death, death on the wave,
And no finger to save,
The blind at the rudder and wild breakers near.

"There's a blush of blood,
On the raging flood,
For cruel the sharp rocks that jut from the shore;—
Death, death on the wave,
And no finger to save!
Oh, who hath a heart let him bend to the oar."

"Show me, oh God! the highest good!"
Hilarion groaned, and doubting stood
A moment, then in doubt no more,
He waved his hand and grasped the oar,
And with his lithe arms' nervous sweep,
Went bounding o'er the billowy deep.
Oh, who can paint the strange surprise,
On parted lips, in lifted eyes,
As dashed the boat toward storm and brine,

While on each side a yeasty line
Curved from the prow, and foamed and curled,
Like snows by wanton breezes whirled.
But sternly, fearlessly, away,
        Away, where still the cry was heard,
Though many strove his course to stay,
        He skimmed the waters like a bird;
While to his passing boat was flung
A chain of pearls by Science strung;
Fair Poesy, her perfume sweet,
In clustering buds cast at his feet;
And Eloquence made haste to bring
A rich, but chastened offering.
On, on he sped, till small and dim,
A speck upon the water's rim,
He paused a moment hoveringly,
A moment more, and he was gone,
And he and his strange fantasy,
Like dews that vanish at the dawn,
Or shadows on the brow of May,
Passed from the minds of men away.
On, on from all that youth ere wiled,
        From joys that seemed with life-strings braided,
From hearts that loved, from lips that smiled,
        From earth's sweet hopes, ere one had faded;
Away to scenes of toil and care,
        He passed to do, and dare, and die,
While few the knees that bent in prayer,
        And many lips curled mockingly,
And darkness grim and shadowy lay,
        On his stern, solitary way.

Source: Emily Judson, *An Olio of Domestic Verses*, 209–32.

Emily C. Judson to Adoniram Judson, April 1849[175]

Contentment

I thank Thee, Father, for so much of bliss,
As makes my heart o'erflow,
The fulness of content, the peacefulness,
Which from Thy blessings grow.

Thanks for those sweet foreshadowings of heaven,
Each passing hour new-born,
Bowing my soul, as added richness given,
Unto the ripening corn.

My life is like a river full and deep,
And glowing with the light,
My other life submerging in its sweep,
As morning buries night.

The pulses of the expanding soul are now
The sands which tell my hours;
And Time's soft hand rests gently on my brow,
As dew upon the flowers.

I know such depth of blessedness as this,
Must even as dew depart,
But still a rich inheritance of bliss,
Lies folded in my heart.

Against no arrow is my bosom steeled,
But one sweet truth I know,—
These hidden waters, day by day unsealed,
Eternally must flow.

Source: Emily Judson, *An Olio of Domestic Verses,* 165–66.

[175] This is the third of four poems Emily wrote in the 1849 time period. The first two were "Love's Last Wish" and "The Choice." The fourth was "The Two Mammas."

Emily C. Judson to the Judson Children (Abby Ann, Adoniram, Elnathan, Henry, Edward), April 1849[176]

The Two Mammas[177]

'Tis strange to talk of two Mammas!
Well, come and sit by me,
And I will try to tell you how
So strange a thing can be.

Years since, you had a dear Mamma,
So gentle, good, and mild,
Her father, God, looked down from heaven
And loved his humble child.

"Come hither, child," he said, "and lean
Thy head upon my breast."
She had toiled long and wearily,
He knew she needed rest.

And so her cheek grew wan and pale,
And fainter came her breath,
And in the arch beneath her brow
A shadow lay like death.

Then dear Papa grew sad at heart,
Oh, very sad was he!
But still he thought 'twould make her well
To sail upon the sea.

He did not know that God had called,
But thought she still might stay,
To bless his lonely Burman home,
For many a happy day.

And so she kissed her little boys,
With white and quivering lip,

[176] This is the fourth of four poems Emily wrote in the 1849 time period. The first three were "Love's Last Wish," "The Choice," and "Contentment."

[177] Looking back on their marriage and trying to explain it all to the children, Emily wrote this poem.

And while the tears were falling fast,
They bore her to the ship.

And Abby, Pwen, and Enna went—
Oh, it was sad to be
Thus parted—three upon the land,
And three upon the sea![178]

But poor Mamma still paler grew,
As far the vessel sped,
Till wearily she closed her eyes,
And slept among the dead.[179]

Then on a distant rocky isle,
Where none but strangers rest ,
They broke the cold earth for her grave,
And heaped it on her breast.

And there they left her all alone—
Her whom they loved so well!
Ah, me! the mourning in that ship,
I dare not try to tell!

And how they wept, and how they prayed,
And sleeping or awake,
How one great grief came crushingly,
As if their hearts would break.

At length they reached a distant shore,
A beautiful, bright land,
And crowds of pitying strangers came,
And took them by the hand.

And Abby found a pleasant home,
And Pwen and Enna[180] too;

[178] Abby Ann, Adoniram, and Elnathan Judson left Burmah for the United States with Adoniram and Sarah Hall Boardman Judson. Henry, Charles, and Edward were too young for the journey and were placed with other missionary families. Charles was to die in August 1845.

[179] Sarah Hall Boardman Judson died on the Isle of St. Helena on September 1, 1845.

[180] Adoniram and Elnathan Judson.

But poor Papa's sad thoughts turned back
    To Burmah and to you.

He talked of wretched heathen men,
    With none to do them good;
Of children who are taught to bow
    To gods of stone and wood.

He told me of his darling boys,
    Poor orphans far away,
With no Mamma to kiss their lips,
    Or teach them how to pray.

And would I be their new Mama,
    And join the little band
Of those who for the Saviour's sake,
    Dwell in a heathen land?

And when I knew how good he was,
    I said that I would come;
I thought it would be sweet to live
    In such a precious home;

And look to dear Papa for smiles,
    And hear him talk and pray;
But then I knew not it would grow
    Still sweeter every day.

Oh, if your first Mamma could see,
    From her bright home above,
How much of happiness is here,
    How much there is of love,

'Twould glad her angel heart, I know,
    And often would she come
Gliding with noiseless spirit-step
    About her olden home.

Much do I love my darling boys,

And much do you love me;—
Our heavenly Father sent me here,
Your new Mamma to be.

And if I closely follow Him,
And hold your little hands,
I hope to lead you up to heaven,
To join the angel bands.

Then with Papa and both Mammas,
And her who went before,
And Christ, who loves you more than all,
Ye'll dwell for ever more!

Source: George Tooze, *Judson Treasures of the First Baptist Church of Malden with A Short Biography of The Life of Emily Chubbuck Judson*.

Emily C. Judson to her Journal, April 7, 1849

The cloud is a little lifted. I am still growing stronger and stronger. Strange that my heart bounds back to earth so joyfully, when I have been accustoming myself to the thought of being with Christ, and being "like Him, for I shall see Him as He is." I do not love the world in one sense; but the thought of leaving it does not make me joyous, nor have I acquired that indifference on the subject which Doddridge makes to be one evidence of growth in grace. It is not so much that my family ties are so strong; but I can not [sic] but feel that my work is unfinished—the shock of corn would be cut down before it was fully ripe. I seem just on the threshold of the very kind of usefulness I have nearly all my life longed for; and I ardently desire the honor of gathering a few sheaves for my Saviour [sic].

"Not of works, lest any-man should boast." Works, indeed! The very privilege of working is only an additional display of grace; but I do so long for this privilege, for it is sweet to receive favors at the hand of Christ. The more I feel indebted to Him, the more I love Him; but I know there are innumerable ways in which to increase my obligations. If He should prefer to take me to Himself rather than let me remain here longer, I shall see the wisdom of it hereafter, and praise Him throughout eternity for removing me from some unseen evil to come. If my Saviour [sic] call, I shall know that my work is finished, and go willingly; but until He call, I pray for length of days, and a wide field of usefulness.

Source: A. C. Kendrick, *Life and Letters of Mrs. Emily C. Judson*, 322; Hanna family files.

Emily C. Judson to her Journal, April 10, 1849

I am feeling very ill. The fever has returned, and my cough is worse. The appearance of recovery might have been one of those delusions to which persons in pulmonary diseases are peculiarly subject. Father in heaven, prepare me for cheerful obedience to Thy will.

Source: A. C. Kendrick, *Life and Letters of Mrs. Emily C. Judson*, 320; Hanna family files.

Emily C. Judson to the Reverend D. G. Corey

"Health of Fanny Forrester [sic] and Family – A letter from Mrs. J. dated April 10, 1849, to her old pastor at Utica says: Mr. J. and the children are quite well. The former able to preach most of the time twice on the Sabbath, and attend two or three meetings in the week in addition to other duties. For myself under the blessing of God, I have rallied a little, and we hope I am slowly improving; though I suppose the danger (if it be not an incongruity for a Christian to talk of danger in connection with death) is not all past. Life especially in my position, seems to me a desirable thing; but my heavenly Father knows what is good for both of us, and for his cause; and I rejoice to be at His disposal."

Source: *Portland Daily Advertiser*, Saturday Morning, September 22, 1849.

Emily C. Judson to her Journal, April 11, 1849

I have been trying to recollect what I have done for Christ in the course of my long and toilsome life, and the prospect is sickening. How soon I may meet my Beloved and my Judge I do not know, but the expectation covers me with confusion. Oh, it is a solemn thing to pass from one's probation—to feel that the last leaf is written and the book about to be sealed for the judgment.

Source: A. C. Kendrick, *Life and Letters of Mrs. Emily C. Judson*, 320; Hanna family files.

Abby Ann Judson to Emily C. Judson, April 15, 1849—Plymouth

My dear Mother

If you will allow me to address you by that endeared name will you do me the favor of accepting a few little tokens of my love which are enclosed with those of my Father in the box. They are not worth much and their only recommendation is in the fact of their coming from me.

The apron for my little sister[181] I cut out and made myself and Aunt Judson[182] sends the white muslin as a dress for her. The handkerchiefs are also a present from her to my dear Father. The toys are from my little brothers[183] and also the cups and saucers which are what remain (sadly injured to be sure) from a whole set which was given to me at St. Helena.[184]

Aunt Judson pays twelve dollars a quarter for my music besides my clothing and extra expense. She pays for everything for me excepting my board and tuition[185] in the English branches.

There is a lady here named Mrs. Harlow who gives Music lessons and I go down and practice every day on the Piano while I am here so as not to forget all that I ever knew.[186] I have now taken lessons four times. My music teacher who instructed me last term has died this vacation. Her name was Miss Noyes.

Mr. Harvey has not been to see Aunt Judson but once [Note: Written and crossed out is "this winter."] since November and never takes the least pain to find out whether my dear brothers are alive or dead when he goes to Boston. [Note: Written and crossed out are five lines as follows: "He has changed very much from what he was when my dear Father was here, and somehow the Baptists are not near so kind to Aunt and me as the other denominations."] I have however been once to spend the afternoon at his house. I have been also to Esq. Loud's.[187]

[181] See vol. 1, "Cast of Characters," s.v. "Judson, Emily Frances."

[182] Abigail Brown Judson, the sister of Adoniram Judson, lived in Plymouth, Massachusetts. A spinster of eccentric character and behavior, she was a beneficiary of her parents' considerable wealth. Her father had wisely invested in land and bank stocks; with the help of Esq. Loud, she had invested that money prudently. She took a strong interest in Adoniram's children and offered them considerable support—though not often without complaint or comment—for their clothing and education in the years to come.

[183] Adoniram and Elnathan Judson were living in Worcester, Massachusetts, with Dr. and Mrs. Calvin Newton.

[184] Abby Ann would have passed through St. Helena in late summer 1845. Adoniram and Sarah Hall Boardman Judson were on their way back to the United States because of Sarah's health; their three oldest children (Abby Ann, Adoniram and Elnathan) were with them. Sarah Judson died and was buried there.

[185] On November 26, 1848, Adoniram Judson wrote a long letter to Abby Ann. One of the admonitions to her in that letter was one of gratitude to the family of Ann Hasseltine Judson in Bradford; Abby Ann was not related to Ann Judson and the Hasseltine family; for this reason their generosity in providing for her education at Bradford Academy, her board, and many of her expenses was beyond all expectation.

[186] On October 22, 1851, Anna Maria Anable, who had Abby Ann as a student in her Philadelphia school, wrote to Emily saying that Abby Ann was a fine pianist and gifted in music.

[187] Esq. Loud lived in Plymouth; apparently, he was a trusted legal and financial adviser to Abigail Judson, for in two letters she mentions his name and suggests that he is advising her on the purchase of some bond or debt instruments.

I some expect to have the company of Mrs. Jones tomorrow as far as Boston on my way back to Bradford. I like her very much. She is a very fine woman.

I must now close which I will do by signing myself

Your very affectionate daughter

Abby A. Judson[188]

How is my little sister Emily. I hope that she is growing up to be a sweet little girl. How I wish that I could see her. Father wrote to me that when she was old enough to come to America that perhaps I should be able to take care of her. I should delight in the task of teaching her young ideas how to ( )!!

Source: American Baptist Historical Society, AJ 10, no. 295.

Emily C. Judson to Miss Jane Kelly, April 17, 1849—Maulmain

My Dear Jane,—

You would have had my congratulations on the promising condition of your school earlier,[189] but for extreme illness which has for a long time prevented me from using my pen. Aunt Cynthia[190] writes that your dear mother and sisters (does your mother remember me?) are all with you,[191] and also that you have Mary Barber,[192] whom I know you love very much. How I should like to step into the dear old house once more and see it in its changes! It would make me melancholy, I know; but still I can rejoice in your bright prospects most sincerely. You have struggled against adversity nobly, and you deserve success.

Does Miss B. remember and speak of me?... Who conducts worship in the dining-room? Who takes charge of the compositions? And who are your music teachers? During my night fevers old scenes have come back to me with peculiar vividness, and O how I have longed to be set down in your school-room with my old composition class once again! Some of the pupils whom I loved have been married since I left, and some have gone down to the grave; the great body of them are scattered widely, while a few may be still with you. I should like to inquire for—,

[188] On November 14, 1846, Abby Ann wrote to Adoniram and Emily, saying, "You will note the change which I have made in the manner of spelling my name. When you write to me please to direct it Abbie." Here, she has returned to "Abby."

[189] When the Sheldon-Anable families gave up their responsibilities at the Utica Female Academy to start the Misses Anable's School in Philadelphia, Miss Jane Kelly was given charge by the trustees. Early letters from Miss Sheldon and Anna Maria Anable from fall 1848 were extremely critical of some of her actions in buying new furnishings, putting the academy in debt, and treating Miss Sheldon poorly. Predictions for her personal success and the continued success of the school were dire; more recent correspondence indicated that the school was prospering.

[190] See vol. 1, "Cast of Characters," s.v. "Sheldon, Miss Cynthia."

[191] See the letter of Miss Cynthia Sheldon to Emily C. Judson dated October 28, 1848.

[192] See vol. 1, "Cast of Characters," s.v. "Barber, Mary."

and—, and—.[193] Are they with you still, or have the older ones *finished* and gone? If you see them, please say for me that I remember them most lovingly; that I recall every feature of their faces, and even the tones of their voices. I shall never see them again in this world; but beg of them to meet me where, I doubt not, friends will recognize each other with more pleasure than we can now conceive—in heaven. Are they beautiful? Tell them to look on those who are but a few years older than themselves, and see how soon beauty will lose its attractive freshness. Are they accomplished? Accomplishments are more enduring; but in the grave, which, since I last saw them, has opened for many as full of health and hope as they, pleasant voices and the tones of music are not heard. There the bounding foot is stilled; the cunning hand is palsied; and there the star of worldly wisdom sets forever. Urge them strongly, dear Jane, to adorn themselves with such Christian graces as shall be transferred with their ransomed spirits to Paradise. Tell them how sweet to the Saviour is the incense of young hearts, and what a precious Friend He is under all the circumstances of life. I wish you would ask each one of them, and any others about you whom I may know, to write me, if but a tiny note. If you please, put all the notes into one envelope and forward to me. Now that our perils by sea, by fire, by robbers, and by a persecuting government, together with our first heavy illnesses, are over, my thoughts revert frequently to old scenes; and though I have a sweet, precious home, and am very happy in it, far happier than ever in my life before, I can not [sic] always keep back the tears. The past—*the past*—has in it a very saddening tone. Then I have to regret that I was not a more meek, prayerful, devoted Christian when with you; and I would gladly retrace my steps, and walk more becomingly as a child of God. Think of my own helpless little children, and of the ignorant heathen women that God has placed me here to guide, and pray for me.

That our Heavenly Father may bless and prosper you ever, is, dear Jane, the prayer of

Yours sincerely and most affectionately,

Emily C. Judson.

Source: A. C. Kendrick, *Life and Letters of Mrs. Emily C. Judson*, 298–300

[193] A. C. Kendrick, in *The Life and Letters of Mrs. Emily C. Judson*, often removed personal names from the letters he included in his biography.

Mrs. Stella K. Bennett to Emily C. Judson, April 17, 1849—Tavoy

My dear Sister Judson,

I was very glad to hear from Br. J's[194] note that your health had improved somewhat since your return to Maulmain.[195] I sincerely hope it may continue to improve. Accept my best thanks for the beautiful cap and gloves you kindly sent me. I now return the two coats of Henry's[196] which I borrowed, I have been uncomfortable about them. The steamer was so long delayed I fear he has needed them. Mr. Bennett[197] has had fever a few times since his last trip into the jungle but I think it has now left him. My own health continues good. The Cross's[198] have been at Monmogon ever since you were here and Mr. C. told me a few days since he thinks sister C. has improved much since she went there. They were anxious to try the change for the poor baby and about three weeks ago I sent it to them, but she still goes on in the same way you saw her here and the Dr. says he doubts if any thing [sic] can be done for her.

Miss VanSomeran was confined last evening with another daughter. The Dr. has Mrs. Inspey [sic] still in hand, I think she is better than when he began treating her. I had a long letter from Mrs. Wade[199] but she had not seen one of our children when she wrote. We rec'd letters from our children by Br. and Sstr Benjamin.[200] All were well but no special news from them.

Hope you have good news from your children at home[201] and that those with you are all well. Thanks for the Memoir of Mr. Crocker. I hope to find time to read it. I was one day telling Mr. B. about your stay in Rangoon. He says that when you get well you should write another book entitled Rangoon in 47. He thinks you might do more in that way to rouse Christians at home about Burmah than has

[194] Adoniram Judson.

[195] Emily earlier experienced a severe illness, and on March 18, 1849, Adoniram wrote to Anna Maria Anable that he despaired that Emily would survive. As part of the treatment, Emily took a ten-day trip to Tavoy, hoping that the change of conditions would be beneficial.

[196] Henry Hall Judson, born July 8, 1842, was the son of Adoniram and Sarah Hall Boardman Judson. Henry was the sixth of their eight children and the fourth of five who survived. He remained in Burmah in 1845 when Adoniram and Sarah returned to the United States with the three older children. He returned with Emily in 1851 and went to live with her family in Hamilton, New York. Henry attended Brown University and Williams Collage; he enlisted in the army at the time of the Civil War in January 1864. Later that year, he experienced a debilitating accident attributed either to sunstroke or a horse kicking him in the head. He was married once—unhappily according to his own correspondence—and he eventually died in a veteran's home in 1918, the last of his siblings to die. Of this, the chaplain noted, "The end was a genuine example of Christian fortitude." See Rosalie Hall Hunt, *Bless God and Take Courage, The Judson Legacy* (Valley Forge: Judson Press, 2005) 291.

[197] Cephas Bennett had arrived in Burmah in January 1830; his wife was Stella Bennett. Mr. Bennett remained the superintendent of the Baptist Press there for more than fifty years. From the Utica area, they sent their children back, and the girls were educated at the Utica Female Academy. The girls included Elsina (April 1828), Mary (November 1829), Ann (August 1833), Ellen (June 1835), and Sarah (June 1837).

[198] See vol. 1, "Cast of Characters," s.v. "Cross, The Reverend Edmund Burke and Julia Ann Putnam."

[199] See vol. 1, "Cast of Characters," s.v. "Wade, Jonathan and Deborah."

[200] See vol. 1, "Cast of Characters," s.v. "Benjamin, The Reverend Judson and Susan."

[201] Abby Ann Judson at Bradford, Massachusetts, and Adoniram and Elnathan Judson, at Worcester, Massachusetts.

[Written across the top margin and text of page 1:] been done for a long time. What say you to it? For as wonder, one Tavoyer who has been two years an inquirer is asking for baptism.

With kindest regards to your husband and children

Affy yrs

S. K. Bennett

Source: American Baptist Historical Society, AJ 12, no. 358.

Emily C. Judson to her Journal, April 18, 1849

Oh God, my Heavenly Father, spare my life I intreat [sic] thee, and grant that I may labour [sic] for many years among these poor heathen. Remove thine afflicting hand and spare me, not for any desert on my part, not for any worth there is in my poor labour [sic], farther than thou shalt deign to give them worth by thy blessing, but as a free gift of grace such as thou dost delight to bestow upon the meanest and most ignoble of thy children. Grant some souls to my hire, some jewels to my heavenly crown—grant me physical strength, intellectual wisdom, prudence and energy, and a holy consecration of heart. Everything that thou givest, it will be my highest privilege to devote to thy cause; and whatever thou withholdest I know is loving withheld so in all things they will be done.

Source: Hanna family files.

Emily C. Judson to Catharine Chubbuck, April 19, 1949—Maulmain

Dear Katy,—

I should hardly write you this month but that you may hear I am ill and so be anxious. The whole truth is, I was attacked by a cough last December which kept growing more and more serious till into January. I strained my breast lifting Emmy Fan[202] during her illness, and for about a week after she got well was considered "in danger," but almost immediately rallied again. We thought I was almost well, and purchased a pony so that I could get exercise on horseback, but I rode him only about a week. After that I went down very rapidly—cough, fevers, and night sweats—until I got to be a mere skeleton and very weak indeed. We then became alarmed, and tried what a trip to Tavoy would do. Mr. J. could not leave very well, so I took Henry[203] and Frances and two servants, and went off under the protection

[202] See vol. 1, "Cast of Characters," s.v. "Judson, Emily Frances."

[203] See vol. 1, "Cast of Characters," s.v. "Judson, Henry Hall."

of a kind English officer, who paid me every attention. Mrs. Bennett[204] noticed my cough at once, and sent for the doctor, who pronounced my case very critical. I spent a week in Tavoy, but did not go out at all, and really I believe they were glad to see me go (though extremely kind), for they were afraid I should die away from my husband. When I reached home again I was in a serious plight; but Dr. Morton[205] (our physician) thought the violent symptoms were to be attributed to congestion of the liver rather than disease of the lungs; in which, thus far, his opinion has proved correct. He overcame the fever, pain in the side, and difficulty of breathing by degrees, so that I now suffer very little from either. I still have some fever, which is kept down by daily doses of quinine, but my cough is slight (I take medicine for it three times a day), the night-sweats have almost entirely disappeared, my appetite has been very much improved, and my strength is daily increasing. We begin now to hope confidently that it is not the will of our Heavenly Father to break up the family again so soon. You may imagine that I have had many sorrowful thoughts about the poor children; but you can not [sic] imagine what a wrenching there was in the case of their dear papa.[206] However, there is every prospect now that my life will be spared; and you may hear of us in a few months, *possibly* at Ava. I don't know—and in truth I am not so very anxious about it as I should be if my hands were not full here. I want the privilege of doing a little for Christ before I die, and I leave it with Him to determine where the work is to be performed—though I must say I have a slight preference in favor of Ava.[207] However, my principal business now is to get well, and every-body seems to be trying to help me. The Houghs[208] send their carriage for me to drive out every morning for the present, and as we find driving very beneficial, we have just made arrangements for purchasing a horse and buggy. And what do you think? just as we were turning the matter over in our minds, in came the mail with a present from Mr. Newton of New York,[209] which enabled us

[204] See vol. 1, "Cast of Characters," s.v. "Bennett, The Reverend Cephas and Stella Kneeland."

[205] See vol. 1, "Cast of Characters," s.v. "Morton, Doctor."

[206] To Emily and the children Adoniram Judson was "dear papa." When Judson was ill in April 1850 and leaving for his ocean voyage, Emily wrote a poem, "Prayer for Dear Papa."

[207] In February 1847, the Judsons moved to Rangoon as a stepping stone for eventual ministry in the royal city of Ava. They were forced to return to Maulmain in September 1847 due to reductions in funding, and when the opportunity arose again, work on the dictionary and illness prevented them from going.

[208] George and Phoebe Hough were the first missionaries to be wholly called by the American Baptist Missionary Union to work in Burmah with Adoniram and Ann Judson. Mr. Hough learned the printing trade from his father, and they set up a print shop to support the work of the mission. They arrived in Burmah in October 1816 and retired from missionary service in 1826; George Hough subsequently worked for the government as an interpreter and school superintendent, and Mrs. Hough worked as an educator. They remained friends with Adoniram Judson and many of the other missionaries. Their independence was problematical at times.

[209] There are six letters in this correspondence from Mr. and Mrs. Newton of New York City. In a June 1846 letter Mrs. Newton indicated that they were "new friends" of Emily. They obviously had considerable wealth, which they shared generously with Adoniram and Emily through packages, and upon Adoniram's death, they immediately sent a check for five hundred dollars to Emily. Mr. Newton called Adoniram his "friend," and one of the letters invited Emily to stay with them in New York upon her return. A later letter indicates that Emily had indeed done that. On May 15, 1846, Adoniram Judson inscribed a dedication to Mrs. H. H. Newton on the fly-leaf of a volume of Burmese hymns that had been compiled by Mrs. Sarah B. Judson: "Mrs. H. H. Newton From A. Judson/ The wings ( ) ( ) /( ) are folded in St. Helena—New York—May 15th, 1846."

to make the purchase. So you see I am quite set up. Tell Mrs. Wade[210] to hurry back before I get so well as to take to walking again; for Mr. J. hates driving so that he usually makes me go out alone—so I shall have a seat for her. (Going out alone is not here as it is in America—we have a groom to lead the horse by the head.)

Did I tell you last month about the nice box I got from Philadelphia? It is valuable, and the articles, which are chosen with great care, are just what we need. We hear by this mail also that we are to have a box from Oliver street church, in New York. The Philadelphians and New Yorkers consulted with each others; so we shall not be overstocked (it is not very easy to be overstocked with wearables in this country) with articles of the same kind. These presents make us doubly glad—glad for their intrinsic value, and glad because we and our work are remembered.

Source: A. C. Kendrick, *Life and Letters of Mrs. Emily C. Judson*, 300—302.

Emily C. Judson to The Reverend Abram Dunn Gillette,[211] April 20, 1849—Maulmain

—"Mamma is as God pleases to have her," a native Christian woman said to me a few days ago, when I was lamenting my inability to perform my usual duties; and it is that consciousness which has, for several months past, kept me from discouragement. If it pleases God to lay me on a bed of sickness, and thus stop my work and break up all my plans, shall I put on a mournful face, and disobey the apostolic injunction to "rejoice evermore?" That would be like a sulky child professing to want to help you, when you prefer it should be quiet—

We don't need a comic almanac to make us laugh sometimes, though we are away in heathendom; we have only to recall scores of funny things some of which you know, and some you do not know. You know we are neither of us *sad* people; perhaps not sad enough; but I believe that work which goes on merrily and without groaning, is quite as acceptable to God as the other. The bearer of glad tidings should not carry a face to spoil his news—a fact of which the natives seem quite aware. However sadness is good, and rejoicings are good; and whether we have a weeping gift or a merry gift, let us strive to use it as we are commanded to use eating and drinking, "to the glory of God." Possibly my doctrine may not be considered orthodox, but it is that of the New Testament.

Source: A. C. Kendrick, *Life and Letters of Mrs. Emily C. Judson*, 302—303

[210] See vol. 1, "Cast of Characters," s.v. "Wade, Jonathan and Deborah."

[211] This is likely a partial letter edited by A. C. Kendrick.

Emily C. Judson to Anna Maria Anable, April 20, 1849—Maulmain

My Darling Ninny,—[212]

I wrote, about two weeks ago, to Aunt Cynthia,[213] but as I then supposed it would be my last letter, it is not suitable to send now. So she will excuse me for not answering her kind notes this month. I am decidedly better than a month ago, and there is now every prospect of entire recovery. The violent symptoms, it seems, were occasioned by congestion of the liver, and not by disease of the lungs, as was at first supposed; though the lungs are not yet perfectly safe from a bronchial affection contracted in December. Did Mr. J. write you that I took a trip to Tavoy in the steamer?[214] I had a charming visit with good Mrs. Bennett,[215] although I was confined to the house, and most of the time, to my bed. I do not wonder that Aunt C. likes her; she is one of the loveliest Christians I ever saw. I feel that I have made a great acquisition in adding her to my list of personal friends. She is a real missionary, always working quietly and noiselessly. "Great will be her reward in heaven."

This illness of mine has been a great interruption to my work. It is now nearly five months since I have been able to read aloud, either in English or Burmese, or to talk continuously, and I find that I have lost very much in the language. It is to be retained only by using the voice, not by the eye. What may be the intention of my Heavenly Father toward me I can not [sic] know, but I think I feel submission to His will. When I was ill in Rangoon, I felt very impatient because I was doing nothing, but I have yielded that point now. I know that I do not deserve the privilege of laboring for Christ, and what right have I to repine? I have a right to pray, however; and I do pray, most earnestly, that I may be allowed to offer my mite, and that it may be accepted. A long life seems very desirable in a place like this; but the All-wise alone can tell whose life to preserve, and whose to take away.

I am not strong enough to mount my pony yet, and the physician says it will be long before the exercise is good for me. But the Houghs[216] kindly send their carriage, and I drive every morning. I am about selling my pony; how I wish I could send him to you—a beautiful, black little creature, smooth and glossy; full of spirit, but gentle and obedient, and gallops, O, so charmingly. Do you not want him? We are negotiating for a horse and buggy, which is to be at my control. Do you think we are extravagant? "All that a man hath will he give for his life," or his wife's life. But just as we were revolving the matter in our minds-what do you think? this very month's

[212] "Ninny" was a name of endearment given to Anna Maria Anable by her most intimate friends at the Utica Female Academy. Emily was "Nemmy."

[213] See vol. 1, "Cast of Characters," s.v. "Sheldon, Miss Cynthia."

[214] Emily gave a complete account of her illness, the trip to Tavoy, and her progress in her April 19, 1849, letter to her sister Catharine Chubbuck.

[215] See vol. 1, "Cast of Characters," s.v. "Bennett, The Reverend Cephas and Stella Kneeland."

[216] See vol. 1, "Cast of Characters," s.v. "Hough, The Reverend George and Phoebe."

mail brought us a present from America which enables us to buy it.[217] To us it seems providential.... May God bless you, dear Ninny, all of you, and grant you much of His presence here, and a place at His right hand hereafter.

Lovingly,

Nemmy

Source: A. C. Kendrick, *Life and Letters of Mrs. Emily C. Judson*, 303—304

Adoniram Judson to Anna Maria Anable, April 20, 1849

Dear Anna Maria—Emily is decidedly better, and as she has been writing you herself, I suppose there is nothing left for me to say—I thought I knew how to take care of the sex pretty well, but this one has proved a real puzzler. All my skill in regimen and exercise seemed unavailing. At length, we hit upon buggy driving—and that is the thing. So I am getting rid of the black saddle pony (that, however, Emily is very sorry to part with), and am procuring a fat backed cream color'd, that streaks through the streets, rapid and steady, with a black man at his head, and a nice pair of wheels at his tail, and her little ladyship perched aloft, and Hon. Capt. Johnson[218] sometimes at her side, but no sooner does a spit of highland or patch of woodland heave in sight, than like the bride-in-the-fable, he turns cat again and is off after the rat, leaving Desdemona and Othello to get home as they can. You see my note smells of the stable and such like—For out of their abundance, etc.

Yours affectly

A. Judson

Emily wants to see Griswold's[219] "five heads"

Source: Hanna family files.

[217] In an April 19, 1849, letter to her sister Catharine, Emily identifies this gift as coming from Mr. and Mrs. Isaac Newton of New York City. Friends of missions and of Adoniram and Emily Judson, the Newtons were generous over the years. Adoniram Judson stayed with them when passing through New York City and gave Mrs. Newton an inscribed collection of Burmese hymns collated by Sarah Hall Boardman Judson. Mr. and Mrs. Newton were the first to send Emily a substantial gift to meet her needs after the death of Adoniram Judson.

[218] Adoniram Judson signed his March 7, 1846, letter to Emily as "Hilarion Johnson." He also uses this again, or variations on it (The Hon. Captain Johnson), on April 20, May 8, and May 14, 1846.

[219] In the correspondence, Mr. Griswold originally appeared in a letter of April 2, 1845, that Emily wrote to her sister Catharine Chubbuck. Emily referred to him as a clergyman who had called upon her when she arrived in Philadelphia and said, "He is a widower what's more and crazy to get married. Don't you think I shall accomplish something?" Then, speaking of her days in Philadelphia, Emily wrote to her brother Walker and said, "I got to be quite a belle while I was gone—gallivanted about with Graham and R. W. Griswold in Philadelphia." The Reverend Griswold was, in addition to an ordained clergyman, a noted anthropologist, editor, and writer, one of the distinguished literary figures of this period; he seemed to be, at least in Anna Maria Anable's eyes, a suitor for the affections of Emily Chubbuck.

Emily C. Judson to her Journal, April 24, 1849

Since my illness I have had some views on the subject of laboring for Christ, which, if not altogether new to me, are stronger and more definite than those I formerly entertained. Glorifying God, doing good to others, and receiving a reflex good, have chiefly occupied my attention, while I have scarcely thought, till now, of the peculiar honor conferred on the individual who is selected to be a co-worker with the Son in adding the declarative glory of the Father. God has no need of us; He could establish His kingdom just as well without us; but, with infinite condescension, He has included our weak, imperfect, sin-polluted labors in His plan. How are we honored by such distinction! and how cheerfully and gratefully should we toil, feeling that our Father bestows a peculiar blessing on us when He trusts the meanest part of His glorious work to our hands. He gives it to us because He loves us—because He wishes to gratify us here, and to enhance our blessedness here-after. And we should *watch* meekly for such work, and pray that it may be given to our hands. It is never sent in an intrusive way; but it ever waits humbly before us; and many is the time we brush it rudely aside, or crush it beneath the bustling foot, because it seems trivial to us, and we do not see that it is from God.

Source: A. C. Kendrick, *Life and Letters of Mrs. Emily C. Judson*, 323; Hanna family files.

Emily C. Judson to her Journal, April 27, 1849

I have just been unpleasantly struck by a remark on the first page of Payson's "Selections;" etc.: "Look back to the time;" he says, "when God existed independent and alone; when there was nothing but God; no heavens, no earth, no angels, no men." What reason have we to suppose that there was ever a point in eternity when God was such a solitary being? Is the idea that He has been creating from eternity more difficult to conceive than the fact of His simple existence? Our finite minds can not [sic] comprehend either. Neither can we conceive how the works of such a powerful and benevolent Being could have had a beginning; for wherever we place the date, however far back in eternity, there is still an antecedent eternity in which He was idle—in which, as far as we can see, many of His attributes could not have existed. So far as we can see!—and how far is that?—the circle described by the sweep of a midget's wing. We know of the existence of God in three persons. —Can we be sure—I am afraid that is not a legitimate subject of speculation. We know God the Father, because He is our Creator and Preserver; we know God the Son, because He is our Redeemer; and we know God the Holy Spirit, because He is our Comforter. We know the angels, because some of them seduced us to evil, and still follow us, heaping evil on our heads, and because those that "kept their first estate" are "ministering spirits" to us; and these are all the beings in the universe of the omnipotent God of whose existence we have been informed. We know nothing here except what concerns our poor, puny selves, but hereafter we shall be taught the things of God. Oh, what a glorious study!

Source: A. C. Kendrick, *Life and Letters of Mrs. Emily C. Judson*, 323–24; Hanna family files.

Emily C. Judson to her Journal, April 28, 1849

To think that a God of infinite benevolence has passed an eternity without *exercising* that beautiful attribute is to me utterly impossible. We know that He delights in seeing His creatures happy, and studies, if we may so speak, to render them happy; and that He has been thus from all eternity is the only view that seems to me consistent with His character. But, on the other hand, if He has been eternally creating, there are eternal creatures; and this seems like an absurdity. How do we know but Lucifer was such a creature; and from this circumstance conceived the possibility of being able to compete with his self-existent Creator? I lose myself in the maze of thought, and my poor, little, narrow mind aches from being stretched so far—Oh, what poor, contemptible creatures we are!—not as God made us, but as we have, through Satan's influence, made ourselves; and yet how we strut and swell, and glory in each other's praises, till, if ridicule could take the place of pity in such benevolent minds, we should have all the hosts of Heaven staring and laughing at us. But no; like their blessed Master, they pity us, and because they know He loved us, notwithstanding all our follies, they hover about us, and whoever among us have truly received His mark, are sure to be continually encircled by unseen angel-wings.

Source: A. C. Kendrick, *Life and Letters of Mrs. Emily C. Judson*, 324–25; Hanna family files.

Emily C. Judson to her Journal, April 29, 1849

I have had evidence to-day that holy angels are not the only "ministering spirits" we have. Satan too sends out his envoys, and they are quite as busy as the others, with the superior advantage of finding an answering voice within us. Little do we dream of the spiritual warfare continually carried on in our presence! The apostle does not represent the enemy of our souls as an inferior being, the dirty, contemptible being that we are accustomed to think him. He says we wrestle "against principalities, against powers, against spiritual wickedness in high places." Our adversary is no shadowy, half-apocryphal being; whose very existence may be suspected to depend on the evil in our own hearts. He is a real living creature, made by the same Hand that made us, and placed far above us at the head of the heavenly hosts. He is fallen now, and the whole strength of his mighty intellect is directed against us: he taxes all his power and all his ingenuity to compass our destruction, because of the bitter hatred he bears to Him who hath loved us from eternity. And with the company of once glorious beings that he drew away from heaven, he has ample resources at his command; and could doubtless at this very moment cope with any and all the beings in the universe, except the omnipotent God. Oh, how humble we should be, and how implicitly we should obey the lowest whisper from heaven, lest we should join our enemy, and try to defeat the benevolent plans of the Great General who has undertaken to conduct our otherwise desperate warfare!

Source: A. C. Kendrick, *Life and Letters of Mrs. Emily C. Judson*, 325; Hanna family files.

Anna Maria Anable to Emily C. Judson, April 29, 1849—Philadelphia

Dear Emily

I wonder where this letter will find you! I cannot learn yet from the papers whether you are on the move to Ava[220] and ( ) ( ) ( ) nothing in your letters since it was first ( ). Mrs. Heman Lincoln[221] called here a few weeks since and she said you were going, beyond that I know nothing. I shall direct this letter to you directly, and not to the care of Uncle Solomon,[222] and I want you to let me know if it arrives safely and what is the better way to direct my letters in future [sic].

So you are as busy, busy, as all Missionaries' wives are! Well! If I did not know that it was in your nature I should feel badly. As it is, and you seem to thrive under such discipline, I suppose we must say nothing, but really three meetings in one day, the baby[223] and a party in the evening, it seems to me require the check. The fact is, I see you want sober and prudent Ninny[224] here to prevent your extravagances. I don't believe you tell me one half of the crazy things you do. Remember, I know

[220] In February 1847, the Judsons moved to Rangoon as a stepping stone for eventual ministry in the royal city of Ava. They were forced to return to Maulmain in September 1847 due to reductions in funding, and when the opportunity arose again, work on the dictionary and illness prevented them from going.

[221] See vol. 1, "Cast of Characters," s.v. "Lincoln, The Honorable Heman."

[222] The Reverend Doctor Solomon Peck was for twenty years the executive secretary of the American Baptist Missionary Union. Many believed him to be hard, stern, and judgmental, and from some of his comments, it is easy to understand that perception. Dr. Peck and Emily did not always have the easiest of relationships. She felt in him the judgment that came from many in the church at the announcement of her impending marriage to Adoniram; that judgment concerned her "secular" past and concern that she was not an appropriate companion for the venerable missionary. On July 18, 1849, Emily wrote a blistering letter of defense to Dr. Peck in response to a letter from him of February 20, 1849; her letter framed how she viewed his perception of her, and her response was meant to set the record straight. There are eleven letters in the collection from Solomon Peck to Emily.

[223] See vol. 1, "Cast of Characters," s.v. "Judson, Emily Frances."

[224] "Ninny" was a name of endearment given to Anna Maria Anable by her most intimate friends at the Utica Female Academy. Emily was "Nemmy."

you of old. When Mrs. Wade[225] comes I shall hear all about you, and your doings. I have a kind of dread of her visit and yet expect to like her. The girls have got in the habit of saying, whenever we get on any article of dress that looks a little *ontrée* [sic], "She looks like Mrs. Wade." I assure you she is quite a bugbear to us teachers, but she writes Sarah sweet letters that notwithstanding old associations I cannot help liking her. We are to entertain at the Convention Mrs. ( ) [Note: Five words of this line are lost to copy quality of the letter.], if he comes on, which is rather doubtful. What do you think cousin Ann Gratiot[226] says? (Her husband has gone to California and she is now at the old Sem. with her children.) Why, that the people in Utica are *confidently* expecting me back there as Domini Corey's[227] wife!! I'll leave it to you to judge of the probability of such a thing.[228] Alonzo Baily has gone with Mr. Gratiot,[229] Horace Hawley[230] and Jane[231] have gone to Hartford, and there is no one to attend the old church from the Fem Sem. but Mary Barber[232] and Mrs. Gratiot. The affairs at Madison University[233] seem to be as far from being settled as ever, and altogether the Baptists seem to be in bad odour [sic] through that section of the country. I do not know a more lamentable thing than the present state of affairs at Hamilton. Dr. Nott[234] says the Baptists never quarrel but what they make something by it. I cannot see anything to be made by this quarrel unless it should be the means of their getting two good universities instead of one

[Written along the right margin of page 2:] which I suppose is what they expected.

We have had a delightful visit from Aunt U.[235] and the Dr. He is much better than he has been for a year past,[236] and Aunt U. is so much encouraged for us that it makes her quite happy to come here. I wish you could know how we look in our present home. You would take more interest in us if you [Note: Several words in

[225] See vol. 1, "Cast of Characters," s.v. "Wade, Jonathan and Deborah."

[226] See vol. 1, "Cast of Characters," s.v. "Gratiot, Charles and Ann."

[227] See vol. 1, "Cast of Characters," s.v. "Corey, The Reverend D. G."

[228] A December 22, 1848, letter from Morven Jones to Emily also mentioned Mary Barber as also a possible suitor for Mr. Corey.

[229] See vol. 1, "Cast of Characters," s.v. "Gratiot, Charles and Ann."

[230] See vol. 1, "Cast of Characters," s.v. "Hawley, Horace H."

[231] Jane Sheldon Hawley was the daughter of John Sheldon and was a niece of Miss Cynthia Sheldon, Mrs. Urania Sheldon Nott, and Mrs. Alma Shelton Anable. She married Horace H. Hawley in 1841. Miss Sheldon was leaving for Wisconsin where the wedding took place, and Emily wrote of this on May 7, 1841. Horace H. Hawley worked in the publishing business and was instrumental in helping Emily with the publication of her earlier books as well as giving her guidance as she struggled with publishers, copyright issues, and other matters relating to publication.

[232] See vol. 1, "Cast of Characters," s.v. "Barber, Mary."

[233] See vol. 1, "Places, Events, Organizations, and Magazines," s.v. "Madison University."

[234] See vol. 1, "Cast of Characters," s.v. "Nott, The Reverend Doctor Eliphalet."

[235] See vol. 1, "Cast of Characters," s.v. "Sheldon, Urania."

[236] Previous letters spoke of severe rheumatism that had incapacitated Dr. Nott for more than a year; see Mrs. Urania Sheldon Nott's letter of March 16, 1849. Also the letters show a strong debate over the doctor's decision to use the homeopathic technique of immersing himself in cold water as a remedy; most of these strong opinions are in the letters of Miss Cynthia Sheldon.

this line are lost due to copy quality.] said she had written to you. [Note: several words in this line are lost due to copy quality.] delighted to get the Dr.'s letter. Did I ( ) ( )?

Mr. Gillette[237] went to ( ) with young Earp who is crazy, but he was obliged to return in the same vessel he went in, staying at Savannah three or four days only. The young man grew worse and Mr. Gillette is now on his way from Charleston. I am sorry on account of the family that this disappointment with regard to Mr. Earp should have taken place, but I am glad to have Mr. G. home at the meeting of the Union. Speaking of lunatics, I saw Hoffman[238] in the street last week. The papers say he is nearly or quite recovered. Fitz Green Halloch is also in an asylum. Many think intemperance has taken him there. Mother[239] who sits in her rocking chair, reading by the same table I am writing on (the parlor center table) sends a great deal of love, and wishes to express her fears about your going to Ava, but is half afraid to for fear she shall be doing wrong. Give my love to Lydia[240] and tell me some news of her ( ) ( ) ( )

[Written along the right margin of the address page:] for she never writes and I have not heard a word from her since I left Utica except what you have told me which is not little. Is she happier than she was? And still teaching in Mr. Howard's[241] school? I am quite anxious about her. Tell me if you like Mrs. Stevens[242] as much as ever.

[Written along the left margin of the address page:] Remember me affectionately to the Dr. and kiss the babies[243] for their Aunty. In the bustle when we first came on I forgot to send them some picture books in Mrs. Robarts'[244] box. I suppose you have plenty of such things in Maulmain but in Ava there'll be a dearth again. Don't forget me Nemmy[245] but remember that I am always ( ) ( )

Ninny[246]

Source: American Baptist Historical Society, AJ 13, no. 481.

[237] See vol. 1, "Cast of Characters," s.v. "Gillette, The Reverend Abram Dunn."

[238] See vol. 1, "Cast of Characters," s.v. "Hoffman, Charles Fenno."In a a letter dated March 17, 1849, Anna Maria mentioned that Hoffman had been committed to an insane asylum.

[239] See vol. 1, "Cast of Characters," s.v. "Sheldon, Alma and Joseph Hubbell."

[240] See vol. 1, "Cast of Characters," s.v. "Lillybridge, Lydia." See also "A Timeline of the Life and Mission of Lydia Lillybridge Simons."

[241] See vol. 1, "Cast of Characters," s.v. "Howard, The Reverend Hosea and Theresa."

[242] See vol. 1, "Cast of Characters," s.v. "Stevens, Elizabeth 'Bessie.'"

[243] Henry Hall Judson, almost seven years old; Edward Judson, almost four and a half years old; and Emily Frances, a year and three months.

[244] See vol. 1, "Cast of Characters," s.v. "Robarts, Mr. and Mrs. W. S."

[245] "Nem" or "Nemmy" was a name of endearment given to Emily by a small group of her intimate friends at the Utica Female Academy. Anna Maria Anable was "Ninny."

[246] "Ninny" was a name of endearment given to Anna Maria Anable by her most intimate friends at the Utica Female Academy. Emily was "Nemmy."

Miss Julia A. Look to Emily C. Judson, April 30, 1849—Belmont

My dear Mrs. Judson,

It has been such an age since I wrote you that I have'nt [sic] any idea what I told you last or which I told you anything at all. Last summer when school closed at Utica I came home and after having been there three weeks, was taken seriously ill with bilious fever, and did not recover until after it was too late to go back. But this place was open to me, within 30 miles of home—a very good salary—which disinterested as they are, school teachers will sometimes mind—and the duties of which are not very onerous, there being four of us teachers and only twenty scholars. Belmont is one of the most beautiful places in the world thirty miles west of Washington. We are six miles from any village, and in sight of no other residences—but we never think of being lonely. Our place, yards, gardens, walks, groves etc. etc. are magnificent, and Mrs. Mercer (our principal) keeps open doors, and the house *is* thronged with company constantly. Mrs. Lewis the grand-daughter of Lady Washington—is with us now. Mrs. Minon has for years been missionary to Africa was here a short time ago and Nemmy[247] it is no exaggeration when I tell you, ( ) would come to my room and sit down and ask questions by the hour about your good Dr. and yourself. I feel myself—and that not infrequently—a very "Lion" to have *seen* and *known* you. But I shall say no more of my present home, for long before—no by the time this teaches you, if we live—I shall be in my new home in Brooklyn. Now dear Nemmy, I know you always used to be interested in my prospects—so I shall tell you every thing [sic] just as I should do it and could find my way into your own home this afternoon and of two having had a nice frolic with Miss Fanny,[248] and sing her to sleep—talk to her mother of my arrangements. Till then—I expect to teach until the last of June—then go to my Fathers where with my dear mother—I shall sew and stitch two months away—and then answering to another name[249] and undertaking new duties start for my new home. On the way I shall of course stop to see our dear friends Miss Cynthia and the Anables[250]—whom I have not seen since they came to Phil—where they are becoming very popular. Nemmy, indeed this writing to you somehow distracts me—I feel as if my letter was going far far away, that I must not say any thing [sic], but of matters of the greatest importance. I want to tell you of little things—and so I will all sorts of things. Sister Susy has gone to Louisville in Ky to live—Mr. S( ) having engaged in business in that

[247] "Nem" or "Nemmy" was a name of endearment given to Emily by a small group of her intimate friends at the Utica Female Academy. Anna Maria Anable was "Ninny."

[248] See vol. 1, "Cast of Characters," s.v. "Judson, Emily Frances."

[249] Julia Look married Mr. Albert B. Casswell.

[250] Miss Cynthia Sheldon—with her sister Alma Sheldon Anable and her nieces Anna Maria, Harriet (Hatty), Mary, and Fanny—moved from Utica to Philadelphia where Anna Maria started the Misses Anable's School.

city, though they keep their home in Aurora to come to in summer. Miss Kelly[251] is getting on very nicely at Utica. Annie G( ) has our composition classes, and Miss K. is very much pleased with her. Col. Gratiot[252] has gone to California and Mrs. G.[253] and family are at the Acad. at Utica. Horace Hawley[254] is in business in New York. You will before this reaches you have heard of the death of poor Mrs. Allen,[255] also of Elizabeth Hoyt,[256] who died as Mrs. Colgate died. Her sister Ellen I mean.[257] Sarah Bell[258] is in Cleveland where she has been since last summer. She spends part of the time with her sister Laura who has a second little daughter. I have just been copying "My Bird"[259] for a lady who is staying with us, and have ( ) it a dozen times over in those days.

[Note: Four words are lost in letter fold.] my dear friend, for your last note. I am truly grateful for those little letters for I know how many claims there are upon your time and pen but *do* not forget mine, slight as it may seem when compared with a Mother's sister's and all your other dear friends. If you were in America, I should ask a word of advice, from you who have had experience, on entering upon a new life. But I have no fears, or a doubt of being happy. I know with our Father's blessings we shall be. Will you and your Dr. come to my wedding, and bring Miss Fanny, and Lydia[260] too? This is my invitation and pray send no regrets. Besides, I claim a woman's prerogative, and have a choice who pronounces the *words* that *make* me ever after "love honor and obey," and have a notion that those "silken fetters" would more firmly bind, and be not less easily worn if ordered on by

[251] See vol. 1, "Cast of Characters," s.v. "Kelly, Miss Jane."

[252] In a letter dated April 29, 1849, Anna Maria Anable told Emily that Mr. Charles Gratiot had gone to California and that his wife Ann was staying with the children at the Utica Female Academy. The letter clearly says "Col. Gratiot"— As far as we can determine, Charles Gratiot did not have an army commission—his father was an army engineer who had done significant work at the port of St. Louis on the Mississippi; he held the rank of colonel. His brother John Gratiot also had a commission as an army colonel and later distinguished himself in the Civil War.

[253] See vol. 1, "Cast of Characters," s.v. "Gratiot, Charles and Ann."

[254] See vol. 1, "Cast of Characters," s.v. "Hawley, Horace H."

[255] Eliza Allen was the editor of the *Mother's Journal* and included material by Emily as early as 1843. Their correspondence went through spring 1846. In December 1848, Emily received a letter from Mrs. Allen's husband, the Reverend Ira Allen, describing in some detail her death. The *Mother's Journal* continued, and in an 1849 letter Anna Maria Anable informs Emily that a piece that she had written had appeared in the publication. In a letter to Emily during their courtship, Adoniram mentioned that he had met Mrs. Allen and went on to say that the *Mothers' Journal* was considered to be a prestigious publication for the church. On May 27, 1846, after a meeting with her, Judson wrote: "I am afraid I shall get to dislike her. She is a woman that I could make some use of. She has a sharp, strong intellect—is a good critic in the rough, but not in the nice. No heart—no amiability—very severe and what is worse, glaringly envious."

[256] See vol. 1, "Cast of Characters," s.v. "Hoyt, Elizabeth."

[257] Miss Cynthia Sheldon first mentions the death of Ellen Colgate in a letter dated November 26, 1847. Anna Maria Anable mentioned the death of Mrs. Hoyt in a letter dated March 17, 1849. Ellen Colgate was the wife of James Colgate, who headed an investment firm in New York; James Colgate was the son of William Colgate, of soap manufacturing fame.

[258] See vol. 1, "Cast of Characters," s.v. "Wheeler, Sarah Bell."

[259] On January 1, 1848, eight days after the birth of Emily Frances Judson, Emily wrote a celebratory poem she called "My Bird." The poem has a total of seven stanzas, and it was widely published in the United States.

[260] See vol. 1, "Cast of Characters," s.v. "Lillybridge, Lydia." See also "A Timeline of the Life and Mission of Lydia Lillybridge Simons."

"Nemmy's" husband. Give my best love to Lydia, and tell her there is less and less competition in school teaching, and I abdicate in favor of those who remain. I do wish she would write to me—the least little bit of a letter would be gladly received, and speedily answered. I want to learn all about her school—and every thing [sic] —and through Anna M.[261] letters will come to just as if we were still at Utica.

[Written along the left margin of page 1:] Present my best regards to your dear Dr. Kiss Fanny and the other children each for me; and believe as ever your sincere and

Affectionate friend

Julia A. Look

Source: American Baptist Historical Society, AJ 17, no. 761.

Emily C. Judson to her Journal, May 3, 1849

I suspect it is not quite right to be strongly desirous of living, even though it be but to do good. True benevolence would make us as glad to see others employed in the active service of the Redeemer as ourselves; and if He chooses others to do the work, what claim have we to prefer? Why should we not go to our graves gladly, and leave our places to those whom He resigns to honor above ourselves? And yet He loves to have us ask all good things of Him; and I know of no higher good than to be an humble instrument in His hands to promote the interests of His most glorious cause, and to save the souls of men.

Source: A. C. Kendrick, *Life and Letters of Mrs. Emily C. Judson*, 325–26; Hanna family files.

Emily C. Judson to her Journal, May 5, 1849

The newspapers say the discoveries in California have made men mad. The same papers said three years ago that poor, little, insignificant "Fanny Forester"[262] was mad—or *romantic*, which is only a pretty word for insanity. I wonder if they would class my madness and that of the gold diggers under the same head. Oh! that I may resemble the Californian madmen in all but the groveling nature of their object; and while they are laying up treasure on earth, may I be gathering gold and jewels which shall outshine the stars, and outweigh all the riches of this lower sphere—materials for a crown in heaven.

Source: A. C. Kendrick, *Life and Letters of Mrs. Emily C. Judson*, 326; Hanna family files.

[261] See vol. 1, "Cast of Characters," s.v. "Anable, Anna Maria."

[262] Emily Chubbuck wrote under the *nom de plume* Fanny Forester. Asked about it once, she said, "Would anyone buy a book written by Emily E. Chubbuck?"

Emily C. Judson to her Journal, May 6, 1849

Mr. J. has been reading to me this evening, Doct. Hopkins' second sermon on Canticles 5:16. At the close he remarked that the true reason why our love for Christ does not partake of the exclusiveness of human love, is that in proportion as His grace is infused into our hearts, we learn not only to obey the golden rule, but our brethren actually become as dear to us as we are to ourselves. And he added, that when we reach heaven we shall love others in precisely the same manner and degree as we love ourselves; so that the joy and happiness we have in Christ individually, will be multiplied by the whole number of redeemed souls that gather round the throne. How strange when we know that "God is love," and heaven is made by loving; and when we see how much bliss a little love creates below—how strange that this source of bliss is cultivated so little by among the children of God!

Source: A. C. Kendrick, *Life and Letters of Mrs. Emily C. Judson*, 326; Hanna family files.

Mrs. Mary H. Brayton to Emily C. Judson, May 20, 1849[263]

My Dear Sister

I rec'd your very interesting letter by the last arrival and I hasten to reply tho I suppose it will not go till the close of this month. I was glad heartily to get your last letter and hear your sentiments upon a subject so often agitated in reference to the children of Miss'ies. The more I see of our native land the more I dread the fashionable fascinating amusements and I should rather say "vices" of this land. I already know the effects upon my own child even under a mother's eye and comparatively little exposure. I know I say "I know by a little what a good deal means." It is astonishing to me to see the number of young people, children of pious parents and ministers of the gospel who give no evidence of a change of heart. I am led inquire [sic] why is it thus? and then I wonder when I think of my own feelings of anguish for my children how so many pious mothers can rest while their children are on the broad road to death. I am glad that I have your approbation in my intention of taking Mary[264] back. Some look on with wonder in as much as if has been stated "that there is an utter impossibility of bringing up children in that country." The awful influence, the many evils etc. etc. May the Lord spare your life and the children He has given you to do as you now intend. I do not know how soon a child may be converted. But I believe very young. I heard a father and mother say of their

[263] There is an addendum to this letter dated June 25, 1849.

[264] Mary Brayton, the daughter of Durlin and Mary Brayton, was born in Burmah on June 5, 1841. At this time, she would have been just shy of eight years old. Many missionaries would have sent her to the United States for her education. George Boardman was six years old when he was sent home. Mrs. Brayton had a very unusual perspective for a missionary family. Of the Judson children, Abby Ann and Adoniram were especially critical when they spoke of this practice in later years.

son 10 years that they thot he was old enough to be converted. But I would begin with a child soon as it can be made to understand, and do my duty in bringing it to the loving Savior and implore that he would lay his hands on them and bless them, and some do understand much sooner than others.

Source: American Baptist Historical Society, AJ 12, no. 353.

Anna Maria Anable to Emily C. Judson, May 25, 1849[265]—Philadelphia

My dear Emily

Your letter of Feb. 20th came on the 14th and in the afternoon of the same day came Mr. and Mrs. Wade's.[266] Dear little Fanny![267] I hope she is well and sweet again, but you Nemmy[268]—weren't you a little imprudent to risk your health so! I suppose it is natural but I shall be anxious about you till I hear again. I wish indeed that I could be there to relieve you of some of your cares, and sometimes I think I may one of these days in some strange sort of mysterious way get smuggled over. From my soul I wish I had gone with you that is, if I could have made myself of any material use to the mission.

The Missionary Union[269] adjourned on the 18th. The meetings were quite interesting I believe, though there was not as much talent engaged as usual. We had quite an idea of creating some D.D.'s to supply the deficiency. The female missionary meetings were exceedingly interesting. Mrs. Wade is ( ) eloquent and Mrs. Vinton[270] I am told speaks very well. Mrs. Bronson wrote a short address which was read. I did not hear any but Mrs. Wade.

We had a houseful of company all that week, and I assure you we were glad to see our friends, for we felt as if we were not yet quite out of the world. Br. Corey[271] was here all the time, and Mr. and Mrs. Bronson[272] have spent two nights with us.

[265] This letter has an addendum added May 28, 1849.

[266] See vol. 1, "Cast of Characters," s.v. "Wade, The Reverend Doctor Jonathan and Deborah."

[267] See vol. 1, "Cast of Characters," s.v. "Judson, Emily Frances."

[268] "Nem" or "Nemmy" was a name of endearment given to Emily by a small group of her intimate friends at the Utica Female Academy. Anna Maria Anable was "Ninny."

[269] Meetings of the American Baptist Missionary Union were held in Philadelphia that year.

[270] Calesta Holman Vinton was the wife of Justus Hatch Vinton. From Connecticut, they first came to Burmah in December 1834. Their main ministry was with the Karens. Mrs. Vinton taught the women and was the author of several hymnbooks in their language. They returned to the United States in 1848, returning to Burmah in July 1850. In 1851, they moved to Rangoon. Mrs. Vinton died in December 1864. Mr. Vinton died in March 1858.

[271] See vol. 1, "Cast of Characters," s.v. "Corey, The Reverend D. G."

[272] Miles Bronson was a graduate of Hamilton University and Seminary and was appointed for missionary service in 1836. His field of service was Assam, and he first reached there in July 1837. He pioneered ministry with the Naga tribes. In 1849. Mr. Bronson returned to the United States and was there for more than a year; he returned to the field in 1851.

We sat table for twenty last week—our usual number is twelve. Mrs. Colby[273] of Boston was here, she and Mrs. Gillette[274] are going to get little daughters to send to our school. Father Bennett, Eld Leonard and his new wife, Mr. and Mrs. Bright,[275] Mr. and Mrs. Kincaid[276] and Mr. Osgood[277] were among the numbers who would drop in to dinner or tea. Our house is only two squares from Sansom St. Church. Mrs. Bronson's health is very delicate, though it seems to me that all she wants is quiet. They have now gone to Wilmington, Del. and on their return will stop with us. We like them very much. The Assamese that they brought with them created quite a sensation among our pupils who had never seen any converted heathen before. One of the daughters of high church parents got permission from them to be excused from school to attend one of the meetings. Mr. Vinton[278] was not here. Mr. Kincaid says that *Solomon the wise*[279] did n't [sic] want him. They say that Solomon has come off victorious from another inspection. Do you want to know how we like the Wade's [sic]? Mrs. Wade is lovely—gentle, affectionate, intelligent and lady-like. I knew her the first day of her arrival as well as I do now. Mr. Wade I could not read so well, and after he had been here a day or two, I told him I wanted to get acquainted with him, whereupon he put his arm round my waist and his hand under my chin and kissed me! as much as to say that's the way that Missionaries get acquainted. Mrs. Wade stood by and told me to let him be a brother to me, and so I straightway fell to talking with them as if I had known them all my life. Mrs. Wade makes much the most interesting speech in public, and is far more engaging in conversation than her husband, but last Sunday eve'g he and I had a good long talk, and I like him right well. He is one of the slow dry and droll sort of men. Don't you think so? His eyes are almost well and his health is much improved than when

[273] Mary Colby was the wife of Gardner Colby, a prominent businessman and active Baptist layman. Mr. Colby was a member of the Board of the American Baptist Missionary Union and an avid supporter of the missionary movement. In a letter after they sailed from Boston to Burmah, Emily mentions the extravagant hospitality extended to them in early July as they waited for the *Faneuil Hall* to embark. Adoniram and then Emily stayed with the Colby family quite frequently over the years. Mrs. Colby was an active correspondent with Emily and supported her, her family, and the cause of missions.

[274] See vol. 1, "Cast of Characters," s.v. "Gillette, The Reverend A. (Abram) D. (Dunn) and Hannah."

[275] Upon her return to America in 1851, Emily Judson was to have a very close relationship with Dr. Edward Bright, the corresponding secretary of the American Baptist Missionary Union. They had known one another previously in New York, as he worked at the time of Adoniram and Emily's marriage with the *Baptist Register*, a prominent regional newsletter. Prior to working as a publisher, he had been, in 1838, the founding pastor of the Bleecker Street Baptist Church in Utica, a church with close ties to the Utica Female Academy. He was appointed corresponding secretary of the Missionary Union the end of May 1846, just prior to Adoniram and Emily's leaving Boston for Burmah. In this role he regularly pleaded with Emily for articles to be published in the missionary magazine, the *Macedonian*. Upon Emily's return from Burmah in October 1851, Adoniram and Elnathan went to live with Dr. and Mrs. Bright for a year. Dr. Bright was to help Emily with many of her business affairs; he carried on the publishing details of the Judson Memoir because of a serious illness in Dr. Wayland's family. He, with Dr. Edward Granger, was to be the executor of the estate of Emily Chubbuck Judson, a responsibility he still carried in March 1869, as reflected in a letter to Anna Maria Anable regarding financial arrangements for Emily Frances Judson.

[276] See vol. 1, "Cast of Characters," s.v. "Kincaid, The Reverend Doctor Eugenio."

[277] See vol. 1, "Cast of Characters," s.v. "Osgood, The Reverend Sewell Mason."

[278] See vol. 1, "Cast of Characters," s.v. "Vinton, The Reverend Doctor Justus Hatch and Calista."

[279] See vol. 1, "Cast of Characters," s.v. "Peck, The Reverend Doctor Solomon."

he came home, but poor Mrs. Wade has been quite ill since the meetings were over. She has a slow fever, something like the jungle fevers they say. What a lovely Christian she is! Her sick room is better than sermons. She is now recovering, but I think it will be some time before she is strong again. Her illness has frustrated our plans for many pleasant excursions while they were here. I am afraid they will go

[Written in the right margin of the address page:] away with rather gloomy recollections of us.

Afternoon. I have just returned with Mr. Wade and some others from visiting the Panorama Rhine. It is a mighty fine thing to sit comfortably on your bench and be carried as if in a vessel across the Atlantic. To witness the grandeur of a storm at sea, without any fear,

[Written in the left margin of the address page:] to visit Liverpool, London and the beautiful villages and castled hills of the Rhine in two hours is quite a feat.

The doctors have been holding a consultation over Mrs. Kincaid's case, to decide if she could live in Burmah. The decision is not made public yet, but I rather think it is favorable—Mr. Wade knows all about it, but I do not like to ask him.

Source: American Baptist Historical Society, AJ 13, no. 480.

Anna Maria Anable to Emily C. Judson, May 28, 1849[280]

[Written in the left and top margins of page 1:] 28th. The doctors have decided that Mrs. Wade[281] has an attack of inflammation of the lungs, but they think there is no danger in her case. I am so glad that she is here, for I do believe that Aunt C.[282] and mother[283] can take care of her better than any except her own family friends. Let me hear from you darling as often as you can—give love to the Dr. and Lydia,[284] and kiss babie[285] from her

Aunt Ninny[286]

Source: American Baptist Historical Society, AJ 13, no. 480.

[280] This is an addendum to a letter written May 25, 1849.

[281] See vol. 1, "Cast of Characters," s.v. "Wade, Jonathan and Deborah."

[282] See vol. 1, "Cast of Characters," s.v. "Sheldon, Miss Cynthia."

[283] See vol. 1, "Cast of Characters," s.v. "Sheldon, Alma and Joseph Hubbell."

[284] See vol. 1, "Cast of Characters," s.v. "Lillybridge, Lydia." See also "A Timeline of the Life and Mission of Lydia Lillybridge Simons."

[285] See vol. 1, "Cast of Characters," s.v. "Judson, Emily Frances."

[286] "Ninny" was a name of endearment given to Anna Maria Anable by her most intimate friends at the Utica Female Academy. Emily was "Nemmy."

Emily C. Judson to her Journal, May 28, 1849

May 28, 1849. I have been very busy since I began to get better—too busy I am afraid for my spiritual good. I have finished notes to the Memoir,[287] and written a great many letters, and taken a short lesson daily in Burmese. To-day I resume my native female prayer-meeting. The women are delighted to see me so well, and expressed their joy both by smiles and tears. They are very anxious to have the Bible class commence again, and I have promised to gratify them as soon as I can use my voice a little better, but they are just like a parcel of children, and yet how vastly superior to the heathen about them! Grace makes a very visible change in them.

Source: A. C. Kendrick, *Life and Letters of Mrs. Emily C. Judson*, 327; Hanna family files.

Emily C. Judson to Anna Maria Anable, June 2, 1849[288]—Maulmain

My Darling Anna Maria,—

I have been thinking of three years ago,[289] when you and I were at the little loggery[290] in Hamilton, and somebody else, not a thousandth part so dear as now, was there too; and we were all anticipating a grand event in the evening. Then good old Dr. Kendrick[291] was able to walk to our house; now he is shut in his coffin—no, not there!—resting in "the bosom of' his Father and his God. Dear grandfather and grandmother[292] occupied the comfortable basement room in Utica, which we used so often to visit of a Sunday evening; and dear Aunt Cynthia[293] was the life of the household. Grandfather and Grandmother have since then found a more comfortable

[287] Emily was working on notes to the previously published *Memoir of Sarah B. Judson, Member of the American Mission to Burmah* (New York: L. Colby and Company, 1848). She started the project, but illness forced her to put it aside. See, for example, Emily's letter to Anna Maria Anable dated April 20, 1849.

[288] This letter has an addendum dated June 18, 1849.

[289] Emily E. Chubbuck and Adoniram Judson were married on June 2, 1846; this letter was written on their third anniversary. Sadly, it will be their last anniversary together.

[290] From A. C. Kendrick, *The Life and Letters of Mrs. Emily C. Judson* (New York: Sheldon and Company, 1831) 166: "Emily reached home—'the loggery,' as she playfully styled her father's humble but very comfortable dwelling—the first week in March."

[291] When Emily Chubbuck was in her teens, Dr. Nathaniel Kendrick was the pastor of the Baptist church in Eaton and also a professor in a local theological school; he eventually became the president of the Hamilton Literary and Theological Institution. At that time in her life, Emily spoke with him about becoming a missionary. Dr. Kendrick gave her the wise counsel of discernment, patience, and waiting. Adoniram and Emily turned to Dr. Kendrick to officiate at their marriage. He married Adoniram and Emily on June 2, 1846. A. C. Kendrick, in *the Life and Letters of Mrs. Emily C. Judson*, says that the marriage of Emily and Adoniram Judson was the last service for which Dr. Kendrick was able to leave his home. Other correspondents mention his continued frailty. He died on September 11, 1848.

[292] Deacon and Mrs. Sheldon were the parents of Cynthia Sheldon, Urania Sheldon Nott, and Alma Sheldon Anable. They had rooms at the Utica Female Academy where two of their three daughters were employed, and they were popular with the students. After she married and moved to Schenectady, Mrs. Nott often wrote to encourage Emily and the other girls to drop in on her parents whenever possible. Isabell Low Sheldon died January 29, 1847, and Deacon Asa Sheldon died in March 1848.

[293] See vol. 1, "Cast of Characters," s.v. "Sheldon, Miss Cynthia."

and a glorious home, where they are more tenderly loved than by us, or even by their own children; and the rest of you have found another home also, but a different one, where you must still encounter the ills of life, and turn over new leaves to be re-read in eternity. I have traveled half the circuit of the globe since then; taken upon myself new toils, new responsibilities, and new enjoyments; added one little spirit to the list of the immortals,[294] and hoped and prayed for the privilege of adding many more of Christ's elect to the list of Christ's redeemed. Every thing [sic] is changed except our hearts; I trust they remain the same, only as they may have gathered spiritual influences about them, and adorned themselves with more beautiful Christian graces. I wish you were sitting by me now, here before my large open window, in a room, I will venture to say, as comfortable and as clean, if not quite so handsomely furnished as yours. The dark, glossy leaves of the Cape Jasmine, just below the balustrade, are sparkling with rain-drops, and it's magnificent white blossoms fill the house with their rich perfume. The trees, too, are all dripping with rain; and gorgeous birds, though not with the rich voices of our robin and bob-o-link, are singing in the branches; while the odd-looking native huts, that peep from the green beyond, add to the picturesqueness of the scene, just as a gnarled tree, or a particularly ugly stump, beautifies an American landscape. The bell has just done ringing, and the gayly dressed natives—the women with bunches of flowers in their black hair, and the men in snowy turbans—go streaming by to the chapel; and—wait a minute!—there, I have had my kiss, and the teacher, as usual of an evening, has gone to spend an hour with his flock. But I am not alone, for there are merry tones rising from the veranda. Nurse is teaching baby the Burmese alphabet, and her curious pronunciation makes her little brothers[295] shout with laughter. But I do not believe you would do it much better; try, and see: *Kah-gyee*, *kah-gway*, *ga-ngai*, *etc*. Finally, the woman comes to *tah-ha-nyen-gyik*, which she pronounces very much as if it contained only one syllable, and baby joins her shrill little voice in the general laugh. She can not [sic] be induced to attempt its pronunciation. I do wish you were here, darling, if only to see how God has blest me with the sweetest of all human homes. True, we lead a life of toil and self-denial; but all that we suffer is for Christ's sake, and we know that our smallest sacrifice does not escape His notice. And for every sacrifice we are receiving, even now, "an hundred fold." I do not know how it is that we are *so* free from every care; nothing can worry us, or make us anxious; and I believe it is because the Saviour is making good His promises. That is why I am not afraid to go

[294] See vol. 1, "Cast of Characters," s.v. "Judson, Emily Frances."

[295] Henry Hall Judson, almost seven years old, and Edward Judson, four and a half years old.

[296] In February 1847, the Judsons moved to Rangoon as a stepping stone for eventual ministry in the royal city of Ava. They were forced to return to Maulmain in September 1847 due to reductions in funding, and when the opportunity arose again, work on the dictionary and illness prevented them from going.

to Ava,[296] or any where [sic]. We *cannot* be *unhappy* while we lie in the hands of God like little children; danger will not be danger, and suffering will be a joy.

We are all getting well again. I drive out as often as the rain will let me, and take my children with me, leaving one at home by turns. I believe I have the trustiest servants in the mission, for others find it very difficult to go out without taking all their children. Mr. J. is looking, I think, much younger than he did in America, and is so well as to be a proverb among Europeans. For myself, I feel as though I had received the same blessing that Hezekiah did, and I am anxious to improve it to the best advantage. There was at one time scarcely the slightest hope of my recovery, and the doctor commissioned Mrs. Bennett[297] to tell me so. But I feel very grateful for that illness. My Heavenly Father revealed Himself to me as He never did in health, and I trust that the influence will remain upon my spirit for ever.[298] I am grateful for recovery too. Even independently of my family, I think that long life in this crisis of the affairs of the world, and especially in a heathen land, is particularly desirable. O, how I wish that you could be here with us! It seems to me that I never loved you quite as well as now, when your new situation and prospects remove the probability of our meeting, except in heaven. But let us strive with all our might to do good, darling, that, when we meet there, we may make glad each other's hearts. Give love to Hatty,[299] Fanny,[300] and Mary,[301] and believe me, darling,

Yours most lovingly,

Emily C. Judson

[Written in the right margin of the address page:][302] We have just been amusing ourselves with a bit of ice sent us by some unknown hand who suppose [sic] had just rec'd it from Calcutta—the first I think that has ever been in this place. I put it in the hand of a sober old native deacon, who screamed and dropped it in an instant. Baby and Ed. both cried, thinking they were hurt, but poor Henry lost the excuse of seeing it; he was out and it melted *so* rapidly under the *touches* of the natives! An electrical machine would be a ( ) ( ) with this bit of ice, in giving shocks.

Source: A. C. Kendrick, *Life and Letters of Mrs. Emily C. Judson*, 304–307; Hanna family files.

[297] See vol. 1, "Cast of Characters," s.v. "Bennett, The Reverend Cephas and Stella Kneeland."

[298] Selections from the entries Emily Judson made to her journal during the time of her severe illness show concern for death, for all that her loss would mean to her family, but also a deep spiritual journey and a resignation to God's will.

[299] See vol. 1, "Cast of Characters," s.v. "Anable, Harriet."

[300] See vol. 1, "Cast of Characters," s.v. "Anable, Fanny."

[301] See vol. 1, "Cast of Characters," s.v. "Anable, Miss Mary Juliet."

[302] Dr. A. C. Kendrick, in *The Life and Letters of Mrs. Emily C. Judson* (New York: Sheldon and Company, 1831), usually edits the letters included in his collection, but this letter shows very little removed or changed. He did not, however, include this addition, nor did he include the addendum dated June 18, 1849.

Catharine Chubbuck to J. Walker Chubbuck, June 10, 1849[303]—Hamilton

Dear Walk.

I got my paper out once last week to write you, but something came that hindered me and so here goes again. I'm as busy as a bee, and a great deal lonesomer I know, for I'm all alone only when father[304] and Wallace[305] are here. We went and carried Mother[306] over to Uncle Bachus Leach's last Friday to stay a week. She was in miserable health, and I thought it would be the best thing in the world for her to get out of the way of the work a while and to visit at the same time if she could. Her health is very poor, but I shall make her as comfortable as I can with care and medicine. She thinks sometimes she must try and do without medicine, but I tell her she shan't [sic] do it for when I use what money I've got I shall send to you for some so you must hold yourself in readiness in case we get run ashore. It isn't likely we shall draw hard enough on you to break you down but I thought I would tell you, so that you would'nt [sic] be too much frightened if we should send for a dollar or two. She is taking Townsend's Sarsaparilla now and I think it is very good for her, but we have to buy it with our money, father never has bought her a bit of medicine to take since she has got so bad. I don't think he realized how she fails at all, and then he feels poor since he has lost his mail route. I guess I have'nt [sic] told you about that, Col. Nye of Madison bid it off, I suppose to put a stage on, he says however that father may carry it if they don't succeed in getting a stage on. He could carry the mail in summer very well, but I don't believe he can, any more winters, and I think perhaps it is for the best that he did'nt [sic] get it. There will be a way provided for us to get along. If Mother's health was as good as his I should'nt [sic]

[303] This letter from Emily's sister Catharine to their brother Walker reveals how Emily's family in Hamilton, New York, went on in her absence. Catharine relays information from Emily's letters home to Walker. This letter describes Emily Frances' near death from cholera.

[304] Emily's father, Charles Chubbuck, was born at Bedford, New Hampshire, on March 3, 1780; he was married to Lavinia Richards in Goffstown, New Hampshire, on November 17, 1805. They were to have seven children. Though he held varying jobs over the years, he failed at many of them, and Emily was the main support of the family after she purchased a home for her family in fall 1842.

[305] Born January 1, 1824, William Wallace Chubbuck was six years younger than Emily. During these years of Emily's correspondence, Wallace lived at or near home and worked at different occupations including printing, office work, and teaching. Emily wrote of him as capable in many areas, but seeming to lack ambition at times. He proved to be a strong support for the Chubbuck family over these years, and at the time of her death in 1854, Wallace had become one of Emily's primary caregivers. After February 1854, she dictated all her letters to him because of her failing strength. Wallace married Julia Allin Throwbridge on July 18, 1854. He died on August 13, 1861, at the age of thirty-seven. The obituary in the Utica *Herald* noted that Wallace had trained as a printer in Morrisville and had gained some very astute political skills. He was "possessed of one of the brightest of intellects, and wield[ed] one of the most trenchant of pens." He had served as a justice of the peace, and as clerk to one of the legislative committees in Albany.

[306] Emily's mother, Lavinia Richards Chubbuck, was born June 1, 1785, at Goffstown, New Hampshire, the eldest of thirteen children. She married Charles Chubbuck on November 17, 1805, at Goffstown, New Hampshire. Four of her children were born at Goffstown, and moved with Charles and Lavinia Chubbuck to Eaton, New York, in September 1816; they were Lavinia, Benjamin, Harriet, and John Walker. Sarah Catharine, Emily, and Wallace were all born in Eaton.

care. Did you lose any thing [sic] by the fire in your city? We of course felt a little afraid that you did. I had a letter from Aunt Holland a few weeks ago. She says you are coming to Michigan this spring to see a—I shant [sic] tell what, important business though I spect [sic] is going to be seen to. Be careful sir how you get yourself into any bad scrape—that's all.

I had a letter from Emily a week or two ago. She has been very sick herself and little Fanny[307] has had the cholera so that they nearly lost her, but they were both getting pretty well again. Wallace is home now and is in poor health. He would have gone to the city to work at the printing business, but we felt afraid to have him go where the cholera rages for he is so bilous [sic] he would be sure to take it, so I guess he will take care of the garden and study law at least at present. He says he answered your letter last spring and don't [sic] see where it went to. He will write you very soon but I was'nt [sic] going to wait for him. I am in a great hurry and so will make my chat short. Write often and come when you can conveniently to see

Your affectionate

Kitty Chub.

Source: Wisconsin Historical Society.

Mrs. Stella K. Bennett to Emily C. Judson, June 12, 1849—Tavoy

My dear Sister Judson

I have after so long a time finished the reading of the Memoir[308] you kindly sent me and now return it with many thanks. [Note: "Br Cross[309] wishes to read it and has it" is written above the line.] I see nothing remarkable about it except the *uncommon* piety of its subject. Mr. C. appears to have possessed these "*best* gifts which are indispensable to the successful missionary." I mean to the Missionary who would win souls. To *me* it is painful to think how much *hard* labor is performed among us that *seems* to have very little to do with the conversion of those about us.

I am very happy to hear from Dr. Morton[310] that you are *quite* well again. He says you said, I frightened you, but I told him I thought it was *you* that frightened me. I shall surely rejoice if time passes that we both had our fright for nothing. We are all in usual health. Sister Cross is always lonely and her two youngest children have been ill most of the time since she returned from ( )mogon. The baby's head has become of a giant size but is apparently unconscious of every thing [sic] but

[307] See vol. 1, "Cast of Characters," s.v. "Judson, Emily Frances."

[308] Fanny Forester, *Memoir of Sarah B. Judson, Member of the American Mission to Burmah* (New York: L. Colby and Company, 1848).

[309] See vol. 1, "Cast of Characters," s.v. "Cross, The Reverend Edmund Burke and Julia Ann Putnam."

[310] See vol. 1, "Cast of Characters," s.v. "Morton, Doctor."

suffering. I begin to think it may outlive the fits. Hope your husband has regained the use of his fingers and that the children[311] are all well.

With kindest regards to Br. J. and the children
I am Yours aff'ly

S. K. Bennett

Source: American Baptist Historical Society, AJ 12, no. 360.

Emily C. Judson to Anna Maria Anable, June 18, 1849[312]

[The following text is written along the left and top margins of the letter written June 2, 1849.]

June 18th. I am sending by this mail Notes to the Memoir[313]—most of them on subjects which will interest you. Those on Boodhism [sic] and Burmese politics, especially the former, have cost me a great deal of study and may be relied on as correct. Boodhism [sic] is a very intricate subject and few missionaries, ever, get to the bottom of it or indeed understand much about it, except stories of the vulgar, which the learned men laugh at.

Source: Hanna family files.

Emily C. Judson to her Journal, June 20, 1849

The notes to the Memoir[314] are finished at last, and are safely deposited in the post-office. To-morrow they will be on their way to Calcutta. I have re-written them all within the last month, and bestowed upon them a great deal of work and some prayers. I think they will give people in America more distinct and definite notions of Boodhism [sic] than they had before, without dragging them through all the rubbish and filth of idolatry.[315] I do not see any use in filling books with the silly vagaries of heathenism, though an outline of the great systems with which the Church has to contend is doubtless useful. What am I to do next?

Source: A. C. Kendrick, *Life and Letters of Mrs. Emily C. Judson*, 327; Hanna family files.

[311] Henry Hall Judson, almost seven years old; Edward Judson, four and a half years old; Emily Frances Judson, a year and a half old.

[312] This was an addendum to a letter written June 2, 1849.

[313] Before she was taken ill, Emily was working on notes to be added to the previously published *Memoir of Sarah B. Judson, Member of the American Mission to Burmah* (New York: L. Colby and Company, 1848). In her letter of April 20, 1849, she spoke of how the illness had limited severely what she could do.

[314] Ibid.

[315] Emily's letter of June 18, 1849, contains similar expressions on the memoir and on "Boodhism."

Emily C. Judson to her Journal, June 22, 1849

[Note: In the original manuscript, the following paragraph was written and then crossed out.]

I think of translating the life of Gandama from the Burmese into the English. It would be a very useful exercise to me, for I would translate literally; and the view of Boodhism [sic] would be valuable also to the Christian world, I have got the volume already on my table, and mean to lose no time in setting about my work.

Source: A. C. Kendrick, *Life and Letters of Mrs. Emily C. Judson*, 327; Hanna family files.

Anna Maria Anable to Adoniram Judson,[316] June 25, 1849[317]—Philadelphia

You letter my dear friend arrived on the 23rd and the sad news which is communicated of dear Emily's sufferings, makes my heart ache both for her and you. At the first reading I felt that the case was indeed a hopeless one—that you were witnessing the final struggles with a disease the first encroachments of which I have often so [Note: "Painfully" is written and crossed out.] anxiously watched.

O! how I longed to be with you to help take care of her! how bitterly I regretted any thing [sic] I had ever said which might have caused her pain. Apprehensions of a fatal termination of this attack, for a few moments overwhelmed me, but on reading your kindly and carefully expressed letter again, I found, as I thought, occasion for hope, and the more I think of it the more sanguine grows my hope. I have seen Emily very ill, when every symptom seemed to indicate diseased lungs, but the doctors thought her difficulty more nervous than pulmonary, and from the remedy your physician is using I imagine he has a somewhat similar opinion of her case. Though these nervous affections may be as distressing as others, they are not I believe apt to be so fatal, at least I will hope for a favorable result.

God grant that she may indeed be restored to you, for though we know that it is better for the children of God to be with Christ, released at once from suffering, temptation and sin, yet our hearts cling to them, and we feel that we cannot be so unselfish as to give them up without a struggle. Blessed be God that he does not condemn this natural feeling! That we are encouraged to pray for the recovery of

[316] This letter, and one of this same date to Emily Judson, was written in response to Adoniram Judson's letter of March 18, 1949, in which he told Anna Maria of Emily's illness and of his despair for her survival. Illness is a recurring issue for Emily, and it imposed years of severe limitations on her, which makes her accomplishments all the more stunning. See vol. 1, "A Timeline of Emily C. Judson as Chronic Invalid."

[317] This letter is undated. It is placed three months after Adoniram's letter because that was about the time it took for a letter to reach the United States, and we believe that Anna Maria would have replied immediately.

the sick, that we may feel that our Saviour [sic] even while he afflicts us, sympathizes with our griefs. But I feel assurance that God has heard our prayer for Emily and that she is now convalescent, and shall wait patiently for the next mail to hear.

I am very much obliged to you for writing so frankly to me; pray do so always and be assured of the most beautiful sympathy in your apprehensions, and the most fervent prayers that our Heavenly Father will have you both in his kind keeping from your affectionate friend

Anna M. Anable

Source: American Baptist Historical Society, AJ 6, no. 79.

Anna Maria Anable to Emily C. Judson,[318] June 25, 1849[319]

Dear Nemmy[320]

I cannot believe but that you will read this letter and that though you have been brought very near the grave, you can now perhaps begin to see why our Heavenly Father ordered it so. Has not the fear of death which used to distress you been taken away? Have you not had a clearer glimpse of the world beyond the grave than you ever had before? Tell me darling, for though we may never see each other again till we meet in that world, which I feel utterly unworthy to hope to enter, all that I can learn of your journey thither will be very precious to me.

We have been very anxious about our dear Mrs. Wade.[321] The attack I spoke of in my last proved to be inflammation of the lungs, and for some days we thought she had come here to die. She thought from the first of her illness and I never saw any one [sic] so happy in the prospect of death as she seemed to be. She is one of the loveliest Christians and sweetest women I ever knew. She talked a great deal about you, and was evidently reminded of you whenever I went into the room.

She is now nearly well again and may expect to leave next week. As for Mr. Wade, we found he did not like to talk much so we read to him and petted him up ( ) I believe we have made him like us[322]—at any rate he talks of adopting me and taking me back with him if Mrs. Wade will consent to take such a good for nothing into her school, and if

[318] This letter, and one of this same date to Emily Judson, was written in response to Adoniram Judson's letter of March 18, 1849, in which he told Anna Maria of Emily's severe illness and of his despair for her survival.

[319] This letter is undated. It is placed three months after Adoniram's letter because that was about the time it took for a letter to reach the United States, and we believe that Anna Maria would have replied immediately.

[320] "Nem" or "Nemmy" was a name of endearment given to Emily by a small group of her intimate friends at the Utica Female Academy. Anna Maria Anable was "Ninny."

[321] See vol. 1, "Cast of Characters," s.v. "Wade, Jonathan and Deborah."

[322] See the letter of Anna Maria Anable to Emily C. Judson dated May 25, 1849.

[Written along the right margin and across the lines of text:] I will promise not to run away to your house as soon as I get over there. Well! I shan't promise, so I don't think they'll take me. How I wish I could fold you to my heart and kiss you good night instead of writing it.

Anna M.

Source: American Baptist Historical Society, AJ 6, no. 79.

Mrs. Mary H. Brayton to Emily C. Judson, June 25, 1849[323]

One month has passed since I commenced this note. For the last eleven weeks I have been down with the fever and ague. I came to see a sister hoping that the change would be favorable. But it still hangs on and I am very much prostrated tho not disheartened to the fullest extent. There were some other items in your letter to which I wish to refer, but as it is not at hand I will defer till another opportunity. I am hoping to be on my way to India by the first of Oct.[324] How gladly would I sail next week or today even with all my weakness. I have been pleading with God to let me go back and labor for and with the heathen tho it may be thro suffering. It is best that I should be kept in the furnace. And O for a heart entirely submissive to the will of God a perfect willingness to suffer as well as to do his will. How I sigh ( ) to be surrounded by the dear sisters among the Karens. I want to see once more the sisters around you. I mean the Burman sisters. Tell Mah Doke I remember her request. They are often remembered in the female prayer meetings which I attend.

[Written along the left margin of page 1:] Fond regards to bro Judson and love for yourself and the children.

Yours aff'ly M. H. Brayton

Source: American Baptist Historical Society, AJ 12, no. 353.

[323] This letter is an addendum to a letter written May 20, 1849.

[324] Durlin and Mary Brayton left Burmah for the United States in February 1847. Mr. Brayton returned to Burmah in November 1847; Mrs. Brayton remained in the United States, leaving in October 1849 and arriving in Burmah in March 1850.

Adoniram "Addy" Judson to Emily and Adoniram Judson,[325] June 27, 1849[326]—Worcester

My dear father and mother,

Capt Hamlin came to see us yesterday and we went to the caravan with him, and I will tell you the animals that we saw there there was an adjutant two black bears one white bear one black tiger four or five lions three young lions a kangaroo two panthers two or three tigers a cage of monkeys and five or six leopards with several others [sic] animals.[327] The performance was as follows. First, a pony came out with a monkey on his back, and galloped round the ring as fast as he could then the monkey stood up on his feet with a flag in his hand and the pony galloped as before, then an elephant came out and took the man up on his trunk and laid him on his tusks then put his trunk round his neck and carried him around the ring, then the elephant took the man's whip and cracked it several times and did many other amusing tricks. Then all the folks went back to the seats and a man and woman went in the lions cages and played with them. The books which Capt Hamlin gave us two volumes of Macauly's [sic] *History of England*, *Guide to Social Happiness* by Mrs. Ellis, *Light and Shadows of Sailor Life*. *Life of Washington* with painted engravings, and *A Kiss for a Blow*. We have heard by news-papers that mother is sick, we hope she is not dangerously so. "We have had our Meeting-house fixed up lately and Isaus Davis has bought an organ.

Source: American Baptist Historical Society, AJ 10, no. 256.

[325] A letter from Dr. Calvin Newton of Worcester, Massachusetts, was added on page 2 of this letter. It appears under the date of June 30, 1849. Adoniram and Elnathan had been living with the Newtons since returning to the United States in 1845.

[326] This letter has an addendum dated June 30, 1849.

[327] The punctuation, or lack of, is exactly as in the letter.

Elnathan "Elly" Judson to Emily and Adoniram Judson,[328] June 27, 1849[329]—Worcester

My dear father and mother.

As it is a very long time since I wrote to you, I now employ the opportunity that is afforded me.

We expect to go and see Abby[330] our next vacation, Abby having invited us. We have lately been poisoined [sic] with dogwood but are not well. Next August our Sunday School is going to have a picnic down to Isac Davis's farm on Long Pond. Dear father if there in [sic] any chance of your ever seeing us will you please write to us about it. We will go to the high school, in a year and three-quarters, and will study Algebra in ten months. We now study History and like it very well. We get along very well at Sunday School, under a new teacher whose name is Mr. Dary, he is preparing for the ministry. I was weighed today and weighed 60 pounds, having gained 11 pounds since I came to this country. Capt. Hamlin came to see us yesterday, and bought us four dollars worth of books, thirty cents worth of confectionary, and two shillings worth of tracts. And we repaid him by paying his fare to Van Amburgh's Caravan which was in the city yesterday.[331] With abundance of thanks.

Source: American Baptist Historical Society, AJ 11, no. 457.

[328] This letter accompanied a letter written by Adoniram "Addy" Judson and two letters written by Dr. Calvin Newton.

[329] This letter has three addenda dated June 28, 29, and 30.

[330] Abby Ann Judson, the first daughter and oldest child of Adoniram and Sarah Hall Boardman Judson, was born September 26, 1835. She saw her mother die on the Isle of St. Helena as they returned to the United States from Burmah. Just before leaving for Burmah with Emily, Adoniram Judson placed Abby Ann at Bradford Academy for her education. The family of Ann Hasseltine Judson was generous to Abby Ann and supportive of her interests and her future. On October 15, 1851, Abby Ann started a course of study at the Misses Anable's School in Philadelphia, and in fall 1853, she moved to New York City to take a teaching position in the home of Mrs. Maria Brown, a former missionary to Siam. She enjoyed a warm relationship with Emily, and her letters show that the two could speak freely with each other.

[331] For a description of this activity, see the letter of Adoniram "Addy" Judson dated June 27, 1849.

Elnathan "Elly" Judson to Emily and Adoniram Judson,[332] June 28, 1849[333]

We expect George[334] every day and have been expecting him for a month. We have lately received a letter from Abby,[335] and answered it. Rev. Mr. Tracy came to see us yesterday. On fourth of July there is to be a match of round ball, to be played on the common, between the young men of Worcester, and the young men of Grafton. And we have high hopes for our players. Aunt Abby[336] has lately sent us some more presents, consisting of handkerchiefs, and some linen cloth for summer clothes. Dear father I know it is my duty to be a Christian, and to do all in my power to promote the Christian cause. Mr. Haswell[337] has arrived in this country, but we have not seen him yet. If it will not cost you any trouble, we would be glad to have you send over two or three pairs of the small green parrots, who exist in that country, by the next missionaries, who come to America, and we will pay the costs of their passage. As the parrots come to such an exorbitant price here we cannot procure any for pets. Mr. Washburn our superintendent sends his love to you.

Source: American Baptist Historical Society, AJ 11, no. 457.

Elnathan "Elly" Judson to Emily and Adoniram Judson,[338] June 29, 1849[339]

Fourth of July comes next week and we expect to have fine times. The city authorities, are having gas pipes laid in all the streets in the city, so as to have gas lights.

Henry Chapin's father is elected mayor of the city. Henry Chapin was our schoolfellow who died. This summer the thermometer has stood and 104, and today it is very rainy and also very cold.

Source: American Baptist Historical Society, AJ 11, no. 457.

[332] Accompanying this letter was one from Adoniram "Addy" Judson and two from Dr. Calvin Newton of Worcester, Massachusetts. Adoniram and Elnathan lived with Dr. and Mrs. Newton.

[333] This letter is the first addendum to a letter dated June 27, 1849. There are two additional addenda dated June 29 and 30, 1849.

[334] George Dana Boardman, the son of George Dana Boardman and Sarah Hall Boardman, was born August 18, 1828, in Tavoy, Burmah. George returned to the United States in 1844 at the age of six and lived with Dr. and Mrs. Calvin Newton in Worcester, Massachusetts. He attended Brown University in Providence, Rhode Island, graduating after taking a few years off for travel in the West. He attended the Newton Theological Institute, and in 1855, he married Miss Ella Covell. He served two churches before settling into the First Baptist Church of Philadelphia, where he served with distinction for thirty years. He formed a close relationship with Emily upon her return in 1851; when she gave him a copy of *An Olio of Domestic Verses*, she addressed it "Georgie—from Mamma."

[335] See vol. 1, "Cast of Characters," s.v. "Judson, Abby Ann."

[336] See vol. 1, "Cast of Characters," s.v. "Judson, Abigail Brown."

[337] James Haswell had sailed for Burmah in 1835, arriving in February 1836 to work with the Talaings. His wife was Jane Haswell. James Haswell became a partner with Adoniram and Sarah Judson, and when Adoniram and Elnathan were born, Sarah turned over the translation of the Peguan Scripture to him. He served as a missionary for more than forty years.

[338] Accompanying this letter was one from Adoniram "*Pwen*" Judson and two from Dr. Calvin Newton of Worcester, Massachusetts. Adoniram and Elnathan lived with Dr. and Mrs. Newton.

[339] This letter is the second addenda to a letter dated June 27, 1849. There are two additional addenda dated June 28 and 30, 1849.

Elnathan "Elly" Judson to Emily and Adoniram Judson,[340] June 30, 1849[341]

This is the last time I shall write, as Uncle Newton[342] is going to Boston today, and it would be best to send it by him, than to pay ten cents. Uncle Newton takes five newspapers now; their names are the *Christian Watchman, and Reflector*, *The New York Recorder*, *The Temperance Standard, or Cataract*, the *Christian Citizen*, and the *Maine Free Will Baptist Repository*. I here bid you farewell.

Your affectionate son.

Elnathan Judson

Source: American Baptist Historical Society, AJ 11, no. 457.

Adoniram "Addy" Judson to Emily and Adoniram Judson,[343] June 30, 1849[344]

Last Tuesday night there was a fire on Green street, a barn was burnt down it belonged to Mr. Dresser leather-dealer. Mr. Washburns our superintendent sends his respects to you. A few Sabbaths ago the proprietor of the painting of Adam and Eve invited our Sabbath School to visit the painting at Brinley Hall the pictures were fourteen feet by twelve. We began to read the bible [sic] through in a year, we read three week-days and five Sundays we now have got most through Psalms. The seventh day of last April I was twelve years old. Elnathan[345] will be eleven years old on the fifteenth of July. Uncle Newton[346] is going this morning to Boston and will carry the letters as far as Boston. We have not seen Mr. Bronson since he returned

[340] Accompanying this letter was a letter from Adoniram "Addy" Judson and two from Dr. Calvin Newton, of Worcester, Massachusetts. Adoniram and Elnathan lived with Dr. and Mrs. Newton.

[341] This letter is the third addendum to a letter dated June 27, 1849. There are two additional addenda dated June 28 and 29, 1849.

[342] Dr. Calvin Newton, after some theological training, went to medical school to become a physician. He apparently had differing ideas about medicine, and he became a part of what was known as the Eclectic School of Medicine; with that background, he established the Worcester Medical Institute. In 1835, Dr. and Mrs. Newton received into their home the young George Dana Boardman, just returned from Burmah for his education. Adoniram and Elnathan went there in fall 1845 when they returned to the United States with their father, and they remained there under the Newton's care until Emily's return in October 1851. At that time, Mrs. Newton had become ill, and the boys went to live with Dr. and Mrs. Edward Bright.

[343] A letter from Dr. Calvin Newton of Worcester, Massachusetts, was added on page 2 of this letter. It appears under the date June 30, 1849. Adoniram and Elnathan had been living with the Newtons since returning to the United States in 1845.

[344] This letter is an addendum to a letter written June 27, 1849.

[345] Elnathan "Elly" Judson was born July 15, 1838, the third child and second son of Adoniram and Sarah Hall Boardman Judson. From November 1845 to October 1851, he lived with Dr. and Mrs. Calvin Newton in Worcester, Massachusetts. He then spent a year with Dr. and Mrs. Edward Bright in Roxbury, Massachusetts, and before entering Brown University, he spent two years at Pierce Academy in Middleboro, Massachusetts. There are strong indications that Elnathan planned to become a minister, and in fact, he did graduate from Union Seminary. In 1860, however, he suffered a serious sunstroke that subsequently caused serious mental impairment. For much of his life, Elnathan was confined to mental institutions. He died after a second paralyzing stroke in 1896; in the last years of his life, Elnathan was lovingly cared for by his sister Abby Ann Judson.

[346] See vol. 1, "Cast of Characters," s.v. "Newton, Doctor Calvin and Mrs. M. I."

[347] See vol. 1, "Cast of Characters," s.v. "Bright, The Reverend Doctor Edward, Jr."

but he is coming here next Wednesday with Mr. Bright[347] from Boston sometime. Last May was our day school Anniversary we marched up to the City Hall and had an address delivered to us. The second Tuesday in June was our S. S. Anniversary our Sabbath School sat in the singer's seats and sang instead of the Choir.

Your affectionate son

Adoniram B. Judson.

Source: American Baptist Historical Society, AJ 10, no. 256.

Dr. Calvin Newton to Adoniram Judson,[348] June 30, 1849—Worcester

Dr. Judson.

My dear brother, I feel ashamed that I do not write you oftener; but, really, my time is all engrossed, and I sometimes get almost worn out. I like medical practice well. Still, I hope and expect the time will come, when I shall not have to depend entirely on my practice for a living, and when I can occasionally, at least, have a respite.

The boys remain kind children; but they are full of play, and sometimes require correction. Religion, in all this region, is quite low; and the children do not feel the interest on this subject which we desire to see in them. They were not, however, without serious reflections, which we hope may be deepened and nurtured into genuine conversion.

Small pox [sic] is now quite extensive in this city, but not generally severe. One or two deaths have occurred. The cholera is not prevailing in several cities of this country, as New Orleans, St. Louis, Cincinnati, somewhat in New York, etc. We may have a *touch* of it here; but I do not expect much, in general. The health of this city (aside from small pox [sic]) is good.

We have not heard *directly* from George,[349] at the west, for some time. By the last letter received from him, he spoke of returning east soon, and we have been looking for him for some time. I have written to make inquiries of Mr. Allen (under whose patronage he went west), in regard to him, and under what circumstances he remains at the west. With a failure in his health before he left college, there seemed *to me* to be a disturbance of his mental powers, and I am feeling seriously concerned in regard to him. I shall to-day, at Boston, make further inquiries in

[348] This is the first part of Dr. Newton's letter; the second part on a separate sheet is dated July 1, 1849. Also accompanying this were letters from Adoniram and Elnathan Judson.

[349] See vol. 1, "Cast of Characters," s.v. "Boardman, George Dana."

regard to him. I felt pained at his leaving college as he did; but he said Dr. Wayland[350] and Dr. Caswell both recommended it; and Mr. Allen, (who had been so good to him) advised his accompanying him to, the west, and engaging in his service there for a time, for his health's sake. I shall probably write you again soon, in regard to him;—that is, as soon as I can get any important information. I shall find out whether Mr. A. has left him, at the west, to take care of himself, or whether he is there in the service of Mr. A. Till recently, I had supposed the latter, and that all was well. *Of late*, I have had suspicions raised, that all is not right in regard to his relation to Mr. A. George, in his letters, has not intimated any such thing; but it has been intimated from another quarter, George's mind and temperament are as peculiar, that, by the existence of unfavorable circumstances, he might be ( ) into a state of insanity. For his sake, for your sake, and the sake of his friends, I shall reach into the past; and if it be found desirable, try to get him home.

Adoniram[351] and Elnathan[352] are well. E. has some ( ) ( ), and A. is more inclined to disease of the chest; but the *doctor*, you know, is always *at hand*. The boys received a letter from yourself a few days since. (See the other sheet. C. N.)[353]

Source: American Baptist Historical Society, AJ 11, no. 457.

[350] Dr. Francis Wayland was the president of Brown University in Providence, Rhode Island. A prominent Baptist leader and active in denominational activities, he was a proponent of missions. In 1851, upon Emily's return from Burmah, Dr. Wayland was asked to write the definitive memoir of Adoniram Judson. Beginning in December that year, Emily moved to Providence to work with him on the project; she was there until June and then returned frequently over the next year before it was finally published in September 1853. A warm friendship developed between Dr. Wayland and Emily.

[351] Adoniram "Addy" Judson was born April 7, 1837, the second child and first son of Adoniram and Sarah Hall Boardman Judson. From November 1845 to October 1851, he lived with Dr. and Mrs. Calvin Newton in Worcester, Massachusetts. He then spent a year with Dr. and Mrs. Edward Bright in Roxbury, Massachusetts, and before entering Brown University, he was two years at Pierce Academy in Middleboro, Massachusetts. After his education and medical school, Adoniram served as a surgeon in the Civil War and became a prominent orthopedic surgeon with several books to his credit. He died in 1916. Over the years, he became vocal about the separation of missionary children from their parents.

[352] See vol. 1, "Cast of Characters," s.v. "Judson, Elnathan 'Elly.'"

[353] The "other sheet" is a reference to the letter dated July 1, 1849.

Letters

July–December 1849

Dr. Calvin Newton to Adoniram Judson,[1] July 1, 1849

(From the other sheet.)[2]

I was called away from writing yesterday morning, and kept engaged, till the time of the cars starting, and I forgot my letter, till I was two or three miles on my way. I saw Dea. Eddy,[3] Mr. Bright,[4] etc. None of them have heard from George,[5] of late. I shall expect to hear from Jamaica Plain in a day or two; and then, if necessary, I shall write to friends in the west. I hope you will not give yourself undue uncariness [sic], till you hear again from me. There may, after all, be nothing, in the case essentially wrong; but I have my fears, and I thought that, in writing you, I ought to express them. Be assured I shall not fail to do what I can to have George ( ) for, and well situated *somehow*, if possible.

We hear by the papers that Mrs. J. is very unwell,[6] and that you have apprehensions in regard to her recovery. Is it so? Your letters to the children give no intimation of it, though of the same date, I believe, of the letter referred to in the papers.

How does the mission prosper? Of what do your labors mostly consist, at present? How is your health? etc. etc. Mr. ( ) is expected here tomorrow. We, of course, will be happy to see him. His trunks arrived yesterday; and even their presence affords some satisfaction. We feel an interest in the cause of missions, and of the cause of Christ generally, even if we are as so situated as to do but little personally to forward the work of God. Mrs. N's health is now about as good as usual. She has been for a few weeks, a good deal unwell, owing to *coal*, labor, etc.

[1] Accompanying this letter were letters from Adoniram and Elnathan Judson; Elnathan and Adoniram were living with Dr. and Mrs. Newton in Worcester, Massachusetts.

[2] The "other sheet" is a letter dated June 30, 1849, a two-page letter in which Dr. Newton had started his thoughts

[3] Richard E. Eddy was the treasurer of the American Baptist Missionary Union.

[4] Upon her return to America in 1851, Emily Judson was to have a very close relationship with Dr. Edward Bright, the corresponding secretary of the American Baptist Missionary Union. They had known one another previously in New York, as he worked at the time of Adoniram and Emily's marriage with the *Baptist Register*, a prominent regional newsletter. Prior to working as a publisher, he had been, in 1838, the founding pastor of the Bleecker Street Baptist Church in Utica, a church with close ties to the Utica Female Academy. He was appointed corresponding secretary of the Missionary Union the end of May 1846, just prior to Adoniram and Emily's leaving Boston for Burmah. In this role he regularly pleaded with Emily for articles to be published in the missionary magazine, the *Macedonian*. Upon Emily's return from Burmah in October 1851, Adoniram and Elnathan went to live with Dr. and Mrs. Bright for a year. Dr. Bright was to help Emily with many of her business affairs; he carried on the publishing details of the Judson Memoir because of a serious illness in Dr. Wayland's family. He, with Dr. Edward Granger, was to be the executor of the estate of Emily Chubbuck Judson, a responsibility he still carried in March 1869, as reflected in a letter to Anna Maria Anable regarding financial arrangements for Emily Frances Judson.

[5] See Calvin Newton's letter of June 30, 1849, concerning problems with George. George Dana Boardman, the son of George Dana Boardman and Sarah Hall Boardman, was born August 18, 1828, in Tavoy, Burmah. George returned to the United States in 1844 at the age of six and lived with Dr. and Mrs. Calvin Newton in Worcester, Massachusetts. He attended Brown University in Providence, Rhode Island, graduating after taking a few years off for travel in the West. He attended the Newton Theological Institute, and in 1855, he married Miss Ella Covell. He served two churches before settling into the First Baptist Church of Philadelphia, where he served with distinction for thirty years. He formed a close relationship with Emily upon her return in 1851; when she gave him a copy of *An Olio of Domestic Verses*, she addressed it "Georgie—from Mamma."

[6] On March 18, 1849, Adoniram Judson wrote to Anna Maria Anable to tell her that Emily was extremely ill and that he feared for her life. In her own diary, Emily wrote that she felt for many weeks that she was looking into the grave. In the letter of March 18, 1849, Adoniram wrote next to the salutation that Emily was better and that she should read the end of the letter first.

We have, at length, obtained a charter for our Medical Institution; and our term, now recently closed, was a very interesting one. We had a first-rate class of 29 students. We hope to have 50 or more next year. I send you a catalogue, which I suppose you will be interested to see.[7]

Mrs. N. joins with me in expressions of the dearest regard for yourself, Mrs. J. and all concerned.

Affectionately I am yours,

Calvin Newton

Source: American Baptist Historical Society, AJ 10, no. 256.

Doctor Edward Bright, Jr. to Emily C. Judson, July 4, 1849—Baptist Mission Rooms, Boston

My dear friend:—

We have heard with deep sorrow of your illness, but we have reason to hope that you have recovered from it. May God spare your precious life for many years!

Our board have [sic] determined to make the *Macedonian*[8] as large as the *American Messenger* or nearly so, and to make it the home agent in our missionary work. Will you allow me to depend on you for a series of short articles for its pages? We intend to give it a circulation of at least 50,000, and our aim will be to make it a powerful auxiliary to the enterprise of Christian Missions. The paper will be enlarged, in December next,—by which time an article from yourself would be received as a Special favor. You need not fear that your communications will come too often.

With the kindest regards to Dr. J. and a kiss for your "little bird"[9] I remain in great haste,

Yours most truly,

Edw. Bright Jr.

Source: American Baptist Historical Society, AJ 14, no. 552.

[7] Calvin Newton came to the medical profession by way of theological education, so he had one foot in the theological field and one foot in the medical field. He practiced a "different" kind of medicine that went against accepted practices and started a medical school in Worcester to train doctors in his beliefs and practices. This school as of this letter is just finishing its first year.

[8] *The Macedonian* was a magazine published by the American Baptist Missionary Union. Emily was often asked to write articles for it.

Emily C. Judson to Catharine Chubbuck, July 18, 1849[10]

—"The goodman" works like a galley slave; and really it quite distresses me sometimes, but he seems to get fat on it, so I try not to worry. He walks—or rather runs—like a boy over the hills, a mile or two every morning; then down to his books, scratch-scratch, puzzle-puzzle, and when he gets deep in the mire, out on the veranda with your humble servant by his side, walking and talking (kan-ing we call it in the Burman) till the point is elucidated, and then down again—and so on till ten o'clock in the evening. It is this *walking* which is keeping him out of the grave.

For myself, I am very well, indeed, though not so strong as before my late attack. We sometimes think that I have received a blow from which I shall never fully recover, though the only thing which makes us think so is continued sore throat and weakness at the chest. The doctor assures us that I am in no more danger from consumption than any other person of equal delicacy of constitution; but physicians are not in general over endowed with frankness.

We are having some encouraging tokens in the Church. Three have been lately baptized; one a trader from Burmah proper, who yesterday returned, in company with a friend, to his home on the Irrawaddy. The friend also is, in all probability, converted, though he can not [sic] bring himself to be baptized. This may be the commencement of a Church (who knows) away up the river. The man appears well.

I should like nothing better than to write such letters as father[11] wishes, about manners, customs, habits, etc., but you can have no conception of the busy life I lead. I am taking a very thorough course in the language, which the natives flatter me by saying I speak elegantly. The other day I turned the "Mother's Litany,"[12] in the memoir, into Burmese, to be sung at my maternal meetings; so you see I have made a beginning in poetry. I do not speak as readily as I write, however.

Lovingly, your sister,

Nemmy[13] C. J.

Source: A. C. Kendrick, *Life and Letters of Mrs. Emily C. Judson*, 307–308.

[9] On January 1, 1848, eight days after the birth of Emily Frances Judson, Emily wrote a celebratory poem that she called "My Bird." The poem has a total of seven stanzas, and it was widely published in the United States.

[10] This letter was edited by A. C. Kendrick for publication in *The Life and Letters of Mrs. Emily C. Judson* (New York: Sheldon and Company, 1831).

[11] Emily's father, Charles Chubbuck, was born at Bedford, New Hampshire, on March 3, 1780; he was married to Lavinia Richards in Goffstown, New Hampshire, on November 17, 1805. They were to have seven children. Though he held varying jobs over the years, he failed at many of them, and Emily was the main support of the family after she purchased a home for her family in fall 1842.

[12] This was a poem written by Sarah Hall Boardman Judson; it was later published in the *Mother's Journal* and in Fanny Forester's *Memoir of Sarah B. Judson, Member of the American Mission to Burmah* (New York: L. Colby and Company, 1848) 214–15. The first stanza appears here: "Lamb of God, enthroned on high, / Look on us with pitying eye, / While we raise our earnest cry, / For our babes, to thee."

[13] "Nem" or "Nemmy" was a name of endearment given to Emily by a small group of her intimate friends at the Utica Female Academy. Anna Maria Anable was "Ninny."

Emily C. Judson to the Reverend Doctor Solomon Peck,[14] July 18, 1849 —Maulmain

My dear Mr. Peck,[15]

I thank you most heartily for your kind way of writing to me, and respect the Christian principle by which I believe you to be activated; but, allow me to suggest that you would sustain the part of mentor to more practical affect, if you knew me better. Truly, whatever you may think, or however good you may believe your reasons are for so thinking, I do not need to be cautioned to tell the truth, in the circumstances under which you propose honoring me with a place in your Magazine.[16] Though, as in the case of the late Memoir,[17] I sometimes embellish my *style*, I never have been guilty of embellishing *facts*, except when I have presented them in the guise of fiction. In the work alluded to (that which a more truthful narrative was never made) I had my reasons, and I believe them good and sound ones, for departing from the beaten track of compilers; but if you will take the trouble to compare my statements with those of other writers, you will find mine always moderate, and where exactness is exquisite, exact.

[Written along the side of page 1 to be inserted here:] **To one who like yourself, has read the pages of inspiration with the eye both of a scholar and a Christian, a popular, practical style, where the subject will admit of it, needs no vindication.**

Moralists have defined falsehood to be anything said or done with an intention to deceive. You do not accuse me of *intending* to deceive; but you hint that I am the victim of some mental obliquity, which makes me see [Note: Here Emily has crossed out "everything in a distorted light."] **things in a different light from sober and prosaic (that is common sense) people—a weakness that has the effect of falsehood though not its moral turpitude. Now, I deny all this, and insist that**

[14] Emily and Solomon Peck had never really hit it off. Peck saw Fanny Forester as a secular writer, and some of his stern, moralistic views in this regard can be seen in his April 30, 1846, letter, as he advocates for her, with a quote from the Bible, a new direction: "Forgetting the things that are behind and reaching forth to the things that are before." On May 8, 1846, in a letter to Anna Maria Anable, Emily reports that Dr. Peck deemed *Allen Lucas* to be an "evil book" and under no circumstances to be reprinted by the denomination. In a February 20, 1849, letter from Dr. Peck asking Emily to write an article for the newsletter on their proposed trip to Ava, the conditions he imposes turn out to be the proverbial straw that broke the camel's back as far as Emily was concerned. He asked her to write in a factual style instead of her more interpretative style. This brought to the surface all of the anger and frustrations about what she experienced as his perceptions of her past, which had been to date buried and unexpressed. In an April 1850 letter, Emily says of this letter, "I will only say that my motive in writing to you as I did was simply to comply with the wishes of my husband, who thought something of the kind was due both to you and myself."

[15] Because of what might be political implications, A. C. Kendrick in his book, *The Life and Letters of Mrs. Emily C. Judson*, has sanitized this letter in a number of ways. He does not identify the fact that it is written to Dr. Solomon Peck, the executive secretary of the American Baptist Missionary Union; instead, he merely says it was written to a "friend." Then, he has edited it rather severely, taking out the passion, the anger, and the righteous indignation. In this letter as presented, the text in normal type appeared in the biography, and the text in bold was omitted by Dr. Kendrick. Additions made by Dr. Kendrick are in parentheses.

[16] Dr. Peck expected Adoniram and Emily to travel to Ava because the Board of the Union had released funds for that long-awaited mission. He asked Emily to write descriptions of the land, country, and culture to be printed in the magazine of the American Baptist Missionary Union.

[17] Fanny Forester, *Memoir of Sarah B. Judson, Member of the American Mission to Burmah* (New York: L. Colby and Company, 1848).

where others see only a rock, I see precisely the same object and nothing more. If I were to attempt a description, it would be my aim, [Note: Here Emily has crossed out "were I called on to describe the rock."] **to transfer the picture from my eye to yours, a task which I could accomplish far better, and with greater facility, by copying the original *exactly*, than by attempting to improve upon it.** You need never fear [Note: Here in the letter the next eight lines are scratched out—these crossed out lines read: "**to avoid confounding it with a tree or hillock, as I might do by giving its bulk and magnitude merely ( ) the ( ) observer perhaps by the use of some learned name, which but a few of my readers would know from any other learned name, and also to transfer the picture from my eye to theirs, by speaking of its ( ).**"] [Note: These lines were written above the eight crossed out lines.] **therefore** that I shall turn a pile of slate stone into granite, but you may be sure, if I ever do delineate a rock for you, that, so far as my power of using language enables me to express myself intelligibly, you will have it as you would see it yourself—not its bulk, magnitude and learned name merely, but everything about it—its stains, seams and fractures, the trailing plant, the pendent lichens, the patches of moss and the spots of sunshine [Note: Here more lines are crossed out. They read, "**On its side. So because I write like a woman rather than a geologist, ( ) a pencil dipped in the colors of nature, instead of geometrical instruments, my work would be regarded with suspicion, I suppose.**"] [Note: These lines were written above the crossed out lines.] playing over its surface. Allow me also to add that however free the use I make of nature's pencil, it does not necessarily follow that my touches lack mathematical precision, but I maintain on the contrary that flowers and herbage, so far from marring the correctness of the naked diagram, are necessary to its completeness.

You would have a tiresome task indeed if you were to set about finding Alderbrook at Hamilton—and why should you expect to find it there? You seem to forget that the Alderbrook tales, being professed fiction, cannot be tried by the same rules as history; nor can they be classed under any of the definitions of falsehood, for they are not only destitute of the *intention* to deceive, but they are actually destitute of the *power*. However, I will acknowledge that I did not make the draft on my inventive powers which was my right. My localities are in the main correct, though as I was under no obligation to be precise, they are sometimes altered and embellished to suit the occasion. My characters and incidents are mostly of the same order, having only a veil thrown about them to prevent their being recognized. About five miles north of Hamilton is the little farm on which I was born, with a trout-stream, bordered by spotted alders running through it, and the very odd looking house ("Underhill Cottage") built by my grandfather, stuck in the side of the hill. **It still belongs to the family and is occupied by an antiquated uncle and a couple of**

maiden aunts. It was one of the last places that I visited before taking a final farewell of my native State; and Mr. J. accompanied me across the creek and up "Strawberry Hill," to gain a better view [sic] of scenery on which twenty years had brought so little change. About three miles north of this, is the village where I was bred, and which, next to the old farm, shared in my memories of that past. I took the liberty in my little sketches, to unite my two early homes; and the brook with its alders, supplied me with a name.

The innocence, or the usefulness of fiction, in at least one of its forms, does not lie open to discussion, for the question has been decided by the Saviour himself. But how far this mode of teaching should be used, at what point it becomes reprehensible, and when it degenerates into a vice, has puzzled too many wise heads, to allow of my venturing an opinion. Justice to myself, however, impels me to say, that although I have indulged somewhat extensively in poetry, novel-reading has never been one of my sins. When I was a child I waded through the voluminous histories of Josephus and Rollin; and afterwards, I took up the principal English prose-writers in course, beginning with the author of Utopia, and ending with Edmund Burke, whom I had not finished when I left America. Pray don't think that I say this boastingly—it is no credit to have read able [sic] authors, unless mental discipline and knowledge combine to produce good results—but in an attempt to meet accusations so grave and at the same time so intangible as yours, a simple statement of seemingly irrelevant facts may be necessary. I seldom more than looked into the light magazines, to which for about eighteen months I contributed,[18] though I must own that my avoidance of them was less to be attributed to principle than taste. Those who have not confined their attention to books or to a select circle of good and intelligent persons, but have had a practical education in the world of men and women, will pay some regard to the wants of weak intellects, and I will venture to assert that where one person is injured by insipid moral tales a hundred persons are benefited. **You may think differently, however, and I will not oppose my opinions to yours. It is not very likely that either of us will have much to do with fashionable magazines, hereafter.**

I suppose some impractical thinkers, (some superficial thinkers), disapproving of the popular magazine literature, unconsciously transfer their opinion of the works to individual contributors; **but I should not think you liable to a mistake of that kind**. If I have written immoral things, let me suffer as I deserve; if not, do not let the odium of such writers as some magazine editors tolerate, rest on me. But even my own productions, though I am answerable for all that is bad in them, furnish no criterion by which to judge by private character. In truth, no two persons could differ

[18] Emily wrote for the *Columbian* magazine, the *New Mirror*, *Knickerbocker*, and *Graham's Magazine*. There was a piece in the *Columbian* as early as March 1844; some material was appearing in 1846, but it was likely written before she met Adoniram Judson, for after that she had little time for writing.

more widely on most points than the fictitious Fanny Forester[19] and the real author of the Sketches. And in this particular, I do not stand alone. Who would believe that the *venerable* author of Proverbial Philosophy was a young and handsome dandy? Or that the poet Young, who was perpetually inveighing against worldly vanities, at the same time crouched to the very dust before the great, in order to gain church preferment, and actually went to his grave crushed beneath a load of mortified ambition? It is well known that Thompson was, to say the least, indifferent to the three things on which he seemed most to dote in his poetry; and Lockhart asserts that L.E.L. who has excited so much sympathy on account of the doleful style of his writings, was an uncommonly light-hearted person. In my own experience as a teacher, I have observed that the gayest of my pupils, usually write religion compositions, while the sober ones frequently chose light topics; as though the effort of expressing the thoughts, threw the mind out of its usual track. One young lady in particular, singularly quiet and demure, and of unquestionable piety, always convulsed the school with laughter. I am not advocating these incongruities, nor will I attempt to explain them; I only mention them as exhibiting a phase of human nature, of which especially in forming an opinion of me through a work professedly fictitious, I ought to have the benefit.

The truth is, my dear Mr. Peck (and you will pardon the assertion, since, under existing circumstances, it is not a very heavy charge) it is yourself that *sees double*, instead of me. Some time ago, certain idle editors, who had nothing else to fill their columns with, took a fancy to write *pretty paragraphs*, about one Fanny Forester, whom they had never seen, and of *whom they knew* positively nothing. Strange to say, the Secretary of the Board seized upon their refracting telescope, and in spite of the united testimony of troops of good people, in spite of ( ) and common sense, in spite of his own eyes even, is actually regarding the poor little missionary through it still. So now, if I conduct myself tolerably well, I am *reforming*, to be sure; and in order to make me a party to the delusion, it is added that the charge is "possibly unnoticed" by myself. I should be sorry not to have improved under the advantages which I have enjoyed for three years past—it would disgrace both my head and my heart—but your allusion evidently points to something beyond this mere matter-of-course advancement. When we first met at Utica, for what did you take me, pray? For a humble school-teacher, shrinking from the public platform to which circumstances had dragged her, or for some gay dancing girl, who cared only to be seen and talked about? Ask those who knew me personally (not those who stood looking on from a distance and *guessed*) if ever I sought society, or if I

[19] Emily Chubbuck wrote under the *nom de plume* Fanny Forester. Asked about it once, she said, "Would anyone buy a book written by Emily E. Chubbuck?"

was not rather proverbial throughout my own circle for avoiding it; ask them if I ever practiced airs and graces for the purpose of winning admiration or if, on the contrary, it was not my aim on all occasions, to conduct myself like a sober common-sense woman. Well might I be sober, for I have had a sober part to act in life; and if I am cheerful now, it is quite as much because I have sounded the depths of human troubles, and know just how much they are to be dreaded, as from natural temperament. After I was sixteen, at which age I was baptized, I never danced in any company, and never attended a theatrical exhibition, unless I should except the opera. I once only attended an Italian opera, [Note: Crossed out here is "in company with a pious friend."][20] but came away [Note: Crossed out here is "before the ballet."] as soon as the music was over, and I never had a wish to go again. It is true that I was sometimes very worldly, that my thoughts and conversation were sadly wanting, and I made spiritually but small advancement in the divine life; but I never went so far as to forget what was due to my Christian profession.

I have written a long letter; and you will have no doubt that I value your esteem, since in order to gain it, I have ventured to impose so far on your patience and good-nature; and have also incurred the danger of finding egotism added to the list of my delinquencies. In conclusion, I can only ask that you will throw aside all illusions, and regard me only as a poor, sinful fellow-travellor [sic] to eternity, with no hope save in the blood of Christ, and no wish, but to devote my few remaining days, small as the offering is, to his service. That I may do this in the wisest and most judicious manner; and that, when I go to the grave, I may leave an influence behind me, better than gold or silver—better even than a good name—allow me to beg an interest in your prayers, and counsels.

Believe me, my dear Mr. Peck,
Ever yours most sincerely and cordially

Emily C. Judson.

P.S. Please accept a copy of the Memoir, which the publisher has been requested to forward to you in my name. I venture to present you with this edition, because some of the Notes, which have been prepared with no small degree of labour [sic], may be of sufficient weight to make the book worthy of your acceptance.

Source: American Baptist Historical Society, AJ 12, no. 382; A. C. Kendrick, *Life and Letters of Mrs. Emily C. Judson*, 308–311.

[20] Emily attended the opera in May 1845 when she stopped in New York City on her way home from Philadelphia to Utica. On that occasion, she accompanied N. P. Willis.

Emily C. Judson to Mr. Alexander Beebee, July 20, 1849—Maulmain

My dear Mr. Beebee,

It is certainly an odd thing for me to apply to you to solve a riddle for one; but my curiosity, (to say nothing of bitter feelings) is so completely roused, that my pen will not keep still any longer. Soon after my arrival here, two and a half years ago, it was vaguely hinted by one of my Utica correspondents, that I had had the misfortune to displease you; but as the writer seemed to take it for granted that I understood all about it, she said nothing intelligible. Another letter came soon after, containing an obscure allusion to "remarks" which it was understood I had made, though I rec'd no information concerning their nature; and finally Miss Sheldon[21] astounded me by writing that, "notwithstanding what had passed," you were still my friend. She added something about the "message" which I sent you, and said she hoped she had explained the matter to your satisfaction. I wished most heartily that she had explained it to me also; and as you will readily believe, did not feel particularly pleased with her having assumed me guilty of some nameless fault, and actually stood in my place to explain or apologize. By the last mail, the mystery, though in no wise lessened, has assumed a more definite form, and I can no longer resist the temptation I feel to ask you what all this does mean. In a letter written by Mr. M. M. Jones,[22] there is an allusion to a "crusty, womanish note," that I sent you on some occasion or other; but beyond this I am left as much in the dark as ever. I do not understand one word of the whole affair—"remarks," "message," "note," or anything else.

Perhaps you are not aware of my position in [name of a place].[23] I was continually toiling, while there—so much so, that I was obliged to keep aloof from all society—denying myself the luxury of morning calls, evening tea-drinkings, and everything of the sort. It was said by some that I was proud, I could go to *other* places, etc. etc. (I *did not* go to "other places," though). Then if I am not positively bashful, I am so near to it, that I did not venture to take that stand among my seniors, which I might perhaps have done—and so again I was *proud*. Lastly came a business transaction, in which I had the misfortune to offend those who would not be conciliated even by the money they so loved; and so a little clique was formed—consisting I

[21] Miss Cynthia Sheldon was in charge of the administrative and financial departments of the Utica Female Academy. Miss Sheldon and her sister Urania, who was literary principal, gave Emily Chubbuck a place at the academy in October 1840. They had deferred any cost to a future time when Emily could afford to reimburse them. Upon Miss Urania Sheldon's marriage in late summer 1842 to the Reverend Doctor Eliphalet Nott, the president of Union College, and her subsequent move to Schenectady, Miss Cynthia Sheldon assumed a larger leadership role at the academy. In the years that followed, Miss Sheldon and Emily developed an even stronger relationship. In 1848, Miss Sheldon moved to Philadelphia to help Miss Anable with the startup of the Misses Anable's School and to assume responsibilities in its operation. Active and well-known in Baptist circles, Miss Cynthia was one of Emily's most important mentors, advisors, and friends until the time of Emily's death in 1854. Miss Sheldon was the aunt of Anna Maria Anable.

[22] See the letter from Morven M. Jones to Emily C. Judson dated December 22, 1848.

[23] With only a Hanna family transcription of this letter, we presume they could not read the name of the place and inserted [name of place] instead.

believe mostly of a single family. Well, a good man whom I love, instigated by—I know not what, and thinking perhaps he was "doing God service," made himself mischievously busy in my affairs as though he had been activated by the bitterest malice. This person was continually laboring to make me distrustful of certain other persons, by hinting that they fashioned their friendship to the company that they chanced to be in; but when the oldest and best friend perhaps that I had on earth was included, and even my intended husband came in for a share in the misrepresentation, I regarded the whole with incredulity. Being thus needlessly annoyed and harassed at a time when I most longed for quiet; I no doubt said many things, which under other circumstances, would not have been spoken; but of one thing I am positive, that I never made a remark concerning you which might not have fallen with perfect propriety from the lips of your own daughter. Furthermore, I never sent you a message of any kind, good or ill; and never (except perhaps in former years when I contributed to the *Register*) penned a note to you in my life. I beg—and I almost venture to *believe*, that you will credit this assertion, however strong you may think your evidence to the contrary; for indeed, the grossness of the charge considering the unprovoked ingratitude which it involves carries, on its face, the marks of falsehood. Please also have the kindness to drop me an explanatory line; and if you have a note in your possession bearing my signature, enclose it, that I may examine the hand-writing.

I have just learned, by a letter from Mrs. Nott,[24] of your second sad loss. The hand of death has been very busy in my circle of acquaintances, since I left America; but nowhere it seems to me, has it fallen so heavily, as on your beloved family. I never knew Mrs. Colgate[25] very intimately, till the time of my delightful visit at her house in the autumn of '45; but Elizabeth[26] was one of the dearest of my pupils. Both of them so young, so intelligent, accomplished, beautiful and good—how strange that they should be singled out to die! But it is *our* father and *theirs*, who had taken them in love; and I doubt not you can with reference to it all say, "Blessed be the name of the Lord."

[24] Urania Sheldon had been the literary principal of the Utica Female Academy in fall 1840 when Emily Chubbuck came to study there. Emily was able to afford this wonderful education through the generous offer of Miss Sheldon and her sister Cynthia, the executive and financial head of the academy, to defer tuition. Urania Sheldon left in late summer 1842 upon her marriage to the Reverend Doctor Eliphalet Nott, the president of Union College in Schenectady, New York. Because of the distance separating them, Emily's relationship with Urania Sheldon Nott did not develop the intimacy that grew between Emily and Miss Cynthia Sheldon. Urania Sheldon Nott remained a mentor, advisor, and friend to Emily in the years of her writing, her missionary endeavors, and upon her return to America in 1851. She was also the aunt of Anna Maria Anable.

[25] Ellen Colgate was the wife of James Colgate and the daughter-in-law of William Colgate of soap manufacturing fame. Ellen Colgate died in fall 1847. Her sister Elizabeth Hoyt died two years later of the same disease that took her sister.

[26] Elizabeth Hoyt was a student at the Utica Female Seminary; according to a July 20, 1849, letter from Emily, Elizabeth was one of her most "delightful" scholars. Anna Maria Anable wrote on March 17, 1849, of the death of Elizabeth Hoyt, saying that she had died of the same disease as her sister Mrs. Ellen Colgate. There is also evidence to connect both of these girls with Alexander Beebee of the *Baptist Register*; Emily writes to him of his terrible loss.

You will receive by Mr. Haswell,[27] a package addressed to Elizabeth, containing a little memento, in the shape of my first Burman book. Please retain it, as a memorial both of your daughter and her friend. I also requested Mr. Colby[28] to send you in my name a copy of an enlarged edition of the Memoir,[29] which I suppose will be published before you receive this letter. I trust you will find the notes which are intended to give a faithful transcript of some few things as they are in Burmah, worthy of perusal.

The operations of the mission are creeping on as usual. All sorts of means are tried—and sometimes one succeeds, and sometimes another, but I believe no one gets discouraged—and why should they? It is a glorious employment, I can assure you; and though it has pleased God to throw upon those now in the field the drudgery of preparation, the day will come when "both sower and reaper shall rejoice together." I am thinking too that a great reaping time is not far distant; for it is not likely that heathen intolerance will long survive that of the Papacy; and the downfall of the latter will probably be the signal for the unloosing of the shackles imposed by the other.

I wonder if you have seen the shocking libel on my poor old father and mother, copied into the Jan'y number of the *Mother's Journal.* Is it not strange that quiet, inoffensive people, who have striven through life to do their duty, both to God and man, and to train up their children in the same ways, must be dropped from their seclusion in their old age, and made such disgraceful puppets of. I had fully resolved never to take notice of any mistaken opinions that people might adopt and propagate with regard to my proceedings and motives; but this praising me at the expense of those I love and venerate is a new feature in the case; and I hope no one will think the few remarks, that I have felt myself under obligation to send to the *Journal* in reply, uncalled for or presuming.

Please give my love to all those who may remember me kindly, and especially to your daughter Clarinda, who I trust has not forgotten the visit we had together in N.Y. Mr. J. sends affectionate regards; and Believe *me*, my dear Mr. Beebee,

Ever yours most sincerely and gratefully,

Emily Judson.

Source: Hanna family files.

[27] James Madison Haswell was born February 4, 1810, in Bennington, Vermont. He was married to Jane Matilda Mason of Cheshire, Massachusetts. The Haswells sailed for Burmah on September 23, 1835, to work with the Talaings, arriving at Amherst in February 1836. When Sarah and Adoniram sailed for America in 1845, it was the Haswells who took care of Henry until Adoniram returned in 1847 with Emily. The Haswells left Burmah in December 1848, arriving in America in 1849; they were to remain in the United States until September 1852, when they again sailed for Burmah. There are five letters in the collection from Mrs. Haswell, beginning with April 19, 1850, and ending in March 1852. A relationship of familiarity and service between the two women is obvious in her letters to Emily—she wrote as though she knew Emily and had worked with her. James Haswell died September 13, 1876, in Maulmain; Jane Haswell died in Maulmain on March 24, 1884. Both had served more than forty years of missionary labor. They were the parents of five children, all born in Burmah.

[28] Lewis Colby was a publisher in New York. In agreeing to publish the *Memoir of Sarah Hall Boardman Judson*, they had also agreed to republish some of Emily's earlier books. Lewis Colby also published *An Olio of Domestic Verses*.

[29] Fanny Forester, *Memoir of Sarah B. Judson, Member of the American Mission to Burmah* (New York: L. Colby and Company, 1848).

Anna Maria Anable to Emily C. Judson, July 27, 1849

Was n't [sic] I glad to see your dear hand writing again Nemmy.[30] I have quite a feast over your letters now a days. Mary Anna Longstreth[31] called to show me hers and Mr. Gillette[32] read me his yesterday. Any body [sic] but me would think you were very strong to be able to write so much, but I know you better darling—and I strongly suspect that you taxed your poor head, hand and side too much last month to make your friends here easy. I was somewhat relieved by your giving so particular an account of your symptoms, but I do hope you are not going to be a ( )tion of liver complaints. Some of the goodies here I was told were quite sure that Mrs. Judson had another little daughter (I should tell the Dr. how they came to *know* anything about it). Is this not a foreshadowed rumour [sic]?

We are getting along quite cosily [sic] here. It is vacation Friday—Fanny[33] and Mary[34] have gone to spend a week in the country with one of our pupils—Hatty[35] is

[30] "Nem" or "Nemmy" was a name of endearment given to Emily by a small group of her intimate friends at the Utica Female Academy. Anna Maria Anable was "Ninny."

[31] Mary Anna Longstreth was a Quaker who lived in Philadelphia and who took an extraordinary interest in Adoniram and Emily Judson. She lived with her extended family, and they are frequently mentioned in her letters. Apparently, she ran a private school much like the one Anna Maria Anable started. Her letter of May 1848 paints a strong picture of her character, her faith, and her sensitivity. In this letter, she remarks on the particular strengths of each of the wives of Adoniram Judson.

[32] The Reverend A. D. Gillette had been, in 1839, following several successful pastorates, the founding pastor of the flourishing Eleventh Baptist Church in Philadelphia. With his wife Hannah and several children (they would eventually have six), they had graciously opened their home to Emily Chubbuck when she came to Philadelphia for her health at the end of March 1845. The connection had been made through Miss Cynthia Sheldon, a family friend of Mr. Gillette and his parents. A prominent Baptist, Mr. Gillette had journeyed to Boston in December 1845 to accompany Adoniram Judson to Philadelphia for meetings and on Christmas Day had introduced Dr. Judson to Emily Chubbuck, with the hope that Fanny Forester could be persuaded to write the Memoir of Sarah Hall Boardman Judson. A. D. Gillette and his wife, Hannah, were to remain valued and trusted friends, not only with Emily, but with the Sheldon and Anable families. He was to move from Philadelphia to New York in 1852.

[33] Fanny Anable was one of nine children born to Joseph and Alma Anable and was a niece of Miss Cynthia Sheldon and Mrs. Urania Sheldon Nott. The correspondence indicates that in April 1845 she was away from home studying and taking music lessons. These spring letters indicate that she was in Philadelphia, working in the home of and with the family of the Reverend A. D. Gillette. See Miss Sheldon's letter to Emily of November 30, 1845, in which she spoke of all that Fanny was doing to improve herself in the field of music, but also her concern for Fanny's interest in the party life and the "vanitie" which surround her." A March 30, 1847, letter from Anna Maria Anable told of Fanny's conversion following her grandmother's death. In September 1847, she was listed as one of the teachers at the Utica Female Academy. Fanny became a teacher with her sisters in the Misses Anable's School in Philadelphia.

[34] Mary Juliet Anable was born February 18, 1830, in Bethlehem, Albany County, New York, one of nine children born to Alma and Joseph Anable. She went to New Orleans with Hatty in 1847, but she returned home early in March 1848, and by 1849, she was working with Anna Maria in the Misses Anable's School in Philadelphia. Writing in March 1849, Hatty said of Mary, "She paints and draws, speaks French, plays the piano, sings, dances and is our mathematician. What should we ever do without her? She laughs from morning till night, and it is really refreshing to be with her." On December 26, 1860, she was married to Pierre Jacques Darey, the officiating minister being the Rev. Dr. Eliphalet Nott, her uncle. Mary died at the age of sixty-eight on April 20, 1898, in Ottawa, Ontario, Canada.

[35] Harriet or "Hatty" or "Hattie" or "Hat" Anable was one of nine children born to Joseph and Alma Anable, and was a niece to Miss Cynthia Sheldon and Mrs. Urania Sheldon Nott. In 1841, she had added a note to a letter written by Miss Cynthia Sheldon to Emily. As early as November 1842 she was away, and a letter from Emily to Catharine Chubbuck said that "she (Miss Sheldon) expected that Hat would return as accomplished as Anna Maria." Her trips away were both educational and employment, as she worked as a private tutor in families that would bring her into their homes. In August 1843, she had just returned from Beonsen, in the vicinity of New Orleans, and was engaged to go again. A letter from Anna Maria on January 6, 1845, said that she would stay South for another year. About this time Miss Cynthia Sheldon mentioned her concern for Hatty's spiritual health. In May 1845 she was in New Orleans. She was home again in summer 1846, but a September 27 letter from Anna Maria said she had been asked by Mr. Roman with some urgency to return and she thought that she should. She was to return home

learning to paint flowers exquisitely and I read to her—sometimes in Macaulay's History and sometimes from William Allen's journal which Miss Longstreth offered to lend me. Our rooms are so large, and our accommodations so useful that though the therm. is at 90 most of the time, we manage to keep very comfortable.

Mrs. Gillette and her dear little Willie spent yesterday with us. Mr. and Mrs. Robarts[36] came to tea and we had quite a sociable time. Mrs. G. expects to be confined in Sept. She looks as sweet as a rosebud malgre [sic] the awkwardness of her "tournure" [sic] at present. I must not forget to tell you that Mary Anna L. was delighted with your letter. She had been a little anxious as to how you would receive what she wrote you.[37] She is a very superior woman—full of kindness and charity, but her sister Susanna is they say a little more perfect. She is a stricter Quaker I imagine but I do not like her as well as M. A. They are both however very kind to us, and I know that is probably because they think you and the Wade's[38] like us. The next best thing to being good is to have good friends.

Now for news. Eugenia Damaux[39] is engaged to Johnny Edmonds and at the very ( ) of felicity. I think you would enjoy reading her letter announcing it. She says she knows they are going to be happy for they have prayed over this matter (both of them) for four years. I wrote to her that she was the first instance I had known of any ( )e's practicing Tipper's [sic] philosophy successfully. It is a great match for both. He is rich and will take Annette to live with them. He is pious and a member of the

from New Orleans in January 1849 after Anna Maria Anable had started the Misses Anable's School in Philadelphia in fall 1848. Harriet was fluent in French, having placed herself earlier in a French environment in New Orleans. Hatty died in 1858.

[36] Mr. and Mrs. W. S. Robarts were active in Philadelphia Baptist circles. They were frequent visitors to the home of the Reverend and Mrs. A. D. Gillette and later to the Misses Anable's School, which Anna Maria Anable and her extended family had started in Philadelphia in 1848. In his biography of his father, Edward Judson mentioned that Adoniram Judson stayed at the. Robarts's home when he came to Philadelphia in December 1845 when he met Emily Chubbuck. A. C. Kendrick said, "(Mr. Gillette and Dr. Judson) arrived in (or out of) due time in Philadelphia, and Dr. Judson was welcomed to the house of Mr. and Mrs. W. S. Robarts, who became warm personal friends, as they were already active friends of the mission cause." (A. C. Kendrick, *The Life and Letters of Mrs. Emily C. Judson* [New York: Sheldon and Company, 1862] 142). In 1846, with the engagement of Adoniram Judson and Emily Chubbuck, the correspondence indicates some hard feelings toward Mrs. Robarts for comments disparaging the coming marriage and missionary service. This is found in Emily's letter to Adoniram dated February 6, 1846; Mrs. Robarts seemed to be accusing Emily of worldliness when all the time, Emily was quick to say, Mrs. Robarts was engaging in the same activity of which she was accused. The correspondence also indicates a satisfactory healing of the relationship. In January 1849, Miss Sheldon told Emily that Mrs. Robarts had placed their daughter Mary in the Misses Anable's School.

[37] See the letter from Mary Anna Longstreth to Emily C. Judson dated May 1848.

[38] Jonathan and Deborah Wade were appointed missionaries to Burmah in 1823. Their relationship with Adoniram Judson was especially dear because of the early experiences they shared, including the death of Ann Judson. When she died and Adoniram returned to Amherst, he never forgot the sight of Deborah Wade standing on the veranda holding little Maria in her arms. Much of their work was spent in the Karen jungle communities following the path of George Boardman. They returned home to America on December 22, 1847, and went back to Burmah in January 1851, just as Emily was returning to the United States. They were from the Hamilton, New York, area. They left for Burmah on July 25, 1850, and were in Maulmain by February 1851. Both died in Burmah; Deborah died at Maulmain in 1868, and Jonathan died in Rangoon in 1872.

[39] Eugenia Damaux had been part of Emily's intimate circle of friends at the Utica Female Academy. Living in New York City, Eugenia suffered from some kind of eye problem that made life difficult at times; this was a matter of comment in many of the letters exchanged between the girls themselves and with Miss Cynthia Sheldon. In 1848, Eugenia was in New York living "at Mrs. Brown's—the same warm-hearted French girl as ever." In 1849, she married Johnny Edmonds, described as rich and pious, and they lived in Utica.

Episcopal ch. She will be surrounded by her dearest friends in Utica and all things look bright and fair for both of them. Elder Corey[40] married this month Jane Backus. Do you remember her? She has improved a great deal within two or three years and will doubtless make him an excellent wife. She has some property, and as the match pleases Mother Hawley,[41] it will probably please the whole church. Mr. Corey is a "rising man" and I am glad he has a wife who will by her accomplishments help to give him influence. Aunt U.[42] says, she hopes she will learn to keep from making faces. Isn't she funny? Do tell me, just between you and me what she says to you now-a-days. I think she would give a good deal if she had not been so foolish, but we have not had a word to say on these old subjects for more than a year.[43] Apparently she is a more sensible woman than she was, but I suspect if the prejudice was not run out in one direction it does in another—somebody has to suffer.

Mary Barber[44] is still in Utica. I have had two affectionate letters from her this Spring and Summer and suppose she would like to spend a month or two here, but I shan't ask her at present for Hatty has been very ill indeed, but is now recovering. They were obliged to dismiss school for a week.

[40] Mr. Corey was the pastor of the Bleecker Street Baptist Church near the Utica Female Academy, and Miss Sheldon and many of the girls from the academy attended worship there. (Cynthia Sheldon, Alma Anable, Deacon Asa and Isabell Sheldon, Edward Bright, and Horace Hawley had been charter members of the church in 1838.) In April 1844, he wrote to Emily expressing dismay that at a school program one of the girls had read a composition justifying dancing as exercise; he spoke of this as a roadblock to the salvation of many. Then, on March 10, 1846, Emily indicated in a letter to Anna Maria that Mr. Corey had been critical of her relationship and impending marriage to Adoniram Judson. Miss Cynthia Sheldon wrote a number of times expressing Mr. Corey's regret and support, and in 1847, there were letters of reconciliation between Emily and Mr. Corey. In spring 1848, letters reveal that Mr. Corey's wife had died of consumption, her condition exacerbated by recent childbirth. She had left behind four children. In July 1849, Anna Maria Anable wrote of his impending marriage to Jane Backus, a good choice for this "rising man." Mr. Corey remained popular with the Sheldon-Anable families even after their move to Philadelphia in 1848. A March 2, 1852, letter from Charles B. Stout told of Mr. Corey's call to the Stanton Street Church in New York City, which Mr. Corey did not accept. Finally, in 1854, there was a pastoral letter from Mr. Corey to Emily on her illness and her possible death. He preached at the Bleecker Street Church as late as January 1867.

[41] The Hawley family was active in the Utica Church; Horace H. Hawley, mother Hawley's son, was in the publishing business and was helpful to Emily.

[42] See vol. 1, "Cast of Characters," s.v. "Sheldon, Urania."

[43] On the Sunday following his marriage to Emily E. Chubbuck, Adoniram Judson baptized Anna Maria Anable by immersion in the Mohawk River in Utica. This was a serious matter for Miss Anable, and her correspondence with Emily and Adoniram in spring 1846 reflects that sincerity. At this time, Mrs. Urania Sheldon Nott, Anna Maria's aunt, was married to a Presbyterian minister who was also the president of Union College in Schenectady, New York. She was vocal in voicing her objections concerning the baptism and the direction the life of her niece was taking. The correspondence reflects that both Emily and Anna Maria were uncomfortable with what had been said, and the relationship with Mrs. Nott was impaired, at least for a time.

[44] Mary Barber was mentioned frequently in the Emily Chubbuck Judson letters; she was a student and then a teacher at the Utica Female Academy. There were ups and downs to that relationship; in fall 1845, apparently Mary had written to someone expressing what Anna Maria Anable called "ingratitude," and Mary had been banned from the academy until she made proper apologies to Miss Sheldon. In a September 7, 1845, letter from Anna Maria, we learn that her remarks had been about Miss Cynthia Sheldon. In November 1847 Jane Kelly remarked that they had not heard from Mary in more than a year. In 1848 Mary Barber was back at the Utica Female Seminary teaching with Jane Kelly. Though at this time Miss Sheldon had moved to Philadelphia, Mary Barber had been able to reconcile with her, and in later years we find Mary very close to the Sheldon-Anable families; later, there was considerable consternation on Miss Cynthia Sheldon's part in her correspondence with Emily about Mary's health, the seriousness of it, and Mary's impending death. These letters were written in April 1852. Miss Sheldon went to help transfer Mary to Albany in June 1852, where she would be better situated and perhaps have access to better doctors. On September 9, 1852, Anna Maria Anable wrote to Emily of Mary Barber's death.

I am glad the "box" contained things that you wanted. It was made up while we were in the midst of "settling" and I do not recollect that we sent you anything. I know Mrs. G. gave me some money and I got you the pins, spectacles, gloves and something else in our excursion.

[Written along the right margin of the address page:] Thanks for all your information about little Fanny.[45] Will and Livy[46] have a little 'Bel, and I suspect those children are destined to live over our early pranks. 'Bel's the cunning ( ) little creature I ever saw. Well, I hope if they come under my influence hereafter, it may be exerted for good, but I am afraid of myself—I see more clearly every day that

[Written along the left margin of the address page:] I have a desperately wicked heart and yet I am quite indifferent about it at times. I wish I were thoroughly good!

[Written along the left and top margin of the first page:] Hatty sends her best love to you. In a letter from Lou Adams, Lou's re-engagement to Arthur Beardsly [sic] is announced. What is Lydia[47] about? If I ( ) given ( ) her any reason I sh'd think she was in a fret with me.

[45] Emily Frances Judson, the daughter of Adoniram and Emily Chubbuck Judson, was born December 24, 1847. Emily married the Reverend Thomas Alexander Thomson (T. A. T.) Hanna in 1870, and they had eight children, two of whom served as missionaries in Burmah.

[46] Born on November 6, 1816, in Albany, New York, William Stewart Anable was the second child and the second son of Joseph and Alma Sheldon Anable. In an August 1844 letter, Miss Cynthia Sheldon reported to Emily that William had returned home, having "doff'd his sailor garb for age." He married Olivia Williams on September 24, 1846, according to a letter written on September 27 by Anna Maria Anable. They moved to Sheboygan, Wisconsin, where Will opened a store. William died February 9, 1863, in Virginia, California. They had one daughter named 'Bel and a son named Judson.

[47] Lydia Lillybridge was one of Emily's closest friends at the Utica Female Academy. When Emily made the decision to go to Burmah as the wife of Adoniram Judson and as a missionary, Lydia wanted to go with them. Emily spoke to Adoniram Judson of Lydia's extraordinary abilities, and Adoniram advocated her appointment before Dr. Solomon Peck and the Board of the American Baptist Missionary Union. Lydia was commissioned to go with them, in spite of the fact that she remained single. Always independent, outspoken, and unafraid to cause ripples in the missionary community, Lydia served on the mission field for twenty-eight years. She married missionary Thomas Simons in May 1851. See the timeline on the life and service of Lydia Lillybridge Simons in vol. 1.

She ought to write to us oftener. The papers this week announced the death of Mrs. Osgood.[48] Mr. and Mrs. Kincaid[49] were appointed for Ava and go out in the Spring. Hamilton Institution[50] has gone clear overboard though I believe they mean to try to keep flourishing a little longer. Another month will tell.

Adios.

Anna M.

[Written along the left margin of page 3:][51] anxious to do so and it will doubtless be a good thing for her. She has improved very much during the last year and makes a very agreeable girl.

Source: American Baptist Historical Society, AJ 13, no. 479.

[48] Rev. Sewall Osgood was a missionary in Maulmain who worked with and lived by Adoniram Judson. Judson and Osgood occupied two of the four homes in the mission compound and lived so close that it "allowed me the pleasure and profit of almost hourly intercourse." He arrived in Burmah in 1834. His first wife Elhira Brown Osgood died on October 5, 1837, in Maulmain. On July 8, 1838, he married Sarah Thomas, the widow of the Reverend Jacob Thomas, with Adoniram Judson officiating at the wedding. He spoke in the letters to Emily, of which there are five between July 1850 and April 1852, of Adoniram Judson as his "most intimate friend." He never personally met Emily, as he had returned from the field prior to 1846. At the time of his letters, he was working with the American Baptist Missionary Union as a district secretary. In 1845, just as they were leaving for the United States, Sarah and Adoniram Judson gave care of Charley, too young to make the trip, to Mr. and Mrs. Osgood. Charley died not long after their departure. Mr. Osgood visted Adoniram, Elnathan, and Abby Ann in the United States. His third wife was Caroline Wait; they were married December 30, 1850, at Saratoga, New York. With all of his suggestions of "intimacy" and "his most intimate friend," Mr. Osgood stated that his life was so busy that he simply did not have the time to look through his papers for anything that would be helpful in writing the Judson memoir.

[49] Born in 1797, educated at the seminary in Hamilton, New York, and ordained in 1822, the Reverend Eugenio Kincaid served several churches before being appointed as a missionary to Burmah in February 1830. His first wife died soon after their arrival. His second wife was Barbara McBain, and they were married in 1833. In these years, they served in Rangoon, Ava, Saduja, and Akyab. The Reverend and Mrs. Kincaid returned to the United States in 1843; because of her persistent health problems, they were not reappointed in 1846. While in the United States, Rev. Kincaid became instrumental in the establishment of the University of Lewisberg (later Bucknell University). Upon Mrs. Kincaid's restoration, they returned to Burmah, arriving in February 1851 just as Emily Judson was embarking for her return voyage. With his knowledge of the language and customs, Rev. Kincaid was able to establish himself in work with the Burmese government at Ava. With one more trip home (in 1857, on an official mission for the King of Burmah to President Buchanan of the United States), they retired to Gerard, Kansas, in 1866. Of Rev. Kincaid, the correspondence indicates a man of convictions and occasional independent action.

[50] The school that became Madison University was founded in 1817 by the Baptist Education Society of New York State for the purpose of educating ministers. Two of its first students, Jonathan Wade and Eugenio Kincaid and their wives, were the first missionaries to join Adoniram and Ann Judson in Burmah. The Wades arrived in 1823, and the Kincaids in 1830. In 1834, the school was organized as a seminary, college, and academy called the Hamilton Literary and Theological Institution. In 1846, it was chartered as Madison University, drawing upon all of the history and good will in its former existence. In 1847, attempts were made to remove the university to the more urban setting of Rochester, and after three years of stressful turmoil that did tremendous damage to the prospects of the university, the courts decided the case in favor of those who wished the university to remain in Hamilton. Letters of the early 1850s show that the university soon made a remarkable recovery, and the university and seminary were later named for philanthropist Samuel Colgate.

Dr. Nathaniel Kendrick was one of the venerated leaders at the school while also serving as the beloved pastor of the youthful Emily Chubbuck. He officiated at the marriage of Adoniram and Emily on June 2, 1846, his last official act in his seriously declining health. After the commitment to stay in Hamilton, Dr. Stephen Taylor was elected as the second president, and later in 1856, George Eaton became the third president. Dr. A. C. Kendrick, the nephew of Nathaniel Kendrick and the biographer of Emily Chubbuck Judson, was one of the professors who left Hamilton in 1850 to teach at the University of Rochester. Numerous graduates were called for service on the mission field, and many churches were blessed through the pastoral ministry of those who had been trained there. One such minister was Courtland Anable, the brother of Emily's best friend Anna Maria Anable; Courtland Anable was there during Emily's final illness and death in 1854.

[51] It is not clear which sentence this fragment was intended to close.

Doctor Edward Bright, Jr. to Emily C. Judson, July 30, 1849—Baptist Mission Rooms, Boston

My dear Friend,

The Board have [sic] instructed the Executive Committee to enlarge the *Macedonian* at the close of the present volume, or to publish a new paper in its stead. The Magazine is to be issued as heretofore but in the words of the report submitted to the Board "things that seem to be essential to the Magazine, the character and length of its articles, its price and postage, will nigh destroy ( ) as an agent in carrying forward the home work of missions among *the masses of our people*. Nor does the *Macedonian*, in its present form, meet the exigency. Its size is that of a juvenile paper. Were it chiefly designed for children, it would be unnecessary to enlarge it; but, to awaken in the hearts of both old and young, a livelier and abiding interest in the Missionary enterprise, it should be printed on better paper and on a larger sheet. A column should be filled with instructive and impressive missionary articles, gathered without restriction from the best sources at home, and from the correspondence of missionaries abroad. Its price should not exceed $12. per 100 copies for the year, and its circulation should be increased to the farthest extent. So far as the periodicals of the Board are concerned, it should be the home agent of our missionary operations."

The support of all our Mission Schools established for the instruction of children and youth has been assigned to our Sabbath Schools at home. Separate monthly acknowledgments are to be made of their contributions on the last page of the *Macedonian* and the balance of the page is to be devoted to such communications from missionaries and members of Mission Schools as will be likely to foster a Missionary Spirit in the hearts of children.

These are our plans; and in prosecuting them, we need your help. I do not ask you for articles or letters which should be published in the Magazine; but for such as might more appropriately be published in a paper ( ) circulation it will be our aim to spread among the masses ( ) people. I trust the Monthly issues will soon reach 50,000 copies—and they must, if possible, be made to do for the cause of missions what those of the *American Messenger* are doing for the Tract enterprise. Allow me to *rely* on your cooperation in this work. At present we find it difficult to get enough from the letters and journals of missionaries, to fill the Magazine and Macedonian. Let me receive, therefore, additional supplies of good things for the monthly sheet. I hope you will favor me with a communication soon and often.

Yours Very cordially

Edw Bright Jr.
Cor. Sec.

Source: American Baptist Historical Society, AJ 14, no. 551.

Doctor Edward Bright, Jr. to Emily C. Judson, July 31, 1849—Baptist Mission Rooms, Boston

My dear friend:—

Did I write you by the last month's mail (?) I intended to do so, but lest it was otherwise I enclose you a circular to which your attention is very earnestly desired. Why might I not depend on you for something about as often as once a month for our new paper? I trust you will thus favor me, and serve the holy cause of Missions.

We learned of your illness with the keenest sorrow and with very sad apprehensions. The Doctor's note to somebody in New York[52] was published in nearly all the papers from the Atlantic to the Pacific, and made multitudes look with painful anxiety for the arrival of the next mail. And, altho' we received nothing from you or the Doctor, at the Rooms—our joy was great when we heard from the papers that the disease had subsided so far as to have the hope of your recovery.

Our Mr. Peck[53] has been obliged to take two months in which to travel and rest. But we trust God will restore his health.

With the kindest regards to Dr. Judson, I remain

Very affec'y Yours.

Edw. Bright Jr.

Source: American Baptist Historical Society, AJ 14, no. 550.

Emily C. Judson to Mrs. Mary L. Colby, August 7, 1849—Maulmain

My very dear Mrs. Colby:

I can scarcely believe it possible that I have not replied. to your letter dated Oct. /48, but I fear I have not. You can conceive what a real gratification it is to get letters from you and others whom I love in America though I cannot always reply as soon as I should be glad to; and will you not "for Charities sweet sake" if nothing else, write me occasionally with out [sic] waiting for a reply? It is a great holiday with us, when the steamer arrives, for I have learned by experience the sweetness of "good news from a far country"!

[52] See the letter of Adoniram Judson to Anna Maria Anable dated March 18, 1849.

[53] The Reverend Doctor Solomon Peck was for twenty years the executive secretary of the American Baptist Missionary Union. Many believed him to be hard, stern, and judgmental, and from some of his comments, it is easy to understand that perception. Dr. Peck and Emily did not always have the easiest of relationships. She felt in him the judgment that came from many in the church at the announcement of her impending marriage to Adoniram; that judgment concerned her "secular" past and concern that she was not an appropriate companion for the venerable missionary. On July 18, 1849, Emily wrote a blistering letter of defense to Dr. Peck in response to a letter from him of February 20, 1849; her letter framed how she viewed his perception of her, and her response was meant to set the record straight. There are eleven letters in the collection from Solomon Peck to Emily.

Yes, I do!! really enjoy a missionary life, and my enjoyment increases as I become more and more absorbed in it. Though I cannot say that my arrangements and employments are in consonance with the refined taste, yet I seldom lay my head upon the pillow at night, with a painful emotion at my heart, or with a wish ungratified. Do not mistake me; we have many causes of sorrows, we do toil (sometimes beyond our strength) and we are familiar with self-denial in many forms, but our troubles are of a nature to be committed to Him in whose cause they are incurred, and I believe they really conspire to make us happier. You would find it the same I have no doubt, if you were here; for I am sure all the world would have picked you out for a happy missionary sooner than me.

Perhaps you have heard of my long illness.[54] Our Heavenly Father has been more kind to us than we can ever express, for when we had fully made up our minds to a parting, the hand of death was stayed. I mean to try to improve the blessing, but I dare not make any promises. May I have help from above.

I am very glad to hear that you like the country and that you are all enjoying such good health[55]—There was a time when we felt very much concerned about yours. How I wish I could have a downright old fashioned romp with you in the fields; or if you decline the unlady-like employment, with your little people. I fancy Henry[56] and Edward[57] would enjoy it too, and even Miss Fanny[58] wouldn't be far behind hand. By the way, what could ever have put it into your head that the child had weak eyes?[59] They are as bright a pair of jet buttons as you ever saw, with a diamond flashing about in them right merrily. I think you must allude to her ankles, which we supposed to have been injured in the birth, and were for a time apprehensive would be very weak. But it has happily quite recovered now, and she runs

[54] See the letter of Adoniram Judson to Anna Maria Anable dated March 18, 1849.

[55] The Colbys lived in a home at Pemberton Square, Boston, and Adoniram and Emily stayed with them before leaving for Burmah. From Pemberton Square, the Colbys moved to Newton Centre and lived in temporary housing at the bottom of the hill from the Newton Theological Institution for a brief period. They lived there until they could move into their new house, which was built on the small farm they purchased.

[56] Henry Hall Judson, born July 8, 1842, was the son of Adoniram and Sarah Hall Boardman Judson. Henry was the sixth of their eight children and the fourth of five who survived. He remained in Burmah in 1845 when Adoniram and Sarah returned to the United States with the three older children. He returned with Emily in 1851 and went to live with her family in Hamilton, New York. Henry attended Brown University and Williams Collage; he enlisted in the army at the time of the Civil War in January 1864. Later that year, he experienced a debilitating accident attributed either to sunstroke or a horse kicking him in the head. He was married once—unhappily according to his own correspondence—and he eventually died in a veteran's home in 1918, the last of his siblings to die. Of this, the chaplain noted, "The end was a genuine example of Christian fortitude." See Rosalie Hall Hunt, *Bless God and Take Courage, The Judson Legacy* (Valley Forge: Judson Press, 2005) 291.

[57] Edward Judson, born December 27, 1844, in Maulmain, Burmah, was the eighth child of Adoniram and Sarah Hall Boardman Judson and the fifth of their children to survive. Only a few months old when Sarah and Adoniram returned to America, Edward's life was saved by the nurture and care he received from Elizabeth Stevens. He loved Emily as the only "Mama" he had ever known and returned with her to the United States in October 1851. Edward, who was Eddy to his family, became a minister; he did mission work with the immigrants in New York City, and with the aid of the Rockefeller Family, he built the Judson Memorial Baptist Church in what is now Washington Park.

[58] See vol. 1, "Cast of Characters," s.v. "Judson, Emily Frances."

[59] See the letter of Mary Colby to Emily C. Judson dated October 9, 1848.

about the house and down on the ground, with rather unusual agility for a child of her age. Yes, it is delightful, notwithstanding all the responsibility, to be a mother; and particularly delightful where husband and children is all we have to love. And I think responsibility delightful too; for that must be an empty useless life that has no cares. If we do not weekly sink down and let responsibilities crush us, or wickedly seek to evade them, they are among our highest blessings—don't you think so?

I thank you for the kind tokens of remembrance, by the Benjamins.[60] My dress is a beauty, and I value it partict1larly for being a little check.

Source: Hanna family files.

Emily C. Judson to Catharine Chubbuck, August 12, 1849[61]—Maulmain

My Dear Katy,—

I told you last month that I could not write the sort of letters father[62] wished, for want of time; but I have thought better of it; and if he will promise not to expect more of me than could in reason be asked of a person who uses the pen on one subject, the thoughts on another, and the tongue on a third, I will see what my unguided " diamond point" will strike out for him of its own accord. First then to the dress, which he will say is always uppermost in a woman's mind, and with certain restrictions and qualifications "I canna althegither denee the truth o't."

The men invariably (to begin at the top) wear turbans, though not always the pure muslin of Moung Shway-moung and Moung Chet-thing, whose head-gear while in America you will doubtless remember. Turbans of that character, except on special occasions, are very scarce. They are a *gentlemanly* article, while those worn by "the great unwashed" are but little above the size of a pocket-handerchief, and disposed of in various fashions. The turban, however, I must say in short, varies from several yards in size to a wisp twisted like a cable, or a small fillet confining the hair around the brow. It is usually white, though sometimes red (which is not so nice); and I have seen some in Rangoon of lace and thin muslin spotted with gold. The hair, which is allowed to grow—the longer the better—is seldom disposed of in the folds of the turban, but confined in a knot or club on the top of the head, of the size

[60] Judson Benjamin was born February 2, 1819, in Rodman, New York. He was baptized in Franklin, Indiana; graduated from Brown University and Newton Theological Seminary; and was ordained on October 13, 1848, in Providence, Rhode Island. He married Susan Ruggles Stone on September 3, 1848, and they departed for Tavoy, Burma, on October 21, 1848. They arrived at Tavoy in April 1849; in March 1850, they were sent to Mergui. Mr. Benjamin collected a vocabulary of 1,200 Salong words. They sailed from Rangoon to Boston on January 21, 1854, and Rev. Benjamin died in Boston of pulmonary disease in February 1855. Susan Benjamin remarried William Ward, and they left from Boston in June 1860 to return to Burmah.

[61] This letter has an addendum dated August 20, 1849.

[62] Emily's father. See vol. 1, "Cast of Characters," s.v. "Chubbuck, Charles."

of which they are very proud. The ears both of men and women have an immense hole bored in the soft part, through which a plug of gold the size of your finger, having a precious stone in each end, is thrust—that is, the wealthy wear this ornament; but the poorer classes use various substitutes, even to a roll of pasteboard or a bit of segar. And here I may as well say that the natives generally, even those who are poorest to appearance, own jewelry more or less! not merely for ornament's sake, but because it is convenient and portable, and they can raise money on it at any moment. Men shave more or less, and wear their beards—of which some of them seem to be as proud as their more civilized brethren—in every variety of fashion.

Their jacket or tunic (*engyee*, they call it), is usually of white long-cloth, with two or three pairs of strings in front by which it is confined at the throat and breast, and then allowed to follow its own way, parting and floating back, to my thinking, in a way very tasteful. There is a sort of stomacher or chemisette crossing the breast. Sometimes the tunic reaches only a little below the waist, sometimes down to the knees—usually it takes a medium between the two. Men seldom wear this when at labor, and frequently dispense with it even when they consider themselves dressed, arranging the waist cloth in a way to remedy the deficiency. The waist cloth is the great article of dress. And when I use this word for want of a better (the Burmans call it a pa-tso), I beg you will not think of the *bit rag* you usually see in pictures of the heathen. This cloth, which is usually of very gay-colored silk, is eight yards long when purchased. The only *making up* it requires is to sew the two sides together without cutting it, so that the width can cover the whole person from the waist to the heel, while the closed end serves as a bag which may hold the betel-box, etc. This garment is worn in a great variety of ways. It is knotted up before; and sometimes falls over each leg like a pair of flowing trowsers, sometimes hangs from the waist like a woman's skirt, and is sometimes twisted into as small a compass as possible to allow free play to the limbs. Very commonly one end is thrown foppishly over the shoulder. A close observer will not unfrequently find in the mode of wearing the pa-tso a clue to the character of its owner. This silk is of Burmese manufacture, coarse, soft, of fast colors, and bears washing well. It is usually woven in checks or stripes. They have a way of making zig-zag stripes to appear like rays of light, a shading in of all the intermediate colors between pale lemon and deep crimson, which almost dazzles the eyes. I went one day to buy one of these for you, but could not get it for less than twenty rupees (about ten dollars), so I had to give it up. Cotton cloths are worn also, but a man would be a poor wretch indeed not to own a silk pa-tso.

The Burmans never wear stockings or any thing [sic] of the kind about the ankles. The most common kind of shoe or sandal is the one I sent father, though they are variously embroidered and sometimes gilded. They have a piece of wood about an inch thick attached to the bottoms to wear as we wear India rubbers. They manufacture umbrellas very much like those of the Chinese, which I think you have seen, but rather coarser. The betel-box is always carried, either by the person himself or a servant, just as an old lady at home carries her snuff-box. Chewing betel and smoking cigars is universal among men, women, and children as soon as they are weaned. The betel grows like a vine. They use both nut and leaf, and spread it with a preparation the ingredients of which I do not know. I believe you have a lacquered box or two. Those used for betel would hold about a pint of liquid. I will for curiosity's sake furnish a betel-box and send it to you by the first opportunity. They put a small metallic box inside to contain the preparation I have mentioned.

Source: A. C. Kendrick, *Life and Letters of Mrs. Emily C. Judson*, 311–14.

Emily C. Judson to J. Walker Chubbuck, August 15, 1849—Maulmain

My very dear brother,

It made me exceedingly sad, I can assure you, to leave America without ever looking on your face again; for you know in "the good old times" we loved each other with rather an uncommon love. But we (my husband and myself) were under the orders of the Board, and could not, without losing several months of precious time, help ourselves. If we had known that the vessel would be detained so long in Boston, we should most certainly have deferred our marriage. But you were a very naughty brother you know, to forsake the family so long; and I should'nt [sic] mind taking a little revenge, but unluckily, in this case, it falls back on my own exiled head. Well—we *shall* meet, I trust, and that where there will be no more partings. I was rejoiced to hear of your conversion,[63] but wish you had yourself written more particulars about it, where it happened, what lead [sic] to it etc. I wish you would tell me, too, how you came to be a Presbyterian. I suppose the Baptists are very weak in the west, but I should hardly think my mother's son would leave them for that. Rightly as I respect the denomination with which you have united yourself, and grateful as I am for the rich mercies shown you, I will own that I should be a *little* better satisfied if my own brother belonged to the same religious sect that I do.

You will wish to know whether I am happy in my new home etc. I am so sorry that you did'nt [sic] see your brother-in-law! I can say to you what perhaps it would'nt [sic] be proper to say to others,—he is the most perfect specimen of a man that I ever saw, visiting in himself (as it seems to me) every virtue. So devotedly pious—so *spiritual* as a Christian—so ( ) and courageous, so generous and self-denying, so humble and yet so independent—so self-sacrificing and yet so full of

[63] See Emily's letter of June 21, 1848. In that strongly evangelistic letter, she writes to Walker about the possibility of his conversion.

consideration for others—such noble firmness of character and yet so yielding and gentle—such an inflexibility of principles, and yet such tenderness and devotion in his domestic relations—in short, he is to me a *mystery of a man*, and you may well believe he has my whole heart. He is a very handsome man too—don't believe the portraits they are all libelous—and though now sixty-two, looks younger than many of his juniors out here, and to my thinking infinitely better than any of them. His hair is black and his teeth perfect. As to manners, his honorary imprisonment in France in former days,[64] and his association with the higher classes of English gentlemen after the Burmese War,[65] have given him a *finish* which I have seldom seen in an American, though my opportunities during the latter part of my story at home were by no means limited. You will naturally wish to inquire into my qualifications for making such a man happy; but I shall not enter on that list—it is enough for you to know that we are just about as happy as we can live. We are happy in each other, we are happy in our precious children, we are happy in our glorious work, and we are happy in the contemplation of that rest which awaits those who labour [sic] here. Our work goes on encouragingly, though from the very nature of it, slowly. I have got enough of the language to be able to conduct formal prayer-meetings, bible [sic] classes etc.—have made one little book and written a few other things.

I will copy for you the first verse of the Burmase hymn I made the other day. It is a translation of the "Mother's Litany"[66] which you will find in the Memoir of Sarah Boardman.

[Note: Here Emily has inserted some script in Burmese.]

We have two fine beautiful boys who are as own children to me—the elder seven,[67] the younger almost five.[68] Miss Emily Frances,[69] your own pretty niece, is almost two years old, and her brothers special pet and plaything. She is a little fat, fair-faced, black-eyed creature, all heart and soul, too sensitive not to suffer a great

[64] In January 1811, frustrated by attempts to form a missionary society in the United States, Adoniram Judson sailed to England to see if the London Missionary Society would accept him and his friends as missionary candidates. On the ocean voyage, a French privateer took the English ship and its passengers prisoner, and Adoniram Judson ended up in a prison in France. He finally obtained release, arrived in England in May, and spent six weeks there pursuing his goals and learning from those who already had invested their lives in missionary service. He realized that asking to be sent by the English society without any American financial contributions made a weak request. Nevertheless, he returned to New York in August with a proposal that he Mr. Newell, Mr. Nott and Mr. Hall would be accepted as missionaries.

[65] In November 1825, Adoniram Judson had been released from prison with the realization of the Burmese authorities that they would need interpreters fluent in Burmese and English to help to negotiate an end to the English-Burmese War. With the defeat of the Burmese, Adoniram Judson was asked by the English authorities to work with them as an interpreter in establishing trade agreements. Adoniram settled Ann and their daughter Maria in Amherst and then went to Ava with the British officials to work on negotiations between the two countries. He was in Ava when in November he received notice of Ann's death on October 26.

[66] This was a poem written by Sarah Hall Boardman Judson; it was later published in the *Mother's Journal* and in Fanny Forester, *Memoir of Sarah B. Judson, Member of the American Mission to Burmah* (New York: L. Colby and Company, 1848) 214–15.

[67] See vol. 1, "Cast of Characters," s.v. "Judson, Henry Hall."

[68] See vol. 1, "Cast of Characters," s.v. "Judson, Edward."

[69] See vol. 1, "Cast of Characters," s.v. "Judson, Emily Frances."

deal in going through the world, but withal, so meek and gentle that she will be sure to make friends for herself. I trust that she will live to be a blessing not only to her relatives, but to the world. She, as well as the boys, are a great comfort to us in our loneliness.

Write me, do, and tell all about yourself. I had a somewhat discouraging letter from Katy[70] this month,—mother[71] low—father[72] lost his mail route—too ill for boarders and yet *must* take them—Melville gone back to his mother, where he is in danger of being ruined etc. etc. I hope you look after them a little. If you want to lay up your earnings in a place to find them beyond the grave, you cannot do better than to help your poor old father and mother while (which will not be long) you have them to help.

[Written in the right margin of the address page:] We remitted a hundred dollars a month or two since, to buy a lot of land for pasturing the cow and perhaps raising corn and potatoes, but we buy it in our own name, as you know father is not very wise about *keeping* that which he can dispose of. I should like to settle on them about ten dollars a month, if I were able; but we have such a troop of children and such a small salary, that we are obliged to practice the most rigid economy. We support three children[73] in America, you know.

[Written in the left margin of the address page:] You will have some curiosity to know how I like the odd world I have come to;—well since it is for Christ's sake that I live in it; but that is the only reason that I can endure it. ( ), and ignorance, and filth! Oh! you cannot conceive half how bad it is.

Write me a long, free letter, full of minute particulars; and don't forget
Your loving sister

Emily C. Judson.

Source: Wisconsin Historical Society.

[70] Sarah Catharine Chubbuck, "Kate," "Kit," or "Kitty" was Emily's older sister by ten months. Outside of the two terms at the Utica Female Academy, which Emily arranged for her, Catharine always lived at home with her parents in Hamilton, New York. The letters indicate opportunities for marriage, but she, for unknown reasons, remained single. She later helped to care for Henry and Edward Judson after their return from Burmah in fall 1851 when they moved into the Hamilton home with their "aunt" and "grandparents," and she was remembered by them as "dear old Aunt Kate—a dear friend."

[71] Emily's mother, Lavinia Richards Chubbuck, was born June 1, 1785, at Goffstown, New Hampshire, the eldest of thirteen children. She married Charles Chubbuck on November 17, 1805, at Goffstown, New Hampshire. Four of her children were born at Goffstown, and moved with Charles and Lavinia Chubbuck to Eaton, New York, in September 1816; they were Lavinia, Benjamin, Harriet, and John Walker. Sarah Catharine, Emily, and Wallace were all born in Eaton.

[72] Emily's father. See vol. 1, "Cast of Characters," s.v. "Chubbuck, Charles."

[73] Adoniram and Elnathan Judson were in Worcester, Massachusetts; Abby Ann Judson was at Bradford Academy in Bradford, Massachusetts.

Emily C. Judson to Catharine Chubbuck, August 20, 1849[74]

I have just come in from my morning exercise, and the whole town is in a stir because it is a Moorman holiday. I wish you could have been with me. The Moguls and other Moormen dress magnificently. One dress will serve to give an idea of the whole, though there is an endless variety of colors, etc. A crimson satin tunic with wide sleeves open on the back and laced-cuff turned up with green satin facing, and edge trimmed with variegated cord. Tunic long, reaching to the ankles, and slashed in a way to display wide striped-silk trowsers, looking for all the world like a pair of rainbows wrought into loose drapery. Sandals—or rather slippers turned up nearly a quarter of a yard at the toes, and glittering with gold and silver embroidery. A gilded cap, or rather rimless hat, appearing as though braided of wide stripes of gold. Buttons, tassels, etc., in keeping with the rest of the finery. The children are all gorgeously dressed, and weighed down with bracelets, anklets, necklaces, finger-rings, toe-rings, etc. The streets are crowded with beggars, lepers, and all sorts of miserable objects, their feet or hands literally eaten off with disease.

Source: A. C. Kendrick, *Life and Letters of Mrs. Emily C. Judson*, 311–14.

Mrs. Elizabeth L. Stevens to Adoniram Judson,[75] September 1849[76]

My dear Mr. Judson

I believe you will confess I have not often troubled you with solicitations for a vote in my husband's favor; but I have this morning to beg your approbation of his going a [sic] voyage for the benefit of his health—and as my wishes are so few and so reasonable "*they ought to be gratified*." This among the rest.[77]

I can anticipate your objections and give answers to them, which cannot but be satisfactory to your mind. You will say—"Why I do not see that bro. Stevens is much of an invalid." True—but then he has been 12 years in Maulmain and in the ordinary course of missionary movements his health will require a voyage ere long—so as "an ounce of prevention is better than a pound of cure," had he not better take a short trip now, and save his going to American by' and bye?

Another objection, I have vanity enough to think would be—his services are too much needed here. He has thought that all over—I arranged it nicely, to tumble

[74] This letter is an addendum to a letter dated August 12, 1849.

[75] The last paragraph contains an interesting comment about Emily Judson—an "I took care of her—so she can take care of me."

[76] This letter is undated. Someone has marked "May, 1850" on it, but that cannot be because Adoniram Judson had gone on his own sea voyage and, in fact, had died by that time. Emily was ill during early and mid-1849, so this letter is placed in September, when she was healthy and before Adoniram took ill in November.

[77] A letter of August 1847 describes Mr. and Mrs. Ranney heading on a sea trip for their health, and Elizabeth Stevens remarked, "Do you know I never was much of a believer in sending off sick folks; I think they need their friends around them."

one burden upon Mr. Simons,[78] another upon Mr. Stilson[79] and take his writing along.

Another idea, if it occurs to you, that his family will miss him, need not weigh at all, as I am so fully competent to filling his place as well as my own; and besides I shall expect Mrs. Judson to help take care of us to pay for my taking care of her and hers.

Hoping for a kind yielding to our united wishing, I remain your humble petitioner

Elizth L. Stevens

Source: American Baptist Historical Society, AJ 19, no. 903.

Mrs. Hannah Gillette to Emily C. Judson, September 15, 1849—Philadelphia

My dear Couzen [sic] Emily

I presume by this time you have nearly given up the idea of ever hearing from me except through friends who I know keep you informed of our prosperity—how long is it since you received a letter from *me*? Mr. G.[80] I know has written but as he does not consider himself responsible for my omissions of duty I cannot face back on him—I might come round you with excuses and apologies as numerous as family cares and baby bornings might suggest—but the fact is, I *might* have written, and I presume you know it whether I confess it or not—if *you* can find time to write to

[78] Thomas Simons was born in Wales. He was ordained on December 18, 1831, after graduation from the Newton Theological Institute and was appointed to missionary service on March 7, 1831. He sailed for Burmah on June 29, 1832, arriving in Maulmain on January 1, 1833. On June 23, 1833, he married Caroline Jenks Harrington in Maulmain, probably the widow of a missionary who had died, and between 1834 and March 1843, they had six children, two of whom died in June 1839. Caroline Simons died on May 1, 1843. Mr. Simons returned to America in May 1846. While in the United States, he visited with Abby Ann Judson at Bradford Academy; she would have known him from her years in Burmah. He returned to Burmah in November 1847, arriving in Maulmain April 19, 1848. His second wife was Lydia Lillybridge, who had sailed to Burmah with Adoniram and Emily Judson; they were married in Maulmain in 1851.

[79] Lyman Stilson was born in Meredith, New York, on January 29, 1805. He attended the Hamilton Seminary and was appointed to missionary service on October 3, 1836. He was married to Lucretia Brownson on August 20, 1837, and both sailed for Burmah on October 28, 1837, along with the Bennetts and the Stevens. Mr. Stilson finally returned to America after Lucretia Stilson's death on August 14, 1851. Mrs. Stilson had been quite ill for some time and the board had authorized her to return to the United States, but as reported in the newsletter of the Missionary Union, "She has been removed to a better country." They worked with Adoniram Judson for thirteen years, and with both Sarah Hall Boardman Judson and Emily Chubbuck Judson. Mr. Stilson's specific responsibilities included the oversight of printing Burmese elementary books for the schools that were maintained by the mission. He also wrote a volume in Burmese on mathematics.

[80] Following several successful pastorates, the Reverend A. D. Gillette was the founding pastor of the flourishing Eleventh Baptist Church in Philadelphia in 1839. With his wife Hannah and several children (they would eventually have six), he graciously opened their home to Emily Chubbuck when she came to Philadelphia at the end of March 1845 for her health. The connection had been made through Miss Cynthia Sheldon, a family friend of Mr. Gillette and his parents. A prominent Baptist, Mr. Gillette journeyed to Boston in December 1845 to accompany Adoniram Judson to Philadelphia for meetings, and on Christmas Day, he introduced Dr. Judson to Emily Chubbuck with the hope that Fanny Forester could be persuaded to write the memoir of Sarah Hall Boardman Judson. A. D. Gillette and his wife Hannah remained valued and trusted friends, not only with Emily, but with the Sheldon and Anable families. He moved from Philadelphia to New York in 1852.

your friends in this country, so many as you have too and so many duties domestic and religious in addition we may not attempt to complain of want of time who have only half your responsibilities. Now what do you suppose dear Emily has settled me down to write just at this time? Well you must know (as all the world seems to by this time, at least the Phil. world) that two weeks ago to day [sic] the Dr. brought us a little girl the greatest wonder of the age; sees, hears, sings (the wrong side of her mouth) has mouth eyes ears and Willie[81] says a wee little nose all *mashed*—the dear friends who have sympathized so much with us in the calamitous event of the birth of our last boy named Willie are rejoicing in earnest now that we have a girl—and such a wonder—and the name oh: so reply every one except our friends in Walnut St. all the Anables[82] and Miss Cynthia[83] (more ( ) than all the rest of the town) say it is just the thing. Yes we have named our Darling G*race* after good Mrs. Bradly—She is very much pleased and the whole Randall family feel not only complimented they say, but reproved for the oversight of now having a child named after her—now when you write again tell me if you do not fancy it—now I remember one of your Heroines is Grace Linden[84]—by the by she has not a middle name. I have a notion to give her the Linden won't it be pretty? Grace Linden Gillette—

We were all made to rejoice when our last letters arrived at the good news of your returning health.[85] There was a grand lamentation not only among your particular friends, but in the public papers both religious and secular concerning you, and we were happy to be able to dispel in some measure *their* fears. Mr. G. from the first intimation he had of your extreme illness would not give you up—was sure the next mail would bring us better tidings. We have heard so much of the Doctor's good nursing that I suppose we may thank him in some measure that you were carried through so serious an attack—you speak of not hearing from Mother in your letter—she is in New York keeping house for my brothers and grand-ma—whom you remember perhaps—she visited here the winter you was [sic] with me—yes the memorable *1846*[86]—the Dr. was here too—and the old lady is now quite infirm and needs the care and attention of a child—Mother has many trials of a domestic nature to contend with—which she says requires more grace sometimes than she feels she has to sustain her. I know she would be infinitely happier with me or at the best with Sister Sue, but her way seems hedged so she cannot form any plan by

[81] Willie, or William, Gillette,was the fifth of the six Gillette children.

[82] Living at the Misses Anable's School were Mrs. Alma Anable and her daughters Anna Maria, Harriet (Hatty), Fanny, and Mary.

[83] See vol. 1, "Cast of Characters," s.v. "Sheldon, Miss Cynthia."

[84] "Grace Linden" is the first story in volume 1 of *Alderbrook* written by Fanny Forester.

[85] See the letter of Adoniram Judson to Anna Maria Anable dated March 18, 1849.

[86] Emily lived with the Reverend and Mrs. Gillette and their family in spring 1845 and again beginning in November that year. She came to Philadelphia hoping that the milder climate would bring an improvement in her health. She met Adoniram Judson in the Gillette's parlor.

which she can be relieved. My brother James the one who accompanied Grand-ma on her visit at that time, has gone to California to search for gold—we are all anxious on his account, but mother misses especially her eldest and most favorite son—she always inquires after you when she has the opportunity and if she was in the labor of using her pen frequently, would write I am sure—but it is such a task that *I* hardly ever receive a line from her—she depends on my brother to keep me informed of affairs in New York.

How I *should* enjoy an evening in your cozy parlor which holds you and yours in such a happy looking circle—Oh: those "three treasures"[87] how I want to see them—and little Fan she will get bored to death if she comes here—how long before we may expect her? Our family is the same plus two it was when you left—oh yes I forget—minus one—old Hannah has left me at last—she I believe is tired of work so desires to work less and designs "*keeping room*" as the colored folk call it—I of course will miss her kind faithful service much—I have one who fills her place much better in real work but I am not

[Written in the right margin of the address page:] yet able to trust her—I never shall feel such confidence in any other servant I am sure—the children will miss her good management and training as ever—

Now about the box—dear Emily—I feared you would think hard of us—we ( ) deposit some ( ) but the fact was we were very poor just at that time much to our annoyance and our efforts were not worth speaking about so long as we could not put our hands deep in our pockets and do something—but if you will tell me when you write again what you want above any thing [sic] else temporal I will see that you have it. I think when Mrs. ( )

[Written in the left margin of the address page:] gets ( ) ( )—we will commence on another box so that we have time to make up our donations as much as we can—you must excuse us this time and trust me for the future.

Walter and Danny[88] have been away all summer in *boarding too long* and will return as soon as Mr. G. goes for them. I presume little Fan will suit Walter first rate—he has grown a grand boy half a head above James who is a quiet studious boy quite under size in every thing [sic] but music—Danny is a fine warm hearted fellow and requires a steady determined hand with him—little Willie is the ( ) of his father and a little loving fond creature—and Sissy Grace—no matter—

Kiss all the children for me and Dr. too—Your affectionate friend and sister
Hannah Gillette

Source: American Baptist Historical Society, AJ 16, no. 716.

[87] This was a reference to Henry Hall Judson, seven years old; Edward Judson, almost five years old; and Emily Frances Judson, almost two years old.

[88] A. D. and Hannah Gillette had six children between 1836 and 1849: Susan, James, Walter, Daniel, William, and Grace.

Emily C. Judson to her Journal, September 17, 1849

What am I to do next? What have I done since (June 20th) that question was asked. Positively nothing, and yet I have been very busy. I concluded not to translate the Life of Gandama[89] for both Mr. J. and myself, each alone and without consulting the other, came to the conclusion that it is not genuine mission work. In some circumstances it might be right and proper to do this thing; but with my limited strength and in my responsible position, it would be inexcusable neglect of the highest good for the minor. I have been trying to fit myself for direct personal effort, but my progress in the language is retarded by the delicacy of my health, and my progress in spirituality by the depravity of my heart.

Source: Hanna family files.

The Reverend Abram Dunn Gillette to Emily C. Judson, September 20, 1849—Philadelphia

My very very dear friend—

Our residence is yet just half way to the publication office and we think the more of it, and felt the stronger attachment to it on that account. We were pained to hear of poor health from your dear circle; but are greatly relieved, by later and more favorable news. May your health and lives and usefulness be prolonged yet many years. We have been favored with visits from the Vintons,[90] Wades[91] and Bronson[92]—arrangements seem now to tend towards the return, as soon as next spring, of all the former and Br. Kincaid[93] and Lady, Dr. Dawson[94] and lady, perhaps even *new recruits*.

[89] See Emily's journal reflection for June 22, 1849 as she speaks on this plan.

[90] Justus Hatch Vinton was born in Willington, Connecticut, in 1806. He attended the theological school at Hamilton, New York, and was ordained in June 1834. In July that same year, he sailed as a missionary to Burmah. His wife was Calista Holman Vinton; they were married April 9, 1834. They worked with the Karens at Chummerah, Newville, and Maulmain, where he had charge of the Karen theological seminary. At the end of 1847, they left for the United States, returning to Burmah and work at Rangoon in July 1850. Justus Vinton died in Kemendine, Burmah, on March 31, 1858. His wife, Calista Holman Vinton, died in Rangoon, Burmah December 20, 1864. Mrs. Vinton taught the Karen women and was the author of several hymnbooks in their language.

[91] See vol. 1, "Cast of Characters," s.v. "Wade, The Reverend Doctor Jonathan and Deborah."

[92] Miles Bronson was a graduate of Hamilton University and Seminary and was appointed for missionary service in 1836. His field of service was Assam, and he first reached there in July 1837. He pioneered ministry with the Naga tribes. In 1849. Mr. Bronson returned to the United States and was there for more than a year; he returned to the field in 1851.

[93] See vol. 1, "Cast of Characters," s.v. "Kincaid, The Reverend Doctor Eugenio."

[94] Miss Cynthia Sheldon called Doctor Dawson a "brother of Mr. (Eugenio) Kincaid." There was some talk of Dr. Dawson going to Ava, but the Board of the American Baptist Missionary Union decided not to appoint him. Miss Sheldon speculated that it was because of lack of funds and not because of any question of his piety or fitness. In March 1850, Anna Maria Anable spoke of a visit from Mr. Bright of the American Baptist Missionary Union to dissuade Dr. Dawson from going to Burmah at least until Mr. Kincaid was settled in Ava. It was increasingly obvious that Dawson would go whether or not he had a board appointment, for there was sufficient funding and interest from the churches in Utica to provide the necessary support. See Emily's letter dated June 20, 1850.

I was sent forth and went to Cuba last spring[95] and returned in July in good health. Should I ever require an extended journey and residence in a tropical region, I should ship for Maulmain. So do not be surprised if you see me walk into your mission premises some of these days "as large as life, and twice as natural." With increasing facilities for traveling it is not out of the range of possibilities for Burmah to be visited, ere long by numerous American Christians. You hope, if so, they may be of the right ( ). May we not hope to see each other yet in time? We will work on and wait on our master's will, and take the allotments of his providence, and fell and say and know that he doeth all things well.

We are delighted to have the dear Annables[96] [sic] among us here—they are indeed an accession to our social circle, our church, and especially to our Female Schools. As I have a *growing* congregation, in more particulars than one—it is a great gain to have a Baptist Female School to which I can recommend my people to send their daughters, and where I know influences unfriendly to truth will not be exerted over their minds—I can trace the departure of many of the *educated* children of Baptists in this City to the seminaries where they were educated.

As most of my families are yet young, and their children small, I can do but little for the school at present in the number of pupils from our own church. But they are succeeding beyond all of their own, and our expectations. They have over thirty scholars, and more are in prospect, and they deserve all they have and many more. But I am writing to those who know them, and I need say no more. They however expect a little pupil from Burmah soon[97]—and one arrived in this house lately as its Mother,[98] while yet panting from the efforts which gave it a place in this world, smilingly said—"Tell Miss A. that my little daughter arrived just in time to enter next term."

She is a welcome little stranger, very bright and mature, may the Lord let us keep her and rear her for usefulness is our earnest prayer. I suppose her happy mother has told you all about her.[99]

Nine months after our great Missionary meeting in which you participated—our Willy was born. I often imagine him, the embodiment of *some* of the excellencies

[95] The Reverend Gillette had previously written of a serious lung condition that prevented him from occupying his pulpit for a number of months.

[96] When Anna Maria Anable started the Misses Anable's School in Philadelphia, she was joined by her mother Alma Sheldon Anable and her sisters Harriet, Fanny, and Mary. They identified themselves and their school with their Baptist faith and heritage.

[97] Anna Maria Anable already wrote to Emily in Burmah to tell her how much she wanted to give Emily Frances Judson her education at her school in Philadelphia. Tragically, Emily Frances did come to the Misses Anable's School after the death of her mother in June 1854; Anna Maria Anable was made guardian of the six-and-a-half-year-old child under the terms of Emily Judson's will.

[98] Within the month, Mrs. Hannah Gillette gave birth to a daughter, whom they named Grace. Mrs. Gillette teasingly told Emily that she would be "Grace Linden" Gillette after a character in a story by Fanny Forester.

[99] See the letter of Mrs. Hannah Gillette to Emily C. Judson dated September 15, 1849.

of that glorious trio, with which our family circle was so highly favored. Dr. Judson and Mr. Dean[100] and Abbott[101]—we sometimes call him our missionary gift.

Our churches in this city and vicinity are gaining, in numbers, intelligence and piety, and I hope in missionary benevolence. But alas, we are far from being what we should long ere this have become. I was absent during the anniversary of the Missionary Union last May—a good influence was left upon the public mind. A very pleasant girl about nineteen years of age in my church wants to be a Missionary. She is small, quite genteel in manners and looks; is lively and prepossessing; her education is deficient, but she is soon to begin study. I want her to obtain a good English education and be ready for some open door in the course of a year or two. Dr. Cote wanted such a girl for Canada a few months ago, but I believe she prefers a foreign field. I think she has no particular wish to marry, but would be guided by providential openings, and the advice of those who are her friends. She is an orphan and will not be high minded about her position or duties in the Lord's vineyard.

You both know that in the Annables [sic], Aunt Cynthia,[102] the Robartses,[103] and our humble selves—you have friends in this City (to say nothing of *hosts* of others elsewhere and here) whom you can *command* at any time. Let us know just what you need and want, for your comfort and usefulness. If it is to be had you shall have it—Do not hesitate to tell us what we can do that will promote your happiness. Please write a joint letter to the Robartses.

Our boys grow and flourish. Walter and Danny[104] are in Washington County, New York and have been several months with my Mother and sisters. James is here—a studious quiet boy—What our "Treasures" are yet to become we know not.

We see the Annables [sic] almost daily and Nelly Bennett[105]—her elder sister has left, and is with Utica friends. Do give our kindest regards to the Dear

[100] The Reverend Doctor William Dean was a distinguished missionary to Hong Kong for more than fifty years. As the pastor of the local church in Morrisville, he baptized Emily Chubbuck when she was seventeen. There are nine letters in the correspondence from Mr. Dean, beginning after Emily's appointment to missionary service. After the death of Adoniram Judson, it was speculated, and not without reasonable support, that William Dean had an interest in taking Judson's place in Emily's life and affections. The later correspondence between Emily and Anna Maria Anable shows that Dr. Dean was often the butt of their ridicule, so something had happened to challenge that relationship. In 1854, when William Dean was courting Mrs. Maria Brown in New York City, Abby Ann Judson was working for Mrs. Brown as an in-house teacher for her children. For the complete story of William Dean's life and the many ways he touched the mission movement and the life of Emily Chubbuck Judson, see vol. 1, "Cast of Characters," s.v. "Dean, William."

[101] Elisha Abbott was born October 23, 1809, in Cazenovia, New York. He graduated from the Hamilton Theological Institute and was ordained August 25, 1835. He wife was Ann P. Gardner, and they were married April 2, 1837. Though they were appointed for work in Telagus, India, that changed upon their arrival, and they went to Maulmain in April 1837. They continued on to Rangoon shortly after that. In March 1840, they established the station at Sandoway. Mrs. Abbott died in Sandoway on January 27, 1845. Mr. Abbott left for the United States in November 1845, returning in August 1847. At one point in the correspondence, Mr. Abbott was mentioned as a possible husband for Lydia Lillybridge.

[102] See vol. 1, "Cast of Characters," s.v. "Sheldon, Miss Cynthia."

[103] See vol. 1, "Cast of Characters," s.v. "Robarts, Mr. and Mrs. W. S."

[104] Between 1836 and 1849, A. D. and Hannah Gillette had six children: Susan, James, Walter, Daniel, William, and Grace.

[105] The Bennett girls were sent from Burmah to be educated at the Utica Female Academy and then at the Misses Anable's School.

Bennetts,[106] Miss Lillybridge,[107] and Howards,[108] and all in your far off land who may remember us.

When you can do so—we shall be exceedingly happy to receive letters. We know your hands and hearts are full. It is sweet to toil for so good a Master as our Redeemer is—May his best blessings ever be your portion is the sincere prayer of Yours most affectionately

A. D. Gillette

Source: American Baptist Historical Society, AJ 16, no. 717.

Emily C. Judson to her Journal, September 20 and 21, 1849

September 20, 1849.[109] *Mem.* To live, not for Time, but for eternity.

September 21, 1849.[110] A person of strong, unwavering faith has already *entered into a rest* which the dissolving of the elements could not disturb.

Source: A. C. Kendrick, *Life and Letters of Mrs. Emily C. Judson*, 327; Hanna family files.

[106] Cephas and Stella Bennett were missionaries to Burmah. They arrived in Burmah in January 1830, and Mr. Bennett remained the superintendent of the Baptist Press there for more than fifty years. He worked with Adoniram Judson on the printing of the Bible into Burmese, but also into the Karen language. Adoniram Judson referred to Mr. and Mrs. Bennett as "his dearest and best of friends." From the Utica area, they sent their children back, and the girls were educated at the Utica Female Academy. The girls included Elsina (April 1828), Mary (November 1829) Ann (August 1833), Ellen (June 1835), and Sarah (June 1837).

[107] See vol. 1, "Cast of Characters," s.v. "Lillybridge, Lydia." See also "A Timeline of the Life and Mission of Lydia Lillybridge Simons."

[108] Hosea and Theresa Howard first sailed for Burmah in 1834, arriving in December that year. Hosea Howard was a recent graduate of the theological seminary in Hamilton, New York. They were stationed in Maulmain as missionaries with Adoniram Judson, and he claimed in a letter to Emily that he worked there with Adoniram longer than any other missionary. Mr. Howard's responsibility was to run schools that the mission maintained, a task in which he was ably assisted by his wife. Lydia Lillybridge was responsible to Mr. and Mrs. Howard when she arrived in November 1846. Mr. and Mrs. Howard left Maulmain for the United States in February 1850.

[109] This is found only in the Hanna Family files.

[110] This is found in both Kendrick's biography and the Hanna family files.

Emily C. Judson to Catharine Chubbuck, September 21, 1849—Maulmain

Dear Katy,—

I am heartily disgusted with all descriptions, and if I had not promised, the Burman women's dress might go to the dogs.[111] But luckily they do not wear much, and, as a stable boy would say, "a short horse is soon curried." They are rather small of stature, so much so that they look upon English ladies with wonder, and say that Mrs. Moore and I are the only women of the mission whose size is at all endurable. Their hair is straight and black; it is carefully oiled, combed directly back from the temples, and confined in a knot on the top of the head. They are fond of decorating the hair with flowers. They wear ear ornaments similar to those of the men, and those who are able to afford it wear a half dozen different necklaces, magnificent ornaments for the head, finger-rings, etc. The chief article of dress is the *ta-ming* (t'mlng), a species of petticoat, of the gayest colored silk, with a deep border at the bottom and a top of crimson cloth, which is gathered in folds about the breast. The *engyee* or tunic is very much like that worn by the men, though sometimes made of thinner material—jaconet, gold-sprigged lace, black lace, yellow gauze, etc. They usually fling a light scarf, silk handkerchief, or small shawl over one shoulder. Their sandals are mostly like those of the men. Burmans always leave these outside the door, for, in their estimation, it is as bad breeding to wear shoes into a house as, in ours, it is to wear their hats. It is curious to see a Burman lady, a bride for instance, magnificently dressed, and her great black feet bare.

The dress of the Burman women is pretty and coquettish, but decidedly objectionable on the score of modesty, if not of decency.... The women are spirited, lively, fond of laughing and talking, and, although shockingly quarrelsome as wives, in the main good-natured. They are as intelligent as could be expected in third circumstances. Boys are always taught to read—girls seldom. Children seldom wear any kind of clothing till seven or eight years old, though they are profusely decorated with necklaces, bracelets, anklets, etc. I have seen children with rich silk velvet jackets just covering the hips, and no other article of dress, aside from jewelry.

Your loving sister,

Nemmy[112]

Source: A. C. Kendrick, *Life and Letters of Mrs. Emily C. Judson*, 315–16.

[111] In a letter from her sister Catharine earlier in the year, Catharine passed on to Emily a request from their father, Charles Chubbuck, that Emily write home about the manners, customs, dress, etc., of the local population in Maulmain. In a reply on July 18, 1849, Emily said that "I should like nothing better than to write such letters—but you can have no conception of the busy life I lead." Then, however, in letter dated August 12 (with an addendum August 20), Emily does exactly that with elaborate descriptions of local dress, including turbans, jewelry, jackets, and more fancy dress, mostly for men. In this letter she continues with a focus on women's dress.

[112] "Nem" or "Nemmy" was a name of endearment given to Emily by a small group of her intimate friends at the Utica Female Academy. Anna Maria Anable was "Ninny."

Emily C. Judson to Anna Maria Anable,[113] September 21, 1849—Maulmain

My Dear Ninny,—[114]

—I will tell you as nearly as I can how I am, and then you will be able to judge as well as we can of the result. I have a slight cough, sometimes with bloody expectorations, and a continued pain in my right side—the latter, Dr. M. says, occasioned by congestion of the liver. My stomach is very weak and so sensitive to the touch that I seldom wear a tight dress, and my throat is shockingly ulcerated. I have a slight difficulty of breathing, and just now can not [sic] read aloud at all. The physician says that my lungs are perfectly sound, but admits that there is more danger of their becoming diseased than there would be if my throat was well, and every fresh attack on my throat is worse than the last, although he succeeds tolerably well in subduing the fever. I am not so thin as I was, and some of my worst symptoms, such as night sweats, have totally disappeared. I work little, study little, walk in the veranda for exercise, drive out every day, and keep in excellent spirits. I suppose it would not be a surprising thing if I were to die in a few weeks, nor be considered a miraculous interposition if I were to live to be eighty years old—so much seemingly depends on accidental causes....

You ask how I felt when looking into the grave. We had expected for some time previous to my going to Tavoy[115] that I was in a fatal decline, and I had endeavored to prepare myself for it. I grew worse on the passage, but still did not think myself in any particular danger till the physician at Tavoy commissioned Mrs. Bennett[116] to tell me what he thought of my case. I was inexpressibly shocked; for it seemed doubtful whether I should ever get back to Maulmain, or see my husband. Mrs. Bennett soon left me alone, and little Frances,[117] who was just beginning to walk, and very proud of it, toddled to the side of my couch, and seemed disappointed that I did not laugh and praise her. I put my arm around her, and she laid her little soft cheek coaxingly on mine, as though she understood that I was in trouble. Then was a struggle; it seemed that my very heart would burst. I tried to tell Henry[118] something about it, but he could not understand, and only tortured me with questions

[113] This letter is the edited version of the original published by A. C. Kendrick in *The Life and Letters of Mrs. Emily C. Judson.*

[114] "Ninny" was a name of endearment given to Anna Maria Anable by her most intimate friends at the Utica Female Academy. Emily was "Nemmy."

[115] See the letter of Adoniram Judson to Anna Maria Anable dated March 18, 1849. He speaks of how Emily was sent by boat to Tavoy, hoping that the sea air and change would be beneficial to her health.

[116] Stella Bennett was the wife of Cephas Bennett; they arrived in Burmah in January 1830. Mr. Bennett remained the superintendent of the Baptist Press there for more than fifty years. From the Utica area, they sent their children back, and the girls were educated at the Utica Female Academy and then the Misses Anable's School. The girls included Elsina (April 1828), Mary (November 1829), Ann (August 1833), Ellen (June 1835), and Sarah (June 1837).

[117] See vol. 1, "Cast of Characters," s.v. "Judson, Emily Frances."

[118] See vol. 1, "Cast of Characters," s.v. "Judson, Henry Hall."

about the funeral, etc, I got a little better before I left Tavoy, and Mrs. B. was somewhat relieved, though I presume she still considered me in a settled consumption. After I reached home I became a good deal calmed, and quite reconciled to leave both husband and children, if it should be the will of God; but still I can not [sic] say that there was any time when I should not have rejoiced at the prospect of recovery. You will think it strange, but it is nevertheless true, that, during most part of the time, I felt greater reluctance to leave my mission work than to leave my family. Yet "we have been so, *so* happy "and the time has been so short!" we used to say to each other with aching hearts many times a day. Then I would watch the poor children at their play, until the tears came and blinded me. Sometimes I had enrapturing views of heaven, and my heart bounded with joy (for I never had any doubts respecting my future state). The horror of death that I used to tell you about was to a great extent taken away; but still death is the curse of sin, and can not [sic] but be dreaded except as its hideous features are lost in the glory of the resurrection. I believe a long life to be a great blessing, and in this age of the world, especially for a missionary, inexpressibly great. I pray daily I may be spared for many years to my husband, to my children, and to my work; and I have no hesitation in putting up this prayer, for you know we are commanded to "be anxious for nothing; but in all things to make known our requests to God." If, notwithstanding this desire to live on my part, my Heavenly Father sees fit to remove me, He will do it in infinite wisdom and in infinite love—for my good and the good of His cause; and I can add most heartily, "His will be done"....

Affectionately,

Nemmy

Source: A. C. Kendrick, *Life and Letters of Mrs. Emily C. Judson*, 316–18.

Miss Lydia Lillybridge to the Reverend Doctor Solomon Peck,[119] September 22, 1849—Maulmain, Burmah

Rev. Mr. Peck,
Dear Sir,

On looking at the date of your last letter to me I am surprised to find that more than a year has passed since it was received. All the reasons of my remissness in not answering it, I cannot well put on paper now; but beg that you will excuse it. I suppose that you were well informed through Mr. Howard,[120] in regard to my employment; else I should not have excused myself on any ground from reporting to you regularly.

Since writing to you, I have experienced some trials (I know of no better term,) which I could not fore-see, not imagine, when I was at home; but I need many more still in order to purge away the dross, and make the pure gold appear.

You will be surprised to hear, and I am ashamed to tell you, that I cannot yet understand, and use, the Burmese language well,—not even ordinarily well. You know, I suppose, that much of my time has been spent in teaching English—perhaps too much.

The daily exercises of the school room have required most of my energies, which are somewhat less than they were in my native climate. Of course, I have not been able to make that progress in Burmese, that I should have done, if I had had nothing to do with teaching another language.

After having been here three or four months, I wrote you that I was very glad to be able to teach in English while acquiring the Burmese; but I now see that it would have been better for me to have spent less time with English the first year.

I have often wished that I could go into the jungle to some Burmese village, and spend six months without hearing a word of my own language.

During the last two years, I have from time to time, felt considerable uneasiness about spending so much of my time with the Eurasian pupils; but they were on my hands—they were, many of them, already in school when I came—those who supported them expected that they would be taught English—and it was in accordance with the design of him who had charge of the school to have them thus taught. I could not, therefore, very well do otherwise than to teach them, even if I

[119] This letter from Lydia Lillybridge to Dr. Solomon Peck, the executive minister of the American Baptist Missionary Union, reveals some of the issues that were active at that time in the Burmese mission. Miss Lillybridge taught with Emily E. Chubbuck at the Utica Female Academy and had sailed for Burmah in July 1846 with Emily and Adoniram Judson.

[120] Hosea Howard first sailed for Burmah in 1834, arriving in December that year. His wife was Theresa, and they had been married just before departure. Hosea Howard was a recent graduate of the Theological Seminary in Hamilton, New York. They were stationed in Maulmain as missionaries with Adoniram Judson, and he was to claim in a letter to Emily that he had worked there with Adoniram longer than any other missionary. Mr. Howard's responsibility was to run schools that the mission maintained, a task in which he was ably assisted by his wife. It was to Mr. and Mrs. Howard that Lydia Lillybridge was responsible when she arrived in November 1846. Mr. and Mrs. Howard left Maulmain for the United States in February 1850.

had wished to. But it was not, and is not, an easy matter to decide positively in my own mind, what course is best to pursue. There are many plausible things to be said on both sides of the question. Even the good brethren here in the Burmese department are not all of the same mind in regard to this thing, as you may possibly know.

You know by the annual reports, the branches that have been taught. It has been my aim to have *every pupil* able to read and write the Burmese language well; and I am happy to say that I believe I have accomplished more in this respect during the present year, than during the two years preceding. The number of pupils in my department has been greater this year, than before, and the proportion of Burmese, greater. The whole number, over fifty, the average number, between thirty-five and forty.

I hope that I shall soon be able to tell you something more satisfactory, in all respects—Whenever there is any cause of dissatisfaction in regard to my proceedings, I beg that you will tell me freely. "Lest the righteous smite me."

Have you received the watch you let me have, from Mrs. Haswell?[121] I will explain hereafter.[122] It is time to close.

With kind regards to Mrs. Peck, as well as to yourself, I am, dear Sir,

Yours respectfully,

Lydia Lillybridge

Anna Maria Anable to Emily C. Judson, September 23, 1849

Dear Nemmy[123]

We have [Note: The rest of line 1, all of line 2, and the first two words of line 3 cannot be read.] I shall devote to you. Your sweet letter of June 2nd came last week, and the memories recalled were both pleasant and painful. Oh! The changes—the changes she[124] changed brought about in Utica [Note: The next line and a half are lost in the letter fold.] chosen to suffer, if need be, with the children of God. You have the satisfaction of feeling that you are engaged in the noblest work which can occupy a human being; and God will bless you for it both in this world and in the world to come. As the years increase my ( ) seems to diverge further and further from yours, but thank heaven! We hope they will terminate at the same point. I no longer feel that to be useful I must ( ) the same ( ) with you; and I come

[121] See vol. 1, "Cast of Characters," s.v. "Haswell, Jane M. and The Reverend James."

[122] See the letter dated October 22, 1849, from Miss Lillybridge to Dr. Peck.

[123] "Nem" or "Nemmy" was a name of endearment given to Emily by a small group of her intimate friends at the Utica Female Academy. Anna Maria Anable was "Ninny."

[124] This is a reference to Miss Jane Kelly, who assumed responsibility for the Utica Female Academy when Miss Cynthia Sheldon moved to Philadelphia to work with Anna Maria Anable and her sisters at the Misses Anable's School. The letters from Miss Cynthia and Anna Maria speak of large expenses for new furnishings with a heavy debt incurred in the process, and there is obvious bitterness at the way that Miss Sheldon was treated by the trustees of the School.

[Note: A line is lost here in the letter fold.] miss my school ( ) ( ) ( ). ( ) I am not satisfied with my manner of life. I feel within such coldness, such barrenness of spirit in religious things that my heart condemns me. With thirty-five girls under my influence to control, direct, and prepare for future usefulness, this ought not to be. I know what I ought to do, but my situation is surrounded by temptations to worldliness, and I am not as much concerned for the religious interests of my girls as I should be. Dr. Ide[125] preached for us this morning a most excellent sermon. As he came out he met Mr. Robarts[126] and said "bro. Robarts I intended to hit you this morning and however hard the blow may be, you may be sure you deserve it." Mr. R. burst into tears and turned away. I should have said the subject was *decision* in religious matters. You will receive by this mail the news of the little daughter in Mr. Gillette's[127] family. [Note: Several words are lost here in the fold of the letter.] school commenced that he had a new scholar for us. Mr. Colby[128] called last Thursday and said his wife told him he must not fail to let me know of her happiness in having her wishes gratified. Mary Frances Colby will be a giant belle in the world I suppose. Mr. C. said she is almost the only girl in Newton. Mr. Roberts,[129] a brother in law (Mr. Colby's) called with him to make inquiries in relation to leaving his little daughter with us for the next six years. He is in business in England and if he can afford it will leave her to [Note: A line is lost here in the letter fold.] of the prevailing ( ) and he has this little girl and three little boys to arrange for. We shall have our full number of scholars as soon as they all return from the country. Our school is

[125] Dr. George Ide was born in Coventry, Vermont, in 1804. Though his father was a minister, George Ide tended toward skepticism and developed a reputation for being quite vocal in sharing his dissident views. After a powerful religious experience of conversion, he gave himself to revivalism, preaching in a number of smaller churches throughout Vermont before being called to Albany, New York. Over the years, he had a series of successful pastorates, including the Clarendon Street Church in Boston. He was at the First Baptist Church of Philadelphia for sixteen years and at the First Baptist Church of Springfield, Massachusetts, for twenty. He was the author of two volumes of sermons and a Sunday school book titled *Green Hollow*. Dr. Ide is mentioned in an October 29, 1848, letter from Anna Maria Anable, and an August 7, 1852, letter of Miss Cynthia Sheldon to Emily Judson. (William Cathcart, *The Baptist Encyclopaedia* [Philadelphia: Louis H. Everts, 1881] 568.)

[126] See vol. 1, "Cast of Characters," s.v. "Robarts, Mr. and Mrs. W. S."

[127] See vol. 1, "Cast of Characters," s.v. "Gillette, The Reverend Abram Dunn." Mrs. Gillette had recently given birth to their sixth child, a daughter, whom they named Grace.

[128] A prominent businessman, Gardner Colby and his family lived in Pemberton Square in Boston before moving "to the country," Newton Centre, Massachusetts. Mr. Colby was a member of the Board of the American Baptist Missionary Union and an avid supporter of the missionary movement. In a letter after they sailed from Boston to Burmah, Emily mentions the extravagant hospitality extended to them in early July as they waited for the *Faneuil Hall* to embark. Adoniram and Emily stayed with the Colby family frequently.

[129] Mr. Roberts was the brother of Mary Colby. A businessman with interests in England, he delivered letters from Emily's friends to her when she arrived in England on her way back to America in late summer 1851. He also offers to render to her every service to ease her journey. He is mentioned in a number of the letters in the following months; he is a widower with at least one child, a daughter Mary, who was a pupil at the Misses Anable's School in Philadelphia. Abby Ann Judson mentions his marriage in her letter of March 7, 1852. See Miss Sheldon's letter of March 8, 1852. This marriage is announced by Miss Sheldon to Emily toward the end of December 1851; the bride was Miss Lynear or Linear of Brooklyn. The wedding took place by the time the March 8 letter was written. Miss Sheldon comments, "He married Miss Linear, who has boarded in the house with him long enough to understand each other at least if she was not quite so deaf—They spent Friday evening here and it was hard telling whether our mighty effort to make it pleasant had any affect—even Mr. Gillette could not get any thing but monosyllables, and half the time the wrong one—I do pity them—except when they are alone—then I doubt not but his children will be well cared for."

prospered, our home is delightful, and we see our friends nearly as often as we did in Utica. Mr. Lincoln[130] called a fortnight since. Julie Look Casswell[131] and her husband spent two or three days with us last week, and next week we expect Eugenia[132] and John Edmunds here. Mary Spencer[133] is coming with him and perhaps some gentleman from Utica, as Sarah Brayton and H( ). Eugenia and her husband and Mary will stay at our house. Sarah Bell[134] is still in Boston with her step-mother. Did I tell you that Mrs. Stow[135] made inquiries of Sarah in relation to our school for Matilda Dean?[136] I offered to make a deduction of fifty dollars for being [Note: Half of this line is lost in the letter fold.] too much. They ought to give the child every advantage, for I am told she is grown up awkward and uninteresting, and as they have no children they can afford to do for her what they think should be done.

I shall be interested ( ) ( ) in the Notes to the Memoir,[137] and ( ) make all such information I get, tell ( ) some of my classes. In ( ) Moral Philosophy the other day I read excerpts from Ro-( )-bye of the creed of the Rasens [sic] to show how safe a guide [Note: The next two lines are lost in the letter fold.] but little about it, but I

[130] This could be Mr. Joshua Lincoln of Boston, a member of the publishing firm Gould, Randall and Lincoln, or it could be Mr. Heman Lincoln, his brother, who was active in Massachusetts Baptist life and in Boston political circles.

[131] Miss Look was a student of Emily's at the Utica Female Academy and then a fellow teacher. A November 22, 1845, letter from Anna Maria, encouraging Emily to stay in Philadelphia for the winter for her health, remarks that Julia had the hardest part because she is teaching Emily's composition class, and the students keep asking for Emily. In a September 1847 letter, she was listed as one of the teachers at the Utica Female Academy. A previous letter of April 30, 1849, spoke of Mr. Casswell coming into her life and of their impending marriage. In that letter she mentioned that they would stay with the Anable family as they went to New York and their new home in Brooklyn. Anna Maria felt it important to let Emily know that he was a man of resources and Julia would be well taken care of.

[132] See vol. 1, "Cast of Characters," s.v. "Damaux, Eugenia."

[133] On February 28, 1848, Anna Maria Anable wrote to Emily saying, "Mary Spencer has just returned from Albany. It is said she is engaged to John James, a handsome young widower with three children, and two or three hundred thousand $'s."

[134] Sarah Bell Wheeler was a teacher at the Utica Female Academy, an intimate of Emily Chubbuck, and one of the few who addressed Emily as Nemmy. In a September 1847 letter, she was listed as one of the teachers at the Utica Female Academy. There are a number of letters from Sarah Bell before and after her marriage to Charles Gould of Boston in October 1850. There are several letters clustered in the year or two after Emily left for Burmah and a number at the time of her return to America. Emily stayed with Charles and Sarah Bell Gould in October 1851 when she arrived in Boston after the long sea voyage from Burmah and then England. She stayed there a number of times following that. In 1851, Anna Maria Anable wrote of Sarah Bell: "Sarah is grown so lovely in person as well as character that she must assert a blessed influence on all with whom she comes in contact."

[135] Born in New Hampshire and educated in Washington, DC, Dr. Baron Stow returned to New Hampshire to become the pastor of the Baptist church in Portsmouth. In November 1832, he became the pastor of the Baldwin Place Church in Boston, where he led a significant revival. With changing social conditions in the North End of Boston and with significant erosion of his congregation as members moved to different areas of the city, Dr. Stowe resigned in 1848. Following a time of rest, he became the pastor of the Rowe Street Church and was there until 1867. The letters of Charles Gould speak of the revival events taking place under the ministry of Dr. Stow. See also the next footnote. Reverend and Mrs. Stow took Matilda Dean, the daughter of William Dean, missionary to Hong Kong, into their home in 1835 when Matilda's mother died on the journey from the United States to Singapore.

[136] William Dean was married to Matilda Cowan on April 10, 1834, and they had one daughter, Matilda, born in February 1835. Mrs. Dean died in March 1835, shortly after her daughter's birth and before they reached their destination in Bangkok. They passed through Maulmain in December 1834 and through Singapore in January 1835. William Dean and his baby arrived in Bangkok in July 1835. Baby Matilda was adopted by Rev. Baron Stow. Matilda was fourteen years old when this letter was written.

[137] Emily recently sent back notes to her memoir of Sarah B. Judson.

take for granted that Paul knew when he said the will of God was manifested to them, and that they were without excuse. This is always in interesting subject to the young, and especially to the unconverted.

Are your papers filled with abuse of Baptist Noel? All denominations join in abusing him here except some cool Baptists who have a little charity for him, though he is not

[Written in the right margin of the address page:] altogether one of us. I do hope his clear head will soon break through the cloud that seems to mystify him at present.

We are kept on the *gin-vioe* [sic] the whole ( ) time by the news from Europe. Does ( ) the doctor think that the "better days" have come? I mean in earnest that the millennium will begin in this century? It seems to me that steam, electricity, missionaries, etc. are doing wonders to bring it about.

[Written in the left margin of the address page:] You know Dr. Pattison[138] was obliged to resign at Covington on account of his anti-slavery principles—well, Dr. Malcom[139] has recently been obliged to resign at Georgetown for the same reason (Kentucky is a grant state for Baptists) and he has received a call to Sansom St. He preaches there to day [sic]. I hope he will accept, for

[Written along the left and top margins of page 1:] mother[140] is obliged to go to Sansom St. a good deal of the time. I forgot to say that Geo. Spencer of Utica is married to Libby ( ) and that he called here about a fortnight since. He says Jane

[138] Dr. Robert E. Pattison had a varied early career. He was pastor of several churches; a tutor at Columbian College in Washington, DC; a professor at Waterville College; the secretary of the Home Department of the American Baptist Missionary Union; and the president of the Western Baptist Theological Institute in Lexington, Kentucky. For six years, he was a professor at Newton Theological Seminary. Following Newton, he became the president of Waterville College, which later became Colby College, named after Gardner Colby of Newton Centre, who was a trustee of both the American Baptist Missionary Union and Newton Theological Seminary. (William Cathcart, *The Baptist Encyclopaedia* [Philadelphia: Louis H. Everts, 1881] 887.)

[139] Dr. Howard Malcom was born in Philadelphia in January 1799. Planning to live as a merchant, he was converted and called to the ministry. Licensed by the Sansom Street Church and educated at Princeton Seminary, he became pastor of a church in Hudson, New York, in 1820. In 1826, he became an agent for the American Sunday-School Union, and in 1827, he became the pastor of the Federal Street Church in Boston. Because of failing health, he toured Europe in 1831 and again in 1835 when his voice failed him and he resigned his parish. He next spent two years in Burmah, and upon his return in 1840, he became the president of Georgetown College in Kentucky. In 1849, he was forced to resign this position because of his anti-slavery views. In late 1849 or early 1850, Dr. Malcolm was called to be the pastor of the Sansom Street Baptist Church, which Alma Anable attended, as did some of the other members on occasion of the Anable-Sheldon families. There are many references to him in the letters of this time period. In 1851, he became the president of the University of Lewisburg and was there until he left in 1857 to resume work on a number of his publications. In this time he became interested in the American Baptist Historical Society and devoted himself to this work until his death in 1879. (William Cathcart, *The Baptist Encyclopaedia* [Philadelphia: Louis H. Everts, 1881] 740–41.)

[140] Alma Sheldon Anable was the sister of Miss Cynthia Sheldon and Urania Sheldon Nott. Genealogy sources show that she married Joseph Hubbell Anable in Troy, New York, on July 28, 1814, and that it was the second marriage for Mr. Anable. Born in 1773, he was forty-one at the time of the marriage, and Alma was likely considerably younger. He died in 1831, which explains why Alma Anable and her family lived and worked first at the Utica Female Seminary and then later at the Misses Anable's school in Philadelphia. Joseph and Alma Anable were the parents of nine children: Henry Sheldon Anable (b. June 21, 1815); William Stewart Anable (b. November 6, 1816); Anna Maria Stafford Anable (b. September 30, 1818), Cynthia Jane Anable (b. January 28, 1820); Samuel Low Anable (b. November 28, 1821); Harriet Isabella Anable, also known as Hatty or Hattie (b. December 18, 1823); Courtland Wilcox Anable (b. July 28, 1825); Frances Alma Anable, or Fanny (b. April 12, 1828); and Mary Juliet Anable (b. February 18, 1830).

Kelly[141] will have to add to her "faculty"—it is altogether too weak. Lilly Kelly has ( ) to the ( ) department—he said it *was time*, and Miss McQueen is more unpopular than ever. He told us a great deal considering that he was Jane's right hand man, and her Latin teacher.

[Written in the bottom margin of the address page:] Give my love to Lydia[142] (she don't [sic] deserve it)—( ) ( )) the dear doctor and kiss the babies[143] ( ) for their Aunt

Anna M.

Source: American Baptist Historical Society, AJ 13, no. 478.

Emily C. Judson to her Journal, September 25, 1849

It is not right for a Christian to be continually thinking of death—the coffin—and the grave. I am determined henceforth to look across this black gulf and keep my eye fixed on Christ. He has trod the ground, and I know that He can, that He *will* lead me safely across; for even now do I feel assured He is preparing a place for me. Why should I fear?—and why should I try to harrow up my mind with fearful pictures, as though the flesh was not weak enough without? No; let ascetics keep their coffins to look at—I will look above the wooden box, and the cast-off clay, clinging, as I hasten onward, with all my might, to the cross. Help me, O blessed Redeemer! and I shall indeed triumph over the grave—triumph most gloriously!

Source: A. C. Kendrick, *Life and Letters of Mrs. Emily C. Judson*, 327–28; Hanna family files.

Emily C. Judson to her Journal, September 29, 1849

This earth is a mere speck in the immensity of God's creations; and yet is as dear to Him, as carefully watched over, and its inhabitants are as precious in His sight, as though this were His all. God is not man, that His interest should be divided and diluted by a multiplicity of objects.—I am less than a speck on the earth—few know of my existence, and soon I shall pass away and be forgotten. But if I have been truly washed in the blood of Christ, I shall not be forgotten of Him. I am as dear to Him

141 These are comments about the Utica Female Seminary; Jane Kelly assumed responsibility when the Sheldon-Anable families moved to Philadelphia to start the Misses Anable's School. Jane Kelly was part of Emily and Anna Maria's intimate circle of friends; in her new position, however, she made some changes and incurred some debt, and there were obvious hard feelings about the way Miss Sheldon had been treated. In all of the subsequent letters, Anna Maria is critical of her, and this paragraph is a good example of that criticism.

142 See vol. 1, "Cast of Characters," s.v. "Lillybridge, Lydia." See also "A Timeline of the Life and Mission of Lydia Lillybridge Simons."

143 Henry Hall Judson, seven years old; Edward Judson, almost five years old; and Emily Frances Judson, almost two years old.

as though I were the only intelligent creature in the universe—as though the only being God created, and the only being for whom the Son of God came into the world and died. If I am truly redeemed, I shall enter into that intimate relation with my Redeemer indicated by the scriptural phrase, "The bride—the Lamb's wife," just as entirely and completely as though, instead of being the minutest infinitesimal part of the Church triumphant, it consisted of me alone. These are overwhelming thoughts, and call for a serious, thoughtful, prayerful line of life. They are at once animating, ennobling, and humiliating.

Source: A. C. Kendrick, *Life and Letters of Mrs. Emily C. Judson*, 328; Hanna family files.

Miss Martha J. Loring to Emily C. Judson,[144] October 13, 1849

Summation: The letter accompanies a box sent by the Bowdoin Square Mission – "It has been, with anxiety, we have watched for tidings from you, since we learned of your failing health, and with deep solicitude and fervent prayer have we commended you to our Father, and to y(our) Father God. It is our hope, and desire, you may soon be fully restored" – they pray for Emily's continued usefulness in the midst of her suffering – hope that "the God of all grace preserve you to assist in advancing his cause" – Miss Loring adds a personal note expressing her own solicitations and prayers – "and when you have passed over Jordan will receive you to reign forever in his kingdom of Light. O pray your life and health be preserved in His sight who notest every sparrow that falleth to the ground! O may he in his great good time restore to you your strength and ( ), that you may continue your Mission of love! I would ask your acceptance of the dress pattern and papers from ( ) personally" – "We should be happy to learn of the safe arrival of this box" – "In behalf of the Bowdoin Square ( ) Circle I am affectionally Martha J. Loring."

[144] The original of this letter is badly stained, and in spite of valiant efforts, the legible copy quality makes up a fraction of the entire text. We have edited it severely, summarized some lines, and put in a couple of complete lines.

Emily C. Judson to Anna Maria Anable,[145] October 21, 1849—Maulmain

My dear Anna Maria,

You have really sent me quite a budget of matrimonial news[146]—Eugenia,[147] and Lou Adams, and Mr. Corey[148]—could'nt [sic] you add the owner of a certain "auburn tressaraet [sic]" to the list? It would be comforting to her friends to know said lady was provided for, in a suitable lady-like sort of a way. By the way, why not set your cap at Mr. [Note: The name has been cut out.] at once, and then come out here, and settle close beside us? You should have the church, and we old ones would turn evangelists—we have a sort of penchant for that business, and you should occasionally look after the picaninnies while we traveled. Then I could help you a deal in getting the language, and give you hints about the people etc. Don't [sic] the bait take?

About Ava[149]—some people have thought we are very imprudent to think of going, Mr. J. being past sixty, and I such an invalid; but when I see people with every luxury about them, and the most skilful [sic] doctor's [sic] in attendance, die down as they do in America, I think we are just as well off in a desert, with God above us, and a loving one beside, as any where [sic] on earth. I would not hesitate one moment on account of my health about going to Ava; but would go, and if I had but a little time to live, try to spend it to the best advantage. No such considerations as that would hinder either of us.

Mr. J.'s objection going to Ava, aside from his dictionary, was to endeavour [sic] to obtain some degree of toleration, if not open, a sort of implied favour [sic]—without which a missionary may sit till doomsday without accomplishing any good. The prospect for obtaining such toleration was never darker than at this moment; but a crisis in the political affairs of Burmah *must* be at hand, and I sincerely hope that the clouds will break away before the arrival of Mr. Kincaid.[150] He will have no difficulty as I thought in *going up* to the capital; but he will find it very hard to get the kind of permission to go, necessary to his being rec'd with favour [sic] when he

[145] This letter has an addendum also dated October 21, 1849. The addendum is a list of items Emily would like to have Anna Maria send to her. It then goes on to comment on her health.

[146] See the letter of Anna Maria Anable to Emily C. Judson dated July 27, 1849.

[147] See vol. 1, "Cast of Characters," s.v. "Damaux, Eugenia."

[148] See vol. 1, "Cast of Characters," s.v. "Corey, The Reverend D. G."

[149] In February 1847, Adoniram, Emily, Henry, and Edward moved to Rangoon as a stepping stone for eventual ministry in Ava. They were forced to return to Maulmain in early September 1847 due to reductions in funding to the mission by the Board of the American Baptist Missionary Union. A February 20, 1849, letter from Dr. Solomon Peck, the executive secretary of the missionary union mentioned to Emily that she would be going to Ava; unfortunately, the opportunity arose when work on the dictionary was more effectively done in Maulmain and when debilitating illness prevented Emily or Adoniram from thinking of making a move. Here, as this is written toward the end of October, those health concerns seem mitigated. She does not know that this will change quickly. Emily will discover that she is expecting once again (she states this at the end of this letter), and Adoniram Judson will begin his final illness toward the end of the year.

[150] See vol. 1, "Cast of Characters," s.v. "Kincaid, The Reverend Doctor Eugenio."

gets there. But "with God all things are possible," and it may be that his time to favour [sic] Burmah is at hand. I am glad on various accounts that Mr. Kincaid is coming—among others, that it relieves us from a duty no person would rashly covet. I would not shrink from duty; neither would I *court* difficulties and dangers, when I saw an able person ready to incur them in my stead. I suppose Mr. J. better calculated to succeed at Ava than any other person, for he has a combined dignity and winningness of manner, which has great power over the natives; but aside from this Mr. K. or any younger man is more suitable, and the rash boldness of the latter may serve him at a pinch where a cooler and deeper judgement [sic] would fail. God understands his own instruments, and may his blessing be upon them wherever they are, and in whatever work they are especially engaged.

Really I cannot sufficiently wonder at and admire the prophetic acumen of the Philadelphia "goodies," for they saw considerably more than a year into futurity and made only one slight mistake—the sex.[151] Master Charley announces his intention of taking a peep into this world of trouble sometime in May next; but I solemnly protest it is the first intimation of the kind I have received since lady Fanny[152] kicked up such a row with my poor stomach in Rangoon.[153] Naughty Charley is following her example, (as it seems to be the delight of these small fry) and the more irritable he finds his subject, the more he seems to glory in tormenting. By the way, we are about as rare a house full as you would care to see. Edward[154] and Frances, the two fat ones, have become mere shadows of what they were, and they still cough incessantly. Their papa too looks more like the "shad that climbed up Niagara," than like his own hearty self. They have been down with fever and influenza, and are just beginning to rally. Henry[155] and I also had the latter, but lightly. But *such* times as I have hopping up in the night and running from one bed to another; at the same time making such interesting demonstrations as one hears the first week of a sea-voyage. Oh! it is rare! Poor Frances has been the worst sufferer. She was cutting her last double teeth and this heightened the disorder. It went to the head, and for several days she lay stupid, and in imminent danger. The doctor says she had uncommon strength of constitution to live through so much. All (all but Charley's mama) are better.

[151] In a previous letter to Emily, she had been told of rumors among the women of Philadelphia about Emily having a second daughter.

[152] See vol. 1, "Cast of Characters," s.v. "Judson, Emily Frances."

[153] Emily is announcing to Anna Maria her second pregnancy. Charles Judson, named after her father, was stillborn in April 1850.

[154] See vol. 1, "Cast of Characters," s.v. "Judson, Edward."

[155] See vol. 1, "Cast of Characters," s.v. "Judson, Henry."

Aunt U[156] has written me only once[157]—an excellent letter, but I fancied a little stiff.[158] I have not answered it yet, I have been so ill and so busy, but mean to next month.

Fanny has given me a kiss for "Aunt Anna" but I can't induce her to give me one for her little cousin 'Bel.[159] She will learn to be less shy one of these days. She is the most beautiful creature that I ever beheld—even more so since her illness than before, and she seems so delicate and spirit-like. Her papa says, as she developes [sic], he feels more and more as though we should not have her long, and sometimes it seems to me as though there was a wonderful look to her; but we neither of us believe much in such whimsies.

The "box" was indeed a treasure—every scrap valuable. *Such* pretty things as I have made for the children and myself from the nice remnants, and such comfortable things from other valuables. There are a few other articles that I want and for which I don't like to send to Boston or New York though it would be nearer. I want three or four caps, light and tasty, but modest sort of dress caps for myself. I have to wear them on account of my head and I have lived thus far on the charity of the mission—principally Mrs. Ranney.[160] She gave me the sweetest little Boston cap that I ever set eyes on. We have to be much more nice [sic] about these things than you would suppose. Then I want a Jenny Lind hat for Frances who is yet bareheaded. Her head is an uncommonly large one, and the hat will not reach her much short of a year after you purchase it. Please also send her a doll. She has got a horrid rag baby which she pets and kisses till it makes me sick.

[Written on the left and top margin of page 1:] Please also send grass-cloth for two skirts, and a little magnifying glass and a prism for the boys. Also a few yards of India rubber cloth. But I will make out a little list on another sheet of paper. Give love to Hatty[161] and all the others. I do long to see you and mean to come over by way of Panama one of these days. The cholera is raging—cases almost at our door last night. No Europeans as yet attacked, but the air is very bad—it almost seems as though I could feel the poison in it.

Au voir de Dieu!

Nemmy[162]

Source: Hanna family files..

[156] See vol. 1, "Cast of Characters," s.v. "Sheldon, Urania."

[157] See the letter of Urania Sheldon Nott to Emily C. Judson dated March 15, 1849.

[158] The Sunday after his marriage to Emily E. Chubbuck, Adoniram Judson baptized her best friend, Anna Maria Anable, in the Mohawk River of Utica. Mrs. Nott, who had married the Reverend Doctor Eliphalet Nott, a Presbyterian clergyman and president of Union College in Schenectady, had been critical, and both Emily and Anna Maria felt that their relationship with Mrs. Nott had been damaged.

[159] 'Bel was the daughter of Anna Maria Anable's brother William and his wife Olivia.

[160] Maria Gager Ranney arrived in Maulmain in May 1844. Her husband Thomas was the superintendent of the printing press and business manager for the missionary compound. A letter from Lydia Lillybridge reveals that Mrs. Ranney had some responsibilities in the mission schools. She had no children; Maria Ranney died on April 26, 1857.

[161] See vol. 1, "Cast of Characters," s.v. "Anable, Harriet."

Emily C. Judson to Anna Maria Anable,[163] October 21, 1849

List of articles desired

1. Three or four lady's caps (Pink trimming is most becoming) I can wear most other colours except straw.
2. A little girl's broad-brimmed straw hat. (Jenny Lind)
3. Gray cloth for two skirts.
4. Two or three yards of India rubber cloth.
5. 1/2 dozen lady's cravats—mostly to match the caps
6. Straw bonnet trimmed with pink.
7. A small magnifying glass. 8th A Basin 9th A Doll.

Please box these things up to send by Mr. Kincaid[164] in the spring, if you have no earlier opportunity. Mr. Newton[165] of New York wrote that he sent a box for us to the mission rooms last Jan'y, and we have not even heard from it, so I suppose it is lying there still. You can judge from this how rapidly we get things, unless some friends are coming immediately. I do not send an order for the money because I think you will venture to trust me, and I don't want to cramp you in your purchases. Spend what money you find necessary, and send the bill—will you? It will be necessary to put up the caps very carefully or the lace will get yellow at sea. Please in making up a box, to throw in some of the cheap publications (no matter if the selection is not nice) with which America is over-run. Sometimes my mind and body are completely worn out and I think I would give anything for the respite from thinking afforded by some of your light trash. Perhaps a better person would'nt [sic] need such kind of rest, but it is peculiarly fitted to the make of my mind; and sometimes when I have over-studied, it takes my mind a whole week to recover its healthful tone; when I know that a little light reading would make it fly back to its old place without any difficulty. And this is no mental peculiarity of mine. Mr. J is precisely the same way, and always has been. He has read five times the novels that I ever did. *Don't tell of it.*

[162] "Nem" or "Nemmy" was a name of endearment given to Emily by a small group of her intimate friends at the Utica Female Academy. Anna Maria Anable was "Ninny."

[163] This letter was an addendum to a letter of the same date.

[164] See vol. 1, "Cast of Characters," s.v. "Kincaid, The Reverend Doctor Eugenio."

[165] There are six letters in this correspondence from Mr. and Mrs. Newton of New York City. In a June 1846 letter Mrs. Newton indicated that they were "new friends" of Emily. They obviously had considerable wealth, which they shared generously with Adoniram and Emily through packages, and upon Adoniram's death, they immediately sent a check for five hundred dollars to Emily. Mr. Newton called Adoniram his "friend," and one of the letters invited Emily to stay with them in New York upon her return. A later letter indicates that Emily had indeed done that. On May 15, 1846, Adoniram Judson inscribed a dedication to Mrs. H. H. Newton on the fly-leaf of a volume of Burmese hymns that had been compiled by Mrs. Sarah B. Judson: "Mrs. H. H. Newton From A. Judson/ The wings ( ) ( ) /( ) are folded in St. Helena—New York—May 15th, 1846."

No, Ninny,[166] I have not got a liver complaint; but there are few persons in this part of the world whose livers are not more or less torpid. This is the case with mine. It needs to be poked with blue pills occasionally. Since I wrote you last, I have had a long talk with Doct. Morton[167] and insisted on his telling me precisely what he thought of my case. He says he believes my lungs to be entirely sound (though weak) and the bronchial tubes to be free from disease. The liver too he said was sound though inactive. He says it took him a long time to decide what was the matter, but he seems as confident now as a clairvoyant would be. It is inflammation of the mucous membranes lining the stomach (not dispepsia, you know). He says the disease is of long standing—probably seven or eight years, and when I told him of my "cachminations" [sic] formerly, he pronounced them spasms of the stomach, and said I should most likely have been ( ) off by them, but for change of scene backed by the voyage.

He says that is a dangerous form of the disease—even more so than the present. He says it is not at all likely that these ulcers in the throat (occasioned by the disease) actually extend into the stomach, thought they are predominately in the esophagus. When I questioned him about the danger he was not quite so communicative—said while it remained in its present form it was not dangerous—but if it should retreat to any vital part, there would be great danger. He several times remarked that I had great reason to be thankful for my sore throat notwithstanding the inconvenience of it. When I asked him if I should ever get rid of it he said that was a great deal to expect from a disease of such long standing, but with proper care and attention it might be ( ) comfortable. He remarked too, what I had already discovered, that it was a very distressing disease. Hav'nt [sic] I given you a long list of ailings—well, I thought it would relieve your mind to know all about it. I place great confidence in what Morton says, for he is acknowledged by every body [sic] to be an uncommonly skilful [sic] doctor, and he *seemed* to be very ( )and honest.

Source: Hanna family files.

166 "Ninny" was a name of endearment given to Anna Maria Anable by her most intimate friends at the Utica Female Academy. Emily was "Nemmy."

167 Doctor Morton was a physician who worked with the missionaries in Maulmain, Burmah. He delivered Emily Frances Judson in December 1847 and was present when Charles Judson ("Angel Charley") was stillborn in April 1850. He was a valued and trusted advisor to the mission families.

Miss Lydia Lillybridge to the Reverend Doctor Solomon Peck,[168] October 22, 1849—Maulmain

Rev. Mr. Peck,
Dear Sir,

In regard to the watch that you so kindly furnished me while in Boston, I had not time to explain when writing to you last month.[169] After running about a year and a half, it stopped; and there being no watch-maker in Maulmain, I found that it would be a troublesome, and expensive business to keep it in repair. I therefore, thought it best to return the watch by Mr. Haswell,[170] and purchase a clock for my school room. I did so, and find the clock more convenient than the watch—I thought that you would not be unwilling to receive the watch again, though I intended to purchase it when I took it. If the watch is found to be injured, I am ready to do anything to give satisfaction.

I am sorry to hear of your ill health, but happy to know that you still retain the office of Secretary.

In regard to my own health, I have much reason for gratitude to the Giver of all good gifts. During the short time that I have been here, which is nearly three years, I have been detained from school by illness, only one half day.

Respecting the health of my soul, I cannot speak as favorably. Oh! that the Holy Spirit would descend upon us like rain.

With affectionate regards to Mrs. Peck, yourself and the little girls, I am
Dear Sir
Yours respectfully,

Lydia Lillybridge

Source: American Baptist Historical Society, Lydia Lillybridge files.

[168] This letter is one of four from Lydia Lillybridge to Dr. Solomon Peck that have been included in the correspondence of Emily Chubbuck Judson. Lydia Lillybridge's story was so intimately connected with Emily's that this gives another window into her life. This also helps to round out the picture of Miss Lillybridge.

[169] See the letter from Lydia Lillybridge to Dr. Solomon Peck dated September 22, 1849.

[170] James Haswell had sailed for Burmah in 1835, arriving in February 1836 to work with the Talaings. His wife was Jane Haswell. James Haswell became a partner with Adoniram and Sarah Judson, and when Adoniram and Elnathan were born, Sarah turned over the translation of the Peguan Scripture to him. He served as a missionary for more than forty years.

Miss Sarah J. Hinckley to Emily C. Judson, November 18, 1849—Versailles, Woodford Co., KY

My very dear Mrs. Judson

Months have passed since the messenger from your "Indian nest"[171] reached me here. It lies before me now, travel-worn—and ( ) with frequent perusal. Those few lines! You did not think as you penned them in your far off home, how very happy their reception would make me—for in the multiplicity of your duties and the demands upon your pen I deemed myself forgotten.

Three years and a half ago! How distinctly I see the halls of the old Sem., the tearful faces, tho' one face so pale with sorrow yet calm in its furrowed composure—on the morning you started for Boston and Burmah. Well change that visits all, has been busy among that tearful group. Some will *weep no more*, some have doubled both joys and sorrows—surely all are separated. You have heard of Nora Westcott's death—Dear Nora, who died triumphantly, beautifully—at Jackson, Miss of the consumption which so long threatened her.

A few months ago a paragraph in the *Home Journal* sent a chill of sorrow to so many hearts.—You were declining in health and Burmah would probably be your grave.[172]

We could only sorrow and pray. Our Father has seen fit to avert the threatened affliction. You are better now—and yesterday the news came that you have another bird—your "nest" will be fuller of song than ever.[173] Little birds! May they long live and with their moving songs and wings keep back the mother bird from flight.—But your dear little babies! how I would love to see them—Are they both like their mother? When *I* gave you up—to go to Burmah, I have often thought it was not an *entire* surrender—for a hope possessed me that you would come back some time. *I am* hopeful yet—and love to be so, except when I think that probably a grave and sorrow lie between you and the *return*. How glad am I and all your many friends that in your exile—your spirit trials—your illness—your dangers—God is nigh you—The hollow of His hand is your refuge—and that gift of God, a hopeful, cheerful heart, turns trials into pure golden blessings.—Thus with more of ( ) we give you up—But your affectionate inquiries shall be answered—The July after you left for Burmah I left Utica with its ties—for wherever destiny called me. The next year I passed in Virginia.

[171] On January 1, 1848, eight days after the birth of Emily Frances Judson, Emily wrote a celebratory poem that she called "My Bird." The poem spoke of a "birdling" that had come to Emily's "Indian nest." It had a total of seven stanzas, and it was widely published in the United States.

[172] On March 18, 1849, Adoniram Judson wrote to Anna Maria Anable to tell her of Emily's illness and that he despaired for her life. Emily's letters also spoke of the severity of this illness, its symptoms, and what God was doing with her and in her through it all.

[173] A rumor had been circulating that Emily had given birth to another daughter. See Emily's letter of October 21, 1849, in which she speaks of this and announces that she is expecting "Charley" in the spring.

Then failing health sent me to my valley-home. Nearly a year I passed alternating between sick bed and lounge—until God blessed medical attention and my dear mother's nursing, by removing the threatened spinal disease and I was restored to health. And apropos of this—What a "Mount of Transfiguration" a sick bed sometimes proves. How soothingly with an altered vision we see the God of Might in the pitying Father "whose frowns are all in love." And sometimes in our deafness to the earth-chords—jangled and out of tune—how stirringly like a trumpet's notes, fall on our ears the voices of the "( ) harping upon their harps"—in the celestial city—

But I am writing to one who knows more of this than I—whose ear needs not the spiritualizing of ( )ness to attune it to heavenly harmonies—who has proven this by self banishment from home to labor in darkness—

Soon after my recovery I came to Ky—where I have been engaged since, teaching a little school of twelve scholars. I am among a noble people—full of kindly sympathies and generous impulses. I like teaching—yet its responsibilities often frighten me. I have not ( ) them much, since I lost you—and have published I believe *nothing*. You know you were my *mama*—and I have never had a *step-mother*—Your question "What am I doing for Christ?" Alas! that I must say *so little*—I find often added to weakness of flesh—want of willingness of spirit.

You hear from Aunt Cynthia[174] and Aunt U.[175]—Their school in Philadelphia[176] is now quite prosperous—as also the Sem.[177] under Miss Kelly's[178] charge. Sister Libby is now in Jackson, Miss. Hannah has been married a year and a half—is living delightfully in Oswego, N.Y. Mrs. Avery and husband have made Louisville their home—where I shall visit them soon and see one whom I know you admire "Amelia Welby." Julia Look[179] is now Mrs. Casswell—and lives in the city of N. Y. Louisa

[174] See vol. 1, "Cast of Characters," s.v. "Sheldon, Miss Cynthia."

[175] See vol. 1, "Cast of Characters," s.v. "Sheldon, Urania."

[176] The Anable-Sheldon families left Utica, New York, to start the Misses Anable's School in Philadelphia. Letters showed an increasing number of students, and after more than a year, it was quite obvious that the endeavor had a solid foundation and a great prospect.

[177] The Utica Female Academy, where Emily had been both a student and a teacher.

[178] Miss Jane Kelly was Emily Chubbuck's friend at the Utica Female Academy, and then she became a teacher with Emily at that institution. Miss Kelly became the literary principal in 1844 with the retirement of Mr. and Mrs. James Nichols from that position. During a period of Miss Kelly's illness in 1844, Emily filled in the position for her. Then, in 1848, when Miss Cynthia Sheldon moved to Philadelphia to help start the Misses Anable's School, Miss Kelly became the "headmistress" of the academy and successfully brought it into the future, though not without some initial disparagement from the Sheldon-Anable families.

[179] Julia Look was a student of Emily's at the Utica Female Academy and later a fellow teacher. A November 22, 1845, letter from Anna Maria encouraged Emily to stay in Philadelphia for the winter for her health and remarked that Julia had the hardest part because she was teaching Emily's composition class, and the students kept asking for Emily. In a September 1847 letter, she was listed as one of the teachers at the Utica Female Academy. On September 23, 1849, Anna Maria wrote that Julia and Albert B. Casswell were married and came to visit with her. In one 1849 letter Julia spoke of another teacher who was teaching "our composition class." On October 27, 1850, Anna Maria Anable noted that she had had a son. She was one of a small number of people who addressed Emily as "Emily" and as "Nemmy" in her letters.

Marble[180] has also married and removed there. Miss Damaux[181] had become Mrs. Edmonds of Utica. Perhaps in retailing [sic] these items I am "carrying coals to New Castle." Willis[182] has become nearly a literary dandy aspiring to be thought the oracle of fashion—taste—etc and I fear becoming heartless. How pitiful—that such God-given talents should be thus frittered away in the baubles of his pursuit. "Poe" the strange poet of "Raven" memory is dead—and his mother-in-law—his earthly guardian angel is represented as suffering in poverty.

Dear friend I have spoken a long yarn—but I know your heart turns with love and fondest memory to America—its people and the heart-circle you left—you promised to write me again—Will you and soon—and tell me all about your Indian home—you cares—your pleasures—your friends and your little ones.

Have you any English society at Maulmain? Where is Miss Lillybridge?[183] Give my most cordial love to her.

You ask what I read? Histories have been my books for a while—Prescott—McCauley—Lamartine—etc. Your life of Mrs. Judson[184] lies before me—which I have reread—and have tried to picture from it your home etc. I have failed to satisfy myself.

I am in a Baptist vicinity—and should I write all the messages of love and kindly wishes they send, my little sheet would be full. Gentlemen—and ladies many say, "tell her I love her"—and all pray for your continued health and usefulness. Now my dear friend need I say how much we all desire your happiness—how much all miss you—but we more who knew you—and with what love I remember your guidance and interest—I do not forget you or yours when my heart looks up for the bestowment of blessings upon its loved ones—or fail to remember with ( ) thanks-

[180] In 1843, Miss Marble was a recent graduate of the Utica Female Seminary and wrote to Emily upon her return to Port Byron. In an 1848 letter to Emily, she was at the academy as a teacher and was fully involved there. According to a letter written by Sarah Hinckley in 1849, Miss Marble married and moved to New York City. In Emily's February 19, 1850, letter she was referred to as "Lou Marble Wright." Then, in April 1851, Anna Maria mentioned that Louisa Marble Wright was now a widow, back living in Utica with her sister.

[181] See vol. 1, "Cast of Characters," s.v. "Damaux, Eugenia."

[182] Nathaniel Parker Willis was the editor, with General George Morris, of the *New Mirror*, a prominent literary magazine in New York. His "discovery" of Emily in the June 8, 1844, edition of the *New Mirror* catapulted her into literary fame and enabled her to command the highest prices for her articles and stories from the major magazines of that period. Over the next two years, he became her friend, mentor, and confidant. His black-bordered letter of March 21, 1846, made it abundantly clear that he had expected to marry Emily upon his return that month from England. He later returned several letters to Emily to demonstrate to her, lest she had forgotten, why he had felt right in that expectation. Within a few months of Emily's departure for Burmah, Willis was married to the ward of a United States senator; one of the letters to Emily from her friends stated that his new bride had significant wealth. The *New Mirror* went out of business as Willis was returning to the United States, and he established another publication, the *Home Journal*, with General George Morris. See vol. 1, "Cast of Characters," s.v. "Willis, Nathaniel Parker (N. P. Willis)." For a detailed examination of his relationship with Emily, see vol. 1, "Timeline," s.v. "The Correspondence and Relationship between Emily E. Chubbuck/Fanny Forester and Nathaniel Parker Willis: A Litany of Unrequited Romance."

[183] See vol. 1, "Cast of Characters," s.v. "Lillybridge, Lydia." See also "A Timeline of the Life and Mission of Lydia Lillybridge Simons."

[184] Fanny Forester, *Memoir of Sarah B. Judson, Member of the American Mission to Burmah* (New York: L. Colby and Company, 1848).

givings that you are spared. My mother and sister desire to be remembered to you with most cordial love. Kiss your children[185] for me. Remember me to Dr. Judson.

I shall be impatient for the time to come when I may hope to hear from you. Till then—and ever—may God bless you with the richest gifts of His providence and grace.

Your most lovingly

Sarah J. Hinckley

Direct: Norwich Chenanys Co. N. Y. I shall return there in June next.

Source: American Baptist Historical Society, AJ 16, no. 669.

Anna Maria Anable to Emily C. Judson, November 24, 1849—311 Walnut St.

Dear Nemmy[186]

It is a rainy Saturday and sha'nt [sic] I have nice time [sic] writing letters? The storm is not as driving as the one you describe in yours of August 1st but only gentle drizzle which makes a good excuse for one staying at home and spending the day as we please. With our many engagements this is a luxury I assure you. Last night the Misses Anable's school had an invitation to visit an Elysian, which for the amusement of the children I will try and describe. In the first place about fifty of us including some friends started from our door, and after a short walk came to a building five stories high. The Elysium rooms were in the fifth story, and by the time we reached it, some of the little ones, not over seven years old were pretty tired but they forgot their fatigue as soon as they entered the first room. Some jumped on the spring boards and immediately bounded up one or two feet in the air, others seated themselves in a little sail car and rode round and round the room which was about sixty feet long, and so gave them a good long ride in going round twice. They were all delighted with this, and wanted to go very fast until while they were going very rapidly the cars went off the track and threw one of the little girls against the wall. She was not much hurt, but a good deal frightened and they learned to be more moderate after that. In the same room were two games, something like nine-pins, a shuffle board, a long pole to walk on, a ladder, upon a scaffolding about eight feet high upon which the boys were to climb underneath with their hands. There was a mattress on the floor underneath, so that if they fell as they were apt to do, they would not hurt themselves. There were elastic bands let down from the ceiling,

[185] Henry Hall Judson, seven years old; Edward Judson, almost five years old; and Emily Frances Judson, almost two years old.

[186] "Nem" or "Nemmy" was a name of endearment given to Emily by a small group of her intimate friends at the Utica Female Academy. Anna Maria Anable was "Ninny."

with rings in them, which the little girls would seize by mounting a staging two or three steps high, and then swing off. When they got tired of play they could go into the next room which was a reading room, with delightful sofas and easy chairs, a piano and books and pictures of all sorts. In the center of the next room was a huge pile of rocks covered with moss, and flowers, on the top of which was a beautiful bronze statue. There were two other statues in the same room, three beautiful little squirrels, three canary birds, a gold-finch and a parrot. One would think that was enough to see at one time, but no, there was one more room nearby, as large as the first one, containing swings of all kinds. There was a large cradle boat which would hold eight little girls, then a boat of nearly the same size swinging in the air. There were large cushioned arm chair swings, in which you could swing yourself by pulling an elastic band, ropes to jump—and battle doors [sic] and graces. We then went down to the next floor where was [sic] a riding school—this seemed odd enough—a riding school on the fourth story! But it was a beautiful room floored with tan bark and the horses looked so fine that Mary[187] and Courtland[188] could not resist the temptation to ride. The three lower stories contained panoramas etc. etc. but we thought we had seen enough for one evening. So we returned home, thinking we had had a nice frolic, and I suspect the little ones were tired enough to sleep soundly at least. Well Nemmy, I rather think you have had enough of this rigmarole. Shall I tell you how gay we have been this fall? How I have had my India number made up[189] and have worn it twice, and how pretty and becoming it is. I christened it at Mrs. Potter's and then wore it to Mrs. Patterson's. Mr. P. is president of one of the great banks here and his wife Dr. Cuyler's daughter is a superb woman. All that family are kindness itself to us—wish us to come in and spend the eve'g or take tea whenever we can, and they always seem to think it a great favor whenever we do so. There are six daughters four of whom are unmarried. The eldest was a pupil of Aunt U's[190] in Sche'd—she is goodness itself, but her life is blighted. Some years ago she was to have been married to a noble young man from Va. The day was appointed, even the supper table spread, all were full of gay anticipation of his arrival, when instead of himself came a letter to Dr. C. from a physician telling of his sudden illness and death on his way to Phila. and containing his last messages to poor Susan. For two years she never was seen to smile; now she tries to be cheerful and even goes into society some. Sarah, who is about twenty-three, is handsome and intellectual. Carrie is playful and affectionate. And Neelie [sic] my pet and

[187] See vol. 1, "Cast of Characters," s.v. "Anable, Miss Mary Juliet."

[188] Courtland Anable was a younger brother of Anna Maria Anable. He held several positions over the years, and he studied at Hamilton College while he boarded for a time with Emily's parents. In 1853, he returned to Philadelphia where he preached his first sermon at the Eleventh Baptist Church. He was "Uncle Court" to Emily Frances Judson. In 1880, Courtland Anable was listed in the Massachusetts Census as an ordained minister serving in a church.

[189] Among the gifts that Emily sent was a dress to be adapted to Anna Maria and cloth to be made into dresses.

[190] See vol. 1, "Cast of Characters," s.v. "Sheldon, Urania."

pupil is bright, pretty, and loving. They have an only brother who is disagreeable as such brothers are apt to be.

While I am in this gossiping mood I will tell you about a great wedding that we attended lately. Miss Bayard, sister to two of our pupils was the bride and Mr. Beck, (according to Bennett's *Herald* the nephew of a *millionaire*) was the bridegroom. Henry Clay, an intimate friend of the family's traveled day and night to get on to the wedding in season and was upset once in the stage coach, which all had to go into the papers, of course. The bride looked lovely in fine lace, embroidered satin etc. and Mr. Clay is as ugly as the pictures make him out to be, but striking and gentlemanly nevertheless. The fashion here is to be married before the family friends, and to send out cards to the "dear five hundred" in a week or two, saying you will be at home to see them at such a day and hour. All *our* folks, that is the church are working their fingers off for a fair. Fanny[191] and Mary are embroidering a superb chair, and the rest of us are doing all sort of little nick-nacks [sic]—Mother[192] knitting baby's shirts, Aunt C.[193] embroidering socks, etc.

Sansom St. has at last got a pastor. Dr. Malcom[194] is determined they ( ) shall do their duty, if he can make them do it by telling it to them. Won't it be a luxury to hear him preach rainy evenings? Hatty[195] and Mary have gone down with young Johnson from Iowa to hear Dr. Ide[196] this afternoon. I have just come up from Bible class, where the dear girls have a chance to learn what they ought to do, but oh! how unfit I do feel to teach them. There is but one of our little number that is a professor of religion, but she may be the means of interesting the others. Nellie Bennett[197] is growing graceful, pretty and interesting, but still I see no indication of any desire for a change of heart. I thought a year ago that she was *very* indifferent, but she does not seem quite as much so now.

There! Mr. Clay, Bishop Potter, Dr. Caylor, Mr. Gillette[198] and some others have just been in to visit the school and Mr. Clay addressed them. It went off beautifully. Can you contrive at what different times this letter is written? I am writing now during recess and as the letter must go this afternoon.

Now for your questions. You say you never received that pair of slippers. I sent them with the wrapper, coffee pot, irons, pie-pans, knives and forks etc. from Boston. I have suspected there were some things in that box that you never appropriated to

[191] See vol. 1, "Cast of Characters," s.v. "Anable, Fanny."

[192] See vol. 1, "Cast of Characters," s.v. "Sheldon, Alma and Joseph Hubbell."

[193] See vol. 1, "Cast of Characters," s.v. "Sheldon, Miss Cynthia."

[194] See vol. 1, "Cast of Characters," s.v. "Malcom, The Reverend Doctor Howard."

[195] See vol. 1, "Cast of Characters," s.v. "Anable, Harriet."

[196] See vol. 1, "Cast of Characters," s.v. "Ide, Dr. George."

[197] Nellie Bennett was the daughter of Cephas and Stella Bennett, who were missionaries to Burmah. As was usual in that period, children were sent back to the United States to be educated, as obviously Nellie Bennett (and her sisters) had been.

[198] See vol. 1, "Cast of Characters," s.v. "Gillette, The Reverend Abram Dunn."

yourself. Did you, or Mrs. Ballard get a set of silver spoons I sent to *you* marked with your initials? Mr. Gillette[199] has given your little poem the "Two Mama's"[200] to Mr. Sartain[201] and he is to give him twenty five dollars for it. We thought it best to spend it here so that you *could* not give it to the Board. What shall we get? I think very likely it will all be expended before we can hear from you. Do you want a new supply of ( ), for gowns, caps etc.? I think I shall send you some at a venture. And the wrapper, I imagine, from your description of yourself that rainy ev'g, would be acceptable.

Mr. and Mrs. Bronson[202] were here yesterday and are to dine with us in company with Dr. Malcom and wife on Thanksgiving day. I like Mr. and Mrs. B. very much. What you said in your note I understand but I think you are a little prejudiced against a certain person who is appointed to the Board to return to Burmah[203] next Spring.

Give a great deal of love to Lydia[204] and tell her I shall answer her excellent note next month—

affect. Anna M. Anable[205]

Source: American Baptist Historical Society, AJ 13, no. 477.

[199] See vol. 1, "Cast of Characters," s.v. "Gillette, The Reverend A. (Abram) D. (Dunn) and Hannah."

[200] In 1849, Emily wrote this poem to explain to the Judson children how she had become Adoniram Judson's wife and their new "mother."

[201] John Sartain was one of the most prominent engravers of the mid-nineteenth century. His works appeared in prominent magazines and books. In 1846, he created an engraving of Emily E. Chubbuck that was used as a plate for *Alderbrook*. The correspondence of spring 1846 reflects meetings with Mr. Sartain on changes thought to be needed. In 1849, Mr. Sartain was publishing a magazine because a letter makes a reference to one of Emily's poems being in it.

[202] See vol. 1, "Cast of Characters," s.v. "Bronson, Miles."

[203] This is probably a reference to the Reverend Eugenio Kincaid.

[204] See vol. 1, "Cast of Characters," s.v. "Lillybridge, Lydia." Also, "A Timeline of the Life and Mission of Lydia Lillybridge Simons."

[205] This may be the only time that Anna Maria Anable uses her last name in a signature. There are more than 150 letters from Anna Maria Anable in the correspondence.

Miss Rebecca Ann "Bessie" Rhees to Adoniram Judson, November 25, 1849[206]—Mount Holly, NJ

I cannot tell you, dear friend, the delight with which I received your letter. I had begun to think before I wrote to you, that I never should hear from you again and sometimes since, when in a desponding mood, I have remembrance, and hoping to find that I had still a place in your regard. The assurance of continued friendship which your letter contained is very precious to me; ah! if an expression of affection from one we love makes us so very happy here, what will be the bliss of that world where all is love, "where the ties we form will be forever unbroken," and no barrier separate us from those whom we hold dear. Next to the service of the sanctuary, I realize in the affection of those I love and honor, the best foretaste of the joys of Heaven.

I should have written sooner, but expect that Brother and Sister Vinton[207] would return to Burmah this fall, have delayed till I should know when they would sail, intending to send my letter by them. But they will not leave now until Spring, and I cannot wait till then to thank you for recollecting and caring for one, who, dear as you are to her, is conscious that she is among the least of those who claim your remembrance. Indeed, I reverenced you so long and so deeply, at a distance, that I can scarcely even now believe that I have a right to call you friend. I never carried my veneration quite so far as my sister Alice, who used to declare, that when she got rich, she "would have the best portrait of you she could find hung in her chamber, and keep wax candles burning before it night and day," an extravagance for which we have often laughed at her, but I recollect that I did say once, when Grand-ma asked me soon after your return to America, if I had ever written to you. "Write to Dr. Judson! That *would* be presumption. I should as soon think of writing

[206] Miss Rebecca Ann Rhees, who wrote this and four other letters to Adoniram Judson, also wrote three letters to Emily C. Judson beginning in September 1850 with the death of Adoniram. Miss Rhees met Adoniram, she said, while he was traveling on deputation in 1846 and transcribed several of his sermons and remarks for publication.

On March 6, 1846, Adoniram wrote to Emily about a letter he had received from a possible suitor and said he would share it with her; then, he added, "And that also of R. A. Rhees, one of the few flames I have had since you left."

In her first letter to Emily, she spoke of her grief at Adoniram Judson's death as inconsolable. A second letter followed in December 1851 in which she commented on meeting Emily briefly at Miss Sheldon's in Philadelphia, probably when Emily traveled there after her return to America. This letter was in response to Emily's request for materials for the Judson memoir. Here, Miss Rhees implored that she be allowed to address her as "Emily," and she obviously was hoping to establish a relationship. Apparently, she was unsuccessful, for in the third letter, she said, "I will not ask you again to write to me." It appears that she had sent something to Emily, who had returned it to her, for after saying the above, she went on to ask Emily to excuse her for sending it along. In not getting what she hoped for from Emily, a hard edge emerges, suggesting that there was more to the request than what was seen on the surface.

The letters of Rebecca A. Rhees ("Bessie") to Adoniram are included in the correspondence to fill in some background information. Their dates are February 19, 1846; May 8 and 10, 1846; October 1, 1848; and November 25, 1849. There are currents emerging that are expressed in a multitude of ways; it seems evident that Miss Rhees would today be called a "groupie" with a strong need for attachment to a famous figure. There is an unfolding story of unrequited love that forms an interesting subchapter to the life of Adoniram and Emily.

[207] See vol. 1, "Cast of Characters," s.v. "Vinton, The Reverend Doctor Justus Hatch and Calista."

to the Apostle Paul." I have contrived to get bravely over all such scruples, you will think, yet I shall never forget the almost awe with which I at first approached you.

I have been for some months past, very anxious about Mrs. Judson's health.[208] I have never prayed more fervently for anything, I think, than for her restoration, and I have felt too as if our God would surely hear the many prayers ascending on her behalf. I rejoice to hear that at the last accounts received, she was so much better, and earnestly hope that she may long, long be spared to you and to the cause.

I am so glad that my rhymes (I shall not call them poetry) gave you pleasure, and though I know you rate them far more highly than they deserve, yet regarding it as a proof of affection, I am more than content, that you should think as well of them as you possibly can. If others judged my productions as favorably as you do and some few beside who love me, my talents, (if talents they are) might be of some benefit, instead of a source of constant disappointment and disquiet, as they now are, giving rise to aspirations which I am compelled to crush, and to visions brightening only to fade.

But you are not mistaken in regard to Mrs. Hemans,[209] when you say of her, "I fear that she was destitute of that spirit, which will, I trust, carry us safely to that blessed world where there is no more sea"? I have always been accustomed to think that it was to this spirit, the spirit of religion and love that her poetry owed its unrivalled sweetness, its exceeding beauty. Do you remember "Christ's agony in the garden," "Christ's stilling the tempests," "Mother's Litany by the bed of a sick child," "The Fountain of Marah" and many other of her pieces which seem to me to prove that she was a Christian, seeking through faith in the same Saviour [sic] whom we love, a home in the same world where we trust to meet, and where I have always looked forward to seeing her whom I regard as the model of a Christian poetess, unequalled in her genius, purity and richness of thought, and melody of expression. I must have you reconsider your judgment dear friend, and if you change your opinion, make the "amende honorable" to Mrs. Hemans, when you write again, will you not? I shall look anxiously for your sanction to my opinion, and to the hope I indulge of meeting her where, in her own beautiful words,

"No tempest e'er shall blow
    No scorching noontide heat,
Where shall be no more snow,
    No weary wandering feet,
And we lift our trusting eyes

[208] See the letter of Adoniram Judson to Anna Maria Anable dated March 18, 1849. That letter was republished throughout the country when it came.

[209] This was Mrs. Felicia Dorothea Browne Hemans, an English poet. Born in 1793 and the mother of five children, she died in 1835.

From the hills our fathers trod,
Go the quiet of the skies,
To the Sabbath of our God."

It is there I look forward to communion with you and all whom I love best; what misery it must be to love one whom you cannot hope to meet in Heaven. I do not care even to become interested in the writings or character of a Stranger whom I can hope to know only as connected with earth.

You kindly inquire for my health, and my "own affairs." I am, I think, better than when I wrote you last; probably as well as I ever shall be in this world, not very strong, but able to accomplish more than those who have less necessity for exertion might imagine. After being for almost two years away from my family and the paternal roof, I have during the last summer, returned to them, and shall remain at least for the winter. It is not pleasant to be away from home, yet while it seemed to be duty, I reconciled myself to it as I best could; but now it seems right to be here, my father having commenced a School in which he requires my assistance. I trust this enterprise may prosper; if it should, it will be the first thing of any kind which I ever attempted, that succeeded. I know not why it is; others who seem no more gifted, and who certainly put forth no more effort, succeed as teachers and as

[Written in the right margin of the address page:] authors, but the blessing is ever held from me. Do you know I sometimes think that there is a meaning in these repeated failures and discouragements, and that the meaning is "thy work is not here; get thee out from thy kindred and thine own land." May it not be so? O! that if it is my Master's will that I should go to the heathen, He would once more open a way for me, and give me strength to walk in it. Your letter discouraged me; I have so long cherished a desire, too faint to be called hope, that I might one day join you. It would be far more of a trial to go into any other field alone, and I will never marry for the sake of going. I have half a mind to persuade Brother and Sister Vinton to take me as a member of their family; I should not be very far from you then, should I? But no! I am not a Baptist, and (conscious as I am that in this country there is no inducement sufficiently strong to lead me to forsake the church

[Written in the left margin of the address page:] of which I am a member, and which I do so dearly love) I dare not profess myself one, (though agreeing with you on all essential points and one in heart with many of you) even for the chance of being sent to Burmah. I have but small space in which to reply to that which forms the burden of your letter—the charge of "inconsistency": a severe accusation, I might have thought it, preferred by another, but you I know mean only kindness, and from my heart I thank you that you care enough for me to tell me when you think me wrong. But indeed, dear friend, I am not inconsistent; I am by no means so thorough a Baptist in sentiment as you appear to think. I do not regard as "unbaptized persons" all who have not received the ordinance by immersion. I have, during the past year, read, thought, and prayed much over the matter, anxiously and humbly desirous of truth, to know the will of the Lord, and my own duty, and I cannot see as you do. Forgive me that! I presume to differ with you who are so much wiser and better than I: it gives me pain to do so, but the time has not yet come when we can see eye to eye. Yet this would surely not affect my usefulness were I with you; our faith is, in all its *essentials*, identical and would not these be all that I should teach? Ah! If I were with you! I have no hope that this will ever be. Yet I will not despair till my 30th birthday which I shall not see for some years to come; I have fixed this as the utmost bound of my anticipations.

Meantime, I will pray for the cause and labor for it so far as I may here, our aim [written in the bottom margin of the address page] now and ever ( ) ( ) ( ) ( ) ( ), now an affection words have no power to utter.

Truly and gratefully yours

Bessie

P.S. Do not cease to pray for me. I need your remembrance. You are never forgotten. Many, many thanks for the Memoir.[210] I need not tell you (if I could) how I value it. My best regards to Mrs. Judson. My parents and sisters unite with me in warm wishes that every blessing may rest upon you. May our God bestow upon you all that we can only ask for you at His hand. *Adieu* in its fullest, deepest meaning.

[Written along the left margin of page 1:] It gives me great pleasure that you wrote to me as "Bessie"; almost all who love me call me by that name. You, I hope, will always do so.

Miss Mary Anna Longstreth to Emily C. Judson, November 27, 1849—Philadelphia

My dear friend,
Emily Judson,

Our hearts were ( ) with sorrow when we heard some months ago of thy severe illness. Can it be our Heavenly Father's will we said, that our dear brother Judson should again be called to drink the cup of bitterness ( ) ( ) ( ) ( ) ( ) were our aspirations that she, who had left all of ( ) ( ) Christ's sake, might be spared to cheer the remainder of his life, and administer those consolations which the tenderness of a wife alone can suggest and bestow. Great thus was our joy and thankfulness in hearing, by a later post, of the improvement in thy health, and still more delighted

[210] Fanny Forester, *Memoir of Sarah B. Judson, Member of the American Mission to Burmah* (New York: L. Colby and Company, 1848).

was I to be assured of this by thy own most welcome letter dated in April and received only three months afterwards. Since then I have continued to hear pleasing tidings of thy welfare through our mutually dear friend, Anna Maria Anable,[211] and I earnestly desire that the blessing of good health may be long continued to thyself and the dear husband. I think we may pray more fervently for the life of *Missionaries* than of other persons, and may be pardoned for less resignation when they are taken from their labors. Their experience is dearly purchased, is invaluable, and can not be bequeathed to others. They have overcome the difficulties of acquiring the language, and they have gained the confidence of the natives. New laborers in the field may be as zealous and devoted, but how little can they accomplish compared with a missionary of ( ) experience. And it does seem to me to be the duty of such a one to take every care to prolong his life, not to labor too constantly, to avoid exposure, to have needed repose, relaxation, and change of air. In many ( ) if one is praying to die, life is not greatly to be desired. "The ( ) ( ) the earliest immortality"—but in the case of missionaries, we feel differently. Would it not be well for *every* missionary's wife to have a pious American female, as an assistant in taking care of and instructing her children, managing domestic affairs, and teaching the natives? If the various duties, which now press so often heavily and laboriously, upon the wives of missionaries, could be lessened by being shared, would not many valuable lives be (saved), which would fall otherwise a sacrifice to overexertion? It would not be necessary for such an assistant to possess all the qualifications which are desirable and perhaps requisite in the *wife* of a missionary, as she would be a subordinate, instead of *principal*, ( ) the school ( ) ( ) such could, therefore, be more readily obtained. I am not pleading for indolence, but it seems to me that even in an economical point of view (the lowest of all considerations, yet sometimes much insisted upon by those who subscribe to missions) it is wisdom to do everything (without regard to expense of money,) to benefit the health and prolong the life of missionaries and their wives. Excuse my being so tedious on this subject, but it is one upon which I feel deeply interested. I would rather be like my dear friend in Burmah telling the poor despised Karens of a Saviour's love than Victoria on her throne; but I feel well-assured that I *am* in my *right niche*, in the one assigned to me by an all-wise Providence, and have never had a desire to leave it. We have greatly enjoyed the Society of our beloved friend D. B. Wade, and her husband.[212] The

[211] Anna Maria Anable was the niece of the Misses Urania and Cynthia Sheldon and the daughter of Joseph and Alma Sheldon Anable. Emily first met Anna Maria in fall 1840 when she went as a student to the Utica Female Academy; both Emily and Anna Maria became members of the faculty there. In these years, Anna Maria became Emily's dearest friend, and the extensive correspondence between the two reflects sensitive, flirtatious spirits and a deep intimacy. Emily was "Nemmy" to Anna Maria's "Ninny." In 1848, Anna Maria Anable, with the help of her extended family, moved to Philadelphia and started the Misses Anable's School in Philadelphia. At Emily's death in 1854, Anna Maria was given guardianship of Emily Frances Judson, daughter of Emily and Adoniram Judson.

[212] See vol. 1, "Cast of Characters," s.v. "Wade, The Reverend Doctor Jonathan and Deborah."

illness of the former, last spring, was very alarming; but her gracious Master has restored her health and strength, and I trust she will be spared yet to see the faces again of her beloved Karens, and to bring many more into the fold of Christ. When she was most ill, her poor husband began to fear he might have to return to Burmah without her, and it was affecting to witness his distress and anxiety, although I doubt not he sought to be fully resigned to the will of God. Our dear friends, the Anables,[213] with whom they were staying and whose house was truly a home for them, live quite near us, (not three squares or blocks distant,) and closely occupied as my time was, by the duties of our school, this proximity enabled me to pay more frequent visits, than I could otherwise have made, to the dear invalid, whose loving, gentle spirit was very precious, diffusing, may I not say, a fragrance like that of "ointment poured forth." A meeting for ladies, at which she gave a great deal of information respecting thy mission, interested me deeply.

I am greatly pleased with the acquaintance I have formed with A. M. Anable, her mother, Aunt and sisters. They are a delightful family and cannot, I think, fail in obtaining as large a school as they wish and people of the most desirable class.

Thy dear husband's settee, of which there is a promise in ( ) ( ) has not yet arrived. Tell him I am anxiously looking for it. He will perhaps, be interested in hearing that since you left America, my youngest brother, who is a farmer, has been very agreeably married ( ) his little boy, about three months old, is a great pet with us. A year ago we were made exceedingly anxious and distressed by the severe illness of our youngest and only married sister—the mother of four sweet children. Her physicians had little, if any, expectation of her recovery and we felt called upon to resign her entirely into the Lord's hands. He, in his mercy, restored the beloved one to her family, and she is now enjoying good health. Before she recovered, our Aunt Collins, who resides with us, became ill, and continued so, with a few intermissions, until the summer, when her health improved and continues to be tolerably good. With the summer came the Cholera, that awful scourge, and although Philadelphia was mercifully and lightly visited in comparison with the cities of the west, the alarm was great; almost every one [sic] was more or less indisposed, and life was felt to hang upon a very slender thread. Thus it was a year of many trials, yet mingled with many unmerited mercies, calling for the live( ) gratitude. My sister Susan who had been for twenty years, my efficient and valuable associate in my school relinquished her arduous ( ) at the vacation. We commenced while we were almost children and have not spared

[Written in the right margin of the address page:] ourselves. The consequence is that my dear sister's strength is so exhausted that she is unable to resume the

[213] Alma Sheldon Anable and her four daughters Anna Maria, Harriet or "Hatty," Fanny, and Mary. Courtland was there at times, although he was working outside the city at this time.

duties of a school; but she still renders me very valuable assistance. I am thankful that my own health permits me, with the aid of hired teachers, to continue my delightful occupation, interesting to myself, and useful, I trust to others. But I generally feel much worn by *evening*, as thou will perceive by the dullness of this letter, which is really not worth sending across the ocean. Yet, poor as it is, it will assure you, I hope

[Written in the left margin of the address page:] that you are often the object of affectionate interest. The message of your little boys[214] was very *sweet*. Tell them their other Aunt Anna does love them, and hopes to send them some more books, when the missionaries return to Burmah. It is delightful to me of thy warm interest in the poor natives, and thy happiness in devotedness to the best of causes. May you both be blessed a hundred fold in this life, as well as receive the cross of righteousness which is promised to the faithful disciple at the end of the race. My mother, aunt, and sister unite with me in warm affection to you both, although *personally* strangers to thyself. Believe me thy sincerely attached and interested friend,

Mary Anna Longstreth

[Written along the left margin of page 3:] Kiss the sweet "Bird" for me. We highly enjoyed thy exquisitely beautiful lines upon her birth.[215]

Source: American Baptist Historical Society, AJ 17, no. 767.

Emily C. Judson to Anna Maria Anable, December 23, 1849[216]—Maulmain

My dear **Ninny**,

I can **only** write you (but) a very short letter this month, for we have just now an unusual number of cares. My poor husband has been ill for the last six weeks. He took cold, which settled on the lungs, and produced a terrible cough, with some fever. This continued three or four days, when he was attacked with dysentery, and the **Doct.** physician had not quite subdued that when a congestive fever set in and took away the remainder of his strength. For about a month he had a burning fever

[214] Henry Hall Judson, almost seven and a half years old, and Edward Judson, almost five years old.

[215] On January 1, 1848, eight days after the birth of Emily Frances Judson, Emily wrote a celebratory poem that she called "My Bird." The poem has a total of seven stanzas, and it was widely published in the United States.

[216] There are two versions of this letter: the original as written by Emily E. Chubbuck and the edited version published by Dr. A. C. Kendrick in his biography, *The Life and Letters of Mrs. Emily C. Judson*. Additions made by Dr. Kendrick are in parentheses, and words in the original left out by Dr. Kendrick have been added in bold. There are significant changes and omissions. In a note in his book, Dr. Kendrick explained that interest, purpose and propriety sometimes led to these changes and exclusions, "I remark here that in giving Miss Chubbuck's letters, I do not always indicate unimportant omissions. Real letters must always contain much which should not meet the public eye; and Emily's were real letters, dashed off hastily amidst pressing cares and duties. Written also after the exhausting labors of the day, they by no means do uniform justice to her epistolary powers."

twice a day, and yet he is now on the gain. So you may imagine that he has something of a constitution to grapple with disease. If he is well enough next week, he will take a trip down the coast. We feel very sad to have him go alone, but it is not absolutely necessary that I go; we could not, (therefore), in conscience ask it of the mission, and we can not afford the expense ourselves. Even Dr. Morton[217] will not say that he can not go without me, though he says that the trip would do *me* immense good, and that I had better go by all means. The English think "Dr. Judson" a sort of Bishop, and supposing our salary to be much greater than that of other missionaries, they never think of expense in our case. Trades-people always charge us higher, and our servant, being known in the bazaar, always expects to pay more for our food than others. **Perhaps** You **don't** do not know, (perhaps), that trades-people always charge the English in proportion to their rank. I have, once in a while, got some Burmese woman to go to bazaar for me, and she **got things** obtained articles for less than a third of what I usually pay. But in a day or two they discovered the ruse, and up went prices again. Are you not interested in my domestic matters?

Mr. J., I say, is better, so much so that I took him a little drive last night (you must know I always hold the ribands [sic] now-a-days), and though he returned excessively fatigued, I do not think it did him any harm. He will be well soon, I trust.

Our children are all on the alert for they are to have three holy days in succession. Tomorrow Edward[218] is five years old, next day Frances[219] is two, and the next day is Christmas. I wish you would just take them to your house and do the needful, for the prospect now is that poor papa will be made crazy and mamma be worn out. Henry[220] is seven only and just like a wild colt; people ask me if I ever saw him *walk*—he is so forever on the jump. He is a clever little fellow though, reads beautifully, writes decently and studies geography and History like a little ( ). He has a pretty Grecian face—people say like his own mamma's.[221]

You speak of the affairs in Europe.[222] Mr. J. does not think that real millennial glory will begin before the year 2000; but thinks that the **1260** twelve hundred and sixty years of the Papacy will end in sixteen or seventeen years. God grant that we may all live to see its downfall! In the meantime—**between now and, say, 1860**, he supposes that Europe will be the theatre of mighty wonders; and though he does not guess what these wonders will be, he thinks we **better all** (may well) observe the caution in Rev. 16:15. Have not the "unclean spirits" already "gone out, " and

[217] See vol. 1, "Cast of Characters," s.v. "Morton, Doctor."

[218] See vol. 1, "Cast of Characters," s.v. "Judson, Edward."

[219] See vol. 1, "Cast of Characters," s.v. "Judson, Emily Frances."

[220] See vol. 1, "Cast of Characters," s.v. "Judson, Henry Hall."

[221] Sarah Hall Boardman Judson.

[222] See the letter of Anna Maria Anable to Emily C. Judson dated September 23, 1849.

is not the world "gathering to Battle?" And *we* may not altogether escape! If England **sh'd** should be involved in a war with Russia, all India would be shaken; and if the latter power **sh'd** should even temporarily gain Constantinople, I tremble for all Eastern missions. But "the Lord God omnipotent reigneth;" and if we should be granted the honors of martyrdom, others will rise up, and the whole East in a few years be flooded with Christianity. **I wish we could have a cozy talk of these things**; it makes my heart swell to *think* of **them** (these things); but my notions are too vague to write down. Yet-have you ever thought of it—*you* may not altogether escape. The **U.S.** (United States) are peopled by Europeans, and, in all but the soil, belong to the old Roman empire. Nobody has yet been able to say who the two witnesses of Rev. 11th. are, and they certainly have not been *slain*. If they were the Waldenses and Albigenses, they have been merged in something greater which (or who) is to be triumphed over for three years and a half. Who knows—(I do not say I think so, for it involves horrors such as I dare not think of)—**but** (that) these two witnesses are not England and America? Well, we have nothing to do but *watch*.

Lovingly,

Nemmy

Source: A. C. Kendrick, *Life and Letters of Mrs. Emily C. Judson*, 332–34; Hanna family files.

Anna Maria Anable to Emily C. Judson, December 28, 1849

Dearest Nemmy[223]

[Note: the copy quality only allows a few words or phrases to be read in the first seven lines of this letter. These include: line 2—"last week"; line 3—"about the approaching"; line 4—"postponed answering"; line 5—"be too late for the"; line 7—"your continued feebleness."]

from the predictions of friends and the hints you have occasionally given in your letters, I had somehow come to think that you were about as well as you used to be. I do not doubt your recovery, but I do hope that you will yet enjoy good health. The next mail after your letters brought us letters from the Wades.[224] They are quite well and laying all their plans for their return next Summer. My sweet little school will never I suppose let me think of going with them[225] ( ) ( ) or else.—Must tell you something about Mr. Wade which interested me exceedingly as an exhibition of his

[223] "Nem" or "Nemmy" was a name of endearment given to Emily by a small group of her intimate friends at the Utica Female Academy. Anna Maria Anable was "Ninny."

[224] See vol. 1, "Cast of Characters," s.v. "Wade, The Reverend Doctor Jonathan and Deborah."

[225] From 1846 through the beginning of 1848, Anna Maria gave serious consideration to joining Adoniram and Emily Judson in Burmah as a missionary. Most of her letters mention her thoughts, and there are several letters to Adoniram and Emily in which she makes specific inquiries. See her letter dated June 29, 1847.

ruling passion. While he was here in the Spring I gave him music lessons, but I did not think he had any particular talent for music, for he was six weeks in learning one tune, but, he got a notion of thorough bass into his head which has worked there all Summer, and his last letter he sent me a "digest of thorough Bass" on one ( ) of letter paper containing all that is ( ) ( ) ( ) in ( ) one hundred of more printed pages, and beautifully and systematically arranged as a Karen alphabet or more like it, fifty problems in Algebra. What is ( ) ( ) he must needs start two or three queries ( ) ( ) musician he had ( ) could ( ), and which I must puzzle my brains over or he will ( ) ( ) ( )—suppose this "digest" will [Note: The next line of the letter is lost in the letter fold.] which is basically for some unknown language.

Mr. and Mrs. Bronson[226] have been here a good deal, and their two little daughters are beautifully provided for in this city. Mr. and Mrs. Haswell[227] I have not seen yet (but when) they come to the city I presume I shall, for the Missionaries are all beginning to find us out.

Mrs. Gillette[228] and the other ladies in the church have been getting up a fair again and I rather think they have had enough of it this time. Aunt C.[229] and some of the rest of ( ) worked night and day almost and after all did not pay for the ( ).

Sartain's[230] magazine is out with your little poem[231] in it and I am told there is an article of yours in the *Mother's Journal*[232] but it has not yet come to this city. Mr. Gillette[233] is getting some books together for you, and we shall have a box of that sort by the first vessel that sails. (Willis')[234] papers you shall have and I will try and get the back numbers of Neal's *Gazette*.[235]

[226] See vol. 1, "Cast of Characters," s.v. "Bronson, Miles."

[227] James Madison Haswell was born February 4, 1810, in Bennington, Vermont. He was married to Jane Matilda Mason of Cheshire, Massachusetts. The Haswells sailed for Burmah on September 23, 1835, to work with the Talaings. They arrived at Amherst in February 1836. The Haswells became partners with Adoniram and Sarah Hall Boardman Judson; Sarah turned over the translation of the Peguan scripture to Mr. Haswell after Elnathan and Adoniram were born, and her energies were focused elsewhere. When Sarah and Adoniram sailed for America in 1845, the Haswells took care of Henry until Adoniram returned in 1847 with Emily. The Haswells left Burmah in December 1848 and arrived in America in 1849; they remained in the United States until September 1852, when they again sailed for Burmah.

[228] See vol. 1, "Cast of Characters," s.v. "Gillette, The Reverend A. (Abram) D. (Dunn) and Hannah."

[229] See vol. 1, "Cast of Characters," s.v. "Sheldon, Miss Cynthia."

[230] See vol. 1, "Cast of Characters," s.v. "Sartain, John."

[231] "The Two Mamas. See Anna Maria's letter of November 24, 1849. There are twenty-four stanzas in this poem.

[232] The *Mother's Journal* was a prominent Christian magazine published by Mrs. Eliza Allen, who died in 1848. Emily wrote for it on occasion and had a contentious relationship with Mrs. Allen due to their differing opinions on writer compensation. Adoniram Judson met with her before they left for Burmah and had declared her to be "difficult."

[233] See vol. 1, "Cast of Characters," s.v. "Gillette, The Reverend Abram Dunn."

[234] See vol. 1, "Cast of Characters," s.v. "Willis, Nathanial Parker (N. P. Willis)."

[235] Joseph Neal was a prominent member of the literary establishment in Philadelphia and became a part of Emily Chubbuck's circle of friends when she was there. Neal was well known and respected as a writer and editor; one of his best known works was the *Charcoal Sketches*. In 1842, he founded the *Saturday Gazette*, a successful publication that contained a great deal of humorous satire. Anna Maria Anable frequently referred to Neal as a beau for Emily. Mr. Neal married Alice Bradley in 1846; he died in 1847.

Shall I (tell you) how we spent Christmas time? At ( ) we girls bought Aunt C. a beautiful pyramid of cake for a Christmas present, and *we* thought we would give them all a Christmas party and have the cake to help ornament the table. We ( ) in our school ( ) on the first floor the most beautiful tableaux and charade that I ever saw. ( ) ascending to the parlors we ( ) a beautiful papier mache stand ( ) ( ) ( ) ( ) our dear girls. They [Note: half of this line is lost in the letter fold.] and Mrs. Gillette who came in[Note: half of this line is lost in the letter fold.] after the fair said she never saw as much beauty in one room before in her life. It is rather remarkable. I have ( ) school ma'am now nearly a year and a half, and I am fast coming to the conclusion that that is what I am made for. Though I make no pretensions to talent, yet I feel that I have the power of calling it forth in others, if *they* have it. My girls have improved—some of them astonishingly—at the same time it is a kind of healthy improvement to which ( ) ( ) ( ) much. ( ) had a night's visit from Aunt U.[236] yesterday. She is doing well with our school. The Dr.[237] is feeble still and she has a great many anxieties. A letter from John Edmonds to day [sic] tells of his and Eugenia's[238] happiness. One from Cousin Ann[239] tells that she is about to change her quarters from the Academy to some other boarding house in the city. She has not ( ) heard from cousin Charles.[240] Jenny and Horace Hawley[241] are in Utica on a visit. They don't like Hartford.

[236] See vol. 1, "Cast of Characters," s.v. "Sheldon, Urania."

[237] The Reverend Doctor Eliphalet Nott was the president of Union College in Schenectady, New York. An ordained Presbyterian minister, he was married to Urania Sheldon Nott, the sister of Miss Cynthia Sheldon and Mrs. Alma Anable and the aunt of Anna Maria Anable.

[238] See vol. 1, "Cast of Characters," s.v. "Damaux, Eugenia."

[239] Ann Sheldon was a younger cousin of Miss Cynthia Sheldon, Mrs. Alma Sheldon Anable, and Mrs. Urania Sheldon Nott. She married Charles Gratiot, the son of a prominent army officer and engineer who opened the port of St. Louis. Because Charles and Ann Gratiot often lived with the Sheldon-Anable families, both at Utica and in Philadelphia after 1848, they were often mentioned in the correspondence. They had six children, one of whom was born very close to the birth of Emily Frances Judson. The letters reveal how Ann coped in her husband's absence when he went west during the gold rush to seek his fortune.

[240] Charles Gratiot grew up in St Louis, where his father was an army engineer responsible for developing the Port of St. Louis. He married Ann Sheldon, who was a cousin of Miss Cynthia Sheldon, Mrs. Urania Sheldon Nott, and Alma Sheldon Anable. Together, Charles and Ann Gratiot had six children. Because they often lived with the Sheldon family, their letters contain a great deal of him. Letters in 1847 speak of his religious awakening; those of 1849 speak of his leaving for the California gold fields. In 1853, Charles Gratiot applied for a grant of 400 acres in Illinois, and he already owned 148 acres.

[241] Mr. Horace H. Hawley enjoyed a family relationship with the Sheldons. A letter Emily wrote on May 7, 1841, reveals that he was to marry a niece of Misses Cynthia and Urania Sheldon and Mrs. Alma Sheldon Anable, the daughter of their brother John Sheldon. Through the help of Miss Cynthia Sheldon, he was introduced into the life of Emily Chubbuck. A member of a publishing firm, he also worked with Alexander Beebee in publishing the *Baptist Register*. Beginning in 1841 with the publication of *Charles Linn*, Mr. Hawley was enormously helpful to Emily Chubbuck as she was publishing her early stories and books. There are numerous references to his help and his generosity.

[Written in the right margin of the address page:] Mary Barber[242] has gone ( ) ( ) ( ) ( ) to Syracuse. Caleb Lyons is in California. Mary Adams[243] ( ) returned from the south and will probably become Mrs. Green next Spring. Miranda Crofts is spending the winter in the city. She looks as youthful as ever. She makes me think of poor Nora Westcott.[244]

Do you recollect that pretty Mrs. Campbell that was in Schenectady that commencement? ( ) ( )

[Written in the left margin of the address page:] an only daughter whom she ( ) ( ) ( ) to us, and she may come on and spend a month with us here. I should like to see her again. Now I must stop and send this off without reading it. All send ( ) of love to yourself, the doctor, and the dear little ones.[245]

Affect'ly

Anna Maria

Source: American Baptist Historical Society, AJ 13, no. 476.

[242] Mary Barber was mentioned frequently in the Emily Chubbuck Judson letters; she was a student and then a teacher at the Utica Female Academy. There were ups and downs to that relationship; in fall 1845, apparently Mary had written to someone expressing what Anna Maria Anable called "ingratitude," and Mary had been banned from the Academy until she made proper apologies to Miss Sheldon. In a September 7, 1845, letter from Anna Maria, we learn that her remarks had been about Miss Cynthia Sheldon. In November 1847 Jane Kelly remarked that they had not heard from Mary in more than a year. In 1848 Mary Barber was back at the Utica Female Seminary teaching with Jane Kelly. Though at this time Miss Sheldon had moved to Philadelphia, Mary Barber had been able to reconcile with her, and in later years we find Mary very close to the Sheldon-Anable families; later, there was considerable consternation on Miss Cynthia Sheldon's part in her correspondence with Emily about Mary's health, the seriousness of it, and Mary's impending death. These letters were written in April 1852. Miss Sheldon went to help transfer Mary to Albany in June 1852, where she would be better situated and perhaps have access to better doctors. On September 9, 1852, Anna Maria Anable wrote to Emily of Mary Barber's death.

[243] Mary Adams was related to the Utica Female Academy. Her letter to Emily in October 1845 was almost a whimsical piece of fantasy with literary pretensions. It would reflect a fairly close relationship. A second letter in December 1845 was similar. The letters were written from New Orleans, and she spoke of Hatty Anable as being near to her. On January 29, 1849, Anna Maria Anable wrote, "Hatty says Mary Adams is going to marry Gardner Green of Norwich,—a very fine young man, of invention, fortune, piety and all that Mary's heart was sighed for." On July 8, 1850, Mrs. Urania Sheldon Nott spoke of attending this wedding in New York.

[244] Nora Westcott was one of the girls from the Utica Female Academy. On January 17, 1847, Anna Maria Anable noted that Nora was in Mississippi, though dying of consumption. In November 1849, Sarah Hinckley spoke of her death.

[245] Henry Hall Judson, age seven and a half; Edward Judson, five years old; and Emily Frances Judson, two years old.

Catharine Chubbuck to J. Walker Chubbuck,[246] December 28, 1849—Hamilton

My dear brother.

I said last fall I never would write you again in the wide world till you answered some of my letters, but I had'nt [sic] the least idea then, that you would neglect me all summer and fall, and so far into winter. Only think you scamp of not writing to me since last April and I sick with fever half of the summer, and have written you twice or three times since then. Perhaps my last letter frightened you[247] cause I asked for some money, but it no need to [sic], for I should'nt [sic] have cared a fig if you had'nt [sic] sent any. I was real vexed with myself as soon as I had done so, it was only one of my weak streaks. I had got out of money being sick so long and not able to earn any thing [sic]. It was for nothing in particular that I wanted it, only to have on hand to buy Mother[248] medicines and such like things in case they were wanted, but I have got along just as well without. We are just now having a terrible time with father.[249] He went to the barn the other evening and went on the scaffold where it was dangerous for a cat to go almost and fell through. Mother heard the racket and called me to go and listen. I did so, and heard groaning, and calling to one of our girl boarders to come with me. I started for the barn and found him lying on his back. I raised him up a little and held him till the girl went and found a man to help me in with him. He could'nt [sic] help himself any, and so I thought there must be some bone out or broken but the doctor said it was an inward hurt but he would get over it in a few days, and I think he might if he was one of the patient sort, but he is so impatient that it seems as if he would worry himself to death. Wallace[250] and I have to do all the lifting of him. I don't let mother take much care of him, she is'nt [sic] able. She and I sleep on the couches in the sitting room nights, and he in the bedroom. I get up every little while, and wait on dad, build a fire and snuff the candle and then back to bed again. He acts like Ned in the night—sometimes will scream murder right in the middle of the night, and that skeers [sic] me you know.

[246] This letter from Emily's sister Catharine to their brother Walker is included because it describes Emily's family in Hamilton, New York, as life went on in her absence. It also contains Catharine's interpretation of letters from Emily and the information that she passes on.

[247] See the letter of Catharine Chubbuck to J. Walker Chubbuck dated June 10, 1849.

[248] Emily's mother. See vol. 1, "Cast of Characters," s.v. "Chubbuck, Lavinia Richards."

[249] Emily's father. See vol. 1, "Cast of Characters," s.v. "Chubbuck, Charles."

[250] Born January 1, 1824, William Wallace Chubbuck was six years younger than Emily. During these years of Emily's correspondence, Wallace lived at or near home and worked at different occupations including printing, office work, and teaching. Emily wrote of him as capable in many areas, but seeming to lack ambition at times. He proved to be a strong support for the Chubbuck family over these years, and at the time of her death in 1854, Wallace had become one of Emily's primary caregivers. After February 1854, she dictated all her letters to him because of her failing strength. Wallace married Julia Allin Throwbridge on July 18, 1854. He died on August 13, 1861, at the age of thirty-seven. The obituary in the Utica *Herald* noted that Wallace had trained as a printer in Morrisville and had gained some very astute political skills. He was "possessed of one of the brightest of intellects, and wield[ed] one of the most trenchant of pens." He had served as a justice of the peace and as clerk to one of the legislative committees in Albany.

It is downright nervousness and sometimes he gets so high that I can't stand it no longer and go and call Wallace. He seems to be pretty well except his hurt has an excellent appetite. I don't know what in the world we should have done if Wallace had been away as he was last winter, for besides all the other things to be looked after father had bought four cows to winter. Wallace had the offer of a school in Rome to teach this winter at thirty dollars a month, and they offered him twenty to edit the new Whig paper here. He hesitated a good while to know what to do I was very glad to have him conclude to stay here but did'nt [sic] like to advise in the matter. We have thought since that it was providential his being here. He will pay his board, and see to the things out doors and then there will be care enough left for mother and me. I think Wallace makes an excellent editor. I kinder [sic] guess he has an idea of working into that office by and by and so you and he can carry it on together;[251] but he keeps it to himself yet if he has. O we had a Christmas present of a dozen copies of the Memoir of Mrs. Judson[252] from the publishers. I shall save one for you. I had a letter from Elizabeth last night and heard by it that you had paid Aunt Catharine a visit. ha! ha! You better tell me something about it Mr. Chub. Emily wrote me not long ago that she had never received a line from you, and the reason she had'nt [sic] written you was that she had forgotten your address. Now while I think of it Emily wants us all to send our Daguerreotype likeness to her by Mrs. Wade.[253] Wallace and I will have ours taken for her, and if I can get father and mother to sit for theirs I shall. I shall get yours copied if I can, but if I can't may I send her the one I have of you? I don't know how to spare it, but don't know when I shall have another so good an opportunity to send. She said in her last letter she guessed she would be home in five years, but the Doc. thought he should wait till he was a hundred years old. I can't write any more now I'm *so* hurried. Mother sends love. Answer this and tell me what you're mad at.

Kitty Chubbuck

Source: Wisconsin Historical Society.

[251] Walker started a newspaper in Milwaukee, the Wisconsin Territory.

[252] Fanny Forester, *Memoir of Sarah B. Judson, Member of the American Mission to Burmah* (New York: L. Colby and Company, 1848).

[253] Deborah Wade was a missionary to Burmah; with her husband Jonathan, they were appointed in 1823. Adoniram Judson called them "his dearest and best of friends." Much of their work was in the jungle communities following the path of George Boardman. They left for the United States on December 22, 1847. From the Hamilton, New York, area, they stayed not far from the home of Emily's parents and sister; they visited the Anable-Sheldon families in Philadelphia. With a large group, they had left Boston on July 25, 1850, and returned to Burmah in February 1851.

The Reverend Doctor Solomon Peck to Emily C. Judson, December 29, 1849—Baptist Mission Rooms, Boston

My dear Mrs. Judson

I find I shall not be able to return an equivalent for your letter of July[254] last, although it has been suggestive of very many thoughts. I thank you for the inner view it gives me of your character and early life. I have read the narrative repeatedly with all the interest you could well desire, free from all admixture of uncharitableness or ungrateful surmisings as to the motives to such an unaffected self-portrayal.

The portraiture itself does not vary so materially from my own previous conceptions of your history and character as you seem to have supposed. These have derived their form and features not so much from vagrant reserve, nor even from published writings of yourself or others, as from our first quiet brotherly interview at Utica,[255] and intercourse with some of your earliest and truest friends. Other influences, it is true, have reached me now and then—but I naturally—unconsciously as it were, cast them off. Nor shall I be likely to allow my earliest impressions to be supplanted by others less agreeable, except by some compulsory process painfully severe and more than once repeated.

But my principal object in writing at this time is to remove a misapprehension as to the meaning of a paragraph in my last letter—a misapprehension I should never have dreamed of and for some time wholly inexplicable. On every reading of your letter I have found myself ready to exclaim—What can this mean? "Cautioned to tell the truth"[256]—"accusations so grave"[257]—"embellishing facts"[258]—Can it be, that I was so misunderstood? I have at length—just to relieve my perplexity poured upon that unfortunate expression—*matter-of-fact*, a very harmless form of speech in my *thought*, little more than a synonym to "prosaic and sober"—but capable, as it would seem, of working sore mischief. All I *designed* by it, was to indicate not so much the

[254] The genesis of this letter goes back to a letter Dr. Peck wrote on February 20, 1849. The Board of the American Baptist Missionary Union had finally opened the door to Ava, and Dr. Peck asked Emily to write some narrative articles for the mission magazine on the sights, people, and culture. Then, he asked her to write sparely and without the embellishment found in some of her other writings. This apparently struck a nerve with Emily, for it prompted a blistering letter, some seven pages of pent up passion written on July 18, 1849. The letter was a defense of her style and, in a sense, her life. This letter is Dr. Peck's response to that impassioned reply.

[255] Solomon Peck traveled to Utica to meet with Miss Lydia Lillybridge as a candidate for missionary service. Such an individual meeting was a requirement of the board. While he was there, he took the opportunity to visit with Emily E. Chubbuck as well.

[256] Emily had said, "Truly, whatever you may think, or however good you may believe your reasons are for so thinking, I do not need to be **cautioned to tell the truth**, in the circumstances under which you propose honoring me with a place in your Magazine."

[257] Emily had said, "Pray don't think that I say this boastingly—it is no credit to have read able authors, unless mental discipline and knowledge combine to produce good results—but in an attempt to meet **accusations so grave** and at the same time so intangible as yours, a simple statement of seemingly irrelevant facts may be necessary."

[258] Emily had said, "Truly, whatever you may think, or however good you may believe your reasons are for so thinking, I do not need to be cautioned to tell the truth, in the circumstances under which you propose honoring me with a place in your Magazine. Though, as in the case of the late Memoir, I sometimes embellish my *style*, I never have been guilty of **embellishing *facts***, except when I have presented them in the guise of fiction"

accuracy of observation sought for, as the *class of objects* to be observed. To borrow part of one of your illustrations, I wished to have the *rock* with its seams and sutures, but could more quietly forgo the moss, and lichens and trailing vines.[259] It seems quite possible for two descriptions to be made with equal ingeniousness and accuracy, and yet the *effect* of each on the reader entirely distinct and peculiar in consequence of its selection and grouping of particulars.—Such a limitation of the meaning of the word may not be s*trictly* accurate, I grant. And yet I think you must have made the limitation, naturally and inevitably, "if you had known *me* better."[260]

The truth is, my dear Mrs. Judson, that with the sincerest Christian affection, with a feeling of an *identity* of personalities with you in the missionary cause, with the keenest sensitiveness to whatever might help or hinder in your work, and not wholly derelict of the spirit of intercession, I have also an habitual confidence and forwardness of *hope*. I may be disappointed—and it would be a grievous disappointment but my hope is in *God*. And in saying that my hope is in God, I betray no singular want of confidence in you. And when I allow myself to hope that God is doing and *will perfect* his work in you, I do by no means insinuate that in you more than in all other missionaries is it needful that his work be done.

To recur to a thought suggested on the first page of my letter—I have been subject to comparatively few influences that should prevent your making on my mind and heart your own proper missionary mark. I have had little to do with "certain idle editors."[261] I do not *remember*—shall I not confess it to you—ever to have read or heard one of those "pretty paragraphs." These many years my head and heart have cared for "one thing." This may have been to my personal loss, but I do not regret it in the review. I think I shall not regret it at the last day. Often and continually, in regard to very much that occupies the busy world around me, I seem to hear One saying—*Let the dead bury their dead.*

I thank you for the Memoir with Notes,[262] and shall look for its coming with pleasure. It will belong, I perceive, to the 20th thousand. What matters my opinion, be it what it may, compared with 20,000. However, *my* opinion is not *made up*. And when it is, it may have its conditions and qualifications. Of one thing be assured, I

[259] Emily had said, "if I ever do delineate a rock for you, that, so far as my power of using language enables me to express myself intelligibly, you will have it as you would see it yourself—not its bulk, magnitude and learned name merely, but everything about it—its stains, seams and fractures, the trailing plant, the pendent lichens, the patches of moss and the spots of sunshine."

[260] Emily had said, "I thank you most heartily for your kind way of writing to me, and respect the Christian principle by which I believe you to be activated; but allow me to suggest that you would sustain the part of mentor to more practical affect, **if you knew me better**."

[261] Emily had said, "The truth is, my dear Mr. Peck (and you will pardon the assertion, since, under existing circumstances, it is not a very heavy charge) it is yourself that *sees double*, instead of me. Some time ago, **certain idle editors**, who had nothing else to fill their columns with, took a fancy to write **pretty paragraphs**, about one Fanny Forester, whom they had never seen, and of *whom they knew* positively nothing. Strange to say, the Secretary of the Board seized upon their refracting telescope, and in spite of the united testimony of troops of good people, in spite of ( ) and common sense, in spite of his own eyes even, is actually regarding the poor little missionary through it still."

[262] Fanny Forester, *Memoir of Sarah B. Judson, Member of the American Mission to Burmah* (New York: L. Colby and Company, 1848).

cannot wish you a kinder critic, or a more generous interpreter, than will be found in

Your faithful friend and brother

S. Peck

[Written in the left margin of the address page:] I have read the *impudent* misrepresentation in the *Mother's Journal*[263] and the correction in the Dec. no. The correction was unquestionably called for.

[Written on the bottom of the address page:] I did visit Hamilton and look for Alderbrook—Of course in vain.[264] But I shall have better success next time.

Source: American Baptist Historical Society, AJ 19, no. 948.

[263] Previous correspondence mentioned an article in the *Mother's Journal* that had been interpreted to be offensive to Emily Judson's family in Hamilton, New York.

[264] For Emily's original remarks that prompted this response, see the third paragraph of her July 18, 1849, letter to Dr. Peck.

Letters

January–June 1850

The Reverend Durlin L. Brayton to Emily C. Judson, January 7, 1850—Mamhsa Karen Jungle

My dear *Sister* Judson

Your kind note of the 3d inst. from Mergui, reached me here in the jungle this morning. No apology whatever was necessary for taking possession of a *mission* house. I certainly cannot rejoice in the necessity, which brought you and your kind husband to Mergui.[1] Still, it would have afforded me very great pleasure indeed to have had the privilege of welcoming you to our quiet home. I exceedingly regret, that you did not think it best to remain at least a month, as I think it would have been beneficial to health, and I then should have had the pleasure of seeing you. But

> "*All* my times are in Thy hand
> All *events* at *Thy* command,"

is a most precious truth. Yes, my dear sister, we are often called to wade through deep waters, but how sweet the promise, "They shall not thee o'erflow." And even tho we may be called to pass through the fire, "The flame shall not hurt thee, I only design Thy dross to consume, and thy gold to refine." *O the sweet wonders of that Cross*!! May its transforming power ever eminate [sic] over hearts and fire us with a holy zeal in our Master's cause!

I had no special news from Am. My family were expecting to sail about the middle of Oct.,[2] and bro. Vinton[3] was not expecting to return the present year.

In regard to my labors here in the jungle, there is much more encouragement among these hardened Prvos, than I have ever before seen. On Pelaw river a few weeks since, had the privilege of baptizing ten individuals, an aged grand-mother, two men and their wives, four young men, and one young woman.

There are quite a number of persons in this vicinity, of whom it may be said, I think in truth, that, they are not far from the kingdom of God.

I called at a house, a few days since where a young woman (not a disciple) showed me a bundle of some fifteen or twenty letters received from different individuals since she and they have learned to read and write here in the jungle. The character of those letters, is an index to the minds of their authors. They were all decidedly religious, and some contained very striking exhortations.

I shall be very anxious indeed to hear from you again, to know how you all are, and especially whether your good husband has recovered. May you know what it is to *rejoice* in the Lord *always*! This is indeed a privilege peculiar to the Christian; and a privilege it *is*, beyond yes—far—far—beyond the price of rubies. What a

[1] Adoniram Judson had taken ill in November 1849, and the symptoms persisted. Emily spoke of Dr. Morton's wanting them to take a sea trip in the hopes that it would be restorative to his health. See the letter of Emily Judson written December 23, 1849, in which she raised the question as to whether or not the expense could justify her taking the trip with him.

contrast between the religion of Jesus, and the withering superstitions about us, or the freezing philosophy of a speculative world!

With much love to yourself and kind husband, with sweet kisses for the little ones[4]—

Affectionately

D. S. Brayton

Source: American Baptist Historical Society, AJ 12, no. 351.

Miss Cynthia Sheldon to Emily C. Judson, January 27, 1850—311 Walnut St., Philadelphia

Jan 27th 1850

My dear Emily,

Your cheerful letters to Anna M.[5] serve to keep us *heart whole* about your future health—and feel although you are still suffering from various causes, that your unshaken faith in God, buoys you up, and that you will find help in every time of need—yes I have ever since your consecration to the good cause of Missions, felt that the Lord hath need of you in a peculiar sense, and that your life would long be precious in His sight—Still whenever the mail is tardy my faith is weak—

We were right glad to have you name some things in good time for the box,[6] which we promised you should come before this. Mr. Hill made returns that he did

[2] Mrs. Brayton sailed from Boston on October 18, 1849.

[3] Justus Hatch Vinton was born in Willington, Connecticut, in 1806. He attended the theological school at Hamilton, New York, and was ordained in June 1834. In July that same year, he sailed as a missionary to Burmah. His wife was Calista Holman Vinton; they were married April 9, 1834. They worked with the Karens at Chummerah, Newville, and Maulmain, where he had charge of the Karen theological seminary. At the end of 1847, they left for the United States, returning to Burmah and work at Rangoon in July 1850. Justus Vinton died in Kemendine, Burmah, on March 31, 1858. His wife, Calista Holman Vinton, died in Rangoon, Burmah December 20, 1864. Mrs. Vinton taught the Karen women and was the author of several hymnbooks in their language.

[4] Henry Hall Judson, seven and a half years old; Edward Judson, five years old; and Emily Frances Judson, two years old.

[5] Anna Maria Anable was the niece of the Misses Urania and Cynthia Sheldon and the daughter of Joseph and Alma Sheldon Anable. Emily first met Anna Maria in fall 1840 when she went as a student to the Utica Female Academy; both Emily and Anna Maria became members of the faculty there. In these years, Anna Maria became Emily's dearest friend, and the extensive correspondence between the two reflects sensitive, flirtatious spirits and a deep intimacy. Emily was "Nemmy" to Anna Maria's "Ninny." In 1848, Anna Maria Anable, with the help of her extended family, moved to Philadelphia and started the Misses Anable's School in Philadelphia. At Emily's death in 1854, Anna Maria was given guardianship of Emily Frances Judson, daughter of Emily and Adoniram Judson.

[6] See the letters of Emily C. Judson to Miss Cynthia Sheldon dated October 21, 1849.

not know of a vessel going from Boston in some time and we heard Mr. Kincaid[7] wished to leave 1st of Ap. which of course would be the best chance—even now we do not know his decision as to time as soon as we can find out that he will defer until the other Missionaries go in June—the box will go to Boston at once—previous to your letter I had been fitting up for Miss Fanny's[8] acceptance—Miss Jenny Lind some two feet high—I do wish she could be transported by telegraph—an extra fine flannel wrapper for yourself should go in the same way cost what it would. If only they could get there before May day—I suppose Anna M. will give you a list of what is not together—and believe you will be satisfied with the out lay of your $25—or from Sartain[9]—some things are added to make the box worth the transportation—but I do hope some additions will be made when the Missionaries go—some effort is now being made in different Churches here to make up garments for the returned Missionaries—but nothing entered upon systematically—It appears necessary to have much done here for the country Churches do not understand how to do the thing properly—Mr. Bronson[10] said they often had inventoried boxes, as so much given by such a Chh to the Board—consequently this sum had been deducted from the salary of the poor Missionary who had previously to sailing acknowledged the contents as personal gifts—I can but feel as I told Mr. B. that some one [sic] should be commissioned to go the length and breadth of our land to set these things in order—We do think very highly of Mr. and Mrs. Bronson, also Mrs. Cutter—they wish much to see you in Maulmain on their way home—The Vintons[11] we have not seen since spring and then only met Mrs. V. an hour or so. They are in Cincinnati, and I learned from a letter yesterday to a friend of Mrs. Vinton's that her nervous system is exceedingly affected—and the subject of leaving her children is quite distracting to her—I know not what led them to vassilate [sic] about leaving them—

[7] Born in 1797, educated at the seminary in Hamilton, New York, and ordained in 1822, the Reverend Eugenio Kincaid served several churches before being appointed as a missionary to Burmah in February 1830. His first wife died soon after their arrival. His second wife was Barbara McBain, and they were married in 1833. In these years, they served in Rangoon, Ava, Saduja, and Akyab. The Reverend and Mrs. Kincaid returned to the United States in 1843; because of her persistent health problems, they were not reappointed in 1846. While in the United States, Rev. Kincaid became instrumental in the establishment of the University of Lewisberg (later Bucknell University). Upon Mrs. Kincaid's restoration, they returned to Burmah, arriving in February 1851 just as Emily Judson was embarking for her return voyage. With his knowledge of the language and customs, Rev. Kincaid was able to establish himself in work with the Burmese government at Ava. With one more trip home (in 1857, on an official mission for the King of Burmah to President Buchanan of the United States), they retired to Gerard, Kansas, in 1866. Of Rev. Kincaid, the correspondence indicates a man of convictions and occasional independent action.

[8] Emily Frances Judson, the daughter of Adoniram and Emily Chubbuck Judson, was born December 24, 1847.

[9] John Sartain was one of the most prominent engravers of the mid-nineteenth century. His works appeared in prominent magazines and books. In 1846, he created an engraving of Emily E. Chubbuck that was used as a plate for *Alderbrook*. The correspondence of spring 1846 reflects meetings with Mr. Sartain on changes thought to be needed. In 1849, Mr. Sartain was publishing a magazine because a letter makes a reference to one of Emily's poems being in it. Mr. Sartain had given twenty five dollars for the poem used in the magazine, and it had been used for items for the box, rather than sent to the board.

[10] Miles Bronson was a graduate of Hamilton University and Seminary and was appointed for missionary service in 1836. His field of service was Assam, and he first reached there in July 1837. He pioneered ministry with the Naga tribes. In 1849. Mr. Bronson returned to the United States and was there for more than a year; he returned to the field in 1851.

[11] See vol. 1, "Cast of Characters," s.v. "Vinton, The Reverend Doctor Justus Hatch and Calista."

but regret exceedingly they should be so misguided either by affections, or advice of others—I was very glad to learn by your good Dr.'s remarks to Mr. Gillette,[12] that he is glad to have Mr. Kincaid assume the responsibility of going to Ava—Mr. K. is as ardent, as a young man of 20—he seems hardy enough to endure long in that climate—Dr. Dawson[13] his brother in Can. I learn does not get appointed by the board, although they have full confidence in his piety and fitness—probably owing entirely on their part to want of funds—or the uncertainty of his success as physician at Ava—he is however going—and I am told will be sustained by individuals—There is wealth enough in this city to reinforce and sustain every department in heathen lands for the furtherance of the Gospel—Mr. Gillette is to baptize three this evening, one is a Medical student native of Switzerland—who is almost settled on becoming Missionary to his native Land—he is said to be a young man of great literary attainments, and sterling character—the other two are young ladies—several others have manifested deep interest in their soul's salvation—our congregations are large and very attentive—Dr. Malcom[14] seems to have resuscitated Sansom St. Chh—it no longer looks like the place where people go, only from a sense of duty—but quite full of attentive hearers—other churches here are progressing—

[12] Following several successful pastorates, the Reverend A. D. Gillette was the founding pastor of the flourishing Eleventh Baptist Church in Philadelphia in 1839. With his wife Hannah and several children (they would eventually have six), he graciously opened their home to Emily Chubbuck when she came to Philadelphia at the end of March 1845 for her health. The connection had been made through Miss Cynthia Sheldon, a family friend of Mr. Gillette and his parents. A prominent Baptist, Mr. Gillette journeyed to Boston in December 1845 to accompany Adoniram Judson to Philadelphia for meetings, and on Christmas Day, he introduced Dr. Judson to Emily Chubbuck with the hope that Fanny Forester could be persuaded to write the memoir of Sarah Hall Boardman Judson. A. D. Gillette and his wife Hannah remained valued and trusted friends, not only with Emily, but with the Sheldon and Anable families. He moved from Philadelphia to New York in 1852.

[13] Miss Cynthia Sheldon called Doctor Dawson a "brother of Mr. (Eugenio) Kincaid." There was some talk of Dr. Dawson going to Ava, but the Board of the American Baptist Missionary Union decided not to appoint him. Miss Sheldon speculated that it was because of lack of funds and not because of any question of his piety or fitness. In March 1850, Anna Maria Anable spoke of a visit from Mr. Bright of the American Baptist Missionary Union to dissuade Dr. Dawson from going to Burmah at least until Mr. Kincaid was settled in Ava. It was increasingly obvious that Dawson would go whether or not he had a board appointment, for there was sufficient funding and interest from the churches in Utica to provide the necessary support. See Emily's comments on Dr. Dawson in her letter dated June 20, 1850.

[14] Dr. Howard Malcom was born in Philadelphia in January 1799. Planning to live as a merchant, he was converted and called to the ministry. Licensed by the Sansom Street Church and educated at Princeton Seminary, he became pastor of a church in Hudson, New York, in 1820. In 1826, he became an agent for the American Sunday-School Union, and in 1827, he became the pastor of the Federal Street Church in Boston. Because of failing health, he toured Europe in 1831 and again in 1835 when his voice failed him and he resigned his parish. He next spent two years in Burmah, and upon his return in 1840, he became the president of Georgetown College in Kentucky. In 1849, he was forced to resign this position because of his anti-slavery views. In late 1849 or early 1850, Dr. Malcolm was called to be the pastor of the Sansom Street Baptist Church, which Alma Anable attended, as did some of the other members on occasion of the Anable-Sheldon families. There are many references to him in the letters of this time period. In 1851, he became the president of the University of Lewisburg and was there until he left in 1857 to resume work on a number of his publications. In this time he became interested in the American Baptist Historical Society and devoted himself to this work until his death in 1879. (William Cathcart, *The Baptist Encyclopaedia* [Philadelphia: Louis H. Everts, 1881] 740–41.)

We are delighted with your article in the Dec. Journal—It is just the thing required—dear Mrs. Wade[15] tells me of a fine visit from your dear parents[16] whom I shall try to see if I can get to Utica in the Spring—business may call me thus far—if so—my plan will be to say to the Wades and Bronsons who are only a few miles off—that *I* will meet them at such a time at your dear cottage—you see big *I* making great demands for distinction—but you may fancy it carried out just about the time this letter reaches you—we often hear from Utica—but I suppose Martha Lillybridge[17] keeps you informed of all important events—and Anna M. writes you so often that I cannot tell you any news about home—Miss Amanda Crafts is spending the winter in the city—she comes in very friendly.—Mrs. Clark of Utica has written to see if we would take her only daughter Jane for a few months—we expect her—and you know Mrs. Clark and Mrs. Crafts[18] are sisters—Miss Augusta designs to visit some friends here next month—she is teaching at the Sem. and only two weeks to spend away—Mrs. Gratiot[19] was very glad to find a new boarding place last month—It appears Mary Barber[20] too is very uncomfortable there—but poor girl has to make the best of it—Jane[21] made a smashing party last month—but poor

[15] Deborah Wade was a missionary to Burmah; with her husband Jonathan, they were appointed in 1823. Adoniram Judson called them "his dearest and best of friends." Much of their work was in the jungle communities following the path of George Boardman. They left for the United States on December 22, 1847. From the Hamilton, New York, area, they stayed not far from the home of Emily's parents and sister; they visited the Anable-Sheldon families in Philadelphia. With a large group, they had left Boston on July 25, 1850, and returned to Burmah in February 1851.

[16] Charles and Lavinia Richards Chubbuck lived in Hamilton, New York.

[17] Martha Lillybridge was the sister of Lydia Lillybridge, who went to Burmah with Emily and Adoniram Judson. Martha was at the Utica Female Academy. On May 28, 1848, Anna Maria wrote, "Martha is a very fine looking girl—but she lacks energy. I think we shall have her take Fanny's (Anna Maria's sister) place at Miss Martin's. It will suit her as she has no desire to shine as a teacher in a school."

[18] Augusta Crafts is mentioned frequently in the letters written from the Utica Female Academy. A number of references chronicle her very strong opinions; many of these were spoken against N. P. Willis and Emily's relationship to him (Mrs. Crafts did not approve of either). In an April 30, 1845, letter Anna Maria Anable said, "The Dr. is not engaged nor isn't going to be to Mary Spencer I imagine, and tho' Mrs. Crafts intimated very strongly that there was *some one* he had his eye upon, he denied it to me strongly and scolded about Mrs. Crafts gossiping tongue."

[19] See vol. 1, "Cast of Characters," s.v. "Gratiot, Charles and Ann."

[20] Mary Barber was mentioned frequently in the Emily Chubbuck Judson letters; she was a student and then a teacher at the Utica Female Academy. There were ups and downs to that relationship; in fall 1845, apparently Mary had written to someone expressing what Anna Maria Anable called "ingratitude," and Mary had been banned from the Academy until she made proper apologies to Miss Sheldon. In a September 7, 1845, letter from Anna Maria, we learn that her remarks had been about Miss Cynthia Sheldon. In November 1847 Jane Kelly remarked that they had not heard from Mary in more than a year. In 1848 Mary Barber was back at the Utica Female Seminary teaching with Jane Kelly. Though at this time Miss Sheldon had moved to Philadelphia, Mary Barber had been able to reconcile with her, and in later years we find Mary very close to the Sheldon-Anable families; later, there was considerable consternation on Miss Cynthia Sheldon's part in her correspondence with Emily about Mary's health, the seriousness of it, and Mary's impending death. These letters were written in April 1852. Miss Sheldon went to help transfer Mary to Albany in June 1852, where she would be better situated and perhaps have access to better doctors. On September 9, 1852, Anna Maria Anable wrote to Emily of Mary Barber's death.

[21] Miss Jane Kelly was Emily Chubbuck's friend at the Utica Female Academy, and then she became a teacher with Emily at that institution. Miss Kelly became the literary principal in 1844 with the retirement of Mr. and Mrs. James Nichols from that position. During a period of Miss Kelly's illness in 1844, Emily filled in the position for her. Then, in 1848, when Miss Cynthia Sheldon moved to Philadelphia to help start the Misses Anable's School, Miss Kelly became the "headmistress" of the academy and successfully brought it into the future, though not without some initial disparagement from the Sheldon-Anable families.

thing is often holed up with headache—Mr. Gratiot[22] writes home in fine spirits from California, sends some gold to her—and says three years there with health, will enable him to live where he pleases—I do hope on more accounts than one that he will get a *big lump*—you remember our Rosina—who went to live with Urania,[23] her husband went to California last spring or rather got there in Oct—he sent two hundred Dollars to Rosina, said he had gathered $900 in 14 days, and should send on the remainder as soon as he learned the remittance was safe with her—It is really wonderful. Mrs. Gillette's[24] eldest brother went on there about Sep. he had cleared $7000 by Nov.—he expects to realize a rapid fortune, and buy a fine house here for Mrs. G.—The most benefit I expect to derive from these diggings is the knowledge of other peoples' prosperity—yes the impulse to the railroad enterprise across the Istmus [sic] will do much for our Mission Cause—perhaps come four years from now you can come home in as many weeks—Then will follow the Telegraph, all distance annihilated—shall we live to see such wonders—and yet not half as wonderful as many improvements in the last 20 years—Anna Bennett[25] is to come back in April and commence teaching a family school some 20 miles from here—she will be in a fine Quaker family—duties very light—at $500 Sal.—we shall be very glad to have her near us, and often here—Nellie[26] is growing up a lovely

[22] Charles Gratiot grew up in St Louis, where his father was an army engineer responsible for developing the Port of St. Louis. He married Ann Sheldon, who was a cousin of Miss Cynthia Sheldon, Mrs. Urania Sheldon Nott, and Alma Sheldon Anable. Together, Charles and Ann Gratiot had six children. Because they often lived with the Sheldon family, their letters contain a great deal of him. Letters in 1847 speak of his religious awakening; those of 1849 speak of his leaving for the California gold fields. In 1853, Charles Gratiot applied for a grant of 400 acres in Illinois, and he already owned 148 acres.

[23] Urania Sheldon had been the literary principal of the Utica Female Academy in fall 1840 when Emily Chubbuck came to study there. Emily was able to afford this wonderful education through the generous offer of Miss Sheldon and her sister Cynthia, the executive and financial head of the academy, to defer tuition. Urania Sheldon left in late summer 1842 upon her marriage to the Reverend Doctor Eliphalet Nott, the president of Union College in Schenectady, New York. Because of the distance separating them, Emily's relationship with Urania Sheldon Nott did not develop the intimacy that grew between Emily and Miss Cynthia Sheldon. Urania Sheldon Nott remained a mentor, advisor, and friend to Emily in the years of her writing, her missionary endeavors, and upon her return to America in 1851. She was also the aunt of Anna Maria Anable.

[24] Hannah Gillette was the wife of the Reverend A. D. Gillette, pastor of the Eleventh Baptist Church in Philadelphia. Emily stayed with them when she came to Philadelphia in spring 1845 for her health, and she returned in November. In the parlor of their home, she met Adoniram Judson on Christmas Day 1845. Mr. and Mrs. Gillette became strong friends and supporters; Mrs. Gillette played an important part in getting Emily's outfit together for her life in Burmah.

[25] Anna Bennett was the daughter of Cephas and Stella Bennett, missionaries to Burmah. She was born in August 1833. An 1850 letter said that beginning in April, she would be teaching at a family school in a private home in the Philadelphia area. By 1853, she was elsewhere, for Miss Cynthia Sheldon was corresponding with her. On September 7, 1853, Miss Sheldon wrote to Emily Judson to say that she had written about Dr. Burton and his interest in her. Dr. Burton was associated with the Southern Missionary Board and was due to leave the country no later than November. Highly thought of, Miss Sheldon said, "I fancy he has found the way to the warm corner of her heart—which is an evidence of tact—probably he is a widower." On September 25, Emily Judson replied, "Anna B's affair strikes me favourably. I never heard of Dr. B. but he probably went out when I was on my way home. It is certainly better to marry a man of established character and expectation than a 'green horn' and Anna would be happier in the east than here." On October 14, 1853, Miss Sheldon wrote again, "The dear girl seemed in a terrible quandary—which she very foolishly thought I could settle—The truth is Anna's heart is *some what* [sic] engaged and I have no doubt but she will decide to go. Mr. Dean told Courtland she would get in the Dr. one of the very best of men." Anna Bennett married Dr. Burton in early November 1853. They sailed in early December 1853.

[26] Nellie Bennett, the daughter of Cephas and Stella Bennett. The Bennett daughters were educated at the Utica Female Academy and then the Misses Anable's School.

girl, very industrious, she has cut and made herself a new dress this week—she is very considerate and amiable exerting a good influence in the house—I am sorry to say we do not succeed in getting boarders—which ties my hands too much for real comfort—still while the girls can get scholars we shall plod along—

Heaven bless you and yours—and keep us all in the straight and narrow path is the fervent wish of your attached friend

C. Sheldon

[Written upside down in the top margin of page 1:] Give love to Lydia[27]—Martha was well the 20th.

Source: American Baptist Historical Society, AJ 20, no. 995.

Miss Cynthia Sheldon to Emily C. Judson, January 27, 1850[28]

Copy
Dr. and Emily Judson
Life of Elizabeth Fry 2 Vols
Memoirs of T. Touvell Buxton
Scrap Book for Henry
Scripture Guide for Henry
Scrap Book for Edward
Here a little, and there a little for Edwd
Doll for Emily Frances[29] and 2 Picture Books
Morocco work Case sissors [sic] pen knife
Pierces, buttons, sewing silk, tape, thread
Bobbins, needles—darning cotton sewing do.
Box of pins 4 sizes 6 pen knives
3 doz lead pencils 1/2 lb sealing wax
Songs in the Night—Castile Soap

[27] Lydia Lillybridge was one of Emily's closest friends at the Utica Female Academy. When Emily made the decision to go to Burmah as the wife of Adoniram Judson and as a missionary, Lydia wanted to go with them. Emily spoke to Adoniram Judson of Lydia's extraordinary abilities, and Adoniram advocated her appointment before Dr. Solomon Peck and the Board of the American Baptist Missionary Union. Lydia was commissioned to go with them, in spite of the fact that she remained single. Always independent, outspoken, and unafraid to cause ripples in the missionary community, Lydia served on the mission field for twenty-eight years. She married missionary Thomas Simons in May 1851. See the timeline on the life and service of Lydia Lillybridge Simons in vol. 1.

[28] This letter is undated, but it obviously was included in a box of supplies sent to Emily and Adoniram in Burmah. It is placed on January 27. Another letter of this same date speculates when the box might be sent, and a letter of January 28, 1850, states that the box was sent the previous morning (January 27).

[29] From a letter of Cynthia Sheldon to Emily, January 27, 1850: "Previous to your letter I had been fitting up for Miss Fanny's acceptance—Miss Jenny Lind some two feet high—I do wish she could be transported by telegraph."

Comb and brush—baby brush and 2 combs
1 bottle of Cologne

This package is from Maryanne Longstreth[30] and family—Do you not think dear Emily—that Aunt C. has some pleasure in packing them for you—yes I do believe there is some thankfulness in this heart in finding others are prompted to do what is not in my power to do at this time—and may never be. These *plain*[31] friends are my admiration to night—they have made many enquiries of late—and this aft'n Maryanne and her sister came in a carriage to bring their packages—For the Wades[32] they had about the same as yourself—and so nicely selected too—I think the children's[33] eyes will dance on seeing the Scrap books [sic]—Mr. and Mrs. Bronson[34] are in the city, were to have come here and staid [sic] till Monday—but Mrs. B. is not able to come—we found many things wanted by them—Mrs. Anable[35] and myself, Nelly Bennett[36] and Mrs. Lee have been busy as bees—just finished off a dress—Mrs. Robarts[37] has run about and had great success I find—Maryanne came again this evening expecting to see the Bronsons and gave me five Dollars for

[30] Miss Longstreth, in her own letters, signed her name as Mary Anna. The references of Anna Maria also refer to her as Mary Anna, but there is one reference in one of the other letters to her as Marianne.

[31] The Longstreths were Quakers in Philadelphia. There are five letters in the collection from them to Emily.

[32] Jonathan and Deborah Wade were appointed missionaries to Burmah in 1823. Their relationship with Adoniram Judson was especially dear because of the early experiences they shared, including the death of Ann Judson. When she died and Adoniram returned to Amherst, he never forgot the sight of Deborah Wade standing on the veranda holding little Maria in her arms. Much of their work was spent in the Karen jungle communities following the path of George Boardman. They returned home to America on December 22, 1847, and went back to Burmah in January 1851, just as Emily was returning to the United States. They were from the Hamilton, New York, area. They left for Burmah on July 25, 1850, and were in Maulmain by February 1851. Both died in Burmah; Deborah died at Maulmain in 1868, and Jonathan died in Rangoon in 1872.

[33] Henry Hall Judson, seven and a half years old; Edward Judson, five years old; and Emily Frances Judson, two years old.

[34] See vol. 1, "Cast of Characters," s.v. "Bronson, Miles."

[35] Alma Sheldon Anable was the sister of Miss Cynthia Sheldon and Urania Sheldon Nott. Genealogy sources show that she married Joseph Hubbell Anable in Troy, New York, on July 28, 1814, and that it was the second marriage for Mr. Anable. Born in 1773, he was forty-one at the time of the marriage, and Alma was likely considerably younger. He died in 1831, which explains why Alma Anable and her family lived and worked first at the Utica Female Seminary and then later at the Misses Anable's school in Philadelphia. Joseph and Alma Anable were the parents of nine children: Henry Sheldon Anable (b. June 21, 1815); William Stewart Anable (b. November 6, 1816); Anna Maria Stafford Anable (b. September 30, 1818), Cynthia Jane Anable (b. January 28, 1820); Samuel Low Anable (b. November 28, 1821); Harriet Isabella Anable, also known as Hatty or Hattie (b. December 18, 1823); Courtland Wilcox Anable (b. July 28, 1825); Frances Alma Anable, or Fanny (b. April 12, 1828); and Mary Juliet Anable (b. February 18, 1830).

[36] Nelly or "Nellie" Bennett was the daughter of Cephas and Stella Bennett, missionaries to Burmah.

[37] Mr. and Mrs. W. S. Robarts were active in Philadelphia Baptist circles. They were frequent visitors to the home of the Reverend and Mrs. A. D. Gillette and later to the Misses Anable's School, which Anna Maria Anable and her extended family had started in Philadelphia in 1848. In his biography of his father, Edward Judson mentioned that Adoniram Judson stayed at the. Robarts's home when he came to Philadelphia in December 1845 when he met Emily Chubbuck. A. C. Kendrick said, "(Mr. Gillette and Dr. Judson) arrived in (or out of) due time in Philadelphia, and Dr. Judson was welcomed to the house of Mr. and Mrs. W. S. Robarts, who became warm personal friends, as they were already active friends of the mission cause." (A. C. Kendrick, *The Life and Letters of Mrs. Emily C. Judson* [New York: Sheldon and Company, 1862] 142.) In 1846, with the engagement of Adoniram Judson and Emily Chubbuck, the correspondence indicates some hard feelings toward Mrs. Robarts for comments disparaging the coming marriage and missionary service. This is found in Emily's letter to Adoniram dated February 6, 1846; Mrs. Robarts seemed to be accusing Emily of worldliness when all the time, Emily was quick to say, Mrs. Robarts was engaging in the same activity of which she was accused. The correspondence also indicates a satisfactory healing of the relationship. In January 1849, Miss Sheldon told Emily that Mrs. Robarts had placed their daughter Mary in the Misses Anable's School.

them—I am too glad to feel ashamed that the Baptists are out done—*in doing*—It is 11 o'clock Saturday night—The box stands in my room yawning for emptiness—as Mrs. Bronson's things with the rest are piled up on my bed—Oh that I could know how it is with you and yours—you will have all prayer to God for restoration—Heaven bless and strengthen you—I shall write you by Mail—Your truly attached

C. Sheldon

Source: American Baptist Historical Society, AJ 20, no. 996.

Miss Cynthia Sheldon to Emily C. Judson, January 28, 1850

Dear Emily—

Anna M.[38] has been prevented from writing to you at this time—I have just found it out 11 o'clock at night—Mr. and Mrs. Gillette[39] were here to a family tea—and have just gone—They are the most cozy friends our girls have—always the same—and interested in every thing [sic] about the school—Mr. and Mrs. Robarts[40] too, although their Mary is rather slow—

Could I have known Anna M. would have come so far short, you should have had a full sheet from me—Mrs. Bennett[41] has a share in this mail not quite finished—all must go in the morn'g. To convince you that my pen moves the same—since 9 o'clock the servant was sent with a package for Utica—to go by Mrs. Dixon the wife of the Pastor of Westminster Church—My share in it is one letter to Mr.

[38] See vol. 1, "Cast of Characters," s.v. "Anable, Anna Maria."

[39] See vol. 1, "Cast of Characters," s.v. "Gillette, The Reverend Abram Dunn."

[40] See vol. 1, "Cast of Characters," s.v. "Robarts, Mr. and Mrs. W. S."

[41] Stella Bennett was the wife of Cephas Bennett; they arrived in Burmah in January 1830. Mr. Bennett remained the superintendent of the Baptist Press there for more than fifty years. From the Utica area, they sent their children back, and the girls were educated at the Utica Female Academy and then the Misses Anable's School. The girls included Elsina (April 1828), Mary (November 1829), Ann (August 1833), Ellen (June 1835), and Sarah (June 1837).

[42] Mr. Corey was the pastor of the Bleecker Street Baptist Church near the Utica Female Academy, and Miss Sheldon and many of the girls from the academy attended worship there. (Cynthia Sheldon, Alma Anable, Deacon Asa and Isabell Sheldon, Edward Bright, and Horace Hawley had been charter members of the church in 1838.) In April 1844, he wrote to Emily, expressing dismay that at a school program one of the girls had read a composition justifying dancing as exercise; he spoke of this as a roadblock to the salvation of many. Then, on March 10, 1846, Emily indicated in a letter to Anna Maria that Mr. Corey had been critical of her relationship and impending marriage to Adoniram Judson. Miss Cynthia Sheldon wrote a number of times expressing Mr. Corey's regret and support, and in 1847, there were letters of reconciliation between Emily and Mr. Corey. In spring 1848, letters reveal that Mr. Corey's wife had died of consumption, her condition exacerbated by recent childbirth. She had left behind four children. In July 1849, Anna Maria Anable wrote of his impending marriage to Jane Backus, a good choice for this "rising man." Mr. Corey remained popular with the Sheldon-Anable families even after their move to Philadelphia in 1848. A March 2, 1852, letter from Charles B. Stout told of Mr. Corey's call to the Stanton Street Church in New York City, which Mr. Corey did not accept. Finally, in 1854, there was a pastoral letter from Mr. Corey to Emily on her illness and her possible death. He preached at the Bleecker Street Church as late as January 1867.

Corey[42]—one to Mrs. Dr. James[43]—Eugenia,[44] Mrs. Ford, Martha Lillybridge[45] and Anna Bennett[46]—Nellie[47] and our Fanny[48] added a few—my mind is much in Utica now—it has been a relief to write my feelings to day [sic] first to Urania[49] this morn'g—three years now, dearest Mother[50] was sinking—all the surroundings are before me, Mr. Corey, Mrs. Ford, and others are grouped in that dear room—then the stillness of death—the grave—but Oh—the long drawn sigh from the inmost recesses of the *dear lone one*—I can now feel it to the heart's core—In six weeks two years will have passed since they were reunited in heaven—there, I love to dwell in thoughts all is peace—yes immortal bliss forevermore—"Shall I among them stand," is often in my heart—Heaven grant that boon to each of us, when life's toils, and joys are over—Most affectionately yours,

C. Sheldon

[43] Dr. James was a trusted physician, who attended the students and faculty of the Utica Female Academy. He is mentioned frequently in the correspondence as having been consulted for varying medical complaints, and his advice was always welcomed and highly regarded.

[44] Eugenia Damaux had been part of Emily's intimate circle of friends at the Utica Female Academy. Living in New York City, Eugenia suffered from some kind of eye problem that made life difficult at times; this was a matter of comment in many of the letters exchanged between the girls themselves and with Miss Cynthia Sheldon. In 1848, Eugenia was in New York living "at Mrs. Brown's—the same warm-hearted French girl as ever." In 1849, she married Johnny Edmonds, described as rich and pious, and they lived in Utica.

[45] See vol. 1, "Cast of Characters," s.v. "Lillybridge, Martha."

[46] See vol. 1, "Cast of Characters," s.v. "Bennett, Anna."

[47] Nellie Bennett was the daughter of Cephas and Stella Bennett. The Bennett daughters were educated at the Utica Female Academy and then the Misses Anable's School.

[48] Fanny Anable was one of nine children born to Joseph and Alma Anable and was a niece of Miss Cynthia Sheldon and Mrs. Urania Sheldon Nott. The correspondence indicates that in April 1845 she was away from home studying and taking music lessons. These spring letters indicate that she was in Philadelphia, working in the home of and with the family of the Reverend A. D. Gillette. See Miss Sheldon's letter to Emily of November 30, 1845, in which she spoke of all that Fanny was doing to improve herself in the field of music, but also her concern for Fanny's interest in the party life and the "vanitie" which surround her." A March 30, 1847, letter from Anna Maria Anable told of Fanny's conversion following her grandmother's death. In September 1847, she was listed as one of the teachers at the Utica Female Academy. Fanny became a teacher with her sisters in the Misses Anable's School in Philadelphia.

[49] See vol. 1, "Cast of Characters," s.v. "Sheldon, Urania."

[50] Isabell Low Sheldon had died January 29, 1847, and Anna Maria Anable had written of her death on February 15, 1847; Deacon Asa Sheldon had died in March 1848. Their daughters were Miss Cynthia Sheldon, Alma Sheldon Anable, and Urania Sheldon Nott.

[Written across the second page, which contains a copy of a newspaper article:] Is this not fine from your old friend—I had copies to send Henry Anable[51]—Willis[52] is a jewel of a friend in time of need—my faith is strong now for more boarders. [Copy of Article from *Home Journal*]

> The Misses Anable's School
>
> At 311 Walnut St., Philadelphia, three very highly accredited teachers have their school for young Ladies, and we have known enough of them through our dear friend and theirs, Fanny Forester,[53] to be sure that under no roof, away from home, would a daughter be subjected to better influences. The testimonials of Dr. Nott,[54] and other equal authorities, are published to the same affect in their printed circular, and their advertisement will be found in another column of this paper.
>
> We may with propriety add, we believe that the climate of Philadelphia is the best in the country, for the period of life employed in education; and there is an atmosphere of taste and elegance about that City, arising from what we do not know, which is very visibly recognized in its ladies, and likely to affect very desirably all who are educated there—
>
> *The Home Journal*
> January 12th, 1850

Source: American Baptist Historical Society, AJ 20, no. 993.

[51] Henry Sheldon Anable was the oldest of the six children born to Joseph and Alma Sheldon Anable. He was born June 21, 1815. In August 1846, he was in the Milwaukee, Wisconsin, area and was thinking of settling there. In a September 27 letter, he said he might leave Utica to join William and Olivia in Sheboygan, Wisconsin. He was married to Rosanna Frick in Sheboygan, Wisconsin, on February 13, 1855, and died September 3, 1887, in Flushing, New York.

[52] Nathaniel Parker Willis was the editor, with General George Morris, of the *New Mirror*, a prominent literary magazine in New York. His "discovery" of Emily in the June 8, 1844, edition of the *New Mirror* catapulted her into literary fame and enabled her to command the highest prices for her articles and stories from the major magazines of that period. Over the next two years, he became her friend, mentor, and confidant. His black-bordered letter of March 21, 1846, made it abundantly clear that he had expected to marry Emily upon his return that month from England. He later returned several letters to Emily to demonstrate to her, lest she had forgotten, why he had felt right in that expectation. Within a few months of Emily's departure for Burmah, Willis was married to the ward of a United States senator; one of the letters to Emily from her friends stated that his new bride had significant wealth. The *New Mirror* went out of business as Willis was returning to the United States, and he established another publication, the *Home Journal*, with General George Morris. See vol. 1, "Cast of Characters," s.v. "Willis, Nathaniel Parker (N. P. Willis)." For a detailed examination of his relationship with Emily, see vol. 1, "Timeline," s.v. "The Correspondence and Relationship between Emily E. Chubbuck/Fanny Forester and Nathaniel Parker Willis: A Litany of Unrequited Romance."

[53] Emily Chubbuck wrote under the *nom de plume* Fanny Forester. Asked about it once, she said, "Would anyone buy a book written by Emily E. Chubbuck?"

[54] The Reverend Doctor Eliphalet Nott was the president of Union College in Schenectady, New York. An ordained Presbyterian minister, he was married to Urania Sheldon Nott, the sister of Miss Cynthia Sheldon and Mrs. Alma Anable and the aunt of Anna Maria Anable.

Mrs. Lucretia B. Stilson to Emily C. Judson, February 12, 1850—Maulmain

My Dear Sister

Be assured your note rec'd last night was very welcome as we had been so long anxiously waiting to hear. Don't I beg of you wait again for something encouraging to write as *no news is bad news* to us. I need not tell you you have our sympathies you know that when one member suffers all the members suffer with it.[55] In the visit of br. and sr. R. you have the expression of the sympathies of the whole mission with a desire to devise some plan for the benefit of your dear husband's health. I have not time to say much and do not need to as you have living epistles. May God direct your future movements and prepare you for all you are to meet.

I venture to send you a few more crackers though I did not succeed as well as I wished and doubted awhile about sending them on that account.

With much love to all

Yours aff't

L. B. Stilson

My health is good. The rest well.

Source: American Baptist Historical Society, AJ 19, no. 891.

Emily C. Judson to Anna Maria Anable, February 19, 1850—Maulmain

My dear Anna Maria,

You did not write me this month, but you are usually so good, that I will not scold. And indeed I am too sad to scold with any kind of spirit—my heart is growing very heavy, and I have almost forgotten how to smile—how I *do* wish you were here! You don't know what trouble I am having—the poor Doct. is as thin as a skeleton, and oh such a face! Then his mind is just like an infant's, occasioned by the weakness of the body. Night and day I am over him all the time—but how can I, who have had so little practice, be a good nurse? I do the best I can, but my hands are weak and awkward, and I am very little accustomed to prepare nice things for the sick. Don't think though that we have no friends—everybody is *so* kind, ready to do anything under the sun, but then a sick man prefers his wife to nurse him though she don't [sic] do it as well as another might.

He was first attacked by a slight dysentery nearly three months ago. This was followed by a slow fever, which has gradually wasted his flesh and strength; and though the doctor has continually maintained that he was in no danger, I have

[55] At the turn of the year, Adoniram and Emily Judson went to Mergui hoping for an improvement in the health of Adoniram Judson. They then spent a month at Amherst.

terrible apprehensions that he will never be like himself again. We first went down to Tavoy and Mergui in the steamer, but it did very little if any good; next we spent a month at Amherst (have just returned) and now we are talking of a long sea voyage. The doctor says medicine is of no use in his case. But a voyage is *so* difficult. He cannot go without me, and my situation added to what I suffer under ordinary circumstances on the water, makes the prospect very dark. Then, the three children![56]—what to do with them. Lydia[57] came and took care of the boys, while we went to Mergui; but they are no *lambs*! I can tell you and they require a firm hand. They almost ran over her, and I would not inflict them on her again. Oh, but you don't know how ruinous it is to children to live in an unsettled way. There never were finer boys, and that is why I fear their getting spoiled. Then to go a voyage [sic], and be confined among strangers, with a sick, perhaps dying husband, and nobody to take care of either of us but these horrid servants, who unless watched every minute get drunk, or rob you, and particularly if they find you are dependent on them run off and leave you in the lurch. Our cook at Amherst, (an old servant and faithful as any) got drunk nearly every night because he knew there was nobody there strong enough to horse-whip him. You think we have turned him off since we came back?—not a bit of it; that would be "jumping out of the frying pan into the fire."

I was just called out. It was to be informed that the Commissioner of Arracan (by a letter which the steamer brought) had invited us to come there, and he would do all in his power to make us comfortable. It is not a good place to go, but it will show you how kind everybody is. The police magistrate here, hearing that we wanted to take the buggy down to Amherst, sent down an order to the jailer to have the roads repaired for our especial benefit. Carriages have never been used there. As for the missionaries—if they were real brothers and sisters they could'nt [sic] be kinder. When I wrote from Amherst saying that Mr. J. was getting no benefit, they rec'd my notes about sundown. One of them went to Doct. Morton[58] immediately—then they called a meeting, voted that Doct. J. should be advised to take a voyage, and the next day's night in the night, one of them with his wife[59] reached Amherst to bring us back. People learn to be kind to each other, in this dreary part of the world.

[56] Henry Hall Judson, seven and a half years old; Edward Judson, five years old; and Emily Frances Judson, two years old.

[57] See vol. 1, "Cast of Characters," s.v. "Lillybridge, Lydia." Also, "A Timeline of the Life and Mission of Lydia Lillybridge Simons."

[58] Doctor Morton was a physician who worked with the missionaries in Maulmain, Burmah. He delivered Emily Frances Judson in December 1847 and was present when Charles Judson ("Angel Charley") was stillborn in April 1850. He was a valued and trusted advisor to the mission families.

[59] A comment made by Lucretia Stilson in her letter of February 12, 1850, reveals that this was Thomas and Maria Ranney. Mr. Ranney was the business manager for the mission, and he accompanied Adoniram on the next voyage and recorded the events of his death on April 12, 1850.

Well, Ninny,[60] I have written you a queer sheet full I know, but I write about that which is on my

[Written in the right margin of the address page:] heart the heaviest. What we shall do I don't know. Another month will decide and then I will write you. I know you pity me, but after all, Ninny, you can't begin to know how miserable I should be but for one consideration—"My Father's at the helm" and he will "bring light out of darkness."

[Written in the left margin of the address page:] I want to answer Aunt C's[61] good long kind letter but have no time. Please tell her, however, not to be in the least concerned about the Karen boy Sheldon nor give a penny more than she feels able for his support. Her supporting him was a mere nominal affair—her moneys went to the Board and the boy has always been and is still supported—the school fund furnished by the Board. I will explain more fully when I write to her.

[Written across the left and top margins of page 1:] I rec'd this month a nice letter from Sarah Hinckley.[62] How it carried me back to those days is sweet, but I would not go back to them for anything notwithstanding all my troubles. Do you ever write to Mrs. Lou Marble Wright?[63] If so, please ask her to write me. I don't know whether I have treated her well or not, about writing, but I know I remember her with a great deal of affection. Julia Casswell[64] too—she wrote me just before she was married and I ought to have replied, and meant to, but it has been *such* a

[60] "Ninny" was a name of endearment given to Anna Maria Anable by her most intimate friends at the Utica Female Academy. Emily was "Nemmy."

[61] Miss Cynthia Sheldon was in charge of the administrative and financial departments of the Utica Female Academy. Miss Sheldon and her sister Urania, who was literary principal, gave Emily Chubbuck a place at the academy in October 1840. They had deferred any cost to a future time when Emily could afford to reimburse them. Upon Miss Urania Sheldon's marriage in late summer 1842 to the Reverend Doctor Eliphalet Nott, the president of Union College, and her subsequent move to Schenectady, Miss Cynthia Sheldon assumed a larger leadership role at the academy. In the years that followed, Miss Sheldon and Emily developed an even stronger relationship. In 1848, Miss Sheldon moved to Philadelphia to help Miss Anable with the startup of the Misses Anable's School and to assume responsibilities in its operation. Active and well-known in Baptist circles, Miss Cynthia was one of Emily's most important mentors, advisors, and friends until the time of Emily's death in 1854. Miss Sheldon was the aunt of Anna Maria Anable.

[62] See the letter of Sarah Hinckley to Emily C. Judson dated December 2, 1849. Sarah Hinckley was one of the girls from the Utica Female Seminary and a student of Emily's; there are some letters from her in the collection. In an 1849 letter Miss Hinckley reminisced about that time and brought Emily up to date on many of those who were there with her. She also spoke of the sad farewell when Emily left for Boston and then Burmah.

[63] In 1843, Miss Marble was a recent graduate of the Utica Female Seminary and wrote to Emily upon her return to Port Byron. In an 1848 letter to Emily, she was at the academy as a teacher and was fully involved there. According to a letter written by Sarah Hinckley in 1849, Miss Marble married and moved to New York City. In Emily's February 19, 1850, letter she was referred to as "Lou Marble Wright." Then, in April 1851, Anna Maria mentioned that Louisa Marble Wright was now a widow, back living in Utica with her sister.

[64] Julia Look was a student of Emily's at the Utica Female Academy and later a fellow teacher. A November 22, 1845, letter from Anna Maria encouraged Emily to stay in Philadelphia for the winter for her health and remarked that Julia had the hardest part because she was teaching Emily's composition class, and the students kept asking for Emily. In a September 1847 letter, she was listed as one of the teachers at the Utica Female Academy. On September 23, 1849, Anna Maria wrote that Julia and Albert B. Casswell were married and came to visit with her. In one 1849 letter Julia spoke of another teacher who was teaching "our composition class." On October 27, 1850, Anna Maria Anable noted that she had had a son. She was one of a small number of people who addressed Emily as "Emily" and as "Nemmy" in her letters.

sorrowful year to me! Please give love to all—your people and the Gillettes[65] etc. and Believe me Lovingly y'rs

ECJ

Source: Hanna family files.

Adoniram Judson to the American Baptist Missionary Union, February 21, 1850[66]

I cannot manage a pen, so please excuse pencil. I have been prostrated with fever ever since the latter part of last November,—and have suffered so much that I have frequently remarked, that I was never ill in India before. Through the mercy of God I think I am convalescent for the last ten days; but the Doctor and all my friends are very urgent that I should take a sea voyage of a month or two,[67] and be absent from the place a long time. May God direct in the path of duty. My hand is failing, so I will beg to remain, &c.

Source: *Missionary Magazine* 30 (June 1850): 189.

Emily C. Judson to Adoniram Judson,[68] February 1850

Watching

Sleep, love, sleep!
The dusty day is done.
Lo! from afar the freshening breezes sweep,
Wide over groves of balm,
Down from the towering palm,
In at the open casement cooling run,
And round thy lowly bed,
Thy bed of pain,
Bathing thy patient head,
Like grateful showers of rain,
They come;

[65] See vol. 1, "Cast of Characters," s.v. "Gillette, The Reverend Abram Dunn."

[66] Adoniram Judson died approximately seven weeks from the time he wrote this letter.

[67] On January 3, 1850, Adoniram and Emily wrote from Mergui, and they were there about a month. Apparently, his health had not improved sufficiently, and a more extensive voyage was to be planned.

[68] This was written to Adoniram Judson during the time of his illness. Taken ill in November 1849, Emily and Adoniram Judson sailed to Mergui and Tavoy and had spent a month in Amherst. About the middle of February, it became clear that his only hope was a trip to sea. Because of her pregnancy and fragile health, Emily was unable to accompany him. As they waited for a ship to be available, Emily penned these words to Adoniram as she sat by his bed.

While the white curtains, waving to and fro,
Fan the sick air;
And pityingly the shadows come and go,
With gentle human care,
Compassionate and dumb.

The dusty day is done,
The night begun;
While prayerful watch I keep,
Sleep, love, sleep!
Is there no magic in the touch
Of fingers thou dost love so much?
Fain would they scatter poppies o'er thee now;
Or, with its mute caress,
The tremulous lip some soft nepenthe press
Upon thy weary lid and aching brow;
While prayerful watch I keep,
Sleep, love, sleep!

On the pagoda spire
The bells are swinging,
Their little golden circlet in a flutter
With tales the wooing winds have dared to utter,
Till all are ringing,
As if a choir
Of golden-nested birds in heaven were singing;
And with a lulling sound
The music floats around,
And drops like balm into the drowsy ear;
Commingling with the hum
Of the Sepoy's distant drum,
And lazy beetle ever droning near.
Sounds these of deepest silence born,
Like night made visible by morn;
So silent that I sometimes start
To hear the throbbings of my heart,
And watch, with shivering sense of pain,
To see thy pale lids lift again.

The lizard, with his mouse-like eyes,
Peeps from the mortise in surprise
At such strange quiet after day's harsh din;
Then boldly ventures out,
And looks about,
And with his hollow feet
Treads his small evening beat,
Darting upon his prey
In such a tricksy, winsome sort of way,
His delicate marauding seems no sin.
And still the curtains swing,
But noiselessly;
The bells a melancholy murmur ring,
As tears were in the sky;
More heavily the shadows fall,
Like the black foldings of a pall,
Where juts the rough beam from the wall;
The candles flare
With fresher gusts of air;
The beetle drone
Turns to a dirge-like, solitary moan;
Night deepens, and I sit, in cheerless doubt alone.

Source: A. C. Kendrick, *Life and Letters of Mrs. Emily C. Judson*, 330–32; Emily Judson, *An Olio of Domestic Verses*, 167–71.

Mrs. Olive Celina Harris[69] to Emily C. Judson, February 23, 1850

Dear Sister Judson

Do not think I have forgotten and that I have no sympathy for you because I so seldom call to see you. Were I sure I could be of any use or even that I should do no harm I should have called often. I am too well aware of the effect of company on a sick person not to take heed and I also know that the Dr. has many old friends who feel that they cannot stay away when he is so ill. We have been peculiarly attached to yourself and that dear husband of yours since our first acquaintance although we have not had the privilege of often enjoying your society. We feel that it is hard to give up that dear brother but when we think of you our trials sink into insignificance.

You my dear sister have trials and those too which are experienilly [sic] but few comparatively.

[69] Norman and Olive Harris sailed to Burmah on the *Faneuil Hall* in July 1846 with Adoniram and Emily Judson.

Had you not an arm of strength to lean upon methinks you would fall. I would say then lean on his arm and it will sustain you. How precious are the promises of our heavenly Father and how tender his care! If He takes from you the Friend of your bosom it is that he may plant him by His own side away from toil and care and pain where joy and bliss forever reigns. Not only will He plant him there but He will reserve a place for you when your work is done that you may enjoy His presence and those you dearly love forever. Now my sister pardon my boldness and believe me when I say that you have our deep sympathy, and prayers. Remember me with affection to your dear husband.

Yours afft

C. C. Harris

Source: American Baptist Historical Society, AJ 16, no. 690.

Mrs. Phoebe Hough to Emily C. Judson, March 1, 1850[70]

My dear Mrs. Judson

How is dear Judson to-day? Do not suppose because I say nothing to you that my heart is not alive to all your sorrows—I do not speak because I wish not to stir the already too deeply agitated fountains—All I can do for you and all my prayers can do for you shall be done—I fear there is no vessel to take Judson away at present and tis [sic] evidently so ordered by God and will be for the best—I still cling to the hope that he may rally and be spared to us. You little know how much my heart clings to him our oldest friend almost, in India, and companion for seven years, of my own age, and more than all of a nature in which I could always sympathize—I could understand him and he me, and we felt our mutual sympathies—I can scarce talk to you

[Written in the top margin of page 1:] on this subject and will only assure you of my love and pray that indeed under any circumstances you may *feel* God to be with you.

Yours affectly

Phoebe Hough

Source: American Baptist Historical Society, AJ 16, no. 665.

[70] This is undated. Adoniram Judson was still alive, and they were looking for a ship to take him to sea. It is placed in early March 1850.

Emily C. Judson to Unknown Recipient,[71] March 1850

"His eyes were filled with tears when I had done reading but still he at first spoke playfully, and in a way that a little disappointed me. Then a look of almost unearthly solemnity came over him, and, clinging fast to my hand, as though to assure himself of being really in the world, he said, 'To love, this frightens me. I do not know what to make of it.' 'What?' 'Why, what you have just been reading. I never was deeply interested in any object, I never prayed sincerely and earnestly for anything, but it came; at some time—no matter at how distant a day—somehow, in some shape—probably the last I should have devised—it came. And yet I have always had so little faith! May God forgive me, and while He condescends to use me as His instrument, wipe the sin of unbelief from my heart.'"

"If ye abide in me, and my words abide in you, ye shall ask what ye will, and it shall be done unto you."

Source: Edward Judson, *The life of Adoniram Judson*, 558.

Dr. J. Taylor Jones[72] to Emily C. Judson, March 11, 1850—Bangkok, Siam

My Dear Sister,

I have been favored to receive your kind letter of Dec. 15th on the 8th inst thro the prince—A lingering fever for several days past in my own person teaches me to sympathize with your husband and yourself. Last Saturday, Mr. and Mrs. Chandler returned (earlier than they designed) from an eastern tour, he having been attacked by fever on his way. He is still feeble but the fever seems broken. Our sympathies and efforts are daily called for by constantly recurring cases of Cholera—among the families connected with us. Even yesterday, Mr. Smith's teacher was taken about 8 o'clk a.m. and died at 4 p.m. and his sister died this morning. Sometimes for weeks we do not hear of it in our immediate vicinity, and then it appears again—but the missionaries have been graciously spared. With the exception of a severe but not

[71] This is about a conversation Emily and Adoniram had when reading about missionary work in Palestine in the *Watchman and Reflector*. According to the article, one of the pieces that had been used there with success had been an article that spoke of Judson's earlier work at Ava.

[72] Dr. John Taylor Jones came out of the New England Congregational tradition. Studying for ministry at Andover Seminary, he came under conviction for baptism by immersion, and went on to finish his theological training at Newton. He was baptized in 1828 by Dr. Malcom. Though his original missionary work was in Burmah where he worked with Adoniram Judson, he found his life's work in Siam when opportunities opened with the Talings. Already fluent in their language because of his work in Burmah, the mission board made Siam his primary focus. One of his first responsibilities was to translate the New Testament into local language. "His associates in missionary labor place Dr. Jones very high on the list of those who have devoted themselves to the services of Christ in the foreign field." (William Cathcart, *The Baptist Encyclopaedia* [Philadelphia: Louis H. Everts, 1881] 616.)

protracted attack of diarrhea in June last, Mrs. Jones has enjoyed almost uninterrupted good health ever since her arrival here.

We have been led to expect soon the arrival here of Hon. J. Balestier, U.S. Envoy to Siam and ( ) China in the Frigate *Plymouth*, accompanied by Mr. Dean[73] from Hong Kong. Also the return of Dr. Bradly accompanied by Dr. Lane, Rev. Mr. Silsbee and their families—and from Scotland, Capt. Peter Brown and Lady—to join his Bro. Capt D. Brown the husband of the late Mrs. Slafter.[74] Such a number of family here will make quite an era in Siam.

We have recently—about a month since—lost our principal, and most valued Chinese assistant by death—and the Church—bereft of Dean, Erddard, Reed and Jencks, by suffering greatly for want of instruction. But we all struggle on in our labors as we can. I have been busy most of the time, since my return, in revising the N. Test. for a 2nd Edn. The revision reaches Titus and the printing Galatians.

Light spreads and so does infidelity. Hundreds, not to say thousands, of Buddhist priests ridicule Buddhism—and yet it furnishes them the most convenient and satisfactory livelihood. We are getting constantly freer access to their views—their arcane—their esoteric doctrine. The *prince* looks upon Buddhism as a mere philosophy: religion properly so called, he does not believe there is any. He was much pleased with the copy of the Mem. of Mrs. S. B. Judson.[75] He is generally upright in life—but ridiculously vain. His brother, of whom frequent mention has been made in time past, we fear, is losing himself in the gulf of intemperance.

It is thought the English will soon call the Siamese Gov't to account for infractions of their commercial Treaty—and the tumult it will occasion cannot be foreseen.

Our hope is in God. His word shall not return to him void. The seed will germinate and bring forth fruit here yet and the sowers and reapers rejoice together in the harvest.

It affords us great pleasure to hear so good account of the health of your little ones.[76] May it be long ere you will be constrained to send any variant ( ).

[73] The Reverend Doctor William Dean was a distinguished missionary to Hong Kong for more than fifty years. As the pastor of the local church in Morrisville, he baptized Emily Chubbuck when she was seventeen. There are nine letters in the correspondence from Mr. Dean, beginning after Emily's appointment to missionary service. After the death of Adoniram Judson, it was speculated, and not without reasonable support, that William Dean had an interest in taking Judson's place in Emily's life and affections. The later correspondence between Emily and Anna Maria Anable shows that Dr. Dean was often the butt of their ridicule, so something had happened to challenge that relationship. In 1854, when William Dean was courting Mrs. Maria Brown in New York City, Abby Ann Judson was working for Mrs. Brown as an in-house teacher for her children. For the complete story of William Dean's life and the many ways he touched the mission movement and the life of Emily Chubbuck Judson, see vol. 1, "Cast of Characters," s.v. "Dean, William."

[74] Mrs. Brown was the wife of an American Baptist Missionary, Corodon H. Slafter. Upon Mr. Slafter's death, she married Captain Daniel Brown, a merchant and sea captain who sailed between Liverpool and Bangkok. When Captain Brown died in September 1850, she returned to New York with her children. In fall 1853, Abby Ann Judson went to live with Mrs. Brown to help with her children, and she wrote to tell her family of Dr. William Dean calling on Mrs. Brown. Dr. Dean and Mrs. Brown were married in May 1854.

[75] Fanny Forester, *Memoir of Sarah B. Judson, Member of the American Mission to Burmah* (New York: L. Colby and Company, 1848).

[76] Henry Hall Judson, almost eight years old; Edward Judson, five years old; and Emily Frances Judson, two years old.

Mine were well when I last heard of them. My eldest was in college. Tell me what news you have from Geo,[77] Abby,[78] Adoniram,[79] Elnathan.[80] I congratulate Miss L.[81] on her excellent health. Assure her of our affectionate remembrance. Mrs. J. sympathizes in your trial, and rejoices in your joys. Though we have no children here she finds ample scope for maternal efforts—and is earnestly struggling to serve her sex among both Siamese and Chinese.

My letter will as much require apology as yours—but as you are quite *aufait* at making them—I crave the privilege of entrusting that to you.

Assure Mr. Judson of my kindest fraternal regards and say I am always glad to hear from him personally or by proxy—only regretting that I can make no more adequate return—for I am neither in good health nor overflowing spirit—*nor*, do I either sink in despondency—but trust that "better times are coming" . But then, or now, I always am, with Mrs. J's kindest regards,

Sincerely
Yours

J. Taylor Jones

Source: American Baptist Historical Society, AJ 16, no. 653.

[77] George Dana Boardman, the son of George Dana Boardman and Sarah Hall Boardman, was born August 18, 1828, in Tavoy, Burmah. George returned to the United States in 1844 at the age of six and lived with Dr. and Mrs. Calvin Newton in Worcester, Massachusetts. He attended Brown University in Providence, Rhode Island, graduating after taking a few years off for travel in the West. He attended the Newton Theological Institute, and in 1855, he married Miss Ella Covell. He served two churches before settling into the First Baptist Church of Philadelphia, where he served with distinction for thirty years. He formed a close relationship with Emily upon her return in 1851; when she gave him a copy of *An Olio of Domestic Verses*, she addressed it "Georgie—from Mamma."

[78] Abby Ann Judson, the first daughter and oldest child of Adoniram and Sarah Hall Boardman Judson, was born September 26, 1835. She saw her mother die on the Isle of St. Helena as they returned to the United States from Burmah. Just before leaving for Burmah with Emily, Adoniram Judson placed Abby Ann at Bradford Academy for her education. The family of Ann Hasseltine Judson was generous to Abby Ann and supportive of her interests and her future. On October 15, 1851, Abby Ann started a course of study at the Misses Anable's School in Philadelphia, and in fall 1853, she moved to New York City to take a teaching position in the home of Mrs. Maria Brown, a former missionary to Siam. She enjoyed a warm relationship with Emily, and her letters show that the two could speak freely with each other.

[79] Adoniram "Addy" Judson was born April 7, 1837, the second child and first son of Adoniram and Sarah Hall Boardman Judson. From November 1845 to October 1851, he lived with Dr. and Mrs. Calvin Newton in Worcester, Massachusetts. He then spent a year with Dr. and Mrs. Edward Bright in Roxbury, Massachusetts, and before entering Brown University, he was two years at Pierce Academy in Middleboro, Massachusetts. After his education and medical school, Adoniram served as a surgeon in the Civil War and became a prominent orthopedic surgeon with several books to his credit. He died in 1916. Over the years, he became vocal about the separation of missionary children from their parents.

[80] Elnathan "Elly" Judson was born July 15, 1838, the third child and second son of Adoniram and Sarah Hall Boardman Judson. From November 1845 to October 1851, he lived with Dr. and Mrs. Calvin Newton in Worcester, Massachusetts. He then spent a year with Dr. and Mrs. Edward Bright in Roxbury, Massachusetts, and before entering Brown University, he spent two years at Pierce Academy in Middleboro, Massachusetts. There are strong indications that Elnathan planned to become a minister, and in fact, he did graduate from Union Seminary. In 1860, however, he suffered a serious sunstroke that subsequently caused serious mental impairment. For much of his life, Elnathan was confined to mental institutions. He died after a second paralyzing stroke in 1896; in the last years of his life, Elnathan was lovingly cared for by his sister Abby Ann Judson.

[81] See vol. 1, "Cast of Characters," s.v. "Lillybridge, Lydia." Also, "A Timeline of the Life and Mission of Lydia Lillybridge Simons."

Emily C. Judson to her Journal, March 12, 1850

The best way to bring the heart into a frame to love a person who has treated me unkindly or is in any way disagreeable to me, is to pray for her. A *general* prayer will not do; I must pray for her success in the things that cross and mortify me most; and if I find my heart too rebellious to offer such a prayer, I have reason to tremble for my spiritual state. If, however, I persevere, I know that God will give me grace to triumph; and then—oh, how I shall love that enemy in heaven!

Source: A. C. Kendrick, *Life and Letters of Mrs. Emily C. Judson*, 328; Hanna family files.

Mr. Thomas Ranney to Emily C. Judson, March 13, 1850

My dear Mrs. J.

Many thanks for the beautiful Purse.

There is a poor old sightless beggar sits by the wayside on the way to Obo. I have passed him a thousand times, perhaps, and always reproached myself that I had not a pice [sic] to give him. Now you have taken away my only excuse for not having money—and if I do not give him an alms hereafter, my sin will be the greater—and if do give [sic], you will have conferred a double blessing by your present.

Affec Yours

Thos Ranney

Source: American Baptist Historical Society, AJ 18, no. 821.

Emily C. Judson to the American Baptist Missionary Union,[82] March 22, 1850

Mrs. Brayton[83] and Miss Wright[84] reached us by the last steamer, both in excellent health and spirits. We thought Mr. Judson's health improving till within a few days; but he is again, I fear, on the decline, and what the result will be our Heavenly Father only knows. My heart is very heavy at our prospects."

Source: Rev. Enoch Hutchinson, ed., *Baptist Memorial and Monthly Record Devoted to the History, Biography, Literature, and Statistics of the Denomination* (New York: Z. P. Hatch, 1850) 9:236.

Anna Maria Anable to Emily C. Judson, March 24, 1850

Dearest Nemmy[85]

I have just been looking over your last letter and dear me! it is two months since it came, and now as this month's steamer is in, I shall not receive one till April. So Master Charley (you are decided on making a Charley of him) is on his way at last.[86] Well, I shall wait till there is a sober certainty, before I present my congratulations. We shipped a box to you last month, which I hope will arrive soon after this letter. It contained a cashmere wrapper for the Dr.—one for yourself, some aprons etc. For the little ones, the caps you mentioned, the bonnet and a few books. We did not dare send the cheap publications[87] knowing that the ship would stop at Calcutta. I

[82] This letter was included in an article that begins, "Dr. Judson declining.—A letter from Mrs. Judson, dated March 22, says—." The article concludes, "Thousands of hearts will sympathize with Mrs. Judson in this affliction, and many prayers will be offered for the life and health of the pioneer of our Eastern missions."

[83] Mary Fuller was born August 17, 1808, in Roxbury, Connecticut. She attended Brandon Academy in Vermont, and the Female Seminary in Warren, Rhode Island. She was married to the Reverend Durlin Brayton on October 2, 1837, and on October 28, 1837, they departed for Burmah. Durlin and Mary Brayton worked in Mergui until their departure for the United States on February 23, 1847. Mary Brayton did not return to Burmah until March 1850. There are several letters from Mary Brayton to Emily; in one of them, she advocated strongly that missionary children should not be separated from their parents. Her only daughter Mary returned with her in 1850. Mary Brayton died on December 16, 1890, at Rangoon.

[84] Hannah Elizabeth Taylor Wright was born September 21, 1820, in Nelson, New Hampshire. She was appointed in 1849 to serve as a teacher at the Karen Normal School in Maulmain, Burmah. She sailed from Boston on October 18, 1849, and arrived in Maulmain on March 18, 1850. She returned to the United States on account of her health on June 29, 1852. In July 1858, she married the Reverend Lyman Stilson, missionary to Burman. Lucretia Stilson, his first wife, had died in Maulmain, Burmah, on August 14, 1851. Lyman and Hannah Wright Stilson had two sons, Charles and Edwin. Lyman Stilson died in Jefferson, Iowa on March 23, 1886; Mrs. Hannah Stilson died in Jefferson, Iowa, in March 1898. There is one letter in the correspondence from Miss Wright. Writing from Newton, Massachusetts, in July 1853, she sent Emily flowers that she "thought had bloomed to shed their fragrance in a sickroom."

[85] "Nem" or "Nemmy" was a name of endearment given to Emily by a small group of her intimate friends at the Utica Female Academy. Anna Maria Anable was "Ninny."

[86] See the letter of Emily C. Judson to Anna Maria Anable dated October 21, 1849. In a previous letter, Anna Maria had spoken of rumors that Emily was to have another daughter. Emily chided Anna Maria's clairvoyance and then suggested that the speculations were wrong in that the child was to be a boy named Charley.

[87] Emily asked for some of the magazines popular in the United States, telling Anna Maria that she and Adoniram liked to read them when they wanted to relax their minds from the seriousness that always seemed to be there.

shall think of it when the Missionaries go. Mr. Bright[88] spent last Sabbath with us and we had a delightful visit from him. He says the Board will probably charter a ship as they did in '46, and send it directly to Maulmain. What do you think Mr. B. was doing here? Trying to persuade Mr. Kincaid[89] that it was best for Mr. Dawson[90] to remain here till he got somewhat established at Ava. Mr. D. is one of your soft smooth canting sort of fellows, who has crept into the affections and sympathies of the people here, until now if the Board does not send him out, I presume he will be sent by the churches here—at least that is what they threaten but of course the Board will manage it. Mr. D. is thought to be very pious and I suppose he is, but you can see more readily than I the difficulty the Board will have in sending him as physician, if he cannot get to Ava.

Mr. B. is a staunch friend and admirer of both you and the Dr. He likes Mr. Kincaid too and so do I. He says Mr. Wade[91] will probably stay in Maulmain. He told Mr. K. slyly at our tea table, that he did not think the Maulmain corps were strong enough, as to *numbers*. Mr. K. looked down at his plate, as though conscious of being played on, and simply said—they were too strong already.

We have rare opportunities to see the under and upper currents of the stream of Missionary life. No, no, Nemmy I shan't set my cap for Mr. Osgood[92] nor any

[88] Upon her return to America in 1851, Emily Judson was to have a very close relationship with Dr. Edward Bright, the corresponding secretary of the American Baptist Missionary Union. They had known one another previously in New York, as he worked at the time of Adoniram and Emily's marriage with the *Baptist Register*, a prominent regional newsletter. Prior to working as a publisher, he had been, in 1838, the founding pastor of the Bleecker Street Baptist Church in Utica, a church with close ties to the Utica Female Academy. He was appointed corresponding secretary of the Missionary Union the end of May 1846, just prior to Adoniram and Emily's leaving Boston for Burmah. In this role he regularly pleaded with Emily for articles to be published in the missionary magazine, the *Macedonian*. Upon Emily's return from Burmah in October 1851, Adoniram and Elnathan went to live with Dr. and Mrs. Bright for a year. Dr. Bright was to help Emily with many of her business affairs; he carried on the publishing details of the Judson Memoir because of a serious illness in Dr. Wayland's family. He, with Dr. Edward Granger, was to be the executor of the estate of Emily Chubbuck Judson, a responsibility he still carried in March 1869, as reflected in a letter to Anna Maria Anable regarding financial arrangements for Emily Frances Judson.

[89] See vol. 1, "Cast of Characters," s.v. "Kincaid, The Reverend Doctor Eugenio."

[90] See vol. 1, "Cast of Characters," s.v. "Dawson, Doctor."

[91] Jonathan Wade was appointed as a missionary to Burmah in 1823. Wade's relationship with Adoniram Judson was especially dear because of the early experiences they shared, including the death of Ann Judson. Much of their work was spent in the Karen jungle communities following the path of George Boardman. They had returned home to America on December 22, 1847, and returned to Burmah in January 1851, just as Emily was returning to the United States. They were from the Hamilton, New York, area. They left to return to Burmah on July 25, 1850, and were in Maulmain by February 1851. Both died in Burmah. Deborah died at Maulmain in 1868, and Jonathan died in Rangoon in 1872.

[92] Rev. Sewall Osgood was a missionary in Maulmain who worked with and lived by Adoniram Judson. Judson and Osgood occupied two of the four homes in the mission compound and lived so close that it "allowed me the pleasure and profit of almost hourly intercourse." He arrived in Burmah in 1834. His first wife Elhira Brown Osgood died on October 5, 1837, in Maulmain. On July 8, 1838, he married Sarah Thomas, the widow of the Reverend Jacob Thomas, with Adoniram Judson officiating at the wedding. He spoke in the letters to Emily, of which there are five between July 1850 and April 1852, of Adoniram Judson as his "most intimate friend." He never personally met Emily, as he had returned from the field prior to 1846. At the time of his letters, he was working with the American Baptist Missionary Union as a district secretary. In 1845, just as they were leaving for the United States, Sarah and Adoniram Judson gave care of Charley, too young to make the trip, to Mr. and Mrs. Osgood. Charley died not long after their departure. Mr. Osgood visted Adoniram, Elnathan, and Abby Ann in the United States. His third wife was Caroline Wait; they were married December 30, 1850, at Saratoga, New York. With all of his suggestions of "intimacy" and "his most intimate friend," Mr. Osgood stated that his life was so busy that he simply did not have the time to look through his papers for anything that would be helpful in writing the Judson memoir.

other man who will take me to India—somehow I find myself completely cured of the India fever[93]—Hatty[94] told me to say that last—I don't know how true it is. Since I wrote you last we have had quite a scare about Mr. Gillette's[95] going away. He received a call to the Berean Church in N.Y. which Dr. Dowling[96] had left and he was some three weeks in making up his mind not to accept it. We were very glad that he at last decided, for he has at length got the same influence over us that he has over the rest of the church. We feel that nobody would do quite as well as Mr. G. Sister Grace[97] is growing pretty every day and Mrs. G.[98] is as lovely and handsome as ( ). We are extending our acquaintances among the members of the church, and out of it, we have as much as we can do to attend to the society we already have.

Last evening we were out (to) a very pleasant party at Mrs. Jos. Patterson's, there we met learning, beauty and wealth. Dr. Darrah[99] a professor in one of the medical colleges, [one] of the most talented, most truly pious and altogether most fascinating of men requested his daughter, a pupil of ours, to introduce him to me. Don't you think Miss Ninny[100] feels awkward when she has to maintain the dignity and manifest the erudition learning in a school ma'am. Well, she does sometimes

[93] For about a year and a half after Emily's marriage to Adoniram Judson, Anna Maria spoke of the possibility of having a call to missions and joining Adoniram and Emily in Burmah. On March 31, 1847, Sarah Bell Wheeler said that Anna Maria was a devoted Christian, and she thought that one day she would go to Burmah. She obviously put a lot of prayer and thought into the matter. The painful medical treatments she underwent in summer 1847 were likely intended to improve her general health (see her letter of June 19, 1847). In summer 1848, she decided that her call was to remain a teacher, and Anna Maria moved to Philadelphia and opened the Misses Anable's School with her family where she raised Emily Francis Judson. Anna Maria remained there until her death.

[94] Harriet or "Hatty" or "Hattie" or "Hat" Anable was one of nine children born to Joseph and Alma Anable, and was a niece to Miss Cynthia Sheldon and Mrs. Urania Sheldon Nott. In 1841, she had added a note to a letter written by Miss Cynthia Sheldon to Emily. As early as November 1842 she was away, and a letter from Emily to Catharine Chubbuck said that "she (Miss Sheldon) expected that Hat would return as accomplished as Anna Maria." Her trips away were both educational and employment, as she worked as a private tutor in families that would bring her into their homes. In August 1843, she had just returned from Beonsen, in the vicinity of New Orleans, and was engaged to go again. A letter from Anna Maria on January 6, 1845, said that she would stay South for another year. About this time Miss Cynthia Sheldon mentioned her concern for Hatty's spiritual health. In May 1845 she was in New Orleans. She was home again in summer 1846, but a September 27 letter from Anna Maria said she had been asked by Mr. Roman with some urgency to return and she thought that she should. She was to return home from New Orleans in January 1849 after Anna Maria Anable had started the Misses Anable's School in Philadelphia in fall 1848. Harriet was fluent in French, having placed herself earlier in a French environment in New Orleans. Hatty died in 1858.

[95] See vol. 1, "Cast of Characters," s.v. "Gillette, The Reverend Abram Dunn."

[96] Dr. John Dowling was born in England in 1807; before coming to the United States in 1832, he established a classical boarding school in Oxfordshire. In the United States, Dr. Dowling had churches in New York before going to the Sansom Street Church in Philadelphia in 1852. While there, Dr. Dowling was active as a leader with the American Baptist Publication Society, and he wrote in great despair in June 1853 that Emily had awarded the publishing contract for Dr. Wayland's memoir of Adoniram Judson to another firm. He said that they had not been given time to prepare a proposal and gave the benefit of keeping the publication within the Baptist family. He returned to New York in 1856 and served churches in New York and New Jersey. He was the author of several books and numerous pamphlets and tracts.

[97] Grace Gillette was born recently to the Reverend and Mrs. Gillette. Mrs. Gillette wrote that she thought of naming the baby Grace Linden Gillette after the "Grace Linden" character in one of Fanny Forester's stories by that same name.

[98] See vol. 1, "Cast of Characters," s.v. "Gillette, The Reverend A. (Abram) D. (Dunn) and Hannah."

[99] Dr. Darrah was a physician in Philadelphia often consulted by the Anable-Sheldon families. He was mentioned frequently in fall 1853 as Harriet was treated for her medical problems, which led to her taking a sea voyage to the West Indies.

[100] "Ninny" was a name of endearment given to Anna Maria Anable by her most intimate friends at the Utica Female Academy. Emily was "Nemmy."

and then again she forgets all about it. When she'll ever get educated she don't [sic] know but this present year closes her metaphysical course with Butler's Analogy.

I shall feel so relieved when I can teach something without so much study before hand.

[Written along the right margin of the address page:] About a fortnight ago, we had a grand Soiree musical, and there were about two hundred persons crowded into our parlors, and all decided that it was the party of the season! Think of that! Those affairs are new for Phil. To give a kind of intellectual character to the affair we keep up the old custom of having compo's, one or two of which I'll send you. I believe I made the same promise last year but forgot it.

[Written along the left margin of the address page:] You ask after mother.[101] If I have not mentioned her, it must be because I am so perfectly free from anxiety on her account. After her long life of toil she has now an old age of rest and comfort—and health such as falls to the lot of few mortals. She reads more than any body [sic] in the house, and sews alternately for each of her daughters. This last occupation she shares with Aunt C.[102]

[Written along the bottom margin of the address page:] After I had done this the girl came up with your note of Dec. 23. The dear Dr. how sorry I am he has been ill. Hope he is quite well by this time. Shall write to Lydia[103] to night [sic] or to morrow [sic]—dear girl.

[Written along the left and top margins of page 1:] A letter from Mary Spencer[104] tells that Eugenia[105] is going to live in the home Horace Hawley[106] occupied on Chancellor Square. Harriet Spencer died in July.

[101] See vol. 1, "Cast of Characters," s.v. "Sheldon, Alma and Joseph Hubbell."

[102] See vol. 1, "Cast of Characters," s.v. "Sheldon, Miss Cynthia."

[103] See vol. 1, "Cast of Characters," s.v. "Lillybridge, Lydia." Also, "A Timeline of the Life and Mission of Lydia Lillybridge Simons."

[104] On February 28, 1848, Anna Maria Anable wrote to Emily saying, "Mary Spencer has just returned from Albany. It is said she is engaged to John James, a handsome young widower with three children, and two or three hundred thousand $'s."

[105] See vol. 1, "Cast of Characters," s.v. "Damaux, Eugenia."

[106] Mr. Horace H. Hawley enjoyed a family relationship with the Sheldons. A letter Emily wrote on May 7, 1841, reveals that he was to marry a niece of Misses Cynthia and Urania Sheldon and Mrs. Alma Sheldon Anable, the daughter of their brother John Sheldon. Through the help of Miss Cynthia Sheldon, he was introduced into the life of Emily Chubbuck. A member of a publishing firm, he also worked with Alexander Beebee in publishing the *Baptist Register*. Beginning in 1841 with the publication of *Charles Linn*, Mr. Hawley was enormously helpful to Emily Chubbuck as she was publishing her early stories and books. There are numerous references to his help and his generosity.

Mr. Colby[107] called to see us the other day. If Hatty and I can afford it we shall make them a short visit next summer. I have heard nothing of the Haswells,[108] tho' I believe they are somewhere in New Jersey.

Give love to the dear Dr.—a kiss to the babies[109]—a warm embrace to Lydia—and a loving heart to yourself

From

Anna M.

Source: American Baptist Historical Society, AJ 13, no. 475.

Mrs. Elizabeth L. Stevens to Emily C. Judson, March 25, 1850[110]

My Very dear Sister

Last night as I lay awake thinking of your watching and anxiety I determined to write this morning and ask if you would not like Edward[111] there tonight and you try as possible to sleep—to make up your mind to care a little for yourself cannot you? It will not do for you to be up night after night—and you know we are all ready to help you.

Would it be of any use for me to go over to your house and attend to the tailor's work? You certainly do not feel like cutting and fitting—and I might pack.[112]

[107] A prominent businessman, Gardner Colby and his family lived in Pemberton Square in Boston before moving "to the country," Newton Centre, Massachusetts. Mr. Colby was a member of the Board of the American Baptist Missionary Union and an avid supporter of the missionary movement. In a letter after they sailed from Boston to Burmah, Emily mentions the extravagant hospitality extended to them in early July as they waited for the *Faneuil Hall* to embark. Adoniram and Emily stayed with the Colby family frequently.

[108] James Madison Haswell was born February 4, 1810, in Bennington, Vermont. He was married to Jane Matilda Mason of Cheshire, Massachusetts. The Haswells sailed for Burmah on September 23, 1835, to work with the Talaings. They arrived at Amherst in February 1836. The Haswells became partners with Adoniram and Sarah Hall Boardman Judson; Sarah turned over the translation of the Peguan scripture to Mr. Haswell after Elnathan and Adoniram were born, and her energies were focused elsewhere. When Sarah and Adoniram sailed for America in 1845, the Haswells took care of Henry until Adoniram returned in 1847 with Emily. The Haswells left Burmah in December 1848 and arrived in America in 1849; they remained in the United States until September 1852, when they again sailed for Burmah.

[109] Henry Hall Judson, who was almost eight years old; Edward Judson, who was almost five and a half years old; and Emily Frances Judson, who was just over two years old.

[110] This is undated; the events are obviously those of Adoniram's illness shortly before his voyage and death. Mrs. Brayton is also mentioned in the letter, and she returned to Burmah on March 18, 1850. The letter is placed a week later and about a week before Adoniram left on his journey at sea.

[111] Edward Stevens arrived in Maulmain in February 1838; his wife was Elizabeth Stevens. Mr. Stevens was responsible for the native churches that were associated with the mission. He took on the work of finishing the dictionary after the death of Adoniram Judson, and he buried "Angel Charley" in the chapel compound after his birth in April 1850. Mr. Stevens was in Burmah for forty-eight years.

[112] Adoniram, seriously ill, was planning to take a trip to sea, hoping that the extended voyage would bring an improvement in his health.

I should think you could trust me to select things out of your chests. I would not tumble up things. If either of us could relieve you and have the privilege of doing something for Dr. J. it would reconcile us more to Edward's not being with him.

Mrs. Brayton[113] was so much disappointed not to see his face yesterday. She wants me to ask if you think we could today if we call early on our way to prayer meeting. I presume you will not wish to have it at your house as you proposed last week. Shall I write so to Mrs. Mason?[114]

Do write me about your own night as well as dear dear Mr. J's. With the most heartfelt sympathy and affection yours

E. L. S.

Would not you bring the boys[115] to come here every day?

Source: American Baptist Historical Society, AJ 19, no. 910.

Dr. J. T. Jones to Emily C. Judson, March 25, 1850—Bangkok, Siam

My Dear Sister,

I wrote you a few days ago[116] in much haste and weakness as but partially recovered from a remittent fever—3 days ago we had notice of the arrival of the British Steamer *Nemesis* on the Bar—with dispatches for the Siamese Gov't—This threw all the officers into great commotion and with hurrying to and fro with boats, flags, ammunition, fort repairs—blocking up rivers etc.—This morg [sic] news has reached us of the arrival of the Am. Frigate—no particulars—Dr. Bradley and his associates at Singapore—Further yesterday morg [sic] my dear wife was seized with a violent attack of Cholera—but thro mercy and the physician the disease is checked and she is convalescent. This morg [sic] Miss. Alorse was seized in a similar way—and is still very ill though, we *hope*, past danger. I am better, but not well. We have every reason to expect exciting times. What will be the result is known only to the All Wise. We trust in Him. Pray for us.

A blessing on you all—

Yours Truly

J. T. Jones

Source: American Baptist Historical Society, AJ 16, no. 654.

[113] See vol. 1, "Cast of Characters," s.v. "Brayton, The Reverend Durlin and Mary."

[114] Ellen Huntley Bullard Mason, the wife of Francis Mason. After the death of his first wife in 1846, Francis Mason and Ellen Bullard were married in September 1847, with Adoniram Judson officiating at the wedding.

[115] Henry Hall Judson, almost eight years old, and Edward Judson, five years and three months old.

[116] See the letter of Dr. J. T. Jones to Emily C. Judson dated March 11, 1850.

Mrs. Johanna C. Bower to Emily C. Judson, Late March 1850

My dear Mrs. Judson

I have the pleasure to send you 1 dozen ( ) for Dr. Judson which if not sufficient for the voyage foray[117] let me know and I will send some more. Should there be anything else you require pray do not hesitate to mentioning it. We ( ) a sea trip will prove beneficial to Dr. Judson's health and that he will be enabled soon to return to you. With our united kind regards,

Bless me
if you will by

Johanna C. Bower

Source: American Baptist Historical Society, AJ 12, no. 314.

Mr. Thomas Ranney to Emily C. Judson,[118] April 7, 1850

My dear Mrs. Judson

Your messenger has just arrived. Before this you have read my chit to Mrs. R. since which Dr. J. has remained about as he was this morning. As you anticipated, he is revived to-day, and I have sat with him for a long time and talked quite freely until I told him we had not better talk any longer. He is asleep now, and—but he has just awoke and calls me. I have read your note to me to him, told him that I had previously informed you of the night etc. etc. and what I now propose doing, which is this. He drank of the coconut milk this forenoon, and likes it well, and now we must have more. They are not to be attained at Amherst. I am supposing this boat will get up to Maulmain in the night-time having stopped to consult the pilot. I find he will be out at sea before 12 tomorrow, and that a boat cannot go to Maulmain and back in season—So I have sent Ko-Shway-Doke with the boat you sent, with letters to Gibson and Legorie, to Amherst, with directions to get as *many* as could be obtained at any price, and as I could not send the money, to look to Mr. Stevens[119] for the pay. The Pilot thinks a few can be had of some of the Burmese, and if so I feel sure Ko-Shway-Doke will not fail in obtaining them. The Captain has just arrived, and I will send this by his return boat. *He* does not return again to M. I should add that Dr. J. remarked in his conversation this morning that he still

[117] Plans were being made to send Adoniram Judson on an extended sea voyage, hoping that it would bring improvement to his health.

[118] This letter from Thomas Ranney was written aboard the *Aristide Marie.* Adoniram Judson had been carried aboard on April 3, 1850, for an extended sea journey, hoping it would bring improvement to his rapidly declining health. Because of her advanced pregnancy, Emily was not able to go with him; however, for the next three days, as the ship passed downriver, Emily was able to be with him each day, returning to her home each evening. This is the first day that she had not been able to reach the ship.

[119] See vol. 1, "Cast of Characters," s.v. "Stevens, The Reverend Edward and Elizabeth."

felt too much life within to make it probable to him that he would die, but he felt that he would have to suffer intensely before the cause of his frequent constipation could be removed, and that such being the will of God, he could not complain.

I shall be able to write you again to-morrow when the Pilot leaves us.

Affec. Yours

T. Ranney

Source: American Baptist Historical Society, AJ 18, no. 815.

Emily C. Judson to Adoniram and Elnathan Judson, April 11, 1850

My Very Dear Children,[120]

I have painful news to tell you—news that I am sure will make your hearts ache; but I hope our heavenly Father will help you to bear it. Your dear papa is very, *very* ill indeed, so much so that the best judges fear he will never be any better. He began to fail about five months ago, and has declined so gradually that we were not fully aware of his danger until lately; but within a few weeks those who love him have become very much alarmed. In January we went down to Mergui, by the steamer, and when we returned, thought he was a little better; but he soon failed again. We next spent a month at Amherst, but he received little, if any, benefit. Next, the doctors pronounced our house—the one you used to live in—unhealthy, and we removed to another. But all was of no use. Your dear papa continued to fail, till suddenly, one evening, his muscular strength gave way, and he was prostrated on the bed unable to help himself. This occurred about two weeks ago. The doctor now became alarmed, and said the only hope for him was in a long voyage. It was very hard to think of such a thing in his reduced state, particularly as I could not go with him; but after we had wept and prayed over it one day and night, we concluded that it was our duty to use the only means which God had left us, however painful. We immediately engaged his passage aboard a French bark bound for the Mauritius; but before it sailed he had become so very low that no one thought it right for him to go alone. They therefore called a meeting of the mission, and appointed Mr.

[120] Though addressed to "Dear Children," apparently this letter was only to Adoniram and Elnathan in Worcester, Massachusetts. Later in the letter, in two laces she addresses them as "my dear boys." We must assume that a separate letter went to Abby Ann Judson in Bradford, New Hampshire.

Ranney,[121] the superintendent of the press, to accompany him. It was a great relief to me, for he is a very kind man, and loves your dear papa very much; and he will do every thing [sic] that can be done for his comfort. The officers of the vessel, too, seemed greatly interested for him, as did every one [sic] else. He was carried on board a week ago yesterday, in a litter, and placed on a nice easy cot, made purposely for him. I staid [sic] on board with him all day, and at dark came home to stay with the children. The next day I found that the vessel had only dropped down a little distance, and so I took a boat and followed. I expected this would certainly be the last day with him; but it was not. Friday I went again; and though he did not appear as well as on the previous days, I was forced to take, as I then supposed, a final leave of him. But when morning came, I felt as though I could not live through the day without knowing how he was. So I took a boat again, and reached the vessel about two o'clock, P. M. He could not speak, except in whispers, but seemed very glad that I came. The natives that I had sent to fan him, till he should get out of the river, came to me, and begged to have him taken ashore again; and so small was my hope of his recovery, that my heart pleaded on their side, though I still thought it duty to do as the doctor had ordered. I came away at dark, and though his lips moved to say some word of farewell, they made no sound. I hope that you, my dear boys, will never have cause to know what a heavy heart I bore back to my desolate home that night. The vessel got out to sea about four o'clock on Monday, and last night the natives returned, bringing a letter from Mr. Ranney.[122] Your precious papa had revived again, spoke aloud, took a little tea and toast, said there was something animating in the touch of the sea breeze, and directed Mr. Ranney to write to me that he had a strong belief it was the will of God to restore him again to health. I feel somewhat encouraged, but dare not hope too much.

And now, my dear boys, it will be three, perhaps four long months before we can hear from our loved one again; and we shall all be very anxious. All that we can do is to commit him to the care of our heavenly Father, and if we never see him again in this world, pray that we may be prepared to meet him in heaven.

Your dear little brothers[123] and sister[124] enjoy excellent health. They are so young that they do not understand much about their papa, though they sometimes cry when

[121] Thomas Ranney was appointed to missionary service in June 1843, arriving in Burmah in May 1844. He was an important part of the Judsons' lives while in Rangoon. He was superintendent of the printing press in Maulmain and business manager for the compound. Thomas Ranney went with Adoniram Judson on his last voyage, and thus was with him when he died. There is a letter in the collection from the *Aristide Marie* written five days before Adoniram Judson's death; one of the things he did at the time of death was to take some locks of his hair to bring to Emily. She later sent one of these locks to Adoniram's sister Abigail in Plymouth. Thomas Ranney provided the accounts of Adoniram's last voyage and his last hours of life. He also handled some of the financial matters for the mission and in the settlement of Adoniram Judson's estate. Thomas Ranney was married to Maria Gager, who died in 1857, and then to Mary E. Bennett, the daughter of missionaries Cephas and Stella Bennett.

[122] See the letter of Mr. Thomas Ranney to Emily C. Judson dated April 7, 1850.

[123] Henry Hall Judson, almost eight years old, and Edward Judson, almost five and a half.

[124] Emily Frances Judson, a little over two years old.

I talk to them about him. I shall write to you just as quick as I hear from your papa, and wish you to write to me, for I love you very much for his sake, though I saw so little of you at Worcester. Give love to Dr. and Mrs. Newton,[125] and believe me

Your most affectionate mamma,

Emily C. Judson

Source: Francis Wayland, *Memoir of the Life and Labors of the Rev. Adoniram Judson, D.D.*, 2:334–36.

Emily C. Judson to Anna Maria Anable,[126] April 15, 1850[127]—Maulmain

My Dear Ninny,[128]

I sit down to write you with a very heavy heart—indeed, heavier than I ever carried in my life before. I do not know whether my precious husband is still living, or whether he may not have already gone **up** to heaven; and I shall have no means of knowing for three or four months to come. After I wrote you last month he continued to decline, but so very slowly that I was not much alarmed, till one evening, all of a sudden, his back gave way as he attempted to go to his cot, and he would have fallen if I had not caught and supported him. From that night he never stood on his feet. About ten days after, he was carried on board a French **barque** bark, bound for Bourbon, and laid on a comfortable cot prepared expressly for him; but poor I was not allowed to go with him. Every body [sic] said it would be madness, and *he* too said I must not go; he would rather stay here and die, than have both our lives endangered. But may you never know the terrible effort which the resolution to separate, under such circumstances, cost both of us. The doctor said that he could not possibly live, if he remained here, but that if he went to sea there was

[125] Dr. Calvin Newton, after some theological training, went to medical school to become a physician. He apparently had differing ideas about medicine, and he became a part of what was known as the Eclectic School of Medicine; with that background, he established the Worcester Medical Institute. In 1835, Dr. and Mrs. Newton received into their home the young George Dana Boardman, just returned from Burmah for his education. Adoniram and Elnathan went there in fall 1845 when they returned to the United States with their father, and they remained there under the Newton's care until Emily's return in October 1851. At that time, Mrs. Newton had become ill, and the boys went to live with Dr. and Mrs. Edward Bright.

[126] This letter has an addendum dated April 18, 1850.

[127] There are two versions of this letter: the original as written by Emily E. Chubbuck and the edited version published by Dr. A. C. Kendrick in his biography, *The Life and Letters of Mrs. Emily C. Judson*. Additions made by Dr. Kendrick are in parentheses, and words in the original left out by Dr. Kendrick have been added in bold. There are significant changes and omissions. In a note in his book, Dr. Kendrick explained that interest, purpose and propriety sometimes led to these changes and exclusions, "I remark here that in giving Miss Chubbuck's letters, I do not always indicate unimportant omissions. Real letters must always contain much which should not meet the public eye; and Emily's were real letters, dashed off hastily amidst pressing cares and duties. Written also after the exhausting labors of the day, they by no means do uniform justice to her epistolary powers." He later added, "In giving a few extracts from his and Miss Chubbuck's correspondence at this time, I have no wish to minister to a prurient curiosity, not to violate that principle which would generally place letters written during the period of an 'engagement' under the shelter of inviolate secrecy."

[128] "Ninny" was a name of endearment given to Anna Maria Anable by her most intimate friends at the Utica Female Academy. Emily was "Nemmy."

a chance—a very small chance, indeed, he acknowledged. So the question became one of duty;—if it had been one of *choice*, all the world **could** (would) not have induced him to go. I had watched over him night and day for five months, and it did seem at first as though we could not breathe apart. "If it *should* be the will of God to let me die here, what a mercy!" he repeated over and over many times a day, as his strength very perceptibly failed. But it was not, and the day before he went on board he revived considerably. The vessel was a long time in going out of the river, and so every morning I took a boat and followed after it, and at evening came back to look after my little ones. In this way I was on board the greater part of four days,[129] and had the privilege of arranging everything for his comfort in the way that I knew he liked. The officers were very kind, and treated me with that delicate, winning politeness **that** (which) the French so well understand, assuring me that everything should he done **for him** in their power—they were entirely at his command. Mr. Ranney,[130] the mission printer, was appointed to go with him, and he took a most faithful Bengallee servant that has been with us for two years. So as far as attendance is concerned, he is quite as well off as if I were with him. The last day I was on board he was much worse—so weak that he could not speak above a whisper, and even that but little. When I parted with him he moved his lips to speak, but made no sound; he did not even open his eyes, though he returned my kiss. When the pilot left, however, he **had again revived**—(he) seemed animated with the prospect of getting out to sea, which he always loved, and told Mr. Ranney to write me that he "felt too much life in him to believe he should die at present, and he had strong hopes of returning to us in as good health as formerly."[131] Mr. Ranney, too, was encouraged, though less sanguine.

Source: A. C. Kendrick, *The Life and Letters of Mrs. Emily C. Judson*, 334–36.

Mrs. Ellen Mason to Emily C. Judson, April 15, 1850[132]

My dear afflicted Sister

I should run in to see you much oftener did I not suppose I would be a great favor to stay away. I do not know that I can do any thing [sic] to aid you, or to sooth your anguish in this trial-hour but to pray for you. This I try to do constantly, and have felt great comfort in prayer. It has seemed to me that God would hear us in

[129] April 3, 4, 5 and 6.

[130] See vol. 1, "Cast of Characters," s.v. "Ranney, Thomas and Maria."

[131] See the letter from Thomas Ranney to Emily C. Judson dated April 7, 1850.

[132] This letter is undated. It is placed on April 15, 1850. Adoniram Judson was absent, so it must be dated after April 3, but there is no mention of the stillborn birth of Charles Judson, so it would be before April 23, 1850.

behalf of your companion, and would yet restore him to you again. But if he should see it best to do otherwise. I feel assured that his *presence* will be with *you both*.

O, he is an all sufficient Comforter, as you have both long known from experience.

If you will feel like letting little Frances[133] go from you a day or two it would afford me real pleasure to take care of her the best in my power. I see your [sic] and the dear children[134] are out or I would beg the privilege of having them with us.

Very affect. Yr.

Ellen Mason

Source: American Baptist Historical Society, AJ 17, no. 736.

Mrs. Stella K. Bennett to Emily C. Judson, April 17, 1850[135]

My dear Sister Judson

I have but a few hurried moments in which to write, and but little to say if I had the time. Under circumstances like yours all words except right ones are vain, and I feel utterly incompetent to say much that would comfort you. I can, and do commend you to the compassion of Him who knows all our sorrows and who will alleviate, or give grace to bear as he sees best.

The state of suspense in which you are placed is one of the ( )nest sufferings, but it is right to hope for the best until we know the worst. Not only for your sake, but for the sake of the cause of Missions and for the Burman Mission in particular I hope the threatened calamity may be averted.

Mr. Bennett[136] has been from home most of the time for four months past and when he told me he was gong away again for another three or four months I felt as though I could not consent to it, but thinking of you makes me ashamed of my rebellion and I am quiet. Had the necessity for his going occurred in the dry season when we have no schools I think I should have accompanied him, but as it is now my duty is plain. Hoping you may soon have intelligence from your dear husband and

[133] See vol. 1, "Cast of Characters," s.v. "Judson, Emily Frances."

[134] This is a reference to Henry Hall Judson, almost eight years old, and Edward Judson, almost five and a half years old.

[135] This letter is undated; the content clearly places it in the middle of April 1850, and thus it is placed on April 17.

[136] Cephas Bennett had arrived in Burmah in January 1830; his wife was Stella Bennett. Mr. Bennett remained the superintendent of the Baptist Press there for more than fifty years. He worked with Adoniram Judson on the printing of the Bible into Burmese, but also into the Karen language. From the Utica area, they sent their children back, and the girls were educated at the Utica Female Academy. The girls included Elsina (April 1828), Mary (November 1829), Ann (August 1833), Ellen (June 1835), and Sarah (June 1837).

that every thing [sic] may be ordered in great mercy for you. With love to yourself and the dear children.[137] Believe me
yours very affy

S. K. Bennett

Source: American Baptist Historical Society, AJ 12, no. 358.

Emily C. Judson to Anna Maria Anable,[138] April 18, 1850[139]

The mail has come in since I commenced this, and my cheerful American letters grated very harshly at first, but on a second reading they make me feel encouraged. I do almost believe that God will yet take pity on us, and let us **see** (have) a few more years of happiness in this world. Oh, you do not know how desolate the house seems, and how I hear his voice calling me by day and by night. The worst of it is the uncertainty of getting intelligence. They arrive in six weeks, and in six weeks more I *might* get a letter, if a vessel should be coming this way—but I may not hear in four, five, or even six months **tho**. Can you imagine a more torturing state of anxiety? Ah, me! are we not brought into terrible straits sometimes?

I shall not write you again probably before my confinement, which is now close at hand.[140] Don't you think I shall miss the tender care, that I had before? Don't feel concerned about me, however. The whole mission take [sic] **care of me, and they are truly like brothers and sisters. It makes people kind to live so far from the world as we do. Please give love to all—remember me to the Gillettes[141] and Robartses[142] and say I wait to write to them, but cannot now. Say to A. Longstreth[143] that I have rec'd her kind letter and if I live will answer it.**

Oh, Ninny,[144] you don't know how I want you to be here—how I want to get into your bosom and cry a week. After being loved and petted as I have been, it is

[137] Henry Hall Judson, almost eight years old; Edward Judson, almost five and a half years old; and Emily Frances Judson, almost two and a half years old.

[138] This is an addendum to a letter written April 15, 1850.

[139] There are two versions of this letter: the original as written by Emily E. Chubbuck and the edited version published by Dr. A. C. Kendrick in his biography, *The Life and Letters of Mrs. Emily C. Judson*. Additions made by Dr. Kendrick are in parentheses, and words in the original left out by Dr. Kendrick have been added in bold. There are significant changes and omissions.

[140] Emily was expecting her second child; that was the reason why she could not go on the sea voyage with Adoniram Judson. She gave birth on April 23 to a stillborn child, whom she named Charles Judson, the "Charles" named for her father.

[141] See vol. 1, "Cast of Characters," s.v. "Gillette, The Reverend Abram Dunn."

[142] See vol. 1, "Cast of Characters," s.v. "Robarts, Mr. and Mrs. W. S."

[143] Mary Anna Longstreth was a Quaker who lived in Philadelphia and who took an extraordinary interest in Adoniram and Emily Judson. She lived with her extended family, and they are frequently mentioned in her letters. Apparently, she ran a private school much like the one Anna Maria Anable started. Her letter of May 1848 paints a strong picture of her character, her faith, and her sensitivity. In this letter, she remarks on the particular strengths of each of the wives of Adoniram Judson.

[144] "Ninny" was a name of endearment given to Anna Maria Anable by her most intimate friends at the Utica Female Academy. Emily was "Nemmy."

so, *so* desolate to be alone! God is disciplining me, however; and I suppose I need something very severe. Sometimes I think it would have been *such* a mercy if I had died during my late illness; but then, who would have taken care of *him* during these tedious five months? No, it was a sweet privilege to be beside him all the time, and he has blest [sic] me over and over again for my care. **Ninny, I am very well and apprehend no danger when I am confined, but if I *should* die, you will take care of Frances[145] and the little stranger[146] won't you? Frances is a bright child and very affectionate, but of a firey temper and very willful. She needs a firm hand—** Good bye, darling; I shall write again as soon as I am able.

Affectionately,

Emily (Nemmy) C. Judson.

Source: A. C. Kendrick, *The Life and Letters of Mrs. Emily C. Judson*, 334–36.

Emily C. Judson to Adoniram Judson, April 19, 1850[147]—Maulmain

My own beloved husband,

It is more than two weeks[148] since you were carried from the house, and how long the time has seemed to me, your own heart will tell you, if you have not been too ill to think of anything but your sufferings. How I wish I could be with you tonight, and kiss your lips, and hands, and feet—do anything for you. I wonder if you wouldn't like a little variety—to have me, instead of Panapah,[149] give you your drink. Oh, darling I didn't half know how sweet the privilege of taking care of you was until deprived of it.

Dr. Morton[150] has been here today, and he always has such an encouraging way with him that I feel better about you after having seen him. I do believe that God will have mercy on us and bring you back again in tolerable health. I wish we had talked over one subject before you left. Dr. Morton says that you must make a long stay at the Isle of France (for he hopes you will cross over there) otherwise your health cannot be firmly established—you will be liable to fall into a similar decline

[145] Emily Frances Judson, born December 24, 1847, was the daughter of Adoniram and Emily Chubbuck Judson.

[146] The expected child of Adoniram and Emily Judson. Charles ("Angel Charley") Judson was stillborn on April 23, 1850.

[147] From the editor: This letter and the letter of May 20, 1850, discovered in the archives of the First Baptist Church of Malden, Massachusetts, where I served for six years as senior minister, touched my heart with a compelling interest in Emily Judson. There was something about the writing, the pathos of her experience, the pain of her suffering, and the articulation of her hope. I remember that day now more than thirty years ago and mark it as the beginning of a journey that has culminated in this project of *The Life and Letters of Emily C. Judson (Fanny Forester)*.

[148] Adoniram Judson had been carried aboard the *Aristide Marie* on April 3. Because of the time it took the ship to reach the open sea, Emily was able to see him on April 3, 4, 5, and 6.

[149] Panapah was one of the Judson's trusted Burmese servants.

[150] See vol. 1, "Cast of Characters," s.v. "Morton, Doctor."

again. So he advises me, as soon as I hear of your safe arrival, and get well enough myself, to take the children and follow after you. The plan strikes me pleasantly, but I should not like to do such a thing without your sanction, so I must think about it and pray over it and try to judge with your judgment. God has been very merciful to me since you went away—I have enjoyed the most perfect health, and everybody is so kind to me! Nancy[151] proves a greater treasure than we anticipated. Ko Een and Bar-John sleep in the verandah, but poor John I was obliged to dismiss and take Chinea in his stead. The children are as well as ever and considerably more civilized. They talk a great deal about "dear papa" and Edward[152] says he knows you will get well because they pray to God about it every night.

We have rec'd a large mail from home this month. Among yours was one, not very important, from Mr. Peck,[153] acknowledging the receipt of two letters from you. The latest [Note: "Latest" is written above a crossed-out "latter."], relative to your going to Ava, he laid before the Ex. Com. and they approved your plan.[154]

There is also a letter from Mr. Osgood,[155] partly on business. You may rest perfectly easy about the little matter he was to adjust—everything is right and safe. I will tell you more, or send you your letters as soon as I know you have any interest in such matters. Ticknor and Co.[156] have sent in their accounts—150.75 due on

[151] Nancy was a Malayan woman who came with Emily from Burmah to America in 1851; she helped Emily with the three Judson children—Henry , Edward, and Emily Frances—and to be there if she was incapacitated by her frequent illnesses. There are numerous references to Nancy in the correspondence, and she continued with her duties with Emily and with the children until Emily's death in June 1854. In her will, Emily left a sum more than sufficient to pay for Nancy's return to her native home.

[152] Edward Judson, born December 27, 1844, in Maulmain, Burmah, was the eighth child of Adoniram and Sarah Hall Boardman Judson and the fifth of their children to survive. Only a few months old when Sarah and Adoniram returned to America, Edward's life was saved by the nurture and care he received from Elizabeth Stevens. He loved Emily as the only "Mama" he had ever known and returned with her to the United States in October 1851. Edward, who was Eddy to his family, became a minister; he did mission work with the immigrants in New York City, and with the aid of the Rockefeller Family, he built the Judson Memorial Baptist Church in what is now Washington Park.

[153] The Reverend Doctor Solomon Peck was for twenty years the executive secretary of the American Baptist Missionary Union. Many believed him to be hard, stern, and judgmental, and from some of his comments, it is easy to understand that perception. Dr. Peck and Emily did not always have the easiest of relationships. She felt in him the judgment that came from many in the church at the announcement of her impending marriage to Adoniram; that judgment concerned her "secular" past and concern that she was not an appropriate companion for the venerable missionary. On July 18, 1849, Emily wrote a blistering letter of defense to Dr. Peck in response to a letter from him of February 20, 1849; her letter framed how she viewed his perception of her, and her response was meant to set the record straight. There are eleven letters in the collection from Solomon Peck to Emily.

[154] Though he had longed to go to Ava for many years, his most recent venture in 1847 had been closed by a lack of funds from the missionary union. The hope had been to use Rangoon as a launching pad. When the board began to reconsider in early 1849, Emily Judson's health was precarious, and the work on the dictionary was entering a critical phase. With the return to Burmah of the Reverend Eugenio Kincaid after some years in the United States, it was decided that Mr. Kincaid would be the one to build the mission in Ava.

[155] See vol. 1, "Cast of Characters," s.v. "Osgood, The Reverend Sewell Mason."

[156] Ticknor and Company, later to become Ticknor, Reed and Fields. They had published *Alderbrook* and later would publish *The Kathayan Slave* and *My Two Sisters*.

two editions of *Alderbrook*.[157] Father[158] had fallen from the scaffold in the barn and rec'd a severe injury[159]—Wallace[160] had charge of a Whig paper and was doing well—Adoniram[161] and Elnathan[162] were well.

The Binneys[163] sail on Monday next. Poor Mrs. Moore[164] was confined last week, and met with another severe disappointment—her child lived only two or three hours. Mr. Mason[165] is very poorly, so his wife tells me, and she speaks as though greatly concerned for him. Darling, I cannot write to you. I was so uncertain in what state my letter will find you, that I feel almost as though sending out into an unknown world. But if you are well enough to think anything about it, you will be a loving interpreter, I know; and if you are not well enough, why, my hope is that we shall have long and sweet communion in heaven. Do you not feel that God is watching over you with tender care? It seems to me as though he is directing us in all things, and it is such a pleasant feeling, that even my anxiety for you yields to it, and I am happier (or, rather, *nearer happy*) than I could have believed I ever should be without you. A thousand blessings on you, my own love! May the "ministering

[157] *Alderbrook* was a collection of Fanny Forester's stories, poems, and sketches and was a sequel to *Trippings in Author-land*. Published by Ticknor and Company (later Ticknor, Reed and Fields), the first edition came out in December 1846, and by April 1847, it was in its fourth edition.

[158] Emily's father, Charles Chubbuck, was born at Bedford, New Hampshire, on March 3, 1780; he was married to Lavinia Richards in Goffstown, New Hampshire, on November 17, 1805. They were to have seven children. Though he held varying jobs over the years, he failed at many of them, and Emily was the main support of the family after she purchased a home for her family in fall 1842.

[159] For the complete story on the fall and the injury, see the letter from Catharine Chubbuck to Emily C. Judson dated December 28, 1849.

[160] Born January 1, 1824, William Wallace Chubbuck was six years younger than Emily. During these years of Emily's correspondence, Wallace lived at or near home and worked at different occupations including printing, office work, and teaching. Emily wrote of him as capable in many areas, but seeming to lack ambition at times. He proved to be a strong support for the Chubbuck family over these years, and at the time of her death in 1854, Wallace had become one of Emily's primary caregivers. After February 1854, she dictated all her letters to him because of her failing strength. Wallace married Julia Allin Throwbridge on July 18, 1854. He died on August 13, 1861, at the age of thirty-seven. The obituary in the Utica *Herald* noted that Wallace had trained as a printer in Morrisville and had gained some astute political skills. He was "possessed of one of the brightest of intellects, and wield[ed] one of the most trenchant of pens." He had served as a justice of the peace and as clerk to one of the legislative committees in Albany.

[161] See vol. 1, "Cast of Characters," s.v. "Judson, Adoniram Brown 'Addy.'"

[162] See vol. 1, "Cast of Characters," s.v. "Judson, Elnathan 'Elly.'"

[163] Joseph and Juliette Binney, missionaries to Burmah. They arrived in Burmah in April 1844. In 1845, Mr. Binney opened the theological school in Maulmain. They sailed to the United States from Burmah in April 1850. There is a single letter in the correspondence from Joseph Binney.

[164] William Moore was from Granville, Ohio, and was a graduate of Dennison University and Covington Institute, Kentucky. He married Elizabeth W. Forbes who was from Cincinnati, Ohio. They departed Boston on November 3, 1847, and arrived in Calcutta on March 18, 1848. They worked with the Karens in Burmah, near Maulmain. Mr. and Mrs. Moore returned to the United States, arriving in Boston December 19, 1853.

[165] Francis Mason arrived in Maulmain in November 1830 and transferred to Tavoy in 1831. His first wife died, and he married Helen Maria Griggs just before leaving the United States. She died in Burmah in 1846; they were the parents of four children. A skilled linguist, Mr. Mason was fluent in twelve languages and translated the Scripture into two of the Karen dialects. In spring 1847, Mr. Mason was seriously ill, and the other missionaries were concerned about him. In September 1847, he remarried, and Adoniram Judson officiated at the ceremony. His new wife was Ellen Huntley Bullard; originally from Vermont, she was the widow of Edwin Bullard, missionary to Burmah. Francis Mason died March 3, 1874, in Rangoon.

spirits" from above hover about you, while you sleep; and may the presence of Christ be continually enjoyed during your waking hours.

So, I commend you to our Heavenly Father, and kiss the paper where I write my Good-bye,

Yours ever

Emily

Source: First Baptist Church of Malden, Massachusetts[166]

Emily C. Judson for the Judson Children, April 1850—Maulmain

Prayer For Dear Papa[167]

Poor and needy little children,
    Saviour, God, we come to Thee,
For our hearts are full of sorrow,
    And no other hope have we.
Out upon the restless ocean,
    There is one we dearly love,—
Fold him in thine arms of pity,
    Spread thy guardian wings above.

[166] This letter originally came from Mrs. Marjorie Carson Hanna Shipman, a great-granddaughter of Adoniram and Emily Judson. Her father was Thomas Carson Hanna. Mrs. Shipman gave this letter and two others, as well as other Judson artifacts, to the First Baptist Church of Malden, Massachusetts, thinking that the Baptist church in the city of Adoniram Judson's birth would be a good repository. These letters and artifacts are now on loan to the American Baptist Churches Board of International Ministries, held by the American Baptist Historical Society.

[167] This appears in Emily Judson's *An Olio of Domestic Verses* ([New York: Lewish and Colby, 1852] 172–74) as "Prayer for an Absent Father." It also appeared in the *Baptist Memorial* (vol. 10 [1851]: 31) with this note: "The following lines, received by a friend in philadelphia, were written after Dr. Judson's departure from Maulmain, to be used by his children as a daily prayer. Their publication is contrary to the expectations and wishes of the writer, but in view of their exceeding beauty, and the light they cast up on the domestic life of Dr. Judson, the friend who received them assented to their publication in the *Macedonian*.

When the winds are howling round him,
    When the angry waves are high,
When black, heavy, midnight shadows,
    On his trackless pathway lie,
Guide and guard him, blessed Saviour,
    Bid the hurrying tempests stay;
Plant thy foot upon the waters,
    Send thy smile to light his way.[168]

When he lies, all pale, and suffering,
    Stretched upon his narrow bed,
With no loving face bent o'er him,
    No soft hand about his head,
Oh, let kind and pitying angels,
    Their bright forms around him bow;
Let them kiss his heavy eyelids,
    Let them fan his fevered brow.

Poor and needy little children,
    Still we raise our cry to Thee;
We have nestled in his bosom,
    We have sported on his knee;
Dearly, dearly do we love him,
    —We, who on his breast have lain—
Pity now our desolation!
    Bring him back to us again!

If it please thee, Heavenly Father,
    We would see him come once more,
With his olden step of vigor,

[168] In the Hanna Family Files we found a separate copy of this second stanza alone, in the handwriting of Emily Judson. It was dated May 28, 1851, and there was a notation that Emily had written while on the *Tudor*. Beneath it she had filled the page with Scripture verses (as follow). We believe the entire poem was written earlier, and this stanza copied with the following thoughts:

"Like as a father pitieth his children so the Lord pitieth them that fear him," and "he that trusteth in the Lord, mercy compass him about."

Not a sparrow "falleth to the ground without leave from your Father—Fear ye not therefore,—ye are of more value than many sparrows."

"He commandeth, and raiseth the stormy wind which lifteth up the waves thereof; they mount up to the heaven, they go down to the depths. Their (men's) soul is melted because of trouble. They reel to and fro and stagger like a drunken man, and are at their wit's end. Then they cry unto the Lord in their trouble, and he bringeth them out of their distress. He maketh the storm a calm so that the waves thereof are still. Oh, that men would praise the Lord for his goodness and for his wonderful works to the children of men!"

"The Lord sitteth upon the flood, yet the Lord sitteth king forever,"—and "As the mountains are round about Jerusalem, so is the Lord round about his people—none of them that trusteth in him shall be desolate."

With the love-lit smile he wore;
But if we must tread life's valley,
Orphaned, guideless, and alone,
Let us lose not, 'mid the shadows,
His dear footprints to thy Throne.

Source: Arabella M. Wilson, *Lives of the Three Mrs. Judsons*, pg. 333, 334; *An Olio of Domestic Verses* (New York: Lewish and Colby, 1852) 172–74.

Emily C. Judson to the Reverend Doctor Solomon Peck, April 19, 1850 —Maulmain

My dear Mr. Peck,

Your two letters addressed to Mr. J. and myself,[169] have been received by the present mail, but I have no heart to pursue the subject of my own, farther. I will only say that my motive in writing to you as I did was *simply* to comply with the wishes of my husband, who thought something of the kind was due both to you and myself.[170] With this consciousness of uprightness of intention, I have no dread of "uncharitable or ungrateful surmisings," even though my danger were much greater than it is.

You will hear from other sources of our severe trials, and I should not have written you at this time, but for a conversation I had with Dr. Morton[171] this morning, in which he gave his opinion of the case very definitely. He says Mr. J. has had no specific disease, though every vital organ has in turn (and sometimes all together) partially refused to perform its office. He spoke particularly of the sluggish action of the heart and lungs, and remarked that the hardships of his past life were now made to tell most fearfully on his failing constitution. He says he had remarked a look of age stealing over him for some months before his illness, and thought it the result of his *short* visit to America. In connection with this he begged me to write to the Wades[172] to postpone their return until Mrs. W's health should be fully re-established; but I suppose a letter would not reach them previous to their embarkation. Dr. Morton told me that if Mr. J. had remained in this place a little longer, he would have lost all chances of life, but that now the probabilities were in his opinion about equally balanced. If I could know that he were living *now*, my hopes would be very strong; but it will be so, *so* long before I can hear!

I will not attempt to describe my own feelings. Those who have suffered will be able to surmise in some small degree, and to those who have not, my words would be an empty sound. I can only be thankful that we are both in the keeping of a Being

[169] See the letter of Solomon Peck addressed to Emily, dated December 29, 1849.

who loves us infinitely, and that we shall ere long find ourselves occupying the places now preparing for us, in that world where "Fear and sorrow, pain and death, / Are felt and feared no more." With these prospects one cannot be very miserable, though the heart must needs sometimes be heavy.

I am glad to hear of the improvement of your health—we were greatly concerned about it at one time. Please present my kind regards to Mr. Bright,[173] whom I claim as an old friend, and

Believe me ever

Yours most sincerely,

Emily C. Judson

Perhaps you would like to hear something of the state of Mr. J's mind. For a long time before he was ill he seemed daily to grow more spiritual and child like [sic] — so much so that even some of the natives remarked the change in his preaching—he was all tenderness and tears. Since his illness he has been singularly resigned. "How sweet to lie entirely helpless asleep in the hands of God" he would often remark. He seemed to have a deep sense of the love of Christ, and sometimes, several times a day, would break out with the exclamation, "Oh the love of Christ! O the love of Christ!" In proportion to this was his love for all who bore the mark of Christ, and I never heard more fervent prayers than he from time to time offered for those, he might under other circumstances have found it difficult to love.

Source: American Baptist Historical Society, AJ 12, no. 381.

Mrs. Jane M. Haswell to Emily C. Judson, April 19, 1850—Fall River

My dear Sister

Your very kind letter was received last month every word of which was very interesting, though we were sorry to hear of Dr. Judson's illness. We shall anxiously wait for another arrival of letters hoping that the trip to Tavoy[174] proved beneficial.

[170] Dr. Solomon Peck wrote to Emily on February 20, 1849, and made a comment about her writing style. Emily wrote back on July 18, 1849; her letter was long, forthright, and even blistering in places. Dr. Peck replied to her letter on December 29, 1849.

[171] See vol. 1, "Cast of Characters," s.v. "Morton, Doctor."

[172] See vol. 1, "Cast of Characters," s.v. "Wade, The Reverend Doctor Jonathan and Deborah."

[173] See vol. 1, "Cast of Characters," s.v. "Bright, The Reverend Doctor Edward, Jr."

[174] When he first became ill, Adoniram took the steamer to Mergui and then to Tavoy, hoping that the change of air would be helpful. Adoniram and Emily then spent a month in Amherst. When he had not improved significantly, the idea of the sea-trip came to the fore.

I was glad to hear particulars about the dear children.[175] Henry[176] you know is my boy. I shall always feel that I have some claim to him.[177]

We have just located ourselves here, where we shall probably make it our home, while we wish for any in this land. My brother has removed from Williamsburg ( ) here which constitutes the chief attraction. Mr. H.[178] is resolved to try to get well, rather than try to *do* anything. We are now making preparations for a visit at the west, attending the meeting of the Union[179] in Buffalo on our way. I intend to leave all our children at home. Hither to in my wanderings, I have had some of them with me. I am for once to try to enjoy myself in going and seeing, yes, and being seen.

I am glad to hear that the Christian women have not forgotten me. Please remember me affectionately to them. I have often thought of the same thing to which you allude, respecting the influence of their prayers in our preservation. If it please the Lord to restore my dear husband's health, and open ways for the satisfactory disposition of our two older children, I fully expect to return. Indeed, Mr. H. has no other thought, but I sometimes find myself continuing to see if there is not some way for me to do a trip with the children.

[Written in left margin, page 2:] With our united love to Mr. Judson and to Henry who I know remembers us.

Very Affectionately yours,

Jane M. Haswell

Source: American Baptist Historical Society, AJ 16, no. 682.

[175] Henry Hall Judson, almost eight years old; Edward Judson, almost five and a half years old; and Emily Frances Judson, almost two and a half years old.

[176] Henry Hall Judson, born July 8, 1842, was the son of Adoniram and Sarah Hall Boardman Judson. Henry was the sixth of their eight children and the fourth of five who survived. He remained in Burmah in 1845 when Adoniram and Sarah returned to the United States with the three older children. He returned with Emily in 1851 and went to live with her family in Hamilton, New York. Henry attended Brown University and Williams Collage; he enlisted in the army at the time of the Civil War in January 1864. Later that year, he experienced a debilitating accident attributed either to sunstroke or a horse kicking him in the head. He was married once—unhappily according to his own correspondence—and he eventually died in a veteran's home in 1918, the last of his siblings to die. Of this, the chaplain noted, "The end was a genuine example of Christian fortitude." See Rosalie Hall Hunt, *Bless God and Take Courage, The Judson Legacy* (Valley Forge: Judson Press, 2005) 291.

[177] When Adoniram and Sarah Judson left Burmah in 1845 because of the serious decline in her health, they had left their three youngest children behind. Henry lived with Mr. and Mrs. Haswell, Charley lived with Mr. and Mrs. Osgood, and Edward lived with Mr. and Mrs. Stevens.

[178] See vol. 1, "Cast of Characters," s.v. "Haswell, Jane and The Reverend James."

[179] The American Baptist Missionary Union.

Mrs. Mary H. Brayton to Emily C. Judson, April 25, 1850

My Dear Sister

You have been so much upon my mind since I left M. that I cannot deny myself the pleasure of writing you a few hasty lines.

I know not from experience the bitterness of your present trials, and therefore cannot sympathise [sic] with you as I could had I ( )ded those similar trials. But I do deeply feel for you and would gladly comfort you with and by kind words or deed.

You have already learned I *trust* the "*habit*" of looking to Jesus, moment by moment and well do I know he will not fail you this trying time. May you come out of the furnace of affliction like gold seven times purified. Jesus is sitting by watching the process and will the very moment he sees *best* say it is *enough*. Commit all into His hands. Can you not with the poet say "It is enough that thou didst come / Why should I the burden bear" So calmly endure the present, and leave the future to Him and with him who cannot fail to do all things well.

I long to hear from dear Mr. Judson. But I suppose you can tell me nothing more than his leaving Amherst.[180]

I wish I could look after your little ones[181] while you are ill, but this cannot be so I will try daily to carry you to the throne of grace. I have recent evidence that God does condescend to hear my poor prayers. I would be humbled in view of His greatness. It is all for Jesus [sic] sake and to him be all the praise.

Yours very affly

M. H. Brayton

Source: American Baptist Historical Society, AJ12, no. 1.

Anna Maria Anable to Emily C. Judson, April 26, 1850

Dear Emily,

Your letter of Dec. is the last that I rec'd but I have heard from you since from Mrs. Bennett[182] and Lydia.[183] I hope the trip to Amherst will do the Dr. good[184]—poor dear man—how he has suffered: I would very gladly acceded to your proposal

[180] Early in the year, Adoniram took the steamer to Mergui and Tavoy, and then he and Emily spent a month in Amherst. With his condition unchanged when they returned, the decision was made for him to take the sea voyage.

[181] Henry, almost eight and a half years old; Edward, almost five and a half years old; and Emily Frances, almost two and a half years old.

[182] See vol. 1, "Cast of Characters," s.v. "Bennett, The Reverend Cephas and Stella Kneeland."

[183] See vol. 1, "Cast of Characters," s.v. "Lillybridge, Lydia." Also, "A Timeline of the Life and Mission of Lydia Lillybridge Simons."

[184] Beginning in early January, Emily and Adoniram took the steamer to Mergui and Tavoy; they then spent the rest of January and part of February in Amherst. When they returned to Maulmain, Dr. Morton insisted that staying there would be catastrophic and that Adoniram Judson's only hope was a lengthy sea voyage.

and taken the children for a few days. Does Willis[185] send you the "Home Journal"?[186] I told him how to direct it etc. Arthur Beardsley who was here a day or two since with his bride Louisa—took Hatty[187] and me to hear Fanny R( ) read Shakespeare. It was a treat I assure you. She has a marvelous voice to begin with—and then she impersonates the characters so entirely that it is to my mind better than a theatrical representation. We also went not long ago to hear the great Ralph Waldo Emerson! We did not get the "Mania" exactly but we thought we'd like to hear the lion growl a little—just to say we had—and I must say, I think he is small pattern of a man sitting up to be—a giant.

We heard old Dr. Baird here also—who used to love us so in Utica. He is delivering the self same lectures he delivered then.

Mr. and Mrs. Wade[188] are I believe I told you going to be near you. Mr. Kincaid[189] is all good about Ava.[190] He is going to take his oldest daughter—a girl of fourteen out with him. She is here now taking drawing and music lessons, what little time we have to devote to her—Mary[191] thinks she has quite a talent for drawing. In music she cannot do much before she sails, but perhaps something. Poor little thing I pity her.

I *must* go to bed now. Hoping to hear next mail that the Dr. is quite strong again and that all are well. I am as ever

Very lovingly

Anna M.

Source: American Baptist Historical Society, AJ 13, no. 474.

[185] See vol. 1, "Cast of Characters," s.v. "Willis, Nathanial Parker (N. P. Willis)."

[186] The *Home Journal* was a new publication, following the *New Mirror*, a collaboration of N. P. Willis and General George Morris.

[187] See vol. 1, "Cast of Characters," s.v. "Anable, Harriet."

[188] See vol. 1, "Cast of Characters," s.v. "Wade, The Reverend Doctor Jonathan and Deborah."

[189] See vol. 1, "Cast of Characters," s.v. "Kincaid, The Reverend Doctor Eugenio."

[190] Mr. Kincaid was to begin the mission in Ava that Adoniram had so longed to start. In 1849, at a time when it was too late for Adoniram and Emily to take on this mission, the board of the American Baptist Missionary Union released the funds. Those same funds had been refused in fall 1847 when Adoniram and Emily were in Rangoon, hoping that their stay there would be but a prelude to a move to Ava.

[191] Mary Juliet Anable was born February 18, 1830, in Bethlehem, Albany County, New York, one of nine children born to Alma and Joseph Anable. She went to New Orleans with Hatty in 1847, but she returned home early in March 1848, and by 1849, she was working with Anna Maria in the Misses Anable's School in Philadelphia. Writing in March 1849, Hatty said of Mary, "She paints and draws, speaks French, plays the piano, sings, dances and is our mathematician. What should we ever do without her? She laughs from morning till night, and it is really refreshing to be with her." On December 26, 1860, she was married to Pierre Jacques Darey, the officiating minister being the Rev. Dr. Eliphalet Nott, her uncle. Mary died at the age of sixty-eight on April 20, 1898, in Ottawa, Ontario, Canada.

Miss Cynthia Sheldon to Emily C. Judson, April 28, 1850—Philadelphia

My dear dear Emily,

It is unnecessary for me to say that you are almost constantly in mind—would that we could know your good Dr. had recovered from sickness, that your own precious life was teeming with the Mother's gush of affection anew.

While I know the reverse of this may have been marked by the unerring hand of providence—I will not, cannot admit it to have taken place—No, I am now thinking it was kind in you to ask dear Lydia[192] to tell us you had gone in the Country, hoping for benefit—and that your most sanguine hopes were realized—ere this the desired change in house is affected—you find it every way advantageous—especially to health.

What a pity you should have been so long exposed to unhealthful surroundings. If it proves so we will with you give thanks to God for your deliverance from it. Anna M.[193] sent off a letter to Lydia yesterday. I could not write then—and hope this will be in time for the same mail—This must be hastily written, for my time this evening has been taken up in writing to dear Mrs. Bennett[194]—and going to Church—Our good Mr. Gillette[195] stands even higher in the affections of his people than before he declined going to new York—and he has full measure of praise from many others—This is as it should be, he richly deserves it all—and no doubt he will have the blessing of Almighty God in staying—Our girls and Courtland[196] think he has greatly improved in sermonizing the last year—and I think they are correct in part, but that their hearing is equally improved—from two to three have been baptized every month for some time—more are expected next Sabbath—and Anna Bennett[197] joins by letter—she is nicely located in West Chester 30 miles from here—I went there with her the 1st inst—She has the teaching of three little girls about four hours a day, in a fine wealthy Quaker's family—Their eldest daughter has been with us almost two years, and she became much attached to Anna—it being mutual Anna scarce feels like being among strangers—she is quite happy—My visit there was very charming—they drove to the celebrated battle ground Brandywine Creek, Painters Bridge etc.—all scenes of interest to me—Anna will enjoy a daily drive through the country which teems with life and beauty—Anna will be here next Sabbath, and again when our dear Missionaries are making their

[192] See vol. 1, "Cast of Characters," s.v. "Lillybridge, Lydia." Also, "A Timeline of the Life and Mission of Lydia Lillybridge Simons."

[193] See vol. 1, "Cast of Characters," s.v. "Anable, Anna Maria."

[194] See vol. 1, "Cast of Characters," s.v. "Bennett, The Reverend Cephas and Stella Kneeland."

[195] See vol. 1, "Cast of Characters," s.v. "Gillette, The Reverend Abram Dunn."

[196] Courtland Anable was a younger brother of Anna Maria Anable. He held several positions over the years, and he studied at Hamilton College while he boarded for a time with Emily's parents. In 1853, he returned to Philadelphia where he preached his first sermon at the Eleventh Baptist Church. He was "Uncle Court" to Emily Frances Judson. In 1880, Courtland Anable was listed in the Massachusetts Census as an ordained minister serving in a church.

[197] See vol. 1, "Cast of Characters," s.v. "Bennett, Anna."

farewell visit—Mrs. Wade[198] is pleased with the appearance of both Maria and Nellie[199]—the dear woman is now I suppose threading the Western New York—we so much feared the journey would prove too much for her that I wrote begging she would seek quiet and six weeks usefulness in this City, where were multitudes to be moved by effective presentation of the necessity laid on each to send "The Gospel to every Creature"—her reply came last week and we are disappointed—although very glad to find her health is improved and that she feels sanguine she can endure—We are all rejoicing in your success with T. S. Arthur[200]—we are so much behind the times as not to have heard of his article until our Mr. Bright[201] told us your article was to come out in the *Macedonian*[202]—he said it was *rich*, and we found it so—do you remember Arthur Beardsley—he is now Editor of "Utica Observer" and Daily [sic]—Well, he brought Louisa Adams here last week as his new bride—we had a fine three days visit from them—they behaved beautifully—but to the point, he had no idea Mrs. Judson could write so *smart* an article—a strong minded touch he said made every word tell—it was conclusive in his mind—I shall try to go to Utica next month—business calls me or I should not afford it—Eugenia[203] is commencing housekeeping in the brick house Mr. Hawley[204] occupied on Chancellor Square—Horace Hawley and wife have got back to Utica—he was here some three weeks since and told us much about Utica, and his want of success where he had been in Connecticut[205]—Mr. Corey[206] is quite out of health, notwithstanding his nice new wife—Morven Jones[207] wrote me the other day—a note only with Anna

[198] See vol. 1, "Cast of Characters," s.v. "Wade, Jonathan and Deborah."

[199] See vol. 1, "Cast of Characters," s.v. "Bennett, Nellie or Nelly."

[200] Timothy Shay Arthur was an active temperance crusader, an editor, and an author of both fiction and non-fiction works. Born in 1809, he was schooled at home by his mother because of his frail health. Around 1833, he started his career as the editor of the *Baltimore Athenaeum and Young Men's Paper*, and by 1839, he was editing the *Baltimore Merchant*. In the next decade, he wrote a number of books, contributed to magazines such as *Godey's Lady's Book*, and published and wrote for *Arthur's Ladies' Magazine* from 1844 to 1846. In 1845, he had been contacted about publishing Emily's *Trippings in Author-land*, but the manuscript was returned to General Morris of the *New Mirror*, who was handling Emily's publishing affairs, with the statement that Emily would profit better with someone else as her publisher. T. S. Arthur continued active in publishing circles until his death in 1885.

[201] See vol. 1, "Cast of Characters," s.v. "Bright, The Reverend Doctor Edward, Jr."

[202] *The Macedonian* was a magazine published by the American Baptist Missionary Union. Emily was often asked to write articles for it.

[203] See vol. 1, "Cast of Characters," s.v. "Damaux, Eugenia."

[204] See vol. 1, "Cast of Characters," s.v. "Hawley, Horace H."

[205] Earlier letters spoke of Mr. Hawley's move to Hartford and of a trip back to Utica where it was reported that they were not happy in Hartford.

[206] See vol. 1, "Cast of Characters," s.v. "Corey, The Reverend D. G."

[207] Morven and Mary Jones were from Utica. They were well acquainted with Miss Sheldon and the Utica Female Seminary affairs; Morven Jones spoke of being present at the Colby's in Boston early in July 1846, just before Adoniram and Emily departed for Burmah. In one letter, Emily called upon them to get some information on the death of her sister Harriet for the book *My Two Sisters*. In another letter, Morven Jones summarized articles about the early mission in Burmah in response to Emily's request for letters from Adoniram Judson in preparation for the memoir. A long letter in 1848 told of news from Utica, Hamilton, and the Baptist church of which Mr. Corey was the pastor. In October 1845, his letter had to do with collecting autographs, her autograph particularly. The 1848 letters (December 9, 21, 22, 1848) also told of a fall that seriously injured Mary Jones; she had been standing on a bridge watching a church baptism by Mr. Corey when the bridge collapsed; her injuries caused her family to fear for her life, and the injuries were persistently disabling.

Bennett's Church letter—that they were getting along finely in the Church—excepting Mr. Corey's ill health, he feared Mr. C. would leave entirely, altho [sic] they had offered to let him be absent six months to recruit is he wished it [sic]—Miss Kelly[208] flourishes but like me wants many new boarders—only one goes to Baptist Church with Miss Barber[209]—Anna M. and Harriet[210] design to see the Missionaries sail about the tenth of July—from there to visit the Green Mountains and Helen Martin now Mrs. Chadwick—return home by Troy—Fanny[211] and Mary[212] visit all the way to Utica—If all things go right they will have a pleasant and profitable jaunt—Heaven bless you and yours is the heart's desire of your truly attached friend

C. Sheldon

Source: American Baptist Historical Society, AJ 20, no. 992.

Emily C. Judson to Adoniram Judson, May 20, 1850[213]—Maulmain

My own dearest love,

It is just six weeks today since you got out to sea,[214] and I cannot but hope, I cannot but *believe* that you are safe at Bourbon, and well enough to read my letter and reply to it. Oh, for one hour—for one little minute only, to be sure, and then I would bear all this loneliness bravely. But it will be a long, long time—long, before I can hear from you, and longer still before we meet. I repeat to myself a hundred times a day the words you formerly put into my ears, "Well, come what will, we *have been* blest [sic]."

Do you observe that my writing is cramped and awkward? I am writing from the bed where I have lain four weeks, and from which the Doctor has not yet given me permission to rise. But you see God has seen fit to spare my life—perhaps for your sake, perhaps for that of the poor children,[215] I am not sure for my own unless

[208] See vol. 1, "Cast of Characters," s.v. "Kelly, Miss Jane."

[209] See vol. 1, "Cast of Characters," s.v. "Barber, Mary."

[210] See vol. 1, "Cast of Characters," s.v. "Anable, Harriet."

[211] See vol. 1, "Cast of Characters," s.v. "Anable, Fanny."

[212] See vol. 1, "Cast of Characters," s.v. "Anable, Miss Mary Juliet."

[213] This letter and the letter of April 19, 1850, discovered in the archives of the First Baptist Church of Malden, Massachusetts, where I served for six years as senior minister, touched my heart with a compelling interest in Emily Judson. There was something about the writing, the pathos of her experience, the pain of her suffering, and the articulation of her hope. I remember that day now more than thirty years ago and mark it as the beginning of a journey that has culminated in this project of *The Life and Letters of Emily C. Judson (Fanny Forester)*.

[214] Adoniram Judson boarded the *Aristide Marie* on April 3, 1850. Emily was able to see him April 3, 4, 5, and 6 as the ship slowly made its way to the open ocean.

[215] The Judson children in Burmah: Henry Hall Judson, almost eight years old; Edward Judson, almost five and a half years old; and Emily Frances Judson, almost two and a half years old.

it could be passed with you. And yet, perhaps I speak wickedly—for my own sake, maybe, in order to purify me by suffering and sorrow. After you left I was not very well, but thought it was the reaction that I might expect. On the 21st and 22nd of last month I was very poorly indeed. On the 23rd towards evening, I was seized with an alarming hemorrhage, and at a little before 12 o'clock was delivered of a dead boy. Poor little fellow; the fatigue and anxiety which aught [sic] to have been borne by me had fallen on his weaker life and crushed it. He was a beautiful boy—my dear little *Charley*,[216] you know—perfect in his formation, and so like you that everyone spoke of it, but very thin—indeed wasted to a skeleton even before he was born.[217] Mr. Stevens[218] and Bar-John[219] took him away and buried him in the Chapel compound by the side of your little Luther.[220] According to previous arrangements, Mrs. Stevens,[221] Mah Zoat, and Mah Boke were here, but when Dr. Morton[222] became alarmed he sent for Mrs. Mason[223] and a couple more Burman women. Mr. Stevens also stayed during the whole, and Lydia[224] hid herself in the children's room. I will not attempt to describe to you how dreadfully I suffered—if we ever meet we shall talk over all these dark passages—we shall certainly talk them over in heaven. Doct. Morton says the rapidity of the labour [sic] saved my life. As it was, I fainted five or six times—indeed, through the whole, one woman stood over me with a fan and another with a glass of water, to keep the breath in me. Dr. M. thought the child had been dead about twenty-four hours, and hastened the burial on that account. Oh, darling, how I have longed to have you here, to whisper one little word of comfort, to pray for me, to take me in your arms, and make me feel there is somebody that loves me exclusively. Everybody is kind to me—the dear good Stevens's especially—but I want someone to love me, and can scarcely be thankful for this kindness born of pity. I wonder if you do think of me much—I know you do if you are well, and if living you must be getting well by this time. I sometimes lie here and fancy our future meeting, until I work myself into a fever of delight, and then—but I will not try to give you the reverse of the picture. I have felt a strong confidence

[216] Charley, or Charles Judson, was named after Emily's father, Charles Chubbuck.

[217] Following the birth of Charles Judson, Emily wrote the poem "Angel Charley," which follows this letter in this volume.

[218] See vol. 1, "Cast of Characters," s.v. "Stevens, The Reverend Edward and Elizabeth."

[219] Bar-John was one of the Judson's trusted Burmese servants.

[220] Luther Judson, a stillborn child born of Adoniram and Sarah Hall Boardman Judson. This occurred on March 8, 1841.

[221] Elizabeth Stevens arrived in Maulmain in February 1838; her husband was Edward Stevens. Elizabeth Stevens took six-month-old Edward Judson into her home when Sarah and Adoniram had to leave for the United States in 1845, and her care and nurture saved his life. She served forty-eight years in Burmah. She had extensive correspondence with Emily Judson, and her letters spoke of everyday life among the missionaries. When Emily returned to the United States, the letters from Mrs. Stevens brought news of friends and colleagues. Mrs. Stevens had a sister, Sarah Haven, in Massachusetts, who wrote a number of letters to Emily asking for information on the Stevens family.

[222] See vol. 1, "Cast of Characters," s.v. "Morton, Doctor."

[223] Ellen Huntley Bullard Mason, missionary to Burmah. The widow of missionary Edwin Bullard, she had married Francis Mason in September 1847.

[224] See vol. 1, "Cast of Characters," s.v. "Lillybridge, Lydia." Also, "A Timeline of the Life and Mission of Lydia Lillybridge Simons."

that you would get well ever since the loss of my little boy—founded perhaps on irrational grounds but still it keeps me from despair.

We had only two letters this month. One was from Lewis Colby[225] with the accounts (he had sold the first edition of the Memoir with Notes[226]), and one from Aunt Cynthia.[227] Doct. Dawson is coming out to be supported by individuals.[228] Poor Abbott[229] writes to Mrs. Stevens in a very discouraged way. His health is miserable. It is not very likely that Beecher[230] will come round—both Abbott and Harris[231] are opposed to it. But my worst news is to come yet. Mr. Stilson[232] was attacked by paralysis the next day after my confinement, and his whole left side is helpless. The doctor says he will not be likely to recover, though he may live in that state many years. Poor Mrs. S. is worse than ever—what will they do? Mr. Mason[233] continues very poorly—only occasionally able to attend his work.

And now, darling, let me again talk about coming to you. Our poor little baby can now be no hindrance, and Mah Zoat says she will go with me. Dr. Morton says I am not strong enough to bear the boisterous passage during the Monsoon, and as he has told it to everybody, I shall not be able to get a note to go till after the Monsoon is over. In the meantime I can hear from you and get all your directions.

[225] Lewis Colby was a publisher in New York. In agreeing to publish the *Memoir of Sarah Hall Boardman Judson*, they had also agreed to republish some of Emily's earlier books. Lewis Colby also published *An Olio of Domestic Verses*.

[226] Fanny Forester, *Memoir of Sarah B. Judson, Member of the American Mission to Burmah* (New York: L. Colby and Company, 1848).

[227] See vol. 1, "Cast of Characters," s.v. "Sheldon, Miss Cynthia."

[228] See vol. 1, "Cast of Characters," s.v. "Dawson, Doctor."

[229] Elisha Abbott was born October 23, 1809, in Cazenovia, New York. He graduated from the Hamilton Theological Institute and was ordained August 25, 1835. He wife was Ann P. Gardner, and they were married April 2, 1837. Though they were appointed for work in Telagus, India, that changed upon their arrival, and they went to Maulmain in April 1837. They continued on to Rangoon shortly after that. In March 1840, they established the station at Sandoway. Mrs. Abbott died in Sandoway on January 27, 1845. Mr. Abbott left for the United States in November 1845, returning in August 1847. At one point in the correspondence, Mr. Abbott was mentioned as a possible husband for Lydia Lillybridge.

[230] Mr. and Mrs. John Sydney Beecher sailed to Burmah with Adoniram and Emily Judson; they served there from 1846 to 1866.

[231] Norman Harris was born on February 19, 1813, in Becket, Massachusetts. He attended Columbia College and Hamilton Literary and Theological School, graduating in 1844. Olive Celina Wadsworth was also born in Becket, Massachusetts, on July 6, 1814. They were married on August 9, 1844, and were appointed to missionary service on October 28, 1844. In July 1846, they sailed to Burmah with the newly married Adoniram and Emily Judson. Olive Harris died in childbirth on November 23, 1853, in Shwegyin, Burma. In 1856, Norman Harris married for the second time; Miranda Harris died of fever in September that same year. Norman Harris left the mission field shortly after the death of his wife Miranda and returned to the United States. There, in June 1858, he married Julia Wadsworth Chapman, the sister of his first wife, Olive Celina Wadsworth. Norman and Julia Harris returned to Burmah in 1858, though not under the auspices of the American Baptist Missionary Union; they were reappointed as missionaries in 1861. Norman Harris died on March 1, 1884, in Hamilton, New York. Julia Harris died in September 1905.

[232] Lyman Stilson was born in Meredith, New York, on January 29, 1805. He attended the Hamilton Seminary and was appointed to missionary service on October 3, 1836. He was married to Lucretia Brownson on August 20, 1837, and both sailed for Burmah on October 28, 1837, along with the Bennetts and the Stevens. Mr. Stilson finally returned to America after Lucretia Stilson's death on August 14, 1851. Mrs. Stilson had been quite ill for some time and the board had authorized her to return to the United States, but as reported in the newsletter of the Missionary Union, "She has been removed to a better country." They worked with Adoniram Judson for thirteen years, and with both Sarah Hall Boardman Judson and Emily Chubbuck Judson. Mr. Stilson's specific responsibilities included the oversight of printing Burmese elementary books for the schools that were maintained by the mission. He also wrote a volume in Burmese on mathematics.

[233] See vol. 1, "Cast of Characters," s.v. "Mason, The Reverend Francis, Helen, and Ellen."

Mr. Stevens[234] has told Shway-loo there is some prospect of his being called after the Monsoon, and the other men will of course be ready. I can bring them or not just as I like. If you are able to go on with your work, you had better do it there, and if not, we had better get the family together and live there. Dr. M. says you must not think of coming back at present.

The children are just now suffering from influenza—otherwise they are very well. The boys pray for "dear papa" every night, and even baby has learned to say "God-take-care-papa." She speaks very distinctly pausing between the words. That God may take care of you, darling, and restore you again to us, is the continual prayer of

Your loving wife

Emily C. Judson

[Written in the left margin of page 1:] Mrs. Stevens thinks you would like to know that the baby was not buried coffinless. He was placed in a neat little box, and buried on the south side of the monument.

Source: First Baptist Church, Malden, Massachusetts[235]

Emily C. Judson, May 1850

Angel Charley[236]

He came—a beauteous vision—
  Then vanished from my sight,
His wing one moment cleaving[237]
  The blackness of my night;
My glad ear caught its rustle,
  Then sweeping by, he stole
The dew drop that his coming
  Had cherished in my soul.

[234] Edward Stevens was working with Adoniram Judson on the English-Burmese dictionary, and he completed the work after Judson's death, making a mark where one had left off and the other had picked it up, as Judson requested.

[235] This letter originally came from Mrs. Marjorie Carson Hanna Shipman, a great-granddaughter of Adoniram and Emily Judson. Her father was Thomas Carson Hanna. Mrs. Shipman gave this letter and two others, as well as other Judson artifacts, to the First Baptist Church of Malden, Massachusetts, thinking that the Baptist church in the city of Adoniram Judson's birth would be a good repository. These letters and artifacts are now on loan to the American Baptist Churches Board of International Ministries, held by the American Baptist Historical Society.

[236] Emily Judson, in *An Olio of Domestic Verses* ([New York: Lewish and Colby, 1852]), has "Angel Charley" as part 3 of a longer poem; "Little Children in Heaven" is part 1, and "The Only Child of His Mother" is part 2.

[237] In the Hanna family files, a copy of "Angel Charley" was found on a single sheet of paper, written in the handwriting of Emily Chubbuck Judson. In that edition, this line reads, "His cherub wing scarce cleaving."

Oh, he had been my solace
    When grief my spirit swayed,
And on his fragile being
    Had tender hopes been stayed;
Where thought, where feeling lingered
    His form was sure to glide,
And in the lone night watches
    'Twas ever by my side.

He came; but as the blossom
    Its petals closes up,
And hides them from the tempest,
    Within its sheltering cup,
So he his spirit gathered
    Back to his brightened breast,
And passed from earth's grim threshold,
    To be the Saviour's guest.

My boy—ah, me! the sweetness ,
    The anguish of that word!-
My boy, when in strange night dreams,
    My slumbering soul is stirred;
When music floats around me,
    When soft lips touch my brow,
And whisper gentle greetings,
    Oh, tell me, is it thou?

I know, by one sweet token,
    My Charley is not dead;
One golden clue he left me,
    As on his track he sped;
Were he some gem or blossom,
    But fashioned for to-day,
My love would slowly perish
    With his dissolving clay.

Oh, by this deathless yearning,
    Which is not idly given;
By the delicious nearness

My spirit feels to heaven;
By dreams that throng my night sleep,
By visions of the day,
By whispers when I'm erring,
By promptings when I pray;-

I know this life so cherished,
Which sprang beneath my heart,
Which formed of my own being
So beautiful apart;
This precious, winsome creature,
My unfledged, voiceless dove,
Lifts now a seraph's pinion,
And warbles lays of love.

Oh, I would not recall thee,
My glorious angel boy!
Thou needest not my bosom,
Rare bird of light and joy;
Here dash I down the tear-drops,
Still gathering in my eyes;
Blest—oh! how blest!—in adding
A seraph to the skies.

Source: A. C. Kendrick, *The Life and Letters of Emily C. Judson*, p. 337–39
Edward Judson, *Life of Adoniram Judson*, p. 528–30.
Emily Judson, *An Olio of Domestic Verses*, p. 186–90.

Miss Mary Anna Longstreth to Emily C. Judson, May 25, 1850—Philadelphia

My beloved friend,

Having heard some time ago of the illness of thy dear husband, we have been waiting with much anxiety for the arrival of the overland mail, ardently hoping it would bring us tidings of his convalescence; but alas! we have been disappointed. As soon as I knew of the arrival of the mail from India, I hastened to our dear Anna Maria,[238] who gave me the contents of thy letter, just received. Sad indeed—my heart bleeds for thee, my dear friend. I feel as if I could fly to thee. I cannot imagine

[238] See vol. 1, "Cast of Characters," s.v. "Anable, Anna Maria."

a more trying position than thine, with a very ill husband, and children needing a parent's watchful care continually, and in thy peculiar situation, requiring rest and quiet—to leave home on a voyage seems impracticable, and on the other hand to allow thy precious invalid husband to sail without thee would be extremely trying, if not impossible. What *will* Emily do? what can she do? we asked of each other again and again. I felt as if, were I only near enough, I would so gladly relieve thee for a season of the care of the *boys*[239] and thy little *girl*.[240] But oh! half the circumference of the globe separated us, and by the time this note reaches thee, how changed must be thy situation. Thy beloved husband can not [sic] long remain in his present state. He will either be restored to health and his family and his usefulness; or he will become an inhabitant of that glorious city, not one of whose inhabitants can say, "I am sick," to rest forever from his labors, and enjoy an exceeding and eternal weight of glory. May it be the Lord's will that he be spared to thee and the church a few years longer! My only consolation in thinking of you in your deep trials, is that the Lord Jesus is with you every moment; you are engraven on the palms of his hand; the very hairs of your head are numbered; he is almighty and his love is as great as his power. No difficulty, no accumulation of obstacles, is too great for Him; he can bid them all to flee in a moment, or he can enable you to bear whatever may be pressing upon you. My prayer continually is that your faith may not *fail*, but that you may *feel* the Everlasting Arm to be always round about you. With dear love to you both, from every member of our family, I am thy sincerely attached friend,

M. A. Longstreth

Source: American Baptist Historical Society, AJ 17, no. 766.

Mrs. Abigail H. Owen to Emily C. Judson, May 25, 1850—Lebanon

My Dear Emily

(If you will pardon my liberty in addressing you as such) I expect to go to Eaton, tomorrow, to bid the beloved Mr. and Mrs. Wade[241] farewell, and this will probably be the last opportunity of sending you any token of remembrance I shall have as I have not been to your father's[242] in some time, and I am afraid it will not be convenient for me to go before Mr. and Mrs. W. will leave.

[239] Henry Judson, almost eight years old, and Edward Judson, almost five and a half years old.

[240] Emily Frances Judson, almost two and a half years old.

[241] See vol. 1, "Cast of Characters," s.v. "Wade, The Reverend Doctor Jonathan and Deborah."

[242] Emily's father. See vol. 1, "Cast of Characters," s.v. "Chubbuck, Charles."

I think I need not tell I was much disappointed in not being able to see you before you left—but thus it seemed to be ordered by providence. Perhaps it has made me think more about you, for I certainly feel a deep interest in your welfare, both spiritual and temporal. I sometimes imagine I see you bending over your books, or pointing not only the tawny skin, but the darkened mind to the Lamb of God. I heard of the illness of the Dr. which gave me much anxiety, for we are yet in ignorance as to the result. But my prayer is that he may be spared to you, a long time yet, and that he may be able to finish the work he has felt so anxious to complete. E. I have more to say to you, than one shred of paper would contain, but my judgement [sic] tells me, a few words from me with all the rest of your letters, must be quite as acceptable as more. You may like to know something about my family and health, which is not very good, for I suffer much from an affection of the lungs and throat at times, and recover again and enjoy pretty good health. I have three children a son and two daughters, the youngest one year old we call Mary, to give you some idea how she looks I will say there is a strong resemblance between her and a penciling you gave me, yes that picture hangs in my sitting room, and often reminds me of one in a heathen land. I think too of your little India bird[243] and imagine to myself how she looks, and sometimes anticipate I may yet see you both. But I must stop and get dinner as it is twelve o'clock, for little Mary is sitting on my lap or pulling my clothes which makes it very hard work to write.

Give my best respects to your husband with a large share to yourself, and if you can find a few leisure moments and in your heart to write me it would be very gratefully received. Mr. Owen joins me in love to you and family.

I remain your sincere friend

Abigail H. Owen

P.S. I send you a few dried plums all I have or I would send more you must eat them and think of Miraett [sic], for I think of her.

A. H. O.

Source: American Baptist Historical Society, AJ 18, no. 822.

[243] On January 1, 1848, eight days after the birth of Emily Frances Judson, Emily wrote a celebratory poem that she called "My Bird." The poem has a total of seven stanzas, and it was widely published in the United States.

Anna Maria Anable to Emily C. Judson, May 26, 1850

My dearest Emily

Your letter of the 19 Feb. has filled me with apprehension—I *know* not what to think either of the Dr. or yourself ( ) ( ) of taking a sea voyage—and yet in your situation I should think it impossible. The critical time for yourself is I suppose soon,[244] and whatever dispensation is in store for you, I do pray that you will be sustained by Him who orders all things well. Would that I could relieve you from some of your anxieties!

But before this reaches you all may be well again. I should hope so, and the more as I see no communication from the Board this month in relation to the Dr.'s health.

The meeting of the Union is just over and Mr. Gillette[245] who was here says it was a most delightful one. They resolved to raise $20,000 more this next year than they have yet done. The missionaries all looked well—Mr. Wade[246] as fat as a porpoise. Mrs. Bronson[247] has settled all her children to her satisfaction. I have not seen the Haswells[248] and do not suppose they have been in the city. The Board have [sic] about decided to appoint Dr. Dawson[249] and wife. The Bible Society in New York had very exciting times. I have not seen the report, but Dr. Cone [sic] has resigned and Dr. Welch is appointed president. All the old managers are turned out and they have an entirely new corps of officers—even Mr. Colgate[250] is laid on the shelf. They passed resolutions which will prevent the recurrence of any such thing* again, letting the Society know that their business was to publish not to translate. The missionaries translate, they publish. It has been a sad thing—but it may result in good.

Since I last wrote, we have had Mrs. Dr. James[251] from Utica to visit us. She with Mr. Warner's little deaf girl Lucy (she is improving in hearing and can talk now tolerably well) spent a week or more with us. Mr. Warner came and took them on to Washington and then returned and feeling a little indisposed Mrs. James asked Aunt C.[252] if *he* could be accommodated in our house. Now, who do you think he is

[244] Anna Maria Anable is referencing the fact that Emily C. Judson was expecting a baby, and that its estimated time of arrival was the month of May.

[245] See vol. 1, "Cast of Characters," s.v. "Gillette, The Reverend Abram Dunn."

[246] See vol. 1, "Cast of Characters," s.v. "Wade, The Reverend Doctor Jonathan and Deborah."

[247] Mrs. Bronson was the wife of Miles Bronson. See vol. 1, "Cast of Characters," s.v. "Bronson, Miles."

[248] See vol. 1, "Cast of Characters," s.v. "Haswell, Jane and The Reverend James."

[249] See vol. 1, "Cast of Characters," s.v. "Dawson, Doctor."

[250] This was William Colgate of soap manufacturing fame. Active in the Bible society, a split took place over whether it should work with missionaries in indigenous languages. Mr. Colgate helped form a new Bible society that would have a broader mandate.

[251] See vol. 1, "Cast of Characters," s.v. "James, Doctor."

[252] See vol. 1, "Cast of Characters," s.v. "Sheldon, Miss Cynthia."

[253] See vol. 1, "Cast of Characters," s.v. "Anable, Harriet."

[254] See vol. 1, "Cast of Characters," s.v. "Anable, Fanny."

[255] See vol. 1, "Cast of Characters," s.v. "Anable, Miss Mary Juliet."

after? It ain't me, nor it ain't Hatty,[253] nor it ain't Fanny,[254] nor 'taint Molly,[255]—nor it ain't mother,[256] but it's *somebody*!! in our family. Mrs. James seems bent on establishing a friend of hers in that beautiful house formerly owned by the Hurlburts [sic] on the hill in Utica. It won't be Mr. Warner's nor Mrs. James' fault if somebody does not yet have a grand house of her own and somebody to take care of her in her old age. Don't laugh now, don't. Mother is fairly scared about it, and so am I beginning to be, but I haven't lisped it to a soul yet, and you must not for the world. It is because you are out of the world that I tell you. Aunt C. has gone to Troy, Schenectady and Utica, and by the time she returns, we should either have invitations to the wedding or she will have gnashed the whole affair. She has not the faintest idea that we suspect anything. Be silent till you hear from me again on this matter.

Dr. Piteher and Rosa with a young friend made us a visit last week. Rosa is pretty as ever, but indolent and some spoiled. We are all getting on well in the school—tho' longing some for the holidays. Mary Anna Longstreth[257] sent me the enclosed note for you. She is a blessed girl—and has longed so for just a few lines from the Dr. I do hope Lydia[258] will write next month to let me know how you all are. With best love to all, yours for ever

Anna Maria

[Written in the left margin of page 2 and corresponding to the asterisk that appears earlier in the third paragraph of the letter:] *You know Mr. ( ) and Mr. Cone wanted the Society to publish a new version of the English Bible—translating the word baptize—immerse etc.

[Written in the space between page 2 and page 3:] All the girls and Mother send dearest love—and sympathy.

Source: American Baptist Historical Society, AJ 13, no. 473.

Doctor Morton to Emily C. Judson, June 7, 1850

My Dear Mrs. Judson

I beg to return you very many thanks, for your kind valuable present of Webster's Dictionary which henceforth I *shall certainly be inclined to adopt as a standard.*

With best regards
Believe Me
Yours Very Sincerely

(Unreadable Signature)

Source: American Baptist Historical Society, AJ 18, no. 874.

[256] See vol. 1, "Cast of Characters," s.v. "Sheldon, Alma and Joseph Hubbell."

Elnathan "Elly" Judson to Emily and Adoniram Judson, June 7, 1850[259] —Worcester

June 7th 1850

My dear father and mother.

It is a long time, since we have written to you, and it is a long time since we have heard from you. Mrs. Wade[260] is coming here on the 10th inst. and she is going to Burmah very soon. She is going to take our letters, and whatever presents we buy for our brothers,[261] and sister.[262] We are going out tomorrow, and [Note: "Bye" is written and crossed out.] buy them something. We get along very well in our Sabbath School, Mr. Davey continues to be our teacher, and Mr. Washburn our Superintendent. We also get along very well in our Day School. We study Reading, Writing, Spelling, Defining, Grammar, Parsing, Analyzing, Geography and Arithmetic. Uncle, and Aunt Newton[263] are very kind to us, they have lately, bought us a flute a peice [sic], and a gentleman, named Professor Parritt gives us lessons, so that we have got to be pretty good players. We have lately written to George.[264] We have received a letter, from our old playmate James Haswell,[265] but we have forgotten to answer it, and I think that we will to-morrow. I [Note: "Think" is written and crossed out.] think that we will write to our friend Eddy Stevens[266] this time, as we have such a good chance, and also to our brothers. A friend of Aunt Newton's was here lately, and she gave Adoniram[267] and I [sic] a handsome bound volume of *Pilgrim's Progress*.

Source: American Baptist Historical Society, AJ 11, no. 456.

[257] See vol. 1, "Cast of Characters," s.v. "Longstreth, Mary Anna."

[258] See vol. 1, "Cast of Characters," s.v. "Lillybridge, Lydia." Also, "A Timeline of the Life and Mission of Lydia Lillybridge Simons."

[259] There is an addendum to this letter dated June 8, 1850.

[260] See vol. 1, "Cast of Characters," s.v. "Wade, Jonathan and Deborah."

[261] Henry Hall Judson and Edward Judson.

[262] Emily Frances Judson.

[263] See vol. 1, "Cast of Characters," s.v. "Newton, Doctor Calvin and Mrs. M. I."

[264] See vol. 1, "Cast of Characters," s.v. "Boardman, George Dana."

[265] James Haswell, the son of Jane and James Haswell, missionaries to Burmah, who had worked with Adoniram and Sarah Judson; it is obvious that the children would have played with each other at that time. James was born in Burmah on September 4, 1836. He was almost two years older than Elnathan.

[266] Eddy Stevens, the son of Edward and Elizabeth Stevens, who were missionaries with Emily and Adoniram in Maulmain. Mr. Stevens ran many of the mission schools and took on the responsibility of finishing the Burmese dictionary upon Adoniram Judson's death. Again, it would be natural for the children to have played together while the families worked together. Eddy Stevens was born in Burmah on December 17, 1838; he was five months younger than Elnathan.

[267] See vol. 1, "Cast of Characters," s.v. "Judson, Adoniram Brown 'Addy.'"

Elnathan "Elly" Judson to Emily and Adoniram Judson,[268] June 8, 1850

We expect to go on a pleasant trip to Maine, where Aunt Newton's[269] sister lives, accompanied by brother George,[270] Abby[271] and Aunt Newton. We expect to go to the high school next Spring. We have been serious for about two months past. And I wish very much that we were Christians. Two ladies and one gentleman were baptized lately at our church. We have read through the Bible, and we now read 1 chapter daily and two Sundays in the Testament. The Anniversary of all the schools came off about two weeks ago, and then all the scholars went to Boston, and while there went into a panorama of the great lakes seven miles long, and then came back all for fifty cents. Our Sabbath school anniversary comes off to-morrow, and then we are going to have a picnic in the hospital grove. We are to write six letters this morning, and I think that we will stay home from school so as to write them. We have been a fishing twice lately, the first time we went to Long Pond, accompanied by Mr. Gifford (one of the students) and Thomas Studley, and caught eleven fish, the second time we went to Stillwater, and caught six fish, and we expect to go again pretty soon.

Adoniram[272] has made a miniature Panorama, with 86 square inches which he is going to send to Burmah, for our little brothers.[273] He has also made a little pair of scales for them. If you approve of it we will send them a few nuts and marbles. We have not got but a little money now to spend for them having lent nearly all of it to brother George, but we will contrive to get them something. Aunt Newton has received a letter from brother George,[274] and he says that he is pretty well, but not so well as he was before vacation. You need not send those parrots I asked you for, I did not think that they would be such a trouble to you.[275] We have been poisoned with dogwood again this summer, but it is now nearly well. [Note: "We anticipate" has been written and crossed out.] We have not heard from Abby for about four months, and we have written her a letter but not sent it yet. Mr. Davis has lately returned from a tour to Cuba, for his health. Professor Parritt has got a canary bird here, now, and he sings very sweetly. Professor Parritt is also an excellent player on the flute, and we frequently sing, while he plays. We go to G. R. Loeland's singing-

[268] This letter is an addendum to a letter written June 7, 1850.

[269] See vol. 1, "Cast of Characters," s.v. "Newton, Doctor Calvin and Mrs. M. I."

[270] See vol. 1, "Cast of Characters," s.v. "Boardman, George Dana."

[271] See vol. 1, "Cast of Characters," s.v. "Judson, Abby Ann."

[272] See vol. 1, "Cast of Characters," s.v. "Judson, Adoniram Brown 'Addy.'"

[273] Henry Hall Judson, almost eight years old, and Edward Judson, almost five and a half years old.

[274] On June 30 and July 1, 1849, Dr. Calvin Newton wrote to Adoniram Judson about George Dana Boardman. George lived with Dr. and Mrs. Newton ever since his arrival in the United States in 1835. George took a long break from his studies at Brown University and went on a trip west with a patron from the college; there was evidence, however, that the relationship had fractured. Dr. Newton said that he was fearful for George's mental condition and saw a "disturbance of his mental powers."

[275] See the letter, dated June 28, 1849, of Elnathan Judson to Adoniram and Emily Judson.

school, and can sing about fifty songs. Tell Eddy Stevens[276] that he may expect a letter from us this time, and also our little brothers and sister Frances Emily.[277] It is I believe the first time they have a letter from me and when brother Eddy[278] can write I will want him to write me a letter. I will also expect one from Henry,[279] as I have a letter which he [Note: "Wrote" is crossed out.] wrote to sister Abby. We did not stay to home from school to-day, but we were dismissed at recessed [sic]. We have read nearly through Romans in the New Testament. If we do not go to Maine this summer, I think that we will go to Bradford[280] to pay sister Abby a visit. We are going to have $1000 worth of fireworks, out on the common Fourth of July night. A Sabbath School from Woonsocket have just arrived in Worcester, and are going to have a picnic in the Hospital Grove, with our Sabbath School. But here I must stop.

Your affectionate son,

Elnathan Judson.

P.S. George arrived here last night on account of ill health. ( ) he has gone to Maine.

Source: American Baptist Historical Society, AJ 11, no. 456.

Mr. Jon Asalun to Emily C. Judson, June 10, 1850

Mrs. Judson

Madam

I deeply regret to hear of Mr. Judsons severe illness and sincerely hope and pray that God would restore him to his ( ) health. I wrote to him some time ago and his silence induces me to believe that my letter might have been mis( ), and as I am particularly anxious to hear from him regarding a question of the greatest importance to us all, you will greatly add to you ( ) kindness to me which I deeply feel and acknowledge by writing to Dr. Judson and communicating my great wish and anxiety of hearing from him before my return to Rangoon as also reminding him

[276] Eddy Stevens, the son of Edward and Elizabeth Stevens, who were missionaries with Emily and Adoniram in Maulmain. Mr. Stevens ran many of the mission schools and took on the responsibility of finishing the Burmese dictionary upon Adoniram Judson's death. Again, it would be natural for the children to have played together while the families worked together. Eddy Stevens was born in Burmah on December 17, 1838; he was about five months younger than Elnathan.

[277] Emily Frances Judson, born December 24, 1847, was the daughter of Adoniram and Emily Judson. She was Elnathan's younger stepsister.

[278] See vol. 1, "Cast of Characters," s.v. "Judson, Edward."

[279] See vol. 1, "Cast of Characters," s.v. "Judson, Henry Hall."

[280] Ann Hasseltine Judson came from Bradford. Her family still lived there, and Abby Ann Judson was attending Bradford Academy at this time. In a letter written November 26, 1848, Adoniram Judson told Abby Ann of the extraordinary generosity of the Hasseltine family in supporting her education.

kindly of his promise regarding the English and Burmese Dictionary which I hope will be ( ) by the first opportunity—three of four of the ( ) copies much as they are finished will be very acceptable—a kind reply by the next steamer is greatly anticipated and anxiously expected ( ) and I ( ) in duty-bound endeavour [sic] to go to Maulmain before my departure to Rangoon, after executing commissions ( ) ( ) ( ) the Sh( ) who is now Governor of the latter town, for the purchase of foods for the Royal household to return my heartfelt thanks to you for your repeated kindnesses ( ) which will be gratefully ( ) by me, hoping you are well by the blessings of God and with best wishes, and compliments to Dr. Judson, Mr. and Mrs. Hough,[281] Bro. Simons,[282] and ( ) and accept the same yourself.

[Note: Signature line is unreadable.]
Pogyan English Royal Interpreter
A letter to my address and care of N. S. ( )
Doonitolah will invariably reach me.

Jan Asalun

Source: American Baptist Historical Society, AJ 17, no. 805.

[281] George and Phoebe Hough were the first missionaries to be wholly called by the American Baptist Missionary Union to work in Burmah with Adoniram and Ann Judson. Mr. Hough learned the printing trade from his father, and they set up a print shop to support the work of the mission. They arrived in Burmah in October 1816 and retired from missionary service in 1826; George Hough subsequently worked for the government as an interpreter and school superintendent, and Mrs. Hough worked as an educator. They remained friends with Adoniram Judson and many of the other missionaries. Their independence was problematical at times.

[282] Thomas Simons was born in Wales. He was ordained on December 18, 1831, after graduation from the Newton Theological Institute and was appointed to missionary service on March 7, 1831. He sailed for Burmah on June 29, 1832, arriving in Maulmain on January 1, 1833. On June 23, 1833, he married Caroline Jenks Harrington in Maulmain, probably the widow of a missionary who had died, and between 1834 and March 1843, they had six children, two of whom died in June 1839. Caroline Simons died on May 1, 1843. Mr. Simons returned to America in May 1846. While in the United States, he visited with Abby Ann Judson at Bradford Academy; she would have known him from her years in Burmah. He returned to Burmah in November 1847, arriving in Maulmain April 19, 1848. His second wife was Lydia Lillybridge, who had sailed to Burmah with Adoniram and Emily Judson; they were married in Maulmain in 1851.

George Dana Boardman[283] to Emily and Adoniram Judson, June 10, 1850 —Worcester

My very dear Parents,

I very gladly embrace the opportunity of writing you and sending by Mr. and Mrs. Wade.[284] I have been out this morning, shopping with Addy[285] and Elly[286] for the little ones in our Burman home.[287] Sister Abby[288] is I suppose, making out her bundle also; we needed her advice very much in making our selections. I saw Sister about six weeks ago. She was then very well, and appeared to be happy. She has grown to be very large, and is progressing finely in her studies. She thinks too a great deal of religious subjects. She very often says that she sometimes gets quite discouraged: for she tries to be as good as she possibly can, and for a few days she succeeds tolerably well, and then suddenly in an evil moment she yields to some temptation. This shows that her mind is seriously disposed. The Misses Hasseltine[289] were well when I was in Bradford last vacation.

My dear brothers here are very happy. They are making decided proficiency in their studies. I hope they will far enough advanced [sic] next Spring to enter the Classical School. About 3 months ago, they were very anxious about the salvation of their own souls. They spent a great deal of time in prayer. In company with several other boys, they had several little prayer-meetings. At this time I could not but help feeling that the prayers of their dear parents were about to be answered. They continued in this anxious state of mind for several weeks. They sent for Mr. Swaim,[290] our pastor, and they voluntarily rose in one of our vestry meetings and asked for the prayers of Christians. After a while these serious impressions in a great degree disappeared: But I am very happy to say, that they have been better boys

[283] See vol. 1, "Cast of Characters," s.v. "Boardman, George Dana."

[284] See vol. 1, "Cast of Characters," s.v. "Wade, The Reverend Doctor Jonathan and Deborah."

[285] See vol. 1, "Cast of Characters," s.v. "Judson, Adoniram Brown 'Addy.'"

[286] See vol. 1, "Cast of Characters," s.v. "Judson, Elnathan 'Elly.'"

[287] This reference is to Henry Hall Judson, almost eight years old, and Edward Judson, almost five and a half years old, the youngest surviving children of Adoniram and Sarah Hall Boardman Judson and stepbrothers of George Dana Boardman. This also refers to Emily Frances Judson, almost two and a half years old, the daughter of Adoniram and Emily Judson. She was not a blood relation to George Boardman.

[288] See vol. 1, "Cast of Characters," s.v. "Judson, Abby Ann."

[289] The family of Ann Hasseltine Judson, who continued to be connected with Bradford Academy in Bradford, Massachusetts. In a letter to Abby Ann written November 26, 1848, Adoniram spoke of the generosity of the Hasseltine family in all that they were doing for her.

[290] The Reverend Doctor Samuel Swaim was born in Pemberton, New Jersey, in June 1809. He finished his college courses at Brown University and then entered Newton Theological Institution. He taught college studies in Granville, Ohio, before receiving a call as pastor of the First Baptist Church in Worcester, Massachusetts. In October 1851, just as she was returning to America, Dr. Swaim wrote Emily about the possible baptism of Elnathan. He spoke of Elnathan's coming to faith and of his meeting with the church requesting baptism, and he was obviously trying to schedule this important event at a time when Emily could be present. Apparently this did not work out, for Elnathan and Adoniram were not baptized until September 1852. The Judson children had all been together in Hamilton, New York, for a number of weeks that summer, and the boys were baptized on September 5. Abby Ann was baptized the following December.

since the time I speak of, than they were before. I cannot help believing that work of grace has been commenced in their hearts, and I fervently pray, that ere long they may give unquestionable evidence of having passed from death unto life.

We think of having a fine time in our next vacation. Grandmother Boardman is very anxious to see us. Our plan now is, for sister, Addy and Elly, Aunt N.[291] and myself to go and spend 4 or 5 weeks in New Sharon.[292] The Misses H. have given their full consent to let Abby go. We hope that the trip will do us good, and we are sure that no tour could be more delightful.

Uncle N.[293] is very busy indeed. His practice is very extensive, and the time which he can spare from his professional duties, is directed to the Medical College. As soon as he has liquidated their debts for the new house, I hope that he will have more leisure.

I came here Saturday, to spend a few days at home on account of ill health. I have found in this country the best of friends. The people of Salem are very generous, and it is owing to their Christian kindness that I am enabled to pursue my collegiate studies.[294] I am particularly indebted to a Miss ( ) and to Mr. Michael Shepherd, whom you probably know, for the generous interest which they take in my welfare. Brown University is about to undergo a revolution. The present system at the advice of President W.[295] is to yield to the system of the German Universities, that is instruction will be imparted mostly in the form of lectures—( ) will be abolished, rooming in college will not be allowed. There seems to be some doubts among the people here, as to the feasibility of the President's plans; time only will determine. I often hear the Dr. speak of you with a great deal of interest.

I suppose you have seen the new edition of mother's Memoir[296]—the notes are spoken of as having much value to the work. I spent several days last vacation with

[291] Mrs. Newton, the wife of Dr. Calvin Newton.

[292] Just before leaving for Burmah in July 1846, Adoniram made a trip to Maine to see the family of George Dana Boardman; he returned with promises that the Boardman family would provide for the education of young Boardman.

[293] See vol. 1, "Cast of Characters," s.v. "Newton, Doctor Calvin and Mrs. M. I."

[294] When Adoniram Judson returned to America in 1845 following the death of Sarah Hall Boardman Judson, he immediately went to Salem, Massachusetts, to meet with some of the members of her family. These family members of young George Boardman's mother are likely giving him this support. We also know from the correspondence that, shortly before his marriage to Emily Chubbuck in 1846, Adoniram Judson made a trip to Maine to speak with the Boardman relatives there. He wrote to Emily on the return trip, saying that he had raised sufficient funds from them to cover the costs of George Boardman's education. See the letter of Adoniram Judson to Emily E. Chubbuck dated April 15, 1846.

[295] Dr. Francis Wayland was the president of Brown University in Providence, Rhode Island. A prominent Baptist leader and active in denominational activities, he was a proponent of missions. In 1851, upon Emily's return from Burmah, Dr. Wayland was asked to write the definitive memoir of Adoniram Judson. Beginning in December that year, Emily moved to Providence to work with him on the project; she was there until June and then returned frequently over the next year before it was finally published in September 1853. A warm friendship developed between Dr. Wayland and Emily.

[296] Fanny Forester, *Memoir of Sarah B. Judson, Member of the American Mission to Burmah* (New York: L. Colby and Company, 1848). An expanded edition with notes written by Emily Judson had recently been published.

Dea. Lincoln[297] in Boston. I rec'd a letter from sister Abby not long since, in which she says that Aunt Abbygail[298] [sic] is as well as usual. I saw Mrs. Cutter a little while ago, and had a very pleasant interview with Mrs. Sutton last Thursday. Mr. ( ) son, who is in college, has just been converted.

[Written in the right margin of the address page:] There is one thing, my dear Parents, that I want to do above all others and that is to visit St. Helena.[299] I would be very willing to go before the mast in any ship bound for that port. I do want to visit my sainted mother's grave. I hope that the day is not far distant when I may be able to do it. All the love I can send, I want you to share between yourselves, and the darling little ones in your family. May He who has ever been my Father, ever be theirs. Your very affectionate son,

G.D.B.

Source: American Baptist Historical Society, AJ 11, no. 409.

Emily C. Judson to Anna Maria Anable, June 20, 1850—Maulmain

My dear Ninny,[300]

I am almost too poorly to write you this month, being too weak to go from the bed to my big chair without assistance. My Heavenly Father is trying me (don't you think so?) very severely, and what will be the end of all these things I do not know. It is eleven weeks today since my husband was carried away from the house, as the dead are carried, and looking more like a dead than a living man—and no news. Oh, you cannot imagine how slowly the days and weeks roll around—if I could only know he is living at this moment! Is not such anxiety torturing? There is reason to hope for a letter next month, but it may not come, and even the month after. I beg of the doctor and the mission to let me follow before hearing, but they will not listen to me. I suppose they have really but *very* little hope for him.

[297] This could be either Joshua Lincoln, partner in the publishing firm of Gould, Randall and Lincoln, or the Honorable Heman Lincoln; both were prominent Baptists from the Boston, Massachusetts, area.

[298] Abigail Brown Judson, the sister of Adoniram Judson, lived in Plymouth, Massachusetts. A spinster of eccentric character and behavior, she was a beneficiary of her parents' considerable wealth. Her father had wisely invested in land and bank stocks; with the help of Esq. Loud, she had invested that money prudently. She took a strong interest in Adoniram's children and offered them considerable support—though not often without complaint or comment—for their clothing and education in the years to come.

[299] St. Helena was where Sarah Hall Boardman Judson, George's mother, died on the way home from Burmah to the United States. The date of her death was September 1, 1845; she was buried there on the Island.

[300] "Ninny" was a name of endearment given to Anna Maria Anable by her most intimate friends at the Utica Female Academy. Emily was "Nemmy."

Did Lydia[301] tell you anything about my confinement? You did well to spare your congratulations[302] on account of poor Charley,[303] for after costing both of us inexpressibly dear, and destroying (I have been greatly reduced by flooding) at least for a time, my hopes of renewed health, he did not stay to comfort the heart of his poor lonely mother. He was a beautiful child, *so* like his dear papa! And full size, only very thin, as though he had pined and died by inches. The suffering, which of right belonged all to me fell upon his delicate little frame, and crushed his life.[304] Mrs. Stevens[305] even imagined she could see of look of sorrow and maturity in the little face, which does not belong to an infant. As I write, it occurs to me that you may not know how to sympathize with me in this loss, which is indeed to me very, very great. It is also enhanced by the circumstances of his poor papa. *His* son!—the other boys[306] are his too, and I love them dearly, but they cannot, you know, be altogether mine.

I was confined prematurely (by fifteen or twenty days) on the 22nd April. I was taken in a very alarming way, and lived almost by a miracle. Did Lydia tell you what a party I had?—people of six different nations, men and women, married and unmarried. How different from Frances'[307] debut when there was none but my husband present. Well, I was so dangerously ill that it was not expected I would recover rapidly, if I did at all, so though very poorly now, I am as comfortable as could be expected. Mr. and Mrs. Stevens come in every day—Mrs. S. sits with me a great deal, and is just like a loving, sympathetic sister. By the way, I am watching the door now lest she should come in and catch me writing. I have her orders not to write any letters this month. All in the mission are very kind to me, but they cannot prevent the house from being very desolate, nor my heart from aching. Oh, Ninny, how I do wish you were here!

I am very glad to hear that you are so happy and prosperous[308]—my thot's are a great deal with you now-a-days, more than when I too was happy. The composition you send is very excellent, indeed,[309]—if I did not love my sorrows, better than joys in which thoughts of *him* have no part, I should almost envy you the task of training

[301] See vol. 1, "Cast of Characters," s.v. "Lillybridge, Lydia." See also "A Timeline of the Life and Mission of Lydia Lillybridge Simons" and the Lillybridge papers in the appendices.

[302] See the letter of Anna Maria Anable to Emily C. Judson dated March 24, 1850.

[303] Charles Judson, named after Emily's father, Charles Chubbuck, was stillborn on April 23, 1850.

[304] See the letter of Emily C. Judson to Adoniram Judson dated May 20, 1850. In that letter, she expressed the same thoughts.

[305] See vol. 1, "Cast of Characters," s.v. "Stevens, Elizabeth 'Bessie.'"

[306] Henry Hall Judson, almost eight years old, and Edward Judson, almost five and a half years old.

[307] Emily Frances Judson was born December 24, 1847.

[308] In fall 1848, Anna Maria Anable left Utica, New York, and the Utica Female Academy and moved to Philadelphia to start the Misses Anable's School with her mother, Mrs. Alma Sheldon Anable; her Aunt Cynthia Sheldon; and her sisters Harriet, Fanny, and Mary. Letters over the previous two years showed a gradual but increasing enrollment.

[309] Emily had been the composition teacher at the Utica Female Academy, and there were many occasions held when the students would read their work. Anna Maria continued that practice with the Misses Anable's School and regularly sent compositions to Emily for her to read and to indicate to her some of the success she was enjoying with her students.

such beautiful minds. Oh, how little can you imagine the degradation, the gross brutality of woman here!

I sh'd like to tell you something of Mr. Dawson,[310] only the least said about people the better. One thing I can perhaps say with safety, that there is not a missionary here but would regret his coming. Moreover, he never was a doctor here, only a very low apothecary—he picked up the title where the English say everybody can get titles, in Yankee-land. The Board knows very well why they don't send him. And now while I am on the subject—Mrs. Kincaid[311] is not the daughter of an officer—that is, a commissioned one, though everybody here says she was uncommonly refined etc. for a person of her class. You think Mr. J. did not like Mr. K. and perhaps he had reasons—but one thing I can assure you, I never heard him pray so fervently for his own prosperity and success, as he did for Mr. K's during the last six months he was with me. Oh, Ninny, how I wish you could know that holy man as I do! But you will know him one of these days in heaven,—and perhaps he is even now there waiting for us. When I think of that I do not regret my present weakness—it would be dreadful to think of living without him. But then the children!—the little things are very well now, and happy too. You say you "shipped a box" etc. in February. Do you mean to say that *you* actually *shipped* it, or that you sent it to the mission rooms to be shipped, because it will probably make some five or six months' difference in the time of my receiving it. If I hear good news, and go to Bourbon I shall stand greatly in need of some of the things. How kind of you to think of the wrappers, they are so comfortable. I wish my poor invalid had his now. Do you know it is my intention to follow Mr. J. with the children and Burmese Assistants, if I hear he is convalescent? By the way, the box reminds me of your apron. We have just heard that the vessel in which the Howards[312] sailed was wrecked off the Mauritius. The passengers and crew were saved, but the cargo, including part of the wardrobe, was lost. Mother[313] and Kate[314] were sufferers to the amount of

[310] See vol. 1, "Cast of Characters," s.v. "Dawson, Doctor."

[311] See vol. 1, "Cast of Characters," s.v. "Kincaid, The Reverend Doctor Eugenio."

[312] Hosea and Theresa Howard first sailed for Burmah in 1834, arriving in December that year. Hosea Howard was a recent graduate of the theological seminary in Hamilton, New York. They were stationed in Maulmain as missionaries with Adoniram Judson, and he claimed in a letter to Emily that he worked there with Adoniram longer than any other missionary. Mr. Howard's responsibility was to run schools that the mission maintained, a task in which he was ably assisted by his wife. Lydia Lillybridge was responsible to Mr. and Mrs. Howard when she arrived in November 1846. Mr. and Mrs. Howard left Maulmain for the United States in February 1850.

[313] Emily's mother, Lavinia Richards Chubbuck, was born June 1, 1785, at Goffstown, New Hampshire, the eldest of thirteen children. She married Charles Chubbuck on November 17, 1805, at Goffstown, New Hampshire. Four of her children were born at Goffstown and moved with Charles and Lavinia Chubbuck to Eaton, New York, in September 1816; they were Lavinia, Benjamin, Harriet, and John Walker. Sarah Catharine, Emily, and Wallace were all born in Eaton.

[314] Sarah Catharine Chubbuck, "Kate," "Kit," or "Kitty" was Emily's older sister by ten months. Outside of the two terms at the Utica Female Academy, which Emily arranged for her, Catharine always lived at home with her parents in Hamilton, New York. The letters indicate opportunities for marriage, but she, for unknown reasons, remained single. She later helped to care for Henry and Edward Judson after their return from Burmah in fall 1851 when they moved into the Hamilton home with their "aunt" and "grandparents," and she was remembered by them as "dear old Aunt Kate—a dear friend."

thirty-five or forty dollars, being the worth of a box I was sending them. Your loss was a splendiferous Chinese apron, which Mr. J. hesitated about letting me send, because he thought it was not a "missionary present." You see he is always right, and my love of finery is punished. It was a Mazarine blue silk, figured, and *so* thick! I never saw anything like it in America. Then it was loaded with the richest kind of white embroidery, not the over shot work, but another stitch—I don't know what they call it. Every one [sic] at the mission had sent some thing [sic], more or less, to friends at home, so we are all in the "same category."

Does Mrs. Gillette,[315] or Mrs. Robarts,[316] or anybody in P. ever speak of me? Give my love to the G's and R's at any rate, and tell them I want to write them very much indeed, but must defer it still a little longer. Dear Aunt Cynthia,[317] too! I owe her two letters, to both of which I am really anxious to reply—especially the one in which she inquires after the Karen boy "Sheldon."[318] Tell her not to trouble herself in the least about him.

Is'nt [sic] this a long letter for a sick woman to write? I have rested a great many times, and so the affair will be very disjointed, I dare say, but, Ninny, you don't know what a relief it is to scratch away to you, even though it is about nothing but Chinese aprons and transmogrified apothecaries. I am heart-sick at the protracted loneliness and desolation. You would pray for me, I know, if you could see me as I am, but *pray* darling, even though you cannot see. I have a sad foreboding that I shall stand greatly in need of your prayers when you read this. Either alone with my helpless little ones upon the ocean, or alone in the wide, cold world. Pray for me, every day,—for there is now nobody on earth to watch over poor

Nemmy

(P.S.) I wish you had sent a bill of the things I wrote for, so that I could give you an order for the money. I hope you will not neglect it next month. I want amazingly to tell you a little secret about Lydia, but don't, pray, allude to it until authorized by something from her. Mr. Simons[319] has been pursuing her for along time, and it would not astonish anyone if he sh'd be successful. Her icy heart certainly begins to thaw. He is too vulgar a man for Lydia, and has no mind whatever, but he is very good-

[315] See vol. 1, "Cast of Characters," s.v. "Gillette, The Reverend A. (Abram) D. (Dunn) and Hannah."

[316] See vol. 1, "Cast of Characters," s.v. "Robarts, Mr. and Mrs. W. S."

[317] See vol. 1, "Cast of Characters," s.v. "Sheldon, Miss Cynthia."

[318] Apparently supporting this Burmese child was problematic for Miss Sheldon, for Emily had also addressed this earlier in a letter to Anna Maria dated February 19, 1850. Emily explained that Miss Sheldon should not be concerned, that sponsoring individual children was a fund-raising technique, that the money raised went into the mission's general fund, and that support for children and children's programs came through the institutional budgets. The issue speaks well to Miss Sheldon's kind and generous heart, as well as less-than-honest efforts to raise funds. See Emily's letter to Miss Sheldon dated August 9, 1850, for Emily's full explanation.

[319] See vol. 1, "Cast of Characters," s.v. "Lillybridge, Lydia." Also, "A Timeline of the Life and Mission of Lydia Lillybridge Simons."

natured and would be kind to her. I think he is very much in love. Now don't mention this so that Martha[320] will hear of it, for if you do it will come straight back.

Source: Hanna family files.

Emily C. Judson to Adoniram Judson, June 21, 1850—Maulmain

My dearest Love,

Still in suspense—still hoping, fearing, longing for news, and trembling lest it should come.[321] If I could only see you—if I could only know for a certainty that I should ever see you again in this world, how happy I should be. I wonder if you think much of me, if you pray for me—oh, what a world of misery this is!

I am not getting up so well from my confinement[322] as I seemed to be a month ago, but still I shall be well enough to come to you as soon as I hear, and the voyage will do me good. About three weeks ago I was attacked by a bowel complaint, which is making me very weak, but I hope the doctor has about overcome it. The doctor is very kind to me, and so are the dear Stevens';[323]—when you come back, I hope you will always love them for my sake. They act as though they could not do enough. The children are in excellent health, and growing finely. They are a great comfort to me. They are much more quiet about the house than they used to be, and both Henry[324] and Edward[325] are very fond of their books. Baby[326] too, every day brings her book to me and says, "Mamma, read me." They all of them remember "dear papa" and never so happy as when talking about you.

I have just heard, this month, of the wreck of the Madura. Is it not strange? Do you remember how we used to talk about it? Next time I send a box[327] I will not send by ( ). Capt. White is so schocked [sic] and conscience-stricken at the thought of

[320] See vol. 1, "Cast of Characters," s.v. "Lillybridge, Martha."

[321] On April 3, 1850, Adoniram Judson had been carried on board the *Aristide Marie*, a ship bound for the Isle of Bourbon; the trip was his only hope of survival. The last time Emily had seen him was April 6, and she would not hear of his death until the middle of August, a long, long four months after he sailed.

[322] On April 23, Emily gave birth to a stillborn son, Charles Judson, named after her father. See her letter of May 20, 1850. Her recovery had been long and slow.

[323] Edward and Elizabeth Stevens were missionaries to Burmah. They arrived in Maulmain, Burmah, in February 1838. There are twenty-four letters in the correspondence from them. Mrs. Stevens took Edward Judson into her home when Sarah and Adoniram had to leave for the United States in 1845, and her care and nurture saved his life. The home of Elizabeth and Edward Stevens burned to the ground in 1847, and two trunks being stored for Adoniram and Emily were destroyed; these trunks held all of their excess clothes and precious mementos, which they had not wanted to bring to Rangoon with them. Mr. Stevens buried Charles Chubbuck (Emily's "Angel Charley") in April 1850. Edward Stevens also accepted the responsibility of finishing the dictionary after the death of Adoniram Judson.

[324] See vol. 1, "Cast of Characters," s.v. "Judson, Henry Hall."

[325] See vol. 1, "Cast of Characters," s.v. "Judson, Edward."

[326] See vol. 1, "Cast of Characters," s.v. "Judson, Emily Frances."

[327] See Emily's letter to Anna Maria Anable dated June 20, 1850; she speaks in detail of a box that was lost on this ship, and some of what was in it for her friends in the United States.

having allowed his wife to go alone that he is going over land to meet her in England. People speak of it as a very mad freak, because if he goes, he will lose his place.

Mr. Stilson[328] has been slowly picking up since last month, and though probably he will never be well, is able to take an occasional short drive. Letters from Mr. Abbott[329] speak very discouragingly of his health. He has had another turn of bleeding—in the throat *he* says. Mr. Simons'[330] and Lydia's[331] affairs are creeping on slowly—I think there is every prospect of its being a match, but doubt whether they will ever be happy. Mr. Moore[332] of Arracan (this is a secret, however,) has offered himself to Lydia and been, of course, rejected. Mr. Bennett's[333] health is not at all good—he has every now and then an attack of fever. It is said they are thinking of another visit to America. There is a suspicion too that the Masons[334] think of going. His health is a very little better. I suppose Mrs. Ranney[335] writes all these things and many more than I know, for I am not in a way to pick up much news.

Our letters from home this month are as uninteresting as they well could be. Nothing from the children.[336] My father[337] was able to get about the house a little, and that was all.[338] Wallace[339] had become editor and proprietor of a *Whig* paper (!) and was boarding at home. [Note: Two words have been marked out.] Kate[340] writes that he is doing well and is very kind to them all. A Circular has come announcing the result of the great meeting in New York. The amount of all is, more attention sh'd be given to preaching, less to books and teaching, and scarcely any *if any* to be teaching English. This last point the Com. do not venture to decide, but it is evident that their leaning is altogether against English. Did I tell you Lewis Colby[341] sent

[328] See vol. 1, "Cast of Characters," s.v. "Stilson, Lucretia and Lyman."

[329] See vol. 1, "Cast of Characters," s.v. "Abbott, The Reverend Elisha Litchfield and Ann P. Gardner."

[330] See vol. 1, "Cast of Characters," s.v. "Simons, Lydia and Thomas."

[331] See vol. 1, "Cast of Characters," s.v. "Lillybridge, Lydia." Also, "A Timeline of the Life and Mission of Lydia Lillybridge Simons."

[332] Calvin Moore was born in Massachusetts in 1818, educated at Madison University and Hamilton Theological Institute, and ordained at Stillwater, New York, in 1848. His first wife was Laura C. Frish, and they arrived at Akyab on March 15, 1849. Mrs. Moore died on November 5, 1849, following childbirth. Mr. Moore's second wife was Emily Frances Whitehead; they were married January 6, 1851, at Calcutta. They had two children, both of whom became missionaries in Assam. Mr. and Mrs. Moore returned to the United States, leaving Burmah on August 9, 1854. Mr. Moore's third wife was Sophia Hubbell Knapp, the widow of missionary H. E. Knapp; they were married in June 1876.

[333] See vol. 1, "Cast of Characters," s.v. "Bennett, The Reverend Cephas and Stella Kneeland."

[334] See vol. 1, "Cast of Characters," s.v. "Mason, The Reverend Francis, Helen, and Ellen."

[335] Maria Gager Ranney arrived in Maulmain in May 1844. Her husband Thomas was the superintendent of the printing press and business manager for the missionary compound. A letter from Lydia Lillybridge reveals that Mrs. Ranney had some responsibilities in the mission schools. She had no children; Maria Ranney died on April 26, 1857.

[336] Abby Ann Judson in Bradford, Massachusetts; Adoniram and Elnathan Judson, in Worcester, Massachusetts.

[337] Emily's father. See vol. 1, "Cast of Characters," s.v. "Chubbuck, Charles."

[338] On December 28, 1849, Catharine Chubbuck wrote that their father, Charles Chubbuck, had suffered a serious fall in the barn.

[339] See vol. 1, "Cast of Characters," s.v. "Chubbuck, W. Wallace."

[340] See vol. 1, "Cast of Characters," s.v. "Chubbuck, Sarah Catharine."

[341] See vol. 1, "Cast of Characters," s.v. "Colby, Lewis."

his acc. last month?—one edition of the Memoir with notes[342] sold. This month your acc'ts from the House in Calcutta have been rec'd.

This is a very stupid letter I know, my darling, but only write and tell me you are getting well, and you shall see how smart and witty I can be. Oh, I think such news would make a new woman of me—both mind and body. Pray for me, darling, continually, and love me, for I have nobody else in the world to love me, nobody. Oh, you don't know how desolate my letters from America make me feel. I have no interest there any longer and here—what is before me I don't know. May God bless you, and restore you to your loving family, is the unceasing prayer of

Yours forever & ever

Emily C.J.

Source: Hanna family files.

[342] Fanny Forester, *Memoir of Sarah B. Judson, Member of the American Mission to Burmah* (New York: L. Colby and Company, 1848). This was a new addition with the addition of nearly sixty pages of notes that Emily had compiled.

Letters

July–December 1850

Mrs. Susan R. S. Benjamin to Emily C. Judson, July 7, 1850—Mergui

Dear Sister Judson,

It is only a few days since the steamer left, that I was disappointed in not sending you a line and now I begin in season to make it sure next time. We are not privileged like you, to know precisely when to expect the steamer, so that we are obliged to do nearly all our visiting beforehand, as she usually comes in one day and goes out the next. But my sister, I have nothing special to write. I only wish to express the deep sympathy I feel for you in your present afflictive circumstances. If I were in your situation I don't know how I should bear it. When *Judson*[1] leaves me, in health, for a short jungle tour I am sad and lonely enough. But, I trust God is strengthening you according to your day and that you are able to commit your dear absent husband to God so perfectly, that no burdensome thought remains. You *feel* that God will do right and are ready to say, "thy will be done." That it may be His will to return your beloved companion in restored health is my earnest prayer for your sake and for the sake of your dear children[2] and for the cause he has so long and faithfully served.

The illness of others of our beloved missionary friends and the prevalence of disease among the people are matters too which should bring us before God. We have had, at this station actually no missionary work this season, in either department. Br. Brayton[3] has had no school and we commenced one a few days ago, with only seven scholars, two or three of these have returned to the jungle and three are sick, leaving a large school of two! Br. Brayton who has been twelve years in the mission, says he never saw such a time. It may be the best thing that could have occurred for him, for he has never been in such poor health. We have greatly feared he would be obliged to try the advantage of a change and we should be left alone, but just now he seems to be better.

My own health which at one time I had nearly given up for lost is becoming quite established and our dear little daughter lives and thrives beyond all our expectations, but she has no teeth though and I fear yet some serious difficulty in

[1] Judson Benjamin was born February 2, 1819, in Rodman, New York. He was baptized in Franklin, Indiana; graduated from Brown University and Newton Theological Seminary; and was ordained on October 13, 1848, in Providence, Rhode Island. He married Susan Ruggles Stone on September 3, 1848, and they departed for Tavoy, Burma, on October 21, 1848. They arrived at Tavoy in April 1849; in March 1850, they were sent to Mergui. Mr. Benjamin collected a vocabulary of 1,200 Salong words. They sailed from Rangoon to Boston on January 21, 1854, and Rev. Benjamin died in Boston of pulmonary disease in February 1855. Susan Benjamin remarried William Ward, and they left from Boston in June 1860 to return to Burmah.

[2] Children in Burmah included Henry Hall Judson, eight years old; Edward Judson, five and a half years old; and Emily Frances Judson, two and a half years old.

[3] The Reverend Durlin L. Brayton was born in Hubbardton, Vermont, on October 27, 1808. He graduated from Brown University and then the Newton Theological Seminary in 1837, at which time he was appointed to missionary service. On October 2, 1837, he married Mary Hawley Fuller, and they sailed for Burmah on October 28, 1837. They arrived in April 1838 and, passing through Amherst and Maulmain, arrived at Mergui in April 1840. In February 1847, they departed Maulmain for America due to Mrs. Brayton's ill health. Mr. Brayton returned to Burmah the following November, and Mrs. Brayton remained in America until arriving back in Burmah in March 1850. They had one daughter, Mary. Mary Brayton died December 16, 1890, in Rangoon; Durlin Brayton died April 23, 1900, also in Rangoon.

consequence.[4] You will remember dear sister that I have but just become a mother and in this near and solemn relation need your prayers. May God be with and grant you strength for the performance of your duties and grace sufficient for every trial is the sincere prayer of your

Affection sister

S. R. S. Benjamin

Source: American Baptist Historical Society, AJ 12, no. 346.

Mrs. Urania Sheldon Nott to Emily C. Judson, July 8, 1850—Union College

My dear Emily

I have heard with deep sympathy of the illness of your dear husband—and feel much for your affliction—I trust he is long before this restored to you—and to his accustomed walks of usefulness—and that you have been safely carried thro' your hour of trial. "Afflictions spring not from the dust" and the Christian should remember that God has said," Whom he loveth he chastiseth." It is thro' such tribulation that the saints are made meet for heaven—I trust you have been supported—and can say "it was good for me that I have been afflicted."

I have known the anguish of seeing my precious husband suffer month after month, and I might almost say year after year, intensely, but it has pleased God to restore him once more to health. Soon after he began to recover—more than a year since, I wrote you a long letter and directed it to Mr. Carr of the Boston Mission Rooms[5]—I trust it reached you in due time—

[4] There is a record of a son born to Judson and Stella Benjamin in August 1851. There is also a note that two other children died in infancy.

[5] See the letter from Mrs. Urania Sheldon Nott to Emily C. Judson dated March 15, 1849.

[6] Harriet or "Hatty" or "Hattie" or "Hat" Anable was one of nine children born to Joseph and Alma Anable, and was a niece to Miss Cynthia Sheldon and Mrs. Urania Sheldon Nott. In 1841, she had added a note to a letter written by Miss Cynthia Sheldon to Emily. As early as November 1842 she was away, and a letter from Emily to Catharine Chubbuck said that "she (Miss Sheldon) expected that Hat would return as accomplished as Anna Maria." Her trips away were both educational and employment, as she worked as a private tutor in families that would bring her into their homes. In August 1843, she had just returned from Beonsen, in the vicinity of New Orleans, and was engaged to go again. A letter from Anna Maria on January 6, 1845, said that she would stay South for another year. About this time Miss Cynthia Sheldon mentioned her concern for Hatty's spiritual health. In May 1845 she was in New Orleans. She was home again in summer 1846, but a September 27 letter from Anna Maria said she had been asked by Mr. Roman with some urgency to return and she thought that she should. She was to return home from New Orleans in January 1849 after Anna Maria Anable had started the Misses Anable's School in Philadelphia in fall 1848. Harriet was fluent in French, having placed herself earlier in a French environment in New Orleans. Hatty died in 1858.

Harriet[6] has been spending a week with me—and leaves tomorrow for Boston—she will be the bearer of this so far—I met her at Mary Adams'[7] wedding in New York—Mary is very well married—Mary Pearson is very well—she has three nice boys—We are enjoying delicious strawberries—which your good husband loved so much—I wish I could send you a nice bucket—but such wishes are vain.

May God bless your and yours and long span the lives of yours and husband—with your little ones.[8]

Ever your affectionate friend

Urania E. Nott

Source: American Baptist Historical Society, AJ 25, no. 1227.

Miss Mary Anna Longstreth to Emily C. Judson,[9] July 15, 1850—Philadelphia

My dear friend,

Emily C. Judson

Our hearts were overwhelmed with sorrow on the arrival of thy last letter to Anna Maria.[10] Such sad accounts of thy dear Husband's health,[11] and your agonizing separation. O the suffering of those four days, while the vessel was delayed, and the daily partings! It seems to me it must have been a daily dying to both. The impossibility of going with him, and the anguish of staying without him—All these things we have thought of again and again, with the deepest, tenderest sympathy. But I must not recall to thee this period of deep affliction. I hope by the time this letter reaches thee, a brighter day will have dawned, and the long night of sorrow be remembered but in thankfulness for its removal. What a blessed thing it is that

[7] Mary Adams was related to the Utica Female Academy. Her letter to Emily in October 1845 was almost a whimsical piece of fantasy with literary pretensions. It would reflect a fairly close relationship. A second letter in December 1845 was similar. The letters were written from New Orleans, and she spoke of Hatty Anable as being near to her. On January 29, 1849, Anna Maria Anable wrote, "Hatty says Mary Adams is going to marry Gardner Green of Norwich,—a very fine young man, of invention, fortune, piety and all that Mary's heart was sighed for." On July 8, 1850, Mrs. Urania Sheldon Nott spoke of attending this wedding in New York.

[8] Henry Hall Judson, eight years old; Edward Judson, five and a half years old; and Emily Frances Judson, two and a half years old.

[9] Though this is a loving letter, it must also have brought considerable pain to Emily. As this was written, Adoniram Judson had already died at sea, and the impending birth of a baby prevented Emily from accompanying him on his journey and had resulted in the stillborn birth of Charles Judson ("Angel Charley"). The assurances in the letter that Adoniram must be spared and the mention of baby articles to be received in another package, surely brought reminders of terrible loss and grief.

[10] Anna Maria Anable was the niece of the Misses Urania and Cynthia Sheldon and the daughter of Joseph and Alma Sheldon Anable. Emily first met Anna Maria in fall 1840 when she went as a student to the Utica Female Academy; both Emily and Anna Maria became members of the faculty there. In these years, Anna Maria became Emily's dearest friend, and the extensive correspondence between the two reflects sensitive, flirtatious spirits and a deep intimacy. Emily was "Nemmy" to Anna Maria's "Ninny." In 1848, Anna Maria Anable, with the help of her extended family, moved to Philadelphia and started the Misses Anable's School in Philadelphia. At Emily's death in 1854, Anna Maria was given guardianship of Emily Frances Judson, daughter of Emily and Adoniram Judson.

although "remembered *joys* are *never past*," our *afflictions* and *trials lose* their bitterness in the recollection and we can think of them calmly, sometimes even joyfully. By this time I trust thy confinement is safely over, an other [sic] sweet *bird*[12] is nestling under they maternal wing. I hope, too, that thy beloved Husband is improving. I can not [sic] think, dear Emily, that it is our Heavenly Father's will to take him from thee during your separation. Even if his health should not be restored, I trust his life will be prolonged to return to thee and gladden once more thy affectionate heart. But let us hope for more than this—even that he is to be spared to his family and the church, and to labor for years to come in the cause that is dearer to him than life itself.

Tell Henry[13] and Edward[14] their "other Aunt Anna" does not forget them, but thinks of them very often. I have made for each of them a Picture Book, which will, I think, please them. I send dear little Emmy[15] a doll with a porcelain head. Tell her she can wash its face as often as she pleases, without spoiling it. I wish Emmy to have her choice of the two dolls sent, and the other to be given to any one of the missionary children you prefer. I was thinking of the little *Masons*[16]—but if there is a missionary's child that is *lame* or in *delicate health*, I should like the preference to be given to *such a one*.

Anna Maria, knowing the heartfelt interest I take in your welfare, and the sympathy that our whole family feel in your joys and sorrows, is very kind in

[11] This refers to Emily's letter to Anna Maria Anable dated April 15, 1850.

[12] On January 1, 1848, eight days after the birth of Emily Frances Judson, Emily wrote a celebratory poem that she called "My Bird." The poem has a total of seven stanzas, and it was widely published in the United States.

[13] Henry Hall Judson, born July 8, 1842, was the son of Adoniram and Sarah Hall Boardman Judson. Henry was the sixth of their eight children and the fourth of five who survived. He remained in Burmah in 1845 when Adoniram and Sarah returned to the United States with the three older children. He returned with Emily in 1851 and went to live with her family in Hamilton, New York. Henry attended Brown University and Williams Collage; he enlisted in the army at the time of the Civil War in January 1864. Later that year, he experienced a debilitating accident attributed either to sunstroke or a horse kicking him in the head. He was married once—unhappily according to his own correspondence—and he eventually died in a veteran's home in 1918, the last of his siblings to die. Of this, the chaplain noted, "The end was a genuine example of Christian fortitude." See Rosalie Hall Hunt, *Bless God and Take Courage, The Judson Legacy* (Valley Forge: Judson Press, 2005) 291.

[14] Edward Judson, born December 27, 1844, in Maulmain, Burmah, was the eighth child of Adoniram and Sarah Hall Boardman Judson and the fifth of their children to survive. Only a few months old when Sarah and Adoniram returned to America, Edward's life was saved by the nurture and care he received from Elizabeth Stevens. He loved Emily as the only "Mama" he had ever known and returned with her to the United States in October 1851. Edward, who was Eddy to his family, became a minister; he did mission work with the immigrants in New York City, and with the aid of the Rockefeller Family, he built the Judson Memorial Baptist Church in what is now Washington Park.

[15] Emily Frances Judson, the daughter of Adoniram and Emily Chubbuck Judson, was born December 24, 1847. Emily married the Reverend Thomas Alexander Thomson (T. A. T.) Hanna in 1870, and they had eight children, two of whom served as missionaries in Burmah.

[16] Francis Mason arrived in Maulmain in November 1830 and transferred to Tavoy in 1831. His first wife died, and he married Helen Maria Griggs just before leaving the United States. She died in Burmah in 1846; they were the parents of four children. A skilled linguist, Mr. Mason was fluent in twelve languages and translated the Scripture into two of the Karen dialects. In spring 1847, Mr. Mason was seriously ill, and the other missionaries were concerned about him. In September 1847, he remarried, and Adoniram Judson officiated at the ceremony. His new wife was Ellen Huntley Bullard; originally from Vermont, she was the widow of Edwin Bullard, missionary to Burmah. Francis Mason died March 3, 1874, in Rangoon.

informing us when she hears from you. She is now enjoying a great treat at Boston in the society of the missionaries[17] who are about to embark for India.

I hope the books, etc. sent, (a list of which I will send in this letter) will arrive safely. I should like to know whether the knives, scissors, and needles, bear the voyage without rusting. Hoping all the articles will be of use to thee, my dear friend, we beg thy acceptance of them as tokens of our affectionate remembrance. May the God of all consolation continually strengthen, support, and comfort thee. Mayst [sic] thou *feel* his arm to be around and underneath thee, while thou art passing through the deep waters, and may he enable thee to sing his praise on the banks of deliverance. Farewell.

Most sincerely and affectionately,

Mary Anna Longstreth

Elizabeth Fry—2 vols.
Songs in the night
T. Fowell Buxton
Picture Book—Scripture Guide—and a small book—Henry
Picture Book—"Here a little" etc. Christmas Tree—Edward
2 dolls—Fanny and Dash—A.B.C. book—Emily Frances
Ladies' Companion—knife—scissors—tape—bobbin—
Pearl buttons—linen buttons—sewing silk—needles
White and black thread—darning cotton—galloon—
Old castile soap—1/2 lb. sealing wax
3 dozen lead pencils
6 penknives
1 box Gillott's pens
from M. A. Longstreth

1 dozen spools of cotton
1 box of pins—4 sizes
Diaper pins—
Comb and brush
Baby's brush and combs—

[17] On July 25, 1850, the *Washington Allston* had sailed from Boston Harbor with a large group of new and returning missionaries, including Mr. and Mrs. Kincaid, Mr. and Mrs. Wade, and Dr. and Mrs. Dawson. The ship was a chartered vessel enabling the American Baptist Missionary Union to send the group directly to Maulmain, Burmah. According to the correspondence, it turned out to be a disastrous trip, with much of the problem the fault of the captain. From Mrs. Hough's letter of May 20, 1851, we gather that there were too many passengers and not enough supplies, among other problems. The ship, according to Emily Judson (February 23, 1851), "entered the mouth of the Salwen [River] just as [her] steamer was leaving it" bound for Calcutta. Emily said that she visited with the Kincaids and Mrs. Vinton in Calcutta, for they had come in on the *Tudor* "from the Cape"—apparently some of the passengers had left the *Washington Allston* en route.

Flask of Farina Cologne Water
from Susan Longstreth

When thy dear husband returns, please give him my love most affectionately. In this message my Mother, aunt, and sister Susan unite, as well as in love to thyself.

Source: American Baptist Historical Society, AJ 17, no. 765.

Mrs. M. I. Newton to Emily C. Judson, July 20, 1850—Worcester

Dear Mrs. Judson

We were *glad* to receive a letter from you (for the last we received from Burmah was dated one year ago the 18th of last March,) although it brought the *sad* intelligence of the sickness of your dear husband. We heard through the papers that Dr. Judson was very ill, but the children[18] thought it could not be so, because you did not write to them. George is unwell.[19] We fear he will not be able to go through with his college course. He has been away from his studies about half of this term. Before he left, the words all run [sic] together, so that he could not do any thing [sic] with his books. The children are growing very fast, and are good *scholars*. Pray for us, for we need *much* wisdom to bring up the *dear* children committed to our care. My health is very poor, I fear I shall not live through the coming autumn. If your husband is living give him my kind regards, and say, we think and talk about him almost every day.

From your unworthy sister

M. S. Newton

Source: American Baptist Historical Society, AJ 18, no. 856.

[18] Adoniram and Elnathan Judson were living in Worcester, Massachusetts, with Dr. and Mrs. Calvin Newton.

[19] George Dana Boardman, the son of George Dana Boardman and Sarah Hall Boardman, was born August 18, 1828, in Tavoy, Burmah. George returned to the United States in 1844 at the age of six and lived with Dr. and Mrs. Calvin Newton in Worcester, Massachusetts. He attended Brown University in Providence, Rhode Island, graduating after taking a few years off for travel in the West. He attended the Newton Theological Institute, and in 1855, he married Miss Ella Covell. He served two churches before settling into the First Baptist Church of Philadelphia, where he served with distinction for thirty years. He formed a close relationship with Emily upon her return in 1851; when she gave him a copy of *An Olio of Domestic Verses*, she addressed it "Georgie—from Mamma."

Emily C. Judson to Catharine Chubbuck, July 22, 1850—Maulmain

My dear Kate

I can write this month only enough to say we have not yet heard from my husband;[20] for I am not yet strong enough to use my pen much. The diarrhea still continues, and I suppose will never be any better while I remain here. If we hear good news, I shall go at once to Bourbon—if bad, I must think of a longer voyage—to America. That was Mr. J's expressed wish before he left, but I shall not come to burden you in any way; I hope if I am not always able to help you I shall never hinder. If God spare me (which is doubtful) it will be for the children's sake—I am good for nothing now, but to look after them. You would be shocked to see what a skeleton I have become. I sit up only a few minutes at a time and the Dr. says even that is injurious—I had better keep my couch [sic] altogether. But then I have a family you know.

It was cheering to me to hear of your getting on so nicely. Tell Father[21] and Mother[22] to keep up good courage, and try to be happy. Tell them to remember Wade's beautiful lines

> "But when he comes nearer to
> Like a fine setting sun he looks richer in grace
> And gives a sure hope at the end of his days
> Of arising in brighter array."

Their race is approaching it's [sic] close (though there may be more years before them than us) but they have bright hopes for the future and though I never see them again in this world, I feel sure that I shall meet both them and you in a world far more beautiful and glorious. Better that than come to you, now a mourner. And yet God knows what is best, and to his hands, do I, in my extremity, commit all my ways.

The children[23] are quite well and more than happy, for they have just rec'd a parcel of toys. If little Charley[24] had lived he would have been just three months

In reference to his "illness," see the letters of Dr. Calvin Newton dated June 30 and July 1, 1849. George Boardman had taken an extensive trip to the American West, and Dr. Newton feared for his health—going so far as to say that George seemed to have "a disturbance of mental powers."

[20] Adoniram Judson left for Bourbon on April 3, 1850, hoping that the sea journey would be beneficial to his health. Unknown to Emily, he died at sea on April 12, 1850.

[21] Emily's father, Charles Chubbuck, was born at Bedford, New Hampshire, on March 3, 1780; he was married to Lavinia Richards in Goffstown, New Hampshire, on November 17, 1805. They were to have seven children. Though he held varying jobs over the years, he failed at many of them, and Emily was the main support of the family after she purchased a home for her family in fall 1842.

[22] Emily's mother, Lavinia Richards Chubbuck, was born June 1, 1785, at Goffstown, New Hampshire, the eldest of thirteen children. She married Charles Chubbuck on November 17, 1805, at Goffstown, New Hampshire. Four of her children were born at Goffstown, and moved with Charles and Lavinia Chubbuck to Eaton, New York, in September 1816; they were Lavinia, Benjamin, Harriet, and John Walker. Sarah Catharine, Emily, and Wallace were all born in Eaton.

[23] Henry Hall Judson, eight years old; Edward Judson, five and a half years old; and Emily Frances Judson, two and a half years old.

[24] Charles Judson, named for Emily's father Charles Chubbuck, was stillborn on April 23, 1850.

old today. He would have saved me many a lonely hour, but God knew best. Your own little niece, Frances,[25] is one of the healthiest happiest little creatures you ever saw—with a heart full of love. She has this minute come in, her eyes dancing, and clapping her little fat hands, to tell me one of the famous feats of "dear Mamma's little daughter."

Love to all inquirers.

Your affectionate sister

Emily C. Judson

Source: Hanna family files.

The Reverend Sewall Mason Osgood to Emily C. Judson, July 24, 1850 —Rochester NY

My dear Mrs. Judson

Your kind letter of April 19 came to hand a few days since. Many thanks for your prompt and satisfactory reply to the business portion of mine of a former date.

May I assure you dear sister that though far away no one can more truly and deeply sympathize with you in your severe trials. I almost fear to take up a paper but my eye shall fall upon the distressing intelligence of Bro. Judson's death. During all my Missionary life till he left for this country Bro. Judson was my most intimate and eternal friend. Our relations to the Mission and the locations of our dwellings allowed me the pleasure and profit of almost hourly intercourse. I look back upon those years with deepest interest,—and the thought that of the four individuals who then made up the little circle of that Mission compound I am perhaps the only one that remains, brings with it an indescribable feeling of desolation. I am not, however, without hope that the influence of the sea air may have proved favorable to his recovery, and that he is by this time with you again and in the enjoyment of comfortable health. But if you are bereaved my dear sister I am aware that all human consolation will be unavailing. We must look to him who has ( ) the cup, for strength and submission. He can heal the wound his own hand hath made. I am thankful to learn that your own health has been so good for the months when your dear husband has needed so much care and sincerely hope that it may be still further confirmed.

I have been very anxious to know how far Bro. Judson has progressed with the Dictionary, and whether it is in a state to be taken up by another if he should not be able to complete it.—If you have any business transactions in this country in which I can be of use to you I hope you will not hesitate to let me know. It will give me great pleasure to aid you in any way in my power.

[25] See vol. 1, "Cast of Characters," s.v. "Judson, Emily Frances."

My family are in usual health. I left home yesterday morning and am spending a few days in this city on public business. I suppose Bro. Wade[26] and the other Missionaries sailed yesterday. I think this is the largest company of Missionaries ever sent out by our Board. But I hope we shall be able to send many more! "The harvest is great, and the laborers are few." I am trying to do what little I can to keep up a healthful time of Missionary feeling in this district. I am expecting to visit some of the Western States again this fall.

I saw Bro. and Sister Starwell a week ago to day [sic] in Lockport. They were well and have now gone east again. They hope to return to Maulmain next year. It is disturbing to see the ravages which sickness and death are making in the Mission circle. We look for Bro. and Sister Howard[27] soon. Bro. Ingalls[28] has arrived, but I have not seen him.

The sudden death of the President[29] has created a great seuration [sic] throughout the land, and I have just noticed the death of Sir Robert Peel in England. Prof. Webster is ( ) to the ( ) on the 30th of August. I should be most gratified to hear from you occasionally. I have been anxious to hear more about the children in this country[30] but seldom either go east or meet with friends from the places where the children reside.

Most sincerely and truly yours

L. M. Osgood

Source: American Baptist Historical Society, AJ 18, no. 828.

[26] Jonathan and Deborah Wade were appointed missionaries to Burmah in 1823. Their relationship with Adoniram Judson was especially dear because of the early experiences they shared, including the death of Ann Judson. When she died and Adoniram returned to Amherst expecting to find her, he learned instead the news of her death. He never forgot the sight of Deborah Wade standing on the veranda holding little Maria in her arms. Much of their work was spent in the Karen jungle communities following the path of George Boardman. They returned home to America on December 22, 1847, and went back to Burmah in January 1851, just as Emily was returning to the United States. They were from the Hamilton, New York, area. They left for Burmah on July 25, 1850, and were in Maulmain by February 1851. Both died in Burmah; Deborah died at Maulmain in 1868, and Jonathan died in Rangoon in 1872.

[27] Hosea and Theresa Howard first sailed for Burmah in 1834, arriving in December that year. Hosea Howard was a recent graduate of the theological seminary in Hamilton, New York. They were stationed in Maulmain as missionaries with Adoniram Judson, and he claimed in a letter to Emily that he worked there with Adoniram longer than any other missionary. Mr. Howard's responsibility was to run schools that the mission maintained, a task in which he was ably assisted by his wife. Lydia Lillybridge was responsible to Mr. and Mrs. Howard when she arrived in November 1846. Mr. and Mrs. Howard left Maulmain for the United States in February 1850.

[28] Lovel Ingalls was born August 21, 1808, in Worcester, New York. He was ordained October 2, 1834, in Boston, New York, and graduated from the Hamilton Literary and Theological Institute in 1837. In September 1834, he married Marcia Dawes of Cummington, Massachusetts; Miss Dawes had been educated at Cummington Academy. They first sailed for Burmah in 1835, arriving at Amherst February 20, 1836. They were stationed at Mergui and then Maulmain in May 1845; Marcia Dawes Ingalls died on November 9, 1845, at Maulmain. Lovel and Marcia Ingalls were the parents of three children. Mr. Ingalls went to Akyab in 1846 and returned to the United States beginning May 1850. He went back to Burmah in December 1851. His second wife was Marilla Amelia Baker, and they married December 23, 1850, at Troy, New York. Mr. Ingalls died at sea on March 14, 1856.

[29] President Zachary Taylor died on July 9, 1850.

[30] Three of the Judson children lived in the United States; Abby Ann lived in Bradford, Massachusetts, where she attended Bradford Academy; Adoniram and Elnathan lived in Worcester, Massachusetts, with Dr. and Mrs. Calvin Newton.

Mrs. E. W. F. Moore[31] to Emily C. Judson, July 27, 1850

My dear Sister

Very many thanks for the lines you so kindly sent me last evening. I have read and reread them with thrilling interest.

Would that I could give vent to my heart's feelings in such sweet living strains. I am very happy to learn that you are feeling better.

With much love aff'ly

Your Sister E. W. F. Moore

Source: American Baptist Historical Society, AJ 18, no. 869.

Anna Maria Anable to Emily C. Judson, July 28, 1850—Roxbury

Dearest Emily

Your last letter was rec'd before I left home, and now, Mr. and Mrs. Lincoln[32] and Hatty[33] having gone to church I can spend a little time in answering it.

What is before you darling I know not—but I fear that before you receive this you will have experienced the greatest sorrow of your life. I know how you love the dear Dr. and can form some idea of how heavily the blow that deprives you of him will fall on you. Oh that I could do something to mitigate your present sufferings! That I could take you to my bosom as of old, and try to sooth all your sorrows there. Dearest Nemmy,[34] my heart is full of sympathy for you, but you have felt the soothing power of a sympathy deeper and truer than mine can be, and that power will still support you. I have but little hope of the Dr.'s recovery, though his last message to you was somewhat inspiring. The dear, noble, devoted man. He has "fought a good fight" and there is without doubt a "crown of glory" and "an eternal mansion" prepared for him.

[31] William Moore was from Granville, Ohio, and was a graduate of Dennison University and Covington Institute, Kentucky. He married Elizabeth W. Forbes from Cincinnati, Ohio. They departed Boston on November 3, 1847, and arrived in Calcutta on March 18, 1848. They worked with the Karens in Burmah, near Maulmain. Mr. and Mrs. Moore returned to the United States, arriving in Boston December 19, 1853.

[32] Joshua Lincoln was a prominent Baptist layman in Boston. Anna Maria Anable lived with Mr. and Mrs. Lincoln in summer 1848 when she went to Boston for medical treatments to correct deficiencies in her shoulder and spine. Mr. Lincoln was active in Massachusetts and national Baptist circles. He also had a brother in Boston, the Honorable Heman Lincoln. The correspondence indicates that both brothers visited with the Anable family in Philadelphia.

[33] See vol. 1, "Cast of Characters," s.v. "Anable, Harriet."

[34] "Nem" or "Nemmy" was a name of endearment given to Emily by a small group of her intimate friends at the Utica Female Academy. Anna Maria Anable was "Ninny."

Our mission friends have sailed the 25th and considering the size of the party I should think might be quite comfortable.[35]

Mrs. Bronson[36] expects to be confined in about six weeks. The poor woman is to be pitied, but I pity the other passengers almost as much. Mr. and Mrs. Wade[37] kept up pretty good courage, and Mr. Kincaid[38] was hopefulness itself. His face is all sunshine homely as it is. Hatty has enjoyed this visit to Boston and Mr. Darling of the Miss. exceedingly. We spent a week with Mrs. Colby[39] at their beautiful new place in Newton, and three days with Mrs. Bright,[40] and now we are at Mrs. Lincoln's but due to leave tomorrow for Vermont, whither we are bound to pay a visit to Helen Martin Chadwick. Thence we go to the White Mountains and return by the Lakes and the Hudson home. Our visit here has been delightful. Every where

[35] On July 25, 1850, the *Washington Allston* had sailed from Boston Harbor with a large group of new and returning missionaries, including Mr. and Mrs. Kincaid, Mr. and Mrs. Wade, and Dr. and Mrs. Dawson. The ship was a chartered vessel enabling the American Baptist Missionary Union to send the group directly to Maulmain, Burmah. According to the correspondence, it turned out to be a disastrous trip, with much of the problem the fault of the captain. From Mrs. Hough's letter of May 20, 1851, we gather that there were too many passengers and not enough supplies, among other problems. The ship, according to Emily Judson (February 23, 1851), "entered the mouth of the Salwen [River] just as [her] steamer was leaving it" bound for Calcutta. Emily said that she visited with the Kincaids and Mrs. Vinton in Calcutta, for they had come in on the *Tudor* "from the Cape"—apparently some of the passengers had left the *Washington Allston* en route.

[36] Mrs. Bronson, the wife of Miles Bronson. Miles Bronson was a graduate of Hamilton University and Seminary, and both were appointed for missionary service in 1836. Their field of service was Assam, and they first reached there in July 1837. They pioneered ministry with the Naga tribes. In 1849, Mr. and Mrs. Bronson returned to the United States and were there for more than a year; they returned to the field in 1851.

[37] See vol. 1, "Cast of Characters," s.v. "Wade, The Reverend Doctor Jonathan and Deborah."

[38] Born in 1797, educated at the seminary in Hamilton, New York, and ordained in 1822, the Reverend Eugenio Kincaid served several churches before being appointed as a missionary to Burmah in February 1830. His first wife died soon after their arrival. His second wife was Barbara McBain, and they were married in 1833. In these years, they served in Rangoon, Ava, Saduja, and Akyab. The Reverend and Mrs. Kincaid returned to the United States in 1843; because of her persistent health problems, they were not reappointed in 1846. While in the United States, Rev. Kincaid became instrumental in the establishment of the University of Lewisberg (later Bucknell University). Upon Mrs. Kincaid's restoration, they returned to Burmah, arriving in February 1851 just as Emily Judson was embarking for her return voyage. With his knowledge of the language and customs, Rev. Kincaid was able to establish himself in work with the Burmese government at Ava.

[39] Mary Colby was the wife of Gardner Colby, a prominent businessman and active Baptist layman. Mr. Colby was a member of the Board of the American Baptist Missionary Union and an avid supporter of the missionary movement. In a letter after they sailed from Boston to Burmah, Emily mentions the extravagant hospitality extended to them in early July as they waited for the *Faneuil Hall* to embark. Adoniram and then Emily stayed with the Colby family quite frequently over the years. Mrs. Colby was an active correspondent with Emily and supported her, her family, and the cause of missions.

[40] Upon her return to America in 1851, Emily Judson was to have a very close relationship with Dr. Edward Bright, the corresponding secretary of the American Baptist Missionary Union. They had known one another previously in New York, as he worked at the time of Adoniram and Emily's marriage with the *Baptist Register*, a prominent regional newsletter. Prior to working as a publisher, he had been, in 1838, the founding pastor of the Bleecker Street Baptist Church in Utica, a church with close ties to the Utica Female Academy. He was appointed corresponding secretary of the Missionary Union the end of May 1846, just prior to Adoniram and Emily's leaving Boston for Burmah. In this role he regularly pleaded with Emily for articles to be published in the missionary magazine, the *Macedonian*. Upon Emily's return from Burmah in October 1851, Adoniram and Elnathan went to live with Dr. and Mrs. Bright for a year. Dr. Bright was to help Emily with many of her business affairs; he carried on the publishing details of the Judson Memoir because of a serious illness in Dr. Wayland's family. He, with Dr. Edward Granger, was to be the executor of the estate of Emily Chubbuck Judson, a responsibility he still carried in March 1869, as reflected in a letter to Anna Maria Anable regarding financial arrangements for Emily Frances Judson.

[sic] we seem to find warm friends. I must tell you a bit of news. Sarah Bell[41] is going to marry Deacon Gould of the book firm.[42] He is a *so so* sort of a man,[43] forty two, and two children; but he is rich and they say very pious, so I suppose Sarah's chances for happiness are tolerably good. The dear child deserves the best man on earth.

I saw Abby Judson[44] at Mrs. Wade's. She is much improved in looks, and seems a fine intelligent girl. Good bye dearest Nemmy. May Heaven shield you under all circumstances. How anxious I shall be to get the next intelligence from you—and the precious little one.[45]

Affec.

Anna M.

[Written along the left and top margins of page 1:] I must not forget to tell you that Aunt C.[46] gave Mr. Warner[47] a turn about ( ), and set him off in directions which will probably lead to the consummation of his wishes. That is, she introduced him to another lady.

Source: American Baptist Historical Society, AJ 13, no. 472.

[41] Sarah Bell Wheeler was a teacher at the Utica Female Academy, an intimate of Emily Chubbuck, and one of the few who addressed Emily as Nemmy. In a September 1847 letter, she was listed as one of the teachers at the Utica Female Academy. There are a number of letters from Sarah Bell before and after her marriage to Charles Gould of Boston in October 1850. There are several letters clustered in the year or two after Emily left for Burmah and a number at the time of her return to America. Emily stayed with Charles and Sarah Bell Gould in October 1851 when she arrived in Boston after the long sea voyage from Burmah and then England. She stayed there a number of times following that. In 1851, Anna Maria Anable wrote of Sarah Bell: "Sarah is grown so lovely in person as well as character that she must assert a blessed influence on all with whom she comes in contact."

[42] Charles Gould was a partner with Joshua Lincoln in the publishing firm of Gould, Kendall and Lincoln.

[43] On September 10, 1850, in a similar letter that Miss Cynthia Sheldon wrote to Emily, she had a bit of a different perspective than Anna Maria on Deacon Gould. She described quite positively the marriage and how happy each was with the other.

[44] Abby Ann Judson, the first daughter and oldest child of Adoniram and Sarah Hall Boardman Judson, was born September 26, 1835. She saw her mother die on the Isle of St. Helena as they returned to the United States from Burmah. Just before leaving for Burmah with Emily, Adoniram Judson placed Abby Ann at Bradford Academy for her education. The family of Ann Hasseltine Judson was generous to Abby Ann and supportive of her interests and her future. On October 15, 1851, Abby Ann started a course of study at the Misses Anable's School in Philadelphia, and in fall 1853, she moved to New York City to take a teaching position in the home of Mrs. Maria Brown, a former missionary to Siam. She enjoyed a warm relationship with Emily, and her letters show that the two could speak freely with each other.

[45] Anna Maria Anable would not yet have heard of the stillborn death of Charles Judson on April 23, 1850.

[46] Miss Cynthia Sheldon was in charge of the administrative and financial departments of the Utica Female Academy. Miss Sheldon and her sister Urania, who was literary principal, gave Emily Chubbuck a place at the academy in October 1840. They had deferred any cost to a future time when Emily could afford to reimburse them. Upon Miss Urania Sheldon's marriage in late summer 1842 to the Reverend Doctor Eliphalet Nott, the president of Union College, and her subsequent move to Schenectady, Miss Cynthia Sheldon assumed a larger leadership role at the academy. In the years that followed, Miss Sheldon and Emily developed an even stronger relationship. In 1848, Miss Sheldon moved to Philadelphia to help Miss Anable with the startup of the Misses Anable's School and to assume responsibilities in its operation. Active and well-known in Baptist circles, Miss Cynthia was one of Emily's most important mentors, advisors, and friends until the time of Emily's death in 1854. Miss Sheldon was the aunt of Anna Maria Anable.

[47] See Anna Maria Anable's letter to Emily C. Judson dated May 26, 1850, on this possible budding relationship between Mr. Warner and Miss Cynthia Sheldon.

Emily C. Judson to Mrs. Elizabeth Stevens, July 30, 1850

To Mrs. Stevens
On Sending Her Carriage for Her

My dear old Bible tells
How the tide of pity swells
    Up above;
And hints at angel forms
That bow amid our storms,
    Lizzie, love.

It puzzles me to know
How these angels come and go
    On our sphere.
Do they cast their wings aside,
When with mortals they abide,
    Lizzie, dear?

I have drunk my cup of tears,
I have known of griefs and fears,
    Pain and care;
Then a footstep sought my bed,
And a form bent o'er my head,
    O, so fair!

But since it can not [sic] fly—
Though I'm sure it's from the sky,
    Lizzie, dear—
If you know, my pretty fawn,
Let the buggy and Bar-John
    Bring her here.

Emily C. Judson

Source: A. C. Kendrick, *The Life and Letters of Mrs. Emily C. Judson*, 339.

Emily C. Judson to Adoniram Judson, August 2, 1850—Maulmain

My dearest, darling Love,

The barque *Monarch*, Capt. Sheppard, leaves for the Mauritius tomorrow, and oh, how I do want to take passage on her, and go to you. You have no idea how long the days and weeks and months seem to me in going by—no, you cannot know, for although I daresay, you long to hear from us, your response cannot be equal to mine. Not a word have we heard from you yet, though in six days more it will be four months since you sailed—four months today since you went on board.[48] I wrote you by the April, May, and June Steamers, so you will have heard long before this, if the letters only go safely, but lest they should not I will recapitulate a little.

On the 22nd of April little Charley[49] was born, under circumstances very similar[50] to those of Luther.[51] I suffered terribly, and was for a long time in great danger. He was buried by Luther's side, and God spared me.[52] A little more than a month after my confinement and when still very weak, I was taken with a bowel complaint, which has wasted me to a skeleton. For about a week now, the disease has disappeared, and I have sanguine hopes of recovery. I am gaining strength too very rapidly. I walk from the bed-room to the sitting room, and there lounge on the couch or the cushioned rocking-chair till evening when I totter back again and Nancy[53] helps me away to bed. I am well enough, however, to exercise a good supervision of the children, and I think you will be pleased with their improvement. They have grown considerably since you left—have improved in their studies and in their manners, and are in the most perfect health. Frances[54] is a fine robust child and

[48] There is a little bit of a difference here on dates. Emily's letter would suggest that Judson boarded the *Aristide Marie* on April 2 and sailed on the eighth. Courtney Anderson, in *To the Golden Shore* [(Valley Forge: Judson Press, 1987) 501], writes that he boarded on April 3 and that Emily saw him through Saturday, April 6. On April 7, the ship reached Amherst, and Judson was sufficiently better, so two of the Burmese faithful returned with the pilot with a letter for Emily from Mr. Ranney. Then, on Monday, April 8, the ship saw the open sea of the Bay of Bengal. The only real difference is on the day of boarding. April 6 was the last time that Emily saw Adoniram. The first dated letter in the correspondence that indicates that Emily learned of Adoniram Judson's death is August 19, 1850; it is addressed to Dr. McKay. Then, another letter dated August 20, 1850, was directed to her sister Catharine. There is another letter to her friend Anna Maria Anable, which is undated, but it was probably also written on August 20. Indications are that word of Adoniram Judson's death reached those in the United States around September 7. A letter from Miss Cynthia Sheldon dated September 10 showed that the story had been in the newspaper the previous Saturday (September 7).

[49] Charles or "Charley" was named after Emily Chubbuck Judson's father, Charles Chubbuck. While she dates the birth as April 22 in this letter, in her May 20, 1850, letter she says, "On the 21st and 22nd of last month I was very poorly indeed. On the 23rd towards evening, I was seized with an alarming hemorrhage, and at a little before 12 o'clock was delivered of a dead boy."

[50] From Emily's letter of May 20, 1850, to Adoniram Judson: "He was a beautiful boy—my dear little *Charley*, you know—perfect in his formation, and so like you that everyone spoke of it, but very thin—indeed wasted to a skeleton even before he was born." Out of this part of her life came Emily's heartfelt poem "Angel Charley."

[51] Luther Judson, the son of Adoniram and Sarah Hall Boardman Judson, was stillborn on March 8, 1841.

[52] All of this information is contained in Emily's letter of May 20, 1850.

[53] Nancy was a Malayan woman who came with Emily from Burmah to America in 1851; she came to help Emily with the three Judson children—Henry, Edward, and Emily Frances—and to be there for Emily if she was incapacitated by her frequent illnesses. There are numerous references to Nancy in the correspondence, and she continued with her duties until Emily's death in June 1854. In her will, Emily left a sum more than sufficient to pay for Nancy's return to her native home.

[54] See vol. 1, "Cast of Characters," s.v. "Judson, Emily Frances."

everybody laughs at the idea of her belonging in any way to me. Dr. Morton[55] says she has got her papa's sanguine temperament. Speaking of Dr. Morton—he has been as kind as a brother, visiting me nearly every day since you left, and showing the deepest interest in our welfare. I gave him your best copy of Webster,[56] after my confinement and he appeared greatly pleased with it. We can send for another if you want it. The Stevenses[57] too have been very kind and attentive. I think I should scarcely have lived without Mrs. S's care. You know how tender she is when one is in trouble.

Everything in the Mission is going on after the old sort. If you have rec'd my letters, you will have heard of Mr. Stilson's[58] illness. He was attacked with paralysis on the 23rd of April, and will probably be a partial paralytic for life, though he is now able to walk (by balancing himself carefully) as far as Mr. Mason's[59] without crutches. He is a pitiable spectacle. Mr. Bennett[60] has a touch of his fever now and

[55] Doctor Morton was a physician who worked with the missionaries in Maulmain, Burmah. He delivered Emily Frances Judson in December 1847 and was present when Charles Judson ("Angel Charley") was stillborn in April 1850. He was a valued and trusted advisor to the mission families.

[56] See the letter of Dr. Morton to Emily C. Judson dated June 7, 1850.

[57] Edward and Elizabeth Stevens were missionaries to Burmah. They arrived in Maulmain, Burmah, in February 1838. There are twenty-four letters in the correspondence from them. Mrs. Stevens took Edward Judson into her home when Sarah and Adoniram had to leave for the United States in 1845, and her care and nurture saved his life. The home of Elizabeth and Edward Stevens burned to the ground in 1847, and two trunks being stored for Adoniram and Emily were destroyed; these trunks held all of their excess clothes and precious mementos, which they had not wanted to bring to Rangoon with them. Mr. Stevens buried Charles Chubbuck (Emily's "Angel Charley") in April 1850. Edward Stevens also accepted the responsibility of finishing the dictionary after the death of Adoniram Judson.

[58] Lyman Stilson was born in Meredith, New York, on January 29, 1805. He attended the Hamilton Seminary and was appointed to missionary service on October 3, 1836. He was married to Lucretia Brownson on August 20, 1837, and both sailed for Burmah on October 28, 1837, along with the Bennetts and the Stevens. Mr. Stilson finally returned to America after Lucretia Stilson's death on August 14, 1851. Mrs. Stilson had been quite ill for some time and the board had authorized her to return to the United States, but as reported in the newsletter of the Missionary Union, "She has been removed to a better country." They worked with Adoniram Judson for thirteen years, and with both Sarah Hall Boardman Judson and Emily Chubbuck Judson. Mr. Stilson's specific responsibilities included the oversight of printing Burmese elementary books for the schools that were maintained by the mission. He also wrote a volume in Burmese on mathematics. In her letter of May 20, 1850, Emily had mentioned Mr. Stilson's paralysis and the seriousness of his condition.

[59] See vol. 1, "Cast of Characters," s.v. "Mason, The Reverend Francis, Helen, and Ellen."

[60] Cephas Bennett had arrived in Burmah in January 1830; his wife was Stella Bennett. Mr. Bennett remained the superintendent of the Baptist Press there for more than fifty years. He worked with Adoniram Judson on the printing of the Bible into Burmese, but also into the Karen language. From the Utica area, they sent their children back, and the girls were educated at the Utica Female Academy. The girls included Elsina (April 1828), Mary (November 1829), Ann (August 1833), Ellen (June 1835), and Sarah (June 1837).

then, and is, I hear, in bed with it today, but it seems not to break him down much. Mr. Simons[61] and Lydia[62] are still billing and cooing but what will be the result of the matter I don't know. I am sure she likes him better than I would once have believed she ever could. Last Sunday a man was baptized—a pure Burman, from a new family, and two or three others are asking for baptism—among them Peter Brady. Mah Doke and some of the others cry when they speak of you. They say they pray for you three times a day. Old Mah Heen is quite ill, and she says all she wants to live for is to see Sayah Gye once more—then she will die content. Old Ko Ban and Mah Men too, say a great many sweet things about you.

Oh darling, if I *could only, only be sure you would* read all this! that I should ever see your dear face again. Oh, how happy, how happy we shall be, Love, if our Heavenly Father brings us together again.

I have told the children[63] that I was writing to "dear papa,"[64] and they go jumping about, and rejoicing as though quite sure you must be getting well. They always remember you in their little prayers. Baby[65] talks a great deal about you. She says the black rocking-chair, and the single cot which she saw you occupy so much are "papa's"; and I frequently find her all alone talking to your engraving, which she calls "little papa." Oh, the children are a great comfort to me, they have got such warm, loving little hearts; and Henry[66] is really growing sympathizing and sensible. I mourn a good deal over poor little Charley, and yet—I have no doubt he was taken to preserve him from future evils. You too will be disappointed, but you will not of course feel as I do—and I shall feel *nothing*—nothing unpleasant—if I am permitted to see you again. I can scarcely think of it without trembling, the blessing seems so

[61] Thomas Simons was born in Wales. He was ordained on December 18, 1831, after graduation from the Newton Theological Institute and was appointed to missionary service on March 7, 1831. He sailed for Burmah on June 29, 1832, arriving in Maulmain on January 1, 1833. On June 23, 1833, he married Caroline Jenks Harrington in Maulmain, probably the widow of a missionary who had died, and between 1834 and March 1843, they had six children, two of whom died in June 1839. Caroline Simons died on May 1, 1843. Mr. Simons returned to America in May 1846. While in the United States, he visited with Abby Ann Judson at Bradford Academy; she would have known him from her years in Burmah. He returned to Burmah in November 1847, arriving in Maulmain April 19, 1848. His second wife was Lydia Lillybridge, who had sailed to Burmah with Adoniram and Emily Judson; they were married in Maulmain in 1851.

[62] Lydia Lillybridge was one of Emily's closest friends at the Utica Female Academy. When Emily made the decision to go to Burmah as the wife of Adoniram Judson and as a missionary, Lydia wanted to go with them. Emily spoke to Adoniram Judson of Lydia's extraordinary abilities, and Adoniram advocated her appointment before Dr. Solomon Peck and the Board of the American Baptist Missionary Union. Lydia was commissioned to go with them, in spite of the fact that she remained single. Always independent, outspoken, and unafraid to cause ripples in the missionary community, Lydia served on the mission field for twenty-eight years. She married missionary Thomas Simons in May 1851. See the timeline on the life and service of Lydia Lillybridge Simons in vol. 1.

[63] Henry Hall Judson, eight years old; Edward Judson, five and a half years old; and Emily Frances Judson two and a half years old.

[64] "Dear papa" was the affectionate name of the Judson children for Adoniram Judson. In April 1850, Emily wrote a poem, "Prayer for Dear Papa."

[65] See vol. 1, "Cast of Characters," s.v. "Judson, Emily Frances."

[66] See vol. 1, "Cast of Characters," s.v. "Judson, Henry Hall."

inexpressively great. I will enclose to you some verses suggested by the loss of little Charley,[67] whose spirit I trust you will believe immortal.

[Written in the right margin of the address page:] I heard from Abby Ann[68] in July, and from the boys[69] indirectly thorough [sic] her. Her letter is dated "Plymouth[70] April 18th." She speaks of loving her teachers better than formerly and of being very happy.[71] There had been a revival in school. She makes no allusion to herself, but I think she has very serious feelings judging from the general tone of her letter.[72] She had not heard of your illness. George[73] was in college. All four of the children had passed the summer vacation previous at their aunt Judson's[74] which I think you had heard before.

[Written in the left margin of the address page:] The last mail bro't but little news. The Wades[75] are appointed to Maulmain—South section. The Memoirs[76] came—fifty with Notes. A small box of things too, that I wrote for to A Maria.[77] It contained *such* a comfortable dressing-gown for you! I long to see you in it, but don't venture to send even the newspapers and letters till I hear. May God bless you, dearest, and bring you back soon to your poor, anxious, loving

Emily C. Judson

Source: Hanna family files.

[67] Emily's poem "Angel Charley" is found in this volume following Emily C. Judson's letter to Adoniram Judson dated April 19, 1850.

[68] See vol. 1, "Cast of Characters," s.v. "Judson, Abby Ann."

[69] Adoniram "Addy" Judson, born April 7, 1837, was the second child and the first son of Adoniram and Sarah Hall Boardman Judson; and Elnathan "Elly" Judson, born July 15, 1838, was the third child and second son of Adoniram and Sarah Hall Boardman Judson. When they returned to America with their father in fall 1845 after the death of their mother on the voyage home, they lived in Worcester, Massachusetts, with Dr. and Mrs. Calvin Newton.

[70] Plymouth, Massachusetts, was the home of Abigail Brown Judson, the sister of Adoniram Judson. A spinster of eccentric character and behavior, she was a beneficiary of her parents' considerable wealth. Her father had wisely invested in land and bank stocks; with the help of Esq. Loud, she had invested that money prudently. She took a strong interest in Adoniram's children and offered them considerable support—though not often without complaint or comment—for their clothing and education in the years to come.

[71] Abby Ann Judson was attending Bradford Academy in Bradford, Massachusetts. Bradford had been home to Ann Hasseltine Judson, Adoniram Judson's first wife, and her ancestors were among the founders in 1639; Ann's father had helped to found the academy in 1803. Abby Ann later to became the headmistress of Bradford Academy.

[72] On interest in such spiritual matters, see the letter of Adoniram Judson to Abby Ann Judson dated November 26, 1848.

[73] See vol. 1, "Cast of Characters," s.v. "Boardman, George Dana."

[74] See vol. 1, "Cast of Characters," s.v. "Judson, Abigail Brown."

[75] See vol. 1, "Cast of Characters," s.v. "Wade, The Reverend Doctor Jonathan and Deborah."

[76] The reference here is to Fanny Forester, *Memoir of Sarah B. Judson, Member of the American Mission to Burmah* (New York: L. Colby and Company, 1848). It had been revised, and Emily had written a number of notes for it. Adoniram Judson desired that "Fanny Forester" write the memoir of his late wife, and that wish brought them together on Christmas Day 1845 in the parlor of the home of the Reverend and Mrs. A. D. Gillette, of Philadelphia.

[77] See vol. 1, "Cast of Characters," s.v. "Anable, Anna Maria."

Mrs. Johanna C. Bower[78] to Emily C. Judson, August 6, 1850

My dear Mrs. Judson

I should have written this morning to thank you for your kind note, and present, but not feeling very well was unable to do so. I can assure you the beautiful little volume[79] will ever be highly valued by me not as a memorial of any ( ) kindness on my part towards Dr. Judson but the esteem I shall always feel for the kind donor and her Husband, whose labours [sic] in the ( ) of the gospel in the Heathen world have been so successful.

We trust soon to hear that Dr. Judson has been restored to you in the full enjoyment of health

With our kind regards
Believe me
yrs sincerely

Johanna Bower

Source: American Baptist Historical Society, AJ 12, no. 315.

Doctor Edward Bright, Jr. to Emily C. Judson, August 6, 1850—Missionary Rooms, Boston

My dear friend:—

Your letter of April 19, was received on the 5th ( ). Its intelligence has awakened the deepest anxiety in the hearts of multitudes throughout this land;—for I ventured to publish all that you say of Dr. Judson in the Magazine and *Macedonian* for August. I could not withhold the full opinion which Dr. Morton[80] had given of his case, when so many desire to know all the facts. We have not the means of knowing when we shall hear from him or Mr. Ranney.[81] But until we hear we shall not cease to

[78] Mr. and Mrs. Bower were missionaries with the Judsons in Burmah. In late March 1850, Mrs. Bower sent items for Adoniram to take on his sea voyage. In August 1850, she wrote to thank Emily for giving her a copy of the revised edition with notes of the memoir of Sarah Hall Boardman Judson.

[79] Emily recently mentioned in a letter that she had received fifty copies of the *Memoir of Sarah Boardman Judson* with notes.

[80] See vol. 1, "Cast of Characters," s.v. "Morton, Doctor."

[81] Thomas Ranney was appointed to missionary service in June 1843, arriving in Burmah in May 1844. He was an important part of the Judsons' lives while in Rangoon. He was superintendent of the printing press in Maulmain and business manager for the compound. Thomas Ranney went with Adoniram Judson on his last voyage, and thus was with him when he died. There is a letter in the collection from the *Aristide Marie* written five days before Adoniram Judson's death; one of the things he did at the time of death was to take some locks of his hair to bring to Emily. She later sent one of these locks to Adoniram's sister Abigail in Plymouth. Thomas Ranney provided the accounts of Adoniram's last voyage and his last hours of life. He also handled some of the financial matters for the mission and in the settlement of Adoniram Judson's estate. Thomas Ranney was married to Maria Gager, who died in 1857, and then to Mary E. Bennett, the daughter of missionaries Cephas and Stella Bennett.

hope or to pray that God will crown the voyage with his blessing and restore to yourself and the mission one who is so justly dear to both.

You have the warmest Sympathy of thousands of Christian hearts in your loneliness and suspense. But the love of Christ, so precious to your absent husband before his departure from Maulmain, has power to sustain him in all the trials of the voyage. His glorious High Priest, though enthroned in heaven, is touched with the feeling of his infirmities; and his High Priest is *yours*. May God help you to confide unwaveringly in His compassion, faithfulness and power. He will do all things well.

Bear to Miss Lillybridge[82] the assurances of my sincere regards, and believe me to,
Yours, most affectionately,

Edw. Bright, Jr.
Cor. Sec

Source: American Baptist Historical Society, AJ 14, no. 549.

Emily C. Judson to Lavinia Richards Chubbuck,[83] August 8, 1850

Sweet Mother

The wild southwest monsoon has risen,
    On broad gray wings of gloom,
While here from out my dreary prison
I look as from a tomb—alas!
    My heart another tomb.

[82] See vol. 1, "Cast of Characters," s.v. "Lillybridge, Lydia." Also, "A Timeline of the Life and Mission of Lydia Lillybridge Simons."

[83] From A. C. Kendrick, *The Life and Letters of Mrs. Emily C. Judson* [(New York: Sheldon and Company, 1831) 340]:

> "Scarcely anything can be conceived more affecting than her present situation. The sods of the valley pressing her new-born child; herself wasted to a skeleton and hardly able to rise from her couch; her friends and relatives divided from her by half the circumference of the globe; her husband withdrawn under circumstances which made it doubtful if he could survive even a week, and yet she compelled to wait four long months before her dreadful suspense can be relieved by the scarcely more dreadful tidings of his death! Rarely are the fountains of sorrow in the human bosom more deeply stirred. Scarcely can we conceive a combination of circumstances more fitted to call forth that wail of a desolate spirit—that shriek of the soul—that cry of intense and concentrated agony which now embodied itself in the following lines to her mother."

From the *Baptist Memorial*, 10:199–200: "These lines first appeared in the *Watchman and Reflector*, and have been copied into other papers; but we think them worthy to be published again. They were penned just before the death of Dr. Judson, after he had left Maulmain on his last voyage." The *Baptist Memorial* had a stanza not published in some of the other presentations. In this copy, that addition appears in bold print. Some of the last stanzas presented here were not in the *Baptist Memorial* issue. Rev. Enoch Hutchinson, ed., *The Baptist Memorial and Monthly Record Devoted to the History, Biography, Literature and Statistics of the Denomination* (New York: Z. P. Hatch, 1851) 10:199–200.

Upon the low thatched roof the rain
With ceaseless patter falls:
My choicest treasures bear its stain,
Mould gathers on the walls—would Heaven
'Twere only on the walls!

Sweet mother, I am here alone,
In sorrow and in pain;
The sunshine from my heart has flown,
It feels the driving rain—ah me!
The chill, and mould, and rain.

Four laggard months have wheeled their round[84]
Since love upon it smiled,
And everything of earth has frowned
On thy poor stricken child,—sweet friend;
Thy weary suffering child.

I'd watched my loved one night and day,[85]
Scarce breathing when he slept,
And as my hopes were swept away,
I'd in his bosom wept.—Oh, God!
How had I prayed and wept!

They bore him from me to the Ship,
As bearers bear the dead;
I kissed his speechless, quivering lip,
And left him on his bed—alas!
It seemed a coffin bed.

When from my gentle sister's tomb,[86]
In all our grief, we came
Rememberst thou her vacant room?
Well, his was just the same—that day,
The very, very same.

[84] Adoniram Judson boarded the *Aristide Marie* bound for the Isle of Bourbon on April 3, 1850; because of delays moving down the river to the bay, Emily saw him for the last time on April 6. She heard nothing since that time except for a hopeful communication on April 7, sent by Mr. Ranney, who had accompanied Adoniram Judson on the voyage.

[85] Of this time, Emily wrote a poem that she titled "Watching." That poem is dated February 1850 in the correspondence.

[86] Emily lost two of her sisters. Lavinia Chubbuck died at Pratt's Hollow in New York on June 22, 1829, just short of her twenty-third birthday. Harriet Chubbuck died in Morrisville, New York, December 6, 1831, in her twentieth year.

Then, mother, little Charley came,[87]
Our beautiful, fair boy,
With my own father's cherished name,-
But O, he brought no joy,—my child
Brought mourning and no joy.

His little grave I can not [sic] see,
Though weary months have fled
Since pitying lips bent over me,
And whispered, "He is dead." Ah me!
'Tis dreadful to be dead!

I do not mean for one like me,
So weary worn and weak,—
Death's shadowy paleness seems to be
Even now upon my cheek,—his seal
On form, and brow, and cheek.

But for a bright winged bird, like him,
To hush his joyous song,
And prisoned in a coffin dim,
Join death's pale phantom throng,—my boy
To join that gristly throng!

O mother, I can scarcely bear
To think of this to-day;
It was so exquisitely fair,
That little form of clay,—my heart
Still lingers by his clay.

And when for one loved far, far more
Come thickly gathering tears,
My star of faith is clouded o'er,
I sink beneath my fears,—sweet friend,
My heavy weight of fears.

Oh, should he not return to me,
Drear, drear must be my night;

[87] Charles Chubbuck, named for Emily's father, was stillborn on April 23, 1850.

And, mother, I can almost see,
Even now, the gather blight,
I stand,
As stricken by the blight.[88]

O but to feel thy fond arms twine
Around me once again!
It almost seems those lips of thine
Might kiss away the pain—might soothe
This dull, cold, heavy pain.

But gentle mother, through life's storms
I may not lean on thee;
For helpless, cowering little forms
Cling trustingly to me.[89]—Poor babes!
To have no guide but me.

With weary foot and broken wing,
With bleeding heart and sore,
Thy dove looks backward sorrowing,
But seeks the ark no more—Thy breast
Seeks never, never more.

Sweet mother for the exile pray,
That loftier faith be given;
Her broken reeds all swept away,
That she may rest in heaven—her soul
Grow strong in Christ and heaven.

All fearfully, all tearfully,
Alone and sorrowing,
My dim eye lifted to the sky—
Fast to the cross I cling—O Christ!
To thy dear cross I cling.

Source: A. C. Kendrick, *The Life and Letters of Mrs. Emily C. Judson*, 340–43; Arabella M. Wilson, *Lives of the Three Mrs. Judsons*, 334–37; Edward Judson, *Life of Adoniram Judson*, 547–49; Emily Judson, *An Olio of Domestic Verses*, 175–81.

[88] This stanza appears in *An Olio of Domestic Verses* ([New York: Lewish and Colby, 1852] 175–81); it is not included in the copy printed in A. C. Kendrick's biography, *The Life and Letters of Mrs. Emily C. Judson*.

[89] Henry Hall Judson, eight years old; Edward Judson, five and a half years old; and Emily Frances Judson, two and a half years old.

The Reverend W. S. MacKay to Emily C. Judson,[90] August 9, 1850—Cornwallis Square, Calcutta

My dear Madam

Although I have not the pleasure of knowing you personally, yet as a friend of your late ( ) husband, I do most deeply and sincerely sympathize with you in your grief for the life of one, whom all Christendom honours [sic] and mourns.

My chief purpose in writing to you is to intreat [sic], that, should you resolve to return to America, and to make Calcutta the first stage on your homeward journey, you will make our house your home, while here.

The acquaintance I have formed with you through your writings (all of which I have read with great pleasure) and through Mrs. Hough's[91] report, and my affection and veneration for Dr. Judson, will, I trust, plead my excuse for what otherwise might be looked on as intrusive.

We have a large house in a pleasant quiet square, away from the noise and bustle of the town; and Mrs. Hough will tell you, that my wife and myself are quiet people, who will do everything in our power to make you feel comfortable and at ease with us.

Go where you will, I am sure that you will find none who valued your husband more highly, or who will more thankfully appreciate the privilege of being permitted to show any kindness to the beloved partner of that noble missionary, whom the Lord so greatly honoured [sic].

If you come by the Steamer I shall endeavor to have a conveyance waiting, to take you at once to our house; but should I not hear of her arrival in sufficient time, the Captain will procure a conveyance for you, and by telling the coachman, or the bearers, my address, "Padre MacKay, Hudwa, Semla," you will easily find us.

Shall you wish to visit Serampore, we can easily take you there at an hour's notice.

Trusting that we may soon have the great pleasure of seeing you among us, and with sincere sympathy in your heavy affection, believe me

Sincerely and respectfully yours

W. S. MacKay

Source: American Baptist Historical Society, AJ 17, no. 751.

[90] In this letter, Rev. MacKay obviously had heard of the death of Adoniram Judson. Here, he invites Emily to stay with him and his wife if they pass through Calcutta on their way to the United States. A second letter reiterates that invitation, and a third letter has to do with providing transportation from the ship to their home.

It is obvious that Emily's stay with the MacKays in Calcutta was deeply meaningful to her. She was later to include in her *Olio of Domestic Verses* a poem, "Wayside Friends," which A. C. Kendrick in *the Life and Letters of Mrs. Emily C. Judson* tells us was dedicated to the MacKays. This poem appears in thif volume dated February 1851.

[91] Phoebe Hough, with her husband George Hough, were the first missionaries to be wholly called by the American Baptist Missionary Union to work in Burmah with Adoniram and Ann Judson. They retired from missionary service in 1826; George Hough subsequently worked for the government as an interpreter and school superintendent, and Mrs. Hough worked as an educator.

Emily C. Judson to Miss Cynthia Sheldon, August 9, 1850—Maulmain

My very dear Aunt Cynthia,

I have not forgotten a letter of yours dated Oct. 24th in which you make inquiries about the boy Sheldon,[92] though I have so long delayed answering you. Let me beg that you will never give yourself any uneasiness about it. Missionaries and agents make use of a great deal of machinery about collecting money, whether wisely or otherwise I will not pretend to judge. But in so much machinery there must be some degree of humbuggery, and allow me to say that this naming and supporting a boy is a small bit of a humbug. There are moneyed people whose fancies are taken with it and for such it is well enough, but I think you ought to know just how the matter stands. No missionary is allowed to appropriate the money he collects to any person belonging to that station. It all goes into the general funds of the Board and is by them doled out without the least regard to the object for which it was given. So the money you give for the support of your Karen boy, may be applied to a Chinese school, or to send home a sick missionary, or to keep me, who do nothing [sic], in broth and gruel. Once break this rule [sic], and allow donors to apply money as they choose, and missions could not be sustained. So you see your boy is supported by the school fund—that is the Executive Com. make out their estimate—so much for schools in Tavoy, and so much in Maulmain,—without the least regard to your thirty dollars, and the boy goes to school *hearing* perhaps that he is supported by good people in America or possibly by a *good lady*, who he thinks has an endless stock of cash, but with a *determined impression* that he is indebted only to teacher Bennett[93] or teacher Binney.[94] As to the name—it is ten to one if the boy knows of his having such a name, though he may have been told—most certainly he is never called by it, for it is not easy to be metamorphosed into Karen. I have now a girl to whom was given the English name of Nancy. She keeps it because it is easily turned into Burmese—or rather the Burmans think that Nancy is only one awkward way of pronouncing Nan-zee, a common name with them signifying fragrant oil. John they can speak for it is Zahn and Peter is Pa-troo, but Sheldon is a nut too hard for their jaws to crack. The Burmans would call it Sel-Don na, or possibly they might be taught to say Sel-dan, but the Karens would certainly render

[92] On this matter of the Karen boy Sheldon, see Emily C. Judson's letters to Anna Maria Anable dated February 19, 1850, and June 20, 1850.

[93] Cephas and Stella Bennett were missionaries to Burmah. They arrived in Burmah in January 1830, and Mr. Bennett remained the superintendent of the Baptist Press there for more than fifty years. He worked with Adoniram Judson on the printing of the Bible into Burmese, but also into the Karen language. Adoniram Judson referred to Mr. and Mrs. Bennett as "his dearest and best of friends." From the Utica area, they sent their children back, and the girls were educated at the Utica Female Academy and later at the Misses Anable's School in Philadelphia. The girls included Elsina (April 1828), Mary (November 1829) Ann (August 1833), Ellen (June 1835), and Sarah (June 1837).

[94] Joseph and Juliette Binney arrived in Burmah in April 1844. He opened the Karen Theological School in Maulmain for training indigenous pastors for the Burmese church. They returned to the United States in April 1850 because of Mrs. Binney's health. He returned in 1859, moving the seminary to Rangoon.

the name unrecognizable. English names are used, but very little among the natives, and are used only as a sort of clap-trap. I should not expose all this to anybody but you, but I do not think it right for you to be deceived, and if Mrs. Bennett had been a little more considerate, or perhaps if she had known you and your resources better, she never would have done it. If you can afford to give money, and feel like giving it, God will no doubt bless you in it, but you ought not to go beyond your means, merely because you feel committed. I dare say no person beyond the Bennetts and those to whom you have mentioned it, know anything about the boy, though if you were to pay in the money and say in your letter that it was intended for this purpose, it would be so published. So you see the Treasurer lends himself to the deception.

I am writing this before the mail comes in, because it is not probable that I shall be strong enough to write all the necessary letters after. I have been gaining, however, for about two weeks and hope to continue so.[95] Oh, how I wish I could be in the midst of you to night [sic]! I wonder if you can begin to imagine how desolate I am.

I thank you very much for your last kind letter, and wish you would write oftener. I thank you too for taking so much trouble about my pretty box. The things are beautiful, but sometimes I think that I shall never wear them. The children are delighted with their things—Frances[96] especially. She says Dolly's name is "Good Lady." Do you receive such young boarders? She is a violent tempered child, saucy as a cub, but perfectly obedient, and oh, *so* affectionate. You have no idea what a comfort the children are to me, though they are a great care too. Give ever and ever so much love to the girls, and to Mrs. Anable,[97] reserving at the same time a large share to yourself. Times have changed with all of us since I bade adieu to the Academy at Utica. Well, it is as God pleases, and he "doeth all things well."

Very aff'y yrs Emily C. Judson

Source: Hanna family files

[95] See Emily's letter to Adoniram Judson dated August 2, 1850, for more information on her illness.

[96] See vol. 1, "Cast of Characters," s.v. "Judson, Emily Frances."

[97] Alma Sheldon Anable was the sister of Miss Cynthia Sheldon and Urania Sheldon Nott. Genealogy sources show that she married Joseph Hubbell Anable in Troy, New York, on July 28, 1814, and that it was the second marriage for Mr. Anable. Born in 1773, he was forty-one at the time of the marriage, and Alma was likely considerably younger. He died in 1831, which explains why Alma Anable and her family lived and worked first at the Utica Female Seminary and then later at the Misses Anable's school in Philadelphia. Joseph and Alma Anable were the parents of nine children: Henry Sheldon Anable (b. June 21, 1815); William Stewart Anable (b. November 6, 1816); Anna Maria Stafford Anable (b. September 30, 1818), Cynthia Jane Anable (b. January 28, 1820); Samuel Low Anable (b. November 28, 1821); Harriet Isabella Anable, also known as Hatty or Hattie (b.

Emily C. Judson to the Reverend Abram Dunn Gillette, August 13, 1850—Maulmain

My Dear Mr. Gillette,

Several months ago I recv'd a paper purporting that I had been made a life member of the Home Mission Soc. by your church. I have long intended to acknowledge the kind compliment, but could not, and more, not being *au fait* to these things, I do not know whether I have done it properly or not. I send the note to you, that you may make what use of it you think proper or suppress it altogether.

I wrote to Mrs. G.[98] a few days ago, and do not now feel like adding many words. I am *so* weak, and *so* tired all the time, and so heavy-hearted! It seems as though my morning never would come, but yet I know it will sometime—a glorious one. How joyfully old friends will greet each other there!

Till then, farewell, and may God bless you!

Aff'y yrs

Emily C. Judson

Source: Unknown.

Emily C. Judson to the Reverend W. S. MacKay, August 19, 1850—Maulmain

My dear sir,

Your kind and truly sympathetic note gave me the first intelligence of this sore bereavement—which has cast so black a shadow over all my future, and left me in the wide world desolate indeed. I do not well know how to express my gratitude for your exceeding great kindness, but it reaches my heart, nevertheless. It comes to assure me, that I have not yet *wholly* lost my sainted husband—that his influence is still hovering about me, since even strangers extend the kindly hand to one who can boast no higher merit, than that she was dear to him.

I thank you most cordially for your generous invitation, and should I visit Calcutta, would gladly avail myself of it. But, as yet, my future course is undecided. The probability however, is, that I shall return to America in the course of a few months, with my children,[99] (whom, by the way, I fear Mrs. Hough[100] did not mention to you) and if so, should most likely embark at Calcutta. In the meantime,

December 18, 1823); Courtland Wilcox Anable (b. July 28, 1825); Frances Alma Anable, or Fanny (b. April 12, 1828); and Mary Juliet Anable (b. February 18, 1830).

[98] Hannah Gillette was the wife of the Reverend A. D. Gillette, pastor of the Eleventh Baptist Church in Philadelphia. Emily stayed with them when she came to Philadelphia in spring 1845 for her health, and she returned in November. In the parlor of their home, she met Adoniram Judson on Christmas Day 1845. Mr. and Mrs. Gillette became strong friends and supporters; Mrs. Gillette played an important part in getting Emily's outfit together for her life in Burmah.

[99] Traveling with Emily would be Henry Hall Judson, a little more than eight years old; Edward Judson; almost six years old, and Emily Frances Judson, almost three years old.

should you know of any family, who would be willing to take me under their protection, during the passage, will you kindly inform me? I should like also to know your opinion of the overland route for a person with three children—eight, six and three years of age-and a native ayah?[101] For several reasons I should prefer returning that way, but fear it is impracticable.

With grateful regards both to yourself and Mrs. MacKay,

Believe me,

Most sincerely yours

Emily C. Judson—

Source: Hanna family files.

Emily C. Judson to Catharine Chubbuck, August 20, 1850—Maulmain

My Dear Kate,—

I suppose you will have heard before this reaches you, that the last blow has fallen upon me—that I am widowed and desolate. Oh, you can not [sic] guess how heavy my heart is—nor how dark and dreary my future appears. God help me! I can not [sic] write particulars now, I am too ill, and Mr. Ranney[102] says he wrote from Mauritius. I can not [sic] say what I shall do. I have no plans, and no expectations. It was my husband's wish that I should go home with my poor little orphans, but the missionaries beg that I will decide on nothing hastily, and I feel as though America could never be a home to me again. Time will tell. In the mean time [sic], pity me, dear Kate, for my poor heart is aching sorely.

Your afflicted sister,

Emily C. Judson

Love to father,[103] mother,[104] and Wallace.[105]

Source: A. C. Kendrick, *The Life and Letters of Mrs. Emily C. Judson*, 345.

[100] See vol. 1, "Cast of Characters," s.v. "Hough, The Reverend George and Phoebe."

[101] See vol. 1, "Cast of Characters," s.v. "Nancy."

[102] See vol. 1, "Cast of Characters," s.v. "Ranney, Thomas and Maria."

[103] Emily's father. See vol. 1, "Cast of Characters," s.v. "Chubbuck, Charles."

[104] Emily's mother. See vol. 1, "Cast of Characters," s.v. "Chubbuck, Lavinia Richards."

[105] Born January 1, 1824, William Wallace Chubbuck was six years younger than Emily. During these years of Emily's correspondence, Wallace lived at or near home and worked at different occupations including printing, office work, and teaching. Emily wrote of him as capable in many areas, but seeming to lack ambition at times. He proved to be a strong support for the Chubbuck family over these years, and at the time of her death in 1854, Wallace had become one of Emily's primary caregivers. After February 1854, she dictated all her letters to him because of her failing strength. Wallace married Julia Allin Throwbridge on July 18, 1854. He died on August 13, 1861, at the age of thirty-seven. The obituary in the Utica *Herald* noted that Wallace had trained as a printer in Morrisville and had gained some astute political skills. He was "possessed of one of the brightest of intellects, and wield[ed] one of the most trenchant of pens." He had served as a justice of the peace and as clerk to one of the legislative committees in Albany.

Emily C. Judson to Anna Maria Anable, August 20, 1850[106]

It is all over, Anna Maria, darling, and oh! do pity me. I am so, *so* desolate. He lived only four days after they left the river, and suffered so intensely that he longed for the release of death. And here for four long months have I been so anxious about him, when he was wearing his crown in heaven? I ought to rejoice and be glad that he is so happy and glorious: sometime, perhaps, I may get strength for it; but now I can think of nothing, and see nothing, but the black shadows that have fallen upon my own heart and life. Oh, it is a terrible thing to lose a friend and guide like him.

I can not [sic] write you any more, darling, for my heart is aching, and I am ill with grief. I do not feel as though I should ever be well again; but perhaps I shall—and then, perhaps—I do not know—I may try to bring my poor little orphans home. Write to me, however; for it is doubtful about my going at all—certainly not at present. It seems to me that I should like to die here, and be buried where my precious husband labored. But no matter; wherever we may be, we shall have no difficulty in finding each other on the resurrection morning. Oh, Anna Maria, you do not know how we have loved one another, and now, *I am alone*. In deep affliction,

Your poor

Nemmy

Source: A. C. Kendrick, *The Life and Letters of Mrs. Emily C. Judson*, 344–45

Mrs. Phoebe Hough to Emily C. Judson, August 20, 1850

My dear Mrs. Judson

I send you a few flowers, and earnestly hope you are stronger to day [sic] and in better spirits. It made me sad to see you yesterday,[107] and I long to so something to make you stronger—Could not come here and enjoy our hill air? I am sure change would do your body good—The spirit I cannot prescribe for—God's promise to the widow is sure but what can fill "the aching void" in your solitary heart! Friends may do much but that they cannot do—

Ever affectionately yours

Phoebe Hough

Source: American Baptist Historical Society, AJ 16, no. 665.

[106] A. C. Kendrick dates this letter as August 15, 1850. A later date is more likely. Emily wrote on August 19 to the Reverend W. S. MacKay that his letter was the first information she had on Adoniram Judson's death. She wrote a similar letter to this on August 20 to her sister Catharine, and it is likely this was written that same day. Her letter to Catharine mentions something Mr. Ranney told her, so we assume that Thomas Ranney, who had accompanied Adoniram Judson on the trip to the Isle of Bourbon, had returned. The information in this letter about when Adoniram Judson died could only have come from Thomas Ranney.

[107] In the few days prior to this date, Emily had learned of Adoniram Judson's death on April 12, 1850. The news had come in a letter from the Reverend W. S. MacKay.

Emily C. Judson to the Reverend Doctor Solomon Peck, August 21, 1850—Maulmain

My dear Mr. Peck,

I am sure that you will acquit me of disrespectful neglect, if in the midst of my sickness and crushing sorrow, I do not write you as I otherwise might. "Stricken, smitten of God and afflicted," my only refuge is the cross of Christ, and I have at present no hope, no feeling, no thought for anything else. It is right to mourn, though not to murmur, and while I say "it is the Lord; let him do what seemeth to him good," my heart must needs be aching with its heavy anguish. And yet, my sorrow is all selfish, for I can and do rejoice, when I think of his having won his crown at last—entered into his rest—a co-heir with Christ in glory; where "the Lamb that is in the midst of the throne shall feed him, and shall lead him into living fountains of pure waters, and God shall wipe away all tears from his eyes."

I beg an interest in your prayers, that God may direct my future course, leading me through the black shadows that have settled on my pathway in the manner [Note: "Way" is crossed out.] that will best conduce to his own glory, and the good of those among whom he may be fit to place me.

With best wishes for your health and prosperity.

Believe me, my dear Mr. Peck,

Your sincere, but sorely afflicted friend,

Emily C. Judson

Source: American Baptist Historical Society, AJ 12, no. 380.

Miss Lydia Lillybridge to The Reverend Doctor Solomon Peck,[108] August 21, 1850—Maulmain, Burmah

My dear Mr. Peck,

Your kind letter of December was received in April, and you will think me rather unfaithful in neglecting so long to answer it. However, you have in the mean time [sic] probably received one from me written in December—49, from which you learned something of my employment during the two years preceding.

108 This letter is one of four letters from Lydia Lillybridge to Dr. Solomon Peck that have been included in this Collection of Emily Chubbuck Judson Correspondence. Lydia Lillybridge's story was so intimately connected with Emily's story as they both made the decision to go to Burmah, as they both settled in and moved in different directions, and as they both faced the issues before them, that this gives another window into those lives and those experiences for our own edification. This also helps to round out our picture of Miss Lillybridge, a most interesting person as we learn from her letters, and from those letters which mention her.

Since the receipt of yours, many sad changes have taken place in the Mission. The venerable Founder, Dr. Judson, has gone to his eternal rest[109]—Mr. and Mrs. Binney[110] have gone home—Mr. Stilson[111] has been laid aside from his work, for nearly four months—and death has entered our dwellings and removed two of our younger pupils—The particulars respecting all these, you will have heard before this reaches you.

There has been more illness among our pupils this year than at any previous time since I have had connection with the school. But all are now in health pursuing their studies with a good degree of diligence. The number in the girls' department is still about thirty five. Though some have left, new ones have come to fill their places.

You wish to know my encouragements, and discouragements—Sometimes, there appears to be such dullness of perception—such a want of retentiveness of memory—such an inclination to pass things by without thought—and such subjection to proud, depraved, and selfish nature, even by those who profess to bear the yoke of Christ, that I feel that my time has been spent in vain—that I have labored for naught—that the Spirit of Christ is scarcely perceptible in them—and sometimes, I reel that it is on account of a want of the right spirit and qualifications in myself, that things are as they are—In short, that I have mistaken my calling—At other times, all manifest so much interest and diligence in their studies,—such attention to religious instruction, and some, such a desire to honor God in all their ways, and to instruct others in the way of righteousness,—that I do indeed feel, that there is reason to bless God and take courage,—that there are not more inconsistencies in their conduct, than in that of their teachers, to say the least. I need not tell you that at such times, I feel that there is not a place in the wide world where I could be happier than I am here. But I *know* that I have not that faith, or patience, and that habitual spiritual mindedness, that ought to exist, and which is always expected to exist in one connected with the missionary work. I often feel that if the Directors of the Mission had been thoroughly acquainted with me, they would never have sent me, and I sincerely tell you (speaking to you as freely as to a brother of my own family) that if, for any cause the Board were dissatisfied with their own action in sending me, I should not wish to retain my connection with the Mission for a single month longer. I might do something here towards supporting myself and instructing the heathen for a few years, and then, I might, possibly wish to return to my native land; (not at the expense of the Union, however.)—But do not imagine that I am habitually gloomy in spirit, for it is far otherwise, as many would testify.

[109] Adoniram Judson had died at sea on April 12, 1850. Emily and the Mission had just heard of his death within the previous few days.

[110] See vol. 1, "Cast of Characters," s.v. "Binney, The Reverend Joseph Getchell."

[111] See vol. 1, "Cast of Characters," s.v. "Stilson, Lucretia and Lyman."

Are the Executive Committee fully decided in their opinions respecting the propriety of having the pupils of this school instructed in the English language? Sometimes they seem to have approved of it, and again to seem to have been dissatisfied with it.—I do *know*, that numbers by learning English in this school, have had a fountain of knowledge opened to them, from which they have sipped deliciously. By means of it, the understanding has been enlightened, and the whole character elevated, and I do not wish to take it upon myself, to shut that fountain against others. Still, I do not feel quite satisfied in regard to the extent to which I should engage in this department of work.—Knowing the difference of opinion on this subject, I should have been much happier during the last three years, if I could have been freed from teaching at all in English, and it would have been much more in accordance with my original ideas of missionary work not to have taught in that language.

You wish to know my ideas of the importance of schools in the work of missions. I never felt the importance of them so much as I do now. If the rising generation are to be instructed in the truths of religion, it appears reasonable that they should be with us day after day, that when a good impression is made, it may be repeated again and again.

Suppose we go from house to house, and from street to street, speaking to the ignorant children the most simple truths of God's word.—They may listen attentively for the time, but without repetition, our words are like water spilt on the ground—like seed sown by the wayside. Without "line upon line, and precept upon precept," we cannot hope to effect much improvement either in the minds or morals of thoughtless degraded children of idolaters. Therefore, if we neglect schools, our efforts must be confined almost entirely to adults, or to a comparatively small number of children.

I leave it to my superiors to decide upon the wiser course.—

I am happy to say that the boys' department of the school as a whole, is in a better state at present, than at any time since my acquaintance with it. The teachers employed are much more efficient than former ones, and if Mr. Stilson's health be spared, there is reason to believe that the school will become what it should be, in all respects.

If you, good people at home, could know how ridiculous it appears to us who are here on the ground, to hear you talk in your reports about the "*Maulmain Burmese High School*," I'm sure that you would not use such lofty terms. The school is in truth, far below many of our common country schools at home.

Mrs. Stilson is very feeble, but still, she "has a mind to work," and does work—often beyond her strength. She is a woman of an excellent spirit, and exerts a happy influence on all around her. Her kindness to me is such, as to make me feel perfectly *at home* in her family.

The loss of dear Dr. Judson is deeply felt by all the Mission. As an individual loss I, perhaps, feel it more than any other besides his own much beloved companion. Still, I should have felt it much more keenly during the first year of my residence here. Long since, "my soul became as a weaned child." Poor Mrs. Judson feels desolate indeed, but exhibits much Christian resignation.—

Not long ago, I requested the brethren of the Mission to release me from the duties of the school for three months to come, that I might make an extraordinary effort to acquire the Burmese Language. Though they did not think it best to grant my request in full, they unanimously consented, I believe, to grant it in part. Therefore, I am excused from teaching in English till the close of the present term, though I continue to oversee, and to watch the interests of the English, as well as the Burmese portion of the School—Mr. Stilson has taken one of my classes, and Mrs. Stilson one. The remainder are taught by the one, a pupil formerly, who has assisted me during the whole of the present year, and under whose instruction, pupils have made good progress. I know of no one among this class of people whose services as a teacher would be so valuable as hers.

We have just commenced a new term, after a vacation of one week, and my arrangements for the Burmese classes are not yet fully completed. I intend to have one in reading the Scriptures, one in First Lessons in Philosophy, one in History, and one in Arithmetic. I am not now capable of teaching all these *well*, but I intend to make myself be.

During my vacation, I took my pupils over to Newton to visit the Normal School; also the other Karen schools. They were much gratified by the visit and were, I hope, excited to greater diligence in their own studies.

That Normal School has been well taught, and is exceedingly interesting.

Miss Wright,[112] I fear, will finish her work in a few years, if she keeps on as arduously as she has commenced.—She calls herself, Miss Vinton,[113] and me, Faith, Hope, and Charity—a threefold cord.

Please remember that whenever I address *Mr. Peck*, I mean *you, yourself*, not the Secretary.

I hope soon to hear that your health is fully restored.

[112] Hannah Elizabeth Taylor Wright was born September 21, 1820, in Nelson, New Hampshire. She was appointed in 1849 to serve as a teacher at the Karen Normal School in Maulmain, Burmah. She sailed from Boston on October 18, 1849, and arrived in Maulmain on March 18, 1850. She returned to the United States on account of her health on June 29, 1852. In July 1858, she married the Reverend Lyman Stilson, missionary to Burman. Lucretia Stilson, his first wife, had died in Maulmain, Burmah, on August 14, 1851. Lyman and Hannah Wright Stilson had two sons, Charles and Edwin. Lyman Stilson died in Jefferson, Iowa on March 23, 1886; Mrs. Hannah Stilson died in Jefferson, Iowa, in March 1898. There is one letter in the correspondence from Miss Wright. Writing from Newton, Massachusetts, in July 1853, she sent Emily flowers that she "thought had bloomed to shed their fragrance in a sickroom."

[113] Calista Holman was born in Union, Connecticut in April 1807. She married Justus Hatch Vinton on April 9, 1834, and they sailed for mission work in Burmah in July 1834. With her husband, she was stationed at Chummerah, Newville, and Maulmain, specializing in work with the Karens. She taught the Karen women and was the author of several hymnbooks in their language. Calista and Justus Vinton were the parents of three children. Mrs. Vinton died in Rangoon on December 18, 1864.

With kindest regards to Mrs. Peck and her honored Father,
Believe me
My dear Mr. Peck,
Yours very sincerely

Lydia Lillybridge

I have deferred writing to my dear Parent till the last moment, and cannot write them a single word. Will you therefore, do me the favor of sending this letter to them as soon as convenient after having read it yourself.

Direct it to James Lillybridge, Pine P.O., Oneida Co., N.Y. By thus doing, you will oblige me exceedingly.

L. L.

[Written in the left margin of the address page:] Mr. Peck will accept my thanks for his favor. Jas. Lillybridge.

Source: American Baptist Historical Society, Lydia Lillybridge file.

The Reverend Edward Stevens to Emily C. Judson, August 26, 1850

My dear Sister Judson,

Very many thanks for the book-stand, which you have kindly sent me, as a memento of the dear departed Brother, with whom I have ever esteemed it an honor to be associated in labor, and into whose labors, in the Providence of God, I am now called more fully to enter. As it falls to my lot to be occupied so much with my pen,[114] the sight of this memento, I am sure will be to me an incentive to diligence in the performance of those labors for which he has been so imminent.

It will also be particularly valuable to me, as a memento of yourself my dear Sister, who have said that the departed *loved me*; and who though smitten by the heaviest affliction, which can beset the heart of woman, I am permitted to see meekly by submission to Him who has appointed it and thereby evincing your interest in that unfading inheritance, which is prepared for all them that love our Lord Jesus Christ in sincerity.

That the riches of Divine Grace may ever be he [sic]—I touch upon you, according to your every need, and upon the dear children[115] who though now left without an earthly father, have a faithful everliving [sic] Father above, shall ever be the Sincere prayer of

[114] Mr. Stevens was to finish the work on the Burmese-English Dictionary started by Adoniram Judson.

[115] This would reference all six Judson Children—Abby Ann, Adoniram, Elnathan, Henry, Edward, and Emily Frances.

Your affectionate brother in Christ

Ed S. Stevens
August 26, 1850

Source: American Baptist Historical Society, AJ 19, no. 904.

The Reverend George H. Hough to Emily C. Judson, August 26, 1850

My dear Mrs. Judson,

I am greatly obliged by your sending me Mr. Judson's cane; I am glad to possess it as a valued memorial of our old friend of 34 years standing.

I am
Very sincerely yrs

G. H. Hough

Source: American Baptist Historical Society, AJ 16, no. 666.

Mr. Thomas Ranney to Emily C. Judson, August 26, 1850

My dear Mrs. Judson

I thank you for the Bible, and shall prize it very highly. When I witnessed your dear husband's death,[116] and his assured hope of immortality, I felt that I was at an infinite distance behind him in attainments in the divine life, and then resolved that I would henceforth endeavor to keep the world at a distance and live for heaven. I am sure this bible [sic] will daily bring to my mind the resolution formed on that solemn occasion.

Affec Yours

Thos Ranney

Source: American Baptist Historical Society, AJ 18, no. 821.

[116] Thomas Ranney had accompanied Adoniram Judson on the *Aristide Marie*, and had been present at his death on April 12, 1850.

Mrs. Jane M. Haswell to Emily C. Judson, August 31, 1850—Framingham

My dear sister Judson,

I am not sure but I am repeating what I wrote last month in writing a line expressing our sympathy for you in your severe affliction. Certain it is that it was in my heart to write and that our hearts have been deeply pained by the intelligence we have received month after month, since last Dec. respecting the failing health of Dr. Judson. It has been our daily prayer with that, I doubt not, of many thousand hearts in this land, that if it be the will of God, he may be spared.[117] Anxiously indeed are we waiting to hear what has been the effects of the voyage upon his health, fearing, from all that we can learn respecting him at the time he embarked, that ere this, he is no more. May our *hopes* rather than our fears be realized.

I am also very anxious to hear how you got along with what you were expecting, at our last received dates from Maulmain.[118] Oh, I do hope to hear that the Lord has been gracious to you and that you have been abundantly blessed. You have one of the best of sisters, to whose kind attentions Dr. J. committed you—Sister Stevens,[119] besides the other sisters equally desirous of doing all in their power to smooth your path or pillow, whose strength or experience would not perhaps admit of their doing as much.

How exalted the privilege of the Christian to cast all his cares upon the Lord, knowing that He careth for him. May his promise support you, my dear sister, under all your trials, present, or yet in store, and keep you in perfect peace. With your united love, believe me,

Yours affect.

Jane M. Haswell

Source: American Baptist Historical Society, AJ 16, no. 681

[117] Mrs. Haswell was writing from Framingham, Massachusetts. Apparently the news of the death of Adoniram Judson had not reached there at this time.

[118] This would be a reference to the birth of Charles Judson on April 23, 1850. The baby was stillborn, and buried in the Chapel Compound next to Luther Judson, the stillborn son of Adoniram and Sarah Hall Boardman Judson.

[119] Elizabeth Stevens arrived in Maulmain in February 1838; her husband was Edward Stevens. Elizabeth Stevens took six-month-old Edward Judson into her home when Sarah and Adoniram had to leave for the United States in 1845, and her care and nurture saved his life. She served forty-eight years in Burmah. She had extensive correspondence with Emily Judson, and her letters spoke of everyday life among the missionaries. When Emily returned to the United States, the letters from Mrs. Stevens brought news of friends and colleagues. Mrs. Stevens had a sister, Sarah Haven, in Massachusetts, who wrote a number of letters to Emily asking for information on the Stevens family.

The Reverend Edward Stevens to Emily C. Judson, September 1850[120]

My dear Sister Judson

The Church Book, Cash, and order, have been received—though not without feelings of sadness. But he who orders all events both joyous and affliction knows and ever does what is *best*.

Mrs. Stevens[121] says she is very glad you are—or were—so bright this morning. As to herself she has walked to monthly concert and back, and is now too tired to write how bright she is.

Yours affect—

E. Stevens

P.S. I found a flower from one of our trees, which I hope you will like.

E. S.

Source: American Baptist Historical Society, AJ 19, no. 904.

The Reverend Cephas Bennett to Emily C. Judson, September 3, 1850 —Tavoy

My dear Mrs. Judson—

I have been on board and got my things that were left, and went on to Mergui and among them was this box that has the ribbons, I now send you the lace, (4 yards for Mrs. Stevens,[122] the remainder for yourself, and any quantity or all of what there is left, you are perfectly welcome to.) As it will be a pleasure to Mrs. B.[123] as well as myself, if you can make use of it, and save buying, and besides, Mrs. B. now does not wish any of what is sent you. Mrs. Cross[124] engaged to send you some Arrow Root, Mrs. Bennett has already sent to me what we had.

[120] This letter is undated. We place it in the time period not long after the news of Adoniram Judson's death had been received.

[121] See vol. 1, "Cast of Characters," s.v. "Stevens, Elizabeth 'Bessie.'"

[122] See vol. 1, "Cast of Characters," s.v. "Stevens, Elizabeth 'Bessie.'"

[123] Stella Bennett was the wife of Cephas Bennett; they arrived in Burmah in January 1830. Mr. Bennett remained the superintendent of the Baptist Press there for more than fifty years. From the Utica area, they sent their children back, and the girls were educated at the Utica Female Academy and then the Misses Anable's School. The girls included Elsina (April 1828), Mary (November 1829), Ann (August 1833), Ellen (June 1835), and Sarah (June 1837).

[124] Mrs. Julia Ann Putman Cross was the wife of Edmund Cross. They were appointed to missionary service in Tavoy, Burmah, on November 28, 1842. Mr. and Mrs. Cross arrived in Maulmain on February 24, 1845, and at Tavoy a month later. They had been married at Morrisville, New York, in August 1843. There are two letters in the Correspondence from Mrs. Cross to Emily; both were written from Tavoy. Both of the letters have to do with helping Emily make preparations for her voyage, and the offering of arrow-root and soojer [sic] as medicines to take for the journey. Mrs. Cross is rather explicit in what soojer is for and how it works. Mrs. Cross died at Toungoo, Burmah in 1875; Mr. Cross died August 14, 1905, in Toungoo, Burmah.

You will regret to hear that Edward[125] was not well, when I returned and I do not know that I can say he is any better. The Dr. thinks his fever will have a run of perhaps 14 or 21 days—Mrs. B. is pretty well. I am getting better, but my head is rather more than common, *muddy*. Hope I shall feel better when I get more settled.

We feel much for you in your loneliness, and if we can in any way add to your comfort, we shall rejoice to do so. With kindest love to the dear children

Yours affectionately

C. Bennett

Source: American Baptist Historical Society, AJ 12, no. 357.

Emily C. Judson to The Reverend Edward Stevens, September 4, 1850—Maulmain

My Dear Mr. Stevens,—

Parting with the manuscripts[126] which were every day before my eyes during three happy years, almost carries me back to that sad morning in April[127] when he passed from the door never again to return. But I well know that my Heavenly Father is ordering all these things, and I have nothing to do but submit—nothing to say but "Thy will, O God, be done!"

A few days before Mr. Judson went away, he told me, if he should never return, to place the Dictionary papers in your hands, and it is in compliance with that request that I now send them. I suppose that he would not have improved the English and Burmese part very essentially while carrying it through the press; and the second part, the Burmese and English is, as far as he had advanced, equally complete. The last word he defined was—, and the corresponding initial vowel—.

The only request he made was that there might be some distinct mark, both in the dictionary and grammar, to indicate where his work ended and yours commenced. The grammar[128] was intended to preface the Burmese and English portion of the dictionary, but is complete only as far as through the cases of nouns—32 manuscript pages. I believe this grammar was on a somewhat different plan from the old "Grammatical Notices"; but I send a printed copy of that, in which he has marked several errors, as it may be of some service to you. In addition to the finished

[125] Edward Bennett, the son of Stella and Cephas Bennett, born in Burmah on June 16, 1837. Edward and Sarah were twins.

[126] This is the manuscript for the English-Burmese Dictionary, to which Adoniram Judson had devoted the last years of his life.

[127] Adoniram Judson had boarded the *Aristide Marie* on April 3, 1850. His hope was that a sea voyage to the Isle of Bourbon would be restorative to his health.

[128] We would note that in 1808, when teaching, Adoniram Judson had compiled an English grammar. (Adoniram Judson, Jun. A.B., *The Elements of English Grammar* [Boston: Cushing and Lincoln, 1808.] 56 pages.) This editor is proud of the copy in his possession. Judson also wrote a manual on mathematics.

parts of the Dictionary, you will find the two old manuscript volumes which he had in use ever after his first arrival in Burmah; and these I beg to have returned to me when the work is completed. Interlined and erased as they are, you will have great difficulty in deciphering them, and will no doubt find some parts quite illegible. I think I mentioned to you the plan of having Moung-Shway-loo make out, from the old printed Dictionary and his own memory, a list of words more or less synonymous, and I send the books, which, although not to be implicitly relied on, are, I believe, quite valuable.

There is one bound volume which I do not recollect having seen before; but I think it must be a vocabulary arranged from an original Burmese one, as I have heard Mr. J. speak of having such a work. The remaining papers, consisting of two or three little vocabularies, and the like, are, I suppose, of no great value; but I thought it best to send every thing [sic] in any way connected with defining words. I also put in with the rest the old proof-sheets, as he sometimes had occasion to refer to them.

And now, may the blessing of God rest upon this work—on you, or whoever else may finish it—on all who, for Christ's sake, study it, and upon poor Burmah, in whose behalf so much time and labor have been expended.

Very affectionately, your sister,

Emily C. Judson

Source: A. C. Kendrick, *The Life and Letters of Mrs. Emily C. Judson*, 345–47.

The Reverend Doctor William Dean to Emily C. Judson, September 5, 1850—Singapore

My dear friend

While at Bangkok I was pained to learn that your good husband was obliged to seek a restoration to health by a voyage at sea but we were not informed what was the place of his destination nor have we since heard the result, but fondly hope that he is again restored to you in health.[129]

I left Siam last Saturday and expect to proceed to Hong Kong next week by the str [sic] wh [sic] brought me here. I came here in company with Sir James Brooke who has been at Siam in behalf of his govt but the object of his mission has not been gained. The old foolish king appears bent on the ruin of his country and the present course of things in Siam is altogether on the down hill road. The missionary friends

[129] Adoniram Judson had died April 12, 1850, on board the Aristide Marie as it made its way across the Indian Ocean from Maulmain, Burmah to the Isle of Bourbon.

at Bangkok were in comfortable health, tho' Mr. Jones[130] was worn down with care and his various labors and needs rest and a change—Mrs. Ch( ) was on the couch but was expected to be about again in a day or two. Mrs. Jones and Miss Morse were well and actually engaged in their duties. Messrs Ch( ) and Smith quite well—the other M( ) friends Mrs. Bradley, Lane, Silsby, Mattoon, House and Bush with their families all in comfortable health. Capt. Brown[131] had been seriously ill for several days and when we left was quite delirious and fears were entertained for his life.

The interests of the Mission are encouraging—particularly in the Chinese department—Four Chinese were baptized during my visit and a few more are promising candidates for church membership. A Chinese assistant who went with me from China is now in charge of the Church under the general superintendence of Mrs. Jones who is attending to the Chinese language with good effect. The Siamese read Christian books with apparent interest but I know of no true conversions among them.

The recent visit of the Embassadors [sic] from U.S. and Great Britain has perhaps awakened some excitement among the Siamese which has resulted in frightening away the Siamese servants and teachers from the Misses. Perhaps as the Mission of those two countries has left Siam apparently at peace, as before matters may resume their old form so far as missionaries are concerned. It may not be surprising to find some important political changes in Siam before many years. If nothing from abroad disturbs their peace civil discord may perhaps be reasonably expected from the two conflicting parties among the Princes and Ministers.

My ( ) at Bangkok though protracted beyond my original expectations has been a pleasant one and perhaps the time etc. not been more profitably spent than with that church wh. [sic] is now destitute of a missionary devoted to its language and interests—a man has been appointed I believe for that post by our Board.

With kindest regards to your husband and associates

Believe me your brother

W. Dean

Source: American Baptist Historical Society, AJ 15, no. 589.

[130] See the letter of Dr. J. Taylor Jones to Emily C. Judson, dated March 11, 1850. In that letter he mentions the anticipated arrival of Dr. Dean with the delegation.

[131] Captain Daniel Brown, from Scotland, owned a ship that traveled from Bangkok to Liverpool. On November 2, 1843, Captain Brown had married Maria Slafter, the widow of a missionary. Captain Brown was to die on September 30, 1850; his wife was to return to New York, where in 1854 William Dean would court and marry her. They were married May 9, 1854.

The Executive Committee of the American Baptist Missionary Union, September 9, 1850

As God in his righteous administration, has been pleased to remove by death the senior missionary of the American Baptist Missionary Union; the Rev. Adoniram Judson, D. D.; and as the event is one of such peculiar importance as to demand of this committee a more than ordinary expression of interest; therefore,

Resolved, That we recognize with devout gratitude, the special grace of the Head of the Church, in providing for us such a pioneer of our missionary enterprise; in endowing him with such eminent qualifications for the service; in preserving him so long through a series of extraordinary labors, sufferings and perils; and in enabling him to execute so much for the glory of Christ, and the welfare of the heathen.

Resolved, That while we bow submissively to the will of Him who has thus in a mysterious way elevated his servant from the work of earth to the reward of heaven, we are happy to cherish a grateful recollection of the many excellencies of our beloved brother, and to place on permanent record our cordial and unqualified testimony to the great purity of his personal character; to the singular uniformity with which he has exemplified the spirit of his vocation; and to the distinguished patience, perseverance, and fidelity, with which, ever since the date of his appointment, May 25, 1814, he has prosecuted his appropriate work.

Resolved, That in the absence of the Foreign Secretary, the Home Secretary be requested to address to Mrs. Judson a letter of condolence, assuring her of the tenderest sympathy of the Committee in her most afflictive bereavement; of the high estimation in which they held the eminently good man of whom she has been thus painfully deprived, and of their readiness, should she so desire, to facilitate the return of herself and family to her native land.

Resolved, That the Home Secretary be requested to communicate to the Mission, with which Dr. Judson was connected, a fraternal expression of our sympathy with them in the severe loss which they have sustained, and of our fervent desire that this dispensation of Providence may be so graciously overruled as to subserve the advancement of that cause to which they and we are mutually pledged.

Resolved, That the Secretaries be requested to take the steps necessary to secure the materials for the preparation of a Memoir of Dr. Judson.

Resolved, That immediate arrangement be made for a public discourse and other religious services appropriate to this afflictive occasion.

Resolved, That copies of these resolutions be forwarded to Mrs. Judson and to the Mission; also to Miss Abigail B. Judson, the only surviving sister of the deceased.

Source: American Baptist Historical Society, AJ 14, no. 548.

The Reverend W. S. MacKay to Emily C. Judson, September 9, 1850[132] —Cornwallis Square

My dear Mrs. Judson,

There are many reasons for your returning, by way of Calcutta, should you decide to return to America. A passage to England for you and your children could be procured in a comfortable passenger ship for about 12 or 1400 R.; and there would be no difficulty in getting an introduction for you to almost any eligible family that might be going at the same time. The overland passage, even you alone, has many advantages but with 3 children, the fatigue and anxiety would be very great, and the expense above 2,000 R.

I think I may venture to say that your passage to England would cost you nothing, for there are many friends of your husband's here, who would most gladly assist you.

One indeed (Major Durand), as soon as he heard of Dr. Judson's death, wrote to me, placing 200 R. at my disposal, if money were wanted for his family. Major Durand says he has met with only 3 men in the course of a ( ) experience, who realized his ideal of true Christian men, and these were Dr. Judson, Bishop Cor( ), and Dr. Duff.

He is anxious that something in the shape of a retrospect of his life and labours [sic] should appear in the *Calcutta Review* (a quarterly periodical now under my management); but until I see or hear from you, I do not wish to decide. Major D. writes admirably, and has much of the enthusiasm necessary to the right accomplishment of such a labour [sic] of love. I think he would willingly undertake it. Such an article would be a mere glance at so much of his public life and labours [sic], as is already known to the world, founded on the two biographies, the Judson offering, and the Society's reports. It would in no respect forestall, or interfere, with a Life of Dr. Judson, which, I trust, as a national monument, the Americans will take care to entrust only to ( ) hands.

You will, I am sure, acquit my indelicacy, or intrusion into your private affairs, when I presume to ask you the state of your circumstances, and what provision you may probably look forward to for the future. There are friends here, as I have already said, who would count it a privilege to be of use to you and your family; but until I know what your plans and ( ) are, I think it better not to move in the matter.

His countrymen, I have not a doubt, will take care of all that belonged to Dr. Judson; but on what scale that may be done, I cannot tell. We at the very least should be allowed to send you to them with as much comfort and in as little trouble to yourself, as may be.

[132] This letter was written in reply to Emily's letter of August 19, 1850.

In regard to the children, I did not know that three were with you. Had I known it, I would have assured you, as I now do, that we have plenty of room for them, and that my children will be delighted to have so many playfellows. I shall look for you this time by the *Enterprize* [sic]; and either I myself, or a friend, will be on board, almost as soon as the arrival off Calcutta to receive you.

I scarcely think sufficient discretion has been exercised in publishing an account of the last hours of your sainted husband. It seems to me cruel, as well as unwise, to note down the chance expressions of pain and delirium, and to give them to the world as if the utterer were responsible for them.

Not that I consider any expression, that fell from Dr. Judson's lips, as requiring apology or defence [sic]; but it is not necessary to give everything to the public. Trusting to see you soon, and with the assurance of our sundery [sic] esteem, and warmest sympathy, believe me

Very truly yours

W. S. MacKay

If you see Mrs. Hough,[133] tell her I will answer her very acceptable letter by next mail.

Source: American Baptist Historical Society, AJ 17, no. 751.

Miss Cynthia Sheldon to Emily C. Judson,[134] September 10, 1850—Philadelphia

My dear dear afflicted one—

Your letter written in weakness and anguish came on Saturday Aft'n two days since and the day long to be remembered—The morning paper had brought to us the dreaded intelligence, our worst fears were realized in regard to your own dear husband—and we were unprepared, yes unreconciled—a gleam of comfort came from your letter a few hours later—we could see you had gained some strength, and was [sic] probably better prepared for this stunning blow—than at the 12th of April—"The Lord reigns, let the earth tremble" was uppermost in my mind for many hours—and this deeply affective providence has been the constant theme of all who know you—unceasing prayer has gone up to the throne of grace for you and the

[133] See vol. 1, "Cast of Characters," s.v. "Hough, The Reverend George and Phoebe."

[134] There is an addendum to this letter dated September 11, 1850.

dear little ones—Mr. Gillette[135] was gone—I have not yet seen him—Anna Maria[136] found him at home just before tea—you may be sure of their deep sympathies—Mary Anna Longstreth[137] too—twice have we mingled the tear since your letter came—The Robarts[138] and others—everyone feels as friends feel when wounded by the same lash—Would that we could mingle tears with yours—and would that the balm of consolation could by us be poured into your bleeding heart—and turn the current of your bitter thoughts to the blessed abode of the saints made perfect in heaven—and the first resurrection of the dead in Christ—Mr. Joshua Lincoln[139] of Boston was here Sabbath Evening—he had heard Dr. Malcom[140] in the morning and at the close of his sermon he presented the melancholy tidings to the Church in this wise—The lamented friend was one of the most distinguished characters of

[135] Following several successful pastorates, the Reverend A. D. Gillette was the founding pastor of the flourishing Eleventh Baptist Church in Philadelphia in 1839. With his wife Hannah and several children (they would eventually have six), he graciously opened their home to Emily Chubbuck when she came to Philadelphia at the end of March 1845 for her health. The connection had been made through Miss Cynthia Sheldon, a family friend of Mr. Gillette and his parents. A prominent Baptist, Mr. Gillette journeyed to Boston in December 1845 to accompany Adoniram Judson to Philadelphia for meetings, and on Christmas Day, he introduced Dr. Judson to Emily Chubbuck with the hope that Fanny Forester could be persuaded to write the memoir of Sarah Hall Boardman Judson. A. D. Gillette and his wife Hannah remained valued and trusted friends, not only with Emily, but with the Sheldon and Anable families. He moved from Philadelphia to New York in 1852.

[136] See vol. 1, "Cast of Characters," s.v. "Anable, Anna Maria."

[137] Mary Anna Longstreth was a Quaker who lived in Philadelphia and who took an extraordinary interest in Adoniram and Emily Judson. She lived with her extended family, and they are frequently mentioned in her letters. Apparently, she ran a private school much like the one Anna Maria Anable started. Her letter of May 1848 paints a strong picture of her character, her faith, and her sensitivity. In this letter, she remarks on the particular strengths of each of the wives of Adoniram Judson.

[138] Mr. and Mrs. W. S. Robarts were active in Philadelphia Baptist circles. They were frequent visitors to the home of the Reverend and Mrs. A. D. Gillette and later to the Misses Anable's School, which Anna Maria Anable and her extended family had started in Philadelphia in 1848. In his biography of his father, Edward Judson mentioned that Adoniram Judson stayed at the. Robarts's home when he came to Philadelphia in December 1845 when he met Emily Chubbuck. A. C. Kendrick said, "(Mr. Gillette and Dr. Judson) arrived in (or out of) due time in Philadelphia, and Dr. Judson was welcomed to the house of Mr. and Mrs. W. S. Robarts, who became warm personal friends, as they were already active friends of the mission cause." (A. C. Kendrick, *The Life and Letters of Mrs. Emily C. Judson* [New York: Sheldon and Company, 1862] 142.) In 1846, with the engagement of Adoniram Judson and Emily Chubbuck, the correspondence indicates some hard feelings toward Mrs. Robarts for comments disparaging the coming marriage and missionary service. This is found in Emily's letter to Adoniram dated February 6, 1846; Mrs. Robarts seemed to be accusing Emily of worldliness when all the time, Emily was quick to say, Mrs. Robarts was engaging in the same activity of which she was accused. The correspondence also indicates a satisfactory healing of the relationship. In January 1849, Miss Sheldon told Emily that Mrs. Robarts had placed their daughter Mary in the Misses Anable's School.

[139] Joshua Lincoln was a prominent Baptist layman in Boston. Anna Maria Anable lived with Mr. and Mrs. Lincoln in summer 1848 when she went to Boston for medical treatments to correct deficiencies in her shoulder and spine. Mr. Lincoln was active in Massachusetts and national Baptist circles.

[140] Dr. Howard Malcom was born in Philadelphia in January 1799. Planning to live as a merchant, he was converted and called to the ministry. Licensed by the Sansom Street Church and educated at Princeton Seminary, he became pastor of a church in Hudson, New York, in 1820. In 1826, he became an agent for the American Sunday-School Union, and in 1827, he became the pastor of the Federal Street Church in Boston. Because of failing health, he toured Europe in 1831 and again in 1835 when his voice failed him and he resigned his parish. He next spent two years in Burmah, and upon his return in 1840, he became the president of Georgetown College in Kentucky. In 1849, he was forced to resign this position because of his anti-slavery views. In late 1849 or early 1850, Dr. Malcolm was called to be the pastor of the Sansom Street Baptist Church, which Alma Anable attended, as did some of the other members on occasion of the Anable-Sheldon families. There are many references to him in the letters of this time period. In 1851, he became the president of the University of Lewisburg and was there until he left in 1857 to resume work on a number of his publications. In this time he became interested in the American Baptist Historical Society and devoted himself to this work until his death in 1879. (William Cathcart, *The Baptist Encyclopaedia* [Philadelphia: Louis H. Everts, 1881] 740.)

the age, in the Christian world—and as if God could set his seal to this mighty eminence, he had given to him the glorious ocean for his winding sheet, the priceless Coral bed for his resting place—This thought to me was so consoling that I have to enlarge upon it—and keep in view the grandeur of the "mighty deep"—do dear Emily cultivate pleasant thoughts on this subject—it will give you a willing mind to say the Lord reigns—I do not suppose this will leave Boston before the 1st of Oct. if I send it now but we send off a package in the morning to dear Sarah Bell[141] who is in Boston and she can give it to Mr. Bright[142]—he will forward all things to you with dispatch. It is settled that dear Sarah will, providence permitting, be Mrs. Gould[143] next month—he has been a widower some two years—They will live in Bennett Street where I do hope dear Emily you will be at home the little time you will want to stay in Boston when in providence your native land is again reached—Mr. G. is Deacon of Rose St. Church—42 years of age and they tell me his house has always been the home of Missionaries—and if possible I will be there too in a few hours after you arrive—all my plans will be made for such meeting then we can talk of the eventful past—also of what we can see in the future—you know our hearts, our hand and our home are open to you and yours—

The school is comeing [sic] up finely—our number of boarders have increased much—we hope to be thankful—

Source: American Baptist Historical Society, AJ 20, no. 991.

Miss Cynthia Sheldon to Emily C. Judson,[144] September 11, 1850

Dear E.—I have not had a moment this morning to write more—Anna M.[145] will write Mr. Gillette[146] too—he intended to write you weeks ago—know dear dear Emily that the fervent prayer is going up to the throne of all grace unceasingly for you—Heaven grant you sustaining grace, and open up the door of providence to return you to our arms in safety—I do feel troubled about your company but think providence indicates the return of the Bennetts[147] by the time our Missionaries arrive there—I beg they will not delay till fell disease removes them from their ardous [sic] field by death—They would prove such props to you on the voyage that I do hope they will embark—but want them to re( ) as soon as they do embark—our greatest joy is to feel that all Christendom now feels right about the return of Missionaries—

[141] See vol. 1, "Cast of Characters," s.v. "Wheeler, Sarah Bell."

[142] See vol. 1, "Cast of Characters," s.v. "Bright, The Reverend Doctor Edward, Jr."

[143] Charles Gould was forty-two years old, a widower with two children, a daughter and an invalid son. He was known to be pious and a friend to missionaries, and he was a deacon at the Rose Street Baptist Church. He was a partner in the publishing firm of Gould, Kendall and Lincoln and was the brother of Mrs. Joshua Lincoln. Charles Gould and Sarah Bell Wheeler were married in October 1850.

[144] This letter is an addendum to a letter written September 10, 1850.

and the board now feel deeply delays, whereby comes protracted suffering—This leaves us in good health—on Saturday evening last Henry Anable[148] arrived from Sheboygan—they are doing pretty well in business—and he is in usual spirits although they were burned out last winter.

May you be encircled by Almighty care—and unwavering trust in the goodness of God pervade your heart—I know it is a great attainment to say from the heart "Altho he slay me, yet will I trust in him"—Love—sympathy, prayers from each are yours—do write—Your friend

C. Sheldon

Source: American Baptist Historical Society, AJ 20, no. 991.

Mr. Lewis Colby[149] to Emily C. Judson, September 14, 1850—New York

Mrs. E. C. Judson

Dear Madam,

We have just heard of the severe blow has fallen upon you [sic] and upon the cause of missions in the death of your honored husband. Although from the news of last month it was generally feared that such might be the result, yet as he has been so wonderfully preserved and for so many years it was hoped his constitution would again rally. But such, it seems was not the will of Providence. His work on earth is done. He has entered upon his rest; and you are left alone in a heathen land, and were not even permitted to be present in his last hours. But I doubt not that the same trust in God which enabled you to enter the missionary field has sustained in this affliction. You will have the sympathy and prayers of thousands in this and other Christian lands.

[145] See vol. 1, "Cast of Characters," s.v. "Anable, Anna Maria."

[146] See vol. 1, "Cast of Characters," s.v. "Gillette, The Reverend Abram Dunn."

[147] See vol. 1, "Cast of Characters," s.v. "Bennett, The Reverend Cephas and Stella Kneeland."

[148] Henry Sheldon Anable was the oldest of the six children born to Joseph and Alma Sheldon Anable. He was born June 21, 1815. In August 1846, he was in the Milwaukee, Wisconsin, area and was thinking of settling there. In a September 27 letter, he said he might leave Utica to join William and Olivia in Sheboygan, Wisconsin. He was married to Rosanna Frick in Sheboygan, Wisconsin, on February 13, 1855, and died September 3, 1887, in Flushing, New York.

[149] Mr. Colby was the publisher of the *Memoir of Sarah Judson* and the *Olio of Domestic Verses*. We note with interest that Mr. Colby uses this letter of sympathy for a business purpose as well, as he suggests to Emily that she write Adoniram Judson's memoir, and he tells her how pleased he would be to print and distribute it. Emily was to receive other similar proposals—one from the publishing firm of Gould, Kendall and Lincoln, through entreaties made to Anna Maria Anable by Joshua Lincoln—and one through her friend the Reverend A. D. Gillette on behalf of the American Baptist Publication Society.

In 1852 there is a letter to Emily from Edward Bright (written December 9)—at this time Francis Wayland has been working on and pretty much finished the Memoir—there is some speculation over the publisher though it is moving towards one of the Boston publishers, and Lewis Colby proves difficult—or rather he is all business for himself—in allowing use for the Memoir of a portrait of Judson to which Lewis Colby owns the copyright. Dr. Bright suggests that Emily use the portrait and let Mr. Colby file suit and let the courts decide ownership.

Dr. Judson's cause has been a very remarkable one. His success, as a missionary has been unparalleled. His name and memory will never die. Not only should the incidents of this remarkable life, however, be written but the strong points in his character which under God contributed so largely to his usefulness in his chosen field should be analyzed and brought out thoroughly for the imitation and benefit of others; and who so well knows those points and is so well qualified to do this as yourself?

It was with this feeling that months ago I ventured to suggest either to him or yourself the propriety of your obtaining from him while living such materials as you might be able to, for the preparation of a memoir, should you in the providence of God survive him.

This I hope you have done, and that whether you return home or remain in Burmah (I know not your determination, though should you conclude to return and be able to use your pen I think I could guarantee you a handsome support from the book you would produce) you may perform for the church this service. I need not say it would give me great pleasure to print and circulate it.

There is, you are aware, in my hand due you and a/c of premiums to last July about $500, which is subject to your order.

Mrs. Colby unites with me in wishing you all Christian consolation and all divine support.

I am, as ever, yours
Most respectfully and truly

Lewis Colby

Source: American Baptist Historical Society, AJ 15, no. 604.

Mrs. Phoebe Hough to Emily C. Judson, September 15, 1850

My dear Mrs. Judson

Many, many thanks for your affectionate note. Though I have all the freshness of feeling of a girl of sixteen yet without her extravagant romance, I am not hurt, nor surprised by being reminded of the fact that my race is nearly run, and my sun nearly set, and I hope I am in a measure though ( ) a full measure than I feel to God for all his mercies to me and mine. His goodness has been truly wonderful, and if we did not know His love, and that He who could give his Son for sinners, and give all superior gifts we should wonder more at such infinite goodness. There is much to encourage the hope of personal recognition in Heaven and one thing is certain as far as our ideas of things go, that without consciousness of what we have been, consciousness of our identity, we cannot be the same beings that were laid in the grave—But then what is a spiritual body? What a body without flesh and blood, "for flesh and blood cannot inherit the kingdom of God." I have always been a dreamer and have had sweet dreams of heaven and oh! how I have enjoyed the thought of recently departed loved ones there. The loved in youth and the fond brother, and gentle sister, and dear parents. May *we* also meet them for short will be ( ) in ( ) him. I believe I feel that I am one with you in spirit. There is a consciousness of feeling, as there was between dear Judson and myself, which I could make no other person understand, and when you are in that dear land I still love, I hope we may still sympathize with and love each other and when a purer, holier, would receive us, may we there perfect our union of spirit.

I have wished to call and see you—Last evening it was near 5 o'clock when Mr. H.[150] came home and there was no getting out. Mr. MacKay's[151] note to me was a sad one—All had been ill, and they had a house of invalids, and he had hardly strength to write a few lines—He bid me remember him to you.

Our dear Ian has been again publicly commended by Gov't for his zeal, and faithfulness—this is very gratifying to a mother's heart.

With love ever
Affectionately yours

Phoebe Hough

Source: American Baptist Historical Society, AJ 16, no. 663.

[150] George and Phoebe Hough were the first missionaries to be wholly called by the American Baptist Missionary Union to work in Burmah with Adoniram and Ann Judson. Mr. Hough learned the printing trade from his father, and they set up a print shop to support the work of the mission. They arrived in Burmah in October 1816 and retired from missionary service in 1826; George Hough subsequently worked for the government as an interpreter and school superintendent, and Mrs. Hough worked as an educator. They remained friends with Adoniram Judson and many of the other missionaries. Their independence was problematical at times.

[151] The Rev. W. S. MacKay, of Calcutta. A Scotch Presbyterian missionary, he wrote Emily of Adoniram's death and was the first to deliver this devastating news. He also invited Emily and the children to live with them in Calcutta when they were there waiting to sail for the United States.

Miss Rebecca A. "Bessie" Rhees[152] to Emily C. Judson, September 15, 1850—Mount Holly, NJ

Do not think that I am intruding on the sacredness of your sorrow, dear Mrs. Judson, by thus addressing you. Were I near you, I would, like the friends of Job, sit down with you in silence, more eloquent than words.—words—ah! what a mocking they seem to a grief like yours! But separated from you, as I am by half the globe, it is by written words of sympathy only I can reach you, and reach you I feel as if I must to-night—would that I could sooth and comfort you.

Oh! Emily! Dear sister! (Suffer me to call you so—it is thus I name you in my prayers to one common Father). I can *sympathize* with you, though I have no power to console you. I yield only to you in my affection for him whom we mourn to-day, or my grief at his departure. I feel that it is impossible for any save yourself to have loved him better than I, or to mourn for him more bitterly, yet what is my love or my grief compared to yours! And what can lighten your heavy sorrow? You have, it is true, the sympathy of many, many Christian hearts, and warm prayers are ascending daily on your behalf. Oh! that they may avail! that He who only can, may comfort you.

My dear, dear Sister, others will speak to you of the useful life, the shining example of the departed of the glorious reward to which he has gone, and the hope of soon rejoining him where the ties we form will remain forever unbroken, but you know all this as well or better than any of us. It is not necessary to remind *you* how good and great he was, for who knew him so well as you, or to point you to the meeting in the world above, for will not your life be henceforth but one anticipation of that home, one pressing forward to that goal?

> "Oh! if no other boon were given,
> To keep our hearts from wrong and stain,
> Who would not strive to ( ) a heaven,
> Where all we love shall live again!
> Hearts *from which* it *was death to sev*er
> *Eyes, this world can* ne'er *restore*
> *There as* warm, *as bright as ever*
> *Shall meet* us and *shall part no more*.

[152] This is the first of three letters from Rebecca A. Rhees to Emily Judson following the death of Adoniram Judson. This letter seems to demonstrate an unrequited love and an inconsolable grief, working toward wanting to establish a "sisterly" relationship with Emily. In her third letter, it is obvious that Emily rebuffed these efforts. There are five letters from Rebecca Rhees to Adoniram Judson dated February 19, May 8, and May 10, 1846; October 1, 1848; and November 25, 1849. On March 6, 1846, Adoniram Judson wrote to Emily about his recent correspondence, including, he said, "that of R. A Rhees, one of the few flames I have had since you left." The story and letters to Adoniram Judson of Rebecca Ann Rhees are found in the correspondence at the time of the dates they were written.

It is not of these topics I would speak, indeed, I *cannot* speak of him now; when any mention his name, his death to me, I feel as Mr. Howard says he does, like saying as did Elisha of old, "Yea, *I know it*; *hold ye your peace*." I am anxious only of the overpowering grief. "My father! my father! the chariot of Israel, and the horsemen thereof." I do not believe I could speak of him, even to you, were you near me but oh! Emily it is my heart that would commune with yours, in all the depth of its grief, the warmth of its affections. Will you let me love you as I loved him? I have loved you long, for your own sake, as well as his, but now that he is gone, that I may no more, even at long, long intervals, claim his remembrance, or receive from him the treasured assurance that he still thinks of and prays for me, I feel as if drawn to you by a closer and holier tie. Let me love you, Emily; let me look upon you as my sister while we both remain on earth, would that I were near you, that I might wait upon you and serve you as a sister for his sake! I dare not look forward to meeting you again, even in Heaven, as I did for a little while on earth, for oh! how many shining ranks will divide him, the tall, bright seraph, bending near the throne, from me, the lowly, the [sic] it may be *scarcely* saved, but you will meet him, for he is yours, and death cannot dissolve nor eternity impair the tie that binds you.

Forgive me I fear I am writing wildly, yet I feel that you can understand me—*he* always did—Oh! he was the only being I ever met by whom I felt that my real feelings were comprehended, the true nature of the affection I felt, understood and returned. And now—oh! that the Lord would open a way for me to devote myself to his work, and become as he wished me to be, a Missionary.

But I shall weary you; I must close; dear Sister, may the Lord, our covenant keeping God, sustain you in this tearful trial, even though heart and flesh fail; may you be enabled to feel that "*Thy Maker is thy husband*," ever near you, ever watching over you to bless. I pray for you constantly; this is all I can do. How strange it seems that I may no longer implore a blessing for him, whose name has been so long blent [sic] with my petitions: oh! he is where no prayer is needed to complete the measure of his perfect bliss; we can in no way minister to him now.

Farewell; forgive the freedom with which one who never saw you writes to you; forgive me, for his sake, who sometimes called me by my familiar household name of Bessie, who permitted me to call myself, what I would most gladly be to you

Your affectionate Sister

R. A. Rhees

Source: American Baptist Historical Society, AJ 18, no. 810.

Anna Maria Anable to Emily C. Judson, September 15, 1850—Philadelphia

Dearest dearest Nemmy[153]

Would that you *could* lay your weary head on my bosom and there see how my heart bleeds for you in your great, unspeakably great, bereavement. O, that I could now reach you, or you me! You have kind friends in M. I know, but it would be such a privilege to take you in my arms again and try to dry your tears. Though my feeling leads me to think that I could be some comfort to you, I know that your only consolation must and will come from God, who, though he has so sorely wounded you is still your kind Heavenly Father who doeth "all things well."

Nemmy darling, the day that we received news of your great loss, I rec'd a letter from you, showing that you were still uncertain of the dear Dr.'s fate. Oh, I feel so thankful that you were kept in ignorance so long—and I so hope that before the sad news reached you, you were recovered from your illness, and that you had some strength to bear up under your affliction. Darling, for our sakes, for the children, and for your own sake, try to overcome any machination to despondency; believe that he who loved you and prayed so for you while on earth, watches over you still. His last thought was of you, and it seemed to me as I read his dying injunction to "take care of poor mistress," that he carried your image with him up to heaven. Oh, Nemmy, if we ever reach that blessed place shall we not rejoice to find the things that are now so dark and [difficult] of comprehension, made plain to ( ) his mysterious dispensation, which caused the beloved teacher to be buried in the ocean within sight of the Burman hills, which caused him to be removed from your affectionate care in his dying moments will all then be understood.

Nemmy darling, I am constantly asked if you will not return to this country, and I sometimes think that you are perhaps now on your way. I have understood that it was the Dr.'s wish that you should return with the children, but of course I can say nothing. Will that not be the best course for you in your delicate health? You have so *many* kind friends here, and so many ways of making yourself useful in this country—and then the children, it is time for them to be here. Remember Phil. had one of the first claims on you, and my home will always be yours, when you will make it so. Mr. Lincoln,[154] who was here last week, begged me to tell you something about his publishing a work for you, whenever you should feel disposed to write. I believe he once wrote you about a work which he thinks would be very popular,

[153] "Nem" or "Nemmy" was a name of endearment given to Emily by a small group of her intimate friends at the Utica Female Academy. Anna Maria Anable was "Ninny."

[154] Joshua Lincoln was a prominent Baptist layman in Boston. Anna Maria Anable lived with Mr. and Mrs. Lincoln in summer 1848 when she went to Boston for medical treatments to correct deficiencies in her shoulder and spine. As early as 1847, Mr. Lincoln was trying to get one of Emily's books for publication. It did seem that the Lincolns and Anna Maria moved into a close relationship. Emily also received similar inquiries from Lewis Colby and from the American Baptist Publication Society.

something like scenes in the east, or in missionary life. He is *very* anxious to publish for you and would pay as well if not better than any one [sic] in the country. He says he will publish anything which you feel disposed to write etc. etc.

I shall be *so* anxious to hear from my own darling now, and to know what you will like to do. Tell me all your own thoughts. I shall understand them. Remember little Frances[155] is mine to educate,[156] and you are mine too, are you not? What would I not give for one hour's talk with you just now. Give a great deal of love to Lydia[157] and all in the Mission ship when it arrives.[158] I have said nothing in reply to what you wrote of the little boy.[159] It must have been a great trial to you to lose him, but is it not well? The widow's God and the Father of the fatherless, lift up the light of His countenance upon you, and evermore bless you and yours, and when this short life is ended bring us all to meet the loved ones who have been gone before in that Heaven where there are no tears—no sighs, but where an eternity of bliss awaits us if we continue faithful to the end.

Ever yours

Anna M.

Source: American Baptist Historical Society, AJ 13, no. 471.

[155] See vol. 1, "Cast of Characters," s.v. "Judson, Emily Frances."

[156] Upon Emily's death in June 1854, Anna Maria became her guardian; she raised and educated her. Emily Frances was six and a half years old at that time.

[157] See vol. 1, "Cast of Characters," s.v. "Lillybridge, Lydia" and the Lillybridge papers in the appendices.

[158] On July 25, 1850, the *Washington Allston* had sailed from Boston Harbor with a large group of new and returning missionaries, including Mr. and Mrs. Kincaid, Mr. and Mrs. Wade, and Dr. and Mrs. Dawson. The ship was a chartered vessel enabling the American Baptist Missionary Union to send the group directly to Maulmain, Burmah. According to the correspondence, it turned out to be a disastrous trip, with much of the problem the fault of the captain. From Mrs. Hough's letter of May 20, 1851, we gather that there were too many passengers and not enough supplies, among other problems. The ship, according to Emily Judson (February 23, 1851), "entered the mouth of the Salwen [River] just as [her] steamer was leaving it" bound for Calcutta. Emily said that she visited with the Kincaids and Mrs. Vinton in Calcutta, for they had come in on the *Tudor* "from the Cape"—apparently some of the passengers had left the *Washington Allston* en route.

[159] This is a reference to the birth of Emily and Adoniram's son, who was named after Emily's father, Charles. Emily called him "Angel Charley" in her famous poem. The baby was stillborn on April 23, 1850, and Emily wondered if all of the events of her illness and Adoniram's illness which would take his life on April 12, 1850, might have been damaging to her child. See the letter of May 20, 1850, which Emily had sent to Adoniram not realizing that he was already dead. Out of her grief, Emily wrote a poem which she called "Angel Charley."

The Reverend Sewall Mason Osgood to Emily C. Judson, September 16, 1850[160]—Indianapolis, Indiana

My dear afflicted Sister

The painful intelligence of the death of your dear husband and my esteemed and intimate friend and Missionary Associate reached me through the public paper at Cincinnati on the 12th inst. I will not attempt to describe my own feelings nor allow myself to stir up the already too troubled waves of sorrow which have been rolling upon your wounded Spirit for these months which have intervened. It is the hand of the Lord which hath done it and it becomes ours to bow with submission to his will.—He has gone beyond the toils and cares and anxieties of Missionary life—to a brighter world where holier ones have long since greeted him to a more exalted sphere of labor,—to higher and more holy enjoyments than earth knows.

Let us travel on and look upward for we shall soon be there. I love to think of him in the Society of those loved ones who have gone before.

Notwithstanding the discouraging accounts in regard to Bro. Judson's health—your letter to me and the one to Adoniram[161] and Elnathan,[162] the stroke has come upon me unexpectedly. I had too fondly relied upon his last message to you before going out to sea. I knew the influence of the clear air and hoped, though it was almost hoping against hope, that he would return and recover, and was waiting with great anxiety for some intelligence from him at the Isle of Bourbon. I am confident my dear Sister that sustaining grace has been meted out to you from the same kind hand which has dealt this severe blow. I am a stranger, but it would give me great pleasure to hear from you, and to have further particulars in regard to yourself, the children, and the departed.

Your sympathizing brother and friend

S. M. Osgood

Source: American Baptist Historical Society, AJ 18, no. 827.

[160] A second letter of this same date accompanied this letter; the second letter concerned business matters Mr. Osgood wanted to with Emily.

[161] Adoniram "Addy" Judson was born April 7, 1837, the second child and first son of Adoniram and Sarah Hall Boardman Judson. From November 1845 to October 1851, he lived with Dr. and Mrs. Calvin Newton in Worcester, Massachusetts. He then spent a year with Dr. and Mrs. Edward Bright in Roxbury, Massachusetts, and before entering Brown University, he was two years at Pierce Academy in Middleboro, Massachusetts. After his education and medical school, Adoniram served as a surgeon in the Civil War and became a prominent orthopedic surgeon with several books to his credit. He died in 1916. Over the years, he became vocal about the separation of missionary children from their parents.

[162] Elnathan "Elly" Judson was born July 15, 1838, the third child and second son of Adoniram and Sarah Hall Boardman Judson. From November 1845 to October 1851, he lived with Dr. and Mrs. Calvin Newton in Worcester, Massachusetts. He then spent a year with Dr. and Mrs. Edward Bright in Roxbury, Massachusetts, and before entering Brown University, he spent two years at Pierce Academy in Middleboro, Massachusetts. There are strong indications that Elnathan planned to become a minister, and in fact, he did graduate from Union Seminary. In 1860, however, he suffered a serious sunstroke that subsequently caused serious mental impairment. For much of his life, Elnathan was confined to mental institutions. He died after a second paralyzing stroke in 1896; in the last years of his life, Elnathan was lovingly cared for by his sister Abby Ann Judson.

The Reverend Sewall Mason Osgood to Emily C. Judson,[163] September 16, 1850

My dear Sister

I wrote you on the 24th of July in reply to yours of April 19, and have now only to say further that if you should find it necessary to draw upon the funds invested here under my direction I will endeavor to make arrangements to accommodate you though the mortgage has I think, a little over three years to run yet.—If there is anything in which I can be of service to you in this country I hope you will not fail to mention it. I am now on a tour of the western and Northwestern States to attend the State conventions of our denomination, but expect to return to my residence in Wyoming, N.Y. about the first of November.

If you feel at liberty to write to me in regards to your plans for the future both for yourself and the children I hope you will feel assured of my sympathy in all, and that so far as desirable your communications shall be confidential. I was very intimate with Bro. Judson, and perhaps knew more of his business arrangements than anyone else—and I would be glad on his behalf as well as for your own sake to render you any service in my power.

Yours truly

S. M. Osgood

Source: American Baptist Historical Society, AJ 18, no. 827.

Doctor Edward Bright to Isaac Newton, Esq.,[164] September 18, 1850—Missionary Rooms, Boston

Dear Brother:—

Your favor of yesterday came this morning, but I cannot give you reliable information as to the course which Mrs. Judson will pursue. She probably did not hear of her great bereavement before Mr. Ranney's[165] return to Maulmain, *about the 1st inst.*[166] Our latest letters from that city are of June 20, at which time Mrs. Judson was very feeble, not having recovered from a premature confinement superinduced

[163] This added letter on business matters was included with another letter of sympathy and condolence dated September 16, 1850.

[164] Though this letter is not to Emily C. Judson, it concerns her plans for the future after the death of Adoniram Judson and tells of friends who rallied around her to provide for her needs.

[165] This report of Thomas Ranney to Dr. Edward Bright, the corresponding secretary of the American Baptist Missionary Union, can be found under the title "The Last Days of Dr. Judson, as Derived from a Letter of Mr. Ranney to the Corresponding Secretary" in Francis Wayland, *A Memoir of the Life and Labors of Rev. Adoniram Judson, D.D.* (Boston: Phillips, Sampson, and Company, 1853) 2:348–52.

[166] On August 19, Emily wrote the Reverend W. S. MacKay of Calcutta to tell him that his letter had been the first to inform her of the death of her beloved husband. Emily stayed with the MacKay family in Calcutta while she waited for the ship to sail on February 24, 1851.

[sic], probably, by the intense anxiety which she felt for her husband in his lonely voyage. Should her health be reestablished, she will be likely to remain in the mission,—for she has been very useful there, and her health has been usually better than before she sailed for Burmah. But the Executive Committee have instructed me to inform Mrs. Judson "of their readiness, should she so desire, to facilitate the return of herself and family to her native land." This information will go to her by the mail which leaves here Oct. 2, and will probably reach Maulmain late in December and it will be sent in accordance with a general rule of the Committee, not because they wish her to return. She may decide that it is her duty to come home;—but *I think* she will not do so unless the state of her health requires it. Her heart is in the mission, and I have reason to know that her missionary [Note: This is the last line on the page and the ink is blurred beyond recognition; seven words are lost.] But it is impossible to form any opinion as to the effect which Mr. Ranney's narrative has had, or will have, on her. She will be satisfied with knowing nothing less than all the particulars of the lonely agony of her husband's last hours, and of his silent burial. The knowledge of all may prove too much for her frail frame and most sensitive nature. But I need not pursue these thoughts. Knowing the deep interest which you and Mrs. Newton[167] have ever felt for Mrs. Judson, I am desirous that you should have all the facts and views which we have. I have, therefore, written freely, and will merely add, that should Mrs. Judson return she will be likely to sail early in January, 1851, as that is the most favorable time. Money sent to her on or before Oct. 2, would almost certainly reach her before her departure, but goods, if sent in October, would not reach Maulmain before February or March.

Cordially yours

Edw. Bright, Jr.

P.S. We have two missionaries to sail for Maulmain about the middle of October. If you send any ( ), it would be desirable to send it at that time.

Source: American Baptist Historical Society, AJ 14, no. 547.

[167] Adoniram Judson always stayed with Mr. and Mrs. Newton when in New York, and Mrs. Newton held a reception for Emily before they sailed to Burmah. They sent Emily a draft for $500 to help with her immediate expenses.

Emily C. Judson to Miss Abigail Brown Judson, September 20, 1850—Maulmain

My Dear Sister,

Last month I could do no more than announce to you our painful bereavement, which, though not altogether unexpected, will, I very well know, fall upon your heart with overwhelming weight. You will find the account of your brother's last days on board the *Aristide Marie*,[168] in a letter written by Mr. Ranney,[169] from Mauritius, to the secretary of the board; and I can add nothing to it, with the exception of a few unimportant particulars, gleaned in conversations with Mr. Ranney and the Coringa servant. I grieve that it should be so—that I was not permitted to watch beside him during those days of terrible suffering;[170] but the pain which I at first felt is gradually yielding to gratitude for the inestimable privileges which had previously been granted me.

There was something exceedingly beautiful in the decline of your brother's life—more beautiful than I can describe, though the impression will remain with me as a sacred legacy, until I go to meet him where suns shall never set, and life shall never end. He had been, from my first acquaintance with him, an uncommonly spiritual Christian, exhibiting his richest graces in the unguarded intercourse of private life; but during his last year, it seemed as though the light of the world on which he was entering had been sent to brighten his upward pathway. Every subject on which we conversed, every book we read, every incident that occurred, whether trivial or important, had a tendency to suggest some peculiarly spiritual train of thought, till it seemed to me that, more than ever before, "Christ was all his theme." Something of the same nature was also noted in his preaching, to which I then had not the privilege of listening. He was in the habit, however, of studying his subject for the Sabbath, audibly, and in my presence, at which time he was frequently so much affected as to weep, and sometimes so overwhelmed with the vastness of his conceptions as to be obliged to abandon his theme and choose another. My own illness at the commencement of the year had brought eternity very near to us, and rendered death, the grave, and the bright heaven beyond it, familiar subjects of conversation. Gladly would I give you, my dear sister, some idea of the share borne by him in those memorable conversations; but it would be impossible to convey, even to those who knew him best, the most distant conception of them. I believe he has sometimes been thought eloquent, both in conversation and in the sacred desk; but the fervid, burning eloquence, the deep pathos, the touching tenderness, the elevation of

[168] Adoniram Judson boarded the *Aristide Marie* on April 3, 1850, bound for the Isle of Bourbon, with the hope that a sea voyage would be restorative to his health.

[169] See vol. 1, "Cast of Characters," s.v. "Ranney, Thomas and Maria."

[170] Emily had been prevented from accompanying Adoniram Judson on his voyage because of her pregnancy; she delivered a stillborn child, named "Charles" after her father, Charles Chubbuck, on April 23, 1850.

thought, and intense beauty of expression, which characterized those private teachings, were not only beyond what I had ever heard before, but such as I felt sure arrested his own attention, and surprised even himself. About this time he began to find unusual satisfaction and enjoyment in his private devotions, and seemed to have new objects of interest continually rising in his mind, each of which in turn became special subjects of prayer. Among these, one of the most prominent was the conversion of his posterity.[171] He remarked, that he had always prayed for his children, but that of late he had felt impressed with the duty of praying for their children and their children's children down to the latest generation. He also prayed most fervently that his impressions on this particular subject might be transferred to his sons and daughters, and thence to their offspring, so that he should ultimately meet a long, unbroken line of descendants before the throne of God, where all might join together in ascribing everlasting praises to their Redeemer.

Another subject, which occupied a large share of his attention, was that of brotherly love. You are, perhaps, aware that, like all persons of his ardent temperament, he was subject to strong attachments and aversions, which he sometimes had difficulty in bringing under the controlling influence of divine grace. He remarked that he had always felt more or less of an affectionate interest in his brethren, as brethren, and some of them he had loved very dearly for their personal qualities; but he was now aware that he had never placed his standard of love high enough. He spoke of them as children of God, redeemed by the Saviour's blood, watched over and guarded by his love, dear to his heart, honored by him in the election, and to be honored hereafter before the assembled universe; and he said it was not sufficient to be kind and obliging to such, to abstain from evil speaking, and make a general mention of them in our prayers; but our attachment to them should be of the most ardent and exalted character: it would be so in heaven, and we lost immeasurably by not beginning now. "As I have loved you, so ought ye also to love one another," was a precept continually in his mind; and he would often murmur, as though unconsciously, "'As I have loved you'—'as I have loved you,'"—then burst out with the exclamation, "O, the love of Christ! the love of Christ!"

His prayers for the mission were marked by an earnest, grateful enthusiasm, and in speaking of missionary operations in general, his tone was one of elevated triumph, almost of exultation; for he not only felt an unshaken confidence in their final success, but would often exclaim, "What wonders—O, what wonders God has already wrought!"

I remarked that during this year his literary labor, which he had never liked, and upon which he had entered unwillingly and from a feeling of necessity, was growing daily more irksome to him; and he always spoke of it as his "heavy work,"

[171] See, as an example of this, the letter of Adoniram Judson to Abby Ann Judson dated November 26, 1848.

his "tedious work," "that wearisome dictionary"' etc., though this feeling led to no relaxation of effort. He longed, however, to find some more spiritual employment, to be engaged in what he considered more legitimate missionary labor, and drew delightful pictures of the future, when his whole business would be but to preach and to pray.

During all this time I had not observed any failure in physical strength; and though his mental exercises occupied a large share of my thoughts when alone, it never once occurred to me that this might be the brightening of the setting sun; my only feeling was that of pleasure, that one so near to me was becoming so pure and elevated in his sentiments, and so lovely and Christ-like in his character. In person he had grown somewhat stouter than when in America; his complexion had a healthful hue, compared with that of his associates generally; and though by no means a person of uniformly firm health, he seemed to possess such vigor and strength of constitution, that I thought his life as likely to be extended twenty years longer, as that of any member of the mission. He continued his system of morning exercise, commenced when a student at Andover, and was not satisfied with a common walk on level ground, but always chose an up-hill path, and then frequently went bounding on his way with all the exuberant activity of boyhood.

He was of a singularly happy temperament, although not of that even cast which never rises above a certain level, and is never depressed. Possessing acute sensibilities, suffering with those who suffered, and entering as readily into the joys of the prosperous and happy, he was variable in his moods; but religion formed such an essential element in his character, and his trust in Providence was so implicit and habitual, that he was never gloomy, and seldom more than momentarily disheartened. On the other hand, being accustomed to regard all the events of this life, however minute or painful, as ordered in wisdom, and tending to one great and glorious end, he lived in almost constant obedience to the apostolic injunction, "Rejoice evermore!" He often told me that although he had endured much personal suffering, and passed through many fearful trials in the course of his eventful life, a kind Providence had also hedged him round with precious, peculiar blessings, so that his joys had far outnumbered his sorrows.

Towards the close of September of last year, he said to me one evening, "What deep cause have we for gratitude to God! Do you believe there are any other two persons in the wide world so happy as we are?" enumerating, in his own earnest manner, several sources of happiness, in which our work as missionaries, and our eternal prospects, occupied a prominent position. When he had finished his glowing picture, I remarked,—I scarcely know why, but there was a heavy cloud upon my spirits that evening,—"We are certainly very happy now, but it cannot be so always. I am thinking of the time when one of us must stand beside the bed, and see the other die."

"Yes," he said, "that will be a sad moment; I felt it most deeply a little while ago, but now it would not be strange if your life were prolonged beyond mine—though I should wish, if it were possible, to spare you that pain. It is the one left alone who suffers, not the one who goes to be with Christ. If it should only be the will of God that we might go together, like young James and his wife! But he will order all things well, and we can safely trust our future to his hands."

That same night we were roused from sleep by the sudden illness of one of the children. There was an unpleasant, chilling dampness in the air, as it came to us through the openings in the sloats [sic] above the windows, which affected your brother very sensibly; and he soon began to shiver so violently that he was obliged to return to his couch, where he remained under a warm covering until morning. In the morning he awoke with a severe cold, accompanied by some degree of fever; but as it did not seem very serious, and our three children were all suffering from a similar cause, we failed to give it any especial attention. From that time he was never well, though in writing to you before, I think I dated the commencement of his illness from the month of November, when he laid aside his studies. I know that he regarded this attack as trifling; and yet one evening he spent a long time in advising me with regard to my future course, if I should be deprived of his guidance, saying that it is always wise to be prepared for exigencies of this nature. After the month of November, he failed gradually, occasionally rallying in such a manner as to deceive us all, but at each relapse sinking lower than at the previous one, though still full of hope and courage, and yielding ground only inch by inch, as compelled by the triumphant progress of disease. During some hours of every day he suffered intense pain; but his naturally buoyant spirits and uncomplaining disposition led him to speak so lightly of it, that I used sometimes to fear that the doctor, though a very skilful [sic] man, would be fatally deceived.

As his health declined, his mental exercises at first seemed deepened; and he gave still larger portions of his time to prayer, conversing with the utmost freedom on his daily progress, and the extent of his self-conquest. Just before our trip to Mergui, which took place in January, he looked up from his pillow one day with sudden animation, and said to me earnestly, "I have gained the victory at last. I love every one of Christ's redeemed, as I believe he would have me love them—in the same manner, though not probably to the same degree as we shall love one another in heaven; and gladly would I prefer the meanest of his creatures, who bears his name, before myself." This he said in allusion to the text, "In honor preferring one another," on which he had frequently dwelt with great emphasis. After further similar conversation, he concluded, "And now here I lie at peace with all the world, and what is better still, at peace with my own conscience. I know that I am a miserable sinner in the sight of God, with no hope but in the blessed Saviour's merits;

but I cannot think of any particular fault, any peculiarly besetting sin, which it is now my duty to correct. Can you tell me of any?"

And truly, from this time no other word would so well express his state of feeling as that one of his own choosing—*peace*. He had no particular exercises afterward, but remained calm and serene, speaking of himself daily as a great sinner, who had been overwhelmed with benefits, and declaring that he had never in all his life before had such delightful views of the unfathomable love and infinite condescension of the Saviour as were now daily opening before him. "O, the love of Christ! the love of Christ!" he would suddenly exclaim, while his eye kindled, and the tears chased each other down his cheeks; "we cannot understand it now—but what a beautiful study for eternity!"

After our return from Mergui, the doctor advised a still further trial of the effects of sea air and sea bathing; and we accordingly proceeded to Amherst, where we remained nearly a month. This to me was the darkest period of his illness—no medical adviser, no friend, at hand, and he daily growing weaker and weaker. He began to totter in walking, clinging to the furniture and walls, when he thought he was unobserved, (for he was not willing to acknowledge the extent of his debility,) and his wan face was of a ghastly paleness. His sufferings too were sometimes fearfully intense, so that, in spite of his habitual self-control, his groans would fill the house. At other times a kind of lethargy seemed to steal over him, and he would sleep almost incessantly for twenty-four hours, seeming annoyed if he were aroused or disturbed. Yet there were portions of the time when he was comparatively comfortable, and conversed intelligently; but his mind seemed to revert to former scenes, and he tried to amuse me with stories of his boyhood, his college days, his imprisonment in France,[172] and his early missionary life. He had a great deal also to say on his favorite theme, "the love of Christ"; but his strength was too much impaired for any continuous mental effort. Even a short prayer, made audibly, exhausted him to such a degree that he was obliged to discontinue the practice.

[At] length I wrote to Maulmain, giving some expression of my anxieties and misgiving, and our kind missionary friends, who had from the first evinced all the tender interest and watchful sympathy of the nearest kindred, immediately sent for us—the doctor advised a sea voyage. But as there was no vessel in the harbor bound for a port sufficiently distant, we thought it best, in the mean time [sic], to remove

[172] In January 1811, Adoniram Judson sailed to England, hoping to find support from the London Missionary Society for appointment to the mission field. He sought help for himself and his companions Newell, Nott, and Hall. On the way over, the ship was captured by a French privateer, and Judson was imprisoned in France with the crew. He received help in escaping from the French authorities and finally arranged safe passage to England. He spent some time here learning from those involved in the English mission, and through conversations with the London Missionary Society, he received a promise of support for him and his friends. He was somewhat handicapped in his discussions as he brought no resources from the United States to help with the expense, and this was exacerbated by the fact that, in spite of a lack of funding, the Americans wanted to maintain control of the mission. Upon returning to the United States in August, he found that interest in missions had increased, and a timely bequest to the Board of Commissioners enabled their appointment through their own denomination.

from our old dwelling, which had long been condemned as unhealthy, to another mission house, fortunately empty. This change was, at first, attended with the most beneficial results; and our hopes revived so much, that we looked forward to the approaching rainy season for entire restoration. But it lasted only a little while; and then both of us became convinced that, though a voyage at sea involved much that was exceedingly painful, it yet presented the only prospect of recovery, and could not, therefore, without a breach of duty, be neglected.

"O, if it were only the will of God to take me now—to let me die here!" he repeated over and over again, in a tone of anguish, while we were considering the subject. "I cannot, cannot go! This is almost more than I can bear! Was there ever suffering like our suffering?" and the like broken expressions, were continually falling from his lips. But he soon gathered more strength of purpose; and after the decision was fairly made, he never hesitated for a moment, rather regarding the prospect with pleasure. I think the struggle which this resolution cost injured him very materially; though probably it had no share in bringing about the final result. God, who saw the end from the beginning, had counted out his days, and they were hastening to a close. Until this time he had been able to stand, and to walk slowly from room to room but as he one evening attempted to rise from his chair, he was suddenly deprived of his small remnant of muscular strength, and would have fallen to the floor but for timely support.

From that moment his decline was rapid. As he lay helplessly upon his couch, and watched the swelling of his feet, and other alarming symptoms, he became very anxious to commence his voyage, and I felt equally anxious to have his wishes gratified. I still hoped he might recover; the doctor said the chances of life and death were, in his opinion, equally balanced. And then he always loved the sea so dearly! There was something exhilarating to him in the motion of a vessel, and he spoke with animation of getting free from the almost suffocating atmosphere incident to the hot season, and drinking in the fresh sea breezes. He talked but little more, however, than was necessary to indicate his wants, his bodily sufferings being too great to allow of conversation; but several times he looked up to me with a bright smile, and exclaimed, as heretofore, "O, the love of Christ! the love of Christ!"

I found it difficult to ascertain, from expressions casually dropped from time to time, his real opinion with regard to his recovery; but I thought there was some reason to doubt whether he was fully aware of his critical situation. I did not suppose he had any preparation to make at this late hour, and I felt sure that, if he should be called ever so unexpectedly, he would not enter the presence of his Maker with a ruffled spirit; but I could not bear to have him go away, without knowing how doubtful it was whether our next meeting would not be in eternity; and perhaps too, in my own distress, I might still have looked for words of encouragement and sympathy to a source which had never before failed.

It was late in the night, and I had been performing some little sick-room offices, when suddenly he looked up to me, and exclaimed, "This will never do! You are killing yourself for me, and I will not permit it. You must have some one [sic] to relieve you. If I had not been made selfish by suffering, I should have insisted upon it long ago."

He spoke so like himself, with the earnestness of health, and in a tone to which my ear had of late been a stranger, that for a moment I felt almost bewildered with sudden hope. He received my reply to what he had said with a half-pitying, half-gratified smile; but in the mean time his expression had changed—the marks of excessive debility were again apparent, and I could not forbear adding, "It is only a little while, you know."

"Only a little while," he repeated mournfully; "this separation is a bitter thing, but it does not distress me now as it did—I am too weak." "You have no reason to be distressed," I answered, "with such glorious prospects before you. You have often told me it is the one left alone who suffers, not the one who goes to be with Christ." He gave me a rapid, questioning glance, then assumed for several moments an attitude of deep thought. Finally, he slowly unclosed his eyes, and fixing them on me, said in a calm, earnest tone, "I do not believe I am going to die. I think I know why this illness has been sent upon me; I needed it; I feel that it has done me good; and it is my impression that I shall now recover, and be a better and more useful man."

"Then it is your wish to recover?" I inquired. "If it should be the will of God, yes. I should like to complete the dictionary, on which I have bestowed so much labor, now that it is so nearly done; for though it has not been a work that pleased my taste, or quite satisfied my feelings, I have never underrated its importance. Then after that come all the plans that we have formed. O, I feel as if I were only just beginning to be prepared for usefulness."

"It is the opinion of most of the mission," I remarked, "that you will not recover." "I know it is," he replied; "and I suppose they think me an old man, and imagine it is nothing for one like me to resign a life so full of trials. But I am not old—at least in that sense; you know I am not. O, no man ever left this world, with more inviting prospects, with brighter hopes or warmer feelings—warmer feelings;" he repeated, and burst into tears. His face was perfectly placid, even while the tears broke away from the closed lids, and rolled, one after another, down to the pillow. There was no trace of agitation or pain in his manner of weeping, but it was evidently the result of acute sensibilities, combined with great physical weakness. To some suggestions which I ventured to make, he replied, "It is not that—I know all that, and feel it in my inmost heart. Lying here on my bed, when I could not talk, I have had such views of the loving condescension of Christ, and the glories of heaven, as I believe are seldom granted to mortal man. It is not because I shrink from death that I wish to live, neither is it because the ties that bind me here, though some of them are very sweet, bear any comparison with the drawings I at times feel towards heaven; but a few years would not be missed from my eternity of bliss, and I can well afford to spare them, both for your sake and for the sake of the poor Burmans. I am not tired of my work, neither am I tired of the world; yet when Christ calls me home, I shall go with the gladness of a boy bounding away from his school. Perhaps I feel something like the young bride, when she contemplates resigning the pleasant associations of her childhood for a yet dearer home—though only a very little like her, for *there is no doubt resting on my future*." "Then death would not take you by surprise," I remarked, "if it should come even before you could get on board ship?" "O, no," he said, "death will never take me by surprise—do not be afraid of that—I feel so strong in Christ. He has not led me so tenderly thus far, to forsake me at the very gate of heaven. No, no; I am willing to live a few years longer, if it should be so ordered; and if otherwise, I am willing and glad to die now. I leave myself entirely in the hands of God, to be disposed of according to his holy will."

The next day some one [sic] mentioned, in his presence, that the native Christians were greatly opposed to the voyage, and that many other persons had a similar feeling with regard to it. I thought he seemed troubled, and after the visitor had withdrawn, I inquired if he still felt as when he conversed with me the night previous. He replied, "O, yes; that was no evanescent feeling. It has been with me, to a greater or less extent, for years, and will be with me, I trust, to the end. I am ready to go to-day—if it should be the will of God, this very hour; but I am not anxious to die; at least when I am not beside myself with pain."

"Then why are you so desirous to go to sea? I should think it would be a matter of indifference to you." No," he answered quietly, "my judgment tells me it would be wrong not to go; the doctor says *criminal*. I shall certainly die here; if I go away I may possibly recover. There is no question with regard to duty in such a case; and I do not like to see any hesitation, even though it springs from affection."

He several times spoke of a burial at sea, and always as though the prospect were agreeable. It brought, he said, a sense of freedom and expansion, and seemed far pleasanter than the confined, dark, narrow grave, to which he had committed so many that he loved. And he added, that although his burial-place was a matter of no real importance, yet he believed it was not in human nature to be altogether without a choice.

I have already given you an account of the embarkation, of my visits to him while the vessel remained in the river, and of our last sad, silent parting; and Mr. Ranney has finished the picture. You will find, in this closing part, some dark shadows, that will give you pain; but you must remember that his present felicity is enhanced by those very sufferings; and we should regret nothing that serves to brighten his crown in glory. I ought also to add, that I have gained pleasanter impressions in conversation with Mr. Ranney than from his written account; but it would be difficult to convey them to you; and, as he whom they concern was accustomed to say of similar things, "you will learn it all in heaven."

During the last hour of your sainted brother's life, Mr. Ranney bent over him, and held his hand, while poor Panapah stood at a little distance weeping bitterly. The table had been spread in the cuddy, as usual, and the officers did not know what was passing in the cabin, till summoned to dinner. Then they gathered about the door, and watched the closing scene with solemn reverence. Now—thanks to a merciful God!—his pains had left him; not a momentary spasm disturbed his placid face, nor did the contraction of a muscle denote the least degree of suffering; the agony of death was passed, and his wearied spirit was turning to its rest in the bosom of the Saviour. From time to time, he pressed the hand in which his own was resting, his clasp losing in force at each successive pressure; while his shortened breath—though there was no struggle, no gasping, as if it came and went with difficulty—gradually grew softer and fainter, until it died upon the air—and he was gone. Mr. Ranney closed the eyes, and composed the passive limbs; the ship's officers stole softly from the door, and the neglected meal was left upon the board untasted.

They lowered him to his ocean grave without a prayer. His freed spirit had soared above the reach of earthly intercession, and to the foreigners who stood around it would have been a senseless form. And there they left him in his unquiet sepulcher; but it matters little, for we know that while the unconscious clay is "drifting, on the shifting currents of the restless main," nothing can disturb the hallowed rest of the immortal spirit. Neither could he have a more fitting monument than the blue waves which visit every coast; for his warm sympathies went forth to the ends of the earth, and included the whole family of man. It is all as God would have it, and our duty is but to bend meekly to his will, and wait, in faith and patience, till we also shall be summoned home.

Source: Francis Wayland, *Memoir of the Life and Labors of the Rev. Adoniram Judson, DD*, 336–48.

Rev. J. Newton Brown and Rev. Dr. A. D. Gillette to Emily C. Judson,[173] September 20, 1850—American Baptist Publication Society, Philadelphia

Dear Sister in Christ,

The tidings of your great bereavement has spread a general sorrow over the Churches of America. For your loss is also ours, and myriads of hearts are daily lifted to God in your behalf in this time of need.

The Board of the American Baptist Publication Society, in this city where you are personally known and loved, shares deeply in the general sympathy and sorrow. And at our meeting yesterday, as a practical expression of this regard, the following Resolution was unanimously passed:

"Resolved, That Rev. J. Newton Brown, Editorial Secretary, and Rev. A. D. Gillette, be appointed a Committee, to correspond with the widow of Rev. Dr. Judson, in reference to the publication by this Society of a Memoir of her distinguished and lamented Husband, so that, being dead, he may yet speak, until 'The earth shall be full of the knowledge of the Lord, as the waters cover the Sea.'"

In obedience to this appointment, we now address you. We hope it may be not to aggravate, but to alleviate your grief. We are persuaded you are equally convinced with ourselves of the importance of such a Memoir. Notwithstanding so much has been published already, in the Memoir of the first and second Mrs. Judson, there is much that yet remains to be written of him personally—of the circumstances, of his early life, his conversion, his call to the Missionary work, his conscientious change of sentiment on Baptism, his labors as a Preacher, Pastor, and Counsellor [sic] of the Native Churches etc. as a Burmese Scholar and Translator, together with his domestic

[173] This letter, sent immediately upon hearing of Adoniram Judson's death, was the opening in the bids for the right to publish the memoir. This letter seems presumptuous and somewhat callous, if not opportunistic, though nicely and warmly expressed by people, if not friends, whom Emily Judson knew and loved. A. D. Gillette created the circumstances that brought Adoniram and Emily together on Christmas Day 1845, and in the parlor of his home, the initial stages of their courtship progressed. This was the third such letter Emily received. It was written in September; a second letter was received from Lewis Colby, publisher of the memoir of Sarah B. Judson, offering to publish a memoir of Dr. Judson; and a third letter came from Anna Maria Anable on behalf of the publishing firm of Gould, Kendall and Lincoln, who had published the biographies of George Dana Boardman and Ann Hasseltine Judson, as well as Judson's book on baptism.

As time passed, Emily became distressed at the scope of the publishing decision. The ABPS assumed that it should automatically be the society's to publish, but Emily wondered what possibilities other options would bring. In the end, it was decided to place the memoir into the hands of a non-denominational publisher, Phillips, Sampson and Company of Boston.

There are several letters from the American Baptist Publishing Society after the publishing contract was signed elsewhere, lamenting that they did not have sufficient time in which to submit a proposal, and there are responses to those letters. In November 1853, there is a gracious letter from Thomas Malcom, corresponding secretary of the ABPS, saying that it seems to have been a wise decision for a non-denominational publisher in that it opened up the market to other denominations. In this letter, he speaks of the success of a ministerial student selling the memoir by calling on Presbyterian and Episcopalian ministers.

Then, of course, there is the bitter, accusatory correspondence with Edward Fletcher, another publisher, who published an unauthorized version of a memoir that sold for a less expensive price but gave Emily no royalties. She pleaded with him in sharp terms to halt publication, but he refused and went ahead with his project. The sharpness of the exchange over the loss of control and financial advantage speaks surely to the pressures felt by Emily, for the memoir was to be a source of future sustenance for the children charged to her care.

life and habits—that the Christian public cannot willingly let die. The interest and value of such a work cannot be easily estimated. Who shall prepare it—what shall be the size, style, price to best adapted to its end, and by whom it shall be published—are questions which, we have thought, it falls to you rightfully to decide. Should you prefer to write it yourself, we would gladly undertake its publication, and would gladly allow you as liberal a compensation as you could obtain from any private publisher.

It seems to us that there are many reasons why such a memoir, by whomsoever written, should be issued by our Society. From all the facts involved, it must be eminently *denominational*, though not sectarian in its character. It would be wrong—would it not?—to hide, or throw into the shade, the great denominational change wrought in his mind by the word and Spirit of Faith—for no ignoble ends surely, but for the honor of Christianity, and the benefit of unborn millions. And our Society was instituted to issue works of this character. The denomination expect [sic] it at our hands. We are now in a condition which enables us to do it, in a style equal to that of any private establishment in this country. In this respect our condition is altogether different from what it was when you left the country. We have now a permanent location, and a beautiful edifice in Arch Street, with a growing business, and funds at our command. Besides, our arrangements for private sale, and supplier to wholesale purchasers and publishing houses in different parts of the Union, we employ between twenty and thirty Colporteurs already (and are constantly increasing the number, as the Lord favors us) in selling our books from house to house—even to California and Oregon. Our publications are also circulated in the West Indies, Canada, and Europe. So that as far as the usefulness of the Memoir depends upon its extended and ever widening circulation, no private publisher could present an equal claim. And while it would thus extensively benefit the public, its issue by *us* would reciprocally tend to aid the Society's influence.

We have thought it our duty and privilege, dear Sister, to lay this subject before you at this time, believing that you have the first right to determine the questions involved. To you and to the fatherless children of our beloved brother, belong the inheritance of his pure and priceless honor, his noble example, his undying memory, by earliest and latest prayers; and to you and them belong whatever pecuniary benefit may accrue from the circulation of his valuable Memoir.

Should you decline writing the work (which we earnestly hope you will not, without the strongest reasons) we should be glad to know to whom (with your knowledge of your husband's wishes) you would prefer to entrust it. We will spare no pains, in any case, to have it all you could desire, all indeed that it should be in order to promote a permanently and widely as possible, the great cause to which he had consecrated his life, as a servant of Christ.

Permit us to add the assurances of our sincere sympathy and esteem. We have the honor to be, in Christian Bonds,

Yours truly,

J. Newton Brown Committee

A. D. Gillette

Source: American Baptist Historical Society, AJ 17, no. 748.

Mr. Thomas S. Malcom to Emily C. Judson,[174] September 21, 1850

Mrs. Judson

Permit me to add a brief expression of my sympathy in your great loss. I have tried to *pray* for you and shall still do so, knowing that God can supply *all you need*, according to his riches in glory by Christ Jesus. Look to Jesus! Hear that voice exclaiming "not as I will, but as thou wilt." May grace help you to say "though he slay me yet will I trust him."

During last year we issued new editions, in an improved form of *John Frink* and *Effie Maurice*.[175]

I enclose a representation of our new building, and an abstract of our last year's operations. God is prospering us and opening wide doors of usefulness. Pray for us!

May God bless you above all I can ask or think

Yours truly

Thomas S. Malcom
Cor. Sec.

Source: American Baptist Historical Society, AJ 17, no. 748.

Emily C. Judson to the Reverend Doctor Solomon Peck, September 22, 1850—Maulmain

My dear Mr. Peck,

If you were not so far distant, I should wish very much to consult your opinion with regard to my future course, for I very much feel the need of advice. I suppose, however, that the Providence of God will eventually decide the matter; and I commit my ways without reserve to his hands. It was the wish of my late husband

[174] This letter accompanied the one sent by J. Newton Brown and A. D. Gillette about the publication of the future Judson memoir by the American Baptist Publication Society.

[175] These are two of Emily's earlier books published in 1844 and 1842.

that I should return to America, collect his scattered family, and assume the guardianship of his children;[176] but I conceive that without disregarding his wishes, I might remain here a few years longer—that is, if it should be the will of God to preserve my health to such a degree that I could be useful. The thought of leaving the mission is very painful to me—I can use the language some—the native Christian women entreat me to stay—and the missionaries approve and encourage, though they do not like to advise. If I have health I can do good, in my small way, while a more competent person would be obliged to spend a long time in learning the language. However, as I said before, God will decide!

My health is improving very slowly, but the doctor says I am not yet strong enough to commence the homeward voyage, even if I should conclude to go. He thinks I might be better in America than here, but does not speak with sufficient positiveness to give much weight to his opinion.

I suppose you know that Mr. J. had finished the first part of the Dictionary, the English and Burmese, and that it had been sent to press. The remainder is now passing through the press, under the supervision of Mr. Stevens.[177] The second part—the Burmese and English—he had completed about three-fourths—perhaps a little less—I cannot say precisely while in its present state.

I fancy it will not be a very serious task for any good Burmese scholar to finish it, having the first part for continued reference and his old manuscripts as a guide.

In compliance with one of my husband's last wishes, I have placed the papers in Mr. Steven's hands, as I believe he considers him better qualified than any one [sic] else to finish the work. I suppose, however, that this will be decided elsewhere.

Concerning that the friends of my sainted husband, and the friends of missions generally, would like to learn something more of those closing scenes in this life of a good man, I have abridged a letter addressed to my sister Judson,[178] in such a manner, that I hope it will not be found inappropriate for publication. I suppose it will be best suited to the columns of the *Macedonian*[179]—so will you kindly hand it to Mr. Bright[180] for that purpose?

I do not attempt to say anything of my own share in these painful afflictions, for God alone knows the bitterness of my cup, and he alone can teach me how to

[176] In a letter written to Dr. Solomon Peck on September 22, 1850, Emily said that it was Adoniram Judson's wish that, if he were to die, she would return to the United States, "collect his scattered family, and assume the guardianship of his children." As early as February 1851, as she began her trip to the United States, Emily Judson began to speak of a time and a place when all of the Judson children could be together. This was something for which each of the children hoped, and there are a number of references and pleadings in their correspondence to indicate this as their heartfelt desire. Work on the memoir of Dr. Judson, as she lived in Providence for most of six months, delayed this possibility. Then, Emily's chronic ill health forced her to the realization that she had neither the strength nor the energy for such an arrangement. The six-week period in summer 1852 was the only time this coming together was to take place. Regarding the future of the Judson children (George Dana Boardman, Abby Ann, Adoniram, Elnathan, Henry, Edward, and Emily Frances), see volume 1, "A Timeline of the Children of Adoniram Judson and Their Desire to Be a United Family."

drink it. Others may mourn a good man, and a useful missionary—I have more than that to mourn—*my world.*

In haste,

Very sincerely and respectfully y'rs,

Emily C. Judson.

Source: American Baptist Historical Society, AJ 12, no. 379.

Mr. Lewis Colby to Emily C. Judson,[181] September 23, 1850—New York

Dear Madam

By the last steamer I informed you that I have in my hand accruing from premiums on your books subject to your order about $500. I also reminded you that some months ago I suggested in a letter that Dr. Judson ought perhaps to furnish you with such materials as he might have for a memoir, that in case he should be called to his heavenly house first you might perform a service for the church. I expressed also in my last the hope that he had done so.

I mentioned to the editor of the *N. Y. Recorder* that I had done so, and he made the enclosed announcement. I did not object to it mainly because I saw that such an announcement might preoccupy the ground in your behalf, and fearing otherwise that something might appear which was should none of us be satisfied with.

Since that the Board have [sic] resolved to secure a memoir, and in connection with their announcement of it in the *Recorder*, I have added my desire to cooperate with them. I have written them to that effect, leaving the matter with them, only asking that I may be allowed to publish the book when ready, provided I will do it on as good terms as any other.

I presume you have been written to on the subject and have been consulted fully. My feeling is that you should prepare the memoir yourself if your health will allow of it, and that Dr. Judson's family should receive the proceeds.

[177] Edward Stevens arrived in Maulmain in February 1838; his wife was Elizabeth Stevens. Mr. Stevens was responsible for the native churches that were associated with the mission. He took on the work of finishing the dictionary after the death of Adoniram Judson, and he buried "Angel Charley" in the chapel compound after his birth in April 1850. Mr. Stevens was in Burmah for forty-eight years.

[178] See the letter of Emily C. Judson to Miss Abigail Brown Judson dated September 20, 1850.

[179] *The Macedonian* was a magazine published by the American Baptist Missionary Union.

[180] See vol. 1, "Cast of Characters," s.v. "Bright, The Reverend Doctor Edward, Jr."

[181] This is a follow-up to his letter of September 14, 1850. Apparently, Mr. Colby allowed an announcement to be placed in the *New York Recorder* that benefited him in terms of the publication of a memoir, when the American Baptist Missionary Union came out with its announcement that the board had authorized a memoir and would be proceeding with its writing and publication. This letter was "damage control."

I have at this time of trial written on this subject with reluctance, but it seemed necessary to explain why I made the announcement I have enclosed, and my present position in relation to it. Assuring you again of sincere sympathy in your affliction

I remain very truly

L. Colby

Source: American Baptist Historical Society, AJ 15, no. 603.

Doctor Edward Bright, Jr. to Emily C. Judson,[182] September 27, 1850—Missionary Rooms, Boston

My dear Sister:—

I have been instructed to transmit to you a copy of the resolutions adopted by the Executive Committee, on receiving the communication from Mr. Ranney[183] giving the mournful particulars of the great affliction which has fallen upon you and them, the mission with which you are connected and the Christian world. In these resolutions the Committee have done no more than to express the cherished convictions of their own hearts concerning the eminently good and great man of whom they speak. Similar expressions have been made by different organizations of Christian men in every part of this land,—for the name of your departed husband was embalmed in the affections of all who knew how to admire the noblest deeds of Christian heroism, to venerate a character whose crowning excellence were a childlike confidence in God and profound submission to His will. The intelligence of your husband's death was, therefore, spread throughout the country with a great rapidity, and all its details were read with intense interest. Denominational lines were forgotten; good men every where [sic] mourned as for the death of one in whom they held a common inheritance.

[182] In the handwriting of Edward Bright, this letter is five pages long. It accompanied the resolution of the executive committee of the American Baptist Missionary Union passed on September 9, 1850. The letter is warm, sensitive, caring, but at the same time, it puts before Emily Judson some of the options and decisions that she will be facing and gives her a remarkable amount of freedom to make those decisions. In a prior letter to Isaac Newton, Dr. Bright suggests that it is his opinion that Emily will stay in Burmah as a part of the mission; here he is quite a bit more circumspect with his opinion.

Ordinarily, this letter would have been written by the executive secretary, Dr. Solomon Peck, but he was traveling and had some health issues. Therefore, the responsibility fell on Dr. Bright. He was on target with many of the issues he raised, particularly as related to the memoir, which eventually was written by Dr. Wayland. Dr. Bright took the memoir through the publication process due to an illness in Dr. Wayland's family.

When she returned to America, Emily Judson wrote a large number of letters to potential sources trying to collect letters written by Adoniram Judson. There are a number of replies to these letters in this correspondence. Her problem of collecting sources was exacerbated by the fact that Adoniram Judson was quite deliberate in destroying all of his own correspondence, for he was quite conscious of how they might be used after his death, and he seemed to want to protect the privacy of his own personal and public life. Kendrick writes, "Dr. Judson's utter disregard, or rather morbid dread of posthumous reputation, had secured the destruction of all papers illustrative of his life, over which he had any control; and time, fire, and water had done an effectual work on the bulk of his correspondence" (Source: A.C. Kendrick, *Life and Letters of Mrs. Emily C. Judson*, 367).

But grateful as these facts must be to you, they have no power to sustain your Spirit under the crushing bereavement which has fallen upon you; and I have no words of sympathy or hope which can heal where God has so severely smitten. I can assure you, however, that what transpired on the barque *Aristide Marie* up to the evening of the 12th of April, has awakened the deepest and tenderest sympathy and solicitude for you. In the closets and around the family altars, and in the sanctuaries of thousands of Christian worshippers, prayer, earnest and I trust prevailing,—has been offered that God would himself prepare you for the statements which our brother Ranney[184] returned to communicate, and to sustain you under the otherwise insupportable grief which those statements must occasion. We cling to the hope that prayer has found acceptance with God thro' Christ Jesus;—and that you think less of your revered husband as a suffering and dying man on the *Aristide Marie*, than as a Seraphic spirit before the throne of infinite majesty and power in heaven. The life which he devoted to the missionary enterprise on earth spanned the entire history of American missions to the heathen;—but it is upon the life which he has now entered, and in the service which now absorbs his capacious soul, that he will hail the sublimest results;—the grand consummation of toil and suffering which once were his. Even now the providence—to us dark, insemtable [sic],—which made the sea the place of his death and burial, is to him radiant with the wisdom and goodness of God; and it will be so to all when the sea gives up its dead, and "death is swallowed up in victory."

The Committee have [sic] not the means to knowing whether you will think it better to remain in the Mission or to return to this country, nor do they wish to decide that question. They have learned so much of your devotion to the holy enterprise, and of your ability to be permanently useful in its service, that they are prepared cordially to respond to your remaining at Maulmain, provided your health will allow you to be actually engaged in some department of missionary work, and that your own deliberate judgment approves the course. But if, on the other hand, you deem it best to return home with your children, The Committee are prepared to authorize all the arrangements necessary to that object, and to give you the most fraternal welcome on reaching these shores. In any event, weather [sic] you remain or return, they will be most happy to do all within their power to subserve [sic] your welfare. In the event of your returning, it would be far better for you to sail from Calcutta direct for this part, than to incur the discomfort and hazard of sailing from Maulmain;—and if the *Washington Allston* equals our expectations, you could not,

[183] This report of Thomas Ranney to Dr. Edward Bright, the corresponding secretary of the American Baptist Missionary Union, can be found under the title "The Last Days of Dr. Judson, as Derived from a Letter of Mr. Ranney to the Corresponding Secretary" in Francis Wayland, *A Memoir of the Life and Labors of Rev. Adoniram Judson, D.D.* (Boston: Phillips, Sampson, and Company, 1853) 2:348–52.

[184] See vol. 1, "Cast of Characters," s.v. "Ranney, Thomas and Maria."

perhaps, avail yourself of better accommodations than her gentlemanly commander would furnish.

You will observe that the Committee have requested the Secretaries to gather materials for a Memoir of Dr. Judson. Their object in so doing was to secure without needless loss of time a biography of the highest order, and in such a way as would make yourself, or the cause of missions, the sharer of the profits of its sales. The Committee knew that publishers would not be wanting to seize so favorable an opportunity to "get up" a book, promising so wide a sale as a memoir of your departed husband; but they hoped the resolution which they adopted would forestall these enterprises, and delay the preparation of a biography until your wishes respecting it could be consulted, and the materials at Maulmain could be made available. The Misses Hasseltines[185] and Miss Abigail B. Judson[186] have been applied to for such materials as they may be able to furnish,—and these will soon be in our possession. Other friends have been invited, thro' the public journals, to forward such papers as they may have. But no individual has been spoken to, on the part of the Committee, with reference to the preparation of the biography, nor has any publisher been encouraged to expect the Ms. nor will any thing [sic] be done with respect to either of these matters, so far as the Committee is concerned, until your own preferences are communicated to them. The impression seems to be general among most of your personal friends with whom I have conversed, that it would not be your choice to undertake the work of writing the biography,—and the conviction is as general that it is a service to which you ought not to be urged. But all feel the great importance of placing the materials in the hands of one of the most gifted writers and judicious men in the denomination, and of giving him sufficient time to elaborate a biography that shall be worthy of its subject and the cause which he served. On learning your wishes with reference to the biographer, the publisher and the style of the work, the Committee will either undertake the supervision of the publication, or place the materials which may then be in their possessions at the disposal of such person or persons as you shall designate. In any event it would be very desirable to secure the earliest transmissions of all the materials, for the biography, at your command.

The Committee have [sic] selected Dr. Wayland[187] to deliver the public discourse provided for in the resolutions. We hope it will be delivered soon, and the effort will doubtless be worthy of the author of the moral dignity of the Missionary enterprise.

[185] The sisters and family of Ann Hasseltine Judson, the first wife of Adoniram Judson.

[186] See vol. 1, "Cast of Characters," s.v. "Judson, Abigail Brown."

[187] Dr. Francis Wayland was the president of Brown University in Providence, Rhode Island. A prominent Baptist leader and active in denominational activities, he was a proponent of missions. In 1851, upon Emily's return from Burmah, Dr. Wayland was asked to write the definitive memoir of Adoniram Judson. Beginning in December that year, Emily moved to Providence to work with him on the project; she was there until June and then returned frequently over the next year before it was finally published in September 1853. A warm friendship developed between Dr. Wayland and Emily.

The Committee have [sic], informally, expressed a wish that a suitable monument might be erected to the memory of Dr. Judson at Amherst, near to hopia-tree.[188] But it is now so late in the season that it will be difficult to provide one and send it out the present autumn. It can be sent, however, next year.

Mr. Ranney's letter reached us on the 6th inst.—and on the following week a slip, embracing the account, which I enclose, was published in nearly all our papers.

With sentiments of sincere respect and affection, I remain

Truly your brother,

Edw. Bright Jr.
Cor. Sec.

Source: American Baptist Historical Society, AJ 14, no. 546.

Mr. Isaac Newton to Emily C. Judson,[189] September 28, 1850—New York

Mrs. Dr. A. Judson

My dear Madam

Your note of March ten ( ) reached us in the late part of June by which we were advised of the protracted illness of Dr. J. since which we have been advised of the necessity of a sea voyage and the very distressing circumstances under which he was compelled to leave the objects of his hearts [sic] affection, and more recently we had the sad intelligence of his decease, on the ocean, alone, the deposit of his body in the deep deep sea. This to us is dark. How dark it must be for you My Dear Sister. And yet it must be right and not only right but nice, for Infinite Goodness and Wisdome [sic] ordered it so. And at some day drops of mercy will be found oozing out from the bitter rod. He rests Good man, where no polluted step will desecrate his grave, his binding sheet the emblem of purification and freedom. He rests where God would have him and believed though he sits where God will find him. I cannot enter in to [sic] the sorrow of a widow, a widow far from home and kindred surrounded with helpless ones. I cannot sooth that troubled breast. But there is *one* who being touched with all the feelings of her infirmities can, *can* turn sorrow into Joy. To that blessed *one* I commend you and pray that his grace may be sufficient for you. About the time your note was rec'd Mrs. N. was confined, and for a long time was in very feeble health, so much so that she has been compelled to be in the

[188] This was the burial place of Ann Hasseltine Judson. In a letter to Emily, Adoniram spoke of passing Amherst on a ship and looking across the horizon for the *hopia tree* by her grave.

[189] See the letter of Dr. Edward Bright to Mr. Isaac Newton dated September 18, 1850. Mr. and Mrs. Newton lived in New York; they considered themselves to be "friends" of Adoniram Judson, and indeed, whenever in New York, he stayed in their home. This warm letter with its enclosed money draft is a symbol of that loving friendly concern that gives birth to practicable necessity.

country the whole summer. Of course she made very slow progress in preparing the few small articles you desired, we had hoped to have got them of [sic] in October, but it will not be possible, and now we are hesitating about sending them with hope of your receiving them, they cannot be sent before Dec. And we are advised by the Board, that if your health fails that you may be expected to return. With these uncertainties, we have thought that a little money certain [sic] would do more good than the articles uncertain and therefore I hereby authorize you to draw on me, eith. [sic] at sight or on time for Five Hundred Dollars ($500) current on the United States, for your own individual use, and trust that you may be able to realize without difficulty or loss. Should it be in order that you leave before the box comes to hand, you can order it disposed of to some of the remaining missionaries. Mrs. N. desires me to remember her to you with much affection. May the Master whom you serve support and comfort you in your affliction.

Truly and affectionately Yrs

I. Newton

Source: American Baptist Historical Society, AJ 18, no. 855.

Mrs. Mary L. Colby to Emily C. Judson, September 29, 1850—Newton Centre Sept 29th 1850

My dear Mrs. Judson

It is so long since you have had a word from me that it would not be strange if you should conclude that I had forgotten or lost all interest in you, but that cannot be, and I know you will excuse me when you know that the partial failure of my sight has obliged me to relinquish writing, reading, and sewing almost entirely for several months past. I am very happy to say that I am now somewhat better and can use my eyes with more comfort than for a long time past, and am constrained to write you a few lines now to assure you of my sympathy and heartfelt sorrow for you in the heavy affliction under which you are now suffering. I am aware that it is impossible for me to realize the weight of sorrow which must now press upon you, but I can pray for you and commend you to Him who is able to sympathize in all trouble and to bind up the broken heart. I trust you have had the support of His Grace during all the trials you have had to pass through during past few months [sic]. We all feel that the missionary cause and the church have sustained an irreparable loss in the death of your dear husband, but for him it has been a glorious change. He has entered upon those joys which it has never entered the heart of man to conceive. O that his death may be sanctified to us and all the professed followers of Christ in this land, and many healed to follow his example of devotion to his Master's work. I have heard by Mrs. Haven[190] of your severe illness and have felt much anxiety on your account; the next letters I sincerely hope will inform us of your recovery. Mr. and Mrs. Binney[191] have recently arrived and are with her brother's family in our neighborhood. We had the pleasure of hearing him preach twice yesterday. Mrs. B. seems quite feeble though she says she is very much better in many respects than before she left Maulmain.

I suppose Anna Maria[192] has written you of her's [sic], and Harriet's[193] visit to Boston[194] and vicinity. We enjoyed their short visit very much, we thought and talked a great deal about you and the trying circumstances in which you were at that time. We had just learned that Dr. Judson had left you and strongly hoped that it was going to restore his health again.

Anna Maria and Harriet gained all hearts in our little circle here, they are such lovely girls none can help loving them. I am so glad they meet with good success in their school. There are many things I would write you my dear Mrs. J of my own family and other matters in our quiet little town, and the Institution[195] in which we feel so much interest but I feel that at this time your heart and mind must be so much absorbed by your own great sorrow that I ought scarcely to intrude a word upon you. I will only say that I have one more added to my little flock of children, a little daughter, a great pet I assure among her four brothers, and with five to look after and care for, I find my heart and hands pretty full. I know not what I should do had I missionary cares beside. My husband unites with me in sympathy and affection in regard for you, and desire if possible in any way to promote your comfort, and should you decide to return to America, be assured we shall be most happy to welcome you to home and hearts, and shall depend, if you come to Boston on your coming immediately to us. We are but a short distance from the city, and but a few minutes ride by railroad. Mr. C's store is 22 Milk St.

Give much love to Miss Lillybridge[196] for me, please tell her I received her good letter and intend to answer it if possible, and now I must close, with much love to you from my sister and mother and from your ever affectionate friend

Mary L. Colby

Source: American Baptist Historical Society, AJ 15, no. 602.

[190] Sarah Haven was the sister of Elizabeth Stevens, Emily's fellow missionary and dear friend. She lived in Massachusetts and wrote a number of times to Emily.

[191] See vol. 1, "Cast of Characters," s.v. "Binney, The Reverend Joseph Getchell."

[192] See vol. 1, "Cast of Characters," s.v. "Anable, Anna Maria."

[193] See vol. 1, "Cast of Characters," s.v. "Anable, Harriet."

[194] Anna Maria wrote from Boston on July 28, 1850. She and her sister Hatty were in Boston to see off the shipload of missionaries who departed on July 25.

[195] The Newton Theological Institution, which was located in Newton Centre.

[196] See vol. 1, "Cast of Characters," s.v. "Lillybridge, Lydia." Also, "A Timeline of the Life and Mission of Lydia Lillybridge Simons."

Mrs. Phoebe Hough to Elisa to Maria Ranney to Emily C. Judson,[197] Fall 1850

Phoebe Hough's Letter:

My dear Mrs. Judson

Rosaldine is the prince of liars, and a good for nothing ( )—Two days lately, when absent from you and probably reporting himself *ill* he was *at work* for Mrs. Barry in C( ) at 10 ans [sic] a day, and he is no doubt at work here for some person getting 10 or 12 ans [sic] a day—I found him very slow but for my distress should not dream of employing him on any terms—What he says of Mrs. B( )'s Tailor is utterly false for he is a first rate Tailor—He is new here and *says illness* has kept him away? Oh that any Christian should be found so absurd as to deny the doctrine of total depravity—If any proof were wanting in countries where children are early taught to find God, it is not wanting in heathen countries. I verily believe the Fakirs of India, and of every other eastern country are incapable of understanding what truth is.

Kindly tell Mrs. Ranney[198] that I have appealed to the highest quarters for a donation towards covering ( ) Sister's *nakedness, and* hope as she is one of the *fair sex* the appeal may be attended to. I am also trying elsewhere.

'Tis only this morning that the Tailor ( ) and I really fear ( ) may prevent his staying with me—At all events I do not intend to employ him since the proof I have of his dishonesty and untruthfulness—I was thinking of you

[Written perpendicular to text in the top margin of page 1:] this morning and that I never hear from you and seldom see you—I have been tied down by work and very often Mr. Hough[199] is not at home before 5 o'clock and 'tis dark ere our dinner is over. I expect to hear

[Written perpendicular to text in the top margin of page 2:] you are ill again.

With love

Ever affec'ly Yours

P. Hough

I've written on the gallop.

[197] This letter was written to Emily by Phoebe Hough. It passed through Elisa's hands, and she added a note. Then, it passed through Maria Ranney's hands, and she added a note. It all is a bit ludicrous, we think! At the same time it does give us a delicious look at life within the missionary community. In the midst of their passion for the proclamation of the gospel, they were eminently human.

[198] Maria Gager Ranney arrived in Maulmain in May 1844. Her husband Thomas was the superintendent of the printing press and business manager for the missionary compound. A letter from Lydia Lillybridge reveals that Mrs. Ranney had some responsibilities in the mission schools. She had no children; Maria Ranney died on April 26, 1857.

[199] See vol. 1, "Cast of Characters," s.v. "Hough, The Reverend George and Phoebe."

Elisa's Note:

My dear sister,

I send this to you because I don't understand the message. Comforting note, isn't it?

Hope you are well.

Aff'y

Elisa

Maria Ranney's Note:

Dear Sister

My little boys are here now, so I have only time to say that I think Mrs. H., wishes you to say to Rosaldine that she will not employ him at least so I understand how can it be that Rosaldine is such a bad fellow?

Aff

M.R.

Source: American Baptist Historical Society, AJ 18, no. 814.

Doctor Edward Bright, Jr. to Emily C. Judson, October 1, 1850—Missionary Rooms, Boston

My dear friend:—

I write to say a few things about the Memoir of your departed husband, as one of your personal friends. But so little time is left that I should be obliged to say them in the briefest manner.

1.—With reference to the author. Several names have been mentioned,—including Dr. Williams, Dr. Hague,[200] Dr. Stow,[201] and Prof. Gammell.[202] Either would probably do the work well,—but I think Prof. Gammell would do it as well or better than any other. His recent preparation of the History of our Missions would give him some very decided advantages.

2.—As to a publisher. The desire to have the book is so great that I am inclined to think the Ms. ought to be put into the market, and let the house publish it. That will furnish the most tasteful work,—and allow the largest percentage for the family or the treasury. S. K. and S. would probably have the book printed in the best style. But it ought to be open to competition.

3.—As to materials,—putting the first last.—I hope special care will be taken to procure all that can be obtained in Maulmain,—not overlooking any documents which may illustrate Dr. Judson's connection with government affairs in the early history of the Mission. Your own knowledge of him, will be an invaluable source from which materials can be drawn.

Now, if I, as a personal friend or as one of the Secretaries, can be of any service to you in helping forward the preparation of the book, do not hesitate to draw upon me. I will gladly assist in carrying out your wishes.

Cordially, your friend,

Edw. Bright Jr.

Source: American Baptist Historical Society, AJ 14, no. 545.

[200] Dr. William Hague was a graduate of the Newton Theological Institution and held a series of distinguished pulpits in Massachusetts and Rhode Island, including First Church in Boston; First church in Providence, Rhode Island; Federal Street church in Boston; Jamaica Plain, Massachusetts; and Wollaston Heights, Boston. He held doctorates from Brown University and Harvard College. He was a well known writer and book reviewer and served as a trustee of Brown University. (William Cathcart, *The Baptist Encyclopaedia* [Philadelphia: Louis H. Everts, 1881] 485.)

[201] Born in New Hampshire and educated in Washington, DC, Dr. Baron Stow returned to New Hampshire to become the pastor of the Baptist church in Portsmouth. In November 1832, he became the pastor of the Baldwin Place Church in Boston, where he led a significant revival. With changing social conditions in the North End of Boston and with significant erosion of his congregation as members moved to different areas of the city, Dr. Stowe resigned in 1848. Following a time of rest, he became the pastor of the Rowe Street Church and was there until 1867. The letters of Charles Gould speak of the revival events taking place under the ministry of Dr. Stow. In his letter of May 1, 1852, Mr. Gould relates, "The religious interest still continues with us. Dr. Stow baptized fourteen last Sabbath, and it was an occasion of deep interest. Hundreds went away unable to find a standing place in the Church." In reply to Emily's request for materials for the memoir, Dr. Stow wrote from Boston in December 1851, sending Emily for the memoir a copy of a manuscript written in 1810 by Adoniram Judson for the ministers' meeting at Bradford, New Hampshire. A second letter in January 1852 accompanies six volumes of early records and reports of the Missionary Union.

[202] William Gammell, a Professor at Brown University, wrote *A History of American Baptist Missions in Asia, Africa, Europe and North America, Under the Care of the American Baptist Missionary Union*. It was published in 1850 by Gould, Kendall and Lincoln.

Elnathan "Elly" Judson to Emily C. Judson, October 6, 1850—Worcester

My dear mother.

As Mr. Thomas and his wife were going to sail next Thursday for Burmah, I thought that it would be the best opportunity I could have, and therefore I determined to write to you and our little brothers and sister, and also to Edward Stevens.[203] I heard of the death of our poor father some time ago, and felt very bad about it, but I am sure that he is enjoying himself in heaven, and is expecting to have us join him soon. Last summer Adoniram[204] and I went on a visit to Farmington, Me. accompanied by Aunt Newton.[205] We went to see a sister of Aunt Newton's there. When we had arrived there we found that our brother George[206] was paying a visit to the same place, and in about a week our sister Abby[207] arrived there though not wholly unexpected. George, Abby, Adoniram, and I then started for our grandmother Boardman's a distance of about seven miles. We staid [sic] there a day and night, and then walked three miles to New Sharon, where our Uncle and Aunt Bullen resided. While there we received a letter from Uncle Newton saying that as Aunt Newton was very ill that all of us had better home at once [sic] except Adoniram, and to leave him at Bethel until Aunt Newton should get better. I parted with them all with a sad heart and returned to Worcester. Before going my friends gave Adoniram, and I [sic] $3.00 apeice [sic]. I have now been separated from Adoniram for a month, but as Aunt Newton is better she is going to send for him to return home by the first opportunity. I was very glad that when she told me of it. I received a letter from Adoniram the 23rd of last month, and he said that he got along very well in Bethel, and by what he wrote, he seemed very much pleased with his new situation. I received a letter from sister Abby last Thursday and was very glad to hear from her. I get along finely in my studies and expect to go into the high-school and to begin the languages on the first of next January. I study Reading, Spelling, Defining, Grammar, Geography, History in the forenoon, and in the afternoon my studies are Arithmetic, and writing. I get along very well in my Sabbath School too. Mr. Davey continues to be our teacher, and Mr. Washburn our superintendent. We do not take books out of the

[203] The references are to his brothers Henry and Edward, his stepsister Emily Frances, and Edward Stevens, the son of missionaries Edward and Elizabeth Stevens in Maulmain.

[204] See vol. 1, "Cast of Characters," s.v. "Judson, Adoniram Brown 'Addy.'"

[205] Dr. Calvin Newton, after some theological training, went to medical school to become a physician. He apparently had differing ideas about medicine, and he became a part of what was known as the Eclectic School of Medicine; with that background, he established the Worcester Medical Institute. In 1835, Dr. and Mrs. Newton received into their home the young George Dana Boardman, just returned from Burmah for his education. Adoniram and Elnathan went there in fall 1845 when they returned to the United States with their father, and they remained there under the Newton's care until Emily's return in October 1851. At that time, Mrs. Newton had become ill, and the boys went to live with Dr. and Mrs. Edward Bright.

[206] See vol. 1, "Cast of Characters," s.v. "Boardman, George Dana."

[207] See vol. 1, "Cast of Characters," s.v. "Judson, Abby Ann."

Library as the trustees are gathering money to replenish the Library, as it has grown rather slim lately. Miss Danforth has sent on some curiosities to our Sabbath School, and they are to be exhibited to-day to the scholars.

The first Sabbath in every month I put in 5 cents into the contribution box now. I am very sorry that Adoniram cannot write to you for as he is so far off it would take two days for the letter to go and inform him of the chance, and even if he wrote immediately on the reception of the letter it would take two days for the letter to reach Boston and by that time Mr. Thomas will have sailed as he is going just 4 days from to-day. The board in Boston[208] have determined to publish a memoir of our father. They have resolved also to help you if you wanted to come to this country, with our family. But ( ) I must stop as I have got to write to Henry, Eddy, and Frances, and also to Edward Stevens.

Your affec

Elnathan Judson

P.S. Excuse this very bad writing as I must write fast as I have so many letters to write in short a time.

Source: American Baptist Historical Society, AJ 11, no. 455.

Emily C. Judson to Mr. Alexander Beebee, October 13, 1850[209] —Maulmain

My dear Mr. Beebee,

Your kind and long letter dated Dec. 1849,[210] ought to have rec'd an answer long since, had it been in my power to write. But it reached me at a time of deep affliction, and since then my heart has been too heavy, and my hand too weak to admit of even this small effort. Our Heavenly Father has seen fit to apportion me a bitter cup, and I must look to him alone for strength to drink it. Disappointment, sorrow, and suffering—but "it is the Lord, let him do what seemeth unto him good."

My loss in itself is crushingly heavy, and then it involves so many disastrous consequences, that did I not know it is all planned and conducted by my best Friend, I should certainly sink down in despair. I had thought that Burmah was my home, but God is teaching me that I am only a poor wanderer—I had hoped to do good among the heathen, but he has seen fit to dispense with my efforts, and send me back to my native land, shorn of my strength, desolate, and sorrowing. I have been

[208] The board of the American Baptist Missionary Union.

[209] This letter is from the archives of the American Baptist Historical Society, though it has no listing there for it.

[210] This letter is not in the correspondence. Emily wrote to Mr. Beebee on July 20, 1849, raising some issues between them that, she hoped, would "clear the air." This letter alludes to some of those issues that Mr. Beebee addressed in his December letter.

suffering during the last five months from the same disease that carried off my predecessor, and there is but little hope of permanent relief except in a return to America.[211] With my three children and feeble health, I could do but little here, and it is better to withdraw and give my place to some person more favoured of God. I have not determined on this course without the deepest pain, for I do love the mission cause, and this mission, where my husband has laboured [sic], and where his associates have shown me so much kindness is particularly dear to me. But with prayers and many tears have I arrived at the conclusion that I can serve the cause of God best by leaving the field, and so it is my duty to yield my own preferences, and follow blindly the hand that is leading me. Perhaps there may be yet other work for me to do—some one [sic] of these children committed to my care may be designed of God for great good. I do not know—but I know that *he* will order all things well. If my life is spared, it is my intention to assume the guardianship of the six children[212] in some place where I can live economically, and furnish them with the means of a useful education.[213] As yet there is no light upon my pathway, my prospects are all dark and doubtful, but I look to the "Father of the fatherless and the widow's God," and I am sure I shall not look in vain. It would have been pleasant if my husband could have seen your letter; but in heaven there will be no need of explanations and I am sure you will love each other there. For my own part, I am guiltless of any thought or feeling toward you but than of respect and Christian affection; and with regard to your authority, I can only say that this was not the only misunderstanding of which he was the author. I do not ( ) he *meant* to do harm, but

[211] To this point, Emily expressed confusion about her future. It was Adoniram Judson's wish that she return to the United States with the children; he had expressed this before his voyage. At the same time, she hoped that she could stay in Burmah for at least a year or two (See her letter to Dr. Solomon Peck dated September 22, 1850). Now, the decision to return home seems clear.

[212] Abby Ann Judson, Adoniram Judson, Elnathan Judson, Henry Hall Judson, Edward Judson, and Emily Frances Judson.

[213] In a letter written to Dr. Solomon Peck on September 22, 1850, Emily said that it was Adoniram Judson's wish that, if he were to die, she would return to the United States, "collect his scattered family, and assume the guardianship of his children." As early as February 1851, as she began her trip to the United States, Emily Judson began to speak of a time and a place when all of the Judson children could be together. Indeed, she purchased a home in Hamilton, New York, where her parents, her sister Kate, and the six children could live as one family.

This was something for which each of the children hoped, and there are a number of references and pleadings in their correspondence to indicate this as their heartfelt desire. Nowhere was this expressed more eloquently than in Abby Ann Judson's letter to Emily dated April 24, 1851. This letter was both beautifully expressed and poignantly painful; her expression of delight was expressed over several pages.

This dream of being together would never come to fruition. Upon Emily's return to the United States, she was physically unable to care for the Judson children. Then, she began work on the memoir of Dr. Judson, and living in Providence for most of six months delayed this possibility. Following that, Emily's chronic ill health forced her to the realization that she had neither the strength nor the energy for such an arrangement. The six-week period in summer 1852 and 1853 was the only time this coming together was to take place.

Abby Ann went from Bradford Academy to the Misses Anable's School to a family teaching position in New York City and then to a career in education. Adoniram and Elnathan stayed with Dr. and Mrs. Bright for a year and then began their college preparation at Pierce Academy in Middleborough, Massachusetts. Henry and Edward stayed in the Hamilton home with Emily's parents and sister and also with various caregivers (see the letters of Mr. A. C. Osborn), though Emily was seldom there. Only Emily Frances was with Emily all of the time.

In her later years, Abby Ann strongly voiced her opinion that one of the great tragedies of missionary service is the necessity of being separated from children at a fairly young age. Adoniram expressed the same feeling.

I think he was too busy, and too much excited to understand what was said to him properly. This is the only way in which I can account for some of the strangest perversions that I ever heard. I think he was *imposed upon*, and that he *misunderstood*; and so I still presume for him the kindest feelings; and would not willingly give him the pain of knowing all the mischief he has done.[214]

I am still very poorly and cannot write much—The mission is enfeebled by sickness and death, but still God is blessing it—it is the favourite cause of his Son.

With kindest remembrances of your family,

Believe me

Ever yours sincerely, Emily C. Judson

Source: American Baptist Historical Society.

Emily C. Judson to Anna Maria Anable,[215] October 20, 1850[216] —Maulmain

My dearest Anna M.

I did not write you last month, for I was perplexed with care, and my heart was so exceedingly heavy that I felt nothing on earth could lighten the burden—now the struggle is over, and my future course decided, **you will not think it is because I do not love you** Ninny,[217] **when I say that it is more painful for me to return to America, to leave all here, than it was to come away originally,—But I have considered the subject prayerfully, have advised with the missionaries, and consulted the wishes of my sainted husband, and I have no doubt with regard to duty—I must go back to America, and if God spares my life try to serve him there,—my heart is *here*,—I love the missionaries, love the work, and love the precious Christians that have been accustomed to gather about me for prayer and instruction—They sobbed like so many children when I announced to them**

[214] We do not know the identity of the individual discussed in this paragraph. We assume it is a reference to someone mentioned in Mr. Beebee's letter of December 1849. He obviously was a source of misinformation, which was to cause pain to Emily and her relationship with Alexander Beebee.

[215] There is an addendum to this letter dated October 22, 1850.

[216] There are two versions of this letter: the original as written by Emily E. Chubbuck and the edited version published by Dr. A. C. Kendrick in his biography, *The Life and Letters of Mrs. Emily C. Judson*. Additions made by Dr. Kendrick are in parentheses, and words in the original left out by Dr. Kendrick have been added in bold. There are significant changes and omissions. In a note in his book, Dr. Kendrick explained that interest, purpose and propriety sometimes led to these changes and exclusions, "I remark here that in giving Miss Chubbuck's letters, I do not always indicate unimportant omissions. Real letters must always contain much which should not meet the public eye; and Emily's were real letters, dashed off hastily amidst pressing cares and duties. Written also after the exhausting labors of the day, they by no means do uniform justice to her epistolary powers." He later added, "In giving a few extracts from his and Miss Chubbuck's correspondence at this time, I have no wish to minister to a prurient curiosity, nor to violate that principle which would generally place letters written during the period of an 'engagement' under the shelter of inviolate secrecy."

[217] "Ninny" was a name of endearment given to Anna Maria Anable by her most intimate friends at the Utica Female Academy. Emily was "Nemmy."

my intention of returning—It would be a real pleasure to me to devote the remnant of my sad life to them—to labour where *he* laboured, and do the work which he loved so much; and then **my knowledge of the language**, though slight, **is too important to be thrown away for a trifle; and my knowledge of the character and habits of the people is probably (from peculiar circumstances) greater than that of others who have been longer in the field—But the state of my health, and the good of the children, require a sacrifice of feeling, which from your position you will be wholly unable to appreciate**[218]—If this sacred charge had not been committed to me, I would gladly stay here and die, willingly, gladly;—But there is great reason to suppose I should not survive another rainy season, and then my helpless little ones would be left a burden on the already over burdened mission—Then if providence has deprived me of the privilege of doing what I consider the *highest good*, would it be right in me to refuse a lower place in the scale of usefulness?—I still feel as though I might be useful to the children, and as Mr. Judson made me their legal guardian, it is my intention to gather them all into one family and try to train them up in a manner pleasing to God[219]—Perhaps, though not the natural mother of their four promising boys, I may become their spiritual mother, and do more good through them than a hundred poor women like me could do directly—I propose leaving here in the January steamer, and returning by way of Calcutta and London. It is thought hazardous for me to return in a merchant vessel ill, and alone, and the extra expenses if nothing more will be defrayed by friends in Calcutta—I have several kind invitations, one of which (from Mr. MacKay, a Scotch Presbyterian Minister, and Editor of the *Calcutta Review*) I have accepted. His house will be my home while I remain in Calcutta—I shall also bring the nurse who has taken care of me the last six months, so you see the undertaking though formidable, may be compassed. When you receive this, I shall probably be on the ocean—pray for me darling, and for my poor little ones—That the "Father of the fatherless, and the Widow's God" may go with us—for the way is very dark and lonely—

Lovingly yours ever

E. C. J.

Source: There is a fragment of this letter in A. C. Kendrick, *The Life and Letters of Mrs. Emily C. Judson*, 348–49; Hanna family files.

[218] This statement is a clear delineation of the issues with which Emily Judson had been struggling since hearing of Adoniram Judson's death: to stay or to return home. Now, in this, the path has been made clear; she will return to the United States.

[219] Regarding the future of the Judson children (George Dana Boardman, Abby Ann, Adoniram, Elnathan, Henry, Edward, and Emily Frances), see volume 1, "A Timeline of the Children of Adoniram Judson and Their Desire to Be a United Family." See also the footnotes to the letter of Emily C. Judson to Mr. Alexander Beebee dated October 13, 1850.

The Reverend Edward Stevens to Emily C. Judson, October 20, 1850[220]

My dear Mrs. Judson

With melancholy interest I looked over the papers of that bundle last evening. They are all notable, some to the church, some to whosoever will have the task of completing the Dictionary[221] so well begun and as far as finished so successfully prosecuted.

The accompanying paper I sent at your request. I hope you do not think of taking it with you. If so, a copy of it I will have taken, as it may prove of importance hereafter in connection with future editions of the Bible. The "Coniguda" [sic] also I have been very glad to get, and will take good care of for future use [sic].

Yours Affec'ly

Ed Stevens

Source: American Baptist Historical Society, AJ 19, no. 904.

[220] This letter is undated. It is placed on October 20, 1850, because there was letter of that date from Emily to Anna Maria saying that she had definitely decided it was best for her and the children to return to the United States,a decision that is reflected in this letter.

[221] On September 4, 1850, Emily sent a letter and the dictionary manuscripts to Edward Stevens, saying that Dr. Judson had directed, if something should happen to him, that Mr. Stevens would finish the dictionary. He asked that there be a mark where his work ended and the new work began.

In a November 15, 1850, letter to the mission board, Emily says:

> In his directions concerning the manuscripts, Mr. Judson did not request Mr. Stevens to finish the work; but by his manner of speaking, it evidently did not occur to him that there could be any other disposition made of it. And in this connection it may not be wholly improper, and I trust will not be deemed officious, for me to mention Mr. J's opinion of the qualifications of his more youthful colleague. He regarded Mr. S. as not only a fluent speaker and writer of the Burmese, but an able scholar also; while his industry, patience and perseverance, as peculiarly fitting him for departments of labor making large drafts on these qualities, were often mentioned in terms of commendation.

Before he would have received Emily's letter, Dr. Solomon Peck wrote on December 20, 1850:

> The action of the Exec. Com. in regard to the Dictionary manuscript, has doubtlessly been anticipated by you. They fully concur in committing them to the care of Mr. Stevens as well as the completing of what remains to be done. They wish him, however, as he will be informed, to defer the execution of the second part of the Dictionary to some future day, when the Mission shall have been reinforced. The labor of completing the work must, without doubt be greatly increased in being passed to another hand, especially if it is true, as has been intimated, that Dr. Judson's later commendations are abbreviated or in cipher.

Miss Mary Anna Longstreth to Emily C. Judson, October 21, 1850—Philadelphia

To Emily C. Judson,

My beloved friend,

Six weeks ago the mournful intelligence of thy *heart-agonizing* bereavement reached us—overwhelming *us* too, with sorrow, and though we have been *daily* with thee in thought and tenderest sympathy, though our hearts have bled with thine, and have longed to tell thee so, still, I have shrunk from addressing thee, knowing how vain must be the attempt of any human being to console. O it must have been a dying daily to visit the Ship[222] and bid farewell to that beloved one, day after day, as the vessel was putting out to sea; surely you felt the *bitterness of death*; and yet the hope of seeing him again was so sweet that it must have been almost impossible not to cherish it, though it was hoping against probability. To lose such a husband, such a friend, guide and guardian, is no common loss. May He who has taken him to Himself, bind up thy bleeding heart, and fill it with confidence, peace and consolation, such as Almighty love alone can bestow. Shielded under His wing, supported by His arms, mayst thou be able to say, "it is well," and from the very depths of Jordan to bring up stones of memorial to the loving kindness of the Lord. "Hitherto hath the Lord helped me." It is the peculiar privilege of His children, that in their sore afflictions, they are not left to themselves or to the broken reeds of earth. O no! it is then that the Lord delights to extend his almighty arm for their support and protection. Though the waves may for a time overwhelm them, they are not permitted to swallow them up. Many prayers have, I doubt not, been offered up to the God of the widow and the fatherless on your behalf; many tears have been shed by hearts sympathizing in your grief. For *him*, who is gone, there is no cause to mourn; his work was finished, and *his rest is glorious*. Try to think of *that*, dear Emily, when oppressed by the weight of thy *own loss*. *He* is forever safe, beyond the reach of pain and sorrow—forever with the Lord he served so well and served so faithfully. May we follow in his steps!

How ill and suffering thou has been, dear Emily! How terrible must the long, long period of suspense have been! I wish dear sister Wade[223] could have been with thee—she is so motherly and so heavenly-minded. But I dare say *all* the missionaries have been very kind. I regret the box sent by the Wades will be so long in reaching

[222] Adoniram Judson boarded the *Aristide Marie*, bound for the Isle of Bourbon, on April 3, 1850. Emily was able to reach the ship each day until April 6; it reached the open ocean on April 7.

[223] Deborah Wade was a missionary to Burmah; with her husband Jonathan, they were appointed in 1823. Adoniram Judson called them "his dearest and best of friends." Much of their work was in the jungle communities following the path of George Boardman. They left for the United States on December 22, 1847. From the Hamilton, New York, area, they stayed not far from the home of Emily's parents and sister; they visited the Anable-Sheldon families in Philadelphia. With a large group, they had left Boston on July 25, 1850, and returned to Burmah in February 1851.

thee. Some of the articles, especially the Cologne water, might have been useful to thee during thy illness.

Thy return to America will be with mingled feelings; but hearts and arms will be open to receive thee.

Kiss the dear children[224] for me, and believe me, most sincerely and

Affectionately thy friend,

Mary Anna Longstreth

Source: American Baptist Historical Society, AJ 17, no. 764.

Emily C. Judson to Anna Maria Anable,[225] October 22, 1850[226]

I am not permitted to raise my self in the bed, for I am suffering from a relapse, bro't on the Doct. says by writing letters, **this however determines me to seize upon the first opportunity for returning to America, for he says medicine is of no use, and delays are dangerous. You must have letters waiting me in London, I will tell you how to address next month, so that I shall not lose the long interval. Do not worry about me, every body [sic] is kind to me for the sake of him whose name I bear—so his precious protection is over me still—and I feel too that God is with me—Give love to all the girls and to Aunt C.[227] and your Mother[228]—is it not strange that I may after all be permitted to see your dear face again.**

Nov. 22nd she writes again—she was able to ride out—and superintend preparations for the voyage—[229]

Source: There is a fragment of this letter in A. C. Kendrick, *The Life and Letters of Mrs. Emily C. Judson*, 348–49; Hanna family files.

[224] Henry Hall Judson, eight years and three months old; Edward Judson, three months shy of six years old; and Emily Frances Judson, three months shy of three years old.

[225] This is an addendum to a letter written October 20, 1850.

[226] See the footnote in the letter of October 20, 1850, about Dr. Kendrick's editing style.

[227] See vol. 1, "Cast of Characters," s.v. "Sheldon, Miss Cynthia."

[228] See vol. 1, "Cast of Characters," s.v. "Sheldon, Alma and Joseph Hubbell."

[229] The letter has a note indicating that it is a copy of Mrs. Judson's letter. It appears that this was a further note added by the copyist.

Mrs. Stella K. Bennett to Emily C. Judson, October 25, 1850—Tavoy

My dear Sister Judson,

You may judge of our disappointment at not receiving a word from Maulmain after a lapse of two months, but the Benjamins[230] have in part supplied the want of letters. We hear from them that you are preparing to leave, and am glad to hear friends have so kindly offered to assist you but fear with all the aid you can obtain that you will scarcely be able to endure all the fatigue and care and sea sickness [sic] between this and America. I think it would almost annihilate *me*, and I don't know how *you* are to bear it. But it is the "Spirit of a man that sustains him" and I trust the Lord will cheer your spirit though your body be ever so unequal to the undertaking. Mr. B.[231] and myself deeply sympathize with you and w'd gladly do any thing [sic] in our power to make your way less rough. Should you think of any thing [sic] we can do, or of any thing [sic] you would like from this place for yourself or children which we can procure we shall be most happy to serve you. I anticipated much pleasure from a visit on the sea shore with you, but as you will be so busy in preparations for your departure you will I suppose have no time or strength for such a visit. I wish you had sent the boys to us for a month as I am intending to go to Monmogon as soon as possible after the steamer leaves and we should all have been very glad of their company, and it would have been such a nice thing for them to remember.

I have been very unwell from one cause or another most of the time since Mr. Bennett's return but dismissed the schools nearly a fortnight since, and hope a change at M. will do me good.

Mr. B. continues to have his fever about as often as he did but the attacks are gradually becoming lighter I think. You will be sorry to hear we lose our good Dr. by the present steamer. This *loss* to us is very great, both as a Physician and friend, Capt. And Mrs. Grant are also superseded now by a single man so that Mrs. Cross[232] and myself will be all the "ladies" left in Tavoy.

Some weeks since Coochil (our old servant, whom you will remember as having formerly been Mr. Judson's servant) put the accompanying paper in my hands, the purport of which you will see on reading. If it be correct as he states, that a part of his wages for the three years of trouble have all this time been in Mr. Judson's hands, we think there will be something found among his papers regarding it, or that he may have sometime said something of the same to you. Coochil took care of little Maria[233]

[230] See vol. 1, "Cast of Characters," s.v. "Benjamin, The Reverend Judson and Susan."

[231] See vol. 1, "Cast of Characters," s.v. "Bennett, The Reverend Cephas and Stella Kneeland."

[232] Julia Ann Putnam Cross married Edmund Cross in Morrisville, New York, in August 1843. They arrived in Maulmain on February 24, 1845, and at Tavoy a month later.

[233] Maria Elizabeth Butterworth Judson, the daughter of Adoniram and Ann Hasseltine Judson, was born January 26, 1825, and died April 24, 1827.

after her mother's death until the Wades[234] arrived. When they came he went into their service, and Mr. J. boarded with them until our arrival, when C. was transferred to us, and Mr. J. boarded with us when in Maulmain, until we went to Rangoon.

The Wades will soon be in M. and will perhaps know something about the wages. It is all new to us. We had never before heard anything of it from any quarter and now know nothing only what the old man states. The troubles of the Burmese War is a topic upon which he always becomes very pathetic. We had a long good letter from Anna Maria[235] by this mail describing her present home, in which she appears very happy. She thinks there is scarcely any body [sic] in the world equal to Aunt Cynthia,[236] and I quite agree with her. The Dr's family are coming here to stop till the return of steamer, and just by way of variety

Written on the first page perpendicular to the text: Mee Yeet has taken it into his head to be married today. Beside I am writing with a pain in my leg which would entirely prevent my doing anything if in my head so please say to Sister Stevens[237] that I *could not* write. Should the steamer be delayed a day longer than is expected. I may be able to say a few words to her before she is off. With love to yourself and children.

Believe me
Aff'y Yours

S. K. Bennett

Source: American Baptist Historical Society, AJ 12, no. 356.

[234] See vol. 1, "Cast of Characters," s.v. "Wade, The Reverend Doctor Jonathan and Deborah."

[235] Anna Bennett was the daughter of Cephas and Stella Bennett, missionaries to Burmah. She was born in August 1833. An 1850 letter said that beginning in April, she would be teaching at a family school in a private home in the Philadelphia area. By 1853, she was elsewhere, for Miss Cynthia Sheldon was corresponding with her. On September 7, 1853, Miss Sheldon wrote to Emily Judson to say that she had written about Dr. Burton and his interest in her. Dr. Burton was associated with the Southern Missionary Board and was due to leave the country no later than November. Highly thought of, Miss Sheldon said, "I fancy he has found the way to the warm corner of her heart—which is an evidence of tact—probably he is a widower." On September 25, Emily Judson replied, "Anna B's affair strikes me favourably. I never heard of Dr. B. but he probably went out when I was on my way home. It is certainly better to marry a man of established character and expectation than a 'green horn' and Anna would be happier in the east than here." On October 14, 1853, Miss Sheldon wrote again, "The dear girl seemed in a terrible quandary—which she very foolishly thought I could settle—The truth is Anna's heart is *some what* [sic] engaged and I have no doubt but she will decide to go. Mr. Dean told Courtland she would get in the Dr. one of the very best of men." Anna Bennett married Dr. Burton in early November 1853. They sailed in early December 1853.

[236] See vol. 1, "Cast of Characters," s.v. "Sheldon, Miss Cynthia."

[237] See vol. 1, "Cast of Characters," s.v. "Stevens, Elizabeth 'Bessie.'"

Mrs. Susan R. S. Benjamin to Emily C. Judson, October 26, 1850—Mergui

Dear Sister Judson,

I regret very much that not a moment was left from my hasty preparation for leaving to call and see you. I fully intended to and did not give it up till almost the last minute. I suppose sister ( ) has told you, that as it was, we barely escaped losing our passage. I am glad to be at home again, and even its entire loneliness is not disagreeable after the hustle and changes we have been through for a month or two past.

I wanted to talk with you about your buggy before we left. As you have concluded not to leave till February, we have concluded not to take the buggy, if you can possibly dispose of it. Nearly the whole use we would make of it for, at least, six months to come would be in the coming two or three, and at the time you leave if you should send it down, there would be no one here to receive it. Bro. Brayton's[238] family and our own would probably be in the jungle. I was perhaps too hasty in engaging it. But I suppose as the circumstance of an agreement change, a change in the agreement also is excusable. I hope you will be able to dispose of it advantageously etc. I think you will perhaps to some of the new comers. We bought a very fine pony of Dr. VanSomerin at Tavoy. You know, we brought his relief down and he was selling off all he could. Sister Bennett[239] had been quite ill with inflammation of the breast but was pretty well again. Mr. B.[240] wishes me to say that he sends you some shells through Mr. Mason[241] and regrets they are not better, but hopes you will find some of interest.

With sincere love your affectionate

Sister S. R. S. Benjamin

Source: American Baptist Historical Society, AJ 12, no. 346.

[238] See vol. 1, "Cast of Characters," s.v. "Brayton, The Reverend Durlin and Mary."

[239] See vol. 1, "Cast of Characters," s.v. "Bennett, The Reverend Cephas and Stella Kneeland."

[240] This could be either Mr. Benjamin or Mr. Bennett.

[241] See vol. 1, "Cast of Characters," s.v. "Mason, The Reverend Francis, Helen, and Ellen."

Anna Maria Anable to Emily C. Judson, October 27, 1850

Dearest Nemmy[242]

Mr. Bright[243] who is staying with us while our state convention sits, says I must write to you, or my letter will not go by the next steamer—you may be on your way home before it reaches you. How my heart rejoices in the thought of seeing you once more. We are already forming plans for the future. Aunt C.[244] is talking of meeting you in Boston, and I am thinking of seeing you in Hamilton next summer vacation—and perhaps going on with you from here ( ), for we think you will have to come thus far south [sic] in the early spring. We have all settled it that you are to live in Phila and Mrs. Gillette[245] has already begun to dispute my claim to you and Fanny.[246] Ah! Nemmy, these plans of ours may make your heart ache for the cause of them, but try to see a light through the gloom of the present and it may shine with unexpected brightness. Mr. Bright will always be a firm friend—he is a jewel of a man. Do you know that the Board are bound to support the widow of a missionary as long as she continues unmarried? By the way Sarah Bell[247] was married last week to Deacon Gould[248] of Boston and, Julia Look[249] has a fine boy. Sarah will be very nicely settled as far as this world's *gear* goes, but her husband—I do not feel very well acquainted with. He is a brother of my friend Mrs. Lincoln[250] and of Dr. Gould. What will poor Lydia[251] do when you come away? I do believe she will have to marry Mr. Simons,[252] though I wish she would wait for Mr. Abbott.[253] I shall not have time to write to her

242 "Nem" or "Nemmy" was a name of endearment given to Emily by a small group of her intimate friends at the Utica Female Academy. Anna Maria Anable was "Ninny."

243 See vol. 1, "Cast of Characters," s.v. "Bright, The Reverend Doctor Edward, Jr."

244 See vol. 1, "Cast of Characters," s.v. "Sheldon, Miss Cynthia."

245 See vol. 1, "Cast of Characters," s.v. "Gillette, The Reverend A. (Abram) D. (Dunn) and Hannah."

246 See vol. 1, "Cast of Characters," s.v. "Judson, Emily Frances."

247 See vol. 1, "Cast of Characters," s.v. "Wheeler, Sarah Bell."

248 See vol. 1, "Cast of Characters," s.v. "Gould, Charles."

249 Julia Look was a student of Emily's at the Utica Female Academy and later a fellow teacher. A November 22, 1845, letter from Anna Maria encouraged Emily to stay in Philadelphia for the winter for her health and remarked that Julia had the hardest part because she was teaching Emily's composition class, and the students kept asking for Emily. In a September 1847 letter, she was listed as one of the teachers at the Utica Female Academy. On September 23, 1849, Anna Maria wrote that Julia and Albert B. Casswell were married and came to visit with her. In one 1849 letter Julia spoke of another teacher who was teaching "our composition class." On October 27, 1850, Anna Maria Anable noted that she had had a son. She was one of a small number of people who addressed Emily as "Emily" and as "Nemmy" in her letters.

250 Mrs. Lincoln was the wife of Joshua Lincoln, a prominent Baptist layman and a partner in Gould, Kendall and Lincoln. Anna Maria Anable boarded with Mr. and Mrs. Lincoln when she stayed in Boston in summer 1847 for medical treatments. Mrs. Lincoln was a strong supporter of missions.

251 See vol. 1, "Cast of Characters," s.v. "Lillybridge, Lydia." Also, "A Timeline of the Life and Mission of Lydia Lillybridge Simons."

252 Ibid.

253 Elisha Abbott was born October 23, 1809, in Cazenovia, New York. He graduated from the Hamilton Theological Institute and was ordained August 25, 1835. He wife was Ann P. Gardner, and they were married April 2, 1837. Though they were appointed for work in Telagus, India, that changed upon their arrival, and they went to Maulmain in April 1837. They continued on to Rangoon shortly after that. In March 1840, they established the station at Sandoway. Mrs. Abbott died in Sandoway on January 27, 1845. Mr. Abbott left for the United States in November 1845, returning in August 1847. At one point in the correspondence, Mr. Abbott was mentioned as a possible husband for Lydia Lillybridge.

this month, but give my dear love to her and say I shall write next mail. Mr. B. thinks you may return in the *Wash. Allston*. I do hope there will be somebody to accompany you. Before the time this reaches you Mr. and Mrs. Wade[254] and all the other dear missionaries will have arrived. Oh, how I should love to be with them for a little while. I suppose I shall never see Mrs. W. again, but her visit to us will never be forgotten. Pray ask Mr. Wade to play you a tune on his Melodion so that you can report progress to me.[255]

Mr. Binney[256] called here day before yesterday, but staid [sic] only a few moments and I had very little conversation with him. Mr. Haswell[257] I met on board ship in Boston and Mr. Howard[258] I have not seen nor heard anything of.

Thank you for the beautiful prayer. I shall try to obey your injunction but I expect Mr. Bright will lay violent hands on it.[259] Adieu dear Nemmy—this letter is not worth sending, but it may be the best I shall send in a long, long while.

Anna M.

Source: American Baptist Historical Society, AJ 13, no. 470.

[254] See vol. 1, "Cast of Characters," s.v. "Wade, The Reverend Doctor Jonathan and Deborah."

[255] When the Wades were home and visiting Philadelphia, Anna Maria Anable gave Mr. Wade music lessons, and she mentions this in former letters to Emily.

[256] See vol. 1, "Cast of Characters," s.v. "Binney, The Reverend Joseph Getchell."

[257] James Haswell had sailed for Burmah in 1835, arriving in February 1836 to work with the Talaings. His wife was Jane Haswell. James Haswell became a partner with Adoniram and Sarah Judson, and when Adoniram and Elnathan were born, Sarah turned over the translation of the Peguan Scripture to him. He served as a missionary for more than forty years.

[258] Hosea Howard first sailed for Burmah in 1834, arriving in December that year. His wife was Theresa, and they had been married just before departure. Hosea Howard was a recent graduate of the Theological Seminary in Hamilton, New York. They were stationed in Maulmain as missionaries with Adoniram Judson, and he was to claim in a letter to Emily that he had worked there with Adoniram longer than any other missionary. Mr. Howard's responsibility was to run schools that the mission maintained, a task in which he was ably assisted by his wife. It was to Mr. and Mrs. Howard that Lydia Lillybridge was responsible when she arrived in November 1846. Mr. and Mrs. Howard left Maulmain for the United States in February 1850.

[259] Dr. Bright, the corresponding or home secretary of the American Baptist Missionary Union, had a voracious appetite for material from the mission fields because of the demands of the mission magazines, including *The Macedonian*, for which he had individual responsibility.

Emily C. Judson to the Reverend Doctor Solomon Peck,[260] November 15, 1850[261]—Maulmain

Rev and dear sir,

I wrote you sometime since, that, in accordance with the directions of my late husband, I had placed the Dictionary manuscripts in the hands of the Rev. Mr. Stevens;[262] but I think I neglected, at the time, to mention several particulars, which may be of interest to you and the Executive Committee.

Mr. Judson finished the English and Burmese Dictionary at the close of the year 1848, soon after which, it went to press. The printing was interrupted by his illness in November 1849, and again resumed, under the supervision of Mr. Stevens, after Mr. Ranney's[263] return from Bourbon, in August last.

The Burmese and English Dictionary—a new compilation from manuscripts, which had been the work of many years—was commenced June 1849, and was probably a little more than half finished, when Mr. J. closed his labours, in November of the same year. If his health had been continued, the whole work, according to his estimation, would have been completed within the present year—at the close of the rainy season. The task, however, will be much more formidable to his successor, involving a greater amount of labour, and doubtless requiring a longer period of time.

While preparing the first dictionary, Mr. Judson was also employed to some extent on the second; so, in his daily discussions with his assistants, something was sure to be elicited, by which the original manuscript might be enlarged and improved; and this accounts for the comparative facility, with which he executed the finished portion if it. The part, however, which remained unfinished is in a very imperfect state; and every word will require to be subjected to the severest scrutiny. Mr. Stevens will not be obliged to puzzle over broken and scattered fragments, for the whole is collected and arranged alphabetically; but a vast deal of critical knowledge will be required in the use of the material, as I know that there was a large portion of it, which the original compiler did not consider reliable. I regret also to add, that the writing is very indistinct, and some parts of it, I fear, wholly illegible. The greater part of Mr. J's Burmese writing was performed with a crayon or pencil, as he fancied an instrument resembling the sylus [sic] better suited to the formation of the Burmese character than our elastic pen.

[260] This letter, dealing with the potential future work to be done on the English-Burmese dictionary that Judson left uncompleted, also appeared as an article in the *Missionary Magazine* (April 1851) 31:106 of the American Baptist Missionary Union.

[261] There is a second version of this letter that appears to be the original. It is dated November 21, 1850; in that copy, there are edits to the last paragraph, and this letter of November 15 reflects those edits. In the original, there were also some additions along the left margin of the first page. Written and crossed out is: "When I say 'commenced' I allude to its preparation for the press—the actual commencement was made when he first began to study the language." Then, written in the margin is: "Was made some thirty-seven years ago, with Mr. J's first knowledge of the language; but its preparation for the first commenced."

[262] See vol. 1, "Cast of Characters," s.v. "Stevens, The Reverend Edward and Elizabeth."

[263] See vol. 1, "Cast of Characters," s.v. "Ranney, Thomas and Maria."

In his directions concerning the manuscripts, Mr. Judson did not *request* Mr. Stevens to finish the work; but by his manner of speaking, it evidently did not occur to him, that there could be any other disposition made of it. And in this connection, it may not be wholly improper, and I trust will not be deemed officious, for me to mention Mr. J's opinion of the qualifications of his more youthful colleague [Note: Crossed out is the phrase "for this or any similar work."]. He regarded Mr. S. not only as a fluent speaker and writer of the Burmese, but an able scholar also; [Note: crossed out is "and was in the habit of deferring to his opinion on difficult questions which implied ( ) ( ) big and his attainments in the language."] while his industry, patience, and perseverance, as peculiarly fitting him for departments of labour making large draughts on these qualities, were often [Note: Crossed out is "the subject of conversation."] mentioned in terms of commendation.

With the highest sentiments of respect and Christian affection,

Believe me

Very sincerely yours,

Emily C. Judson

Source: American Baptist Historical Society, AJ 12, no. 378.

Emily C. Judson to Mrs. Urania Sheldon Nott,[264] November 16, 1850—Maulmain

My Dear Mrs. Nott,

I can not [sic] recollect positively whether I replied to your letter, written long since, or not, but I know it was in my heart to do so, though I may have failed in the accomplishment. For the last two years, "sickness and sorrow, pain and death," have been my constant attendants; and, in consequence of this, I have neglected many social duties and been deprived of many pleasures, among which correspondence with those I formerly loved is not the least. And now, though my hands are full of cares, and my heart heavy with its accumulated burden of sorrows, my thoughts still turn back to other days, and, even in the midst of pain, and weakness, and desolation, I find something not unlike a ray of sunshine left me from the dreadful wreck of all those bright hopes. God has given me a bitter portion, and yet, through all, even in the heaviest of my trials, His loving-kindness and tender mercy have never failed; and now, though my path in life is darkened forever, He yet condescends to guide me, and I can not [sic] be wholly miserable. Heaven seems very dear to me, and very near, indeed, since it contains my sainted husband and the precious, precious little

[264] This letter is the edited version of it which appeared in *The Life and Letters of Mrs. Emily C. Judson* by A. C. Kendrick.

one that I had hoped to receive in his stead.[265] And then, my own feet have been treading, for the last six months, close on the verge of eternity, so that trust in Christ has been my only resource, both for myself and my poor little orphans,[266] and I have found it, indeed, a sweet dependence. Now my health is a little better, and the doctor says that if I return to America, I have a good prospect of recovery from the disease contracted here, though, on other accounts, a cold climate will be less favorable to me than a warm one. It is very painful to me to leave the mission just as I began to be prepared for usefulness, but it is of God's ordering, and I know that He will do what is best, both for me and for His cause. If I stay here I can not [sic] live; if I go to America I may be permitted to be of some use to the children; so, there is no ground for question. I shall leave here for Calcutta in January, I think, and then take a passenger ship for England—I shall probably reach England in June or July.

—It is my intention, if God spares my life, to gather the poor children (six in all) under one roof, and make a home for them in some place where they can have the advantage of good schools, and we can live economically.[267] I can not [sic] yet decide where that will be. The three children here[268] with me enjoy excellent health, and are delighted with the prospect of the voyage, but more especially the wonders they expect to meet in America. I shall also bring with me the Indian girl[269] I have employed of late as a nurse, and a little son of Mr. Stevens, a brother missionary. So my party will consist of six, and don't you think they need a more efficient head than I? How different when I came out! Friends in America prepared my outfit and packed it, and my husband put everything in its place and watched me all the way, as mothers watch their infants. But the "Father of the fatherless and the widow's God" will go with us now, and I do not think I shall be afraid.

We heard of Dr. Nott's[270] illness with much sorrow, and there was a time when my husband did not expect to precede him to heaven; but God had work for one and not the other, and "He doeth all things well."

With much love to yourself and Dr. Nott, as well as the Pearsons,

Very affectionately yours,

Emily C. Judson

Source: A. C. Kendrick, *The Life and Letters of Mrs. Emily C. Judson*, 349–51.

[265] This is a reference to Charles Judson, stillborn on April 23, 1850, a little over two weeks after Judson had departed on the *Aristide Marie*.

[266] Henry Hall Judson, Edward Judson, and Emily Frances Judson were in Burmah with Emily.

[267] Regarding the future of the Judson children (George Dana Boardman, Abby Ann, Adoniram, Elnathan, Henry, Edward, and Emily Frances), see volume 1, "A Timeline of the Children of Adoniram Judson and Their Desire to Be a United Family."

[268] Henry Hall Judson, Edward Judson, and Emily Frances Judson.

[269] See vol. 1, "Cast of Characters," s.v. "Nancy."

[270] The Reverend Doctor Eliphalet Nott was the president of Union College in Schenectady, New York. An ordained Presbyterian minister, he was married to Urania Sheldon Nott, the sister of Miss Cynthia Sheldon and Mrs. Alma Anable and the aunt of Anna Maria Anable.

Emily C. Judson to the American Baptist Missionary Union,[271] November 22, 1850

As this fragment was published in the *Baptist Memorial*, an introduction to it stated: "Mrs. Judson, under date of Nov. 22, informs us that the state of her health has decided her, in accordance with the advice of Dr. Morton,[272] and the concurrence of the mission, to return to this country, but the time of her departure was not fixed. She says:

"The three children[273] are in excellent health, and scarcely know, poor things! That they are orphans. They talk tenderly of 'dear papa'[274] who is 'now with Christ in heaven,' but they are just as happy, (and I would not have them otherwise,) as though I could be happy with them. Pray for them and for me, while we are on the ocean."

Source: Rev. Enoch Hutchinson, ed., *The Baptist Memorial and Monthly Record Devoted to the History, Biography, Literature and Statistics of the Denomination* (New York: Z. P. Hatch, 1851) 10:199–200.

Mrs. J. A. P. Cross to Emily C. Judson, November 23, 1850—Tavoy

My Dear Mrs. Judson

I have felt most sincerely to sympathise [sic] with you in your late most heavy affliction though I have hesitated to say so to you on paper. It has seemed to me that common words of sympathy expressed in a common way must seem so *cold* to one whose heart was bleeding at every pore and besides I have supposed that you would receive a multiplicity of condolences from so many of your friends and acquaintances who would understand how to endeavor to soothe and comfort your sad heart much better than I a comparative stranger could. I have no doubt you have found your chief source of consolation in Him who has wisely no doubt seen fit thus heavily to lay his hand upon you. I have found it "sweet to lie passive in his hands and know no will but his."—I am glad to learn through Mrs. Stevens[275] that your health has a little improved and hope as the cold weather comes on it will continue to improve much more. I hope your children are all well too.—I have much pleasure in sending you the half dozen canisters of arrow-root as you requested

[271] This is a fragment from a letter written by Emily to the American Baptist Missionary Union dated November 22, 1850; it was published in the *Baptist Memorial* (Rev. Enoch Hutchinson, ed., *The Baptist Memorial and Monthly Record Devoted to the History, Biography, Literature and Statistics of the Denomination* [New York: Z. P. Hatch, 1851] 10:199–200). The rest of that letter is lost; apparently, it was not preserved with many of the other archives.

[272] See vol. 1, "Cast of Characters," s.v. "Morton, Doctor."

[273] Henry Hall Judson, Edward Judson, Emily Frances Judson.

[274] "Dear papa" was the affectionate name of the Judson children for Adoniram Judson. In April 1850, Emily had written a poem, "Prayer for Dear Papa."

[275] See vol. 1, "Cast of Characters," s.v. "Stevens, Elizabeth 'Bessie.'"

in your note to Mr. Bennett.[276] It has been kept perfectly free from moisture since it was made in the first place and I hope you may find it all good and useful. I got the idea from Mrs. Benjamin[277] that the canisters I sent before were both spoiled so as to be useless to you but am glad to hear it was a mistake in part. I hope you will have milk on board ship from goats or cows to use with the arrow-root for it is very insipid without. Also let me commend you to take a quantity of good kiln dried soojer [sic]. I think if I recollect right you are apt to be troubled with sea-sickness and if so you will find th( ) soojer gruel seasoned with nothing but a little salt to taste a very good antidote. I have never tried any thing [sic] which quieted the stomach so much as this. The longer the soojer is boiled the better.

Many thanks for the book[278] and habit-shirt I received from you some time since. I hope you will see some of my family friends when you get home. My father lives in Billerica Mass. But his health is so bad at present that I should not be surprised to hear of his death at any time. My mother also is in very bad health. I have one sister whose husband is pastor at Chickopee Falls, Mass. His name is Bellamy. Do you know if Lucy A. Tillinghast still lives? Should you live to visit Hamilton and vicinity please remember me with love to any of my numerous friends there who may inquire. Your parents are there yet I suppose. The voyage must seem an immense undertaking to one in your health but I can but hope it may prove useful to you. I hope you will feel the All sustaining Arms ever underneath you and be enabled to cast all your care on him who careth for you.

With love and kisses to the children[279]

Yrs affly

T. A. P. Cross

Source: American Baptist Historical Society, AJ 15, no. 617.

Mrs. L. M. Elliott to Emily C. Judson, November 23, 1850

My dear Mrs. Judson

You have most kindly anticipated my wishes, in presenting me with another Copy of your deeply interesting Memoir of the late Mrs. Judson—and a History of Your Missions. I shall value them both exceedingly.

[276] See vol. 1, "Cast of Characters," s.v. "Bennett, The Reverend Cephas and Stella Kneeland."

[277] See vol. 1, "Cast of Characters," s.v. "Benjamin, The Reverend Judson and Susan."

[278] Fanny Forester, *Memoir of Sarah B. Judson, Member of the American Mission to Burmah* (New York: L. Colby and Company, 1848). This probably would have been a more recent edition with notes that Emily had added.

[279] Henry Hall Judson, Edward Judson, and Emily Frances Judson.

The success which God has granted to the labors of your late esteemed husband has indeed been wonderful. May it please the Great Head of the Church to pour out his Spirit more abundantly upon those who remain to carry on the Work! I sent home to my parents a Copy of your Memoir of the late Mrs. Judson with which they were much interested, and my Father, Dr. Pearson, sent you his Memoir of the venerable Missionary Schwartz, thinking you might be interested by the similar work of God in another part of the Vineyard. I never heard if the Volumes reached you—and were read by Dr. Judson. I should like to be able to tell my father so.

With many thanks for your kind wishes on my behalf, and every sentiment of esteem—

Believe me
Dear Mrs. Judson
Yours most truly

L. M. Elliott

Source: American Baptist Historical Society, AJ 16, no. 1528.

Mrs. Mary H. Brayton to Emily C. Judson, November 25, 1850—Mergui

My Dear Sister Judson

I found four days since on coming from the jungle very unexpectedly a note from you, tho *very* acceptable I will assure. So deep have been your afflictions and so aggravating that I even did not ever think you could bestow one tho't upon *me*. And the only reason I have not written you again, and since the lamentable but joyful intelligence of the father of this Mission having gone home to glory was because I feared I should aggravate rather than comfort. A lady once told me (who had been recently bereaved of a lovely infant) that she could not endure to have one who had never buried a child attempt to sympathise [sic] with her. It seems so heartless! You have more than once, twice or thrice even been remembered by me in my feeble but most comforting approaches to the throne of grace. And even before I dared raise my pen this morning to reply to your kind note I felt that I must go and again name the blessing of God upon you and the souls He has so directly given into your charge. I do feel for you and the tears will flow as I write and I will continue to carry you before the ( ) of every good and perfect gift and wish I could do even more—For the sake of the children[280] I hope your life *will* be spared and your health restored that you may carry out your plans and bring the scattered ones

[280] Ibid.

together that they may not be destitute of that affection which is so desirable in brs and sisters, that you may train them for usefulness here and happiness above. Much should I love to learn how you succeed. Tell Henry Mary[281] has been baptized, and I hope he will soon if he has not given his heart to God and followed Jesus in the same precious ordinance. And the others also have much I do wish to hear that all have chosen wisdom's ways and are walking in the same.

I am sure my dear Sister God designs that you shall shine in heaven and what more can we ask? May you ever from the heart say "Thy will be done" and try to teach the dear children to do the same.

I am sorry to say I shall be unable to send you any shells ( ) and as for the Mergui pearls I have never seen them tho I have often heard of their existence. The nutmegs I beg you will accept and hope you will find them nice.

My health is very good for me and I never loved my work i.e. of winning souls to Christ more than at the present time. May our kind Father bless you and yours ever,

Very aff'ly
Yours

Mary H. Brayton

Source: American Baptist Historical Society, AJ 12, no. 349.

Anna Maria Anable to Emily C. Judson, November 26, 1850

Dearest Emily

This mail has brought me the first intelligence from you since your great loss though we long ago felt your loss. I *do* pity you darling, and I hope and pray that God will sustain and comfort you, that "thy Maker will be thy husband," and that He will give consolation to your stricken soul. Would that you were here now that you could lay your weary head on my bosom as of old. I suppose your feelings are right about staying in Maulmain for a while, they are certainly natural. But I am disappointed. I will say nothing about it now, but I am afraid that, if you stay long abroad, Nemmy,[282] I shall never see you again. Your letters, though you evidently try to be cheerful, show that you are far from well—and I do believe it would do you good to see your native land and your early friends again, to say nothing of the children. By this time Mr. and Mrs. Wade[283] will have arrived, and I am *so* glad that they are to be stationed in Maulmain. She can tell you something about us in P. and whether or no [sic] she

[281] Mary Brayton, the daughter of Durlin and Mary Brayton. She was born June 5, 1841, so she would have been a year older than Henry.

[282] "Nem" or "Nemmy" was a name of endearment given to Emily by a small group of her intimate friends at the Utica Female Academy. Anna Maria Anable was "Ninny."

[283] See vol. 1, "Cast of Characters," s.v. "Wade, The Reverend Doctor Jonathan and Deborah."

thinks you could be happy with us. You have such a delightful circle of warm—beautiful Christians in M. that I know you would miss them here. We are in a sadly cold state—I myself particularly. I never, or not for many years have felt so sluggish and cold in my religious affection as during the past year.

Dearest Nemmy, pray for your friend, that her hopes may be resting on a sure foundation, and that she may not find at last that she had been deceiving herself.

Mrs. Gillette[284] and family are well, and the Robarts[285] have moved down to Pine St. several blocks below us. The Earps have just returned from abroad and Annie is to be married in Feb. George will be married in Jan. Please darling give my dear love to Lydia,[286] Mr. and Mrs. Wade and kiss the little ones[287] for their Aunt Anna—

faithfully A.M.

Source: American Baptist Historical Society, AJ 13, no. 469.

The Reverend Lyman Stilson to Emily C. Judson, November 28, 1850

My dear Mrs. Judson.

In behalf the school [sic] including teachers pupils and patrons I would express my most sincere thanks for the very fine and valuable present and I would that it may the source [sic] of great improvement to all who will be privileged with the presence of the books. A sight of these books will make the Children's eyes sparkle and I hope they will learn their value and treasure up from them much valuable knowledge. We shall remember with much satisfaction the Donor and pray the Lord to grant his blessing upon her in all her ways.

Yours aff'ly

L. Stilson

Source: American Baptist Historical Society, AJ 19, no. 891.

[284] See vol. 1, "Cast of Characters," s.v. "Gillette, The Reverend A. (Abram) D. (Dunn) and Hannah."

[285] See vol. 1, "Cast of Characters," s.v. "Robarts, Mr. and Mrs. W. S."

[286] See vol. 1, "Cast of Characters," s.v. "Lillybridge, Lydia." Also, "A Timeline of the Life and Mission of Lydia Lillybridge Simons."

[287] Henry Hall Judson, eight and a half years old; Edward Judson, almost six years old; and Emily Frances Judson, almost three years old.

Mrs. Frances L. Waldo[288] to Emily C. Judson, December 1850—Belle Grove Sunday School

Mrs. Judson

Perhaps you may think it rather presuming for me to address you now, when your heart is sore distressed, and bowed down with that desolation which can only be felt when *the* object of our dearest affection is called away and life is thus made to us one "*night* of sorrow" save the light that cometh from beyond the tomb.

Many expressions of sympathy in your very great affliction are continually reaching your "Indian home"—but I doubt whether any one [sic] has borne the kind wishes and sincere prayers of more true hearts than this little Missionary Article which I am now commissioned to present to you.

About a year since my husband and myself established a little Sabbath school in a destitute portion of the suburbs of our city—Tis not on heathen ground, but truly it seemed to us a missionary field and often have we lifted our hearts in prayer feeling *most* deeply that "God *alone*" can give the increase. Yet in his own good time, he has smiled upon our humble efforts and crowned them with great success.

As these little ones have been taught from Sabbath to Sabbath of Christ as the first great missionary, and of those who following his example have gone to carry the blessed tidings of salvation through Christ to their benighted heathen, a flame of missionary feeling has been kindled in their hearts, which for a time only glimmering in the socket now begins to burn with a steadier light. By their request I present to you this little token of their sympathy—not from children rich in the things of earth, but from a band destitute of many of the comforts of life and to whom their *penny* contributions seemed a great offering when prized by the effort necessary to obtain it—that their mite might be added to the treasure of the Lord.

If in the multitude of cares that must often press heavily upon your heart you should find time to send them a few words of encouragement it would be gratefully received by them if directed to their superintendent—F. A. Waldo, M.D., Cincinnati, Ohio.

One request more—that you will remember at the throne of grace this humble effort of one upon whom I trust your influence ceased not—with her school days.

Frances L. Waldo

$10 enclosed, for support of Mrs. Judson and so acknowledged in the Magazine.

R. E. Eddy[289]

A. B. M. Union

Source: American Baptist Historical Society, AJ 22, no. 1116.

[288] The postscript indicates that Mrs. Frances Waldo, the wife of Dr. F. A. Waldo, was once a student of Emily's at the Utica Female Academy and that Emily had touched her life.

[289] Richard Eddy was the treasurer of the American Baptist Missionary Union.

Emily C. Judson to Anna Maria Anable, December 2, 1850—Maulmain

My darling Ninny,[290]

I have received my September letters this month, and my table is almost piled with them—some eloquent heart-letters, on which my poor heart can rest, like yours and Aunt C's,[291] Mr. Newton's,[292] Mr. Osgood's[293] etc.—Others kindly sympathetic in their dignity—Others commonplace condolences from hearts that felt *some* but lacked expression—Others relating to the Memoir,[294] for which the book-sellers are scrambling like a parcel of hungry heirs—other pure business annoyances—and, one, (oh, "tell it not in Gath!") offer of marriage! Do you wonder that I am ill—that I have been obliged to call a doctor, and pill and poultice, and that I cannot write you more than a few lines from sheer weakness. Oh, darling, how I wish you were here!—I have done almost nothing but cry the whole week. The time draws near for me to leave the Mission and you don't know how I cling to it.

Oh Ninny, much as I love you all I would not go home now, if I could help it. I *could* be useful here—the church loves me and I know a little of their language and a good deal of their character, and then it is the place where *he* lived and the work *he* loved. Still I have his approbation[295] in leaving, and the approbation of my Heavenly Father also, otherwise he would not so have ordered it.

One month more, and then I go to pass a half year among strangers, and not merely strangers, but people of another nation, another mode of thinking, and almost another religion. Well, God will carry me through it, or take me home, I

[290] "Ninny" was a name of endearment given to Anna Maria Anable by her most intimate friends at the Utica Female Academy. Emily was "Nemmy."

[291] See vol. 1, "Cast of Characters," s.v. "Sheldon, Miss Cynthia."

[292] There are six letters in this correspondence from Mr. and Mrs. Newton of New York City. In a June 1846 letter Mrs. Newton indicated that they were "new friends" of Emily. They obviously had considerable wealth, which they shared generously with Adoniram and Emily through packages, and upon Adoniram's death, they immediately sent a check for five hundred dollars to Emily. Mr. Newton called Adoniram his "friend," and one of the letters invited Emily to stay with them in New York upon her return. A later letter indicates that Emily had indeed done that. On May 15, 1846, Adoniram Judson inscribed a dedication to Mrs. H. H. Newton on the fly-leaf of a volume of Burmese hymns that had been compiled by Mrs. Sarah B. Judson: "Mrs. H. H. Newton From A. Judson/ The wings ( ) ( ) /( ) are folded in St. Helena—New York—May 15th, 1846."

[293] Rev. Sewall Osgood was a missionary in Maulmain who worked with and lived by Adoniram Judson. Judson and Osgood occupied two of the four homes in the mission compound and lived so close that it "allowed me the pleasure and profit of almost hourly intercourse." He arrived in Burmah in 1834. His first wife Elhira Brown Osgood died on October 5, 1837, in Maulmain. On July 8, 1838, he married Sarah Thomas, the widow of the Reverend Jacob Thomas, with Adoniram Judson officiating at the wedding. He spoke in the letters to Emily, of which there are five between July 1850 and April 1852, of Adoniram Judson as his "most intimate friend." He never personally met Emily, as he had returned from the field prior to 1846. At the time of his letters, he was working with the American Baptist Missionary Union as a district secretary. In 1845, just as they were leaving for the United States, Sarah and Adoniram Judson gave care of Charley, too young to make the trip, to Mr. and Mrs. Osgood. Charley died not long after their departure. Mr. Osgood visted Adoniram, Elnathan, and Abby Ann in the United States. His third wife was Caroline Wait; they were married December 30, 1850, at Saratoga, New York. With all of his suggestions of "intimacy" and "his most intimate friend," Mr. Osgood stated that his life was so busy that he simply did not have the time to look through his papers for anything that would be helpful in writing the Judson memoir.

[294] Fanny Forester, *Memoir of Sarah B. Judson, Member of the American Mission to Burmah* (New York: L. Colby and Company, 1848).

[295] Before his death, Adoniram Judson indicated that Emily would do best to return to the United States if he were to die.

cannot tell which, but it will end some way. Oh darling, if I ever *do* see your dear face again! The Indian papers are almost as enthusiastic as ones own in their praises of our precious saint. One writes—"Tried by every vicissitude of humanity, he came out like pure gold; chained in a dungeon, and face to face with the executioner, or swimming on the topmost wave of popularity, the idol of all that was good and holy in his native land—in the extremes of household happiness, and household bereavements—driven again and again (as it seemed forever) from the Mission field, or rejoicing over his little flock and his completed Bible—in the pulpit, or the platform or in cheerful, social intercourse, Adoniram Judson was always true to his own high nature, combining the warm affections of a man, with the strength, simplicity and directness of an apostle of the living God." Then after complimenting his wives, saying that "they rose to his height, and shine even beside him," he adds, "Such a noble group warms our hearts to America, and make us feel proud that the same blood runs in our veins." You will not think that I have much reason to fear such strangers, but then you know, darling, he has not seen me, and I am one of that "noble group," and I am invited to his house.

It is not probable that I shall make any stop in England as I know no one there, but you must have letters waiting for me. Address "Care of Joseph Symon Esq., 2 Turnwheel Lane, Cannon St. London." This is our agent.

[Written in the right margin of the address page:] I must not write any more [sic] —I am too tired. Think of me, darling, and pray for me, and love me and ask Aunt C. and your Mother,[296] and Hatty[297] and Fanny[298] and Mary[299] to do the same. Do you know—I am *living* on

[Written in the left margin of the address page:] the prayers of good people in America I think; for my life, considering all I have passed through is little less than a miracle. Love to the Gillette's,[300] the Robartses,[301] and Miss Longstreth.[302] I shall try to write next month

Goodbye, darling—Nemmy[303]

[296] See vol. 1, "Cast of Characters," s.v. "Sheldon, Alma and Joseph Hubbell."

[297] See vol. 1, "Cast of Characters," s.v. "Anable, Harriet."

[298] Ibid.

[299] Mary Juliet Anable was born February 18, 1830, in Bethlehem, Albany County, New York, one of nine children born to Alma and Joseph Anable. She went to New Orleans with Hatty in 1847, but she returned home early in March 1848, and by 1849, she was working with Anna Maria in the Misses Anable's School in Philadelphia. Writing in March 1849, Hatty said of Mary, "She paints and draws, speaks French, plays the piano, sings, dances and is our mathematician. What should we ever do without her? She laughs from morning till night, and it is really refreshing to be with her." On December 26, 1860, she was married to Pierre Jacques Darey, the officiating minister being the Rev. Dr. Eliphalet Nott, her uncle. Mary died at the age of sixty-eight on April 20, 1898, in Ottawa, Ontario, Canada.

[300] See vol. 1, "Cast of Characters," s.v. "Gillette, The Reverend Abram Dunn."

[301] See vol. 1, "Cast of Characters," s.v. "Robarts, Mr. and Mrs. W. S."

[302] See vol. 1, "Cast of Characters," s.v. "Longstreth, Mary Anna."

[Written in the left margin of page 1:] It will be a great comfort if Aunt C. will meet me in Boston, but yet I don't like to put her to the trouble. Mrs. Colby[304] has invited me to her house, so I have two strings and [Note: the line ends here in mid-sentence.].

Source: Hanna family files.

Mrs. Emma Relief Keyes Knapp[305] to Emily C. Judson, December 1850[306]

My dear Sister,

Many thanks for the engraving you so kindly sent me. I shall preserve it, and value it as a likeness and memorial of one whose name I have loved to hear from my childhood. I rejoice, tho' I have never been permitted to see him that I have at last been permitted to see the field of his toil, and the dear family from which he has been taken.

Husband is also much pleased with the picture, wishes you to accept his thanks.

I am happy to say I am much better, think I shall be quite well when we are ready to leave. I shall see you again, I trust, if it be only a few moments.

Yours ever Affec'ly

E. R. K. Knapp

Source: American Baptist Historical Society, AJ 17, no. 781.

[303] "Nem" or "Nemmy" was a name of endearment given to Emily by a small group of her intimate friends at the Utica Female Academy. Anna Maria Anable was "Ninny."

[304] See vol. 1, "Cast of Characters," s.v. "Colby, Mary."

[305] Emma Knapp and her husband Harvey, were appointed in 1849 as missionaries to Burmah and arrived at Akyab in March 1850. Harvey was a graduate of Madison University and Hamilton Theological Seminary, both of which were near Emily's home in Hamilton, New York. Emma Knapp died May 24, 1851.

[306] This letter is undated; it is one of three in the correspondence. It is placed first because the last paragraph speaks of leaving; in her December 12, 1850, she speaks of leaving and never seeing Emily again.

Mrs. Emma Relief Keyes Knapp[307] to Emily C. Judson, December 12, 1850—Akyab

My dear Sister Judson

I was disappointed in not seeing you once more before I left Maulmain, as I shall not probably have the privilege again in this world. But I am glad I have been permitted to become acquainted with you in this world, to enjoy Christian intercourse, and bow together before the throne of grace; for I trust the tie that unites the hearts of all the friends of Jesus has thereby been strengthened between us, and that hereafter there will be a mutual interest and sympathy which we should not otherwise have known.

I hope your health is still improving, that your strength may sufficient [sic] for you, during the exciting and wearisome task of starting on your long journey. And may the God of all grace and strength, be your support, your guide and protector on the sea and on the land, and under all circumstances in which you may be placed.

I am happy to say we arrived safely, at our home, and are now enjoying our work very much. Our healths are good. We are busy just now in preparing for our jungle tour, shall leave early next week. So you will excuse a hasty note. I shall be happy to have a line from this month, also to know whether you go to C. by Steamer or ship.

Our united regard to yourself and dear family and believe me

Your affect sister in Christ

E. R. K. Knapp

Source: American Baptist Historical Society, AJ 17, no. 781.

Mrs. Emma Relief Keyes Knapp[308] to Emily C. Judson, December 13, 1850

My dear sister

I send a small package which I hope may not make you much trouble.

You doubtless remember I asked you once if you c'd take a little parcel with your things which wd go to Hamilton soon after your arrival. If you can dispose of it in that way you will favor me, but any other way most convenient for you will answer my purpose.

Affectionately Yours

E. R. K. K.

[307] See vol. 1, "Cast of Characters," s.v. "Knapp, Emma Relief Keyes and The Reverend Harvey."

[308] Ibid.

P.S. I learn that the Burman by whom I tho't to send the parcel has no trunk or chart and I do not like to trust it to go on deck. If you stop at Akyab on your way to C. I will have it handed to you there.

E.R. K.

Source: American Baptist Historical Society, AJ 17, no. 781.

Mr. A. L. Cutten to Emily C. Judson, December 13, 1850

My dear Mrs. Judson,

I beg you will accept my warmest thanks for your kindness in sending me the "Miniature Bowie Knife" as a keepsake. I shall prize it very highly, and preserve it most carefully, as a Memento of your beloved and now sainted husband. I was most *anxious* to obtain possession of some little article, however trifling, that once belonged to that great and good man, for whom I have always entertained the highest respect and esteem—and the warmest affection one could cherish towards a revered and beloved father.

It will be my aim to see that "the knife conducts itself with propriety"—which I doubt not will be the case, as it is not likely ever to see much active service.

Believe me
My dear Mrs. Judson
Yours most truly

O. T. Cutten

Source: American Baptist Historical Society, AJ 15, no. 614.

Emily C. Judson to Right Rev. Bishop Wilson of Calcutta, December 17, 1850—Maulmain

My Beloved Father in Christ,—

I was so much overcome yesterday, both by a sense of the condescension of your lordship's visit, and also by the flood of mournful reminiscences which it generated; that I failed to say how warmly my now sainted husband reciprocated the affection you were pleased to express for him, and how deep were his respect and veneration. I also neglected to fulfill one of his last requests, made only a few days previous to our final earthly parting. It had been his intention to send you a copy of the memoir of his late wife, but the first editions were so defaced by typographical errors that he deferred it until we should receive a revised edition.[309] This was expected daily when he went away, and he commissioned me to beg your lordship's acceptance of a copy in his name, so soon as I should receive it. My subsequent illness, together with my anticipated visit to Calcutta, has prevented the fulfillment of his wishes until now.

I also do myself the pleasure to add another memento—the accompanying engraving, from a portrait taken five years since in America. Those who loved him do not think it correct, but it is a very good representation of the face he wore in public.

Permit me again to express my warmest thanks for your kind gift—the Book of books—and to assure your lordship that this will be the copy which I shall hereafter read in my closet, and preserve among my choicest treasures.

Praying that our Heavenly Father may have you in His holy keeping, and spare you to the Church of Christ for many years to come; and trusting that when you sometimes think of a saint in glory, you may remember also the widow and the fatherless in their desolation, believe me, my lord, with reverential affection,

Most sincerely yours,

Emily C. Judson

Source: A. C. Kendrick, *The Life and Letters of Mrs. Emily C. Judson*, 351–52

Mrs. E. W. F. Moore to Emily C. Judson, December 18, 1850

My dear Mrs. Judson

Will you accept of a tiny bit of butter from my dairy. I want to see you and tell you how gratified the Bishop was with your note and gift[310] but probably Mrs. Hough[311] has mentioned it to you. His Lordship presented my husband with a vol. of his sermons yesterday, and as husband was absent it devolved upon me to say thanks, but I presume my note did no [sic] call forth any such encomiums as yours.

With much love
Yours affectionately

E. W. F. Moore

Source: American Baptist Historical Society, AJ 18, no. 869.

[309] Fanny Forester, *Memoir of Sarah B. Judson, Member of the American Mission to Burmah* (New York: L. Colby and Company, 1848).

[310] See Emily's letter of December 17, 1850, written to Right Reverend Bishop Wilson of Calcutta.

[311] See vol. 1, "Cast of Characters," s.v. "Hough, The Reverend George and Phoebe."

The Reverend Doctor Solomon Peck to Emily C. Judson,[312] December 20, 1850—Baptist Mission Rooms, Boston

My dear Sister

You will have received before this, I presume, the letter addressed to you last Sept. by the Home Soc during my late sickness, and have learned from it the reply which the Exec. Com. would give to your intimations in regard to your future course. Whatever you finally determine, the Com. will cordially accede to it, and will do all in their power to promote your carefulness and your welfare. I will not repeat the sentiments contained in that letter. They have my most hearty conscience [sic]. I only regret, and at the time it was a heavy affliction to me, that at such a season of public calamity and private grief I was unable to be at my post, and to bear my part in those expressions of mourning and sympathy which abounded on every side. You have indeed been "smitten of God and afflicted," and in a way and degree we had little thought of. Among the sorrows which I foreshadowed in your past, and to which I made some allusion before you sailed for the East, this had no place. I was confident you would *share* in the common heritage of God's people, but had not anticipated for you so *early* and so *large* a portion. But God knows best his own plan and how to bring it to pass. He knows too how to sustain. He has pierced you through with many sorrows; but He has also, I feel assured, poured into your heart his exceeding grace and precious consolations.

I have just been reading again your most deeply interesting narrative of the closing scenes of Dr. Judson's life.[313] They were scenes most befitting the termination of such a life of such a missionary. I bless God for such a testimony to the elevation of his piety and to his social virtues, and to His own grace and faithfulness. I bless the Providence that has put those scenes on record. It was not only fitting but needful. Too much might otherwise have been left to empirical conjecture to fill out *justly* the complement to his public character. Removed so early from his native home and country, and afterwards secluded generally from social intercourse by residence or taste or occupation, we knew him more as a missionary of Christ than as a fellow labour [sic] and brother. These "closing scenes" bring out the excellencies of his character more dearly. We now can speak, not presumptuously, but the things we *know*.

[312] Due to Dr. Peck's illness, all of the correspondence to Emily from the Missionary Union at the time of Adoniram Judson's death came from Dr. Edward Bright. This included a proclamation from the Board, and Dr. Bright's communication as to what the board would be prepared to do to help Emily as she explored her future options for herself and her family. This is Dr. Peck's first correspondence at hand after Adoniram Judson's death. It is both tender and heartfelt.

[313] See Emily's letter of September 20, 1850, to Abigail Brown Judson, the sister of Adoniram Judson. This letter was widely circulated, as Emily outlined the events which had begun with the onset of Judson's last illness in November 1849, and which had culminated with his boarding the Aristide Maria for a lengthy ocean voyage to the Isle of Bourbon.

The letter agreeably to your suggestion passed into the hands of Mr. Bright,[314] who intends to publish it in the *Macedonian* for Feb. It will appear also, simultaneously, in the Magazine—no repository more suitable for it—and I cannot distrust your cordial acquiescence

The action of the Exec. Com. in regard to the Dictionary manuscript, has doubtlessly, been anticipated by you. They fully concur in committing them to the care of Mr. Stevens[315] as well as the completing of what remains to be done. They wish him, however, as he will be informed, to defer the execution of the second part of the Dictionary to some future day, when the Mission shall have been reinforced. The labor of completing the work must, without doubt be greatly increased in being passed to another hand, especially if it is true, as has been intimated, that Dr. Judson's later commendations are abbreviated or in cipher.

My dear Mrs. Judson, I do very clearly apprehend, as I think, the bitterness of the cup which God has given you. It is my sincerest wish to assure you of my truest and tenderest sympathy. I feel powerless to administer consolation. Yet I know, He who has provided is able to accomplish—who also will do it. To Him I earnestly commend the widow and the fatherless children. A father of the fatherless and a judge of the widow is God in his holy habitation.

Most truly
Your friend and brother

S. Peck Cor. Sec.

Source: American Baptist Historical Society, AJ 19, no. 944.

Emily C. Judson to Doctor Edward Bright, December 23, 1850—Maulmain

My Dear Mr. Bright,

I have no words with which to express my gratitude for the kind sympathy of yourself and the executive committee in my afflictions, nor the pleasure with which I have regarded your manifest appreciation of a character now made perfect in glory.[316] I would also, were it in my power, extend my thanks to all those Churches and individual Christians who have given me the support of their prayers during these dark months of trial; for surely the everlasting arms have been about me, and God—even the God in whom *he* trusted—has led me. In sorrow, in anxiety, in weak-

[314] See vol. 1, "Cast of Characters," s.v. "Bright, The Reverend Doctor Edward, Jr."

[315] See vol. 1, "Cast of Characters," s.v. "Stevens, The Reverend Edward and Elizabeth."

[316] See the action of the Executive Committee of the American Baptist Missionary Union in a letter written September 9, 1850; also the letter that accompanied the action, written by Edward Bright, on September 27, 1850.

ness, in the depths of desolation and affliction, I have found the blessedness of clinging to the cross of Christ, and though I have had my hours of trembling and despondency, I have also had glimpses of the eternal world, and of a crown radiant with the glory of the redeemed, which have made me rejoice that I am permitted thus to suffer, while the suffering is *mine alone*.

After my illness of 1849 (by which my prospects of usefulness in the mission were greatly impaired), my husband expressed his desire that, in case of his death, I should return to America and assume the guardianship of the children. A few days previous to his embarkation I took occasion to allude to the subject, inquiring if he had any objection to my remaining here until I had accomplished certain objects for which I had been striving to prepare myself, provided it should seem in my own eyes the wisest course, and should meet the approval of the Mission and the Board. After some little hesitation he replied that it would be very sad to leave me in such circumstances, and he should feel far happier to think of me in the position he had so often pictured in my native land, but added, "I do not wish you to feel under the least restraint from any thing [sic] I have said; act as your judgment dictates, and I am sure that God will guide you to a wise decision." I felt, therefore, that it would not be a violation of his wishes for me to remain until the age of the children made my return necessary; and for a little time, with the kind concurrence of the Mission, I decided accordingly. But God ordained it otherwise, and, as you have already learned, left me without a choice. The physician who has attended upon me for the last three years has expressed his decided conviction that I shall never be equal to the performance of active missionary duties; and there is much reason to fear that loss of life might be the penalty of remaining through another rainy season. The manner of effecting my return has been a subject of great anxiety to me. A merchantman, with no female friend or medical adviser on board, presents but a forbidding prospect; and I have not felt at liberty (looking to your treasury for disbursement) to incur the additional expense of more suitable accommodations. Even in this, however, God has fulfilled His promise to those who put their trust in Him. A few friends in Bengal have proposed making up a small purse as a tribute to the departed, which I hope will be sufficient to defray all expenses over and above those usually incurred by returning missionaries. I therefore propose leaving here in the January steamer for Calcutta, and thence taking an English passenger ship to London, which port I hope to reach early in May. May I be assured of your prayers, both in my own behalf and in behalf of my fatherless children?

I need scarcely say that the action of the Board on the subject of the proposed memoir[317] meets my most cordial concurrence....

[317] On September 27, Dr. Bright had spoken forthrightly on the need for a memoir of Doctor Judson, and of those who might be well qualified to write it.

The choice of a biographer I consider to be a question of great difficulty and delicacy, and one on which I can not but hesitate to express a decided opinion. The common tendency, I think, would be to place the subject at a cloudy distance, and divest him of those attributes of humanity the lack of which no heroism or saint-like quality should ever be thought sufficient to compensate. Besides, Dr. Judson possessed a strongly marked character, and one writer might seize upon one view, another upon another, and a third upon still another; while each representation would be as incomplete as the description of a multiform edifice from the survey of a single side. He needs a biographer capable of grasping his whole character at once, and of reconciling and harmonizing its singularly diverse elements—its delicacy with its strength, its almost unparalleled tenderness with its uncompromising sternness, its sensibility with its stoicism, its ardent enthusiasm with its cool severity of judgment, its frank, genial socialness with its tendency to asceticism, its discreet and quiet caution with its bold fearlessness, its patience in study with its promptitude in action; its impetuous earnestness, its graceful play of fancy, its humor, with its serene dignity, its mock seriousness, the simplicity of its devotion, and its constant aspirations after holiness. The work had better never be performed than marred by weak hands; the character had better remain undelineated till the judgment day than be crippled to suit the powers of a mind less capacious than his own. In addition to this, his life has been such a complete exposition of the age in which it began and ended, that a rapid but comprehensive glance at these times will be an essential requisite to a full development of the subject. The unseen influences which had been so long in operation, and gradually tending to the finally bold conjuncture; the Spirit of God brooding upon the dark waters until they were finally stirred beneath it; the new-born light, flashing forth in the Old World, to be caught up and reflected from the walls of Andover; the progress of the wondrous work, girdling the whole earth with its slowly advancing glory; all this requires to be connected and interwoven in such a manner as to exemplify the dealings of God in the mightiest movement which marks this age of wonders.

Pardon me if I write too earnestly. I do not wish to overstep the bounds of modesty, but it is a subject on which I have a right to feel the deepest interest; and yet I can truly say that I am less solicitous for my husband's honor (which I believe would be safe in any hands) than desirous that his death should subserve the interests of the noble cause to which his whole life was devoted.

The Committee will be pleased to learn that the mission so far anticipated their wishes with regard to the monument at Amherst as to obtain a grant of the ground from government, so that whatever changes occur, the spot marked by the hopia tree[318] will remain undisturbed.

[318] There had been action towards erecting a monument by the hopia tree that marked the grave of Ann Hasseltine Judson, who was buried at Amherst.

Again thanking both you and the Committee for your courteous consultation of my wishes, your kind sympathy, and your expressed interest in my welfare, believe me, my dear Mr. Bright, with the highest respect and esteem,

Most sincerely yours,

Emily C. Judson

Source: A. C. Kendrick, *The Life and Letters of Mrs. Emily C. Judson*, 352–55

Mr. A. L. Cutten to Emily C. Judson, December 23, 1850

My dear Mrs. Judson,

With very many thanks I return the intensely interesting little volume you was [sic] so kind as to lend me,—"The Old Man's House." Never before was I so interested in a narrative, and in spite of myself I could not commend my feelings. It is truly beautiful. "Home, Sweet Home" of the Christians? Truly, "there's no place like *Home*."

May "the soft notes of Music and the Whispering Winds" of which sweet little Annie spoke, cheer you, on your lonely journey through this vale of tears, till you also at last reach your home above, and enter into the "rest which remaineth for the people of God."

( ) you are feeling quite well this morning, after the rest and quietness of the Sabbath, believe me,

My dear Mrs. Judson,

Yours affecly,

A.L. Cutten

Source: American Baptist Historical Society, AJ 15, no. 614.

Letters

January–June 1851

Reverend W. S. MacKay to Emily C. Judson, January 6, 1851—Hoosy Gunge, ( ) ( )

My dear Mrs. Judson,

Being out of Calcutta during our vacation for a week or two, I was late in receiving your letter, and have barely time to answer it, as the steamer leaves Calcutta early on the morning of the 10th. I am glad for your sake it is to be the *Tenasserem* [sic] as it is a much larger, swifter and more comfortable vessel than the *Enterprize*, [sic] and may give us 2 or 3 days more of you in Calcutta. We shall be quite ready and truly delighted to receive you. If I were in Calcutta, I should ask the Captain to send or take you on to us; but, as I cannot do so, the best thing you can do is wait quietly on board, until I, or some one [sic] from me, come to fetch you at the vessel in Semaphore, and I shall have friends on the watch, you will not, I think, have to wait long.

We would all like you to go in the *Lucen* [sic] as both captain and doctor are personal friends of ours, and would be sure to do everything in their power for your comfort. She is ( ) a splendid ship. I shall endeavor to get a good upper cabin for you in her conditionally. She will probably sail about the 10th of February. You speak too kindly of any thing [sic] I am attempting to do for you; but though we have never met, I do not look upon you as a stranger and I truly feel a deep interest and sympathy (I might say affection) for you, not only for your husband's sake, but from all I can gather about yourself. I regret much that our personal acquaintance is likely to be so short; but I venture to anticipate (should God spare us) much pleasant epistolary intercourse hereafter.

The Judson Testimonial, as I ought to have called it from the first, is not going on as I could have wished; but as soon as the *Review* has been read containing Major Durand's ( ) tribute to your husband and your own most beautiful, elevating, and touching letter, I think we shall succeed to the extent that I contemplate.

I am sorry, that I fall into the mistake, or rather advertency, which you mention; but it is of little consequence as the error is wholly mine, and only not literally and strictly correct. I mean now to propose it as a testimonial on the part of Judson Christians to their value for him, his services, and his family. I will not say any more [sic] at present; indeed I am so overburdened with work at the moment that I cannot; but I hope in about three weeks to see you face to face, and to try at least to show you that in my dear wife and myself you will find a brother and a sister.

I have ordered a copy of the *Review* to be sent to you; but I fear it will not be ready in time. Believe me, my dear Mrs. Judson, with much sympathy and high esteem,

Your sincere friend

W. S. MacKay

Give my kindest regards to Mrs. Hough[1] and tell her I shall write and tell her all about *you* next time. I am living with the Bren( )s, and heard of her through him a day or two ago. He also will write bye and bye [sic].

Source: American Baptist Historical Society, AJ 17, no. 750.

Emily Judson's Will,[2] January 9, 1851

Be it known that I, Emily C. Judson, Widow, of the town of Maulmain, in the Tenasserim Provinces, being about to commence a voyage to America, and being also in feeble health, make, publish and declare this instrument to be my last Will and Testament, in the manner following, to wit:

1. I give and bequeath to my sister, Catharine Chubbuck, all the real estate of which I shall die seized, to be held by her, for the use of my parents during the natural lives of both or either one of them, and afterward to revert to her and to her heirs and assigns forever.[3]

2. I give and bequeath to my said sister Catharine for her own use and that of my parents, all my personal property in America, including my right and title to certain books published by George D. Ticknor[4] and Co. Boston,[5] and by Lewis Colby and Co.[6] New York, and also including all that may be due to me from the American Baptist Missionary Union at the time of my death.

3. I direct that the right I possess in the Memoir of Sarah B. Judson, be placed at the disposal of the said Missionary Union; and also that the sum of One Thousand rupees be paid into the treasury of said union, being the amount of certain sums devoted by my late husband to Missionary purposes.

4. I give and bequeath to Nancy,[7] the East Indian girl who accompanies me to America Three hundred and fifty dollars, to enable her to return with a comfortable

[1] Phoebe Hough and her husband George were the first missionaries to be wholly called by the American Baptist Missionary Union to work in Burmah with Adoniram and Ann Judson. They retired from missionary service in 1826; George Hough subsequently worked for the government as an interpreter and school superintendent, and Mrs. Hough worked as an educator.

[2] Emily Judson wrote a later will; see January 20, 1854.

[3] In late summer 1842, Emily used the proceeds from her writing to purchase a house in the village of Hamilton, New York, for her parents and her sister Catharine, who never married. She incurred a debt of $400 for this purpose; over the years, she added improvements and said in one letter that she would not "take a thousand dollars for it." Adoniram Judson helped with some of the final payments as they were being married.

[4] The name of Emily's publisher was William D. Ticknor.

[5] Ticknor and Company had published *Alderbrook* and would later publish The *Kathayan Slave* and My *Two Sisters*.

[6] Lewis Colby was a publisher in New York. In agreeing to publish the *Memoir of Sarah Hall Boardman Judson*, they had also agreed to republish some of Emily's earlier books. Lewis Colby also published *An Olio of Domestic Verses*.

[7] Nancy was a Malayan woman who came with Emily from Burmah to America in 1851; she helped Emily with the three Judson children—Henry , Edward, and Emily Frances—and to be there if she was incapacitated by her frequent illnesses. There are numerous references to Nancy in the correspondence, and she continued with her duties with Emily and with the children until Emily's death in June 1854. In her will, Emily left a sum more than sufficient to pay for Nancy's return to her native home.

outfit to her native land; and if she should not wish to return, or should be able to obtain a passage gratis, I direct that the above mentioned sum be still paid her in consideration of her faithful service.

5. I direct that the books, clothing, and other articles which I have reserved as memorials of my late husband, be distributed among his six children,[8] at the discretion of the Executors; and that my own private property of a similar character, be placed at the disposal of Miss Anna Maria Anable,[9] of Philadelphia, Pennsylvania, whom I hereby appoint the guardian of my daughter, Emily Frances Judson.[10]

6. I appoint Dr. Calvin Newton[11] of Worcester, Massachusetts, and Miss Abigail B. Judson[12] of Plymouth, Massachusetts, the executors of my will, and joint guardians of the children left to my care (with the exception of the above mentioned daughter), begging that they will accept the sum of five hundred dollars each, as a token of my esteem and confidence.

7. If, after deducting the above specifications, and meeting the various liabilities to which the estate may be subject, any other property should yet remain to me, I direct that the same be equally divided among the six children left to my guardianship, to supply any deficiency in the sum devoted by their late father to their support and education; and if such deficiency be found not to exist; or if it shall be made up from any other source, that the funds be reserved to be equally divided among the said surviving children, when the youngest shall have reached the age of twenty one years.

In testimony whereof I hereunto set my hand and seal, this ninth day of January in the year of our Lord, One Thousand Eight Hundred and Fifty one.

[8] Abby Ann Judson, Adoniram Judson, Elnathan Judson, Henry Hall Judson, Edward Judson, and Emily Frances Judson. George Dana Boardman was not included in the guardianships that were given to Emily, nor was he included in this will or in the later will of January 20, 1854.

[9] Anna Maria Anable was the niece of the Misses Urania and Cynthia Sheldon and the daughter of Joseph and Alma Sheldon Anable. Emily first met Anna Maria in fall 1840 when she went as a student to the Utica Female Academy; both Emily and Anna Maria became members of the faculty there. In these years, Anna Maria became Emily's dearest friend, and the extensive correspondence between the two reflects sensitive, flirtatious spirits and a deep intimacy. Emily was "Nemmy" to Anna Maria's "Ninny." In 1848, Anna Maria Anable, with the help of her extended family, moved to Philadelphia and started the Misses Anable's School in Philadelphia. At Emily's death in 1854, Anna Maria was given guardianship of Emily Frances Judson, daughter of Emily and Adoniram Judson.

[10] Emily Frances Judson, the daughter of Adoniram and Emily Chubbuck Judson, was born December 24, 1847. Emily married the Reverend Thomas Alexander Thomson (T. A. T.) Hanna in 1870, and they had eight children, two of whom served as missionaries in Burmah.

[11] Dr. Calvin Newton, after some theological training, went to medical school to become a physician. He apparently had differing ideas about medicine, and he became a part of what was known as the Eclectic School of Medicine; with that background, he established the Worcester Medical Institute. In 1835, Dr. and Mrs. Newton received into their home the young George Dana Boardman, just returned from Burmah for his education. Adoniram and Elnathan went there in fall 1845 when they returned to the United States with their father, and they remained there under the Newton's care until Emily's return in October 1851. At that time, Mrs. Newton had become ill, and the boys went to live with Dr. and Mrs. Edward Bright.

[12] Abigail Brown Judson, the sister of Adoniram Judson, lived in Plymouth, Massachusetts. A spinster of eccentric character and behavior, she was a beneficiary of her parents' considerable wealth. Her father had wisely invested in land and bank stocks; with the help of Esq. Loud, she had invested that money prudently. She took a strong interest in Adoniram's children and offered them considerable support—though not often without complaint or comment—for their clothing and education in the years to come.

Emily C. Judson

Signed, sealed and declared by the above named Emily C. Judson to be her last Will and Testament, in the presence of us, and we, at her request, in her presence and in the presence of each other, hereto subscribe our names as witnesses.

A. L. Cutten
Thos. L. Ranney[13]

Source: Hanna family files.

Mrs. J. A. P. Cross to Emily C. Judson, January 10, 1851—Tavoy

My Dear Mrs. Judson,

I received your very kind note yesterday and as mail by Burman boat closes tomorrow I hasten to reply thinking it possible you will not be in Maulmain when the mail by steamer closes. I was very sorry that you paid Mr. Ranney[14] for the arrow-root, as it was far from my thoughts or intention to receive any pay for it.[15] I should indeed esteem it a great privilege to contribute in any way in my power to making your voyage more comfortable by any such helps in regard to food. I shall accordingly request Mr. Ranney to return you the six rupees and beg you to accept the arrow-root as a small indication (I) feel most sincerely in your course. (I am sorry) soojer disagrees with you but it might not do so on board ship when you were laboring under sea-sickness. I believe it has an effect with many to produce diarrhea and as sea-sickness has a tendency to produce constipation it might still be useful to you under such circumstances. But you are of course the best judge. I suffer so dreadfully from sea-sickness myself that I feel a very great sympathy for any one [sic] who suffers similarly and the last time I was out at sea the soojer was a great help to me.

I do not wonder that your heart is sad and desolate but he who has wounded alone can heal, and I doubt not you are much of the time enabled to feel the "he doeth all things well." He does not willingly afflict. Reflections upon the infinite bliss in which your dear departed husband is now a blessed participator must be comforting to you, and in how short a time we shall all have done with earth. I have

[13] Thomas Ranney was appointed to missionary service in June 1843, arriving in Burmah in May 1844. He was an important part of the Judsons' lives while in Rangoon. He was superintendent of the printing press in Maulmain and business manager for the compound. Thomas Ranney went with Adoniram Judson on his last voyage, and thus was with him when he died. There is a letter in the collection from the *Aristide Marie* written five days before Adoniram Judson's death; one of the things he did at the time of death was to take some locks of his hair to bring to Emily. She later sent one of these locks to Adoniram's sister Abigail in Plymouth. Thomas Ranney provided the accounts of Adoniram's last voyage and his last hours of life. He also handled some of the financial matters for the mission and in the settlement of Adoniram Judson's estate. Thomas Ranney was married to Maria Gager, who died in 1857, and then to Mary E. Bennett, the daughter of missionaries Cephas and Stella Bennett.

[14] Ibid.

[15] See the letter of Mrs. Cross written November 23, 1850.

no doubt in your loneliness you sometimes feel it necessary to pray for reconciliation to remaining on earth all your appointed time but I trust you will ever feel underneath you the Almighty Arms as your unfailing support.

My husband is now absent in the jungle. You will be happy to hear that a greater blessing has attended jungle efforts in this region this season than for many years previous. In one village where there was not a single Christian before six ( ). These six with 12 others connected with Christian f( ) leading inhabitants have been baptized and numbers more are nearly ready.

We can but hope God has great mercies in reserve soon to be bestowed upon these people.

With love to all your dear children[16] and the most sincere sympathy and regard for yourself yrs very affly

J. A. P. Cross.

Source: American Baptist Historical Society, AJ 15, no. 617.

The Reverend Cephas Bennett to Emily C. Judson, January 11, 1851—Tavoy

My dear Sister Judson,

I have been hesitating, whether to write you or not by this Burman boat, as I fear she will not arrive until you have departed for the shores of the "far west"—but I having a moment will run the risk of missing you, as what I write will not be a great loss, even if you never meet it.

Thanks for your kind note, and lest I forget it, I would say all the letters I have of our late dear friend,[17] I will look over soon, and what I find, if I find anything which I have not much expectation of doing, which will be worth printing in the memoirs of one whose memory will even be first to us all, while life lasts, and would that we could all be more like the pattern he has set us, or in other words, that we

[16] Henry Hall Judson, Edward Judson, Emily Frances Judson.

[17] Mr. Corey was the pastor of the Bleecker Street Baptist Church near the Utica Female Academy, and Miss Sheldon and many of the girls from the academy attended worship there. (Cynthia Sheldon, Alma Anable, Deacon Asa and Isabell Sheldon, Edward Bright, and Horace Hawley had been charter members of the church in 1838.) In April 1844, he wrote to Emily expressing dismay that at a school program one of the girls had read a composition justifying dancing as exercise; he spoke of this as a roadblock to the salvation of many. Then, on March 10, 1846, Emily indicated in a letter to Anna Maria that Mr. Corey had been critical of her relationship and impending marriage to Adoniram Judson. Miss Cynthia Sheldon wrote a number of times expressing Mr. Corey's regret and support, and in 1847, there were letters of reconciliation between Emily and Mr. Corey. In spring 1848, letters reveal that Mr. Corey's wife had died of consumption, her condition exacerbated by recent childbirth. She had left behind four children. In July 1849, Anna Maria Anable wrote of his impending marriage to Jane Backus, a good choice for this "rising man." Mr. Corey remained popular with the Sheldon-Anable families even after their move to Philadelphia in 1848. A March 2, 1852, letter from Charles B. Stout told of Mr. Corey's call to the Stanton Street Church in New York City, which Mr. Corey did not accept. Finally, in 1854, there was a pastoral letter from Mr. Corey to Emily on her illness and her possible death. He preached at the Bleecker Street Church as late as January 1867.

could be more like *his* pattern. If I find anything I will forward it to you care of Br. Bright,[18] and as I shall send overland, the letters will probably be in Boston before you. I would have sent them now, but I have not had time to look at them.

I am glad the children were pleased with the shells, but I hope next year if I am spared to send home a box, I shall be able to send them much prettier ones, and add considerably to their variety, as since I packed theirs, we have found many *living* varieties, and far more perfect shells—It is even a pleasure by me to encourage in the young what I fancy will be a pleasure to them in after life, and dissipate, if possible or rather destroy that tendency all naturally have to vanity, and vexation of spirit—Think of the misery of the world is caused by a vacancy of mind and the not having proper *subjects* for reflection, and being *happy* in such subjects. As to myself, I am but a child yet—and can see where, if I were to live over my life I should, I think, avoid some of the rocks and quicksands of life. If in my own children I am not permitted to see what I desire, it is a pleasure to see in others, what is more praiseworthy.

Be assured, you will often be remembered by Mrs. B. and myself, we are of the domestic kind of animals, and though the old adage is too true very often, "Out of sight, out of mind," it is not so with us, in all cases at least, as we often talk over past scenes and past friends.

May the widows [sic] God ever shield you, and preserve you from all harms, and give you to see much good—and experience it too in person—The God of the fatherthelless [sic] *will* take care of the children, to his care we can commit you all in safety. I would write more, but I have been called off more than half a dozen times since I began this note, and must now close it as the time for closing the mail has arrived. Please give my best regards to the dear children, and to all friends you may meet who shall enquire after our welfare—

Your affectionate Brother

C. Bennett

Source: American Baptist Historical Society, AJ 12, no. 357.

[18] Upon her return to America in 1851, Emily Judson was to have a very close relationship with Dr. Edward Bright, the corresponding secretary of the American Baptist Missionary Union. They had known one another previously in New York, as he worked at the time of Adoniram and Emily's marriage with the *Baptist Register*, a prominent regional newsletter. Prior to working as a publisher, he had been, in 1838, the founding pastor of the Bleecker Street Baptist Church in Utica, a church with close ties to the Utica Female Academy. He was appointed corresponding secretary of the Missionary Union the end of May 1846, just prior to Adoniram and Emily's leaving Boston for Burmah. In this role he regularly pleaded with Emily for articles to be published in the missionary magazine, the *Macedonian*. Upon Emily's return from Burmah in October 1851, Adoniram and Elnathan went to live with Dr. and Mrs. Bright for a year. Dr. Bright was to help Emily with many of her business affairs; he carried on the publishing details of the Judson Memoir because of a serious illness in Dr. Wayland's family. He, with Dr. Edward Granger, was to be the executor of the estate of Emily Chubbuck Judson, a responsibility he still carried in March 1869, as reflected in a letter to Anna Maria Anable regarding financial arrangements for Emily Frances Judson.

Mrs. Stella K. Bennett to Emily C. Judson, January 11, 1851—Tavoy

My dear Sister Judson

As mail closes suddenly this morning for Maulmain and I hasten to write you a few words fearing I should not have another opportunity before you leave.

[Note: the next paragraph—12 lines—is lost.]

You kindly inquire about my health. I am happy to tell you it is as good as it has been for years, and so far as I am concerned, I have no idea of ever returning to America. Mr. B. is now in comfortable health. His fever returns occasionally but we have every reason to hope that with common prudence about exposing himself he will in time over come [sic] it.

My children at home at ( ) ( ) [Note: the next eight lines are lost.] I thought much of you and your departed husband on New Years day. You will recollect that last N. Years day was the last and only time I had seen Mr. J. for many years. I have many times thought of the few moments I saw you both on the steamer and been thankful. I have even thought with pleasure and gratitude on the short visit you made us two years since and believe it ( ) to have been much to my advantage if I could have seen you( ). It is a blessed hope we have of again soon meeting [Note: line is lost] ( ) eternity. Neither Mr. Bennett or myself can forget You and your dear children and so far as our poor prayers will avail to secure you every blessing you will have them I don't wonder you feel that it would be better for you to dep( ) and hope you will *try* to live for the sake of your children and I trust you may not only be permitted to do for them what nobody else would do, but that you may also do much yet for the cause of Christ. You have the ability, and you may have the opportunity of recommending religion and Missions where few Missionaries can. May God aid you to seek His glory wherever you may be. I am oppressed at the thought of what you have before you in getting home, but pray that you may be carried through all ( ). Miss Cynthia says she is to greet you in Boston at Sarah Bell Wheeler's alias Mrs. Gould's.[19] She seems to think we are coming "for certain". Dear dear Aunt Cynthia. I ( ) bless her forever. If you can possibly give us a line before you leave Calcutta we shall be very thankful.

[Written across the text on page one:] Sorry to hear Henry[20] had had fever but Hope he is well again. With much love to all the children from myself and Edward and with the prayer that God may keep you in all your ways and ( ) the light of this countenance ( ) to shine upon you.

[19] The references are to Miss Cynthia Sheldon, Emily's mentor and friend from the Utica Female Academy, and Sarah Bell Wheeler, a friend from those same days when both were students there. Sarah Bell married Charles Gould, a widower, and lived in Boston at this time.

[20] Henry Judson, the next to youngest surviving son of Adoniram Judson and Sarah Hall Boardman Judson, whom Emily had embraced as her own.

( ) you an affect fare well

S. K. Bennett

Source: The American Baptist Historical Society, AJ 12, Number 355.

The Reverend Lyman Stilson to Emily C. Judson, January 20, 1851

To Mrs. E. C. Judson

Dear Madam

Will you please pay to R. E. Eddy[21] Esq the sum of Companys Rupees one hundred or forty five Dollars and forty five and a half cents, being the amt of an order I ran by yourself or Nu [sic] in favor of Rev. E. A. Stevens[22] but which item was omitted in my account with you on settlement just previous to your departure for America

L. Stilson

Source: American Baptist Historical Society, AJ 12, no. 365.

Emily C. Judson to Anna Maria Anable,[23] January 20, 1851—Maulmain

Weary and desolate—weary, worn, and desolate—oh! Anna Maria,[24] my path is mantled over by the very "blackness of darkness." I am on the eve of embarkation—one day more and I leave my loving, sympathising [sic] **friends here, to plunge into the midst of strangers. How well fitted I am for this long and lonely voyage, you will imagine when I tell you that I have not been able to enter even the nearest mission house since that fatal April but once, and then,**

[21] Richard Eddy was the treasurer of the American Baptist Missionary Union.

[22] Edward Stevens arrived in Maulmain in February 1838; his wife was Elizabeth Stevens. Mr. Stevens was responsible for the native churches that were associated with the mission. He took on the work of finishing the dictionary after the death of Adoniram Judson, and he buried "Angel Charley" in the chapel compound after his birth in April 1850. Mr. Stevens was in Burmah for forty-eight years.

[23] There are two versions of this letter: the original as written by Emily E. Chubbuck and the edited version published by Dr. A. C. Kendrick in his biography, *The Life and Letters of Mrs. Emily C. Judson* (New York: Sheldon and Company, 1831). Additions made by Dr. Kendrick are in parentheses, and words in the original left out by Dr. Kendrick have been added in bold. There are significant changes and omissions. In a note in his book, Dr. Kendrick explained that interest, purpose and propriety sometimes led to these changes and exclusions, "I remark here that in giving Miss Chubbuck's letters, I do not always indicate unimportant omissions. Real letters must always contain much which should not meet the public eye; and Emily's were real letters, dashed off hastily amidst pressing cares and duties. Written also after the exhausting labors of the day, they by no means do uniform justice to her epistolary powers." He later added, "In giving a few extracts from his and Miss Chubbuck's correspondence at this time, I have no wish to minister to a prurient curiosity, not to violate that principle which would generally place letters written during the period of an 'engagement' under the shelter of inviolate secrecy."

[24] See vol. 1, "Cast of Characters," s.v. "Anable, Anna Maria."

(two weeks since) it brought on a relapse from which I am still suffering. My Calcutta friends, however, write me very kindly, even tenderly, and though they are *stranger-friends,* God may *see fit* to turn their hearts toward me—I don't know. It is better of course to look altogether above the world, but that is scarcely possible when in it. Oh! For the rest of the people of God! Sometimes I think it would be delightful to share *his* grave—but then—the children.[25]

Lydia[26] came and interrupted me—then Mrs. Stevens[27]—then the Houghs,[28] and finally Mr. Stevens.[29] I have been talking over with him the affairs of the church, and have almost lost sight of my personal troubles in these precious interests. Think how I knew all the members, and how sad I must feel to leave them to those that I think do not fully understand them. Mr. S. is an educated, gentlemanly man, a persevering labourer [sic], and a thoroughly conscientious Christian. But he is a man of narrow views, strong prejudices, inclined to favouritism [sic], a miserable judge of character, and humbly and meekly self-willed. He is intellectually a miniature man, wrought in iron, and venured [sic] with wax—yet I love him dearly, and so did Mr. J. for he has the kindest of hearts and the best of brotherly feelings. He only lacks flexibility and expansion. But the poor church! Oh, Ninny[30] you don't know what they have lost, but the old members do, and when they come to see me, can only sit and sob.

[25] Emily C. Judson now had guardianship of Abby Ann Judson, Adoniram Judson, Elnathan Judson, Henry Hall Judson, Edward Judson, and Emily Frances Judson.

[26] Lydia Lillybridge was one of Emily's closest friends at the Utica Female Academy. When Emily made the decision to go to Burmah as the wife of Adoniram Judson and as a missionary, Lydia wanted to go with them. Emily spoke to Adoniram Judson of Lydia's extraordinary abilities, and Adoniram advocated her appointment before Dr. Solomon Peck and the Board of the American Baptist Missionary Union. Lydia was commissioned to go with them, in spite of the fact that she remained single. Always independent, outspoken, and unafraid to cause ripples in the missionary community, Lydia served on the mission field for twenty-eight years. She married missionary Thomas Simons in May 1851. See the timeline on the life and service of Lydia Lillybridge Simons in vol. 1.

[27] Elizabeth Stevens arrived in Maulmain in February 1838; her husband was Edward Stevens. Elizabeth Stevens took six-month-old Edward Judson into her home when Sarah and Adoniram had to leave for the United States in 1845, and her care and nurture saved his life. She served forty-eight years in Burmah. She had extensive correspondence with Emily Judson, and her letters spoke of everyday life among the missionaries. When Emily returned to the United States, the letters from Mrs. Stevens brought news of friends and colleagues. Mrs. Stevens had a sister, Sarah Haven, in Massachusetts, who wrote a number of letters to Emily asking for information on the Stevens family.

[28] George and Phoebe Hough were the first missionaries to be wholly called by the American Baptist Missionary Union to work in Burmah with Adoniram and Ann Judson. Mr. Hough learned the printing trade from his father, and they set up a print shop to support the work of the mission. They arrived in Burmah in October 1816 and retired from missionary service in 1826; George Hough subsequently worked for the government as an interpreter and school superintendent, and Mrs. Hough worked as an educator. They remained friends with Adoniram Judson and many of the other missionaries. Their independence was problematical at times.

[29] See vol. 1, "Cast of Characters," s.v. "Stevens, The Reverend Edward and Elizabeth."

[30] "Ninny" was a name of endearment given to Anna Maria Anable by her most intimate friends at the Utica Female Academy. Emily was "Nemmy."

The boys[31] are almost crazy about going to America. You and Mrs. Gillette[32] forget, darling, that I have three children, instead of one; and you don't know that I mean to have six, if they will consent to live with me, and then try to make a home too for my poor old father[33] and mother,[34] where they can see smiling faces.[35] I did *not* know that the Board was bound to support widows, and Mr. J. thought they were not. But it makes no difference. I could not accept of their support without conforming to certain *rules* which would trammel me in my intentions with regard to the children. It would be wrong for them to support me very liberally and under existing circumstances, it would be wrong for me to accept of the *contributions of the churches*. I do not feel so, however, about certain other incidental matters, to which it is, to say the least, questionable whether they or I have the best right; but even if they should decide these points less generously than I could wish, I still have other resources. God grant that sick or well I may live a life of usefulness

[Written in the right margin of the address page:] though he has seen fit to call me from the dear, dear Mission;—I should like amazingly to set up house-keeping in Philadelphia, but fear I shall be obliged to go to some less expensive place. My first object will be to secure good schools to the children.

[Written in the left margin of the address page:] Give my love to dear Mrs. Gillette. Tell her I am very *old* now, and a matronly establishment would be more suitable (even though it involves heavy cares) than to her pretty home. Perhaps I shall want to take board in P. the first winter, and bring Abby Ann[36] to your school. My biggest boy is now eight years old and the other six—Would you have insuferable objections to the *sex*?

[31] Henry Hall Judson, eight and a half years old, and Edward Judson, six years old.

[32] Hannah Gillette was the wife of the Reverend A. D. Gillette, pastor of the Eleventh Baptist Church in Philadelphia. Emily stayed with them when she came to Philadelphia in spring 1845 for her health, and she returned in November. In the parlor of their home, she met Adoniram Judson on Christmas Day 1845. Mr. and Mrs. Gillette became strong friends and supporters; Mrs. Gillette played an important part in getting Emily's outfit together for her life in Burmah.

[33] Emily's father, Charles Chubbuck, was born at Bedford, New Hampshire, on March 3, 1780; he was married to Lavinia Richards in Goffstown, New Hampshire, on November 17, 1805. They were to have seven children. Though he held varying jobs over the years, he failed at many of them, and Emily was the main support of the family after she purchased a home for her family in fall 1842.

[34] Emily's mother, Lavinia Richards Chubbuck, was born June 1, 1785, at Goffstown, New Hampshire, the eldest of thirteen children. She married Charles Chubbuck on November 17, 1805, at Goffstown, New Hampshire. Four of her children were born at Goffstown, and moved with Charles and Lavinia Chubbuck to Eaton, New York, in September 1816; they were Lavinia, Benjamin, Harriet, and John Walker. Sarah Catharine, Emily, and Wallace were all born in Eaton.

[35] Regarding the future of the Judson children (George Dana Boardman, Abby Ann, Adoniram, Elnathan, Henry, Edward, and Emily Frances), see volume 1, "A Timeline of the Children of Adoniram Judson and Their Desire to Be a United Family." See also the footnotes to the letter of Emily C. Judson to Mr. Alexander Beebee dated October 13, 1850.

[36] Abby Ann Judson, the first daughter and oldest child of Adoniram and Sarah Hall Boardman Judson, was born September 26, 1835. She saw her mother die on the Isle of St. Helena as they returned to the United States from Burmah. Just before leaving for Burmah with Emily, Adoniram Judson placed Abby Ann at Bradford Academy for her education. The family of Ann Hasseltine Judson was generous to Abby Ann and supportive of her interests and her future. On October 15, 1851, Abby Ann started a course of study at the Misses Anable's School in Philadelphia, and in fall 1853, she moved to New York City to take a teaching position in the home of Mrs. Maria Brown, a former missionary to Siam. She enjoyed a warm relationship with Emily, and her letters show that the two could speak freely with each other.

[Written across and perpendicular to the text on page 1:] I think you will love baby[37] dearly—she is so loving and warm-hearted. She thinks we are "going to heaven to find her papa" because she knows that he went away in a ship and that he is now in heaven. Poor thing! How little can she imagine all she has lost.—Pray for me dear Ninny, while I am on my desolate way and ask Aunt C.[38] and all the others to do the same.

Yours ever aff'y

Nemmy

Source: Hanna family files.

Mrs. Olive Celina Harris[39] to Emily C. Judson, January 21, 1851[40]

Dear Sister Judson

I did intend to go down with the children this evening they seemed so anxious to see your boys before they left, but concluded to send them down on foot tomorrow morning as I was so much fatigued. I do not like the idea of not being able to see you again and again in the flesh but as that being who rules in infinite wisdom has seen fit to thus direct your steps it would be very unwise in me to complain. Could we have all our wishes granted us we no doubt should see many more unhappy hours than we now see. Though our trials at first seem to be grievous yet when we can trace a Father's hand we can kiss the rod that smote for we know that it has power to heal. You my dear Sister have already passed through several afflictions but I trust you are not in despair. You have a sweet hope to rest on and that hope is that you will soon at the longest join that loved one in recounting the dealings of God with you and with him be permitted to cast your crowns at the feet of Him who has bought you. Can we not value this hope after being permitted to see those who know nothing of this hope. [sic]

[37] See vol. 1, "Cast of Characters," s.v. "Judson, Emily Frances."

[38] Miss Cynthia Sheldon was in charge of the administrative and financial departments of the Utica Female Academy. Miss Sheldon and her sister Urania, who was literary principal, gave Emily Chubbuck a place at the academy in October 1840. They had deferred any cost to a future time when Emily could afford to reimburse them. Upon Miss Urania Sheldon's marriage in late summer 1842 to the Reverend Doctor Eliphalet Nott, the president of Union College, and her subsequent move to Schenectady, Miss Cynthia Sheldon assumed a larger leadership role at the academy. In the years that followed, Miss Sheldon and Emily developed an even stronger relationship. In 1848, Miss Sheldon moved to Philadelphia to help Miss Anable with the startup of the Misses Anable's School and to assume responsibilities in its operation. Active and well-known in Baptist circles, Miss Cynthia was one of Emily's most important mentors, advisors, and friends until the time of Emily's death in 1854. Miss Sheldon was the aunt of Anna Maria Anable.

[39] Norman and Olive Harris came to Burmah on the *Faneuil Hall* in July 1846 with Adoniram and Emily Judson as fellow passengers.

[40] This letter is undated. It is placed on January 21, 1851, the evening before Emily departed from Maulmain to Calcutta, there to sail to England.

My dear Sister you have my sympathys [sic] at this hour of trial but they are of little worth. I cannot sympathize with you as one who has been through the same furnace. No. I know you will say that I know nothing about it. I do not my sister. I hope I never may. But if I should be called to the same trial in this land and among strangers I shall then remember you. I am exposed and would wish to be prepared but I do not think it an easy matter to prepare ones self [sic] when all is well.

The duties and responsibilities which are now resting on you are almost insurmountable in your feeble health; therefore I would say try to make them as easy as you can. I know it will be impossible to roll them off but do so as far as possible. You are now bereft of an arm of flesh to sustain you or a bosom companion to shelter or protect you. You must therefore look and take refuge under a divine arm. This arm will never leave you for one single moment. You have already felt its sustaining power.

When you get out to sea and especially when you pass near the spot where the remains of that loved one was consigned to its resting place you will no doubt live over again the first pang of parting but my sister do not let these things over come [sic] you. Try to think what that kind heart would say could he speak to you. Would he not say (be calm my love) you will soon be near my side and in my embrace. Think of his happy exchange and let him rest in quiet. When you get on board the ship methinks you will feel your loneliness more than ever. It has been so short a time since you came out and under peculiar circumstances that you will be carried back to those days and you will feel at times almost ready to sink under your troubles. The first year of ones [sic] married life is often more vivid before the minds eye than after years. Our situation is so new, so altered, so changed, that many little incidents are remembered. These will all come up before you and then you will contrast the difference in your outward and homeward bound.

O my sister I feel sad and wish I could in some way comfort you but all I can do is to pray the Lord for you that he will sustain you under your severe trials. If you have any company on board who take an interest in your welfare (which I trust you will have) make them your friends and do not hesitate to let them know your wants or to speak to them of your sorrows. It sometimes relieves one to speak of their ( ) dejection. Be free in making your wants truly to those who are to assist you and have as ( ) care as you possibly can. If you have trusty men on board let them now and then look after your children and do not be afraid of troubling them. Again I would say cast your care on the Lord for he cares for you. We are left behind to labor a little longer in the fields and though you leave us yet I trust we shall have your prayers for our success. Trust you will not forget us though you may be far away. You leave us under peculiar circumstances and with us leave mementos of your love and affection which cannot soon be forgotten by you. You will leave not only the many scenes connected with your loved ones [sic] labors and the place you so long enjoyed with him but you leave a bledge [sic] of your hearts [sic] affection that infant's dust so fondly cherished in your bosom. Therefore methinks we need not fear that you will forget Burmah. No my sister. I know you will not nor his sons either. If possible I think you will feel more anxious that they may be redeemed then whilst with them. When you are away how you will long for one more opportunity with them but my sister you can still pray for them.

Now my dear sister if I never see you again in the flesh may we be permitted to meet above. Let us often hear from you. Yours in the bond of love

O. C. H.

[Written along the left margin of page 4:] I have wanted to give the children[41] something for my boys but have succeeded in getting only a few shells. I hope they will not forget my boys. They may be called to the same trial.

[Written along the left margin of page 2:] If it is possible I hope you will see some of our friends and if you see mother Bonny in Hamilton tell her all about us with much love.

Source: American Baptist Historical Society, AJ 16, no. 674A.

Mrs. Ellen Mason to Emily C. Judson,[42] January 22, 1851

My dear Sister

I cannot forbear putting *a good bye* upon paper, especially as I am not permitted the pleasure of being with you today. I hope you are getting rested a little after your great fatigue.

Be assured you have our warmest sympathies on your long voyage. May the God of the widow, and the fatherless ever support, comfort, and bless you, shall be the constant prayer of Your affectionate friend

Ellen Mason

P.S. I hope if you can spare time to write me a line occasionally that we shall have the happiness of hearing from you direct. Direct letters to Tavoy for I intend leaving Maulmain by the February steamer.

Source: American Baptist Historical Society, AJ 17, no.737.

[41] Henry Hall Judson, Edward Judson, Emily Frances Judson.

[42] The first part of this letter is undated. The postscript is dated January 22, 1851.

Mrs. Deborah Wade to Emily C. Judson, January 23, 1851

My very dear Sister

Here in the midst of conf( ) ( ) that you are in the steamer *leaving* us, and that we *may not meet*. My heart is too full for utterance—I had expected to be much with you and no heart could sympathize with you as I do—but here come the ( )ants to take us off and Mr. Wade is calling me—Oh cannot I give you one sisterly kiss? Cannot I hug those precious little ones[43] to my heart? But this will not do.—I will write you when I get on land—We are in good health but eternity seems *near*. Mr. Wade unites in kindest love to you, and kisses for the dear children.

Your ever affectionate sister

D. R. L. Wade

I was much with your precious mother and family[44] before leaving Hamilton[45] and enjoyed it highly.

Source: American Baptist Historical Society, AJ 22, no. 1120.

Miss Cynthia Sheldon to Emily C. Judson, January 28, 1851[46]—Philadelphia

My dear dear Emily

The *Macedonian*[47] has this evening reached us—Oh with what deep feeling have we traced the working of your spirit and the effort of your hand in that article which redounds so much to the Glory of God[48]—Heaven be praised that you were strengthened for this vast work—Thousands will see the end of the good man to joy in the Holy Ghost—and you cannot think how much every word concerning him from your pen is prized—O I am so glad you could write it—and that it is sent

[43] Henry Hall Judson, eight and a half years old; Edward Judson, six years old; and Emily Frances Judson, three years old.

[44] Living in Hamilton were Emily's parents, her sister Catharine Chubbuck, and occasionally her brother Wallace Chubbuck.

[45] Jonathan and Deborah Wade just returned from time in the United States; originally from the Hamilton, New York, area, they spent considerable time there. They also visited Philadelphia, and the letters from Anna Maria Anable and Miss Cynthia Sheldon contain references of visits and activities shared. Obviously, they had hoped to see Emily and the children, but the scheduling made that impossible.

[46] The original of this letter was dated 1850. However, the content demands that it be 1851.

[47] *The Macedonian* was a magazine of the American Baptist Missionary Union.

[48] This was the long article Emily sent to Adoniram Judson's sister, Abigail Brown Judson. It detailed the onset of Adoniram Judson's illness in November 1849 and went through his boarding the *Aristide Marie* on April 3, 1850. The letter was dated September 20, 1850, and it was widely published.

forth—this copy is in advance to Mr. Gillette[49]—When ours come, or we can get them they shall go forth to such of our friends as do not take that paper.

This has been an eventful day to me, altho' most all the time confined to my room—Yet whatever is important generally finds its way here by some means—A friend sent me a copy of letters this morning from the Kincaids[50]—Dr. Dawson[51] and the Scottish Clergyman at Capetown, giving us the most thrilling account of sufferings on ship board [sic] —It haunts me like a spectre [sic]—how wonderful that any of them lived through it, and how deplorable that they could not all leave the ship—I sent a letter to dear Mrs. Wade[52] yesterday—Anna Maria[53] wrote to Lydia[54] and yourself—I told her that yours would probably come back—as it has seemed to me that you would take the *Washington Allston* home—now I am sure you will not[55]—

[49] Following several successful pastorates, the Reverend A. D. Gillette was the founding pastor of the flourishing Eleventh Baptist Church in Philadelphia in 1839. With his wife Hannah and several children (they would eventually have six), he graciously opened their home to Emily Chubbuck when she came to Philadelphia at the end of March 1845 for her health. The connection had been made through Miss Cynthia Sheldon, a family friend of Mr. Gillette and his parents. A prominent Baptist, Mr. Gillette journeyed to Boston in December 1845 to accompany Adoniram Judson to Philadelphia for meetings, and on Christmas Day, he introduced Dr. Judson to Emily Chubbuck with the hope that Fanny Forester could be persuaded to write the memoir of Sarah Hall Boardman Judson. A. D. Gillette and his wife Hannah remained valued and trusted friends, not only with Emily, but with the Sheldon and Anable families. He moved from Philadelphia to New York in 1852.

[50] Born in 1797, educated at the seminary in Hamilton, New York, and ordained in 1822, the Reverend Eugenio Kincaid served several churches before being appointed as a missionary to Burmah in February 1830. His first wife died soon after their arrival. His second wife was Barbara McBain, and they were married in 1833. In these years, they served in Rangoon, Ava, Saduja, and Akyab. The Reverend and Mrs. Kincaid returned to the United States in 1843; because of her persistent health problems, they were not reappointed in 1846. While in the United States, Rev. Kincaid became instrumental in the establishment of the University of Lewisberg (later Bucknell University). Upon Mrs. Kincaid's restoration, they returned to Burmah, arriving in February 1851 just as Emily Judson was embarking for her return voyage. With his knowledge of the language and customs, Rev. Kincaid was able to establish himself in work with the Burmese government at Ava. With one more trip home (in 1857, on an official mission for the King of Burmah to President Buchanan of the United States), they retired to Gerard, Kansas, in 1866. Of Rev. Kincaid, the correspondence indicates a man of convictions and occasional independent action.

[51] Miss Cynthia Sheldon called Doctor Dawson a "brother of Mr. (Eugenio) Kincaid." There was some talk of Dr. Dawson going to Ava, but the Board of the American Baptist Missionary Union decided not to appoint him. Miss Sheldon speculated that it was because of lack of funds and not because of any question of his piety or fitness. In March 1850, Anna Maria Anable spoke of a visit from Mr. Bright of the American Baptist Missionary Union to dissuade Dr. Dawson from going to Burmah at least until Mr. Kincaid was settled in Ava. It was increasingly obvious that Dawson would go whether or not he had a board appointment, for there was sufficient funding and interest from the churches in Utica to provide the necessary support. See Emily's letter dated June 20, 1850.

[52] Deborah Wade was a missionary to Burmah; with her husband Jonathan, they were appointed in 1823. Adoniram Judson called them "his dearest and best of friends." Much of their work was in the jungle communities following the path of George Boardman. They left for the United States on December 22, 1847. From the Hamilton, New York, area, they stayed not far from the home of Emily's parents and sister; they visited the Anable-Sheldon families in Philadelphia. With a large group, they had left Boston on July 25, 1850, and returned to Burmah in February 1851.

[53] See vol. 1, "Cast of Characters," s.v. "Anable, Anna Maria."

[54] See vol. 1, "Cast of Characters," s.v. "Lillybridge, Lydia." Also, "A Timeline of the Life and Mission of Lydia Lillybridge Simons."

[55] On July 25, 1850, the *Washington Allston* had sailed from Boston Harbor with a large group of new and returning missionaries, including Mr. and Mrs. Kincaid, Mr. and Mrs. Wade, and Dr. and Mrs. Dawson. The ship was a chartered vessel enabling the American Baptist Missionary Union to send the group directly to Maulmain, Burmah. According to the correspondence, it turned out to be a disastrous trip, with much of the problem the fault of the captain. From Mrs. Hough's letter of May 20, 1851, we gather that there were too many passengers and not enough supplies, among other problems. The ship, according to Emily Judson (February 23, 1851), "entered the mouth of the Salwen [River] just as [her] steamer was leaving it" bound for Calcutta. Emily said that she visited with the Kincaids and Mrs. Vinton in Calcutta, for they had come in on the *Tudor* "from the Cape"—apparently some of the passengers had left the *Washington Allston* en route.

therefore am writing hurriedly that this may be put in the office this evening, and overtake the package in Boston, which we sent yesterday morn'g—do tell dear Mrs. Wade we little thought of their great troubles—their protracted voyage had troubled us much—I had thought that was ended, which gave me spirits to write her—I have been dear E. more than anxious they should arrive on your account—this long letter in the *Macedonian* explains sufficiently why we did not get a note from you last mail—you will I know write whenever you can—but that was all important—Mr. Gillette brought the paper and we have been talking over all these matters until tea was ready. My room has got to be a general rendezvu [sic]—this week particularly we are fitting off Anna Bennett[56] for Georgia. She and Nelly[57] are serving by my stand. Mrs. Anable[58] has a lamp by herself at another table plying the needle for the same purpose—All send abundance of love to you—and from all eyes have the tears fallen this evening while reading, and talking about you—It has taken a load from my heart. I see how wonderfully you was sustained [sic]—under accumulated woes—and I find too some resources which we knew not off [sic]—That readiness to depart, how beautiful—Those expressed visions of Deacon Graves—how strikingly prophetic of the close—Yes every thing [sic] which you have so fully noted, leads us to wonder, admire, and adore the Almighty hand which was beneath, around, and upon you—Strengthening, filling you for a great work—

[Written in the top margin of the address page:] Dear Emily when we can know whether you remain there for a time, or design to come home the first opportunity then will our minds be more fixed on your surroundings—we do so long to see you and the dear children here—that I can hardly bear to think of your remaining there—

[56] Anna Bennett was the daughter of Cephas and Stella Bennett, missionaries to Burmah. She was born in August 1833. An 1850 letter said that beginning in April, she would be teaching at a family school in a private home in the Philadelphia area. By 1853, she was elsewhere, for Miss Cynthia Sheldon was corresponding with her. On September 7, 1853, Miss Sheldon wrote to Emily Judson to say that she had written about Dr. Burton and his interest in her. Dr. Burton was associated with the Southern Missionary Board and was due to leave the country no later than November. Highly thought of, Miss Sheldon said, "I fancy he has found the way to the warm corner of her heart—which is an evidence of tact—probably he is a widower." On September 25, Emily Judson replied, "Anna B's affair strikes me favourably. I never heard of Dr. B. but he probably went out when I was on my way home. It is certainly better to marry a man of established character and expectation than a 'green horn' and Anna would be happier in the east than here." On October 14, 1853, Miss Sheldon wrote again, "The dear girl seemed in a terrible quandary—which she very foolishly thought I could settle—The truth is Anna's heart is *some what* [sic] engaged and I have no doubt but she will decide to go. Mr. Dean told Courtland she would get in the Dr. one of the very best of men." Anna Bennett married Dr. Burton in early November 1853. They sailed in early December 1853.

[57] Nelly Bennett was another of the daughters of Cephas and Stella Bennett.

[58] Alma Sheldon Anable was the sister of Miss Cynthia Sheldon and Urania Sheldon Nott. Genealogy sources show that she married Joseph Hubbell Anable in Troy, New York, on July 28, 1814, and that it was the second marriage for Mr. Anable. Born in 1773, he was forty-one at the time of the marriage, and Alma was likely considerably younger. He died in 1831, which explains why Alma Anable and her family lived and worked first at the Utica Female Seminary and then later at the Misses Anable's school in Philadelphia. Joseph and Alma Anable were the parents of nine children: Henry Sheldon Anable (b. June 21, 1815); William Stewart Anable (b. November 6, 1816); Anna Maria Stafford Anable (b. September 30, 1818), Cynthia Jane Anable (b. January 28, 1820); Samuel Low Anable (b. November 28, 1821); Harriet Isabella Anable, also known as Hatty or Hattie (b. December 18, 1823); Courtland Wilcox Anable (b. July 28, 1825); Frances Alma Anable, or Fanny (b. April 12, 1828); and Mary Juliet Anable (b. February 18, 1830).

[Written in the bottom margin of the address page:] This must go to the office—Anna M. and the others have gone to a Historical Lecture this evening except Hattie.[59] She is not well enough to go out evenings except when very pleasant—Anna M.'s letter I suppose will give you any news—may the blessings of heaven abide with you—I feel more to need your prayers dear E.—that my own heart may be more alive to the goodness of God in restoring mercies—

Most affectionately and sincerely yours,

C. Sheldon

Source: American Baptist Historical Society, AJ 20, no. 994.

Mrs. M. Thomas to Emily C. Judson,[60] February 1, 1851

My dear Mrs. Judson,

Your kind note from the Steamer came duly to hand, and had it been practicable I should ere this have called upon you, but my present circumstances will not admit of my taking so long a ride.

I should have experienced a melancholy pleasure in receiving for a season yourself and dear children had it been needful, but Mr. Mackay's invitation you could not do otherwise than accept and my only wish was that you might not feel the want of a home here in your painfully trying circumstances.

I trust you have found a gracious God faithful to his promises to the widow and the fatherless and have experienced those consolations in your affliction which He alone can give.

I hope we shall have the pleasure of seeing you shortly. Mr. Thomas will take the earliest opportunity of calling but has been much engaged the past week.

Accept our united Christian affection and sympathy, and, Believe me

Your friend and sister in Christ,

A. Thomas

Source: American Baptist Historical Society, AJ 21, no. 1066.

[59] Harriet or "Hatty" or "Hattie" or "Hat" Anable was one of nine children born to Joseph and Alma Anable, and was a niece to Miss Cynthia Sheldon and Mrs. Urania Sheldon Nott. In 1841, she had added a note to a letter written by Miss Cynthia Sheldon to Emily. As early as November 1842 she was away, and a letter from Emily to Catharine Chubbuck said that "she (Miss Sheldon) expected that Hat would return as accomplished as Anna Maria." Her trips away were both educational and employment, as she worked as a private tutor in families that would bring her into their homes. In August 1843, she had just returned from Beonsen, in the vicinity of New Orleans, and was engaged to go again. A letter from Anna Maria on January 6, 1845, said that she would stay South for another year. About this time Miss Cynthia Sheldon mentioned her concern for Hatty's spiritual health. In May 1845 she was in New Orleans. She was home again in summer 1846, but a September 27 letter from Anna Maria said she had been asked by Mr. Roman with some urgency to return and she thought that she should. She was to return home from New Orleans in January 1849 after Anna Maria Anable had started the Misses Anable's School in Philadelphia in fall 1848. Harriet was fluent in French, having placed herself earlier in a French environment in New Orleans. Hatty died in 1858.

[60] This was addressed to Mrs. Judson, care of Rev. W. S. MacKay, Cornwallis Square (Calcutta).

Mrs. F. C. Sykes to Emily C. Judson, February 8, 1851[61]

My dear Mrs. Judson,

I have much pleasure in sending our conveyance for you. I send it early that you may avoid coming in the heat of the day; but if you think it will be too trying to your strength to come before breakfast pray retain the carriage as long as you please; we breakfast soon after 8 o'clock. I hope you will bring the dear children[62] if you can do so with comfort to yourself, and if you have any work in which I or my young ladies can assist you we shall be delighted to do so if you can bring any with you. I have another proposal to make my dear madam: we fear as the journey is a long one you may find it too fatiguing to return at night, will you therefore consent to remain all night? My dear friend Mrs. Yates[63] has kindly offered to accommodate you in her room if you will stay, and we shall be able to find sleeping rooms for the children. Please therefore make your arrangements as you think will be most for your comfort and best for your strength.

I have had a great desire to see you since reading your Memoir[64] of my beloved friend (whom I first knew as Mrs. Boardman[65]), and I did not think I should so soon have the pleasure.

With Christian regards I am
Yours most affectionately

F. C. Sykes

Source: American Baptist Historical Society, AJ 19, no. 878.

The Reverend Eugenio Kincaid[66] to Emily C. Judson, February 10, 1851—Steamer Enterprise

My Dear Mrs. Judson

It was in my heart to call and see you on Saturday, but we had promised to dine on the *Tudor* with our kind Captain and his Officers at half past two and contrary to my expectations it cost me the entire forenoon to procure the necessary papers from the Marine Office and from the Custom House and then I had to take our

[61] This letter is undated. It is placed about a week after Emily's arrival in Calcutta.

[62] Henry Hall Judson, Edward Judson, Emily Frances Judson.

[63] See letters of February 18 and 20, 1851, from Mrs. Yates.

[64] *The Memoir of Sarah Boardman Judson*.

[65] Sarah Hall Boardman Judson was the second wife of Adoniram Judson.

[66] The Reverend Eugenio Kincaid, his wife, and other missionaries sailed from Boston on July 25, 1850, and were just reaching their destination. Mrs. Wade, also in this group, wrote earlier that they had hoped to see Emily Judson, but that the ship schedules had prevented it.

luggage to the Steamer. We had the pleasure of meeting Mr. M( ) 's daughter—as well as many others on the *Tudor*.

We are much gratified to learn that you have decided on taking your passage in the *Tudor* for London. You will have every possible comfort and every thing [sic] is as free as air—The Captain anticipates the wants of his passengers—all the Officers are gentlemen and the Steward and cuddy servants are prompt and attentive—

In your extremely feeble state of health, you need the accommodations and comforts of such a ship. The room you have selected will constantly have a circulation of sweet pure air.

A voyage to London under such circumstances will, we trust, greatly contribute to the restoration of your health. We feel deeply for you in your loneliness and pray that the Shield of Heaven may be round about you and your orphan children on the deep, as heretofore on the land—You will, I know, find warm Christian hearts in the Fatherland—

Should you remain, as you probably will, your days at the Cape of Good Hope, I hope you will see Mr. Maigan, the Pastor of the Dutch Church and Mr. Thompson, Pastor of the Church at Union Chapel.

From Christian friends at the Cape you will receive a most cordial welcome.

I have no time to write. Mrs. Kincaid,[67] Mrs. Vinton,[68] Miss McKaine wish to be remembered in Christian love.

Yours ever affec'ly

Eugenio Kincaid

Source: American Baptist Historical Society, AJ 17, no. 786.

Mrs. A. M. Wood to Emily C. Judson, February 10, 1851[69]

Dear Mrs. Judson

I send to see if you would like to take a drive this pleasant day. My husband is lamenting that his engagements will not allow him, to day [sic], to go with you—and I am such a "special coward" with horses that I do not dare to offer to drive. But Philip will call for you, at whatever hour will best suit you, and will take you wherever you would like to go. He is often my attendant in my chaise driving; and I have always found him a very careful driver.

[67] Barbara McBain Kincaid was the second wife of Eugenio Kincaid; they were married in 1833.

[68] Calista Holman Vinton was the wife of Justus Hatch Vinton. From Connecticut, they first came to Burmah in December 1834. Their main ministry was with the Karens. Mrs. Vinton taught the women and was the author of several hymnbooks in their language.

[69] This letter is undated. It fits the time that Emily was in Calcutta waiting for the *Tudor* to sail; it is placed in the approximate middle of her stay.

I send you a little drop of honey from Mr. Hymeltin—a part of a little glass which Professor Boise brought me from Athens. I think it will be much more at home with you than it is with me, for with all my genealogical pains and anxieties, I am not able to establish even the most remote affinity between my ties and the "Hymeltin" family.

Do let me know just how you are today. I have been every day wanting to see you—and am looking forward with much pleasure to that warm pleasant day when you will feel as if you could come over and take that great home dinner with us.

With much love—Yours

A. M. Wood

Source: American Baptist Historical Society, AJ 22, no. 1109.

Unknown[70] to Emily C. Judson, February 11, 1851[71]—Allipore

Dear Mrs. Judson

I have been so continually in attendance upon a sick niece that I have never left home but to go to her and to Church for many weeks—or I should have called upon you. Will you excuse the formality of a visit—and come and spend a few hours with me any day most convenient to yourself? I will send the carriage for you and send Jon back again and I hope you will bring your children if you are able to come—I should feel great interest in talking of Maulmain friends belonging to the Mission of whom I often think with affection.

Believe me

( ) ( )
( ) ( )

Source: American Baptist Historical Society, AJ 15, no. 630.

Mr. C. B. Lewis to Emily C. Judson, February 15, 1851

My dear Mrs. Judson

Please accept my best thanks for the verses and the copies of Dr. Judson's Sermon. I shall feel great pleasure in sending the latter to the brethren for whom they are intended.

[70] The signature on this letter is unreadable.

[71] This letter is undated as to the year. Alipore was an affluent suburb of Calcutta, India; this would place the letter in February 1851 when Emily was there preparing for her journey back to the United States.

I sent to Mr. Thomas of our Mission Press for some paper of the kind you wish to have and have great pleasure in forwarding what he has sent.

Mrs. Lewis unites with me in many kind regards. Our hope and prayer is that the good hand of our Heavenly Father may guide you over the ocean and be ever with you for your comfort and defence [sic].

Believe me
Very affectionately yours

C. B. Lewis

Source: American Baptist Historical Society, AJ 16, no. 777.

Emily C. Judson to Anna Maria Anable, February 16, 1851[72]—Calcutta

My dear Ninny,[73]

I have rec'd your sweet letter enclosing Miss Longstreth's[74]—the last I shall know of you for many lonely months to come. I have been here now over two weeks, in the family of the Rev. W. S. Mackay, missionary of the Scotch Free Church, and one of the finest specimens of manhood I have ever met. He is more than a brother to me, and his family and friends gather about me as though they had known me all their lives and could not express too much affection and sympathy. I do feel grateful to God for this great mercy of turning the hearts or strangers toward us in our loneliness and desolation. I have been out once here—to visit the Baptist missionaries, who have also shown me great kindness, but it was quite too much for my strength, and brought on a relapse from which I am still suffering. I wish very much to visit Serampore and was to have done so last Friday, but was not well enough. I have still a little hope of seeing that interesting spot, as the trip is made in a boat instead of a carriage.

The "friends and admirers of the late Dr. Judson," in this place have got up what they call "the Judson Testimonial" and have raised nearly 3000 R's. When it is considered that these are neither Americans nor Baptists—but that ministers and others of almost every denomination have contributed to the Testimonial, and that, as Mr. Mackay tells me, without any solicitation, the whole is peculiarly gratifying.

[72] This letter has an addendum dated February 20, 1851.

[73] "Ninny" was a name of endearment given to Anna Maria Anable by her most intimate friends at the Utica Female Academy. Emily was "Nemmy."

[74] Mary Anna Longstreth was a Quaker who lived in Philadelphia and who took an extraordinary interest in Adoniram and Emily Judson. She lived with her extended family, and they are frequently mentioned in her letters. Apparently, she ran a private school much like the one Anna Maria Anable started. Her letter of May 1848 paints a strong picture of her character, her faith, and her sensitivity. In this letter, she remarks on the particular strengths of each of the wives of Adoniram Judson.

Major Durand, formerly Commissioner of the Tenasserim Provinces and a Churchman, gave 200 R's and also wrote a fine article for the *Calcutta Review* which I should be glad to send you if I can get it. A single copy of the *Review* costs 8 R's or $4, so one looks at the purse twice.

I have a very few letters to friends in England, among which is one to the Dr. Nealy who formerly visited America, and one to the Rev. Shepard, who baptized Baptist Noel. I also have one to Noel himself, but though I long to make his acquaintance, I shall not present it—it is given by a *rather* inimitable person, and I do not like to venture on troubling a man who has so many visitors.

I have taken passage on the ship *Tudor*, Capt. Lay, bound for London. She is a passenger ship of 1200 tons. My cabin (for myself, 3 children and servant) is about 9 ft. (10 ft. is crossed out) square. I shall be crowded but much more comfortable than most poor Am. Missionaries who go home. I pay 1500 R's for my passage to England. The *Tudor* is advertised to sail on the 20th, but it is generally thought she will not get off before the 25th. My way does not appear quite so dark as it did at one time—it would be ungrateful to feel discouraged when I have thus far been so wonderfully assisted, and tenderly cared for. Pray for me, darling, and write to me in London.

Give love to all—I will write to Miss Longstreth if I can, but if I do not, you will know the reason, and please tell her. I am very weak and overburdened with cares.

Lovingly

Nemmy[75]

Source: Hanna family files.

Mrs. W. H. Yates to Emily C. Judson, February 18, 1851—N 11 Circular Road

My dear Mrs. Judson,

Much as I should like to see you once more before your departure, yet I think I must deny myself that pleasure, as I do not feel quite competent to day [sic] to take so long a ride. My good friend Mrs. Sykes however, will be the bearer of this, and with it I send two notes of introduction for you to some of my kindest friends, who should they be at home will be delighted to see you. I have left the notes open in case you might not be able to go yourself and might wish therefore to write a note yourself which you could put inside the envelope.

[75] "Nem" or "Nemmy" was a name of endearment given to Emily by a small group of her intimate friends at the Utica Female Academy. Anna Maria Anable was "Ninny."

I regret to find you were so poorly after your kind visit to us, but hope you are now better. It was a great gratification to me to have spent one day in your dear society—may we thro' grace and the love of our Redeemer be permitted in God's good time, to spend a happy eternity together.

And now permit me to thank you for your much valued present—( ) Mrs. S. will acknowledge hers in person.

I trust you will have a safe and pleasant passage to my native isle, and afterwards to your own fine country, as well as your dear children. Remember us affec'y to them, and very kindly to the friends with whom you are residing. I was glad to hear a good account of ( ) Mrs. M. and trust she with her little one are still going on well.

Farewell my dear friend. Believe me

Your truly affectionate

W. H. Yates

Source: American Baptist Historical Society, AJ 22, no. 1108.

Mrs. W. H. Yates to a Friend in London, February 20, 1851—Calcutta

My dear Friend,

The bearer of this is the widow of the late Dr. Judson, who with three little children is returning to America by way of England. I believe she has no Christian friends in my native land, and I feel sure that both you and your dear husband, will be much pleased to see her and pay her what attentions you may be able during her stay in London.

Yrs Affec.

W. H. Yates P. T. O.

She goes to their American agent in London whose direction is as follows

J. Symans Esqr.
2 Turnwheel Lane,
Cannon Street,
London

Source: Hanna family files.

Emily C. Judson to Anna Maria Anable, February 20, 1851[76]

[Note: Post script is written in the margins.] I must write to Mr. Bright[77] and that is all I can hope to do. I have been very ill and am now only a *little* better. The doctor here says my only hope is to get off soon. I am sorry not to see Serampore, but of course I cannot visit it. I must go aboard on the 24th—Monday next—it will not do me much harm as I can be carried in a palanquin and once on board, I trust all will go well. Shall I really see your face again in this world? God knows and His will be done!

Source: Hanna family files.

Mrs. Lucretia B. Stilson to Emily C. Judson,[78] February 20, 1851—Maulmain

My Dear Sister Judson,

[Note: Parts of the first three lines are blotted out by the wax seal used on the letter.] ( ) ( ) ( ) ( ) ( ) ( ) to me than I ( ) ( ) ( ) ( ) you would be ( ) ( ) ( ) ( ) such a *long* letter by the Steamer. I need not assure you however that it was very very welcome. Nancy[79] did not fully understand me in regard to writing by the pilot. I did not wish you to write to *me* particularly but to *someone* so that we might hear which you did and with which I was satisfied. I was sorry to hear that you suffered so much on the Steamer but feel encouraged that you gained so much before your last date. How much I do hope that that passage of Scripture which you read to me one day may prove applicable to your case and that you may be able to do a great deal of good in our own dear native land. I was very glad you spoke so particularly about the dear children.[80] I hope you will continue to do so. You must know I shall feel interested in hearing every item you feel able to write.

You speak of thinking of me when in Akyab harbor and speak of jewels which will probably be added to my crown from that place. I have ventured to hope that I might have been the means direct [Note: On page 2, the greater parts or all of nine lines are lost where the seal was fixed.] How can I expect such a rich reward as jewels in my crown when I have left undone *so much* that I ought to have done, and have done *so little* that I ought to have done? O that I had lived more to God's glory and O for the Spirit's influences to bring me even now where I should be.

[76] This letter is an addendum to a letter dated February 16, 1851.

[77] See vol. 1, "Cast of Characters," s.v. "Bright, The Reverend Doctor Edward, Jr."

[78] This letter mentions virtually every missionary under the sponsorship of the American Baptist Missionary Union who was serving anywhere in Burmah.

[79] See vol. 1, "Cast of Characters," s.v. "Nancy."

[80] Henry Hall Judson, eight and a half years old; Edward Judson, six years old; and Emily Frances Judson, three years old.

Sr. Stevens[81] is so good about telling news that I suppose you will know particulars the new missionaries from her. We were much pleased with them. I hope you will see the Assam Missionaries. They left here with Mrs. Ranney[82] on the 3rd inst. The whole company suffered so much from improper food and impaired air that the invalids to say the least are not near as well as when they left Boston. How strange that there should have been such a mistake made in providing for the miss.[83]

It will probably be an *everlasting* disgrace to the Board for miss. to go home for their health, and then lose it by ( ) ( ) coming back is a difficult thing to be reconciled to. I have seen Sr. R. and the Kincaids[84] but little since their arrival. Br. Brayton[85] has returned from the jungle. Went into Siam and had as good success as [Note: At the top of page 3, ten lines are all or partially lost from the wax seal.] (—He left—and don't—source and—save that—with S.—from trying—). I have been gaining strength lately so that I have driven out ( ) about half a mile or so. I commenced taking cod liver oil a week or two after you left (which Dr. Dawson[86] kindly let me have) and I think it increases my appetite and I hope it is going to do me good. Mr. Stilson[87] has been driving himself lately in order to get his ( ) off by this steamer but has finally given it up and gone to bed with a hard head-ache. A day or two of rest however, I trust will remove it. He can bear very little company

[81] See vol. 1, "Cast of Characters," s.v. "Stevens, Elizabeth 'Bessie.'"

[82] Maria Gager Ranney arrived in Maulmain in May 1844. Her husband Thomas was the superintendent of the printing press and business manager for the missionary compound. A letter from Lydia Lillybridge reveals that Mrs. Ranney had some responsibilities in the mission schools. She had no children; Maria Ranney died on April 26, 1857.

[83] On July 25, 1850, the *Washington Allston* had sailed from Boston Harbor with a large group of new and returning missionaries, including Mr. and Mrs. Kincaid, Mr. and Mrs. Wade, and Dr. and Mrs. Dawson. The ship was a chartered vessel enabling the American Baptist Missionary Union to send the group directly to Maulmain, Burmah. According to the correspondence, it turned out to be a disastrous trip, with much of the problem the fault of the captain. From Mrs. Hough's letter of May 20, 1851, we gather that there were too many passengers and not enough supplies, among other problems. The ship, according to Emily Judson (February 23, 1851), "entered the mouth of the Salwen [River] just as [her] steamer was leaving it" bound for Calcutta. Emily said that she visited with the Kincaids and Mrs. Vinton in Calcutta, for they had come in on the *Tudor* "from the Cape"—apparently some of the passengers had left the *Washington Allston* en route.

[84] See vol. 1, "Cast of Characters," s.v. "Kincaid, The Reverend Doctor Eugenio."

[85] The Reverend Durlin L. Brayton was born in Hubbardton, Vermont, on October 27, 1808. He graduated from Brown University and then the Newton Theological Seminary in 1837, at which time he was appointed to missionary service. On October 2, 1837, he married Mary Hawley Fuller, and they sailed for Burmah on October 28, 1837. They arrived in April 1838 and, passing through Amherst and Maulmain, arrived at Mergui in April 1840. In February 1847, they departed Maulmain for America due to Mrs. Brayton's ill health. Mr. Brayton returned to Burmah the following November, and Mrs. Brayton remained in America until arriving back in Burmah in March 1850. They had one daughter, Mary. Mary Brayton died December 16, 1890, in Rangoon; Durlin Brayton died April 23, 1900, also in Rangoon.

[86] See vol. 1, "Cast of Characters," s.v. "Dawson, Doctor."

[87] Lyman Stilson was born in Meredith, New York, on January 29, 1805. He attended the Hamilton Seminary and was appointed to missionary service on October 3, 1836. He was married to Lucretia Brownson on August 20, 1837, and both sailed for Burmah on October 28, 1837, along with the Bennetts and the Stevens. Mr. Stilson finally returned to America after Lucretia Stilson's death on August 14, 1851. Mrs. Stilson had been quite ill for some time and the board had authorized her to return to the United States, but as reported in the newsletter of the Missionary Union, "She has been removed to a better country." They worked with Adoniram Judson for thirteen years, and with both Sarah Hall Boardman Judson and Emily Chubbuck Judson. Mr. Stilson's specific responsibilities included the oversight of printing Burmese elementary books for the schools that were maintained by the mission. He also wrote a volume in Burmese on mathematics.

with what he once could. ( ) ( ) ( ) from the Knapps[88] by the Steamer in regard to the Kemmies were not encouraging. He found them all engaged in feasting and drinking even the disciples going with them. Even Pai Tong ( ) was there and whom we esteemed so highly seems to have gone far astray. I hope this is the darkest time among them and that after long continued effort they will throw aside their heathen astons, and "become clothed and in their right minds." They seem pleased with Mrs. Moore.[89] Mrs. Moore and Miss Wright[90] were thrown out of their buggy a short time ago by the horse's falling down. Sr. M's ancle [sic] was badly sprained, but no serious consequences. We prize our good pony very much, *so gentle* and yet *so strong*. I hope now ( ) I am strong enough to ride to be ( ) benefited through this means (or I might) [Note: On page 4, ten lines are lost partially or in total from the wax seals.] (—consider it—the buggy and—is I crawl—book—love and kisses—I—house—again. Sister Emily—me. Dear child I—) and do as much good in her life as you would have done by remaining here if you hadn't bad health. (I don't mean to insinuate by this remark that I do not think you'll do good at home. You know that I believe you will be useful anywhere.)

Remember me to Nancy. The children give their love to all. Mr. Stilson is a little better this morning (21st) and will write a note on business but says "the love must all go into my letter" so you will accept a share from him also.

The Harris'[91] called here this morning. He came down to see the Dr. Has had a cold for two or three months. From what he said I don't think the Dr. considered it

[88] The Reverend Harvey Knapp, and his wife Emma, were appointed in 1849 as missionaries to Burmah and arrived at Akyab in March 1850. He was a graduate of Madison University and Hamilton Theological Seminary, both of which were near Emily's home in Hamilton, New York. Emma Knapp died May 24, 1851.

[89] William Moore was from Granville, Ohio, and was a graduate of Dennison University and Covington Institute, Kentucky. He married Elizabeth W. Forbes from Cincinnati, Ohio. They departed Boston on November 3, 1847, and arrived in Calcutta on March 18, 1848. They worked with the Karens in Burmah, near Maulmain. Mr. and Mrs. Moore returned to the United States, arriving in Boston December 19, 1853.

[90] Hannah Elizabeth Taylor Wright was born September 21, 1820, in Nelson, New Hampshire. She was appointed in 1849 to serve as a teacher at the Karen Normal School in Maulmain, Burmah. She sailed from Boston on October 18, 1849, and arrived in Maulmain on March 18, 1850. She returned to the United States on account of her health on June 29, 1852. In July 1858, she married the Reverend Lyman Stilson, missionary to Burman. Lucretia Stilson, his first wife, had died in Maulmain, Burmah, on August 14, 1851. Lyman and Hannah Wright Stilson had two sons, Charles and Edwin. Lyman Stilson died in Jefferson, Iowa on March 23, 1886; Mrs. Hannah Stilson died in Jefferson, Iowa, in March 1898. There is one letter in the correspondence from Miss Wright. Writing from Newton, Massachusetts, in July 1853, she sent Emily flowers that she "thought had bloomed to shed their fragrance in a sickroom."

[91] Norman Harris was born on February 19, 1813, in Becket, Massachusetts. He attended Columbia College and Hamilton Literary and Theological School, graduating in 1844. Olive Celina Wadsworth was also born in Becket, Massachusetts, on July 6, 1814. They were married on August 9, 1844, and were appointed to missionary service on October 28, 1844. In July 1846, they sailed to Burmah with the newly married Adoniram and Emily Judson. Olive Harris died in childbirth on November 23, 1853, in Shwegyin, Burma. In 1856, Norman Harris married for the second time; Miranda Harris died of fever in September that same year. Norman Harris left the mission field shortly after the death of his wife Miranda and returned to the United States. There, in June 1858, he married Julia Wadsworth Chapman, the sister of his first wife, Olive Celina Wadsworth. Norman and Julia Harris returned to Burmah in 1858, though not under the auspices of the American Baptist Missionary Union; they were reappointed as missionaries in 1861. Norman Harris died on March 1, 1884, in Hamilton, New York. Julia Harris died in September 1905.

any thing [sic] serious at present. He leaves for Laming today below Amherst. He has just heard of the death of his father for whom he has no hope.

Yours Aff'y

Lucretia B. Stilson

P.S. I thought you wd be likely to visit our friends. I wd give you their names etc. If however you should stray off into Franklin or Meredith Delaware Co. N.J. you would find Stilsons and Brownsons ( ) ( ) you. Stilsons also are in Mt. Morris N.Y.

Source: American Baptist Historical Society, AJ 19, no. 890.

Mrs. F. S. Sykes to Emily C. Judson, February 21, 1851

My dear Mrs. Judson

I have now much pleasure in sending this silk jacket and two pairs of boots for your dear little girl,[92] and I shall feel gratified by your kindly accepting them as a slight expression of my sincere regard for yourself and the interest I feel in the dear child, as well as esteem and affection for her father's memory. I wish to present you with some trifle as a token of my love, and was glad to find out something that would be really useful.

I trust our short acquaintance dear Mrs. Judson will not end when you leave the shores of India but that you will favour [sic] me with a letter to inform us of your welfare, and that our friendship will, (as you said in your note to Mrs. Yates) "be perfected in another world."

You will have our best wishes and prayers while on the mighty ocean; we trust the Lord will be very gracious to you not only there but as long as you sojourn in this wilderness and that we may be permitted to meet in our Father's house in peace.

[92] See vol. 1, "Cast of Characters," s.v. "Judson, Emily Frances."

Mrs. Yates[93] unites with me in kindest love and with many kisses to dear little Emily and my love to Henry[94] and Edward.[95]

I am, my dear Mrs. Judson
Yours very affectionately

F. C. Sykes

Source: American Baptist Historical Society, AJ 19, no. 879.

M. Ryan to Emily C. Judson, February 22, 1851

Dear Madam,

I have much pleasure in sending the little articles of Indian manufacture of which I spoke last evening. I had hoped Edward[96] would have been the bearer of them to his Mamma, but he left so quietly, as to disappoint me in the matter.

Though a stranger, I trust my sincerely kind wishes for the future may not prove intrusive or unacceptable. May it please the Lord to guide you and yours in safety over the mighty deep—and make you an honoured [sic] instrument in His hands for carrying on His work in the earth—and whether be assigned the field of labour [sic] in the benighted realms of the East, or the far more privileged ones of the West—May proofs not be wanting, that your labour [sic] for Him has not been in vain.

May He who has graciously declared Himself to be the "Husband of the widow, and the Father of the fatherless," be with, watch over, and bless you.

Believe me,
Dear Madam
Yours in sincere respect;

M Ryan

Source: American Baptist Historical Society, AJ 18, no. 808.

[93] See the two letters from Mrs. Yates dated February 18 and 20, 1850.

[94] Henry Hall Judson, born July 8, 1842, was the son of Adoniram and Sarah Hall Boardman Judson. Henry was the sixth of their eight children and the fourth of five who survived. He remained in Burmah in 1845 when Adoniram and Sarah returned to the United States with the three older children. He returned with Emily in 1851 and went to live with her family in Hamilton, New York. Henry attended Brown University and Williams Collage; he enlisted in the army at the time of the Civil War in January 1864. Later that year, he experienced a debilitating accident attributed either to sunstroke or a horse kicking him in the head. He was married once—unhappily according to his own correspondence—and he eventually died in a veteran's home in 1918, the last of his siblings to die. Of this, the chaplain noted, "The end was a genuine example of Christian fortitude." See Rosalie Hall Hunt, *Bless God and Take Courage, The Judson Legacy* (Valley Forge: Judson Press, 2005) 291.

[95] Edward Judson, born December 27, 1844, in Maulmain, Burmah, was the eighth child of Adoniram and Sarah Hall Boardman Judson and the fifth of their children to survive. Only a few months old when Sarah and Adoniram returned to America, Edward's life was saved by the nurture and care he received from Elizabeth Stevens. He loved Emily as the only "Mama" he had ever known and returned with her to the United States in October 1851. Edward, who was Eddy to his family, became a minister; he did mission work with the immigrants in New York City, and with the aid of the Rockefeller Family, he built the Judson Memorial Baptist Church in what is now Washington Park.

[96] Ibid.

Emily C. Judson to Doctor Edward Bright, February 23, 1851—Calcutta

My Dear Mr. Bright,—

I am just now on the point of embarking for England, after spending some three weeks in this place, waiting for the sailing of the vessel. I am in the family of the Rev. W. S. MacKay, missionary of the Free Church of Scotland, a fine scholar, a warm hearted Christian, and altogether one of the most noble and chivalrous characters I ever met. Through him, I have made the acquaintance of a large circle of friends, not only of his own church, but Episcopalians, Independents, ete., and have also met with all the English Baptist missionaries in town. I have been too ill to visit Serampore, which I regret exceedingly, for I consider it, apart from family associations, a place of deep missionary interest. "The Judson Testimonial," a subscription by "the friends and admirers of the late Dr. Judson" (as they style themselves), for the benefit of his family, amounted to about three thousand (Company's) rupees; and from this it is my intention to defray all the expenses of my passage home, above what the Board would have to pay in the *Washington Allston*. That somewhat unfortunate vessel entered the mouth of the Salwen just as the steamer was leaving it.[97] I, however, saw Dr. Dawson,[98] and received a very hurried note[99] from Mrs. Wade,[100] whom I was distressed to pass without seeing. At this place I had the pleasure of meeting the Kincaids[101] and Mrs. Vinton;[102] the latter looking very well, but poor Mrs. Kincaid had almost a ghostly appearance. They seemed very glad to learn that I was going in an English vessel, and the very one which brought them from the Cape. I have taken my passage (a small upper-deck cabin) on the *Tudor*, Captain Lay,[103] bound for London, *via* Madras, Masulipatam, and the Cape. As she touches at so many places, I anticipate rather a long voyage, but there is every prospect of its being a pleasant one, at least so far as accommodations and society are concerned.

[97] On July 25, 1850, the *Washington Allston* had sailed from Boston Harbor with a large group of new and returning missionaries, including Mr. and Mrs. Kincaid, Mr. and Mrs. Wade, and Dr. and Mrs. Dawson. The ship was a chartered vessel enabling the American Baptist Missionary Union to send the group directly to Maulmain, Burmah. According to the correspondence, it turned out to be a disastrous trip, with much of the problem the fault of the captain. From Mrs. Hough's letter of May 20, 1851, we gather that there were too many passengers and not enough supplies, among other problems. The ship, according to Emily Judson (February 23, 1851), "entered the mouth of the Salwen [River] just as [her] steamer was leaving it" bound for Calcutta. Emily said that she visited with the Kincaids and Mrs. Vinton in Calcutta, for they had come in on the *Tudor* "from the Cape"—apparently some of the passengers had left the *Washington Allston* en route.

[98] See vol. 1, "Cast of Characters," s.v. "Dawson, Doctor."

[99] See the letter of Deborah Wade to Emily C. Judson dated January 23, 1851.

[100] See vol. 1, "Cast of Characters," s.v. "Wade, Jonathan and Deborah."

[101] See vol. 1, "Cast of Characters," s.v. "Kincaid, The Reverend Doctor Eugenio."

[102] Calista Holman was born in Union, Connecticut in April 1807. She married Justus Hatch Vinton on April 9, 1834, and they sailed for mission work in Burmah in July 1834. With her husband, she was stationed at Chummerah, Newville, and Maulmain, specializing in work with the Karens. She taught the Karen women and was the author of several hymnbooks in their language. Calista and Justus Vinton were the parents of three children. Mrs. Vinton died in Rangoon on December 18, 1864.

[103] When the passage had been booked, Captain W. J. Lay gave Emily a map showing the route they would be taking. As Emily noted in this letter, there would be a number of stops, and in this letter, she is optimistic as to when she is to reach England. On the map was a drawing of the *Tudor*; it is shown as a three masted sailing ship in full sail.

There will be at least two pious families on board, perhaps more. I pay for myself, three children,[104] and a servant girl,[105] fifteen hundred rupees, which is thought to be a very moderate sum. I was very much benefited by the change when I first came to Calcutta, but it soon passed away, and since then I have been growing more and more poorly every day. The doctor whom I have consulted here says there is no hope for me but in a long voyage, and thought it a matter of regret that the vessel should be so long delayed. Then, although I have received company here mostly on my couch, I know it has injured me, and I anticipate great benefit from the quiet of the vessel. I know it is on account of the respect for my sainted husband that I am received so well here; and I can assure you the evidences of esteem for him which meet me on every hand are deeply gratifying to me.

The Missionary Conference (Scotch Free Church) has addressed me a beautiful letter, and private testimonials are almost numberless. I send you with this the *Calcutta Review*, a quarterly edited by Mr. MacKay,[106] and containing an article from the pen of Major Durand, formerly commissioner of the Tenasserim provinces. He was a personal friend of my husband and the second Mrs. Judson,[107] and has also shown great kindness to me. Through Lord Ellenborough, with whom he is a favorite, he possesses much influence, and the whole of it is exerted in favor of pure, genuine Christianity. It will be a blessed thing for missionaries, and for the heathen, when there are more such men in the East.

I feel like setting up an Ebenezer in this place before I go, for surely the Lord has thus far helped me; but I still go on my way with fear and trembling, not knowing what is before me; though I do know that God, even *my* God, is on the sea as on the land. It is not very probable that I shall reach England before the end of June, which will bring me to America at a very favorable season—the hottest of the year. Do not forget to pray for me while on my trackless way, and also for my poor little ones, that however desolate in other respects, we may have the presence of our Heavenly Friend.

Sincerely and affectionately yours,

Emily C. Judson

Source: A. C. Kendrick, *The Life and Letters of Mrs. Emily C. Judson*, 357–59.

[104] Henry Hall Judson, eight and a half years old; Edward Judson, six years old; and Emily Frances Judson, three years old.

[105] See vol. 1, "Cast of Characters," s.v. "Nancy."

[106] The Reverend W. S. MacKay was a missionary for the Free Church of Scotland; he also edited the *Calcutta Review*, which Emily described as a prestigious magazine. Rev. MacKay was the first to inform Emily of Adoniram's death in his August 9, 1850, letter, and he also insisted that she stay with him and his wife while she was in Calcutta on her way to the United States.

[107] Sarah Hall Boardman Judson, Adoniram Judson's second wife.

The Reverend W. S. MacKay to the Reverend Doctor Cunningham, February 24, 1851[108]—Calcutta

My dear Dr. Cunningham,

Should she have time to visit Scotland, this note will be delivered to you by Mrs. Judson, the widow of the lamented Dr. Judson, the Apostle of Burmah. She is in very delicate health, and, as you will perceive when you know her, a gifted unassuming and interesting woman. So she will be a strength in Edinburgh, I am sure, should your engagements permit, that you will have pleasure in showing her such attention, as may be in your power, both for her late husband's sake and for her own.

I retain a grateful remembrance of your kind wife to myself, and therefore feel the more confidence in recommending Mrs. Judson to your attention.

Yours sincerely

W S MacKay

Source: Hanna family files.

Mrs. Emily C. Judson to The Reverend and Mrs. W. S. MacKay, February 1851

Wayside Friends

A stranger and ye took me in;
A stranger sad and lone,
By Time's cold, ever-beating surf,
One moment hither thrown;
And by your gentle ministry
And by your words of love,
Ye've forged a chain whose golden links
Will gather strength above.
Oh, oft my weary feet grow faint,
With longings for that strand;
So very dear and beautiful
Is yonder spirit-land!
But howe'er long your homeward path,
Whatever tide ye breast,
Our Father's love-smile light the way!
His blessing on ye rest!

Source: Emily C. Judson, *An Olio of Domestic Verses*, 195–96.

[108] Written on this letter of introduction: Envelope / Forwarded by Mrs. Judson / The Reverend Dr. Cunningham / Principal of the Free ( ) College / Edinburgh.

Mary Eliza Leslie to Emily C. Judson, February 24, 1851

Allow me to express to you my deep sense of all the kindness you have shown to me—and especially my thanks for the very beautiful volume[109] you have so kindly sent me. Much—very much—as I prize it for its intrinsic merit, the value of it is to me considerably enhanced by its having been given me by its very talented authoress, and as containing her hand writing [sic].

And I cannot but also express the gratification I have experienced in seeing you and the dear children,[110] especially your loving little "birdling."[111] It was a pleasure I had long desired, and which when felt was even greater than I had anticipated, larger as were my expectations.

( ) unites with me in best [wishes] and prayers that [you] may have a safe, pleasant, and speedy voyage, and may reach the land of your fathers with fully restored health and strength.

With kind love to yourself and the dear children
I am
Yours very sincerely

Mary Eliza Leslie

Source: American Baptist Historical Society, AJ 17, no 777.

Mrs. Olive Celina Harris to Emily C. Judson, February 26, 1851[112]

Dear Sister Judson

How are you this morning? Methinks I see a smile on your brow. Have you got all things arranged in your cabin to your liking? Where is your bed and is that comfortable. Where do you put the children and how do they like being so couped [sic] all away from their play mates [sic]. Little Fanny[113] or I might say Emily tries to keep a cheerful countenance on her mother for children are always sad if they see mother cast down. Do you suffer from seasickness as you did when I was one of your ship's company.[114] Methinks I hear you say no, at least I hope this is not the case for I do not see the dear one by you to administer a cordial when needed. Oh how miss

[109] This is likely a copy of the memoir of Sarah Boardman Judson.

[110] Henry Hall Judson, eight and a half years old; Edward Judson, six years old; and Emily Frances Judson, six years old.

[111] On January 1, 1848, eight days after the birth of Emily Frances Judson, Emily wrote a celebratory poem that she called "My Bird." The poem has a total of seven stanzas, and it was widely published in the United States.

[112] This letter is undated. We place it just as Emily is preparing to sail from Calcutta for Liverpool.

[113] See vol. 1, "Cast of Characters," s.v. "Judson, Emily Frances."

[114] Norman and Olive Harris sailed with Adoniram and Emily Judson on the *Faneuil Hall* in July 1846.

that one do you not [sic]. You have children[115]—but they can fill only the children's place. You have plenty of company on board but they can fill only their own place. If you have a kind and attentive Capt and physician they can fill only their own place. So my sister you will say notwithstanding you have as many around you yet you feel that you are alone. You must feel it more than ever for when you left your parents and all that was dear you was not alone [sic]. You had one to bear with you these little trials and to speak a consoling word. You go to bed and how lonely the pillow. You go to the table and there is one wanting to make up the number. Shall I imagine you on deck alone also. If there is one by your side it will be a stranger. I shall not hear that endearing word I sometimes heard when I was one of your numbers so soft and so sweet to attract your attention or catch your smile.

Well dear sister methinks you have every thing [sic]for your comfort and I hope it will be so to the end of your voyage. That you are lonely I cannot doubt for I miss that dear one and feel lonely too; but my sister will you not be comforted with the fact that you have his angels to hover around you and to keep him appraised of all your joys and sorrows too. Then what tidings will you let them bear to the sainted one during this long voyage which is before you. How soon that bright guardian will conduct you to the portals of peace where that ( ) is waiting to greet you is yet unknown. Be patient a little longer and the ( ) will be passed. Oh the hope of the Christian and the encouragement to endure as good soldiers. This hope is yours. Let it support you. You have immortal treasure committed to your care. For these you will be willing to spend a few more wearisome days and nights and I hope you may be permitted to see them all rejoice in the same hope which bears your spirits upon this hour of trial. A double responsibility is resting on you. May you have grace and wisdom given you sufficient to your day is my prayer.

Now sister do not think that this visit was intended to instruct you for I am aware of your pen and your high thought of future bliss. I only designed it for a little comforter and to express my sympathy for and ( ) ( ) you. Pardon all and believe me your sincere sister and friend.

That the good lord will be around you to protect you and carry you safely to our mother land shall be our daily prayers.

Yours in love

O. C. Harris

Source: American Baptist Historical Society, AJ 16, no. 688.

[115] Traveling with Emily were Henry Hall Judson, eight and a half years old; Edward Judson, six years old; and Emily Frances Judson, three years old.

Mrs. Charlotte Haberlin to Emily C. Judson, February 26, 1851—Calcutta

Farewell dear dear friend and sister. May the Lord keep you as the apple of his eye and make you feel and enjoy his gracious presence continually—give you to realize that you are with the precious treasures entrusted to your care *in deed* and *in truth* in *His own hand* and that not a hair can fall from your head without His will.

You have vanished from my sight—we no sooner met than we had to part again to pursue separately our pilgrimage thro' the seemingly pathless waste of our lonely future which so much would have drawn us to do jointly; or the heart would at least fain have enjoyed for a little while longer the sweet intercourse which had its beams with such congenial warmth and clear depth from your soul to mine. But it must not be thus—and no doubt it is best as the Lord decrees.—We shall move inward under the shadow of the same guardian hand, we have *one* ( ) *one* ( ) in view, we are hastening to *one* house to join *one* circle which shall no more be broken up. In looking back ( ) in meeting—I ( ) feel it as making a new acquaintance but rather as a *recognition*. Known the soul ( ), your words—feelings—experiences not merely found a ready *echo* but were felt as my own often before you fully expressed them; such I suppose will be the case tho' in a much higher, fuller, and exalted sense in the finding of kindred spirits above and it is delight to look forward to our ending in glory what we began under the cross, to mingling ( ) of everlasting joy on the subject which first made our tears flow together—to see the sunbeam rising from the little brightened spool of earth and time's dark vale merge in the glorious light of the eternal sun—and above all to be One in Him our head—Him who loved us and redeemed us, that a possibility of separation from Him—without sin—without any other thought or wish ( ) but His. Why then with such glorious hopes before us should we mourn for ( ) homes below—the treasure of earthly tho' the dearest ties—why should our hearts cling bleeding in times fleeting forms, memory cleave to earth and imagination even dwells beneath its ( ) besides Earth's charm will soon be done—when our real life—the long reality of bliss—shall appear. Let us fix our hearts and look on this reality secured to us and for us in the Rock of Ages—which nothing on this ( ) ( ) world can [Note: A line is lost in a tear at the bottom of the page.] more and tho' outwardly we shall walk—the midst of ever wakeful storms—joy unspeakable and full of glory shall be ours—deep deep peace within—too deep for any storm to reach.

When I left you on Monday Evening[116] my feelings were undesirably sad—it was a painful disappointment not to spend the quiet longed for, hoped for hour with you, with which I was soothing my mind in the wonderful prospect of parting—it was a sacrifice to be hurried away without uttering one word of all my heart full and

[116] This would have been February 24, 1851.

hearing one word from you of all I should have wished to hear—without seeing you comfortably retired to your own little cell and feeling the feeling with which you were at the last able to view the next future lying before you—I would have liked to linger and know if you felt ( ) comforted for having accomplished one more soul's trying step and were starting on the one which is to bring you nearer your object of present life and duty with less ( ) hope and expectation—but the rail was drawn and even when stepping on shore my eye might vainly thro' the dimmed atmosphere to distinguish your form on the vessel—One assurance only was left me and partly did I avail myself of it. I fled to the throne of grace and in pouring out my full heart there in intercession, submission and faith I found the reality and bliss of spiritual union and communion of the Lord's own—I miss you very much and so do more or less all the inmates of our house—dear little Emily[117] with her shy look often steals upon my memory and honest Edward[118] and sensible Henry[119] I long to receive a line to hear how you progress—how your health is—what sort of company you have—your impressions of the Captain[120] and the many ( ) of the ship. You spirits I trust are raised joyful—hope your strength equal to your days—and the support suited to your wants—every way and measure. O He is a faithful covenant keeping ( ), and our Lord a faithful High Priest touched with our infirmities—a hearer and answerer of prayer.

Once more farewell my beloved friend—found in affliction—parted in sorrow to visit again in strength. Kiss your dear children for me and let mine have a little place in your prayerful memory. Every one [sic] here requests to be remembered to you—

With fond love and prayers which will follow you faithfully and breathe many a greeting to ( ) ( ) ( ) for you.

Yours in the best of bonds

Charlotte Haberlin

[Written in the left margin of page 1:] Mrs. MacKay[121] ( ) pretty well and so does the baking. I feel ( ) for ( ) ( ) ( ) ( ) ( ).

Do not forget to send me your address in America and England. I ( ) Mr. MacKay can direct me.

Source: American Baptist Historical Society, AJ 16, no. 686.

[117] See vol. 1, "Cast of Characters," s.v. "Judson, Emily Frances."

[118] See vol. 1, "Cast of Characters," s.v. "Judson, Edward."

[119] See vol. 1, "Cast of Characters," s.v. "Judson, Henry Hall."

[120] W. J. Lay, captain of the *Tudor*, on which Emily was sailing from Calcutta to England.

[121] Reverend W. S. MacKay first informed Emily of the death of Adoniram Judson through a letter of August 9, 1850. See vol. 1, "Cast of Characters," s.v. "MacKay, The Reverend W. S."

Mrs. Elizabeth L. Stevens to Emily C. Judson, February 28, 1851[122]—Maulmain

My poor, dear Sister

How grieved I am you left Calcutta so poorly! We all prayed for you at *Mrs. Stilson's*[123] *yesterday*. She is in pain though and what do you think? She hopes she is ... but I fear her hope is founded on an evidence of increased weakness. I'm not going to write you this *month* as I'm very busy and have been *threatened* though just not better. I wrote by Calvin and again last Steamer. I've only to say now Calvin carries to Boston for you some sheets of extracts wh. you had copied[124] and which Mr. Hough[125] found in (page two) the book you borrowed—Crawford's Embassy.

Emma broke her arm a fortnight since—the rest of the children are well.

We really are rejoiced about the Wades[126] having the church. Don't let the Board oppose his keeping it. We have not had a volcanic eruption yet—Matters are not discussed enough between *opposite* parties. Mr. K.[127] and Dr. D.[128] have been over to Rangoon and enjoyed your house for *the rains*. Mrs. Moore[129] is threatened with repetition of past and presence.

Aff'ly Yrs

E.L.S.

Source: The American Baptist Historical Society, AJ 19, Number 908.

[122] A letter of March 22, 1851 states that Mrs. Stevens had sent a prior letter a month before. We believe that this is that earlier letter, and so we have given it a date of February 28. The date on the letter is clearly March 21, 1851, but that is an obvious error as the contents of both letters do not allow it. This is not the first occasion in the correspondence that such an error has occurred.

[123] See vol. 1, "Cast of Characters," s.v. "Stilson, Lucretia and Lyman."

[124] Preparing for the Memoir of Dr. Judson which was to be written, Dr. Edward Bright, Corresponding Secretary for the American Baptist Missionary Union, had suggested that she gather as much material as she could before leaving Maulmain, and bring it back with her.

[125] See vol. 1, "Cast of Characters," s.v. "Hough, The Reverend George and Phoebe."

[126] See vol. 1, "Cast of Characters," s.v. "Wade, The Reverend Doctor Jonathan and Deborah."

[127] See vol. 1, "Cast of Characters," s.v. Kincaid, The Reverend Doctor Eugenio."

[128] See vol. 1, "Cast of Characters," s.v. "Dawson, Doctor."

[129] See vol. 1, "Cast of Characters," s.v. "Moore, The Reverend William and Elizabeth W. Forbes."

Emily C. Judson to Anna Maria Anable, March 5, 1851—Ship Tudor

My dear Ninny[130]

We are drawing near to Masulipatum, and as there will be an opportunity to send letters on shore, I thought I would let you hear a word from my floating home. We have now been more than a week on board, and wind and wave is altogether in our favour, so much so that even I am ashamed to own to sea-sickness, though I cannot help feeling a little of it, as I should in a common rocking-chair. I have been so well the greater part of the time, as to get into the cuddy to dinner, which is more than I could do in Maulmain. Beyond that, I stay in my cabin, which, although crowded is very light and airy. The captain is very kind and accommodating, and the cuddy servants civil and obliging. The passengers too seem all very good natured sort of people—they play whist and drink wine of an evening in the cuddy which adjoins my cabin, but I have as yet heard no profane word spoken and they are all very kind and respectful to me.

I do not think there are any decidedly pious people on board, but they are all outwardly religious. One of the gentlemen (Capt. Burton) told me that one of the other passengers had lent him the *Calcutta Review*,[131] and he had just been reading Maj. Durand's article, so he felt quite acquainted with me and my "bird."[132] Precious little Birdy! She is so shy that no one can speak to her unless by stealth, and yet she makes a great many friends for me with her amusing little ways. Her brothers[133] too are dear good little fellows, but I sometimes feel very anxious about them. The Capt. and passengers say that they behave beautifully when out of my sight, but I already have found some new phrases added to their vocabulary, and occasionally they become pert and flippant—not to me of course, but to others. It is a place for spoiling children unless one keeps a double watch over them.

We have everything that we could ask for on the table, even to milk, and we can ask for anything we want and have it brought to our cabins at any hour of the day.

So Ninny you see that poor Nemmy[134] is very comfortable in her loneliness, but ah me! me! how very lonely it is, no human heart can know. *To flyaway and be at rest*—but then my children! I do not wish to go away from them, until it shall please God to call me.

[130] "Ninny" was a name of endearment given to Anna Maria Anable by her most intimate friends at the Utica Female Academy. Emily was "Nemmy."

[131] The *Calcutta Review* was under the leadership of her host in Calcutta, the Reverend W. S. MacKay, who had published a number of articles on the life of Adoniram Judson, including the one by Major Durand.

[132] On January 1, 1848, eight days after the birth of Emily Frances Judson, Emily wrote a celebratory poem that she called "My Bird." The poem has a total of seven stanzas, and it was widely published in the United States.

[133] Henry Hall Judson, eight and a half years of age, and Edward Judson, six years of age.

[134] "Nem" or "Nemmy" was a name of endearment given to Emily by a small group of her intimate friends at the Utica Female Academy. Anna Maria Anable was "Ninny."

Do you recollect how we used to laugh about my coming home, an old woman, and how missionaryish I should be. Well, darling, I am very old, and very missionaryish, though I have not yet been away from you five years,—a change I should scarcely have looked for, in so short a time; and even now I am often half startled out of my propriety, and rub my eyes, and wonder if it is I, when gay people lower their voices as I come near, and those who can think of nothing but dancing and the like either remain dumb, or make a spasmodic effort to speak of sober matters for my sake. I am treated as though I was some stately madam—with the greatest respect and deference ever, but with a sort of favor that to me would be amusing. The *Washington Allston* reached Calcutta, just as we were coming off again, but not in time for me to get off my two boxes—one I believe from Miss Longstreth,[135] the other from Kate.[136] The Assam missionaries, however, came on board, but under such circumstances that I could scarcely be glad to see them. They spoiled my parting with my Calcutta friends and my friends spoiled my visit with them. I wonder what you will hear about the troubles of the missionaries coming out—I find there are two very different versions.[137]

Did you ever wonder what I did with my pretty bonnet and caps etc. etc. rec'd last July [Note: "April" is marked out.] when I went into mourning? I distributed them among the missionaries, who had been so kind to me;—and the beautiful dressing gown which *he* had never seen, went to Mr. Ranney.[138] I could not get very decent mourning in Maulmain but I scarcely needed it there; and I have been able

[135] See vol. 1, "Cast of Characters," s.v. "Longstreth, Mary Anna."

[136] Sarah Catharine Chubbuck, "Kate," "Kit," or "Kitty" was Emily's older sister by ten months. Outside of the two terms at the Utica Female Academy, which Emily arranged for her, Catharine always lived at home with her parents in Hamilton, New York. The letters indicate opportunities for marriage, but she, for unknown reasons, remained single. She later helped to care for Henry and Edward Judson after their return from Burmah in fall 1851 when they moved into the Hamilton home with their "aunt" and "grandparents," and she was remembered by them as "dear old Aunt Kate—a dear friend."

[137] The *Washington Allston* had left Boston on July 25, 1850, chartered by the American Baptist Missionary Union for passage of a large number of new and returning missionaries to Maulmain and India. Correspondence indicates a difficult passage with shortages of supplies. It was approaching Maulmain as Emily was departing for Calcutta. Here Emily indicates that the ship had moved on to Calcutta with the missionaries going to Assam.

[138] See vol. 1, "Cast of Characters," s.v. "Ranney, Thomas and Maria."

to supply myself with everything I wanted in Calcutta. Give love to all the family also the Gillettes,[139] the Robartses,[140] and Miss Longstreth, and believe me, darling

Ever yours lovingly—

E. C. J.

Source: Hanna family files.

Mrs. Ellen Mason to Emily C. Judson, March 21, 1851

My dear Mrs. Judson

I was delighted to hear so good an account of yourself in your first letter, and that Mr. MacKay[141] was indeed a brother though less we could not have expected from what we know of his character.

I did not write you by last mail thinking every body [sic] else would, and that too many communications from one source would deprive you of all the pleasure of perusal.

Your last letter to us all caused us much grief and fear for your health, but Doctor Morton[142] told us that he inferred from your letter to him that you were very much improved, which I hope for your sake, for the sake of those dear babes, and for our own sakes, may really be true.

I assure you dear sister, it grieves me to go into your old house. There sits the couch just as you left it—and I sit and gaze upon it almost expecting to see your pale yet cheerful face on the wall but the reality will press itself upon me telling me you are not there but far away upon the waters—and that we shall not probably

[139] See vol. 1, "Cast of Characters," s.v. "Gillette, The Reverend Abram Dunn."

[140] Mr. and Mrs. W. S. Robarts were active in Philadelphia Baptist circles. They were frequent visitors to the home of the Reverend and Mrs. A. D. Gillette and later to the Misses Anable's School, which Anna Maria Anable and her extended family had started in Philadelphia in 1848. In his biography of his father, Edward Judson mentioned that Adoniram Judson stayed at the. Robarts's home when he came to Philadelphia in December 1845 when he met Emily Chubbuck. A. C. Kendrick said, "(Mr. Gillette and Dr. Judson) arrived in (or out of) due time in Philadelphia, and Dr. Judson was welcomed to the house of Mr. and Mrs. W. S. Robarts, who became warm personal friends, as they were already active friends of the mission cause." (A. C. Kendrick, *The Life and Letters of Mrs. Emily C. Judson* [New York: Sheldon and Company, 1862] 142.) In 1846, with the engagement of Adoniram Judson and Emily Chubbuck, the correspondence indicates some hard feelings toward Mrs. Robarts for comments disparaging the coming marriage and missionary service. This is found in Emily's letter to Adoniram dated February 6, 1846; Mrs. Robarts seemed to be accusing Emily of worldliness when all the time, Emily was quick to say, Mrs. Robarts was engaging in the same activity of which she was accused. The correspondence also indicates a satisfactory healing of the relationship. In January 1849, Miss Sheldon told Emily that Mrs. Robarts had placed their daughter Mary in the Misses Anable's School.

[141] See vol. 1, "Cast of Characters," s.v. "MacKay, The Reverend W. S."

[142] Doctor Morton was a physician who worked with the missionaries in Maulmain, Burmah. He delivered Emily Frances Judson in December 1847 and was present when Charles Judson ("Angel Charley") was stillborn in April 1850. He was a valued and trusted advisor to the mission families.

meet again until we awake on the morning of the resurrection. Mr. Wade[143] has placed a melodeon just where your book side-table stood, and he frequently plays for me when I go in, and plays very well too, but I cannot heed the music for there you be looking upon us, with little Emily[144] hiding her eyes on your bosom; and when I sit down to the tea-table I see only before me your dear husband pale, and emaciated, just as he looked the last time he sat at table. So I don't often go in there much as I love the Wades.

I rejoice that your stay in Calcutta has been pleasant for you, and trust that He who watcheth all his children will abundantly bless those who bless the widow and the fatherless.

I suppose you have had all the news concerning the missionaries, the ship *Washington Allston*, her captain, and the tasteful addition over the hatchway etc. etc. They had a bitter six months certainly whoever may have been the cause.[145]

Our furniture etc. has been nearly all sent down to Tavoy, and Mr. Mason[146] with Mr. Abbott[147] shall leave for that place on Monday next but I remain a month or two longer in Maulmain to read proofs for his book still in the press.

Helen and the boys talk much about your children, and want to see them, but they console themselves with the *confident* expectation of sometime seeing them in America, and I suppose they anticipate sport with them there just as they used to have together here.

[143] Jonathan Wade was appointed as a missionary to Burmah in 1823. Wade's relationship with Adoniram Judson was especially dear because of the early experiences they shared, including the death of Ann Judson. Much of their work was spent in the Karen jungle communities following the path of George Boardman. They had returned home to America on December 22, 1847, and returned to Burmah in January 1851, just as Emily was returning to the United States. They were from the Hamilton, New York, area. They left to return to Burmah on July 25, 1850, and were in Maulmain by February 1851. Both died in Burmah. Deborah died at Maulmain in 1868, and Jonathan died in Rangoon in 1872.

[144] See vol. 1, "Cast of Characters," s.v. "Judson, Emily Frances."

[145] The *Washington Allston* had left Boston on July 25, 1850, chartered by the American Baptist Missionary Union for passage of a large number of new and returning missionaries to Maulmain and India. Correspondence indicates a difficult passage with shortages of supplies. It was approaching Maulmain as Emily was departing for Calcutta. Here Emily indicates that the ship had moved on to Calcutta with the missionaries going to Assam.

[146] Francis Mason arrived in Maulmain in November 1830 and transferred to Tavoy in 1831. His first wife died, and he married Helen Maria Griggs just before leaving the United States. She died in Burmah in 1846; they were the parents of four children. A skilled linguist, Mr. Mason was fluent in twelve languages and translated the Scripture into two of the Karen dialects. In spring 1847, Mr. Mason was seriously ill, and the other missionaries were concerned about him. In September 1847, he remarried, and Adoniram Judson officiated at the ceremony. His new wife was Ellen Huntley Bullard; originally from Vermont, she was the widow of Edwin Bullard, missionary to Burmah. Francis Mason died March 3, 1874, in Rangoon.

[147] Elisha Abbott was born October 23, 1809, in Cazenovia, New York. He graduated from the Hamilton Theological Institute and was ordained August 25, 1835. His wife was Ann P. Gardner, and they were married April 2, 1837. Though they were appointed for work in Telagus, India, that changed upon their arrival, and they went to Maulmain in April 1837. They continued on to Rangoon shortly after that. In March 1840, they established the station at Sandoway. Mrs. Abbott died in Sandoway on January 27, 1845. Mr. Abbott left for the United States in November 1845, returning in August 1847. At one point in the correspondence, Mr. Abbott was mentioned as a possible husband for Lydia Lillybridge.

Tell Henry[148] and Edward[149] that it makes me feel just like weeping when I look around and see the seats in the Sunday School all vacant, and I think the children feel so too. Tell them I wish they would keep a journal and send me of the voyage home and I will read it to the children or if I am in Tavoy will get someone else to do it.

I don't wonder little Emily wants to be taken home—I should think she would, dear child.

With kindest wishes, and sincere love
believe me, dear Sister
ever yours

Ellen Mason

[Written along the left margin of page 2:] Mr. Mason desires kindest regards, and the children all send love.

Source: American Baptist Historical Society, AJ 17, no. 738.

Mrs. Elizabeth L. Stevens to Emily C. Judson, March 22, 1851[150]

My dear Sister

This morning back came posting the bundle containing the extracts[151] from Crawford's "Embassy" wh. I wrote you a line last mo. to say I was sending it by Calvin. Like every thing [sic] connected with going home affairs, since you commenced the game in the river, it just missed him. As Calvin *went* out the Steamer went in. His going in the Saratoga made him off sooner than I expected—I'm *so* disappointed for him not to have received my parting gifts. If we could have foreseen all when making our plans, we should not have done as well, as we have. Undoubtedly it is best just as it is and we may sometime know *why* and *how* it is best. Even now you may be sure we are glad to have Eddy,[152] and Sarah[153] here with us.

I suppose Miss Lilly[154] is writing you all the particulars of the interesting scene when she said *yes* last Saturday—the happiest of men (and would he but or ought to be, he happens just now to be really very poorly, from exposure to the sun, eating pork, etc.) is this moment over there trying to dissuade her from the plan of wait to

[148] See vol. 1, "Cast of Characters," s.v. "Judson, Henry Hall."

[149] See vol. 1, "Cast of Characters," s.v. "Judson, Edward."

[150] This is a follow-up letter to Mrs. Stevens's letter of February 28, 1851.

[151] Emily was collecting materials for the proposed Judson memoir. See the prior Elizabeth Stevens letter dated February 28, 1851.

[152] Edward O. Stevens was born December 17, 1838, the son of Edward and Elizabeth Stevens.

[153] Sarah Stevens was born December 3, 1840, the daughter of Edward and Elizabeth Stevens.

[154] See vol. 1, "Cast of Characters," s.v. "Lillybridge, Lydia." Also, "A Timeline of the Life and Mission of Lydia Lillybridge Simons."

the end of the year as the Stilson's[155] wish on account of the school. The children send love to yrs and Edward[156] much to you.

Most Affly

Bessie

Source: American Baptist Historical Society, AJ 19, no. 902.

Emily C. Judson, "The Southern Cross,"[157] April 1851[158]

To the Southern Cross

Sweet empress of the southern sea,
    Hail to thy loveliness once more!
Thou gazest mournfully on me,
    As mindful we have met before.

When first I saw the Polar Star
    Go down behind the silver sea,
And greeted thy mild light from far,
    I did not know its mystery.

My Polar Star was by my side,
    The star of hope was on my brow;
I've lost them both beneath the tide,—
    The cross alone is left me now.

Not such as thou, sweet Thing of stars,
    Moving in queenly state on high;
But wrought of stern, cold iron bars,
    And borne, ah me! so wearily!

Yet something from these soft warm skies
    Seems whispering, "Thou shalt yet be blest!"

[155] See vol. 1, "Cast of Characters," s.v. "Stilson, Lucretia and Lyman."

[156] See vol. 1, "Cast of Characters," s.v. "Stevens, The Reverend Edward and Elizabeth."

[157] Emily came home to America in 1851 on the ship *Tudor*. As she left the shores of India in February, Kendrick wrote, "once more the southern cross looked down upon her—but with a deeper, sadder meaning than when she first gazed on it through the glowing atmosphere of hope. It's strange blended lesson of severity and kindness she thus sweetly interpreted" (Kendrick, *The Life and Letters of Mrs. Emily C. Judson* [New York: Sheldon and Company, 1831] 359).

[158] In *An Olio of Domestic Verses*, Emily dates this poem "Indian Ocean, April, 1851."

And gazing in thy tender eyes,
The symbol brightens on my breast.

I read at last the mystery
That slumbers in each starry gem;
The weary pathway to the sky—
The iron cross—the diadem.

Source: A. C. Kendrick, *The Life and Letters of Mrs. Emily C. Judson*, 360; Emily Judson, *An Olio of Domestic Verses*, 191–92.

Mrs. Sarah Bell Wheeler Gould to Emily C. Judson, April 8, 1851—Philadelphia

My dear Emily

I have been enjoying my visit with the loved ones here so much—and we have talked so often about dear Emily—Aunt Cynthia[159] and I have decided that the better plan for you when you come to Boston, will be to make your home at our house—I assure you Emily that we can in a very quiet way but shall be *so* happy to have you come immediately to our house and make yourself at home—Dear Aunt Cynthia will come on to meet you—

I hope and pray that you will have a comfortable journey if possible and be returned to us in health—I cannot tell you what a delightful school the girls have.[160] Providence has smiled on all their plans, and I trust that we are truly grateful to our Heavenly Father for all His omens.

Aunt Urania[161] came to P. on Friday and returned to New York yesterday. She has not altered since you left—Indeed Nemmy[162] I trust you will not find your friends changed at all.

[159] See vol. 1, "Cast of Characters," s.v. "Sheldon, Miss Cynthia."

[160] The Misses Anable's School in Philadelphia was started by Anna Maria Anable and involving her sisters Harriet, Fanny, and Mary; their mother, Alma Anable; and their Aunt, Miss Cynthia Sheldon.

[161] Urania Sheldon had been the literary principal of the Utica Female Academy in fall 1840 when Emily Chubbuck came to study there. Emily was able to afford this wonderful education through the generous offer of Miss Sheldon and her sister Cynthia, the executive and financial head of the academy, to defer tuition. Urania Sheldon left in late summer 1842 upon her marriage to the Reverend Doctor Eliphalet Nott, the president of Union College in Schenectady, New York. Because of the distance separating them, Emily's relationship with Urania Sheldon Nott did not develop the intimacy that grew between Emily and Miss Cynthia Sheldon. Urania Sheldon Nott remained a mentor, advisor, and friend to Emily in the years of her writing, her missionary endeavors, and upon her return to America in 1851. She was also the aunt of Anna Maria Anable.

[162] "Nem" or "Nemmy" was a name of endearment given to Emily by a small group of her intimate friends at the Utica Female Academy. Anna Maria Anable was "Ninny."

You shall be just as quiet at our house as you wish Nemmy—I wish you were already here—I'll have the children to care for, and I have thought of you many times since I was married.[163]

The weather is changing from—but you know all about it—Mr. and Mrs. Gillette[164] came in a short time last evening. They are just the same—

My good husband[165] came for me yesterday and we leave for home this afternoon—The thought of leaving these loved ones makes me sad, but I have been with them more than two weeks—quite a long time for "Mother" to be away the children think—Aunt Cynthia is disappointed in not having a letter from you this morning—maybe one will come this afternoon—

I trust dear Nemmy that you shall be preserved in health, and that we shall all have the pleasure of seeing you once more—Our house is No. 8 South Bennet St—but drop a line to me if possible before you come and believe me till then your loving friend

Sarah B. Gould

Source: American Baptist Historical Society, AJ 16, no. 698.

Miss Cynthia Sheldon to Emily C. Judson, April 9, 1851—311 Walnut St., Philadelphia

Dear Emily,

We learn by Mr. Gould[166] that you had arrived in Calcutta—The ship letters were in Boston on Monday—were due here this morning—we feel sadly disappointed but hope on for the next mail—our dear Sarah[167] has written you—The papers say you will arrive early in June—if so dear E. and providence continues to smile on us—I shall meet you at Sarah's[168] on your arrival—I do hope you will accept her

[163] Sarah Bell Wheeler and Charles Gould were married in October 1850.

[164] See vol. 1, "Cast of Characters," s.v. "Gillette, The Reverend Abram Dunn."

[165] Charles Gould was forty-two years old, a widower with two children, a daughter and an invalid son. He was known to be pious and a friend to missionaries, and he was a deacon at the Rose Street Baptist Church. He was a partner in the publishing firm of Gould, Kendall and Lincoln, and was the brother of Mrs. Joshua Lincoln. Charles Gould and Sarah Bell Wheeler were married in October 1850.

[166] Ibid.

[167] Sarah Bell Wheeler Gould was a teacher at the Utica Female Academy, an intimate of Emily Chubbuck, and one of the few who addressed Emily as Nemmy. In a September 1847 letter, she was listed as one of the teachers at the Utica Female Academy. There are a number of letters from Sarah Bell before and after her marriage to Charles Gould of Boston in October 1850. There are several letters clustered in the year or two after Emily left for Burmah and a number at the time of her return to America. Emily stayed with Charles and Sarah Bell Gould in October 1851 when she arrived in Boston after the long sea voyage from Burmah and then England. She stayed there a number of times following that. In 1851, Anna Maria Anable wrote of Sarah Bell: "Sarah is grown so lovely in person as well as character that she must assert a blessed influence on all with whom she comes in contact."

[168] Sarah Bell Wheeler invited Emily and her children to stay with her while in Boston upon her return.

invitation—and assure you it is most cordially given by Mr. Gould as well as herself—we like him much and Sarah is very happy—which should satisfy all her friends—

I am writing now because I want she should take to you a little book—on seeing it you will know it was written in the fullness of Mr. Gillette's[169] warm heart—and it does really touch the hearts of all readers as far as I know—the public want, yes need truths circulated until the time for writing fully on the subject—and good judges say this little book seems to fill the niche better than any other out of press—or likely to be this year—every one feels that your views only should guide the writer, if you do not write the record of that *best* of men, whose record is on high—

Mr. Roberts[170] (Mrs. Colby's[171] brother) will hand you this in London—he leaves New York next week—and I send it on by Mr. Gould to him for fear another opportunity will not present—we shall send letters by Mail to reach you in time—

We are well—heaven grant to encircle you with journeying mercies, and that you may have abundant cause to joy in the God of your salvation ever more—

Yours ever

C. Sheldon

This will be handed or left for you by Mr. Roberts—his address will be

E. G. Roberts and Co.
13 Kings Arms Yard
London

he wishes to serve you—do let him know how he can do it.

Source: American Baptist Historical Society, AJ 20, no. 989.

[169] See vol. 1, "Cast of Characters," s.v. "Gillette, The Reverend Abram Dunn."

[170] Mr. Roberts was the brother of Mary Colby. A businessman with interests in England, he delivered letters from Emily's friends to her when she arrived in England on her way back to America in late summer 1851. He also offers to render to her every service to ease her journey. He is mentioned in a number of the letters in the following months; he is a widower with at least one child, a daughter Mary, who was a pupil at the Misses Anable's School in Philadelphia. Abby Ann Judson mentions his marriage in her letter of March 7, 1852. See Miss Sheldon's letter of March 8, 1852. This marriage is announced by Miss Sheldon to Emily toward the end of December 1851; the bride was Miss Lynear or Linear of Brooklyn. The wedding took place by the time the March 8 letter was written. Miss Sheldon comments, "He married Miss Linear who has boarded in the house with him long enough to understand each other at least if she was not quite so deaf—They spent Friday evening here and it was hard telling whether our mighty effort to make it pleasant had any affect—even Mr. Gillette could not get any thing but monosyllables, and half the time the wrong one—I do pity them—except when they are alone—then I doubt not but his children will be well cared for."

[171] Mary Colby was the wife of Gardner Colby, a prominent businessman and active Baptist layman. Mr. Colby was a member of the Board of the American Baptist Missionary Union and an avid supporter of the missionary movement. In a letter after they sailed from Boston to Burmah, Emily mentions the extravagant hospitality extended to them in early July as they waited for the *Faneuil Hall* to embark. Adoniram and then Emily stayed with the Colby family quite frequently over the years. Mrs. Colby was an active correspondent with Emily and supported her, her family, and the cause of missions.

Dr. Calvin Newton to Emily C. Judson, April 12, 1851[172]—Worcester

Dear Mrs. Judson,

Your letter to the children, dated, Jan. 15th, 1850 (1851), is received this morning, and I hasten to reply. Mrs. N's health has been poor, for the past year; and, though considerably improved just now, there is still some uncertainty whether she will continue to amend or not. Considering this fact, and knowing your late husband's wish, we are expecting that you will take charge of the boys, after your return; and I would commend, to your attention, Worcester, as one of the most desirable places, in which you can find a house. It is a beautiful place and delightfully located. The advantages of its School, too, are superior. Why not then decide, at once, permanently to come immediately to our house, on your arrival in the country, and make *ours your* house, till you can find a better.[173]

The boys are essentially as well as usual. Of late, Adoniram's[174] health is not *very* good. He is growing rapidly.

Any assistance, which it shall be in our power to render you, will be rendered most cheerfully; and I hope you will not hesitate a moment to come directly here.

George's[175] health is quite good, of late. He is at Brown University; and spends a portion of his vacations with us. While his health was poor, he was out of College near two years,[176] and, therefore, *fell back* two classes.

( ) have of late had some special religious interest in this city. In our pastor's society, it is hoped, that there have been, within a short time, almost 30 conversions.

Please receive Mrs. N's kindest regards and sympathies for you; and may God conduct you safely over the deep, to your native land and future home.

With Christian regard I am yours

Calvin Newton

Source: American Baptist Historical Society, AJ 12, no. 452.

[172] This letter had a second page containing the letter of the same date written by Elnathan "Elly" Judson.

[173] Regarding the future of the Judson children (George Dana Boardman, Abby Ann, Adoniram, Elnathan, Henry, Edward, and Emily Frances), see volume 1, "A Timeline of the Children of Adoniram Judson and Their Desire to Be a United Family."

[174] Adoniram "Addy" Judson was born April 7, 1837, the second child and first son of Adoniram and Sarah Hall Boardman Judson. From November 1845 to October 1851, he lived with Dr. and Mrs. Calvin Newton in Worcester, Massachusetts. He then spent a year with Dr. and Mrs. Edward Bright in Roxbury, Massachusetts, and before entering Brown University, he was two years at Pierce Academy in Middleboro, Massachusetts. After his education and medical school, Adoniram served as a surgeon in the Civil War and became a prominent orthopedic surgeon with several books to his credit. He died in 1916. Over the years, he became vocal about the separation of missionary children from their parents.

[175] George Dana Boardman, the son of George Dana Boardman and Sarah Hall Boardman, was born August 18, 1828, in Tavoy, Burmah. George returned to the United States in 1844 at the age of six and lived with Dr. and Mrs. Calvin Newton in Worcester, Massachusetts. He attended Brown University in Providence, Rhode Island, graduating after taking a few years off for travel in the West. He attended the Newton Theological Institute, and in 1855, he married Miss Ella Covell. He served two churches before settling into the First Baptist Church of Philadelphia, where he served with distinction for thirty years. He formed a close relationship with Emily upon her return in 1851; when she gave him a copy of *An Olio of Domestic Verses*, she addressed it "Georgie—from Mamma."

[176] See the letters of Dr. Calvin Newton to Emily C. Judson, dated June 30 and July 1, 1849, in which he speaks of George Boardman's absence and the problems George was addressing.

Elnathan "Elly" Judson to Emily C. Judson, April 12, 1851[177]—Worcester

Dear mother.

We received your kind letter this morning and were very glad to hear from you as we were in a state of great anxiety. Aunt Newton[178] was much frightened at first when she saw the black seal. Our Annual examination came off Thursday before last with great credit to Adoniram[179] and myself as we did not miss a single question. I received a letter from sister Abby[180] yesterday. She thought that you could not bear the care and trouble of six children[181] at one time but then she said that she was sure that she would help you as much as she could.[182] Did you receive our box of presents before starting for this country. I shall be almost enchanted when I see you and my dear little brothers and sisters and Eddy Stevens.[183] I shall hardly believe my senses. I have begun a letter to sister Abby today. The examination which I shall have to undergo previous to entering into the High School comes off next Monday. I hope that I shall get in, for it would be a great disappointment if I should not. With many prayers for your safe arrival I ever remain,

Your affectionate son

E. Judson

Source: American Baptist Historical Society, AJ 12, no. 452.

George Dana Boardman to Emily C. Judson, April 13, 1851—Brown University

My dear Mother,

Your very kind letter of Jan. 11th, was gratefully received yesterday. I am delighted at the prospect of so soon welcoming you home. I now fondly look forward to many a happy day wh. we may spend together. In an epistolary respect, I have to confess that I have been a very undutiful son. To write a letter is to me the most irksome of tasks. I verily believe that my antipathy to letter writing is inborn, and I am sure that this innate antipathy has only grown with my growth. But now that we are likely to

[177] This letter was an addendum to an April 12, 1851, letter written by Dr. Calvin Newton.

[178] This is the wife of Dr. Calvin Newton, of Worcester; Elnathan and Adoniram lived with them beginning with Adoniram Judson's return to America in fall 1845.

[179] See vol. 1, "Cast of Characters," s.v. "Judson, Adoniram Brown 'Addy.'"

[180] See vol. 1, "Cast of Characters," s.v. "Judson, Abby Ann."

[181] At this time, the six Judson children included Abby Ann, Adoniram, Elnathan, Henry and Edward, who were all born to Sarah Boardman Judson and Adoniram Judson, and Emily Frances Judson, daughter of Emily and Adoniram Judson.

[182] Regarding the future of the Judson children (George Dana Boardman, Abby Ann, Adoniram, Elnathan, Henry, Edward, and Emily Frances), see volume 1, "A Timeline of the Children of Adoniram Judson and Their Desire to Be a United Family."

[183] Though there was earlier mention of Eddy Stevens traveling to the United States with Emily, he does not show up in the letters that she wrote in February and as they boarded the *Tudor*.

be united together by the endearing ties of family intercourse, I hope that I shall furnish many a convincing proof that I am an affectionate though unworthy son.

Many of our reminiscences will be full of sorrow. We shall miss the wise and tender counsels of one whose smiling face will never beam on us again. But the rich legacy of his loves, and his prayers, and his Christian example will be to us a foundation of all consultation. After all, these sorrowful reminiscences can but awaken emotions of gratitude. The thought that the loved one who toiled so earnestly for his divine master, is now reaping the fruits of his abundant labors, has in it more of joy than of sorrow: and I am confident that the interchange of our remembrances of the past, sad, very sad, tho' it be, can scarcely fail to be a source of delight to each of us.

Tonight I rec'd a letter from Addy[184] and Elly.[185] They tell me that they are just entering the High School. They can hardly contain themselves, (nor can I,) at the delightful idea that we are all to live together, mother and brothers and sisters.[186] ( ) spend the joyous hour when the same roof will cover a bereaved yet happy family. I hardly know what to say to you about this—so often are our most precious plans defeated in this world of disappointments. I *will* say however, that all *I* can do towards the accomplishment of our long cherished plans shall be soon speedily and right earnestly. I long to see you, and the precious little ones with you, and to be to you, my dear Mother, a dutiful and affectionate son, and to the others a tender elder brother. I long for the hour, when you may lean upon me for support, when you may tell me all your sorrows and joys, when I may look to you as my fond Mother, and you upon me as a son not unworthy of your love. I earnestly pray, that it may please our Heavenly Father, to grant us this richest of all earthly blessings.

Brothers tell me that Dr. Newton has already written you respecting this. I don't know what he has said: but I am sure that however much he and Mrs. Newton may love the boys, they would cheerfully part with them on condition of their living with their dear mother. I shall write to Dr. Peck[187] at once, and learn his plans. He

[184] See vol. 1, "Cast of Characters," s.v. "Judson, Adoniram Brown 'Addy.'"

[185] Elnathan "Elly" Judson was born July 15, 1838, the third child and second son of Adoniram and Sarah Hall Boardman Judson. From November 1845 to October 1851, he lived with Dr. and Mrs. Calvin Newton in Worcester, Massachusetts. He then spent a year with Dr. and Mrs. Edward Bright in Roxbury, Massachusetts, and before entering Brown University, he spent two years at Pierce Academy in Middleboro, Massachusetts. There are strong indications that Elnathan planned to become a minister, and in fact, he did graduate from Union Seminary. In 1860, however, he suffered a serious sunstroke that subsequently caused serious mental impairment. For much of his life, Elnathan was confined to mental institutions. He died after a second paralyzing stroke in 1896; in the last years of his life, Elnathan was lovingly cared for by his sister Abby Ann Judson.

[186] Regarding the future of the Judson children (George Dana Boardman, Abby Ann, Adoniram, Elnathan, Henry, Edward, and Emily Frances), see volume 1, "A Timeline of the Children of Adoniram Judson and Their Desire to Be a United Family."

[187] The Reverend Doctor Solomon Peck was for twenty years the executive secretary of the American Baptist Missionary Union. Many believed him to be hard, stern, and judgmental, and from some of his comments, it is easy to understand that perception. Dr. Peck and Emily did not always have the easiest of relationships. She felt in him the judgment that came from many in the church at the announcement of her impending marriage to Adoniram; that judgment concerned her "secular" past and concern that she was not an appropriate companion for the venerable missionary. On July 18, 1849, Emily wrote a blistering letter of defense to Dr. Peck in response to a letter from him of February 20, 1849; her letter framed how she viewed his perception of her, and her response was meant to set the record straight. There are eleven letters in the collection from Solomon Peck to Emily.

probably will communicate them to you himself. Meanwhile I shall do my uttermost to secure the object wh. we all so earnestly desire to be effected.

When you arrive at London, will you be kind enough to write me a letter, detailing to me your wishes and plans? Possibly you may see a dear friend of mine, who is just graduating, and who is soon to start for Greece, his native home, by way of London. If I think that there is any prospect of his seeing you, I will write by him. How long do you expect to remain in London, and how will you cross the Atlantic? Please write me all about this. Meantime my fervent prayers will be that God will grant you, and my dear little brothers and sister, a prosperous voyage and a speedy and happy home for us all. Kiss those dear little ones for me, whom never having seen, I tenderly love, and believe me, that I will try to be to them all that the tenderest brother can be. And now, my dear Mother, I fervently pray that He, who tempers the wind to the shorn lamb, may guide you and comfort you and be to you far more than the most loving father or husband.

Your very affectionate son,

Geo. Dana Boardman.

Source: American Baptist Historical Society, AJ 11, no. 408.

Mrs. H. H. Newton to Emily C. Judson, April 16, 1851—New York

My dear Mrs. Judson, Mr. Newton[188] informed me this morning that my letter to you must be sent tomorrow. I have accordingly seated myself to write you a few lines—but what can *I say* that will in any way comfort you and so I have thought and thought again and again—I have desired to write months since, but it seems as if my words and ideas were frozen—to say to you I sorrow for you and that "all things work together for good, to those who love me" etc. etc. seems cold and common-place—so I feel my dear Mrs. Judson that I must be still—I take up my pen at this late period to inform you, that though I have been so long silent, I have not ceased to remember you—and love you—and sincerely hope you, with *yours*, will on your arrival in New York come immediately to our house—we will do all in our power to comfort you and relieve you of care—I must say a word with regard to the boxes last summer—when I heard of failing health I stopped making articles for you—but what I prepared I preferred saving until I saw you or heard something of your future plans. I have a few articles, under clothes for you, ready on your arrival here.

[188] When they first heard of Adoniram Judson's death, Mr. and Mrs. Isaac Newton wrote immediately and enclosed a draft for $500.00 to meet the immediate needs of Emily and the children.

And now My Dear Mrs. Judson, that the God of all afflictions and mercies may keep and return you and your little ones to us in safety is the sincere and heartfelt prayer of

Your aff friend

H. H. Newton

Our no. is 29 Market St.

Source: American Baptist Historical Society, AJ 18, no. 857.

Mrs. Elizabeth L. Stevens to Emily C. Judson, April 18, 1851

My dear Sister

I wrote you a note, wh. you missed by going from Calcutta just at the Steamer's time for getting in and lost a month. I wrote another wee bit of one for Miss Lilly[189] to enclose, but she did not send—Now I ought not to write much besides to Mother and Calvin. Tomorrow Mrs. Powers is to spend here and next day is laundry so our mail time will go.

My little Henry Ripley was born the first day of this month, a nice big boy—looks like Mr. ( )pey!! so Eddy[190] and Mrs. Ranney[191] say—Eddy sings little Heman's hymns over him—I don't know how we would get on without him; he and I each are principal sub-assistant nurses. There was Providence in his not going home[192]—I keep saying for want of something else to say. How extraordinary that after all Calvin sho. have gone via England! The W. A's Capt. got angry, because C. would not work Sunday and told him in a fit he had better go back in another ship, wh. C. accordingly did.

We were *so* glad to hear as favorable accounts as you sent from Masulipatum may better far reach us from England.

Mrs. Moore's baby is 10 days older than mine after all! but a frail feeble little thing. We hope it will live as it seems improving.

[189] See vol. 1, "Cast of Characters," s.v. "Lillybridge, Lydia." Also, "A Timeline of the Life and Mission of Lydia Lillybridge Simons."

[190] Edward Stevens was born December 17, 1838, and was the son of Edward and Elizabeth Stevens.

[191] See vol. 1, "Cast of Characters," s.v. "Ranney, Thomas and Maria."

[192] The original plans were for Edward Stevens to travel to the United States with Emily and her children.

The Kincaid's[193] and D's[194] are all gone to Rangoon. We never alluded to the troubles in conversation with them nor have we except once a little with the V's[195]—so things have been quiet for us. They have made Mr. and Mrs. Hough[196] strong converts to their story. Mrs. H. think wonde( ) [Note: A line is lost in the ragged edge of the page bottom.]

[Written in the right margin of the address page:] of his age!!!

Did I tell you Dr. Dawson's ( ) at English chapel a kind of chemical explanation of the Book of Daniel? Calvin says he was all the way out preparing it to astonish the meeting with! The worth of all was Major Boyle and daughter among other big folks, were there; their first and only attendance there. Apropos of Major B. and Miss B. they

[Written in the left margin of the address page:] called here when baby was three days old—not knowing what had happened—so after all I must call there.

What a providence that you did not go in the Buckinghamshire! It was burnt to the water's edge off Diamond Harbor! All lives but two spared, but nothing else.

If you stop in London you may see Calvin there. Oh if he could only have gone with you. All the *W. A.*[197] company love him as a dear

[Written in the bottom margin of the address page:] kind brother. In Calcutta he kept with the missionaries all the time and was a lovely good boy. I enjoyed him exceedingly while here. Go to Framingham[198] when you first get home *do*.

Lovingly

E. L. S.

Source: American Baptist Historical Society, AJ 19, no. 902.

[193] See vol. 1, "Cast of Characters," s.v. "Kincaid, The Reverend Doctor Eugenio."

[194] See vol. 1, "Cast of Characters," s.v. "Dawson, Doctor."

[195] Justus Hatch Vinton was born in Willington, Connecticut, in 1806. He attended the theological school at Hamilton, New York, and was ordained in June 1834. In July that same year, he sailed as a missionary to Burmah. His wife was Calista Holman Vinton; they were married April 9, 1834. They worked with the Karens at Chummerah, Newville, and Maulmain, where he had charge of the Karen theological seminary. At the end of 1847, they left for the United States, returning to Burmah and work at Rangoon in July 1850. Justus Vinton died in Kemendine, Burmah, on March 31, 1858. His wife, Calista Holman Vinton, died in Rangoon, Burmah December 20, 1864. Mrs. Vinton taught the Karen women and was the author of several hymnbooks in their language.

[196] See vol. 1, "Cast of Characters," s.v. "Hough, The Reverend George and Phoebe."

[197] This is a ship, the *Washington Allston*, which recently had arrived in Maulmain and Balcutta carrying a number of the Missionary Union missionaries. There was some thought of Emily going to England on it.

[198] Mrs. Stevens is referring to Framingham, Massachusetts, just to the west of Boston, not far from Worcester. It was where her mother and sister, Sarah Haven, lived.

[199] See vol. 1, "Cast of Characters," s.v. "Anable, Anna Maria."

Miss Cynthia Sheldon to Emily C. Judson, April 18, 1851—311 Walnut St., Philadelphia

My dear dear Emily,

Your letter to Anna M.[199] date Jan. 20th came to hand last evening—need I say dear E. that although it confirmed our hope about your sailing at the appointed time, it really increased our apprehension about your health—so very weak at that date—We feel deeply—yes weighed down with the thought of your unfitness for the voyage—I do trust our cry is unto *Him* who only can give strength and every needed good to your fainting, drooping, yet ardent spirit—you are in the path of duty dearest when you pray, and put forth means to prolong your precious life—it is marking heaven's blessing on the children confided to your care—and by the eye of faith in God's promises, I now see you raised up—and the dear ones grown up—*brought up* to call you blessed—do be of good cheer—when you get this side of the big waters you will find some helping hands—be assured dear E. there is many a heart panting for the privilege *to do* in this big city as well as other places—we know providence seems to point very distinctly to your selecting this for your abiding place—we are rejoicing in it more than you can tell—Well do I know that to your overburdened heart it is of little use to talk of happy days to come—yet dear E. we are by the principles of our holy religion bound to enjoy the things of this life as unto God—he is our all, and in all—we can rejoice that He directs all things—and in all his appointed ways, feel assured He is leading us by the right way to join the happy loved ones in Heaven.

We have waited for the time to come that letters would meet you in England—I shall enclose to you now the receipt of your drafts—they are in a way to draw interest from the 15th of this month—and to come at your bidding—whenever you say the word—I am so glad dear E. to find your money matters better than we feared.

You will have Sarah Bell's[200] letter or note[201] with this—you may be certain that both herself and Mr. Gould[202] are hearty in the invitation—and will be disappointed if you decline entirely—I am sure of what I say—it may be as some say that Mr. G. is rather close in money matters generally—but in having friends at his house there is nothing of it—I do believe the implication has come from the sickness of his first wife and his consideration for her, making an excuse for living much alone—for Sarah insists that Mr. Gould likes to have company as well as she does, and she means to have her house open to friends—the more the better—she has plenty of room for you and yours and one to share for me too—My heart is quite set on

[200] See vol. 1, "Cast of Characters," s.v. "Wheeler, Sarah Bell."

[201] See letter from Sarah Bell Wheeler Gould to Emily C. Judson dated April 8, 1851.

[202] See vol. 1, "Cast of Characters," s.v. "Gould, Charles."

meeting you there—Mrs. Colby's[203] brother E. G. Roberts[204] leaves N. York this week for London—he has a little package by way of introduction to you—he will call and render you all the service in his power—do not not [sic] hesitate to let him know what he can do—If you should conclude to come in a New York Steamer—I will be there the first train after the telegraph reaches here—if not in waiting—if we can know before hand what Steamer you take I shall be in waiting for it either in Boston or New York—My Brother is about settling at Williamsburg nearly opposite N. York to be Bookkeeper for a company there, in which Dr. Nott[205] is interested—we are rejoicing in it—for it promises a good salary—and improvement in his circumstances—we shall feel almost neighbors—I have forbore to mention to you that on the 15th of Dec. by a mis-step coming home from Church in the evening—the large bone was broken short <u>off</u> just above the ankle—This to be sure was serious business—weeks passed with me on the bed in a brace—but I was surrounded with so much watchful kindness—O you cannot know how good they all were—yes, vieing [sic] with each other to do most for poor me—all that skill and kindness could do, was done continually—and from my inmost soul went forth thanksgiving for encircling mercies—I have seen enough to convince me if in providence my shattered frame should render me useless—our dear ones would never cast me by—but God has seen fit to give me the use of my feet again—and in one month more probably the full use without weakness—I desire to praise *Him* continually who hath done all things well—

Dear Emily your disease has been hidden from us—we knew your strength was prostrated but we did not know (*as* we now understand) that the difficulty was in the bowels—will you dear E. if that difficulty is still there, or you have a reoccurrence make use of the simple prescription which I shall give—it has done wonders to heal such cases—and cannot do harm—Heavens grant we may meet to recount together all the past way—and have wisdom to form future plans for the best good of all concerned—I do believe the Board will meet your views about your claims and interest in some matters which will relieve your mind from anxiety for the future—All send a heaping measure of love to you—do *have* the darling one know us—ever your truly

sympathizing friend

C. Sheldon

[203] See vol. 1, "Cast of Characters," s.v. "Colby, Mary."

[204] See vol. 1, "Cast of Characters," s.v. "Robarts, E. G."

[205] The Reverend Doctor Eliphalet Nott was the president of Union College in Schenectady, New York. An ordained Presbyterian minister, he was married to Urania Sheldon Nott, the sister of Miss Cynthia Sheldon and Mrs. Alma Anable and the aunt of Anna Maria Anable.

[Written on a separate page:] Recipe for bowel complaints—Dysentery—or Cholera Morbus—1 gill of good vinegar ½ gill of water—add six tablespoonful of loaf sugar and 1 of fine salt—simmer together and take a spoonful every few minutes till relieved—take it warm—the feet must be kept warm—if inflammation is settled in the bowels—flannel wrung from boiling water and applied often will subdue it.

[Written on a separate page:] Received from Mrs. Emily C. Judson by two drafts the sum of One Thousand Dollars—in trust on interest until she calls for the same

Philadelphia April 15th, 1851

C. Sheldon

Source: American Baptist Historical Society, AJ 20, no. 990.

Anna Maria Anable to Emily C. Judson, April 20, 1851

Dearest Emily

I wonder where you are now and how you are. We have heard here that you are thinking some of taking the overland route, and yet it seems so uncertain and your stay in Calcutta seems so indefinite as to time that I do not know whether to think of you as there, sailing down the Mediterranean, or round the Cape of Good Hope. Won't you feel that you can rest after "scooting" about the world so long, if you could only once more sit down in the little "Snuggery" at Hamilton. Ah me! how many assinations [sic] does that word recal [sic] of the loved and departed. I felt so sure at one time that I should see him again, again hear his voice in prayers that I can only at times realize that he is really gone. Abby[206] sent me your letter to her aunt, and though I had read the most of it in print,[207] the entire letter was very acceptable, as developing more fully your plans. From that dear Emily I understand that it was *your* proposition to gather the children together in one family.[208] Most of your friends here think that will hardly be a possible project unless your health should be much better than it ever yet has been. But you can judge best, after all, and you cannot tell well what will be best until you get home again. We have had a delightful visit from Sarah Bell,[209] who seems very happy or rather very satisfied in her marriage. Until I saw her I was not a little anxious about her happiness, but I am convinced that she will pass along through life without feeling many wants,

[206] See vol. 1, "Cast of Characters," s.v. "Judson, Abby Ann."

[207] The majority of letters sent home by Emily and Adoniram Judson were published in the public press; such was the interest in their life and activity.

[208] Regarding the future of the Judson children (George Dana Boardman, Abby Ann, Adoniram, Elnathan, Henry, Edward, and Emily Frances), see volume 1, "A Timeline of the Children of Adoniram Judson and Their Desire to Be a United Family."

[209] See vol. 1, "Cast of Characters," s.v. "Wheeler, Sarah Bell."

which her good husband[210] will not meet. He is much more of a man than he appeared to be before his marriage, indeed he appears with her like an intelligent, conscientious, and good meaning man. Sarah is grown so lovely in person as well as character that she must assert a blessed influence on all with whom she comes in contact. They say her little daughter and invalid boy are dotingly fond of her. She holds a very good position in Society in Boston, and has some relations there who are charming people. Mr. ( ), her step brother has a lovely family, and he and they have done every thing [sic] for Sarah that an own brother and fam. could have done. Their being in Boston makes us feel that dear Sandy [sic] is not quite away from all connections. She wants to have you stay with her very much and I shall enclose a note which she left for you to that effect. Do you know dear Nemmy[211] that I expect to see you almost as soon as our quarter closes, and that seems ( ) close at hand. I am promising myself a visit to Utica this vacation and I do not think I shall be so near Hamilton without running over first thing. I must not forget to give you Mr. Robert's[212] address. It is, E. G. Roberts and Co., 13 Kings Arms Yard, London. He has got one of the dearest, brightest little girls in our school, that I have seen in a long while, and I think he himself is a mighty nice man, so you must write him a note and let him know when you arrive in London, for he said he should be happy to do anything for you, and perhaps should return to this country about the time that you would. I have never told you that poor Louisa Marble Wright[213] is left a widow. She is now in Utica with her sister Fanny Mattson.

Sarah Hinckley[214] will be returning from Kentucky next summer and you will probably see her too. She has kept up her correspondence with Molly and has been a very successful *Music* teacher! Ellen Bennett[215] will probably be on her way south by the time you get here. She is grown very lovely. I don't think I shall write you darling, but in the strong hope of seeing you soon I am

Lovingly as of old

Anna Maria

Source: American Baptist Historical Society, AJ 13, no. 468.

[210] See vol. 1, "Cast of Characters," s.v. "Gould, Charles."

[211] "Nem" or "Nemmy" was a name of endearment given to Emily by a small group of her intimate friends at the Utica Female Academy. Anna Maria Anable was "Ninny."

[212] See vol. 1, "Cast of Characters," s.v. "Roberts, E. G."

[213] In 1843, Miss Marble was a recent graduate of the Utica Female Seminary and wrote to Emily upon her return to Port Byron. In an 1848 letter to Emily, she was at the academy as a teacher and was fully involved there. According to a letter written by Sarah Hinckley in 1849, Miss Marble married and moved to New York City. In Emily's February 19, 1850, letter she was referred to as "Lou Marble Wright." Then, in April 1851, Anna Maria mentioned that Louisa Marble Wright was now a widow, back living in Utica with her sister.

[214] Sarah Hinckley was one of the girls from the Utica Female Seminary and a student of Emily's; there are some letters from her in the collection. In an 1849 letter Miss Hinckley reminisced about that time and brought Emily up to date on many of those who were there with her. She also spoke of the sad farewell when Emily left for Boston and then Burmah.

[215] Ellen Bennett was born in Burmah on June 8, 1835, and was the daughter of Cephas and Stella Bennett, missionaries.

Miss Lydia Lillybridge to Emily C. Judson, April 21, 1851—Maulmain

Oh, Emily!

You cannot imagine how much I feel the want of the beaming light of your countenance, nor how lonely it was here while Mrs. Ranney[216] was gone. She did not come till this month.

I wish I could know where you are now, and how you are. How I should enjoy being with you—being your *ayah*.

Mrs. Wade[217] is kind, *very* kind and *good*, and I am [Note: "Liking her" is written and crossed out.] loving her more and more, but she is not *Emily* after all.

I showed her the letter I wrote to the Ex. Committee respecting my going to Amhest [sic]; but she, nor Mr. Wade[218] did not at all think it best for me to be so much alone. They thought it would wear upon my health and spirits—said they had been so much alone that they knew how it would be.—Besides, they did not wish to advise me to do anything in opposition to the mind of the Mission, and thought that the Committee would not either. I finally concluded to let the matter *lie on the shelf* a while. I *guess* they were afraid that I wanted to get too much power into my hands, but they do not think so now if I judge correctly.

What do you think I did about three days ago?—I concluded to stop quarrelling with Mr. Simons[219] and go and live with him! Mrs. Stevens[220] has told all the funny things about it,[221] I presume, and I will not repeat. Do tell me what she has written—don't forget.

Some will think that because you are gone forever that I have done what I should not have dared to do if you had remained. Now you will boast of being a true prophet for you said that you expected to hear such news on your arrival home.

[216] See vol. 1, "Cast of Characters," s.v. "Ranney, Thomas and Maria."

[217] See vol. 1, "Cast of Characters," s.v. "Wade, Jonathan and Deborah."

[218] Ibid.

[219] Thomas Simons was born in Wales. He was ordained on December 18, 1831, after graduation from the Newton Theological Institute and was appointed to missionary service on March 7, 1831. He sailed for Burmah on June 29, 1832, arriving in Maulmain on January 1, 1833. On June 23, 1833, he married Caroline Jenks Harrington in Maulmain, probably the widow of a missionary who had died, and between 1834 and March 1843, they had six children, two of whom died in June 1839. Caroline Simons died on May 1, 1843. Mr. Simons returned to America in May 1846. While in the United States, he visited with Abby Ann Judson at Bradford Academy; she would have known him from her years in Burmah. He returned to Burmah in November 1847, arriving in Maulmain April 19, 1848. His second wife was Lydia Lillybridge, who had sailed to Burmah with Adoniram and Emily Judson; they were married in Maulmain in 1851.

[220] See vol. 1, "Cast of Characters," s.v. "Stevens, Elizabeth 'Bessie.'"

[221] For information on the marriage of Lydia Lillybridge to Thomas Simons, see the letter of Elizabeth Stevens to Emily C. Judson dated May 20, 1851. See also the letter of Lydia Lillybridge to Emily C. Judson dated May 11, 1951; the letter of Phoebe Hough to Emily C. Judson dated May 20, 1851; and the letter of Lydia Lillybridge Simons dated May 22, 1851. See also in vol. 1, "A Timeline of the Life and Mission of Lydia Lillybridge Simons."

You and Anna Maria[222] and Aunt C.,[223] will grow stout by laughing over it, but I do not care so much about that as I did once.

It is time to send the letters. It is too bad that I should have been so hindered by company today.

Much love to the children and much for yourself.

Very affectionately yours

Lydia Lillybridge

Source: American Baptist Historical Society, AJ 17, no. 772.

Miss Lydia Lillybridge to Emily C. Judson,[224] April 27, 1851[225]

[Note: This portion of the letter is from the 924 file.]

O! Emily, I must tell you about the change in the school.[226]

Pascal wanted his salary raised, and had had communication with Mr. Howard[227] in regard to it. Mr. H. tho't the Board would grant it if the Mission asked it, and said that he should be willing himself. But, (amazing to tell!) the *whole mission* had found out that his "price was not above rubies," and unanimously agreed in council assembled, to refuse any addition to his salary—telling him (by the mouth of Mr. Simons)[228] that if he could do *better* for himself, he was at liberty to leave.—

[222] See vol. 1, "Cast of Characters," s.v. "Anable, Anna Maria."

[223] See vol. 1, "Cast of Characters," s.v. "Sheldon, Miss Cynthia."

[224] This letter was likely written six days after the letter of April 21, 1851, with news of the school and teaching situation; these items had filled her previous letters, and nothing was said of them in the April 21 letter. This letter is a compilation from several different files, but it is possible that it is actually one letter.

The first section of the letter came as file 924, and this is obviously the start of the letter.

The second section of the letter came marked as coming from the file 896, a section of letters from Mrs. Stevens. The letter is obviously not from Mrs. Stevens—along one of the pages is written "From Lydia," and the handwriting, content, and paper size make it a continuation of the April 27 letter from file 924.

The third section of the letter came in file 922, which is dated July 19. This seems misplaced, for the paper size is different, and it is unlikely that this fragment written on May 11 would go with a letter written two months later; rather it makes more sense to have been a final note to the April 27 letter. The content about the missionaries in Rangoon and it being no place for ladies ties in with the April 25, 1851, letter, which speaks of the war and the destruction of Rangoon. There is also some print bleed-through on the May 11 page, and it is obvious that this is written on the back page of the second segment marked the file 896. The "Kiss Frances and Edward and Henry" can clearly be read backwards on the May 11 page.

[225] There is an addendum to this letter dated May 11, 1851.

[226] Both Lydia and Mrs. Stevens spoke of differences of opinion amongst the missionaries; this letter seems to outline whatever portion of the difference had to do with the schools, and certainly advocates Lydia's rather firm opinions.

[227] Hosea Howard first sailed for Burmah in 1834, arriving in December that year. His wife was Theresa, and they had been married just before departure. Hosea Howard was a recent graduate of the Theological Seminary in Hamilton, New York. They were stationed in Maulmain as missionaries with Adoniram Judson, and he was to claim in a letter to Emily that he had worked there with Adoniram longer than any other missionary. Mr. Howard's responsibility was to run schools that the mission maintained, a task in which he was ably assisted by his wife. It was to Mr. and Mrs. Howard that Lydia Lillybridge was responsible when she arrived in November 1846. Mr. and Mrs. Howard left Maulmain for the United States in February 1850.

[228] See vol. 1, "Cast of Characters," s.v. "Lillybridge, Lydia." Also, "A Timeline of the Life and Mission of Lydia Lillybridge Simons."

Accordingly he left about a month since. The Mission gave R's 60 and house rent. He now gets 110, with the prospect of an increase some time or other.

I am glad he has left, for, he was not what one ought to be in that place, though the best to be had in these parts. Mr. Simons is now obliged to be in school most of the day, in order to keep it "*lingering*" on till some one [sic] comes. But Mr. Howard says in a letter just received that he does not see any probability of a teacher's being appointed this year—But—but I think they will not find me teaching English after the end of this year, even if it be necessary to make a division in this household[229] to prevent it, and if Mr. Simons persists in serving Eurasian scholars after that time, you may expect to hear of a rupture, perhaps a*n open o*ne—for, I am bound by no law human or Divine to submit in this respect (*Am* I?) If the Board were to withdraw their support from me, I might be glad to teach such a school—Perhaps I should have refused *obstinately* to have *anything* to do with it this year if it had not been for those excellently judicious, and experienced women, Mrs. Wade[230] and Mrs. Bennett,[231] who seemed to think it would not be wise for me to refuse altogether, considering the circumstances.

[Note: This portion of the letter came from the 896 file] Aside from this I think Mrs. Wade's opinion agrees with yours precisely. Perhaps she would not go so far as to say that *no* person whatever receiving support from the Board, should engage in teaching a Eurasian school.

I wonder if you'll convert Mr. Bright.[232] He said to Mrs. Haswell[233] while speaking of my having left the school "*But surely she will not let the school suffer*." Do ask him and others if *they* think it wise for us to spend our energies in teaching this class to eat, and drink, and act, and think in English, to this neglect of these Burmese multitudes of children that are taught nothing but idolatry and superstition.

I do wish that I had a mind that could see clearly, reason correctly, rise above everybody's opinions, and decide independently for its self [sic]. But I did not intend to trouble you more with this same old jargon—and thought I had closed my letters without doing so, but—Oh dear me! Do pardon me this time.

In regard to "my son," if you have any bad reports of him do have the kindness to let me know. Judging from his letters, I have an idea that he is a pretty decent

[229] Mr. Thomas Simons and Miss Lydia Lillybridge were to be married on May 13, 1851.

[230] See vol. 1, "Cast of Characters," s.v. "Wade, Jonathan and Deborah."

[231] Stella Bennett was the wife of Cephas Bennett; they arrived in Burmah in January 1830. Mr. Bennett remained the superintendent of the Baptist Press there for more than fifty years. From the Utica area, they sent their children back, and the girls were educated at the Utica Female Academy and then the Misses Anable's School. The girls included Elsina (April 1828), Mary (November 1829), Ann (August 1833), Ellen (June 1835), and Sarah (June 1837).

[232] See vol. 1, "Cast of Characters," s.v. "Bright, The Reverend Doctor Edward, Jr."

[233] Jane Haswell sailed for Burmah in 1835, arriving in February 1836 to work with the Talaings. Her husband was James Haswell. She served as a missionary for more than forty years. Mrs. Haswell took in Henry Hall Judson when Adoniram and Sarah sailed for the United States in spring 1845. The correspondence between Emily and Jane Haswell reflects a warm relationship between the two.

lad, thoroughly "*a chip of the old block*." Of course he is what they call a "green one." But he may get repened [sic] there under such auspicious influences.

Tell Nancy[234] that we shall be very glad to see her back again.

I wonder if she would like to live with me. Kiss Frances[235] and Edward [236]and Henry[237] for me.

Source: American Baptist Historical Society, AJ 19, no. 924.

Abby Ann Judson to Emily C. Judson,[238] April 29, 1851—Bradford

April 29th, 1851

My dear Mother,

It was with the greatest pleasure that I received your letter dated Maulmain Jan 10th. I have been afraid that if you came to this country that you would not be able to have us all live together but I feel almost sure from what you said in your letter that you intend to collect us all into one family[239]—My only trouble now is that something will happen before you arrive here. Adoniram[240] and Elnathan[241] laugh at me because I always see the worst of everything but on the whole I think that it is a good plan for if any thing [sic] bad happens I shall be prepared for it and if any thing [sic] good that it will be an agreeable disappointment.

It makes me so happy that I can scarcely realize that it is so when I think that you are coming to this country. It will seem so strange for Adoniram and Elnathan and myself to have a home for though we have been with those we love and who have been kind to us yet we could not feel as if we really had a house. I had a letter from Elnathan a little while ago and he mentioned that he had received a letter from you and copied it off for me. I found that you expressed yourself to them in even stronger terms than you did to me with regard to our living together. Oh! I feel almost certain that it can be accomplished in some way. I would be willing to do any thing [sic] in the world that I can to assist you. By the time you are prepared to settle down in a real home I shall be old enough to earn a good deal of money.

[234] See vol. 1, "Cast of Characters," s.v. "Nancy."

[235] See vol. 1, "Cast of Characters," s.v. "Judson, Emily Frances."

[236] See vol. 1, "Cast of Characters," s.v. "Judson, Edward."

[237] See vol. 1, "Cast of Characters," s.v. "Judson, Henry Hall."

[238] This letter was addressed to: Mrs. Emily C. Judson / Care of Joseph Symon Esq. / No. 2 Tremwheel Lane. Cannon St. / London Eng. There is a postal stamp from Bradford, and a second stamp, above which is written "ABMU US" and under which is written "Rec. 9/5/51."

[239] Regarding the future of the Judson children (George Dana Boardman, Abby Ann, Adoniram, Elnathan, Henry, Edward, and Emily Frances), see volume 1, "A Timeline of the Children of Adoniram Judson and Their Desire to Be a United Family."

[240] See vol. 1, "Cast of Characters," s.v. "Judson, Adoniram Brown 'Addy.'"

[241] See vol. 1, "Cast of Characters," s.v. "Judson, Elnathan 'Elly.'"

Aunt Hasseltine[242] seems to think that you will not be able to keep house on account of the expense but indeed for my part I would be willing to work very hard rather than forgo that pleasure. Nancy[243] says that she thinks that I know enough now to teach a common school and I intend to pay a good deal of attention to my music till you come and perhaps I may be able [Note: Abby Ann wrote "afraid," crossed it out, and wrote "able" over it.] to teach some beginners on the piano. Oh! how I love to build "castles in the air" which after all generally vanish as soon as completed. Very often when I should be studying or doing something else I find myself dreaming of what we shall do when you come here. I have imagined it all over a hundred times our meeting [sic]. Generally when I think of anything a good deal it does not happen as I wish and I try not to think so much of our living together but the thought *will* come if I try *ever* so hard.

Elnathan told me in his last letter that he and Adoniram had just been examined to enter the high school and were admitted. It delighted me exceedingly for I have been dreading the trial for some time for fear they would not be able to pass successfully. But all my anxieties with regard to that have been removed. He wrote in very good spirits and seemed to be very happy at the idea of your coming to this country.

Perhaps you would like to know something of my studies. This term I am attending to Physiology, Virgil, English Grammar, and taking lessons on the Piano. I do not know whether I ever wrote anything about Miss Crocker—one of my teachers. Excepting the Hasseltines I love her better than anyone else connected with the school. It is one of my darling schemes to have you acquainted with her when you come here so that she might come and see us when I go away from here.

I have not heard from George[244] for some time but I suppose that he is very much engaged in his studies. Mr. Allen of Jamaica Plain has lost all his property I believe, but there is a very benevolent lady residing in Salem who has undertaken to carry him through college. Her father is a sea captain and he gives her so much every year and by being very economical she is able to save enough. She educated one young man who has since died and on his deathbed he asked her to take some one [sic] else and educate them so she has taken George. He is now at Providence at college but I do not know how near he is to the end of the course.[245] Elnathan said in his latest letter that he had written to him and requested him to write to me, which I hope he will do soon.

242 Probably the reference is to Abigail Hasseltine, the sister of Ann Hasseltine Judson.

243 Nancy Hasseltine addressed Abigail Hasseltine as "aunt"; with this, Nancy would be one of the nieces of Ann Hasseltine Judson, also there with the family at Bradford Academy.

244 See vol. 1, "Cast of Characters," s.v. "Boardman, George Dana."

245 Because of illness and his trip west, George had been forced to drop out of college for almost two years, thus throwing off his schedule of studies. After the absence, he did go back to Brown to finish his course before going on to seminary at Newton. See the letters of Calvin Newton of June 30 and July 1, 1849.

Last summer vacation I went to Deacon Hill's in South Boston to see Uncle and Aunt Wade.[246] I had a letter from Mary Hill their daughter yesterday and she wanted me to go there again next vacation. I had a letter from Sarah Haven[247] a little while ago and she spoke of my going to see her. I have five places where I can visit next vacation but if you come here before I suppose I shall not go.

[Written in the right margin of the address page:] We are going to have tomorrow for a holiday as it is May-day and we are all anticipating a deal of pleasure in gathering May flowers. I had a letter from Aunt Judson[248] and a bundle a day or two ago. She is very kind indeed to me and does a great deal for me. She spoke of your coming to this country with a good deal of pleasure but I do not believe that she

[Written in the left margin of the address page:] will be happier than I shall. I hope that you will arrive before the close of the term because the girls want to see you. Hoping to see you *very very* soon I am

Your affectionate daughter

Abby

[Written along the left and top margins of page 1:] My Aunts and cousins send their love to you and say that they would be very happy to see you here when you come and would like a long visit. They also want me to tell you that symaphize [sic] with you in the loss we have sustained. Please kiss little Henry[249] and Edward[250] and Fanny[251] for me and give my love to them and accept a great deal for yourself from me. You said that they talked a good deal of seeing their "big sister Abby." I am afraid they will not find me half so big as they expected at any rate not too big to play with them. It frightens me sometimes when I think how much you expect of me but I can only do as well as I can. I always tell Miss Crocker that when I go somewhere else that I shall be a most perfect little body and she always insists upon it that I shall not be a bit better. I believe almost everything she says but I hall not

[Written along the left margin of page 3:] believe that till I learn it from experience.

Source: American Baptist Historical Society, AJ 10, no. 293.

[246] Jonathan and Deborah Wade were appointed as missionaries to Burmah in 1823. Adoniram Judson called them "his dearest and best of friends." Much of their work was spent with the jungle communities following the work of George Boardman. They returned to America on December 22, 1847, and returned to Burmah in January 1851, just as Emily was returning to the United States. They were from the Hamilton, New York, area. They returned to Burmah on July 25, 1850, and were in Maulmain by February 1851.

[247] Sarah Haven was the sister of Elizabeth Stevens, Emily's fellow missionary and dear friend. She was also the niece of Frances Wayland, who worked with Emily over the next several years to write the Judson memoir.

[248] See vol. 1, "Cast of Characters," s.v. "Judson, Abigail Brown."

[249] See vol. 1, "Cast of Characters," s.v. "Judson, Henry Hall."

[250] See vol. 1, "Cast of Characters," s.v. "Judson, Edward."

[251] See vol. 1, "Cast of Characters," s.v. "Judson, Emily Frances."

Emily C. Judson to Catharine Chubbuck, May 1851

I beg that you will never call the English cold-hearted any more [sic]. So far as I have seen here, they are *all* heart; and even you and Mrs. Stevens[252] could scarcely be kinder to me than six or eight of the prominent passengers on the *Tudor*.[253]

Source: A. C. Kendrick, *The Life and Letters of Mrs. Emily C. Judson*, 361–62.

Mrs. Maria Gager Ranney to Emily C. Judson, May 1, 1851[254]

My dear Mrs. Judson

I just begin to feel that I ought to have written you before for I this morning learned that Mrs. Stevens[255] has written three or four times. I have thought often of you and yours since I left you on the deck of the *Tudor*[256] and followed your course through the reckless ocean and in our little meeting you have been made the frequent subject of our prayers.

I was disappointed when your chits from Marsulipitan [sic] came to others and I received none, but I suppose your hands and heart were full of other matters of more importance. Perhaps however had you known I was still in Calcutta when your chits came you would have put in a line in the letter which Sarah Thomas received from the young lady under your charge. Don't you know I was detained six long weeks in that dreadful city, just because I could not get a passage in the ship. I think of it now at this distance of time with horror. The city of Calcutta to me was not agreeable to my feelings or my bilious tendencies, but I am better now ( ) our nice new airy house has quite set me up again. If I am to live in the East give me the climate of Maulmain. My little school is going nicely, never so well before. I have got a new teacher, and sent off the old one for his inefficiency.

I shall have to close with a great deal of love for you and the dear children.

Affectionately

Maria

[Written in the bottom margin of the address page:] P. S. Please try and have the gold ( ) the most elastic kind whatever it may cost, and a ( ) one end.

Source: American Baptist Historical Society, AJ 16, no. 665.

[252] See vol. 1, "Cast of Characters," s.v. "Stevens, Elizabeth 'Bessie.'"

[253] The *Tudor* is the ship on which Emily sailed from Calcutta to Liverpool beginning in February 1851.

[254] This letter is undated, and signed simply by "Maria." It is likely from Maria Ranney, for other correspondence reveals that she was in Calcutta for a period of time. She was there when the ship *Tudor* sailed; in the letter, she says she was there six weeks before she could book passage. With time to get back to Maulmain, May 1, 1851, is a reasonable date. The letter was certainly written in this time period.

[255] See vol. 1, "Cast of Characters," s.v. "Stevens, Elizabeth 'Bessie.'"

[256] Emily sailed from Calcutta to Liverpool, England on the *Tudor*.

Miss Cynthia Sheldon to Emily C. Judson, May 4, 1851—311 Walnut St., Philadelphia

Dear dear Emily,

Yours of Jan. came to hand, and the replies sent to the care of your agent in London—this was done some ten days since. Yesterday yours from Calcutta[257] came to hand. Would that you could know our feelings on such occasions—every word you say is weighed in the balance of hope—and with breathless anxiety we see the scale of *fear* rising but a little—then a little more hope preponderate you are again on ship board—we trust now nearing London—Oh that we could take a peep into to that [sic] 9 feet square cabin room—this Sabbath afternoon—see that weeks on the Ocean had given you strength—and the strong arm of the Lord upholding you with your dear charge, altogether leaning on that Almighty never failing support of him you so deeply mourn—we all mourn—yet as knowing his pure spirit is in glory—Our family are well—have mostly been to Church this morning although it rained a little then—now it is raining fast, preventing the well ones from going out—early morn was bright, my calculations were made for going to our own Church (three were baptized)—dining with the Gillettes,[258] and attending communion this aft'n—but not so—Mrs. Anable[259] and myself ventured to Sansom St. Chh this morn'g ( ) ( ) must suffice—If it should clear off I shall not dare walk it in the evening—We are to have an English Missionary from ( )—whom I should like much to hear—The twin Mission and Publication Societies hold their Anniversaries Tuesday and Wed'y evenings to give us a little spice of the Anniversaries just entering on in New York—Boston—some of the good Ministers are really expecting you will arrive there before the Meeting closes—but as I have before said—do let us know when the prospects are bright for meeting you as the boat lands, if we can know what boat—My plan is to stay while you stay in B.—then go with you as far as necessary, if even to your own cottage home in Hamilton—

[Written in the left margin of the address page:] I shall write to Catharine[260] this week in answer to a sweet letter received not long since—They will know my plan for meeting you—Anna M.[261] will join you in Hamilton when the school closes first of July—

Mary Anna Longstreth[262] called yesterday to enquire all about *our dear Emily* (as she always says in speaking of you) and had just gone before your letter came.

[257] See Emily Judson's letter to Anna Maria Anable dated February 16, 1851.

[258] See vol. 1, "Cast of Characters," s.v. "Gillette, The Reverend Abram Dunn."

[259] See vol. 1, "Cast of Characters," s.v. "Sheldon, Alma and Joseph Hubbell."

[260] See vol. 1, "Cast of Characters," s.v. "Chubbuck, Sarah Catharine."

[261] See vol. 1, "Cast of Characters," s.v. "Anable, Anna Maria."

[262] See vol. 1, "Cast of Characters," s.v. "Longstreth, Mary Anna."

Mrs. Robarts[263] came a few minutes afterward—she is all on tip toe about your future arrangements and comfort—she is sure most any thing [sic] can be done that you might wish—I think the same, but very gravely told her—

[Written in the right margin of the address page:] we all stood ready to help you carry out plans, all could be right—you must know dear E.—the hearts of the people are turned in your behalf "as the rivers of waters are turned"—Schenectady[264] even is in the current—do hope you will be able to see the Miniature World—do use your privilege which the God of providence has made peculiarly yours—the two fold [sic] weight of name—let it be sent to whom you will—and you will have attention—Baptist Noel—by all means, through him Victoria if you please—you may wish to shun rather than court attention—but material for use must be in the account—

[Written in the bottom margin of the address page:] Mr. Roberts[265] has been much in England—he wishes to serve you—I send this to his care in a letter his little daughter has written—If your time is taken up—he will tell us of your intended movements homeward—he will give you a note written before you sailed—do not disappoint Sarah Bell[266] about going to her house first—then to Mrs. Colby[267]—you will see by Sarah's note to you how[268] much she desires it. I am sure you must come in a Steamer—if not arranged for, do not hesitate taking the passage—it would be made up here, if the Board cannot do it—Mr. Roberts may assist you much in the matter.

All send love in abundance—Heaven uphold and comfort you ever—

Yours

C. Sheldon

Source: American Baptist Historical Society, AJ 20, no. 988.

[263] See vol. 1, "Cast of Characters," s.v. "Robarts, Mr. and Mrs. W. S."

[264] Schenectady was the home of Mrs. Urania Sheldon Nott and her husband the Reverend Doctor Eliphalet Nott, the president of Union College in that city. Mrs. Nott was the sister of Miss Cynthia Sheldon.

[265] See vol. 1, "Cast of Characters," s.v. "Roberts, E. G."

[266] See vol. 1, "Cast of Characters," s.v. "Wheeler, Sarah Bell."

[267] See vol. 1, "Cast of Characters," s.v. "Colby, Mary."

[268] See the letter from Sarah Bell Wheeler Gould dated April 8, 1851.

Miss Lydia Lillybridge to Emily C. Judson, May 11, 1851[269]

[Note: This portion of the letter came in the 922 file.]

Mr. Kincaid,[270] and Mr. Vinton[271] are at Rangoon and intend to spend the rains there. Mr. Dawson[272] has been, and is going again. No place for ladies there just at present—I presume you will hear particulars from some other one.

Source: American Baptist Historical Society, AJ 19, no. 924.

Miss Lydia Lillybridge to Emily C. Judson, May 11, 1851[273]—Maulmain, Burmah

O! Emily! My dear Emily!

I would have given worlds to have had you here during the week just past. It has been one of great excitement and vexation to me. I believe that there has been nothing equal to it since the days of Mrs. Howard.[274]

When I wrote you last month I thought that the public ceremony which is to fix my destiny for life would have been completed before this time. But Mr. Simons[275] has been ill ever since that time, and is now just getting strong again, and the affair will probably be finished in two or three days. But this delay is not what has vexed me.—Ever since the return of Mr. Simons from America I have heard over and over from various sources, that "his heart has always set on having a boarding school"—and almost everyone in the Mission seemed fixed in the belief that he *would* have one sometime or other, though he was sent back for the express work of *Burmese preaching*. Perhaps you know that having *charge* of a *boarding school* does not suit my fancy—and that the idea that I should be obliged if connected with him, has been one of the severe huge mountains in the way of my being married, for more than a year. (I mean all the time, a boarding school for Eurasians.)[276] Whether you know it or not, it is so; and for some months weeks [sic], I have been thinking that I should eventually become a fixture in this school if *I* acceded to Mr. Simon's proposals—I

[269] For an explanation on dating this letter, footnote on the date of the letter dated April 27, 1851, Miss Lydia Lillybridge to Emily C. Judson.

[270] See vol. 1, "Cast of Characters," s.v. "Kincaid, The Reverend Doctor Eugenio."

[271] See vol. 1, "Cast of Characters," s.v. "Vinton, The Reverend Doctor Justus Hatch and Calista."

[272] See vol. 1, "Cast of Characters," s.v. "Dawson, Doctor."

[273] This letter has an addendum dated May 22, 1851.

[274] Theresa Howard was born in New York; with her husband Hosea, she arrived in Burmah on December 26, 1834. They worked in Maulmain and Rangoon for sixteen years before sailing for the United States on February 28, 1850. Theresa Howard worked with her husband in the schools established by the mission. She died in Bloomington, Illinois on July 14, 1868.

[275] See vol. 1, "Cast of Characters," s.v. "Lillybridge, Lydia." Also, "A Timeline of the Life and Mission of Lydia Lillybridge Simons."

[276] While no reason is given for her making this distinction, in a letter written July 21, 1851, Lydia comments, "She is a Eurasian—very intelligent for one of that class."

therefore told him plainly and repeatedly, that I understood his wishes to be in regards to those things, and expressed to him my aversion to that particular charge—whereupon he assured me that he wished to have nothing to do with the school, and that I should not have anything to do with this, or any other school any further than I chose—that I might take my own course in regard to the choice of my work, and the manner of doing it, and that he would afford me every facility in his power. It was with this view of things that I consented to join Mr. Simons.[277]

Source: American Baptist Historical Society, AJ 19, no. 928.

Mrs. Phoebe Hough to Emily C. Judson,[278] May 20, 1851—Maulmain

My dear Mrs. Judson

I received your short note written from Calcutta and was thankful for it, though I should have liked to have heard more of your opinion of our friends the MacKays[279]—I know almost nothing of Mrs. MacKay—him you would be sure to like—I am almost daily thinking of your arrival in England, and what will be your feelings, parting perhaps because a few became dear from Christian sympathy and kindness during the voyage and meeting others unknown, and entering in strange and untried scenes—Then your arrival in your native land, under circumstances so ( )! I fancy all this, and pray that you may know the presence, and support, of the widow's God and feel assured that you will be sustained under every case, and trial—You must tell me every thing [sic] interesting about your voyage—whether you favored any acquaintances who ( ) ( ) ( ) and how your health was, and how the dear children fared and ( ) than this, let me know how England appears to you as compared with America and ( ) let me know all you can find to communicate.

The only *remarkable* event here is the marriage of Mr. Simons[280] and Miss Lillybridge.[281] It took everybody by surprise, for I hear she rejected him, so decidedly, that the ( ) of feeling which took place could not be accounted for—I think her reasons for so strange a step obvious enough. The Stilsons[282] are daily declining in health, and a change of house could not be far distant and other future changes must come. The school had become to her a laborious task without much to encourage her in the results and besides she labored under the direction of others, ( ) ( ) ( ) of feeling ( ) to unmarried ( ) of her age—A house and *independence* ( ) ( ) ( ) disadvantages appeared more

[277] Thomas Simons and Lydia Lillybridge were married shortly after this letter was written on May 11, 1851, and before the addendum of May 22, 1851.

[278] The blank spaces in the transcription of this letter are due to the wax seal, which bled through, obscuring two sections on each page.

[279] See vol. 1, "Cast of Characters," s.v. "MacKay, The Reverend W. S."

[280] See vol. 1, "Cast of Characters," s.v. "Simons, Lydia and Thomas."

[281] See vol. 1, "Cast of Characters," s.v. "Lillybridge, Lydia." Also, "A Timeline of the Life and Mission of Lydia Lillybridge Simons."

desirable than her present condition, and though the man she consented to take as a husband would not command her respect he might win her regard, by kindness and affection and he become her protector and I think we can never judge correctly in such cases as ( ) ( ) we ( ) know all the material which influence a woman's decision. Miss Lillybridge (Mrs. Simons) is a very good, amiable person but her education and her acquaintances with the world have not been such as to force her into comparisons unfavourable [sic] to her husband, and since she came to this country she has lived in families the head of which are not well polished in manners nor more refined in feelings than Mr. Simons—as I have said so much on this subject I shall leave Mrs. Stevens[283] and others to give you an account of the wedding.

The Wades[284] are exceedingly liked by the members of the Burmese Church and enter into the subject of pastoral care with much zeal—Mrs. Wade visits all the women, and looks into their moral and domestic condition, and as some of them have told me, *preached* to them in their own houses, which means that she talks, reads, and prays with them, which she has health, strength, and time to do as she has no children. Mr. Wade can never be an eloquent preacher, but will be a good pastor.

The Kincaids[285] left for Rangoon on the 12th of last month, and on their arrival met with most decided opposition—they were scarcely permitted to land their goods and when landed opposed at every step so that they scarcely obtained a house to shelter them. The gov. ( ) to put Mr. Kincaid in irons, and imprison him but Mr. K. is the last man in the world to be ( ) as to yield to threats even from Authority—He stood firm, and the result is permission from Ava, so the gov. says, to remain, and carry out his work unmolested. He does everything openly and without a shadow of concealment, and at the date of his last letter, had preached both in English and Burmese to both audiences.—"This is the Lord's doing and wonderful in our eyes." The Gospel may yet change that great moral desert into a fruitful field.

Mr. and Mrs. Thomas who arrived lately for the Tavoy Mission are rather interesting persons—Mrs. Thomas particularly—The American ( ) ( ) who came out as Missionaries are ( ) less polished than their wives and they may appear so from the fact that what we ( ) ( ) is ( ) simplicity and ( ) in a man awkward bashfulness. The "instruments" for Assam, which came out in the unfortunate *W. Allston*,[286] were certainly a credit to "*our country*"—you will hear of the bountiful provisions made by the Boston Committee for the Missionaries on that vessel. Putting all statements

[282] See vol. 1, "Cast of Characters," s.v. "Stilson, Lucretia and Lyman."

[283] See vol. 1, "Cast of Characters," s.v. "Stevens, Elizabeth 'Bessie.'"

[284] See vol. 1, "Cast of Characters," s.v. "Wade, The Reverend Doctor Jonathan and Deborah."

[285] See vol. 1, "Cast of Characters," s.v. "Kincaid, The Reverend Doctor Eugenio."

[286] The *Washington Allston* had left Boston on July 25, 1850, chartered by the American Baptist Missionary Union for passage of a large number of new and returning missionaries to Maulmain and India. Correspondence indicates a difficult passage with shortages of supplies. It was approaching Maulmain as Emily was departing for Calcutta. Here Emily indicates that the ship had moved on to Calcutta with the missionaries going to Assam.

together there appears to have been very gross neglect, as well as ignorance and parsimony—and no other blame could attach to the Captain short of taking a vessel out of Port with such a number of passengers, and such a deficiency of stores, and stock is enough to condemn him—common humanity should have made him insist on a proper precaution for his passengers, and common civility should have made him behave towards *all* of them with respect and attention—you were wise to go home in an English vessel where you are always sure of attention and comfort.

We go see the "( ) ( ) of our way" without any but the silent changes of time. George[287] has a ( ) ( ), and ( ) ( ) ( ) children the *noble* name of Hough not likely to be soon lost—Sally and all hers excepting her boy, were well when she last wrote—She was sending ( ) ( ) for a change.

I am reading the lines of Mrs. Fry, *the* Mrs. Fry, and her brother-in-law Sir T. T. Buxton and recommend them to you—A hundred women like Mrs. Fry would change the moral aspect of the world—In the first place God gave her the means of doing good, and in the second, His grace supplied the motive which directed her to use these means, and devote all the energies of body, and spirit, to his service. Buxton, you know, was one of the great leaders in the slave emancipation case and in revising the criminal code of England—He was the bosom friend of Wilberforce, and of others of that character.

We have a family staying with us who came in the steamer—Mr. Chase is to act in the ( ) here—Under such circumstances, I have really very little time for writing, and none for reading—I hope you will make all allowance for this hurried letter, and not act as

[Written in the top margin of page 1:] the tit for tat principle—your ( ) must of ( ) here—( ) while people are daily ( ) on some new ( ). Let me know how you find your children at home etc. etc. Mr. Hough ( ) we have and if Didd( ) were here she would send kisses to the children.

Yours very affectionately

Phoebe Hough

Source: American Baptist Historical Society, AJ 16, no. 662.

[287] George Hough was the husband of Phoebe Hough.

Mrs. Elizabeth L. Stevens to Emily C. Judson, May 20, 1851—Maulmain

My dear Sister

Mrs. Simons![288] is writing you a long letter and I can't help putting in a line to tell you how many more times than usual I have thought of "The Judsons" today because news came this morning of the dismasting of the "*W. Allston*"[289] in a hurricane which made two other ships off Mauritius at the time utter wrecks. I fear the *Saratoga* was in the same vicinity but we hear nothing of her having received injury. You were beyond that danger but how many others you may have experienced and may even now be in the midst of we cannot know. My poor darling how are you at this very moment? Worn out with anxiety and desolateness added to many aches? Sarah's[290] letter this mail is full of questions about you. You must go to F[ramingham] and answer them yourself. "Aunt Cynthia"[291] will hurry you to Phila. "Anna Maria"[292] will be waiting ( ) [Note: A section of the page is torn out, and the ends of eight lines are missing.] impatiently. I dare say you will stop in Boston a minute. ( ) ( ) what great difference will ( ) ( ) ( ) time make to them? None ( ) ( )ed with the difference it will ( ) make to me and my mother ( ) sister for you may not again be in their vicinity for years.

I wonder if Lydia has left anything for the rest of us to tell you about her affairs—I did so want you here to help part of the time. None of us here could influence her at all. It was a real trying time to us for a while. She had the "tantrums worst kind" because the brothers voted to request Mr. Simons to take that school after her employment. Mr. Stilson[293] has failed *very* much of late from dysentery, and when they found she was going, he and Mrs. S. felt unable to go on with the school. After the vote, she circulated the news that the affair was given up—sent back wedding presents—stopped preparations. You can imagine how she flounced about. We all patted her and coaxed and she consented to be married and then things went on nicely. She looked extremely well—quite a majestic bride as she walked up the aisle of the crowded Burmese chapel—a plain muslin dress and Mrs. Thomson's veil. She behaved well there and at the tea party at Mrs. Stilson's. Today it is a week and she

[288] Lydia Lillybridge and Thomas Simons married on May 13, 1851. See vol. 1, "Cast of Characters," s.v. "Lillybridge, Lydia." Also, "A Timeline of the Life and Mission of Lydia Lillybridge Simons."

[289] On July 25, 1851, the *Washington Allston* sailed from Boston for Burmah with a large group of new and returning missionaries under appointment of the American Baptist Missionary Union. It had been a disastrous trip according to the correspondence, and much of it the fault of the captian. Mrs. Hough's letter of May 20, 1851, reveals that there were too many passengers and not enough supplies, among other problems.

[290] Sarah Haven was the sister of Elizabeth Stevens, Emily's fellow missionary and dear friend. She lived in Framingham, Massachusetts, and wrote a number of times to Emily.

[291] See vol. 1, "Cast of Characters," s.v. "Sheldon, Miss Cynthia."

[292] See vol. 1, "Cast of Characters," s.v. "Anable, Anna Maria."

[293] See vol. 1, "Cast of Characters," s.v. "Stilson, Lucretia and Lyman."

commenced superintending schools after putting Mr. S's old deeds to right. Oh dear me! who'd a thought it. ( ) [Note: The bottom right corner of this page is torn away, and the bottom has a ragged edge. The endings of eight lines are lost, as are two complete lines at the bottom.] she came and told me she had said "( ) after *her week's final* deliberations" ( ) was *sure* she was in ( )—he can ( ) ( ) had seemed to increasingly offi( ) ( ) now believe it was *ordered* ( ) ( ) and will end well and I think ( ) ( ) ( ) on the course of time ( ) ( ) ( ) [Note: two lines are lost here] to ( ). She intends superintending the girls department and visiting other schools and going to native ( )—a good work may she be blessed in it.

As to housekeeping her servant says "She is Mrs. Hough's[294] Sister." I told her of it today with some advice about expecting too much of the poor lazy cheating creatures.

We enjoy Mr. and Mrs. Wade[295] *much* and we do hope the church is getting pretty good. He is just the thing for them to be pastor.

We get along nicely with Newton—no allusions made. Mr. V.[296] is seeming like himself again. Mr. ( ) is at Martaban and our Comm. is now Col( ).

We are all well and my baby[297] big and good.

Mary's[298] love to Edward[299]—and also from the rest [Note: the page is torn out here—the end of two lines and the signature is lost] ( ) ( ). Mr. Stevens[300] is making a trip to Amherst.

Most ( )

Source: American Baptist Historical Society, AJ 19, no. 901.

Mrs. Ellen H. B. Mason to Emily C. Judson,[301] May 21, 1851—Maulmain

My dear Sister Judson

We were rejoiced to hear that your health was improving and do pray earnestly that ( ) ( ) Father may smile upon you, and ( ) ( ) ( ) with his protecting being. How *peaceful* the soul that reposes in Him. And what bright visions of the upper world are given to those whose hearts are linked to heaven! Oh, that we might ever keep

[294] See vol. 1, "Cast of Characters," s.v. "Hough, The Reverend George and Phoebe."

[295] See vol. 1, "Cast of Characters," s.v. "Wade, The Reverend Doctor Jonathan and Deborah."

[296] See vol. 1, "Cast of Characters," s.v. "Vinton, The Reverend Doctor Justus Hatch and Calista."

[297] Henry Ripley Stevens was the son of Edward and Elizabeth Stevens, born April 3, 1851.

[298] Mary Stevens, daughter of Edward and Elizabeth Stevens.

[299] See vol. 1, "Cast of Characters," s.v. "Judson, Edward."

[300] See vol. 1, "Cast of Characters," s.v. "Stevens, The Reverend Edward and Elizabeth."

[301] The original of this letter was damaged by the wax seal bleeding through all of the pages, and this is responsible for the unusual number of lines and words lost.

a firm hold on those delicate cords flung down by God's angels to draw our lingering souls to Christ.

I felt much ( ) I assure you dear sister in being compelled to leave this pagan land around which your guardian angel's spirit will ever seem to linger, and where you would so gladly have spent the remainder of your days in teaching these wayward daughters of idolatry. But we do not know what purposes have been formed in the courts of the blessed—we cannot know what is designed for you to do yet in this glorious course. I often hear a whisper that you have a work to do in the Home Department! I mean among the [Note: A line is lost at the bottom of page 1, and seven lines are lost to the top of page 2.] which might listen to you of ( ) the cross and the great work of redemption which might not be accessible to the holy evangelical divine. I feel much for those great and noble minds which sit in such serene eminences that they are almost left without the ( ) of instruction. Oh, how much you may do by putting forth all your vigorous power for the gifted irreligious! Who can tell how many golden spirits may thus be won to the mission enterprise! I thought Mr. ( ) suggestion opportune when he called on *Christians to pray* particularly and earnestly for the conversion of Jenny Lind. Would that she might be brought and truly ( ), and her angelic powers of song be consecrated to the glorious work of mission. But I must close. Ellen[302] sends a little letter to Henry[303] and a great deal of love to Edward[304] and Emily[305] and Franky[306] says "tell them I love" [Note: Eight lines are lost at the top of this page.]

Ellen H. B. Mason

P.S. If you strike off any poetic effresions [sic] on your passage home and have such time to send me them, I shall feel great obliged. And if when you reach home you see Mrs. Robinson—"The most learned lady in America"—Doct. Robinson's lady, please tell me about her. I hope you will see Baptist Noel in England, and all the other good men.

Others will tell you the news so I leave that off my list. Indeed I am no great news-gatherer. What will you say to Lydia[307] now? I was very greatly ( ) towards ( ) ( ) she told me her decision.

Source: American Baptist Historical Society, AJ 17, no. 747.

[302] Ellen Bullard was born May 5, 1843; she was Mrs. Mason's daughter from her first marriage.

[303] See vol. 1, "Cast of Characters," s.v. "Judson, Henry Hall."

[304] See vol. 1, "Cast of Characters," s.v. "Judson, Edward."

[305] See vol. 1, "Cast of Characters," s.v. "Judson, Emily Frances."

[306] This was Francis Mason, born June 24, 1846, the son of Francis Mason and his second wife, Helen Maria Mason.

[307] See vol. 1, "Cast of Characters," s.v. "Lillybridge, Lydia." Also, "A Timeline of the Life and Mission of Lydia Lillybridge Simons."

Mrs. Lydia Lillybridge Simons to Emily C. Judson, May 22, 1851[308]

Though I had talked my plans over freely with Mrs. Stilson from time to time, telling her that I would assist thus and so in the school, if I should go, and she communicated the same to Mr. Stilson,[309] yet when he found that I had really decided the question affirmatively, and that I intended to go soon, seemed to be amazed; and began to talk about dismissing the boarding department altogether. It seems that he had thought that if I should accede to Mr. Simons's[310] proposals, I should stay until they could get another teacher, or at least until the end of the year. He called a meeting of the brethren to consult with them in regard to dismissing the boarders in the girl's department and I thought they would probably be dismissed—but, I believe that they thought it would be a disgrace to dismiss it, and as Mr. Stilson told them that he and Mrs. Stilson felt unequal to the task, they unanimously invited Mr. Simons in view of his proposed union with Miss Lillybridge to take the charge of the school. This vexed me exceedingly, for they knew some of them, if not all, the aversion that I felt to such a measure. If I could have imagined that such a thing would have come so soon, I should not have said yes at all, and then said, that if Mr. S. would give up the engagement I would stay in school till I was thoroughly gray—and indeed, I felt willing to stay *unmarried* but could not bring my mind to consent to take the charge I had so long had an aversion to, immediately upon being married. I really felt that the brethren did not treat me very handsomely, and the subject made quite a ferment among us. I must either go on and take the charge that (I) had resolved not to do, else be considered as acting in opposition to the united judgment of the *Mission*, and as causing my husband to do so too—for, though Mr. S. told them that he wished to have nothing to do with the school, they would think that it was only because I influenced him to refuse. Indeed, Mrs. Stevens[311] told me, that every body [sic] thought him just the man for the place, that if he did not or would not accept it he would be acting in opposition to the wishes of the Mission, the Board and every body [sic] else. Don't you see I had reason to be vexed?

The time for closing is come, and I cannot tell you the particulars about the wedding. It occurred on the 13th inst. at 6 o'clock at the Burmese Chapel—tea at Mrs. Stilson's.

[308] This letter is an addendum to a letter dated May 11, 1851.

[309] See vol. 1, "Cast of Characters," s.v. "Stilson, Lucretia and Lyman."

[310] See vol. 1, "Cast of Characters," s.v. "Lillybridge, Lydia." Also, "A Timeline of the Life and Mission of Lydia Lillybridge Simons."

[311] See vol. 1, "Cast of Characters," s.v. "Stevens, Elizabeth 'Bessie.'"

More next time—I have a letter for you from A. M. Anable[312]—unsealed—nothing very special.

Yours very affectionately

Lydia Simons

Source: American Baptist Historical Society, AJ 19, no. 928.

Emily C. Judson to Mrs. Elizabeth Stevens, May 26, 1851

Would you not be astonished to see me getting ready for a dinner party, three miles out of town, at the fashionable after-dark hour? They have a joke on board the ship that the fairies have changed me; for I am not the same person that came on board at Calcutta. And they are right. I am not fat yet, as you will readily believe, but my complexion is entirely changed, my appetite is enormous, and nothing that I can eat or drink does me the least harm. I did not improve much until we got in sight of land which was about five weeks before we actually landed. The first gale, which was frightful, nearly killed me while it lasted; but as soon as it was over, I came out a new creature, and from that moment up to this, I have been steadily improving. You never saw me when I was so well as I am now. Dear, good Captain Lay[313] watches my face and notices every change, and it is "now you have a head ache," or " I shall not ask you how you are this morning—your face tells," or "now you need this," etc. His kindness is almost incredible. Every morning after I got well enough to go on deck, he would come to my cabin door, and tell me whether I had better come out or not, what shawl to wear, etc., and during the gales, when we were all shut up in our darkened cabins, he took my boys[314] and Mrs. Thomas's[315] into his cabin to relieve us, and—but there is no use in trying to enumerate—he does every *thing* [sic]. His attentions to us who have no protectors, are not merely the attentions of a courteous gentlemanly commander, but the thoughtful watchfulness of a brother or husband.

Source: A. C. Kendrick, *The Life and Letters of Mrs. Emily C. Judson*, 361.

[312] See vol. 1, "Cast of Characters," s.v. "Anable, Anna Maria."

[313] W. J. Lay, Captain of the *Tudor*, the sailing ship that was taking Emily from Calcutta to England.

[314] Henry Judson, almost nine years old, and Edward Judson, almost six and a half years old.

[315] Mrs. Thomas was a fellow passenger on the *Tudor*. The two formed a bond with each other on the voyage.

Mrs. Olive Celina Harris to Emily C. Judson, May 29, 1851—Newton (in Burmah)

Dear Sister Judson,

Many days and even months have passed away since you left us for America, yet you have not been forgotten by us, especially when we have bowed around the mercy seat to ask for protecting care. We were too well acquainted with your outward bound to forget the homeward and often have I wished I could slip in [sic] to your cabin as I have been wont to do in days past in order that I might know more particularly concerning your prosperity. I am rejoicing in knowing that you are comfortably situated and hope you will realize more joy than you anticipated. Notwithstanding all your fine company and kind attentions yet you will have many gloomy hours and perhaps no confidential friend to whom you can breathe a word of sorrow. Well my sister though this may be the case yet you will not be comfortless because you can hold intercourse with a friend who has been touched in the feelings of our infirmities and knows how to hear our sorrows. Were it not for this dear friend I should despair of your being comforted. May the Lord protect you and the dear little ones in our prayers. Trust Sister Stevens[316] has kept you appraised of all the news since you left therefore I will not go into particulars. Our own family have been ill some of the time since you left though not seriously so. Judson had a very hard time with the scarlet fever in consequence of taking cold and I fear he will feel the effects of it for some time. Joseph has been very well until within a few days past he was troubled with those complaints. He is better now. Lydia is suffering from teething and looks rather thin. My own health is very good. The children[317] do not forget the little Judsons and want to see them very much.

The Vintons[318] have returned and appear very much as they used to. Br Vinton is not as well but sister V. I think is improved in health. They have the theol school and Sister V. is translating. Sister Wright's[319] health is very poor yet shoulders the whole charge of the school and Sis Miranda assists very little. Sis M. is translating and appears to have some classes in Karen. Our school has commenced and now numbers over one hundred scholars. So you see my sister that we shall have something to do this season. Br and Sister Grover are very well. They have a fine little boy and a school of thirty-five scholars. Thus far union and harmony seems to prevail

[316] See vol. 1, "Cast of Characters," s.v. "Stevens, Elizabeth 'Bessie.'"

[317] The three Harris children were Judson Wade, born June 18, 1845; Joseph Nathan, born April 22, 1847; and Lydia Amanda, born May 30, 1849.

[318] See vol. 1, "Cast of Characters," s.v. "Vinton, The Reverend Doctor Justus Hatch and Calista."

[319] See vol. 1, "Cast of Characters," s.v. "Wright, H. E. T."

[320] Joseph and Juliette Binney, missionaries to Burmah. They arrived in Burmah in April 1844. In 1845, Mr. Binney opened the theological school in Maulmain. They sailed to the United States from Burmah in April 1850. There is a single letter in the correspondence from Joseph Binney.

in our ( )ions. We have heard from Mr. Binney.[320] Mrs. B's health not much improved but br B was quite well. We fear they will never return. The Thomases arrived in April and went to Tavoy. We've since heard they were sick with fever.

[Written in the left margin of page 2:] I have learned that Brother Bonney is in Philadelphia. If you have any means of getting the box to their place do so but do not put yourself to any trouble.

[Written in the left margin of page 3:] We shall feel very anxious to hear of your arrival not only in England but in America. Now Sister let us know all about how you and the children have enjoyed the passage.

Affy yr O. C. Harris

[Written in the right margin of page 3:] Judson and Joseph wish to be remembered—both send love to your children.[321]

Source: American Baptist Historical Society, AJ 16, no. 687.

Emily C. Judson to Mr. Thomas,[322] June 1851—Atlantic Ocean

Alone Upon the Deep

The song is on my lip, Love,
The sunlight in my eye,
But there's a shadow at my heart—
I need not tell thee why;
For could I steal some fairy's power
To wing the upper air,
I'd look into thy heart and find
It's fellow nestled there.

Alone upon the deep, Love!—
The low winds softly call,
And solemnly, upon the waves,
Dark shadows rise and fall;—
I watch the twilight gathering round,
I list the billows' moan,
And wonder if thy heart, like mine,
Is desolate and lone.

[321] Henry Hall Judson, Edward Judson, and Emily Frances Judson.

[322] Mr. Thomas was the husband of Abby Grace Thomas, a fellow passenger with Emily on the ship *Tudor*, which was sailing from Calcutta, India, to England. Emily wrote this poem for Mrs. Thomas' absent husband.

I'll sing the song thou lovest,
        I'll kneel in solemn prayer;
—'Tis sweet to know the same high Power
        Hath both of us in care;—
I'll ask rich blessings on thy head,
        Then seek my silent rest,
And try to dream my pillow still
        Thy true and loving breast.

Source: Emily C. Judson, *An Olio of Domestic Verses*, p. 193–94.

Mrs. Charlotte Haberlin to Emily C. Judson,[323] June 3, 1851—Calcutta

My beloved Friend—

I have been longing for this moment ever since you left—and now that I know you will be within reach of a written communication and I sit down to give words to all that have for months filled my heart and mind for you and drawn me times without reminder to follow your track on the ( ) deep and send you my love's greeting with the dewy morn'y breeze and the soft evening breath—I feel as if I had better be silent—as if I should prefer this silent wordless sleep inward communion to my poor half intelligible, indifferently impressive mode of expression—and a want and desire I have often been sensible of ( )lands out more prominently than usual, that of a more perfect language to convey the energy of thought the glow of feeling the vividness and fullness of our soul's yearnings—the hidden blessings of experience to a sister being [Note: A line is lost here because of blurring.] you all the ( ) of hope and faith and comfort which the Lord plants along my lonely path thro' the wilderness and take my share of your cup of affliction—soothe your pains and tho' with a feeble hand it may be point to our ( ) glorious prospects—to the hope with like the midnight flame charts its constant progress and tells of its inward vitality in the darkest hour—and ends in rejoicing with you that we are every day nearing the port, with every vanishing hour approaching closer to the longed for—Eternity. O that we may get a deeper more lasting and all prevailing impression of Eternity—to our hearts and think speak and act more in reference to it. How it would lighten all burdens and temper all our feelings—tune our minds for its celestial strains. Dearest Friend accept the long delayed thanks for the welcome sweet messages you sent me from Masulipitan it made my heart *rich* and glad—and sad I fancied you suffering

[323] Mrs. Haberlin wrote in a tight handwriting style, and many of the words were not clearly written. The individual letters were undistinguishable.

and comparatively alone—at all events I know there was not a heart near that loved you as I do, that would have missed you with true affection tho' others may have done it better in other respects—how often since have I caught my imagination in making plans to follow you and perhaps be united again here ( ) in my work tho' I know perfectly what gulf lies between the plan and its fulfillment—and that our paths thro' this vale of imperfections must lie apart to meet in our heavenly home. I long now to hear from you, to learn how your dear form has borne all the trouble and fatigue and insomnia of the voyage—how your dear children quest thro' it. Emily[324] still clinging to your dress and looking like a frightened bird from under the protecting covering in the consciousness of perfect safety there? and sensible Henry[325] I trust he has given you satisfaction and him a comfort to you.

I have just seen the arrival of the *Tudor*[326] at the Cape mentioned in the paper with the addition "all well on board"—What would I not have given had there been one word to assure me of your well being—satisfactory tho' the other was in one respect—one little message to tell us how you fared, for we all often and often want to move out with the asking exclamation—I wonder where or how Mrs. Judson is—and vague and manifold muse the surmises and possibilities that present themselves to my mind affective ( ) soaring over the sunrise and alighting here and there bring back after all very unsatisfying accounts—By this time however I trust you are ( ) ( ) on firmer ground and more accessible to fond enquiries, of which I have a heart full—but I am sure you will anticipate them and answer them *fully*—I wish as fully as I would love to reach.—However your interest in all these members of the family whose hospitality you shared with me, reminds me to return to the time you left and give you a short history of what you remember of its ( ) striking features. Mrs. MacKay[327] when you left recovering from her late trial—remained for a considerable period in an indifferent state of health—her little girl however grew strong tho' no body [sic] would call her pretty, or make a favorite of her—she was more looked upon as an infliction and cause of Mrs. M's bad health, ( ) however has since mended considerably and with her Mama's better health and spirits little Annie enjoys more affection attentions she is beginning to show a more decided likeness to Jane. Mr. MacKay promotes his labors as usual with the additional self-imposed task of love in unbounded hospitality—we have usually been *alone*, if this word may be used at all—for we are a host in ourselves. At present we have four young people and officers with one interested and the other with his married wife, some remote

[324] See vol. 1, "Cast of Characters," s.v. "Judson, Emily Frances."

[325] See vol. 1, "Cast of Characters," s.v. "Judson, Henry Hall."

[326] Emily was sailing on the *Tudor*, a ship bound from Calcutta to Liverpool, England.

[327] Mrs. MacKay was the wife of the Reverend W. S. MacKay, who was a missionary for the Free Church of Scotland; he also edited the *Calcutta Review*, which Emily described as a prestigious magazine. Rev. MacKay was the first to inform Emily of Adoniram's death in his August 9, 1850, letter, and he also insisted that she stay with him and his wife while she was in Calcutta on her way to the United States.

acquaintance dating from the time of Mr. MacKay's residence—VanD( )land; the wedding is to take place from this house and Jane to be brides' maid. She talked of—no! it was begun before you left—Observatory is completed at least and the top of it affords a pleasant note in the Evenings to breathe more fresh air, raised above all the neighborhood; the instruments are not put up yet and we are all expectations to look on the glorious stars. The *Calcutta Review*[328] has got a rival in a *Calcutta Quarterly*—which with a wider range of ( ) subjects and light literature will not easily interfere with the field of the *Review.*—for which it becomes more and more difficult to find writers—Mr. M. has been thinking of resigning the Editorship—the Free Church Institution goes on as usual flourishing—tho' no conversions have taken place of late. There have been several ( ) ( ) with the London Miss Society which have occasioned a great consternation amongst the native gentlemen, who called a meeting to deliberate on the means to prevent the spread of Christianity—they ( ) however found that it would be no easy matter and confessed that not much can be done. One zealous member proposed to give up English Education, which was the root of this evil—but with almost one voice he was put down—what shall we do without English—if it is not the way to ( ) bliss hereafter it is the road to wealth and riches! but the arguments proved all overwhelming—to open schools equal to the missionary institutions was ( ) proposition made and abandoned for want of funds—and the third means debated on, was an easier process that has hither-to been informed by the ( ) to ( ) ( ) into the Hindu communion as had left its tenets for a time—After much deliberation it was agreed upon to change the hard ( ) of 12 years solitary banishment into a ( ) of money—after which the president with rather a worried smile put the question for whom in fact they had been legislating and if double apostates were worth the trouble of being taken back with so much ( )—I suppose this effort has exhausted all the active orthodoxy and patriotism and every thing [sic] will flow on its apathetic stagnant morning—O that the Lord would rush His spirits [sic] breath at last and make the dawn for this poor country. Native female education progresses slowly and quietly—another school is to be opened to assist in its spread—a normal school for training teachers to make them available for any Nature you may prefer ( ) tuition for the females of his family—I'm still continuing under my trying charge hoping for deliverance; of our endeavoring to ( ) my mind into not prescribing the how and when, but to wait and be still and be faithful with the entrusted talents. From my dear treasures at home I am thoughtful to say I continue to receive ( ) ( ) my sweet little girl does my heart good with her feeling endearing little sayings—her deeply personal recollections of her sainted Papa—the signs of the Spirit's work in her heart and tender conscientiousness with which she lately confessed to me that she had been telling some untrue words in fun to her little brother to make him believe some little nonsense—

that she had since felt it was wrong and would not do it again. My eldest goes on vigorously with his studies and is all pleasure and energy in his work and at the same time acting Papa. O how my heart often longs—to see them and serve them and give some expression to the tenderness the desire to devote myself to them and to feel the return of their affection; my sister acts in this respect a singularly faithful part, directing all their interest and feeling—and putting all ( ) ( ) in reference to my pleasure and displeasure so that in all they do they live as it were with me.—Mary and Wally MacKay have now begun regular lessons with one of the young converts. I wish much for Mr. M's comfort they would be sent to Scotland—Mr M's 2nd daughter and Mr M's eldest are likely to move out at the end of the year, I suppose you will see them before. Mr. M's eldest son Ogilair [sic] has just returned here on account of a severe attack of illness which has caused much anxiety to his mother, he is very delicate and seems unlikely ever to be able to stand this climate. I feel much for him.

One party that occupied your apartment was a strange couple—Dr. and Mrs. Poor missionaries from Ceylon and countrymen of yours—they have been about 30 years in Ceylon and have grown quite original—they seemed as if of an antiquated race and other generation; his graciousness of speaking—public ( ) much hilarity and made at all events lasting impressions—I trust for good when the comical tinge has worn off.—All the missionary friends here, whom you saw during your stay are well—Mrs. MacKay sends her love to you and would have written if not in such which ( ) calls on her time and strength. Mr. Cauble and Jane join in affectionate remembrance the former is now very strong—Mr. MacKay no doubt will write himself soon. Please give my kisses to your dear children and tell them not to forget their former land. I must bid farewell to you my loved Friends—another grateful kiss for the sweet little ( )—Angel Charlie [sic], you and ( ) in your lad—I do share your feelings on the subject, dearest Friend. God bless you—let us cling closer and closer to Him, who loves better than any friend and ( ) closer than any brother can, loves better than father and mother; let us take His own promises to Him, remind Him of our right to expect what our Lord and Saviour [sic] has worked out for us with his blest

Written perpendicular to the text on page 5: and not ( ) Him until He bless and give us Himself and all with Him; May He bless richly your ( ) over all and make us all much ( ) ( ) ( ) before Him. Rememberance dearest Friend where your path may lead I trust you finish first the ( ) ( ) ( ) providing for you and yours—How I long to see your ( ) again. Where may you be?

Adieu
Ever yours in the ( ) ( )

Charlotte Haberlin

Source: American Baptist Historical Society, AJ 16, no. 685.

George Dana Boardman to Emily C. Judson, June 15, 1851—Brown University

My dear Mother,

About a month since I wrote you a letter which I directed to London:[329] but some time [sic] after I had sent it, I was reading over your letter again, and noticed that I had made a mistake in the direction of my letter. For "( ) ( )" I read ( ) ( ) and for "Can( ) St." I read Cannon St.: and so I am afraid that you will never receive the letter. I hope this may reach you in season.

I cannot but hope that joyous days are before us. I know that it must have been a sad hour when you felt that it was your duty to suspend your missionary labors. Still, mingled with the assurance that it was your duty, the thought that you were about to return to your native land must have cheered you, and made the sacrifice less painful. And now while you are on the wide ocean, I can sympathize with you in your happy prospects. Nor is the prospect happy to you alone: be assured, dear Mother, that I long, I am afraid impatiently, to welcome you home. I long ( ) to speak the name, *mother*. I long to have one to whom I can tell my joys and sorrows, of whom I can ask advice, and to whom I may fondly hope, I may be an affectionate and dear son. With the blessing of Heaven, I hope to see our widely scattered family united in a quiet and happy home.[330] Heaven grant that this delightful prospect may be realized. I do not know how this will be. It is not in man to direct his footsteps. If there be anything which I can do to secure this dearest object of my earthly wishes, I shall not leave it undone.

Since the day when we parted, you, dear Mother, have been called to pass through many fiery trials. But He, who knows how to "temper the wind to the shorn lamb" has graciously sustained you. It has afforded me the sincerest comfort to know, that when God's hand was heaviest upon you, your trust was still in Him. I fervently pray that He who has thus far sustained you in the darkest hours, may ever be to you more than you have ever lost.

You will be delighted to learn that dear Elly[331] now gives great evidence of being a child of God. Dear fellow, he is very conscientious, and strives hard to be a faithful

[328] This was a paper published by the Reverend W. S. MacKay.

[329] On her return from Burmah, Emily reached London in August 1851 and sailed for America toward the end of September; she arrived October 1, 1851.

[330] George Dana Boardman had been returned to America at the age of six, shortly after his mother, Sarah Hall Boardman, married Adoniram Judson. He never saw her again. All of his life, he was cared for by those who loved him and yet who were also strangers. It was Sarah's choice that he not stay with family members as she felt they would be too indulgent with him. He would have seen Adoniram and then Emily briefly at the end of 1845 and the beginning of 1846, and then when they left, he never saw Adoniram again.

Regarding the future of the Judson children (George Dana Boardman, Abby Ann, Adoniram, Elnathan, Henry, Edward, and Emily Frances), see volume 1, "A Timeline of the Children of Adoniram Judson and Their Desire to Be a United Family."

[331] See vol. 1, "Cast of Characters," s.v. "Judson, Elnathan 'Elly.'"

Christian. I received a letter from him the other day which I shall keep as rich trust for you. He will probably be baptized as soon as it is convenient after your arrival. I am sorry that I cannot tell the same cheering news about brother Addy.[332] I sincerely hope that the Christian influence of his younger brother will not be lost upon him. I hear that there is an extensive revival in Haverhill, the town adjoining Bradford, but I have not learned yet whether sister Abbie[333] is one of the happy converts. It cannot be that the child of so many prayers should long persist in refusing to give her heart to the Savior. How glorious it would be, if all the children here should be prepared to exert upon the little ones coming with you, the sacred influence of Christian examples.

Mr. and Mrs. Haswell[334] have been spending the past week in Providence. They hope to set sail by October. Mrs. Binney[335] is coming here in a few days to make a visit: I am very anxious to see her.

As vacation is drawing near (the term closes in four weeks,) if you should write me from London, please to direct to the care of Dr. Newton[336] at Worcester. I presume you may meet in London, my American friends who have gone to attend the world's fair. At any rate, don't stay long, for we are very anxious to see you. Do write me if possible from London, and tell me your plans as far as they are determined, for I shall try to regulate my own course by your plans. If there be anything I can do for you, tell me the whole of it; and I will most gratefully do it. Do lean upon me as a most affectionate son. I have a thousand things to tell you when you come, but it ( ) them to put them on paper. Kiss the dear little ones for me, and tell them about their elder brother, who often thinks of them, and tenderly loves them, and longs for them; and accept for yourself the sincere and warmest love [Note: "Affections" is crossed out, and "love" is written over it.] of

Your affectionate Son

Geo. Dana Boardman

Source: American Baptist Historical Society, AJ 11, no. 407.

[332] See vol. 1, "Cast of Characters," s.v. "Judson, Adoniram Brown 'Addy.'"

[333] See vol. 1, "Cast of Characters," s.v. "Judson, Abby Ann."

[334] James Madison Haswell was born February 4, 1810, in Bennington, Vermont. He was married to Jane Matilda Mason of Cheshire, Massachusetts. The Haswells sailed for Burmah on September 23, 1835, to work with the Talaings. They arrived at Amherst in February 1836. The Haswells became partners with Adoniram and Sarah Hall Boardman Judson; Sarah turned over the translation of the Peguan scripture to Mr. Haswell after Elnathan and Adoniram were born, and her energies were focused elsewhere. When Sarah and Adoniram sailed for America in 1845, the Haswells took care of Henry until Adoniram returned in 1847 with Emily. The Haswells left Burmah in December 1848 and arrived in America in 1849; they remained in the United States until September 1852, when they again sailed for Burmah.

[335] Juliette Binney arrived in Burmah in April 1844. Her husband was Joseph Binney, who opened the Karen Theological School in Maulmain for training indigenous pastors for the Burmese Church. They both worked in establishing general education possibilities for the Burmese people. She returned to the United States in 1850 because of her health. He returned in 1859, moving the seminary to Rangoon.

[336] See vol. 1, "Cast of Characters," s.v. "Newton, Doctor Calvin and Mrs. M. I."

Mr. Thomas Ranney to Emily C. Judson, June 21, 1851—Maulmain

My dear Mrs. Judson

I am certainly guilty of a fault on not having written to you before now. I have been hoping for a month to get in the little balance still due so that I could square up our accounts—but I am not yet able to do it, as our brethren have only had enough lately to defray current expenses. After a few things had been taken by Mr. Stevens[337] and others, brother Wade[338] took all that remained in the house, and gave me one hundred rupees. I don't know who had the best bargain, but at the same time the Amer. Ship was here, and I was so fully occupied that I could not attend to the removal and sale at Auction, and if I had, I doubt whether a larger amount would have been realized. Mrs. Ranney's[339] trip to Calcutta did her good, but she had a sorry time of it, being compelled to wait a whole long month because unable to get a passage on the trunk steamers [sic]. We are both delighted with our new house, but a thought of someone often comes up when we think of the time when we were proposing to be neighbors in our new dwellings. How dark and unknown the future! Who would have supposed that in one short year such distances were to separate us as the world of heaven, and the setting suns? Our ways and our interests are in the hands of the Lord, and all is well.

Still our little circle changes—Lydia[340] is no longer a [Note: There is a word here in the Burmese language.], nor a [Note: There are several words here in the Burmese language.], but an [Note: There are several words here in the Burmese language.]. There are some points about this ( ) not quite pleasant to speak of, for which I am really sorry. I will say to you a word or two about them only. Lydia it was understood contemplated leaving the school entirely when married, and required a sort of pledge that Simons[341] would not take the school if she took him. And it so happened that the Mission, on being consulted, saw no other way, to secure the prosperity of the school other than of putting Mrs. Simons into it. They with great unanimity invited Mr. Simons, before he was married, to take charge, and relieve br. Stilson,[342] who, with Mrs. S., is dying by inches. About a month after the marriage, br. S. gave his answer, declining to take the school, and we have referred the matter to the Ex. Committee. I am not sure that Mr. Simons' refusal arises from Lydia's dislike altogether. Indeed I am inclined to think not. I do not believe he would be willing to engage in any thing [sic] involving the necessity of removal from his *too much* loved dwelling. I should say they are both equally averse to the under-

[337] See vol. 1, "Cast of Characters," s.v. "Stevens, The Reverend Edward and Elizabeth."

[338] See vol. 1, "Cast of Characters," s.v. "Wade, The Reverend Doctor Jonathan and Deborah."

[339] See vol. 1, "Cast of Characters," s.v. "Ranney, Thomas and Maria."

[340] See vol. 1, "Cast of Characters," s.v. "Lillybridge, Lydia." Also, "A Timeline of the Life and Mission of Lydia Lillybridge Simons."

[341] See vol. 1, "Cast of Characters," s.v. "Simons, Lydia and Thomas."

[342] See vol. 1, "Cast of Characters," s.v. "Stilson, Lucretia and Lyman."

taking. This I think peculiarly unfortunate, as both are better fitted to the work of school teaching than any thing [sic] else, and the Exec. Com. will dislike to require them to what they themselves dislike. Lydia has imbibed a notion that she can be more useful in stimulating, overseeing and frequently visiting the Day Schools, and this is well, so far as it goes. In fact the Mission have no claim whatever upon her now, as she has entered into a new relation, but we feel to regret that she could not have seen it to be her duty to urge instead of discourage br. Simons from engaging in the Boarding School. I mention this much to you as her friend, and as still sympathising [sic] in our difficulties and trials, but do not let what I have said work to the injury in any way whatever of Lydia, whom I esteem as highly as ever.

Affec Yours

Thos Ranney

Source: American Baptist Historical Society, AJ 18, no. 820.

Doctor Edward Bright, Jr. to Emily C. Judson, June 30, 1851—Boston

My dear Mrs. Judson:—

We shall look with much anxiety for the tidings of your arrival in London. It is possible that our Dr. Peck[343] who leaves bound for Liverpool in the *Europa*, on Wednesday the 8th ( ) may meet you in London, on his way from Liverpool to Paris. We all hope it may be so. But as his chief object in leaving home is to visit the French and German Missions, he will be under the necessity of spending only a short time in London before proceeding to the Continent. In the event of your not seeing Dr. P. our agent, Mr. Symon, will do all in his power to meet your wishes, and to facilitate your return to this country. I trust you will not fail to take passage for this part. Many hearts and homes will be open to receive you and yours.

The arrangements for the Memoir[344] have all been suspended agreeably with your request. When you come I doubt not it will be found practicable to adopt a course which will secure a biography, of the highest order. No individual has been appointed to prepare the work;—all thought it desirable to delay the appointment until after your arrival.

Favor us with early intelligence of your arrival in London, and of the effects of the voyage upon your health, and believe me to be

Affectionately yr. brother,

Edw. Bright, Jr.

Source: American Baptist Historical Society, AJ 14, no. 543.

[343] See vol. 1, "Cast of Characters," s.v. "Peck, The Reverend Doctor Solomon."

[344] The proposed memoir of Adoniram Judson was eventually written by Dr. Francis Wayland, the president of Brown University in Providence, Rhode Island. Emily Judson worked with him on collecting the materials for it.

Letters

July–September 1851

Mrs. Elizabeth "Bessie" Stevens to Emily C. Judson, July 16, 1851—Maulmain

My dear Sister,

As you may suppose from the date we are today watching the flagstaff and thinking of home. I have counted the months and cannot but hope we may hear of you from the Cape. I have so many things to say to [sic]! But when can I write them? I am now, can you fancy it? quite a "keeper at home" and act the school ma'am all day long, as busily as though I were a believer in the doctrine. "*Delightful*! task!" When I could not find Eddy[1] home I knew I must set myself vigorously at work—besides, Sarah[2] *will* keep growing tall, and Emma and Mary[3] ought, at least, to know their a-b-c-and d. Once a week I go over to sit an hour or two with poor, dear Mrs. Stilson.[4] She sends over the same old hippy poney [sic] you used to (ride). She is *very* much weaker than when you left—has given up the *hope* I wrote you of—her feet are swollen—her mouth sore and altogether *I* think her symptoms those of an approaching termination of her ( ) with us. Would you suppose it of one so good? She doubts her preparation for heaven—that gives me some hope she will not ( ) be taken—I believe her ( ) will [Note: One line is lost at the bottom of the page, and two lines are lost at the top of page 2.] ( ) bright. We now have our prayer meetings regularly in her sick room as we used to do in yours. Our day is changed to Thursday to accommodate Mrs. Wade[5] who feels too weary to attend Wednesdays after having the women with her all the early part of the day. Besides ( ) going to Mrs. Stilson I go about once a fortnight to Newton. You know I sort of feel the case

[1] Edward Stevens was the son of Elizabeth and Edward Stevens; he was born on December 17, 1838.

[2] Sarah Stevens was the daughter of Elizabeth and Edward Stevens; she was born on December 3, 1840.

[3] Emma and Mary Stevens were the daughters of Elizabeth and Edward Stevens.

[4] Lucretia Brownson was married to Lyman Stilson on August 20, 1837, and both sailed for Burmah on October 28, 1837, along with the Bennetts and the Stevens. Mr. Stilson returned to America after Lucretia Stilson's death on August 14, 1851. Mrs. Stilson had been quite ill for some time, and the board had authorized her to return to the United States, but as reported in the newsletter of the missionary union, "she has been removed to a better country." They worked with Adoniram Judson for thirteen years and with both Sarah Hall Boardman Judson and Emily Chubbuck Judson.

[5] Deborah Wade was a missionary to Burmah; with her husband Jonathan, they were appointed in 1823. Adoniram Judson called them "his dearest and best of friends." Much of their work was in the jungle communities following the path of George Boardman. They left for the United States on December 22, 1847. From the Hamilton, New York, area, they stayed not far from the home of Emily's parents and sister; they visited the Anable-Sheldon families in Philadelphia. With a large group, they had left Boston on July 25, 1850, and returned to Burmah in February 1851.

of Mrs. Moore[6] and my grandson Charles John, who is a frail wee bit of a boy—and then poor Miss Wright[7] thinks it so kind in anybody to go and sit with her. I go there for an hour or 2 besides calling at Mrs. K's[8] and Mrs. H's. It is about two months that Miss W. has *been entirely* confined to the house and lately she has been able to sit up but little. She received some internal injury from over exertion 10 years ago and after suffering 4 or 5 years from it thought herself cured [Note: Several lines are lost at the bottom of the page.] again by riding on ( ) on an elephant. I do not know what the injury was and am not sure whether Dr. M.[9] has told what ( ) has suffered the inflammation. She still hears 6 or 7 recitations daily, in her rocking couch, but suffers very much—( ) state of mind is interesting—willing to suffer—ready to go home or to the grave as the will of the Lord is.

I do not go to see Mrs. Simons[10] often for fear of trespassing on her time. I could not think of attempting to tell you what wonderful strokes of business are going on—schools without number—new plans—sewing—English etc. One school on each veranda of the Welsh palace—one begun before the rest of us are up. I find that one would not wish to go where there was so much bliss that the sight of an old friend could not add to it. It would all be very amusing and delightful to us to see so much usefulness and happiness if we could keep good natured about it that so much strength and energy should not be expended when it is so much needed, now. Mr. and Mrs. Stilson are so feeble—L. is just the wife for Mr. Simons—but dear me ( ) are too many other things to say to go on with this. [Note: A line is lost at the bottom of the page.]

Source: American Baptist Historical Society, AJ 19, no. 894.

[6] Elizabeth Moore was the wife of William Moore. They departed Boston on November 3, 1847, and arrived in Calcutta on March 18, 1848. Their work was with the Karens in Burmah, near Maulmain. Mr. and Mrs. Moore returned to the United States and arrived in Boston on December 19, 1853.

[7] Hannah Elizabeth Taylor Wright was born September 21, 1820, in Nelson, New Hampshire. She was appointed in 1849 to serve as a teacher at the Karen Normal School in Maulmain, Burmah. She sailed from Boston on October 18, 1849, and arrived in Maulmain on March 18, 1850. She returned to the United States on account of her health on June 29, 1852. In July 1858, she married the Reverend Lyman Stilson, missionary to Burmah. Lucretia Stilson, his first wife, had died in Maulmain, Burmah, on August 14, 1851. Lyman and Hannah Wright Stilson had two sons, Charles and Edwin. Lyman Stilson died in Jefferson, Iowa on March 23, 1886; Mrs. Hannah Stilson died in Jefferson, Iowa, in March 1898. There is one letter in the correspondence from Miss Wright. Writing from Newton, Massachusetts, in July 1853, she sent Emily flowers that she "thought had bloomed to shed their fragrance in a sickroom."

[8] Mrs. Eugenio Kincaid, who was working at Ava.

[9] Doctor Morton was a physician who worked with the missionaries in Maulmain, Burmah. He delivered Emily Frances Judson in December 1847 and was present when Charles Judson ("Angel Charley") was stillborn in April 1850. He was a valued and trusted advisor to the mission families.

[10] Lydia Lillybridge was one of Emily's closest friends at the Utica Female Academy. When Emily made the decision to go to Burmah as the wife of Adoniram Judson and as a missionary, Lydia wanted to go with them. Emily spoke to Adoniram Judson of Lydia's extraordinary abilities, and Adoniram advocated her appointment before Dr. Solomon Peck and the Board of the American Baptist Missionary Union. Lydia was commissioned to go with them, in spite of the fact that she remained single. Always independent, outspoken, and unafraid to cause ripples in the missionary community, Lydia served on the mission field for twenty-eight years. She married missionary Thomas Simons in May 1851. See the timeline on the life and service of Lydia Lillybridge Simons in vol. 1.

Mrs. Elizabeth "Bessie" Stevens to Emily C. Judson, July 18, 1851

The *Tennessarin* [sic] brought no tidings of you as I hoped. A letter from Edward's Uncle Ripley spoke of the kind reception which awaits you from Christian friends at home. Let Sarah[11] know as soon as you reach Boston and she says she will go there immediately. She wrote me of Mr. Gillette's[12] sermon with Miss Reeves letter and poetry.[13] You wont [sic] want me to talk over things with, when you get to "*your own*"—yet there are some things I fancy I could understand and enter into, better than they even. I shall much wait to know if you have a trying time about the Memoir[14] and if your poor dear crushed heart is bruised anew by difficulties about the children. Oh I do hope Abby[15] will be a comfort to you. The way looks "great and desolate before you but I do believe the Lord will be better to you than your fears—remember how you dreaded Calcutta and how much later [Note: The last lines of the letter are lost.]

Source: American Baptist Historical Society, AJ 19, no. 894.

[11] Sarah Haven was the sister of Elizabeth Stevens, Emily's fellow missionary and dear friend. She lived in Massachusetts and wrote a number of times to Emily.

[12] Following several successful pastorates, the Reverend A. D. Gillette was the founding pastor of the flourishing Eleventh Baptist Church in Philadelphia in 1839. With his wife Hannah and several children (they would eventually have six), he graciously opened their home to Emily Chubbuck when she came to Philadelphia at the end of March 1845 for her health. The connection had been made through Miss Cynthia Sheldon, a family friend of Mr. Gillette and his parents. A prominent Baptist, Mr. Gillette journeyed to Boston in December 1845 to accompany Adoniram Judson to Philadelphia for meetings, and on Christmas Day, he introduced Dr. Judson to Emily Chubbuck with the hope that Fanny Forester could be persuaded to write the memoir of Sarah Hall Boardman Judson. A. D. Gillette and his wife Hannah remained valued and trusted friends, not only with Emily, but with the Sheldon and Anable families. He moved from Philadelphia to New York in 1852.

[13] We believe this to be Miss Rebecca Rhees. Miss Rhees was enamored with Adoniram Judson, and there are five letters in the correspondence from Miss Rhees to him. In one of them she wrote that she had attended Mr. Gillette's church and was heart-broken when, while reading a letter to the congregation from Judson, there was no mention of a special greeting to Miss Rhees. In 1846 Rebecca Rhees wrote a poem, "Farewell to Judson," which she included with a letter. That poem resurfaced after Judson's death and was to be published in 1852. For more information see vol. 1, "Cast of Characters," s.v. "Rhees, Rebecca Ann or 'Bessie.'"

[14] The pending memoir of Adoniram Judson was written by Dr. Francis Wayland, president of Brown University in Providence, Rhode Island.

[15] Abby Ann Judson, the first daughter and oldest child of Adoniram and Sarah Hall Boardman Judson, was born September 26, 1835. She saw her mother die on the Isle of St. Helena as they returned to the United States from Burmah. Just before leaving for Burmah with Emily, Adoniram Judson placed Abby Ann at Bradford Academy for her education. The family of Ann Hasseltine Judson was generous to Abby Ann and supportive of her interests and her future. On October 15, 1851, Abby Ann started a course of study at the Misses Anable's School in Philadelphia, and in fall 1853, she moved to New York City to take a teaching position in the home of Mrs. Maria Brown, a former missionary to Siam. She enjoyed a warm relationship with Emily, and her letters show that the two could speak freely with each other.

Mrs. Lydia Lillybridge Simons to Emily C. Judson, July 21, 1851—Maulmain

My dear Emily,

Do you remember that you used to tell me that if you were in my place you should like to have the superintendence of all the day schools? Well, I have as much of that kind of work now as I can attend to. There is the school at Dine (?) Woon Quin with from sixty to seventy-five pupils that come to me, some of them, every week, and the others once in two weeks—The School at Mapoon consisting of about a dozen boys and as many girls that have lately entered; I visit about once in two weeks, and they will come to me about as often. You know, I suppose, that there have never been any girls in that school because the teacher had no wife. Lately through the efforts of Mr. and Mrs. Wade,[16] the Burmese assistants, and my own, these twelve have been induced to attend, and they are learning finely. I took some sewing down for them one day and engaged Mary Ann Rawlinson one of our old school girls who lives near, to teach them sewing an hour every day. This sewing, I suppose you know, is one of the greatest inducements for them to come to school.

For the last month I have had from twenty to thirty pupils here at my own home, learning on my back veranda—pupils that have never had any Christian instruction before. I got most of them by going from house to house inviting them to come, and hope to make it a permanent and efficient school. Frances Roohe from the boarding school, assists me from 9 o'clock till 3. I have the children an hour before breakfast and teach them myself.—Jessie and Jane Cotton are the principal assistants in the female department of the boarding school. I go there once a week to hear their review lessons, and to encourage the pupils. Some of them, Capt. Crisp's children in particular, wished to leave soon after I came away; but I tried to make them think that Jessie was a very good teacher—and she is, really so. But she will be married I suppose at the close of the year, and then the school will go down probably if some one [sic] is not sent by the Board to take charge of it. Poor Mrs. Stilson[17] is beat just out of her grave, and he too.—She is obliged to be carried to and from the carriage when she drives though she can walk about the room a little.

[16] Jonathan and Deborah Wade were appointed as missionaries to Burmah in 1823. Adoniram Judson called them "his dearest and best of friends." Much of their work was spent with the jungle communities following the work of George Boardman. They returned to America on December 22, 1847, and returned to Burmah in January 1851, just as Emily was returning to the United States. They were from the Hamilton, New York, area. They returned to Burmah on July 25, 1850, and were in Maulmain by February 1851.

[17] Lucretia Brownson and Lyman Stilson were married August 20, 1837, and they sailed for Burmah on October 28, 1837, along with the Bennetts and the Stevens. Mr. Stilson returned to America after Lucretia Stilson's death on August 14, 1851. Mrs. Stilson had been quite ill for some time, and the board had authorized her to return to the United States, but as reported in the newsletter of the missionary union, "she has been removed to a better country." They worked with Adoniram Judson for thirteen years and with both Sarah Hall Boardman Judson and Emily Chubbuck Judson.

We are trying to get up a new school at Noeing [sic] ( ) village. The wife of the assistant there has lately been baptized and began teaching last week with seven girls. She is a Eurasian—very intelligent for one of that class—dresses in the Malay style. She was formerly the mistress of an Eng. officer who used to send the ( ) and pray with her every night before retiring—and she considers him as the means of her [Note: This is the last line of the page, and just over half of it is lost to a tear.]

[Written in the bottom margin of the address page:] but she looks upon her former practice with great abhorrence, more so, Mrs. Wade says, than any one [sic] she has ever met with—I have been trying to have Caroline Forster get up a little school and teach in her mother's house—She got the promise of sixteen but only seven have been. I am going ( ) with her from house to house, so she if I [Note: Two thirds of this bottom line is lost.] them to come

[Written in the left margin of the address page:] [Note: Two thirds of this line is lost because of the torn edging.] meeting—(she has all the ( ) ( ) ( ) ( ) neither have I been out to call on anyone. I had a joyous escape the other day—Mrs. Hough[18] invited all of the Missionaries except ( ) ( ) ( ) to tea. Mrs. Stevens[19] will tell you everything curious or interesting.

[Written in the center section between pages 2 and 3:] I have now been here less than two months and have never been so much ( )ied since I have been in this country. I have not been out to tea or to

[Written along the left and top margin of page 1:] ( ) as much work here, I suppose as I should at Amherst. It seems ( ) ( ) like "( ) ( ) work," than teaching English, but still I think it a good thing to teach these Eurasians English as well as Burmese. But the time has nearly come for them to be taught in day schools.

Affectionately Yours

Lydia Simons.

Source: American Baptist Historical Society, AJ 19, no. 928.

[18] George and Phoebe Hough were the first missionaries to be wholly called by the American Baptist Missionary Union to work in Burmah with Adoniram and Ann Judson. Mr. Hough learned the printing trade from his father, and they set up a print shop to support the work of the mission. They arrived in Burmah in October 1816 and retired from missionary service in 1826; George Hough subsequently worked for the government as an interpreter and school superintendent, and Mrs. Hough worked as an educator. They remained friends with Adoniram Judson and many of the other missionaries. Their independence was problematical at times.

[19] Elizabeth Stevens arrived in Maulmain in February 1838; her husband was Edward Stevens. Elizabeth Stevens took six-month-old Edward Judson into her home when Sarah and Adoniram had to leave for the United States in 1845, and her care and nurture saved his life. She served forty-eight years in Burmah. She had extensive correspondence with Emily Judson, and her letters spoke of everyday life among the missionaries. When Emily returned to the United States, the letters from Mrs. Stevens brought news of friends and colleagues. Mrs. Stevens had a sister, Sarah Haven, in Massachusetts, who wrote a number of letters to Emily asking for information on the Stevens family.

Captain W. J. Lay[20] to Emily C. Judson, August 1851—Royal Exchange Buildings

My dear Mrs. Judson

I leave town tomorrow and by chance I may be in again one day next week but I do not know your direction so it is the only way I can hear any thing [sic] of you by note. My ( ) went to Doughty St. with your parrot but found that you had left. Mr. Thomas[21] told me that you were at a Mr. B. Gurney, Denmark Hill, but to be certain I send this through your agents to know whether all your things are right and whether I can do anything for your ( ) and when you are off for your own land, and the chance of my seeing you again or not—

Trusting this will find you all well and your little girl quite recovered from her indisposition.—

I am My dear Mrs. Judson
Yours Sincerely

W. J. Lay

Source: American Baptist Historical Society, AJ 16, no. 779.

The Reverend Edward B. Underhill to Emily C. Judson,[22] August 13, 1851

My dear Mrs. Judson

I just write a line to bid you welcome to England and to say that only very pressing occupation has prevented me calling upon you today. I hope, however, to have that pleasure tomorrow morning.

Believe me to be
Yrs most truly,

Edw B. Underhill

Source: American Baptist Historical Society, AJ 21, no. 1046.

[20] Captain Lay was the Captain of the ship *Tudor*, on which Emily booked passage from Calcutta to England as she returned in 1851 to America. We are told in her biography by A. C. Kendrick that Captain Lay was unusually solicitous of Emily's needs during that voyage, and this letter certainly reflects that solicitude. See the letter of Emily C. Judson to Mrs. Elizabeth Stevens dated May 26, 1851, for Emily's personal description of the kindness of Captain Lay.

[21] Mr. Thomas was the husband of Abby Grace Thomas, who had sailed from Calcutta to England as a fellow passenger with Emily on the *Tudor*. It was for the absent Mr. Thomas that Emily had written the poem "Alone upon the Deep."

[22] This letter was written on the stationary of the Baptist Mission House, Moorgate Street, London.

Miss Cynthia Sheldon to Emily C. Judson,[23] August 14, 1851—311 Walnut St., Philadelphia

My dear dear Emily,

Heaven be praised for this evenings *Telegraph*—you were safe the 29th of May. I shall not take up time nor paper in telling you our anxieties and fears—about you and the dear ones—but now we look forward for your letters tomorrow evening—sleep will be sweet to night [sic] at least when I get sleepy—I have just closed a letter to Anna M.[24] now in Utica, or may be [sic] with your dear parents—the paragraph of joyful news was enclosed to her—although I presume the same is in Utica to night—shall I tell you how it reads—

> Safety of Mrs. Judson
> Boston Aug. 13th
> Letters have been received here, stating that Mrs. Judson ("Fanny Forester")[25] for whose safety fears had been entertained, was at Capetown in good health on the 29th of May, to sail for England.

This dear E. I had read and reread—before the "good health" was thought of—safety—safe—were enough now for our family—Mrs. Anable[26] and myself are the house hold [sic] except servants—but day after tomorrow we expect Courtland[27] will appear having in charge Nellie Bennett[28] and Mary Gratiot[29]—the first has been

[23] There is an addendum to this letter dated August 15, 1851.

[24] Anna Maria Anable was the niece of the Misses Urania and Cynthia Sheldon and the daughter of Joseph and Alma Sheldon Anable. Emily first met Anna Maria in fall 1840 when she went as a student to the Utica Female Academy; both Emily and Anna Maria became members of the faculty there. In these years, Anna Maria became Emily's dearest friend, and the extensive correspondence between the two reflects sensitive, flirtatious spirits and a deep intimacy. Emily was "Nemmy" to Anna Maria's "Ninny." In 1848, Anna Maria Anable, with the help of her extended family, moved to Philadelphia and started the Misses Anable's School. At Emily's death in 1854, Anna Maria was given guardianship of Emily Frances Judson, daughter of Emily and Adoniram Judson.

[25] Emily Chubbuck wrote under the *nom de plume* Fanny Forester. Asked about it once, she said, "Would anyone buy a book written by Emily E. Chubbuck?"

[26] Alma Sheldon Anable was the sister of Miss Cynthia Sheldon and Urania Sheldon Nott. Genealogy sources show that she married Joseph Hubbell Anable in Troy, New York, on July 28, 1814, and that it was the second marriage for Mr. Anable. Born in 1773, he was forty-one at the time of the marriage, and Alma was likely considerably younger. He died in 1831, which explains why Alma Anable and her family lived and worked first at the Utica Female Seminary and then later at the Misses Anable's school in Philadelphia. Joseph and Alma Anable were the parents of nine children: Henry Sheldon Anable (b. June 21, 1815); William Stewart Anable (b. November 6, 1816); Anna Maria Stafford Anable (b. September 30, 1818), Cynthia Jane Anable (b. January 28, 1820); Samuel Low Anable (b. November 28, 1821); Harriet Isabella Anable, also known as Hatty or Hattie (b. December 18, 1823); Courtland Wilcox Anable (b. July 28, 1825); Frances Alma Anable, or Fanny (b. April 12, 1828); and Mary Juliet Anable (b. February 18, 1830).

[27] Courtland Anable was a younger brother of Anna Maria Anable. He held several positions over the years, and he studied at Hamilton College while he boarded for a time with Emily's parents. In 1853, he returned to Philadelphia where he preached his first sermon at the Eleventh Baptist Church. He was "Uncle Court" to Emily Frances Judson. In 1880, Courtland Anable was listed in the Massachusetts Census as an ordained minister serving in a church.

[28] Nellie Bennett was a daughter of Cephas and Stella Bennett, missionaries to Burmah.

[29] Mary Gratiot was the daughter of Charles and Ann Sheldon Gratiot; Ann Sheldon Gratiot was a cousin of Miss Cynthia Sheldon. Mary Gratiot was born in 1839.

in Utica—Courtland has been there too—Mary G. visiting her friends in Troy—we had a letter from Anna M. yesterday—she has been with Eugenia Edmonds[30] some three weeks and has greatly enjoyed this her first visit at Utica—she was going to Hamilton this week—and I trust the good news will gladden the hearts of our own dear home tomorrow's mail—I have enclosed to Anna M. a sweet letter from Mary[31] at Detroit—she and Hattie[32] have had a charming visit at Sheboygan[33]—now the week in Detroit has been charming—they are likely at this time in Cleveland—Sunshine has been around each thus far on their journey—Fanny[34] writes in extasies [sic] about Boston too—she boasted of seeing you first when she went on—but the dear girl will of course leave there in two weeks from this—at which time they all design to be at home—Sarah Bell[35] is making great calculation on your stay with

[30] Eugenia Damaux had been part of Emily's intimate circle of friends at the Utica Female Academy. Living in New York City, Eugenia suffered from some kind of eye problem that made life difficult at times; this was a matter of comment in many of the letters exchanged between the girls themselves and with Miss Cynthia Sheldon. In 1848, Eugenia was in New York living "at Mrs. Brown's—the same warm-hearted French girl as ever." In 1849, she married Johnny Edmonds, described as rich and pious, and they lived in Utica.

[31] Mary Juliet Anable was born February 18, 1830, in Bethlehem, Albany County, New York, one of nine children born to Alma and Joseph Anable. She went to New Orleans with Hatty in 1847, but she returned home early in March 1848, and by 1849, she was working with Anna Maria in the Misses Anable's School in Philadelphia. Writing in March 1849, Hatty said of Mary, "She paints and draws, speaks French, plays the piano, sings, dances and is our mathematician. What should we ever do without her? She laughs from morning till night, and it is really refreshing to be with her." On December 26, 1860, she was married to Pierre Jacques Darey, the officiating minister being the Rev. Dr. Eliphalet Nott, her uncle. Mary died at the age of sixty-eight on April 20, 1898, in Ottawa, Ontario, Canada.

[32] Harriet or "Hatty" or "Hattie" or "Hat" Anable was one of nine children born to Joseph and Alma Anable, and was a niece to Miss Cynthia Sheldon and Mrs. Urania Sheldon Nott. In 1841, she had added a note to a letter written by Miss Cynthia Sheldon to Emily. As early as November 1842 she was away, and a letter from Emily to Catharine Chubbuck said that "she (Miss Sheldon) expected that Hat would return as accomplished as Anna Maria." Her trips away were both educational and employment, as she worked as a private tutor in families that would bring her into their homes. In August 1843, she had just returned from Beonsen, in the vicinity of New Orleans, and was engaged to go again. A letter from Anna Maria on January 6, 1845, said that she would stay South for another year. About this time Miss Cynthia Sheldon mentioned her concern for Hatty's spiritual health. In May 1845 she was in New Orleans. She was home again in summer 1846, but a September 27 letter from Anna Maria said she had been asked by Mr. Roman with some urgency to return and she thought that she should. She was to return home from New Orleans in January 1849 after Anna Maria Anable had started the Misses Anable's School in Philadelphia in fall 1848. Harriet was fluent in French, having placed herself earlier in a French environment in New Orleans. Hatty died in 1858.

[33] William Anable, Anna Maria Anable's oldest brother, had gone to Sheboygan after his marriage in 1846 to open a store. Henry Anable, a year younger than William, had gone to join him.

[34] Fanny Anable was one of nine children born to Joseph and Alma Anable and was a niece of Miss Cynthia Sheldon and Mrs. Urania Sheldon Nott. The correspondence indicates that in April 1845 she was away from home studying and taking music lessons. These spring letters indicate that she was in Philadelphia, working in the home of and with the family of the Reverend A. D. Gillette. See Miss Sheldon's letter to Emily of November 30, 1845, in which she spoke of all that Fanny was doing to improve herself in the field of music, but also her concern for Fanny's interest in the party life and the "vanitie" which surround her." A March 30, 1847, letter from Anna Maria Anable told of Fanny's conversion following her grandmother's death. In September 1847, she was listed as one of the teachers at the Utica Female Academy. Fanny became a teacher with her sisters in the Misses Anable's School in Philadelphia.

[35] Sarah Bell Wheeler was a teacher at the Utica Female Academy, an intimate of Emily Chubbuck, and one of the few who addressed Emily as Nemmy. In a September 1847 letter, she was listed as one of the teachers at the Utica Female Academy. There are a number of letters from Sarah Bell before and after her marriage to Charles Gould of Boston in October 1850. There are several letters clustered in the year or two after Emily left for Burmah and a number at the time of her return to America. Emily stayed with Charles and Sarah Bell Gould in October 1851 when she arrived in Boston after the long sea voyage from Burmah and then England. She stayed there a number of times following that. In 1851, Anna Maria Anable wrote of Sarah Bell: "Sarah is grown so lovely in person as well as character that she must assert a blessed influence on all with whom she comes in contact."

her—and I do not yet give up greeting you first on Ship board—The Gillettes[36] have been traveling north—they are expected this week—Mary Robarts[37] is with them.

Mr. and Mrs. R.[38] are home—and have talked much about your protracted voyage—soon after your letter written ten days out reached us—we learned from England that the vessel was expected from the 9th to the 15th of June—and ever since that date we have looked most anxiously for each Steamer not for yourself—but the letters telling us when you would leave London. Now dear E. you are well enough to enjoy London delights—and I hope you will take time for it notwithstanding we are half crazy to see you.

Source: American Baptist Historical Society, AJ 20, no. 987.

Miss Cynthia Sheldon to Emily C. Judson,[39] August 15, 1851

Friday Morning—Our own paper this morning adds to the last nights communication that you are probably now in England.

I shall send this enclosed in one to Mr. Gould[40]—he will forward it if by your letters to the Board you are likely to remain in London a little—Heaven direct you in all things—and preserve us all to recount together the varied providences—sorrows and joys of this five years absence—long long five years so fast have you lived—You will of course let us know what steamer you take passage on—Then the time is regular that I can be at either port if blessings continue to us at home—do avoid the equinoctial gale if you can—I must stop to say a word to Fanny[41] and Sarah B.[42]—

[36] See vol. 1, "Cast of Characters," s.v. "Gillette, The Reverend Abram Dunn."

[37] Mary Robarts was a student at the Misses Anable's School, the daughter of Mr. and Mrs. Robarts.

[38] Mr. and Mrs. W. S. Robarts were active in Philadelphia Baptist circles. They were frequent visitors to the home of the Reverend and Mrs. A. D. Gillette and later to the Misses Anable's School, which Anna Maria Anable and her extended family had started in Philadelphia in 1848. In his biography of his father, Edward Judson mentioned that Adoniram Judson stayed at the. Robarts's home when he came to Philadelphia in December 1845 when he met Emily Chubbuck. A. C. Kendrick said, "(Mr. Gillette and Dr. Judson) arrived in (or out of) due time in Philadelphia, and Dr. Judson was welcomed to the house of Mr. and Mrs. W. S. Robarts, who became warm personal friends, as they were already active friends of the mission cause." (A. C. Kendrick, *The Life and Letters of Mrs. Emily C. Judson* [New York: Sheldon and Company, 1862] 142.) In 1846, with the engagement of Adoniram Judson and Emily Chubbuck, the correspondence indicates some hard feelings toward Mrs. Robarts for comments disparaging the coming marriage and missionary service. This is found in Emily's letter to Adoniram dated February 6, 1846; Mrs. Robarts seemed to be accusing Emily of worldliness when all the time, Emily was quick to say, Mrs. Robarts was engaging in the same activity of which she was accused. The correspondence also indicates a satisfactory healing of the relationship. In January 1849, Miss Sheldon told Emily that Mrs. Robarts had placed their daughter Mary in the Misses Anable's School.

[39] This letter is an addendum to a letter written August 14, 1851.

[40] Charles Gould was forty-two years old, a widower with two children, a daughter and an invalid son. He was known to be pious and a friend to missionaries, and he was a deacon at the Rose Street Baptist Church. He was a partner in the publishing firm of Gould, Kendall and Lincoln, and was the brother of Mrs. Joshua Lincoln. Charles Gould and Sarah Bell Wheeler were married in October 1850.

[41] See vol. 1, "Cast of Characters," s.v. "Anable, Fanny."

[42] See vol. 1, "Cast of Characters," s.v. "Wheeler, Sarah Bell."

Mrs. Anable[43] joins in love to you and dear ones with gratitude to God for the glad news

ever your affectionately
attached friend

C. Sheldon

Source: American Baptist Historical Society, AJ 20, no. 987.

Mrs. Abby Grace Thomas to Emily C. Judson, August 16, 1851—18 ( ) Terrace

My dearest Friend

I heard from Mr. Lyall yesterday that your sweet little Emmy[44] was almost herself again. I was delighted to hear this. He also mentioned that you meditated a visit to Gurneys in the Country, is this so? and when do you go?

I have been so engaged with old, and new friends, that I could not write a line before. I felt certain you would let me know if any thing [sic] particular happened. I met Capt. Th( ) in Oxford Street after we left you on Thursday. Mrs. Selwood was to leave London today, for Dorsetshire. I am so flurried, I know not whether I told you that Mary:shhe [sic] had written me a long letter! Why don't you come and see me? I hope you liked some of the things we selected for you. We must all go to the Exhibition together next week, and would you like to go to the Opera one night before it closes? Captain and Mrs. Lay[45] have taken apartments close to us, opposite the Kensington Gardens. I saw him yesterday he has consulted Dr. Latham phd [sic], I believe he is advised to remain quiet, and not to go to sea yet awhile.—He is looking so ill I think! ( ) excellent ( ), how terrible is it not? I must now conclude they are talking to me every moment, and I scarcely know what I am saying.

My daughter is to be here on Tuesday. With kindest love ever believe me yours most affectedly

Abby Thomas

Source: American Baptist Historical Society, AJ 21, no. 1065.

[43] See vol. 1, "Cast of Characters," s.v. "Sheldon, Alma and Joseph Hubbell."

[44] Emily Frances Judson, the daughter of Adoniram and Emily Chubbuck Judson, was born December 24, 1847. Emily married the Reverend Thomas Alexander Thomson (T. A. T.) Hanna in 1870, and they had eight children, two of whom served as missionaries in Burmah.

[45] W. J. Lay was the captain of the *Tudor*, which brought Emily and Mrs. Thomas from Calcutta to England. Other letters tell us that he gave her exceptional attention on the voyage, making it easier on her than it might have been. See the letter from Emily C. Judson to Mrs. Elizabeth Stevens dated May 26, 1851, for Emily's personal observations on the kindness of Captain Lay.

Mr. J. A. Hinton to Emily C. Judson, August 20, 1851—City

Dear Mrs. Judson,

I have the pleasure of forwarding to the [sic] ticket which you allowed me to procure for you. The act itself is trivial, but not trivial is the heartfelt gratification it has afforded me to be even in this slight degree linked with you, and those with whom you are identified.

Most truly yours,

J. A. Hinton

Source: American Baptist Historical Society, AJ 16, no. 668.

Mr. Joseph Symon to Emily C. Judson, August 21, 1851—2 Turnwheel Lane, Common Street

Mrs. Judson

Dear Madam,

I wrote you on 19th, in enclosing the first halves of Bank of England notes for £20 and requested to hear from you of their due receipt, as I am without this advice for you, I fear to send the 2nd halves lest the former not have reached your hands.

The cards are ready and I will send them per carrier during this morning together with the keys of your luggage which has been examined and will be here by tomorrow or Saturday. Mr. Haven[46] arrived ( ) *Saratoga* fm Calcutta yesterday.

I am dear Madam
Yrsmoobed[47]

Joseph Syman

Source: American Baptist Historical Society, AJ 18, no. 848.

[46] On the address page is the note, "with parcel ( ) by C. Haven Jr. Esq." Apparently, Mr. Haven had brought some letters for Emily from Calcutta on a ship that left after the *Tudor*. Earlier, there had been some talk of Emily sailing on the *Saratoga*.

[47] We presume this is a variation on "Yours most obedient" or "Yours most obediently."

Mrs. D. C. Beeby to Emily C. Judson, August 27, 1851—15 Gloucester Place, Greenwich

My dear Mrs. Judson

Cannot you spend a day with us before you leave Mr. Gurney's? I should be greatly pleased to have your company either on Friday or Saturday. We shall be very glad to see the dear children too, and the servant[48] must come too also [sic]. If you take an omnibus to the "Elephant and Castle," I think you won't get one to Greenwich—or the more sure way would be to take the omnibus to the Greenwich Railway Station London Bridge and come by Railway to Greenwich. The omnibus would put you down just outside the station and you must ask your way to the *Greenwich* Railway, as there are others to Boylton Dover etc. After leaving the omnibus you pass through some gates when you go through a covered Archway, then keep to your left and walk on till you see "Greenwich Railway" where you will take your tickets and get into one of the carriages—take a return ticket. I wish I had a son that I could send to you; but I have not, and am obliged to manage as well as I can in going about. My eldest son is on this Railway but he has no time however to give to any thing [sic] except business. He has not even been to the Exhibition yet! I hope you have recovered from the fatigues of yesterday. Charlotte and I reached home safely last eveny [sic] and chatted awhile about yourself and dear children; also about those of our dear ones who are gone to a better world, and are rejoicing in the presence of *Jesus*; whom not having seen I trust *we* love, and can look forward with joy to the time when we hope to serve him without weariness and without sin. I pray that God may ever be with you and grant you the best of his blessings. With our united love to yourself, also to Mrs. Smith, Believe me

My dear friend
Yours Affectionately

D. C. Beeby

Source: American Baptist Historical Society, AJ 12, no. 323.

[48] Nancy was a Malayan woman who came with Emily from Burmah to America in 1851; she helped Emily with the three Judson children—Henry , Edward, and Emily Frances—and to be there if she was incapacitated by her frequent illnesses. There are numerous references to Nancy in the correspondence, and she continued with her duties with Emily and with the children until Emily's death in June 1854. In her will, Emily left a sum more than sufficient to pay for Nancy's return to her native home.

Mrs. Ellen H. B. Mason to Emily C. Judson, August 30, 1851—Tavoy

My dear Mrs. Judson,

I have not heard a word from you yet since your departure from the Madras Coast, and I need not tell you how solicitous we all feel to hear of your safe arrival among sympathizing friends. I long to hear how you are—where you are—how you like old Albion, and the Crystal what—Empire? What you think of the great world there after years of eremitism—and how your own desolate spirit bears up under all the ills, and exposures that must attend you. Be so good as tell me how the children[49] got on during the voyage, and where you will be located, for I assure you, dear sister, I feel a deep interest in everything that affects your happiness.

I am here you see at last in Tavoy, but it is not the rosy Tavoy I once saw—the rains are very heavy, and everything is wet, mouldy [sic], and gloomy. Our bungalow is on very low ground, and green mould under it makes it seem like a cavern. Then it is haunted with white ants. Have you ever in Rangoon or Maulmain had their attentions? How exquisite! Such silent devourings [sic]! all without a single warning rap. Rats too, those celebrated ancients, (they must have been dacoits in a former state) dispute possession of every chest, and drawer. I fancy I have got a *little* farther into the realm of barbarism for as Hindu Marz said of the Irish—"They are hathens [sic]"—not half as civilized as Maulmain *mures*.

But these are trifles, and I cannot find a heart for gaiety under present depressing circumstances. I am sure you will grieve with me when I tell you that my dear Mason[50] has been very ill since you left us. For five months past he has been but just alive. I was detained in Maulmain nearly four months, during most of which time he was ill here in Tavoy. One day we think him convalescent, and perhaps the very next he has a renewed attack more violent than before. How many times I have thought of you during the past two months. Doctor Judson's last, long, lingering illness and your changes—watchings—and forebodings, are ever before me; and I can't half fear that the same dark dreadful night that fell upon you, and whose bitterness I know too well—is again approaching. I am convinced that Mason cannot remain here and live many months longer—we must, therefore, seek a change of climate, or I must see him laid aside his sainted Maria.[51] All here are urgent for us to make no delay—but how hard it is? We do not feel as though we

[49] Henry Hall Judson, Edward Judson, Emily Frances Judson.

[50] Francis Mason arrived in Maulmain in November 1830 and transferred to Tavoy in 1831. His first wife died, and he married Helen Maria Griggs just before leaving the United States. She died in Burmah in 1846; they were the parents of four children. A skilled linguist, Mr. Mason was fluent in twelve languages and translated the Scripture into two of the Karen dialects. In spring 1847, Mr. Mason was seriously ill, and the other missionaries were concerned about him. In September 1847, he remarried, and Adoniram Judson officiated at the ceremony. His new wife was Ellen Huntley Bullard; originally from Vermont, she was the widow of Edwin Bullard, missionary to Burmah. Francis Mason died March 3, 1874, in Rangoon.

[51] Helen Maria Griggs Mason, the second wife of Francis Mason, died in Burmah on October 8, 1846.

could bring ourselves to such a resolution. All fears for future usefulness are frustrated—and you know what that means, for you have felt all its bitterness. I had anticipated doing a good deal for the Karens here in school and jungle, and if husband were well I might have as many about me as I could teach. But my dear Mason's disappointment is greater if possible than mine, for he had got hard at work in the revision and printing of the Bible. But, oh, "We will be patient," and try to labour [sic] or wait with submissive hearts as our Master bids.

Be so good as to remember me affectionately to Miss Sheldon[52] if you be with her when this reaches you and believe me dear Mrs. Judson,

Ever truly and affectionately yours

Ellen H. B. Mason

P.S. Mason desires his kind interest and regards to you and to your children. Tell Henry[53] and Edward[54] we do not forget them, but want to see them very much, and little sister too. The children frequently speak of them and ask about them.

Mrs. Bennett[55] is about and returning home—Mrs. Cross[56] is intending to leave in the spring—and what will become of Tavoy? The Thomases [sic] are making good progress in the language, and are a lovely couple. Dear sister Stilson[57] as you

[52] Miss Cynthia Sheldon was in charge of the administrative and financial departments of the Utica Female Academy. Miss Sheldon and her sister Urania, who was literary principal, gave Emily Chubbuck a place at the academy in October 1840. They had deferred any cost to a future time when Emily could afford to reimburse them. Upon Miss Urania Sheldon's marriage in late summer 1842 to the Reverend Doctor Eliphalet Nott, the president of Union College, and her subsequent move to Schenectady, Miss Cynthia Sheldon assumed a larger leadership role at the academy. In the years that followed, Miss Sheldon and Emily developed an even stronger relationship. In 1848, Miss Sheldon moved to Philadelphia to help Miss Anable with the startup of the Misses Anable's School and to assume responsibilities in its operation. Active and well-known in Baptist circles, Miss Cynthia was one of Emily's most important mentors, advisors, and friends until the time of Emily's death in 1854. Miss Sheldon was the aunt of Anna Maria Anable.

[53] Henry Hall Judson, born July 8, 1842, was the son of Adoniram and Sarah Hall Boardman Judson. Henry was the sixth of their eight children and the fourth of five who survived. He remained in Burmah in 1845 when Adoniram and Sarah returned to the United States with the three older children. He returned with Emily in 1851 and went to live with her family in Hamilton, New York. Henry attended Brown University and Williams Collage; he enlisted in the army at the time of the Civil War in January 1864. Later that year, he experienced a debilitating accident attributed either to sunstroke or a horse kicking him in the head. He was married once—unhappily according to his own correspondence—and he eventually died in a veteran's home in 1918, the last of his siblings to die. Of this, the chaplain noted, "The end was a genuine example of Christian fortitude." See Rosalie Hall Hunt, *Bless God and Take Courage, The Judson Legacy* (Valley Forge: Judson Press, 2005) 291.

[54] Edward Judson, born December 27, 1844, in Maulmain, Burmah, was the eighth child of Adoniram and Sarah Hall Boardman Judson and the fifth of their children to survive. Only a few months old when Sarah and Adoniram returned to America, Edward's life was saved by the nurture and care he received from Elizabeth Stevens. He loved Emily as the only "Mama" he had ever known and returned with her to the United States in October 1851. Edward, who was Eddy to his family, became a minister; he did mission work with the immigrants in New York City, and with the aid of the Rockefeller Family, he built the Judson Memorial Baptist Church in what is now Washington Park.

[55] Stella Bennett, with her husband Cephas, arrived in Burmah in January 1830. Five of their seven children were born in Burmah, but they returned to the United States for education. The girls attended the Utica Female Academy, so Mrs. Bennett is frequently mentioned in the correspondence.

[56] Julia Ann Putnam Cross married Edmund Cross in Morrisville, New York, in August 1843. They arrived in Maulmain on February 24, 1845, and at Tavoy a month later.

[57] Lucretia Stilson was the wife of Lyman Stilson, and they were missionaries to Burmah. They arrived in Burmah in February 1838. There are five letters in the correspondence from them. Lucretia Stilson died in Maulmain, August 14, 1851.

will have heard, is at rest, above. We grieve and mourn for her—but those four young children with an invalid father—who will care for them? Poor orphans—my heart bleeds for them.

[Written in the bottom margin on the back of the address page:] What a shame! Here are Morton's four children taught to worship idols like the heathen around them! They are just beginning to learn English and break off from such degradation—but not through the father's influence for he seems to care nothing for them. Dreadful, is it not?

[Written in the right margin of the back of the address page:] Mrs. Benjamin[58] has a fine boy and is well. His health is much improved. The Braytons[59] were well by last accounts.

[Written in the left margin of the address page:] Your poor empty box sits before me still waiting patiently to be filled, and it is really too bad that I have been so dilatory but it will appear at your door by and by I hope.

Source: American Baptist Historical Society, AJ 17, no. 742.

Mrs. Eliza Rutherford[60] to Emily C. Judson, August 30, 1851—Belthornton

My dear Mrs. Judson

I received your card of address just previous to our coming to Balthornton which has prevented our calling upon you as we so fully intended doing. We are staying with Mrs. Foulger, my husband's sister and next week we are to go into Buckinghamshire to visit my own relatives so that I almost fear we shall not have the pleasure of meeting you before you leave this country.

The Rev. Mr. Freeman whom Mr. Rutherford wished to introduce to you is gone into Germany for the benefit of his health—We were at a meeting of the Evangelical Alliance last evening which greatly interested us. I regret that our time has been so much occupied since our arrival as to prevent our going before.

It would give me great pleasure to hear from you, how long you are likely to remain in England and what your plans are.

[58] Susan Ruggles Stone married Judson Benjamin on September 3, 1848, and they departed for Tavoy, Burma, on October 21, 1848. They arrived at Tavoy in April 1849; in March 1850, they were sent to Mergui. They sailed from Rangoon to Boston on January 21, 1854, and Rev. Benjamin died in Boston of pulmonary disease in February 1855. Susan Benjamin remarried William Ward, and they left from Boston in June 1860 to return to Burmah.

[59] Durlin and Mary Brayton sailed as missionaries to Burmah in October 1837. While there, they worked mainly with the Karens. They left Burmah in February 1847 for health reasons and became advocates for the mission cause at home. Mr. Brayton returned in November 1848, and Mrs. Brayton in March 1850.

[60] Eliza Rutherford was a passenger with Emily on the ship *Tudor* as she journeyed from Calcutta to England on her way back to the United States.

With our united kind regards, believe me dear Mrs. Judson
Very sincerely Yours

Eliza Rutherford

A letter directed to the care of Messrs John Foulger and Son, Netcliffe Highway would always reach me.

I say loves to Edward,[61] my frequent little visitor on board the *Tudor*.

Source: American Baptist Historical Society, AJ 18, no. 809.

Mrs. S. A. Newell to Emily C. Judson, September 1851

My dear Mrs. Judson

We have both felt very sorry not to be able to talk ( ) you but we have had scarcely ( ) ( ) ( ) ( ) ( ) ( ) ( ) to London. We called yesterday on Mr. Showld [sic] thinking he should hear that you were staying near him but finding that we ( ) ( ) ( ) we had no time for ( ) ( ) had an appointment at 2 o'clock. I feel very sorry not being able to see you before we left. Our dear Parents have been waiting for our arrival the last seven weeks, and they almost despair of seeing us. Our precious boy was not with our parents. They thought the west of London would be to [sic] much for him. I quite long to see him. We propose leaving town tomorrow morning. I shall be very glad to hear from you when you have spare time. Mrs. Lay[62] called on me today. I was pleased with her. I was sorry to hear that your dear children have been so unwell. I do trust when you are finally settled in your native land your dear children will be better. When ( ) the Lord's great mercies to us how very much ( ) ( ) ( ) ( ) thankfulness. It has been a great disappointment to be not seeing you. I shall be glad to hear from you. Our address ( )

[Written across the top text of page 1:] Country is ( ) ( ). ( )

[Written across the bottom text of page 1:] has left a few little presents for your dear children. Now dear Mrs. Judson may the Lord bless and keep you and be with you when again our ( ) ( ) ( ) ( ) ( ) ( ) ( )

( ) Christian. Love to you. ( ) ( ) ( ) yours
I am thankful ( ) ( ) ( ) ( ) ( ) ( ) ( ) ( )

S. A. Newell

Source: American Baptist Historical Society, AJ 18, no. 853.

[61] See vol. 1, "Cast of Characters," s.v. "Judson, Edward."

[62] Mrs. Lay was the wife of W. J. Lay, the captain of the *Tudor*.

Miss Mary Esther Smith to Emily C. Judson,[63] September 1, 1851

My dear Mrs. Judson

You have indeed added to my treasures. That the purse is in itself pretty and curious, is its least recommendation, but any keepsake from you will ever retain with me a high value.

As a friend is with me I hasten to give Mama's message but any interruptions should prevent me from finishing and sending this note.

We have a houseful now and I believe our friends do not leave us til the end of next week so that mama is sorry to say she could not give you a bed till then. If however about that time it would suit you to spend a few days with us we should be very happy to see you for we are both quite longing for further communication with you.

In the meantime, the friends at present with us, had friends (I think relations) among the English forces who were appointed to obtain the release of the prisoners at Ava. And as far as Mrs. Hopkins recollects were one of Dr. Judson's convoy when the liberation was effected[64] and she is quite anticipating the pleasure of seeing you if it would not be too great a demand upon your strength to give us a day either Saturday or Monday. We do not wish to be unreasonable, but if you can do so we shall be so pleased—so very glad to see you.—If any to us, unfortunate circumstances should prevent our meeting with you kindly direct us where we shall send the little parcel you are good enough to take charge of for Mrs. Sigourney[65] for us, that it may reach you.

Do excuse a very hurried and I am afraid abrupt note, but I don't like to keep my visitor waiting

[Written perpendicular to text on page 1:] any longer.

Please present our kind regards to Mr. and Mrs. Angus;[66] and believe me dear Mrs. Judson

Yours very affectionately

Mary Esther Smith

Source: American Baptist Historical Society, AJ 19, no. 914.

[63] This letter is undated; it was obviously written during Emily's stay in England as she traveled from Calcutta to the United States. It is placed about halfway into her stay there. Mary Ester Smith was the daughter of Mary Anna Smith; this letter is related to the letter from her mother dated September 6, 1851.

[64] Adoniram Judson was moved from prison to the British camp on February 21, 1826.

[65] Lydia Huntley Sigourney was one of the first American women to succeed at a literary career. A teacher, she moved to Hartford, Connecticut, at the invitation of Daniel Wadsworth to open a school for the daughters of his friends. In 1819, she married Charles Sigourney, and the financial stability this brought to her allowed her to devote herself full time to writing and publishing anonymously. She used the proceeds from her writings to fund a number of charities, among them the cause of missions at home and abroad.

[66] On her return to America, Emily stayed in England for about a month; for a part of that time she was with the Rev. and Mrs. Angus and their children at Stepney College.

Mrs. Mary Anna Smith[67] to Emily C. Judson, September 6, 1851—Denmark Hill

We so appreciated my dear friend all the kindly feelings you have evinced towards us and the adverse circumstances which arise on all sides to our prolonged social intercourse are to me quite a discipline. I hope I may be led the more earnestly to direct my eye to our Father's house—where we may hope to meet and know no parting.

I would on no account have had you risk any painful fatigue to come hither and quite acquiesce in the decision—to give up dear Mrs. Angus'[68] kind and beautiful alternative is very difficult to us all—yet with all my laguness [sic] I have been obliged to confess the thing impracticable. The hearts of our friends are with you—and they wd gladly avail themselves of such a kind offer if they could. I am not writing a farewell—I fancy your "business" will require a longer time than can ( ) be seen in advance—so I shall hope on.

You do not say whether it will be in London or Stepney that your cases must be packed.

My Mary[69] is an excellent packer and would joyfully come to your aid at Nevorgate [sic] Street or anywhere you appointed. Do not hesitate to accept her

[Written in the left and top margin of page 1:] if she can be of the ( )alleble service.

Mr. and Mrs. Hopkins have not yet the letters which decide their return.

I must now unwillingly ( ) off—God bless you dear friend.

Every very affectionately yours

Mary Anna Smith

Source: American Baptist Historical Society, AJ 19, no. 917.

[67] Mary Anna Smith was active in mission circles in England. She was well acquainted with Amelia Angus, with whom Emily stayed for a portion of the time that she was in England on her way from Burmah to America. Her three letters to Emily in September 1851 and early 1852 have to do with trying to see her while she was there (they seem to have connected only through correspondence) and trying to find materials at the later date that would be of use in the memoir. Apparently, Adoniram Judson had considerable contact with British mission leaders. In the letter, she remembers the time that she met Ann Judson. There is a fourth letter from 1854 in which she gives her impressions from her initial reading of the memoir of Adoniram Judson. There is also an earlier letter of September 1, 1851, from her daughter, Mary Esther Smith, writing on behalf of her mother. They hoped to have Emily and the children stay with them, but other visitors, and perhaps the desire of Emily to preserve her strength by not having to travel so much, did not allow these plans to work out.

[68] Emily stayed with Amelia Angus and her family at Stepney College. There are five letters in the correspondence from Mrs. Angus.

[69] Mary Esther Smith had written Emily on her mother's behalf on September 1, 1851.

[70] There is an addendum to this letter dated September 8, 1851.

Mrs. Charlotte Haberlin to Emily C. Judson, September 7, 1851[70]

My dear dear Friend, so fondly so frequently remembered, where can my thoughts find you? My soul has been wandering forth and would fain alight in a less unknown region beside you, but there is nothing to guide the fluttering wings of my imagination.

I must ( ) content myself ( ) ( ) ( ), that our spirits meet before the mercy seat—to know of the union and communion in our Lord and master and to know and rejoice in the prospect of a more real reunion in His presence for Evermore. We all heard with deep sympathy the news of your boisterous dangerous passage to the Cape, and the uncertainty of your subsequent progress, your arrival at home, your state of suffering health—the anxiety for your children all these circumstances have given a sad impress to the remembrance of you and much increased my longing to hear from you, to have something positive to cling to.—Life is at best and in its most stable form but a floating cloud but ours is indeed a restless ( ) sea ( ) rising and falling—and our frail bark is cast here and there—sometimes in the midst of rolling waters and at others in the dry burning strand drifting apart ( ) so—without knowing where the magnet points or where the haven of rest is—for in vain do I look for the beloved one who directs its searching to the magnet—Still the great helmsman moves its unknown influence and in looking to him is safety—and the holding him fast will surely land us in the heavenly home.—This is Sunday afternoon. I was much refreshed by the sermon I heard this morning from Mr. Bosenell—on Ps. 73.27. "Whom shall quick us with thy counsel, and afterward receive us into glory." The ways of God frought with wisdom and love and ( ) to our ( ) wants, all ending in glory—A sublime theme who may well inspire us to exclaim with the Psalmist in the next verse—"Whom have I in heaven but thee? And there is none upon Earth that I desire beside Thee!" I thought of you and made me long to sit down and write to you—enjoy an hour of Sabbath's evening with you, whilst all is hushed around and each one in his or her own closet seeking the required food—or rest—or blessing for the heavenly inmate. Mr. MacKay[71] is in his "upper chamber"—the Observatory preparing himself for the Evening when he is to conduct the divine service in the Free Church and preach to us. I know you would enjoy sharing with us—his answers are really as the opening breezes laden with Eden's spring breath; and leave these gentle but deep touches in ( ) in the world; you will be glad to hear that his health is very good and his appearance much stronger than last winter. Mrs. MacKay with a former ( ) ( ) goes thro' her usual *full* tack of labors of love—for all kinds of protégés—her young flock give her considerable trouble, from baby—whose servant Annie was a perfect martyr to boils—Johny

[71] The Reverend W. S. MacKay was a missionary for the Free Church of Scotland; he also edited the *Calcutta Review*, which Emily described as a prestigious magazine. Rev. MacKay was the first to inform Emily of Adoniram's death in his August 9, 1850, letter, and he also insisted that she stay with him and his wife while she was in Calcutta on her way to the United States.

the ( ) only now they are recovering from them. Willy and Mary go on as usual. ( ) ( ) I could assist in their being sent home. Jane has lost ( ) of her fresh blooming appearance thro' delicate health during our trying hot and rainy season; Mrs. M's eldest son is recovering from a sickly state of health to acquire a more robust constitution; he is and will be more and more a comfort to his mother, he is truly pious and such an affectionate son that it rejoices my heart, tho' at times with a tear of anticipation in my eye, to observe him. The two younger daughters are not coming out this year—a painful disappointment to Mrs. M. Mrs. Cork is still now and then a sufferer from nervous head-aches—she mentions you with sincere affection and was ( ) ( ) together of you, to me the process ( ) ( ) during ( ) on my path by her affectionate ( ) and looks.

[Note: Pages 4 and 5 are missing. Page 3 ends as a complete paragraph, and the next page starts in the middle of a sentence.]

her better ( ) with—thus far the local ( ) which no doubt will ( ) be more completely and better givers [sic] by Mr. MacKay who proposes writing to you as soon as he hears from you. We all long for news from you and D.V. to join in your ( ) of ( ) that you have been safely brought to your journey's end.—( ) ( ) ( ) will make me happy with the sight of your handwriting.—The last mail enriched my heart with many a loving trials letter from my own dear children and relations and for the time being it seems as if nothing lacking—no ( ) was tilled—yet all the tick of friendship—affection love may flow in full ( ) over a heart bereaved of its own beloved one—it will be left dry and parched the moment the flood retires.—Often very often I feel myself a complete ( ) ( ) I have sometimes experienced—earnestly realized the truth that God writes His best messages on our ( ) hearts—that the finest spiritual enjoyments are ( ) in those moments.

My duties continue much the same; the gentleman who founded and supported the school hitherto, Mr. Beth( ) died last month rather suddenly and I fear not prepared for the ( ) change—it seems the more sad to reflect that a mind so capable of ( ) ( ) noble failings—of ( ) in kindness and generosity of ( ) ( ) ( ) ( ) beauty of our glorious religion should not have found rather ( ) accepted the *saving* truth—the school has now passed into the hands of Lord Dal( ) still as a private institution and I continue in it for the present as I have some hope of seeing a better system introduced; at all events I think it my duty to do all I can to bring it about—A pleasing encouraging ( ) stands connected with my school is that one of my former, now married pupils come to me privately every Even'y for instruction ( ) merely in secular knowledge and her husband's expressed wish in Christianity. May God grant His blessing and His Spirit to the salvation of a precious world.

Source: American Baptist Historical Society, AJ 16, no. 684.

Anna Maria Anable to Emily C. Judson, September 7, 1851—Philadelphia

Dearest Emily

It is so *so* long since I have heard from you that I must write and relieve my heart by keeping up a communication even though it be all on one side. I never received your letter from Cape Town though I know you wrote—but there is a strange and funny story about that letter which I must reserve till I see you, for as it was not made plain to me on paper so I despair of making it plain to you till I can tell it verbally which I hope will be before long. By the way when and how will that be? I am *fixed* here in Phil. for the year to come. My wanderings for this season are over and my friends will have to come and see me, and must I wait till you have been to Boston and New York and Hamilton and the cold weather drives you at last to Phil. I cannot bear to think of it. Now I will tell you what I learned this last week. Mr. Roberts[72] (Mrs. Colby's[73] brother) says that if you take the "City of Glasgow" or some other Phil. steamer, you will probably come a good deal cheaper than in the Collins or Canada[74] lines and you will be out only a few days longer. Don't you think you had better do it? For more reasons than one I wish you would, for the principal one I acknowledge is selfish, but I don't want you, the minute you set foot in your native land again to face into the hands of the Boston Board and the Boston booksellers. They are well enough in their times, but they are very fierce to have everything settled as soon as possible. It is just three weeks tomorrow darling

[72] Mr. Roberts was the brother of Mary Colby. A businessman, with primary business interests in England, he delivered letters from Emily's friends to her when she arrived in England on her way back to America in late summer 1851. He also offers to render to her every service he can so as to ease her journey. He is mentioned in a number of the letters in the following months; a widower with at least one child, a daughter Mary, who was a pupil at the Misses Anable's School in Philadelphia. Abby Ann Judson mentions his marriage in her letter of March 7, 1852.

[73] Mary Colby was the wife of Gardner Colby, a prominent businessman and active Baptist layman. Mr. Colby was a member of the Board of the American Baptist Missionary Union and an avid supporter of the missionary movement. In a letter after they sailed from Boston to Burmah, Emily mentions the extravagant hospitality extended to them in early July as they waited for the *Faneuil Hall* to embark. Adoniram and then Emily stayed with the Colby family quite frequently over the years. Mrs. Colby was an active correspondent with Emily and supported her, her family, and the cause of missions.

[74] Emily eventually sailed on the *Canada* from Liverpool to Boston.

since I saw your dear Mother[75] in Hamilton. Your father[76] and Kate[77] and Wallace[78] had all gone to the evening exercises before the Commencement and your mother was home all alone when the stage landed me at her gate. Didn't we have a nice talk over our cup of tea? and didn't we keep it up until half past ten when the rest of the family came home and didn't I read your letters from the Cape and for the first time have my anxiety about you relieved? Well I did. And I had the nicest visit that you can think of—and we all had the finest Commencement that old Hamilton has boasted these many years, and all over *nice* graduates. How Dr. Eaton[79] did cry over those new graduates. He told them they had rendered their Divine Maker a service which no other graduates ever had or even could render her. They had stood by her when she was in the dust of her humiliation, by their constancy they had kept life in her bosom; yes, he told them, in the great chain of events connected with that beloved Institution they had constituted the golden link which bound the

[75] Emily's mother, Lavinia Richards Chubbuck, was born June 1, 1785, at Goffstown, New Hampshire, the eldest of thirteen children. She married Charles Chubbuck on November 17, 1805, at Goffstown, New Hampshire. Four of her children were born at Goffstown, and moved with Charles and Lavinia Chubbuck to Eaton, New York, in September 1816; they were Lavinia, Benjamin, Harriet, and John Walker. Sarah Catharine, Emily, and Wallace were all born in Eaton.

[76] Emily's father, Charles Chubbuck, was born at Bedford, New Hampshire, on March 3, 1780; he was married to Lavinia Richards in Goffstown, New Hampshire, on November 17, 1805. They were to have seven children. Though he held varying jobs over the years, he failed at many of them, and Emily was the main support of the family after she purchased a home for her family in fall 1842.

[77] Sarah Catharine Chubbuck, "Kate," "Kit," or "Kitty" was Emily's older sister by ten months. Outside of the two terms at the Utica Female Academy, which Emily arranged for her, Catharine always lived at home with her parents in Hamilton, New York. The letters indicate opportunities for marriage, but she, for unknown reasons, remained single. She later helped to care for Henry and Edward Judson after their return from Burmah in fall 1851 when they moved into the Hamilton home with their "aunt" and "grandparents," and she was remembered by them as "dear old Aunt Kate—a dear friend."

[78] Born January 1, 1824, William Wallace Chubbuck was six years younger than Emily. During these years of Emily's correspondence, Wallace lived at or near home and worked at different occupations including printing, office work, and teaching. Emily wrote of him as capable in many areas, but seeming to lack ambition at times. He proved to be a strong support for the Chubbuck family over these years, and at the time of her death in 1854, Wallace had become one of Emily's primary caregivers. After February 1854, she dictated all her letters to him because of her failing strength. Wallace married Julia Allin Throwbridge on July 18, 1854. He died on August 13, 1861, at the age of thirty-seven. The obituary in the Utica *Herald* noted that Wallace had trained as a printer in Morrisville and had gained some astute political skills. He was "possessed of one of the brightest of intellects, and wield[ed] one of the most trenchant of pens." He had served as a justice of the peace and as clerk to one of the legislative committees in Albany.

[79] See vol. 1, "Cast of Characters," s.v. "Eaton, The Reverend Doctor George W."

glorious past to the still *more glorious future*.[80] And the people rapped their canes and clapped their hands and stamped their feet, and I almost expected to hear them shout, Amen.

Your mother looks a little more feeble than she did when I last saw her, but your father looks better. Kate and Wallace about the same—and so with the house, the village—never looked so nice as now, and it certainly is in my opinion the prettiest little village I ever saw.

Hattie's[81] old friend (Mr. Bondousgive) [sic] has just come in to tea and I must close my letter for the mail steamer. I think it is strange I did not receive any letter from you last week, as you usually are so good about writing. I have almost a mind to get up a quarrel and make you come this way to settle it. Won't it do? Miranda Crafts has happened in to tea too, so I must stop and see the folks. Adieu.

10 1/2 at night. I have not time now dear Nemmy[82] to tell you about my visits and the journeys of

[Written along the left top margins, and across the first three lines of the text of page 1:] the girls this summer. May is still in Utica tho our school has begun. I did not want her to come back until she was perfectly settled and she will not be here until October. Mother[83] and Aunt C.[84] have been well all summer ( ). The season is by no means over here yet for the ther. is at 80 today. Don't hurry home darling till your visit is made in England, but let us see you here as soon after as possible.

Anna M.

Source: American Baptist Historical Society, AJ 13, no. 467.

[80] The school that became Madison University was founded in 1817 by the Baptist Education Society of New York State for the purpose of educating ministers. Two of its first students, Jonathan Wade and Eugenio Kincaid and their wives, were the first missionaries to join Adoniram and Ann Judson in Burmah. The Wades arrived in 1823, and the Kincaids in 1830. In 1834, the school was organized as a seminary, college, and academy called the Hamilton Literary and Theological Institution. In 1846, it was chartered as Madison University, drawing upon all of the history and good will in its former existence. In 1847, attempts were made to remove the university to the more urban setting of Rochester, and after three years of stressful turmoil that did tremendous damage to the prospects of the university, the courts decided the case in favor of those who wished the university to remain in Hamilton. Letters of the early 1850s show that the university soon made a remarkable recovery, and the university and seminary were later named for philanthropist Samuel Colgate.

Dr. Nathaniel Kendrick was one of the venerated leaders at the school while also serving as the beloved pastor of the youthful Emily Chubbuck. He officiated at the marriage of Adoniram and Emily on June 2, 1846, his last official act in his seriously declining health. After the commitment to stay in Hamilton, Dr. Stephen Taylor was elected as the second president, and later in 1856, George Eaton became the third president. Dr. A. C. Kendrick, the nephew of Nathaniel Kendrick and the biographer of Emily Chubbuck Judson, was one of the professors who left Hamilton in 1850 to teach at the University of Rochester. Numerous graduates were called for service on the mission field, and many churches were blessed through the pastoral ministry of those who had been trained there. One such minister was Courtland Anable, the brother of Emily's best friend Anna Maria Anable; Courtland Anable was there during Emily's final illness and death in 1854.

[81] See vol. 1, "Cast of Characters," s.v. "Anable, Harriet."

[82] "Nem" or "Nemmy" was a name of endearment given to Emily by a small group of her intimate friends at the Utica Female Academy. Anna Maria Anable was "Ninny."

[83] See vol. 1, "Cast of Characters," s.v. "Sheldon, Alma and Joseph Hubbell."

[84] See vol. 1, "Cast of Characters," s.v. "Sheldon, Miss Cynthia."

Mrs. Charlotte Haberlin to Emily C. Judson, September 8, 1851[85]

I came back to bid good bye—to give you the shower if I could of kind regards and remembrances from all the inmates of the house, and their wishes for your welfare. May the Lord guide your steps and smooth your path before you. Kiss your dear dear children for me and accept a kiss of warmest affection from

Yours in the best of love

C. Haberlin

Source: American Baptist Historical Society, AJ 16, no. 684.

Mrs. Eliza Davies to Emily C. Judson, September 8, 1851—Grove Hill Globe

My dear Mrs. Judson,

The accompanying book must belong to you I think, as it was found in the bedroom you occupied here, a day or two after you left. I should retain it to return to you when you pay your promised farewell visit, but that I hear your time is still so much occupied that it is uncertain whether we shall see you again. I shall *hope* however to see you, but whether I do or not, be assured I shall follow you and your dear children with my prayers and best wishes. I shall look with anxiety for news of your safe arrival in your native land. There I doubt not God will bless you, not only for His own mercy's sake and in fulfillment of His promises, but also for the sake of His servant, who had so long and so arduously fulfilled His bidding. I shall always ( ) with much pleasure to the few short hours we have spent together. They refreshed and cheered me much.

My father and sister desire their kind regards to you, and my children send their love to yours. Accept the assurance of a sister's love from

Your very affectionate

Eliza Davies

Source: American Baptist Historical Society, AJ 15, no. 596.

[85] This is an addendum to a letter dated September 7, 1851.

Emily C. Judson to the Reverend Doctor Solomon Peck, September 9, 1851—Stepney College

My dear Mr. Peck,[86]

A line from Mr. Ogan[87] Symon has just favoured me with your address; and also informed me that you will not leave Donai at least before Friday. We were expecting you here this week, and I still hope that you will come before I leave. **I find my health very much improved by the voyage, long and stormy as it was and the sallow Indian cheeks of my children are beginning to glow with English roses.**[88] It is now four weeks since I arrived in England, and I am beginning to feel some anxiety to finish my wanderings. It is my present intention to leave this for Liverpool on Monday next (the 15th) and take the Steamer which I believe leaves on the 20th for Boston. It would be almost too pleasant a thing to hope for, to have your company across the water.

My short stay in England has been exceedingly pleasant and I have found many friends, and formed many ties which I am sure not even death will have the power to dissever. Most of my time has been spent at Mr. B. Gurney's Esq'r and the Rev. Joseph Angus,[89] and they have introduced me to a very wide circle of friends and acquaintances. I have met some "men who have hazarded their lives for Christ" and others who have hazarded their still dearer reputation. Will you be kind enough to drop me a line letting me know whether there is a prospect of our meeting.

Your kind letter awaiting my arrival was more than welcome and the sympathy no less needed *now*, than when the shadow was new and more strange. The shadow is still there, and has lost none of its heaviness, though I have learned perhaps to wear it better. But I have no thought of murmuring—the question oftener comes home to my heart—"What shall I render unto the Lord for all his mercies."

Hoping to hear soon from you,

Believe me,

Yours with Chr'n affection, Emily C. Judson.

Source: American Baptist Historical Society, AJ 12, no. 376.

[86] The Reverend Doctor Solomon Peck was for twenty years the executive secretary of the American Baptist Missionary Union. Many believed him to be hard, stern, and judgmental, and from some of his comments, it is easy to understand that perception. Dr. Peck and Emily did not always have the easiest of relationships. She felt in him the judgment that came from many in the church at the announcement of her impending marriage to Adoniram; that judgment concerned her "secular" past and concern that she was not an appropriate companion for the venerable missionary. On July 18, 1849, Emily wrote a blistering letter of defense to Dr. Peck in response to a letter from him of February 20, 1849; her letter framed how she viewed his perception of her, and her response was meant to set the record straight. There are eleven letters in the collection from Solomon Peck to Emily.

[87] There is a letter in the correspondence from Mr. Ogan Symon that follows this letter; it has to do with transferring banknotes, and we conclude he was likely a financial agent for the mission.

[88] A. C. Kendrick quoted these lines in his biography, *The Life and Letters of Mrs. Emily C. Judson* (New York: Sheldon and Company, 1831) 362.

[89] On her return to America, Emily stayed in England for about a month; for a part of that time she was with the Rev. and Mrs. Angus and their children at Stepney College.

Mrs. Amelia Angus to Emily C. Judson, September 11, 1851[90]

My dear Mrs. Judson

It really seems so *very very* dull without you here tonight, that I am *obliged* to seek relief in gossiping to you by letter, and so my heart trouble will in this end make trouble to you, in receiving and reading my poor little epistle—but don't be afraid. I am not going to sentimentalize though in sadness have: and though I might tell an "over time tale" of the "*many* thoughts that flit to thee a thousand in number": but can really find a good *business* excuse for my very early intrusion.

I find two or three little things left behind, which I will send to you: the *Calcutta Review*,[91] Henry's and Edward's[92] toothbrushes, and some marbles and your paper of pins—besides these: Mr. Nelson has sent your books today: so that altogether I shall be able to make up a pretty large parcel: I should *like* to send it by Mr. Golbert if I could be sure of his direction: Joseph thinks it is Warwick Lane Holborn but he is not sure: if however I cannot find him ( ), I will send it by Dr. Peck[93] or Mr. Howe.

My chicks Miss their merry companions *very* much. I scarcely know whether Charlie misses the boys or Milly her dear little Emmy[94] the most: and I—but no. I *cannot* tell you how my heart aches to see and hear you again: and yet how warmly, even amidst its sadness, it *thanks you* for the *happin*ess of the last ten days.

I hope you had a pretty comfortable journey today, and are not *too much* tired tonight—though I sadly fear you are looking very *very* pale.

Source: American Baptist Historical Society, AJ 17, no. 754.

[90] This letter is undated and unsigned. It is from Mrs. Amelia Angus. In her other letters, she mentions her children Charlie and Milly, as mentioned here. It would be from Emily's time in England on her return to America; a letter dated September 15 by Mrs. Angus makes it clear that Emily had been gone from their home for several days. Thus, it is placed in the September 11 timeframe.

[91] The *Calcutta Review* was published by the Reverend W. S. MacKay; Emily stayed with the MacKay family while she was in Calcutta waiting for passage to England. Mr. MacKay had placed a lot of material in the magazine on the life and work of Adoniram Judson.

[92] Henry Hall Judson, nine years of age, and Edward Judson, six and a half years of age. They were the two youngest surviving children of Adoniram and Sarah Hall Boardman Judson.

[93] See vol. 1, "Cast of Characters," s.v. "Peck, The Reverend Doctor Solomon."

[94] See vol. 1, "Cast of Characters," s.v. "Judson, Emily Frances."

The Reverend Doctor Solomon Peck to Emily C. Judson, September 11, 1851—Donai

My dear Mrs. Judson

It was fully my purpose to be in London as early as yesterday, but having missed of seeing Mr. Oncken[95] in Germany, I am awaiting his arrival here. I shall now be detained until Monday, possibly Tuesday, of next week. On Wednesday at the latest I shall hope to call at Mrs. Lyman's and unless you leave word to the contrary proceed immediately to Stepney.[96] If you have *engaged* your passage for the 20th, will you need to leave for Liverpool before Thursday? It would give me great pleasure to see you, if it would not too much disarrange your plans.

I do not see that it would be possible for me to accompany you to Boston, unless you could defer your departure one week, and *provided* also that I could obtain a release from my engagement to sail in the *Ocean Queen*; which last is little to be expected. She sails on the 28th or the day following. I would make the attempt however most earnestly, on my arrival in London, unless indeed you would incline to take passage also in the same (*Ocean Queen*.)

I rejoice to know of your safe arrival at London and the improvement of your health; as also of the kind attentions you have received from Christian friends. May God mercifully prosper your way to America.

Allowing myself to hope that I may see you next week, I am truly
Your brother

S. Peck

Source: American Baptist Historical Society, AJ 19, no. 946.

[95] Reverend John Oncken was called the "apostle of the German Baptists." He was baptized in the river Elbe near Hamburg, Germany, on April 22, 1834, by Professor Barnas Sears, and this was considered to be the beginning of the German Baptist Mission. Under great prosecution in his native land because of his conviction on believer's baptism by immersion, he had gained the respect of his peers through his love, courage, and firm determination, which could not be intimidated or silenced. Always a local church pastor, he was traveling in the United States at the invitation of the American Baptist Missionary Union in 1853, and it is quite obvious that Emily met him as a part of this tour. Dr. Wayland wrote in July 1853 that this tour seemed providential as the release of the Judson memoir was projected for the fall. In a letter dated October 7, 1853, Anna Maria mentioned Reverend Oncken as a possible suitor for Emily, contrasting him with Dr. William Dean. Emily's reply on October 13 was rather blistering.

[96] Stepney College was the home of Joseph and Amelia Angus; Emily stayed with them for a part of the time that she had been in England.

Mr. C. M. Bissell to Emily C. Judson, September 12, 1851—Wavertree Liverpool

My dear friend,

I was favored with your note this morning and am happy to learn we are to see you so soon.

I find that a ( ) at Mr. Cropper's is to come on a week sooner than was anticipated so that we have as( ) ed to ask you to come direct to us. A cordial welcome must stand in the loom of larger domain. I only regret that you propose to be here so short a time. I shall not however do anything in the way of ( ) a berth till you come. I suppose you will send your sea luggage direct by luggage train to await your directions. This would be the more economical plan as on the traveling trains they charge beyond a certain form.

Perhaps you will oblige and write another note to answer to say by what *train* you propose to leave on Monday, that you my be met at Edgehill.

Mrs. Bissell joins me in kind regards ( ).

I am ( ) truly yours

C. M. Bissell

Source: American Baptist Historical Society, AJ 12, no. 320.

Mrs. Mary Anna Smith to Emily C. Judson, September 15, 1851[97]—Denmark Hill

Will you pardon me my dear dear friend for approaching you once more when your thoughts ( ) be very occupied with many things but Mrs. Angus'[98] visit seems to open the way and the temptation is irresistible. I could not speak a farewell tho' others dare—nor did I say anything of what I wished to say to you—I was partly oppressed with over weariness still more with disappointment and sorrow to give up the hope of giving you some evidence of our interest and friendship.—It will not be thus when we meet in our Father's house. I have been dwelling with intense feeling this morning on our Lord's prayer John 17.24. Father I will that they also whom thou hast given me may be with me *where I am*, that they may behold my glory etc. The uncertainty of your *future* had pained me and it came as a passage of love explaining how he who had secured a home in his own presence and run his

[97] This letter is undated. There is an earlier letter from Mary Esther Smith that was written on behalf of her mother, and it has to do with meeting Emily. Emily planned to stay with them, but because of the presence of friends, the visit would have to be delayed. A September 6 letter from Mary Anna Smith acknowledges that for unfortunate reasons, the meeting will not take place at all. This letter comes after that, and since Emily is to leave for America of September 20, it is dated September 15.

[98] On her return to America, Emily stayed in England for about a month; for a part of that time she was with the Rev. and Mrs. Angus and their children at Stepney College.

heart as our final portion—would surely guide and guard us all the way—and place us just where we may receive the visits of his grace and the highest culture for such an exalted destination. I dare not ask you to let me hear from you—you will have so many claims and the dear children will be enough to fill your hands and heart—but I shall hear of you—and at the throne of grace I trust we may often meet, there at present we plead for you many promises and especially for your journey and voyage. That solacing for—"My presence shall go with thee, and I will give thee rest."

Believe me my beloved friend
Ever faithfully yours

Mary Anna Smith

My husband and Mary are not here or wd join me in all that is kind—the former is improving but the attention requisite for his sad boil kept him at home and me also—or I co'd have forgotten my weariness and found my way

[Written along the left and top margins of page 1:] to Stepney—sure of Mr. A's and Amelia's welcome.

Mary has a severe cold.

Perhaps a warmer neck ribbon may be comfortable as the weather becomes cool.

Source: American Baptist Historical Society, AJ 19, no. 919.

Mrs. Amelia Angus to Emily C. Judson, September 15, 1851[99]

My very dear Mrs. Judson

Many, many thanks to you, for your kind and very welcome note: and you think I don't miss you? No, no. I don't and won't believe that—indeed, indeed I seem more sad hearted than ever, as the lapse of time makes me realize that I could scarcely believe at first that you really are far away: still amidst all the pain of parting, I feel only too thankful to have been allowed to know and *love* you so well: and in future days, as many a pleasant daydream will the happiness of these past hours return again. Many thanks too for your kind present of books: I feel though rather unwilling to take them out, it seems so greedy: however I have done so: and shall value them much as your gifts: I have taken out too the Memoir[100] for Mrs. L( ) Smith: the rest of the books I have sent off to you by *railway* today: I was intending to do before your note arrived: and therefore did so at once: it is to come by a *fast* train, as I was told that was no dearer than a luggage train and therefore ought to

[99] There is an addendum to this letter dated September 18, 1851.

[100] Fanny Forester, *Memoir of Sarah B. Judson, Member of the American Mission to Burmah* (New York: L. Colby and Company, 1848).

reach you early tomorrow: perhaps if you do not see it in that time you will kindly ask Mr. Bissell[101] to send and see about it. I did not pay for it, as I think it will be delivered more quickly if unpaid for. I have put into the parcel two or three little books which—my children wish to send to yours and also: another little book of Mr. Hamilton's—"the happy home" which perhaps you will like to see. I have tried for "the Vine. Pslm. Ced( )" but cannot get them in time: the other two sermons I now enclose. I am only sorry that the children's books are not all quite new—but I could not procure new ones in time to send.

We saw your friend Dr. Peck[102] yesterday, and were very much pleased with his appearance, and with the little we could see of him in such a bustle: we are to go to Papa's tomorrow to dine with him, and other friends at 3 o'clock: if you could only meet us there too!!

Our busy day passed off pretty comfortably yesterday: we had a very large gathering here to tea and Mr. Kennedy's large chapel filled in the morning. Mr. Sawin (is that right) was here but not Deacon Gilbert or Mr. House.

There are certainly some tender love passages between Emmy's[103] and Milly[104] [sic] hearts: ( ) ( ) ( )—Milly's eyes watered sadly this evening when I told her Emmy wanted to see her again: and she wishes much to go in the ship with her. Oh, will they ever meet again?

But I find I must close my letter or I shall make it too late for the post—but I don't mean to promise you not to trouble you again by letter for I have a strong conviction that I shall certainly want to pen an epistle to America by way of relief to my own feelings: and indeed I shall sadly long to hear something about you: and yet I feel too that nothing I can write is worth your receiving, and reading, and that amidst your numerous duties there I ought not to trouble you to write to me: still I cannot give up the idea now: perhaps in time I may grow not *less loving*, but less selfish.

My husband desires to be very kindly remembered: be assured my own *dear dear* friend, that we shall *very constantly*, and *affectionately* remember you, and more especially so when bowing before our Father's footstool—Oh, may "the Lord indeed bless thee and keep thee: make his face shine upon thee and give thee peace."

Charlie[105] and Milly send love and kisses to the boys[106] and Emmy. I hope they will not soon forget as all ( ) shall often talk of them—and though you would laugh at my wine bottle, I cannot help fancying you have found it a pleasant and useful

[101] While in Liverpool before her departure for the United States, Emily was staying with Mr. and Mrs. Bissell. It appears that Mr. Bissell was an agent responsible for securing Emily a ship berth for her return to the United States.

[102] See vol. 1, "Cast of Characters," s.v. "Peck, The Reverend Doctor Solomon."

[103] See vol. 1, "Cast of Characters," s.v. "Judson, Emily Frances."

[104] Milly Angus was the daughter of Joseph and Amelia Angus.

[105] Charlie Angus was the son of Joseph and Amelia Angus.

[106] Henry Hall Judson and Edward Judson were the youngest two surviving sons of Adoniram and Sarah Hall Boardman Judson.

companion—I scarcely like to *ask* you to write but if you have a few leisure moments, a wee note would be very very welcome.

Please give my love to the boys and a kiss to Emmy, and a large portion of love to Emmy's dear mamma, and with very kind regards to Mr. and Mrs. Bissell from my husband and myself and kind remembrances from him to you

Believe me to be in haste

Yours very affectionately

Amelia Angus

Source: The American Baptist Historical Society, AJ 12, Number 331.

Mrs. Abby Grace Thomas to Emily C. Judson, September 16, 1851—( ) ( ) Terrace

My dearest Friend

It does seem strange, that our friendships, commenced under such peculiar circumstances, should thus be ( ).[107] Captain Young's prognostications have been quite ( ), of this fact however. You must be perfectly aware, it little heeds therefore, that I should enlarge on the subject—I am truly glad that your visit in My Motherland has been so agreeable, and that you have tho unexpectedly, met with so many delightful, and healthy friends. I cannot but regret with yourself that our meetings have been so like "( ) Visits." I could not control circumstances, had a Carriage been at my command I should not have lived in the ( ) ( ) without seeing you much oftener.

I return the enclosed with many thanks for your truly kind and friendly intentions in sending it. ( ) you have expressed your appreciation of my husband's[108] ( ). You may perhaps be disposed to possess a likeness of the ( ). I only wish the accompanying did fuller justice to the original.

With every wish for your health and happiness in this World and a blessed portion in that better one to come.

Believe me always ( ) true and unchanging friend

Abby Grace Thomas

[Written on page 1, perpendicular to and across the text:] P.S. I sent the boxes on Saturday as you directed and hope they reached you safely. I am going to write to Mr. Newell soon. ( ) ( ) Adieu.

Source: American Baptist Historical Society, AJ 21, no. 1065.

[107] Mrs. Thomas and Emily Judson had been passengers together on the *Tudor*, sailing from Calcutta to Liverpool.

[108] It was for the absent Mr. Thomas that Emily, on the voyage from Calcutta to Liverpool, had written the poem "Alone upon the Deep." This poem can be found in this correspondence in June 1851.

Mr. Alfred Ogan to Emily C. Judson, September 17, 1851— 2 Turnwheel Lane, London

Mrs. Emily Judson

Dear Madam

Enclosed I have now the pleasure of handing you 1( ) halves of Bank of England notes asunder

JQ 17100/5—9 July 1850 ea: L20	-	L100
JT41700/3—11 August 1850 ea: L10	-	30
JX21147/40—13 Aug. 1850. ea. L5	-	20
		£150

The Receipt of which be good enough to acknowledge when the 2nd halves shall be sent.

I wo have forwarded before but Mr. Syman is out of town. Mr. Peck[109] arrd yesterday.

Yrsmorespy[110]

Alfred Ogan

Source: American Baptist Historical Society, AJ 18, no. 847.

Mrs. Amelia Angus to Emily C. Judson, September 18, 1851[111]— Stepney College

Joseph wishes me to mention that Nelson's address is

Thomas Nelson
Paternoster Row

and that a line from you would no doubt be very highly prized, if you were inclined so far to favor him. There are two copies of each book, making a dozen volumes besides those you have with you[112]—My husband looks rather covetously at the

[109] See vol. 1, "Cast of Characters," s.v. "Peck, The Reverend Doctor Solomon."

[110] Presumably an abbreviated form of "Yours most respectfully."

[111] This is an addendum to a letter dated September 15, 1851.

[112] Thomas Nelson was an English publisher. We would gather from this that some of their inventory had been sent to Emily as a gift. Thomas Nelson was later to publish *Tales For All Seasons*, a collection of Fanny Forester's stories that had appeared in the anthologies *Trippings in Author-land* and *Alderbrook*. As this volume was receiving its final edit, this editor received from the David Hanna Family a copy of *Memoir of Sarah B. Judson of the American Mission to Burmah*, by Fanny Forester. It was published by Thomas Nelson, Paternoster Row, London, 1851. The inscription on the inside cover reads "To Mrs. Judson with the publisher's respectful compls. London, Sep. 12, 1851."

unknown volumes, and seems anxious to make their acquaintance, which however I intend to do before long—pray excuse pencil—it is eleven o'clock and I am upstairs—

Good night my own very dear kind friend—sweet sleep pleasant dreams and our Father's own rich blessing of peace every around you.

A. A.

[Written across the text on page 1:] I think you have managed extremely well about your passage—I am very glad for your sake that you are going to ( ), and trust you will have a happy meeting with all your friends.

Written across the text on page 8: With kind regards to Mr. and Mrs. Bissell[113]

Believe me to be

Ever more lovingly yours

Amelia Angus

Source: American Baptist Historical Society, AJ 12, no. 331.

Emily C. Judson to the Reverend Doctor Solomon Peck, September 19, 1851[114]—Wavertree[115]

Dear Dr. Peck,

It would have given me great pleasure to stop and see you in London, but the arrangements had been so made with Mr. Bissell that I could not well remain without disappointing, and perhaps annoying him. I have taken my passage in the *Canada*—Mail Steamer, which leaves here tomorrow.

I did not venture to wait for a packet, it would have made me so late in the season, and I have very much to do before the cold winter sets in. I am feeling the cold very much, but still continue to improve in health. Mr. Bissell remarks a wide difference between my present face, and the one I first showed in London.

Mrs. Angus[116] writes me you are to be at Denmark Hill[117] today, and I almost envy you. They made it a very delightful home to me after my long wanderings.

I am told that I must close my letters and dress for a little drive into the country.

Wishing to meet you in America, and begging your prayers for myself and my little ones

[113] Emily stayed with Mr. and Mrs. Bissell in Liverpool before her voyage home. Mr. Bissell was in charge of arranging her passage.

[114] See the letter of Solomon Peck to Emily C. Judson dated September 11, 1851.

[115] This is the home in Liverpool of Mr. and Mrs. Bissell; Emily was staying with them before her departure. Mr. Bissell made the arrangements for her journey.

[116] On her return to America, Emily stayed in England for about a month; for a part of that time she was with the Rev. and Mrs. Angus and their children at Stepney College.

[117] Denmark Hill was the home of the Smith Family. See the letters from Mary Anna Smith (mother) and Mary Esther Smith (daughter). The Smiths were active in British Baptist mission circles, and Mary Anna Smith mentions having met Ann Judson.

Believe me
Yours most sincerely,

Emily C. Judson

Source: American Baptist Historical Society, AJ 12, no. 375.

Mrs. Elizabeth L. Stevens to Emily C. Judson, September 22, 1851—Maulmain

My dear Sister

I have just this moment of our *last* mail day met with an awkward accident, which has made the fore finger [sic] of my right hand so lame I am quite in doubt about being able to finish my pacquet [sic] for this month. It is swollen and painful, but if it would only keep itself out of the way of the other fingers "I guess" they could manage.

We are all overjoyed that you were in such fine health and spirits when you wrote from Cape Town May 30th that we cannot say a sympathizing word about the long passage, 5 weeks in sight of land, hurricanes etc. Rather will I tell how disappointed I am not to have a letter dated *London*. I am so thankful Capt. Lay[118] was so good and the passengers so kind and some agreeable—but you know "*I told you so*" did'nt [sic] I? Mrs. Newton is vastly delighted. She somehow feels almost as though she had been extolled herself as she thinks herself and Mr. Kincaid[119] the means of your going on the *Tudor*.

Oh so many things to write! which first? I must take the subject now uppermost day and night. Eddy and Sarah[120] may soon leave us. Arrangements are being made for Mr. Stilson[121] and his motherless children to go as soon as possible, but as Dr.

[118] W. Lay was the captain of the *Tudor*, the ship on which Emily sailed from Calcutta to England.

[119] Born in 1797, educated at the seminary in Hamilton, New York, and ordained in 1822, the Reverend Eugenio Kincaid served several churches before being appointed as a missionary to Burmah in February 1830. His first wife died soon after their arrival. His second wife was Barbara McBain, and they were married in 1833. In these years, they served in Rangoon, Ava, Saduja, and Akyab. The Reverend and Mrs. Kincaid returned to the United States in 1843; because of her persistent health problems, they were not reappointed in 1846. While in the United States, Rev. Kincaid became instrumental in the establishment of the University of Lewisberg (later Bucknell University). Upon Mrs. Kincaid's restoration, they returned to Burmah, arriving in February 1851 just as Emily Judson was embarking for her return voyage. With his knowledge of the language and customs, Rev. Kincaid was able to establish himself in work with the Burmese government at Ava. With one more trip home (in 1857, on an official mission for the King of Burmah to President Buchanan of the United States), they retired to Gerard, Kansas, in 1866. Of Rev. Kincaid, the correspondence indicates a man of convictions and occasional independent action.

[120] Edward Stevens, born December 17, 1838, and Sarah Stevens, born December 3, 1840.

[121] Lyman Stilson was born in Meredith, New York, on January 29, 1805. He attended the Hamilton Seminary and was appointed to missionary service on October 3, 1836. He was married to Lucretia Brownson on August 20, 1837, and both sailed for Burmah on October 28, 1837, along with the Bennetts and the Stevens. Mr. Stilson finally returned to America after Lucretia Stilson's death on August 14, 1851. Mrs. Stilson had been quite ill for some time and the board had authorized her to return to the United States, but as reported in the newsletter of the Missionary Union, "She has been removed to a better country." They worked with Adoniram Judson for thirteen years, and with both Sarah Hall Boardman Judson and Emily Chubbuck Judson. Mr. Stilson's specific responsibilities included the oversight of printing Burmese elementary books for the schools that were maintained by the mission. He also wrote a volume in Burmese on mathematics.

M.[122] thinks his health in such a state, and *prospects* such that it is hardly safe to allow *his own* children to go with him unless there is some one [sic] else in the party, who could take of them in event of his having another stroke. Of course we cannot send ours unless Mrs. Bennett[123] goes, which is now probable. Some of Eddy's outfit is outgrown and worn out so I am barely replenishing it and getting dear Sarah ready. If they go I wish they could be where you could sometimes see them. I think you would write me of them better than my own dearest mother and sister even, having known them as they are *here* and understood just how they seem to us every day. Write me your own experience about your children and specifically about Abby;[124] dear girl! may she be a comfort to you and you a rich blessing to her. Write me too your experience about outfit. Give advice and hints to help us when we go home. I cannot say how long that may be. Edward[125] began to be troubled with neuralgic pain in his eye and face like Mr. Wade[126] and Mr. Haswell[127] and was reminded of *the back* of the latter—but rest restored him soon and he is now well with care, yet I cannot but think it premonitory—I want him certainly to finish the Dictionary first,[128] that is, if he is allowed. I wrote you the Board wished him to lay it aside and preach till somebody shd be sent ( ) of that work. The Board wish to do right, but at such a distance cannot understand our circumstances and duties. They sent us a note of censure for moving into this house without consulting them. They cannot comprehend why a man cannot live at a distance from his work just as ministers at home can—neither can they see how our houses differ from those at home so two

[122] See vol. 1, "Cast of Characters," s.v. "Morton, Doctor."

[123] Stella Bennett was the wife of Cephas Bennett; they arrived in Burmah in January 1830. Mr. Bennett remained the superintendent of the Baptist Press there for more than fifty years. From the Utica area, they sent their children back, and the girls were educated at the Utica Female Academy and then the Misses Anable's School. The girls included Elsina (April 1828), Mary (November 1829), Ann (August 1833), Ellen (June 1835), and Sarah (June 1837).

[124] See vol. 1, "Cast of Characters," s.v. "Judson, Abby Ann."

[125] Edward Stevens arrived in Maulmain in February 1838; his wife was Elizabeth Stevens. Mr. Stevens was responsible for the native churches that were associated with the mission. He took on the work of finishing the dictionary after the death of Adoniram Judson, and he buried "Angel Charley" in the chapel compound after his birth in April 1850. Mr. Stevens was in Burmah for forty-eight years.

[126] Jonathan Wade was appointed as a missionary to Burmah in 1823. Wade's relationship with Adoniram Judson was especially dear because of the early experiences they shared, including the death of Ann Judson. Much of their work was spent in the Karen jungle communities following the path of George Boardman. They had returned home to America on December 22, 1847, and returned to Burmah in January 1851, just as Emily was returning to the United States. They were from the Hamilton, New York, area. They left to return to Burmah on July 25, 1850, and were in Maulmain by February 1851. Both died in Burmah. Deborah died at Maulmain in 1868, and Jonathan died in Rangoon in 1872.

[127] James Madison Haswell was born February 4, 1810, in Bennington, Vermont. He was married to Jane Matilda Mason of Cheshire, Massachusetts. The Haswells sailed for Burmah on September 23, 1835, to work with the Talaings. They arrived at Amherst in February 1836. The Haswells became partners with Adoniram and Sarah Hall Boardman Judson; Sarah turned over the translation of the Peguan scripture to Mr. Haswell after Elnathan and Adoniram were born, and her energies were focused elsewhere. When Sarah and Adoniram sailed for America in 1845, the Haswells took care of Henry until Adoniram returned in 1847 with Emily. The Haswells left Burmah in December 1848 and arrived in America in 1849; they remained in the United States until September 1852, when they again sailed for Burmah.

[128] Edward Stevens, at the suggestion of Adoniram Judson, picked up on the work of the English-Burmese Dictionary after the death of Adoniram Judson.

families cannot live together. At first I thought I would write a full letter of explanations to Uncle Lin Martabon [sic].

Good bye again Darling
Ever Aff'ly Yrs

Bessie

Source: American Baptist Historical Society, AJ 19, no. 900.

Mrs. Lydia Lillybridge Simons to Emily C. Judson, September 22, 1851—Maulmain

Maulmain, Sept. 22 1851

My dear Emily,

I have now so much as head and heart can do in the way of superintending schools, if not all that heart could wish. However, the warmth of any pleasure is somewhat dampened by being obliged to take the whole charge of the Boarding School for a time. But this charge will not last always, for I will not let it. When Jess Cotton is married, I think she will take most of the girls department to instruct in her own house. She will take three or 4 of the boarders and I hope most of the day scholars.

And the boys boarding department must come down for I *will not pay the money* for the support of those that can be retained as day-scholars without.

Mrs. Stevens[129] will write all the news, of course.

I intended to write to Anna Maria,[130] but am hindered wonderfully to day.

Ever affectionately [page 3] Yours

Lydia Simons

Source: The American Baptist Historical Society, AJ 19, Number 927.

Mrs. Amelia Angus to Emily C. Judson, September 23, 1851—Stepney College and Stepney Green

My dear Mrs. Judson

The temptation you have put in my way is quite too strong to be resisted: for although I *am not* clever, and therefore *ought* to be afraid to write—to one—so far my superior in mind and intellect: still I must confess your talent is so happily blended with sweetness and kindness that I only admire and love, instead of fear

[129] See vol. 1, "Cast of Characters," s.v. "Stevens, The Reverend Edward and Elizabeth."

[130] See vol. 1, "Cast of Characters," s.v. "Anable, Anna Maria."

you. Many many thanks for your last kind note which with all—the most pleasant and tender emotion—gives me a vast deal of *amusement*. I can trace no agitation however in *your* note and therefore am at no loss to conclude how you yourself laughed at the "idle tale" you tell: but two things surprise me: first that *such* a thing should be *ever* reported though doubtless by somebody who knows my *husband only*: and then that *Mrs. Bissell*[131] (sensible woman as I have always thought her) should think it worth while to repeat it: well, well, let it pass—my husband and I have laughed heartily at the idea. By the bye, you have not told me how you liked Mr. Bissell:[132] pray forgive my curiosity: but after all the various opinions given to you here, I was anxious to know what you thought of him.

I saw the departure of your steamer notice in the Times. I shall look out eagerly for notice of its arrival at Boston and hope you have got comfortable accommodations, pleasant fellow passengers, etc. second Capt. Lay[133] if possible. I think it is certainly well you have not waited[134] for Dr. Peck:[135] for it seems just now by no means certain *when* he will come exactly except that he wishes to be in Boston early in November: he was here last night and seems to feel so vexed to have so short a time to see London and England and Scotland that we talked together of the feasibility or otherwise of changing his passage from the *Ocean Queen* to a steamer a fortnight or so later; whether he will try to do it or not I cannot tell. We have much enjoyed his company when we have seen him: my husband and he had a long chat last evening upon the strict and open communion question: this morning they went into the Tract Society Committee breakfast together. I fear we shall not see him again. I find although he has no weakness for Sherbrook he has one for music: he has heard Jenny Lind in America and sets aside one of his very few evenings here to attend the ( ) ( ) oratorio—Elijah etc. Mr.Howe has been down to see us again too: he drank tea with us on Saturday.[136]

[Written perpendicular to the text on page 3:] to you. Charlie and Milly[137] send their love and kisses to Henry,[138] Edward[139] and Emmy:[140] they *flatter* themselves that Edward and Emmy the least if not Henry too would like to come here again.

[131] Mrs. Bissell wrote one letter to Emily dated December 30, 1851.

[132] Mr. Bissell wrote to Emily C. Judson on September 12, 1851, suggesting that he had something to do with acquiring her boat tickets for the trip from Liverpool to Boston.

[133] W. Lay was the captain of the *Tudor*, the ship on which Emily sailed from Calcutta to England.

[134] See the letter of Dr. Solomon Peck to Emily C. Judson dated September 11, 1851.

[135] See vol. 1, "Cast of Characters," s.v. "Peck, The Reverend Doctor Solomon."

[136] A page of this letter may be missing. The writing perpendicular to the text begins with the end of a sentence ("to you"). Page 3, the last page available, ends with the close of a complete paragraph ("Mr Howe has been down to see us again too: he drank tea with us on Saturday.")

[137] Charlie and Milly were the children of Joseph and Amelia Angus.

[138] See vol. 1, "Cast of Characters," s.v. "Judson, Henry Hall."

[139] See vol. 1, "Cast of Characters," s.v. "Judson, Edward."

[140] See vol. 1, "Cast of Characters," s.v. "Judson, Emily Frances."

Believe me to be dear dear Mrs. Judson
Evermost affectionately and gratefully yours

Amelia Angus

Source: American Baptist Historical Society, AJ 12, no. 333.

Mrs. Abby Grace Thomas to Emily C. Judson, September 24, 1851[141]—Richmond

I have received your last, dated the day before you left Liverpool, and believe me dearest, that I feel as much pained as it possible for you to be—I am staying with my Sister in the Country, or I would have written by today's mail, but I had not your letter in ( ). I am indeed truly rejoiced to find that I am still cared for; it is a dreadful thing to feel that one you loved dearly should prove the very reverse of what your heart desired. Do you not think so? I cannot express to you dearest, what my feelings were, until I received your last letter—but that I can say they were far *from enviable*. I shall get the book you recommended and I doubt that I shall be repaid by reading it. I *know* I shall be pleased with *Alderbrook*[142] and I will write and tell you exactly what I think of it.

My Lyall returned from Scotland on Friday last—he called on Saturday and he is looking so well—better than I have ever seen him. I will get ( ) direction from ( ) and send it to you—Captain Lay has gone out again on the "*Tudor*"[143]—he sailed from Portsmouth, on Monday I believe. Mrs. Lay called to see me, and brought her lovely child Mary to see me also. Only fancy Coll Marshall calling! I was quite astonished. We were gone to the Expedition and had not therefore the pleasure of seeing the ( ) ( ) that, for which I was very

Written across all four pages of text: glad. I still adhere to my old intention of visiting America in the Summer and I shall be *so happy* to see you again, *one quarter of an hours'* [sic] *talk* will do more than *ten letters*. We should immediately understand one another again. The Newells are somewhere in Wales. I have mislaid their address, but when I return to May's ( ) I will look for it and you shall have it, if I am so fortunate to find it.

Source: American Baptist Historical Society, AJ 21, no. 1065.

[141] There is an addendum to this letter dated September 30, 1851.

[142] *Alderbrook* was a collection of Fanny Forester's stories, poems, and sketches and was a sequel to *Trippings in Author-land*. Published by Ticknor and Company (later Ticknor, Reed and Fields), the first edition came out in December 1846, and by April 1847, it was in its fourth edition.

[143] The *Tudor* was the ship on which Emily sailed from Calcutta to England, and Captain Lay was most attentive to her during that journey. There is a letter in the correspondence (August 1851) indicating his attempt to be in touch with her during her stay in England.

Mrs. Abby Grace Thomas to Emily C. Judson, September 30, 1851[144]

Missed the mail, and I now send by this one Mr. Lyall's address is "26 Orsett Terrace" ( ). I am very sorry I cannot find Mrs. Newell's card. I have looked every where [sic] for it, but unsuccessfully!—I hope you reached your own dear land well and safely and that you found all there as you wished and desired. My darling "( )" has not been well and both she and Alice have bad coughs and colds. I had not seen any thing [sic] of Mr. Lyall for some time, his time is too much occupied I suppose and our quiet cottage cannot offer any great inducement to a young man, even to one so good and kind as our dear friend Mr. Lyall. We are going to the Exhibition for the last time ( ) ( ) it closes altogether on the 11th of October. I wish you had seen Richmond my birthplace; it is so lovely! I lived there until I went ( ) to India first as a very young girl. I shall not forget my feeling on Sunday ( ) ( ) ( ) ( ) I attended divine service at the ( ) old church where I had knelt *so often many years ago*—Oh, it was a sad, and solemn feeling dearest, and we heard such a beautiful sermon. I *think* these were the words of the Text: "The harvest is past, the Summer is gone and I am not saved."[145] I shall not attempt to describe what I felt. I am *sure* I could not do so! Good bye. God bless you and with every sincere wish for your happiness here and hereafter ( ) ( ) believe me your affectionate and attached friend.

Abby Grace Thomas

Source: American Baptist Historical Society, AJ 21, no. 1065.

[144] This is an addendum to a letter started September 24, 1851.

[145] Jeremiah 8:20: "The harvest is past, the summer is ended, and we are not saved."

INDEX